Ethnic Continuity
in the
Carpatho-Danubian Area

Ethnic Continuity
in the
Carpatho-Danubian Area

Elemér Illyés

FIRST EDITION:
EAST EUROPEAN MONOGRAPHS, NO. CCXLIX
1988

SECOND EDITION:
HUNYADI ÖCS. MK.
HAMILTON, ON.
STRUKTURA PRESS

E. Illyés: Ethnic continuity in the Carpatho-Danubian Area.

2nd (revised) edition, 1992.
A multi-disciplinary study, with the main emphasis on linguistics.

Copyright © 1988 by Elemér Illyés
ISBN 0-88033-146-1
Library of Congress Catalog Card Number 88-80384

Printed in Hungary

CONTENTS

III LINGUISTICS

PREFACE

This work examines the ethnic and linguistic history of the various peoples in the Carpatho-Danubian area (Southeastern Europe) from ancient times until the early Middle Ages. The ultimate fate of these peoples is also taken into consideration, as well as some aspects of the current historiography of the area. The research for this book has required an eclectic approach, based on historical materials, archaeology, and philology; the scanty and fragmentary nature of written historical records (indeed, the often total lack of documentary evidence), together with the not always reliable archaeological data, has made scholarly research on this area extremely difficult. The most reliable knowledge has been gleaned from Balkan philology.

This book deals with the ethnogenesis of the Romanian people and the question of whether a Romanized population lived north of the lower Danube and has maintained continuity there, ethnically, linguistically, and in its settlements, since Roman times. This theme has been the subject of a spirited and long-standing controversy; and a great many of the works on the history of Southeastern Europe have been colored by political and ideological considerations.

The introductory chapter gives a general picture of the ethnic and historical relationships in Southeastern Europe in ancient and early medieval times. Chapter II discusses the archaeological remains of peoples who lived or are still living in the Carpatho-Danubian area. Standard publications that appeared until the year 1986 inclusively have been considered here. It was, however, impossible to discuss all the work done in this area; and new writings on the subject are appearing continually. Chapters III and IV deal with main linguistic problems, with an emphasis on the importance of East and Late Latin on the early development of the Romanian language. The philological data derived from place and river names are also considered.

The appendix contains an index of names and a list of place names in three languages. The place names given here are those officially in use today; the Hungarian and German names are in part the major historical forms and in part those most generally used. There is also a selective bibliography and, at the end of each chapter, basic references to useful sources.

The author would like to express his appreciation to the copy editor of the manuscript, John R. Clegg, as well as to a colleague whose contributions helped make this book possible.

Lago di Garda   *E. I.*
June 1987

ABBREVIATIONS

Acta Ant. Hung.	Acta Antiqua Academiae Scientiarum Hungaricae, Budapest
Acta. Arch.	Acta Archaeologica Academiae Scientiarum Hungaricae, Budapest
AMN	Acta Musei Napocensis, Cluj-Napoca
AIESÉE	Assotiation International d'Études Sud-Est Européennes
AIIA	Anuarul Institutului de istorie şi arheologie, Cluj-Napoca
CIL	Corpus Inscriptionum Latinarum
DEX	Dicţionarul explicativ al limbii române, Bucureşti,
Gesta	Gesta Hungarorum, Budapest
ILR	Istoria limbii române, Bucureşti
MCA	Materiale şi cercetări arheologice, Bucureşti
MGH	Monumenta Germaniae Historica
RE	Realencyclopädie der klassischen Altertumswissenschaft, Stuttgart
Reallexikon	Reallexikon der Germanischen Altertumskunde, Berlin, New York, 2nd edition
RER	Revue des études roumaines, Bucureşti
RRH	Revue Roumaine d'Histoire, Bucureşti
SCIV	Studii şi cercetări de istorie veche
SCIVA	Studii şi cercetări de istorie veche şi arheologie, Bucureşti
SCL	Studii şi cercetări lingvistice, Bucureşti
SF	Südost-Forschungen, München
SRH	Scriptores Rerum Hungaricarum, I-II. Edited by E. Szentpétery, Budapest 1937–1938.
TIR	Tabula Imperii Romani, Budapest, Bucureşti, Ljubljana

I

HISTORY

ABOUT THE EARLY HISTORY OF THE PEOPLES OF SOUTHEASTERN EUROPE BEFORE AND DURING THE ROMAN CONQUEST

Introduction

Southeastern Europe, especially the Balkan Peninsula, has been subject to centuries of historical and ethnic turbulence. In the course of its history some of the oldest peoples, such as the Thracians, Illyrians, Getae, and Dacians, became extinct. The scarcity of written records about the ancient and early medieval history of Southeastern Europe is well known. Although the texts in Latin and those by the Byzantine authors about historical events and the populations of the area do offer researchers a starting point, they are frequently contradictory and unreliable in many areas, such as chronology and the designation of the names of individual peoples. In general, these texts are difficult to interpret, because they are vague and fragmentary. Too often, they have been interpreted in a one-sided way, in order to support an author's particular prejudices.

The lack of historical records, philological theories based on insufficient and unreliable data, and, finally, speculative and arbitrary analyses of archaeological discoveries make it difficult to give a clear picture of the ethnic relationships in Southeastern Europe in ancient and medieval times.

There are no written records about the early history of the autochthonous inhabitants of the Balkan Peninsula, the Illyrians and the Thracians. Some were Romanized or semi-Romanized and probably retreated from the Slavs into the mountainous regions. Only fragments of their languages have survived, and these cannot be appraised with any degree of certainty.

Rome conquered part of the southern Balkan Peninsula including Macedonia in about 168 B.C. and Dalmatia in 156–155 B.C. A second

1

period of conquest subdued the Balkan peoples on the Sava in 35
B.C.; a quarter of a century later the Balkan Peninsula as far as the
Danube belonged to Rome. In 395 A.D., after the death of Emperor
Theodosius I, the Roman Empire split into two parts and was never
to be reintegrated. The Western Empire (Rome) collapsed less than a
century later following the German conquest in 476 A.D.; the smaller,
yet stronger Eastern Roman, or Byzantine, part lasted, however, for
another thousand years. The Byzantine Empire (Byzantium), with
Constantinople as its capital, was thus the organic continuation of
the Roman Empire. The Byzantine Empire itself fell in 1453. The
Byzantines called themselves Romans (*Rumi, Romanoi*), while the Slavs
identified them as Greeks. In the sixth century, particularly during
the reign of Justinian (527–565) Latinity became evident in court life,
in the army, and in public life of the Byzantine Empire. From the
time of Mauritius Tiberius (582–602), however, the second element
got the upper hand; and the empire became more and more Greek.
The Latin language, however, preserved its influence to some extent
as late as the seventh century. After the seventh century the main
sources of information about the early Middle Ages were provided
by Byzantine writers, chroniclers, hagiographers, and letter writers,
writing in Greek; and there are no extant Latin sources, until the
ninth century. Besides the Byzantine sources there are Muslim historical
narratives, the reliability of which, however, is generally assumed to
be questionable.

    In Roman times the northwestern part of the Balkan Peninsula,
inhabited by various tribes, was a territory administrated by the
Romans and was designated as *Illyricum* by Greek and Roman authors.
At the beginning of the first century A.D. this territory was divided
into Dalmatia [*Illyricum Superior*], Pannonia, and Moesia [*Illyricum
Inferior*]. Fragments of the Old Illyrian language are preserved in the
form of personal names in inscriptions of Roman times. Latin was
the principal liturgical language and Dalmatian the main vernacular
one. The Slavic invasions of the seventh century eliminated to a large
extent the Latin-speaking element of *Illyricum*.

    The territory north of the lower Danube (the Wallachian Plain) was
inhabited by the Getae and part of modern Transylvania and the Banat by
the Dacians. The only peoples of the Balkan Peninsula, other than the
Greeks, to survive the turbulences of Balkan history were the Vlachs (the
ancestors of the Romanians) and the Albanians. Tenth and eleventh
century documents, mostly Byzantine, mention these two peoples. The

Vlachs inhabited the southern part of the Danubian region, that is, Moesia Superior and Dardania, as well as Macedonia and Thessaly, which was known at the end of the Middle Ages as Grand Wallachia.

The basic religious terminology of Rumanian is Latin, which suggests that the Vlachs were Christianized during the Roman epoch, in an environment of Latin. They were organized by the Bulgarians in the Orthodox Church probably in the early tenth century, and borrowed from them the Slavic liturgy and the Cyrillic-Methodian church tradition.[1] The Slavonic Council decreed Slavic the official language of the church in 893 A.D.

The ethnic identity of the peoples mentioned in the early medieval records of Southeastern Europe is still of central importance. Unfortunately, the few surviving written materials, except when they deal with the most important subjects, have only caused great confusion. Ethnic names, for instance, are used inconsistently by the various authors: The name Scythian, for example, was often applied indiscriminately to Cumanians, Pechenegs, and Tatars; the Hungarians were often referred to as Turks, Paeonians, Sarmatians, and Pannonians; and Bulgarians were called Moesians and Scythians. Similarly, the Romans were called Bulgarians, or Ausonians; the Scythians, Uzes or Carps; the early Romanians, Vlachs or Dacians; the Germanic tribes, Alemanni and Franks; and the Getae, Cumanians and Uzes. The Pechenegs were called Moesians, Sarmatians, and Scythians; and the Huns were referred to as Hungarians, Uzes, or Scythians. The sixth century Gothic historian Jordanes called the Goths Slavs, and the Huns Goths, while the fifth century Byzantine historian Priscus designated the Huns nearly always as Scythians. The Byzantines regarded all their northern neighbors as Slavs. Furthermore, writers of antiquity could not distinguish clearly between Dacians and Getae, the northern neighbors of the actual Thracians, who spoke either Thracian or a Thracian-related language. The Greek sources identify the Dacians also as Getae, which also include the actual Getae who lived on the lower Danube. This makes it difficult to differentiate between the Dacians of Dacia Traiana and the Getae to the south of the Danube.

The Thracians

The name Thracian is a collective designation for several Balkan groups and for some of the peoples of Asia Minor. The Thracians succumbed to Greek influence in the eighth and seventh centuries B.C. and, later, during the second century B.C., the Thracians were under Roman rule. In 46 B.C. the Roman Emperor Claudius made

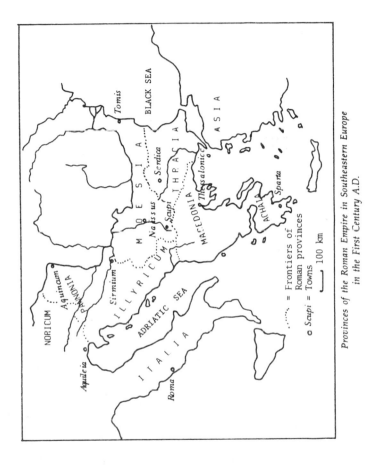

Provinces of the Roman Empire in Southeastern Europe
in the First Century A.D.

Thracia a Roman province. The territory of old Thracia was broken up into several districts stretching from south of the Balkan Mountains to Moesia Inferior and Scythia Minor (Dobrudja). Because the Thracians had at least partly lost their identity under Greek and Roman rule, they were assimilated into other peoples during the age of the peoples' migration.

The Thracian language belongs to the Indo-European group spoken in ancient times in the eastern part of the Balkan Peninsula. In the sixth century A.D. the Thracian language became extinct. The area in which Thracian was spoken is difficult to ascertain, since only few linguistic remnants still exist. In all probability, however, Thracian dialects were used at one time or another in Thracia, in parts of Macedonia, in Lower Moesia, by the Getae on the Danube, and in Dacia as far as Asia Minor.[2]

The Scythians

The Scythians came as nomadic tribes from Inner Asia in about 1500 B.C. and settled on the lower course of the Don and Dnieper rivers. This territory was known as Scythia, a name also given to Dobrudja (Scythia Minor) and to the territory to the north of the Danube. Their language was akin to the extinct language of the Iranians. The Danubian Scythians were known alternatively as Goths and Huns.

Moesia (Misia)

Moesia, the territory between the lower Danube and the Haemus (Balkan) Mountains was a Scythian domain in ancient times. The inhabitants belonged to the Thracian family of peoples (Getae and others) who fell under Roman rule in 29 B.C. At the end of the first century Moesia was divided into *Moesia Superior* (the western part) and *Moesia Inferior* (the eastern part). *Moesia Superior* disintegrated later into Dardania, whose capital was Scupi (modern Skoplje), while *Moesia Inferior*, in turn, disintegrated into Dacia Mediterranea, whose capital was Serdica (modern Sofia). Following the division of the Roman Empire, Moesia became part of the Eastern Roman Empire. In the sixth and seventh centuries Slavs and Avars passed through Moesia. By 681 the land was under Bulgar domination, and it became a Slavic-Bulgarian territory.

ABOUT THE EARLY HISTORY OF THE ROMANIANS

Even though the early history of the Romanians is still obscure, contemporary scholarship indicates that the center of their ethnogenesis should be sought south of the Danube, on the Balkan Peninsula. This conclusion is not new;[3] indeed, it has long been the subject of much controversy. Nevertheless, in the past few decades new information has come to light that could lead to a solution of the problem. The field of linguistics offers the most valuable evidence; but historical records and the knowledge supplied by place names and, to some extent, by archaeology can also help lead to a conclusion.

The medieval history of the Romanians will be discussed in the analysis of ancient and early medieval peoples and in the history of the languages of Southeastern Europe in subsequent chapters. Special attention will be accorded to archaeology and linguistics in that process. Likewise, Romanian historiography from the beginning to the present will be examined and evaluated.

The First Written Sources About Early Vlachs
The Testimony of Byzantine Authors

Medieval written records first mention Vlachs (Vlahi) south of the Danube between Kastoria and Prispa in the second half of the tenth century (976) and in the first half of the eleventh century, in the time of the Byzantine Emperor Basileios II. An anonymous Byzantine chronicler referred to Vlachs south of the Danube in 980: the Emperor Basileios II entrusted the ruling of the Vlachs of Elada (northern Greece, Thessaly, and Enbeea) to Nicoulitza.[4] In the second half of the tenth century the Vlachs were mentioned by Byzantine and West European authors as being in the central and southern parts of the Balkan Peninsula, south of the Sava and Danube rivers.[5] The twelfth century Byzantine author, Ioannes Kinnamos, described an expedition against Hungary in 1166 A.D. in *Historia*.[6] He wrote, among other things, that "Leon, also known as Vatatzes, brought many soldiers from other areas, even a large number of Vlachs, about whom it is said that they are the descendants of colonists from Italy."[7] There are divers' theories about the geographical origins of the Vlach recruits in the army of Leon Vatatzes: J. Ch. Engel, R. Roesler, B. P. Hasdeu, J. Jung, N. Bănescu, and the Hungarian Byzantine scholar Gyula Moravcsik argued that they came from south of the Danube, that is, from the Balkan Peninsula or Paristrion (Dobrudja), while Th. Uspenskij, L. Pić, D. Onciul, Nicolae Iorga and others assumed that these Vlachs were from north of the Danube.[8]

It is still of concern to Romanian historians whether the Vlachs mentioned in the texts of the Byzantine chroniclers were Romanians from north or south of the Danube.[9]

Byzantine historical writing enjoyed a renaissance under Anna Komnena, Niketas Choniates, Kekaumenos, and others who followed the example of great historians of antiquity such as Priskos, Prokopios, and Theophylaktos Simokatta, in the sixth century, the last of the ancient historians of the Greeks. Anna Komnena (1083–1148), a daughter of the Byzantine Emperor Alexios I Komnen (1081–1118) and the author of the *Alexiade* (*Alexias*),[10] which deals with the events during her father's rule from 1081 to 1118, mentioned Vlachs on the Balkan Peninsula near the village of Andronia (modern-day Nezeros) in Thessaly. She also described the Pechenegs' crossing the Danube from the north to fight against the Byzantines. Komnena's *Alexiade* described the Vlachs as a nomadic population, and several passages tell about their presence between the Balkan Mountains and the Danube. Komnena, like other Byzantine authors, generally refers to the Hungarians as Dacians.

Niketas (Nikhetas) Choniates,[11] a Byzantine chronicler of the mid-twelfth century, mentioned that on their way to Galicia (Halicz) after escaping from prison the Vlachs had captured Andronic Komnen. Opinion is divided about whether these Vlachs were living north of the Danube or south of the river: Wilhelm Tomaschek, Robert Roesler, the Romanian Alexandru D. Xenopol, Dimitrie Onciul, and Constantin C. Giurescu argued that the Vlachs who captured Andronic Komnen were from north of the Danube, while the Romanian Haralambie Mihăescu, Constantin Daicoviciu, and others assume that these Vlachs were from south of the Danube.[12] In a series of articles published in the periodical *Tribuna* (Cluj),[13] the prominent Romanian scholar and foremost expert on Dacia Traiana, Constantin Daicoviciu, set forth the false interpretation of Byzantine sources: "We are persuaded that the Vlachs who captured Andronic on their way to Galicia were pursuing officers of the Byzantine army set up especially for such missions; in other words, they were Vlachs from the Haemus (Balkan) Mountains."[14] Thus, "the Vlachs mentioned in Choniates' text were those Vlachs who lived in Moesia, south of the Danube, at the time of the arrival of the Slavs and Bulgars."[15]

Around the turn of the twelfth century, Georgios Kedrenos,[16] a Byzantine monk, described events beginning with the rule of Emperor Isaac I Komnen (1057–1059). He frequently referred to the Goths from the north bank of the Danube and the Avars as being at war with the Byzantine Empire; the Gepidae and the Slavs were among the allies of the Avars. Reference was also made both to the Bulgarians, who, after their victory over the Byzantines, established their rule south of the Danube, and to the Hungarians, who were allies of Byzantine Emperor Leon VI. Kedrenos also made the first mention, in 976, of nomadic transhumant Vlachs in their early homeland on the Balkan Peninsula.

Niketas (Nikhetas) Conchitas mentioned the beginning of the 1185 revolt of the Vlachs, under the brothers Asên and Peter, against the Byzantine Emperor Isaac II Anghelos. This, as well as the founding of Grand Vallachia, which was approximately the size of Thessaly, is evidence that a large number of Vlachs lived south of the Danube, on the Balkan Peninsula. In the same period, Niketas Conchitas mentioned "the barbarians of the Haemus Mountain, who formerly called themselves Misians but now Vlachs and are enemies of the Romans." These Vlachs destroyed whole cities and also at times defeated the Byzantine armies. As late as the fourteenth century, the Vlachs still played an important political role and were instrumental in bringing Bulgarian Czar Michael III Sisman in 1323 to the throne. The Vlachs fought with the Bulgarians on the Balkan Peninsula as well as with the Cumanians north of the Danube (1186), against Byzantium, an indication that few, if any, Vlachs lived north of the Danube at this time. As already noted, the medieval Byzantine authors reported Vlachs only south of the Danube, on the Balkan Peninsula; they mentioned only Pechenegs and Cumanians north of the Danube.

One Byzantine document was discovered in 1881 in a Moscow library and contains two eleventh century writings by the Byzantine general and author Kekaumenos: a book called the *Strategicon*, written between 1075 and 1078[17] giving important advice on both military and political matters of the time; and a smaller book that its discoverer named *Logos Nudetetikos*. Kekaumenos's *Strategicon* gives a good picture of Byzantine and Balkan history. It contains a passage about the early Vlachs in the tenth and eleventh centuries and is often described as the first and most important record of the connection between the Vlachs and the Dacians. The author described the Vlachs who were living in the southern parts of the Balkan Peninsula as peasants and townsmen. Besides the Vlachs in his own territory (Thessaly), he also knew about Vlachs living in Epirus and Macedonia. These passages are based upon documents and family tradition and should be considered reliable; they include the first mention of Vlachs in 976 A D between Kastoria and Prispa (the Annals of Bari with information about Vlach soldiers in the Byzantine army in 1027, and the edict of Emperor Basileios II from 1020 in which the "Vlachs throughout Bulgaria" are subordinated to the archbishop of Ochrida).

The relevant passages of Kekaumenos's *Strategicon* as interpreted by Romanian historians will be given here. According to *Istoria Romániei*, the Byzantine general and author Kekaumenos correctly associated the Vlachs of the Balkans with the Dacians of Decebal, showing the connection between these Romanians and the ancient Daco-Thracian population of the Carpatho-Danubian-Moesian territory.[18] With respect to the three branches of Romanians (that is, Arumanians, Meglenorumanians, and Istro-Rumanians), it has been assumed that certain historical sources, such as the Byzantine author Kekaumenos and the anonymous geographer from the beginning of the fourteenth century, justify the opinion that these three branches of Romanians arrived relatively recently in groups in the areas in which they are still living today. "They came in shepherds' migrations from the masses of Daco-Moeso-Romans and thereby had avoided Slavization."[19] In the third edition of the same treatise (1974), the explanation about the detachment of Arumanians, Meglenorumanians, and Istro-Rumanians was changed to read: "as a result of the pressure by the last waves of horsemen."[20]

As can be seen from the interpretation of Kekaumenos's text, contemporary Romanian historiography (since 1960) puts the emphasis on the Dacian component of "Daco-Roman" rather than the Roman. The Byzantine chronicler Kekaumenos in his *Advice and Stories* mentioned that the Vlachs were the descendants of the Dacians.[21] Furthermore, it is assumed that Kekaumenos described some displacements of population from the North to the South and not the reverse.[22]

A superficial reading of these texts would give the impression that Kekaumenos described a popular tradition among the eleventh century Vlachs of Thessaly, whom he must have known well from personal contact, about their origin from the Dacians, the Bessians, and the Romans. Closer analysis reveals, however, that this impression is false in several respects. It is an example of how historical records can be misinterpreted in the absence of rigorous analysis of sources. The interpretations of Kekaumenos's passages by contemporary Romanian historians are characterized first of all by omissions of key parts of Kekaumenos's text; vague assumptions; and data inserted by modern authors into Kekaumenos's text. Indeed, all these records ignore the fact that Kekaumenos described the territory of the Dacians and the Bessians (whom he identified with the Vlachs) as entirely to the south of the Sava [Saos] and Danube rivers, in Serbia. Instead, the geographical areas are made vague (for example, "Carpatho-Danubian-Moesian" area); and the periods in which the migrations of the Dacians and Bessians may have taken place are also referred to only vaguely as "centuries earlier" or "at relatively late periods." The most serious distortion, however, is the way in which the authors treated the crucial question of the location of the ancient Dacian and Bessian areas. The text of Kekaumenos does not, in fact, even mention the Carpathians or the areas north of the Danube.

It is obvious that a correct interpretation of the passages about the Vlachs in the *Strategicon* presupposes a critical analysis of the whole texts and the circumstances under which it was written. Kekaumenos's data about the Vlachs must be divided into two categories: records about the Vlachs who were living in Hellas in his own time, and a passage about the early history of the Vlachs. Kekaumenos must have possessed several letters and other documents written by Byzantine Emperors Basileios II and Constantine X to relatives and members of the Nikoulitza family. He described to them the June 1066 revolt in Hellas by Greeks, Bulgarians, and Vlachs because of increasing taxes.[23] Kekaumenos's passage on the Vlachs living in his own time in Hellas and their part in the revolt against the Byzantine Emperor was based on personal experience, family tradition, and letters from the Byzantine emperors. What he wrote about the origin of the Vlachs, however, was of questionable reliability: "[The Vlachs] never kept their word to anyone, not even to the ancient Roman Emperors. Having been attacked in war by Emperor Trajan and having been defeated totally, they were subdued and their King, named Decebal, was killed and his head was put on a pike and brought to the city of the Romans. These [Vlachs] are, in fact, the so-called Dacians, also called Bessians [*Bessoi*]. Earlier they lived in the vicinity of the Danube and Saos, a river which we now call Sava, where the Serbians live today, and [later] withdrew to their inaccessible fortifications. Relying upon these fortifications, they feigned friendship and submission to the ancient Roman Emperors and then swept down from their strongholds and plundered the Roman provinces. Therefore, the exasperated Romans crushed them. And these left the region: some of them were dispersed to Epirus and Macedonia, and a large number established themselves in Hellas."[24] It had long been assumed that Kekaumenos wrote this on the basis of a Vlach tradition with which he was acquainted. The Byzantist Mátyás Gyóni summarized the opinions of the following nineteenth century authors about what Kekaumenos meant by Dacians and Bessians: Wilhelm Tomaschek (who believed that the Vlachs were of Bessian origin), Josef Ladislav Pić, Alexandru D. Xenopol, Dimitrie Onciul, and Bogdan Petriceicu Hasdeu.[25] It is most likely, however, that Kekaumenos did not derive his data about the origin of the Vlachs from popular traditions but rather from the Byzantine literature of his own time. The story about Athénodore and the Emperor Augustus when he was advising the Byzantine Emperor against relying on flatterers shows that he did use contemporary literature when writing the *Strategicon*. This history could hardly have been taken from popular tradition but is found in several Byzantine texts, such as the *Excerpta* of Emperor Constantine VII Porphyrogenetos (or Porphyrogenitus, 905–959),[26] written between 945 and 959; the *Epitome* of Léon Grammaticos; and the abbreviated version of the *Historia Romana* by Dio Cassius Coccineus (Cocceianus, 155–255). At the time of Kekaumenos the Byzantine historians' main source about the history of Rome and the history of Trajan's wars with the Dacians was the second century *Historia Romana* (translated into Greek by Ioannes Xiphilinos between 1071 and 1078).[27] It should be mentioned that the passages and excerpts of Dio Cassius's Roman History were the source of errors and erroneous explanations (Decebal, for instance, was not killed but committed suicide). The descriptions of the carrying of Decebal's head to Rome are similar to those in the abbreviated version in the *Strategicon*,[28] except that Dio Cassius did not call Decebal an "emperor." There were, however, four places in the *Historia Romana* in which "emperor" [βασιλεως] was used.[29]

Furthermore, the text itself has nothing to do with the essence of the theory of continuity: namely the intermingling of the Romans and the Dacians in Dacia. On the contrary, the "Dacians" and "Bessians" were described as the Romans' enemies, who were defeated and dispersed by the Roman Emperors and were later decimated, after which they left the area, wandering to Epirus, Macedonia, and Hellas. The description of the territory in which these Dacians and Bessians were living was not north of the Danube but was clearly defined as being "in the vicinity of the Sava and the Danube rivers, where the Serbians are living today." In contemporary Byzantine texts, Serbia was described as the territory between the Morava River in the east, the Drin in the south, and the Drina in the west, in other words, south of the Sava on the Balkan Peninsula. Thus, if Kekaumenos's text is to be believed, it is actually evidence against the theory of continuity north of the Danube. An analysis of the *Strategicon* shows, however, that Kekaumenos really had no idea about the original territory of the Vlachs; nor did he even know where Dacia Traiana was situated. This is not surprising because many Byzantine authors confused Dacia Traiana and Dacia Aureliana. Errors about the areas in which the other non-Greek peoples were living were also frequent in Byzantine literature. The twelfth century scholar Ioannes Tzetze, for example, placed the Hungarians in the Balkan Peninsula (south of the Sava and Danube rivers), because he mistakenly identified this population with the Moesians.

In the second half of the passage about the Vlachs, Kekaumenos described the situation in Dacia before the Roman conquest: the Dacian fortifications in the high mountains, Dacian incursions and the plundering of the Roman provinces before 106 A.D.; and the treacherous character of the Dacians, all of which was available to Kekaumenos in Dio Cassius's Roman History or in its abbreviated version. He also described the incursion in 10 A.D. of the Dacians into Pannonia.

Kekaumenos apparently believed that these events had occurred south of the Danube, in Serbia, or in other words, that Dacia was situated there and that the Dacians and Bessians were living there until Trajan dispersed them to Epirus, Macedonia, and Hellas.

Why, then, did Kekaumenos identify the Vlachs with the Dacians and the Bessians? The Byzantine authors' love of the archaic is well-known. As previously mentioned, they often designated contemporary peoples by antique names, in most cases on the basis of the territory in which they were living or some ethnographical similarity between the different populations. In this respect, two contemporaries of Kekaumenos, Michael Psellos and Anna Komnena, founded a kind of literary custom, with the principle of not designating any contemporary people by its barbarian [contemporary] name.[30]

MEDIEVAL CHRONICLERS. THE RUSSIAN PRIMARY CHRONICLE. THE GESTA HUNGARORUM.

As already mentioned, although the written sources about the early medieval history of Southeastern Europe do offer researchers certain indications of the contemporary situation, they are frequently contradictory and confused in many areas, such as chronology and the designation of the names of individual peoples. This is repeatedly shown by critical analyses of the texts. Moreover, subjective factors, such as the historical biases of the chroniclers, make it even more difficult to arrive at a balanced and objective view. An investigation should also be made to determine whether the chroniclers wrote the texts themselves and, if so, to what extent they went back to earlier historical records or whether they relied on secondary sources.

The early historians, of course, had a propensity to distort their writings about the past by using contemporary facts and ideas. As classic examples, one may cite the *Gesta Hungarorum* and the *Russian Primary Chronicle*, which are, as the only written sources, extremely important for their commentaries about the ethnic and historic relationships of Southeastern Europe in the ninth and tenth centuries.[31] At the same time, however, they are responsible, through their inaccuracies, for the controversy between two neighboring peoples, the Romanians and Hungarians, over the meaning of "Roman" and "Vlach." An attempt will therefore be made to give as objective an analysis as possible of the problem. (It should be remembered that since these texts refer to the 9th - 10th centuries, thus at least five centuries after the Romans abandoned Dacia Traiana, they have no relevance for the question of Daco-Roman-Romanian continuity /see chapter IV/).

The *Russian Primary Chronicle*, which allegedly corroborates the *Gesta Hungarorum*, should be mentioned before a closer analysis of Anonymus's work. The *Russian Primary Chronicle*, formerly called

Nestor's Chronicle after one of its supposed compilers (died 1112), is called *Povest' vremenykh lyet* [Tale of Past Years][32] in Russian and was probably written by anonymous Russian monks in Kiev in the eleventh and early twelfth centuries. It deals chiefly with the founding of Russia and the deeds of its leaders until about 1110. The authors of the chronicle used various Greek, Bulgarian, Russian, and other sources as well as oral information. It contains 93 chapters; the Romanian translation[33] is 203 pages. A short passage in this chronicle mentions Slavs, Vlachs, and Hungarians in the Carpathian Basin at the end of the ninth century:

> in 6396, 6397, 6398,   6400, 6401,   6403, 6404, 6405, and 6406 [888–897 A.D.] the Hungarians passed near Kiev, near the mountain that is still called Ugers Koie; and when they had reached the banks of the Dnieper, they set up their tents there, for they were nomads, as the Polovitsi still are today. Coming from the east, they marched in haste over the high mountains, which are called the mountains of the Ougri, and began to fight against the Volochi and the Slavs who inhabited these countries. The Slavs had originally lived there, and the Volochi had subdued the country of the Slavs. Later, however, the Hungarians drove out the Volochi, subdued the Slavs, and settled in their country. Since then, that region has been called Hungary.[34]

Transylvania is not mentioned in this text, a fact that makes any conclusions about this territory only hypothetical. Consequently, the *Russian Primary Chronicle* cannot confirm anything the author of the *Gesta Hungarorum* wrote about Transylvania.

The beginning of the Hungarian chronicles dates to the second half of the eleventh century. The first, early chronicle, the *Gesta Ungarorum*, from the time of Saint Ladislaus 1040–1095 in its original form, has not been preserved but was continued in the twelfth century. An anonymous chronicler used the early chronicle in writing his own *Gesta Hungarorum*, which dealt with the early history of the Hungarians, especially the conquest.[35] Research has determined that the anonymous author, Master P. (P [etrus] Dictus Magister), was the notary of King Bela III (reigned from 1173 to 1196) and that the work was written in about 1200.[36]

The Hungarian historian György Györffy[37] has listed the main works on this subject, the first of which was published in 1802.[38] Although the text was written in Latin, it contains some isolated Hungarian words with certain archaic characteristics (especially final vowels) that began to disappear in the twelfth century. They were still found in the Hungarian words of the *Regestrum Varadiensis* (1208–

1235) but disappeared completely by the second half of the thirteenth century.

Györffy collected the names of the small localities, estates, rivers, and so forth, that are mentioned in Anonymus's work and marked them on a map. Most of them are in the region of Buda and along the middle course of the Tisza River. A few appear along the Vág River in northwestern Hungary, in Transylvania, in the region of Kolozsvár (Cluj), and in the Banat. He pointed out that an awareness of small, insignificant geographical names generally indicates a more thorough knowledge of the area in question than would the names of large rivers and places that could be known to people who never even lived in those areas. The area around Buda, as Györffy's map testifies, was one of the regions the author of the *Gesta Hungarorum* (*Gesta*)[39] knew best and where he might well have lived. These and certain other circumstances brought Györffy to the conclusion that the *Gesta* was written by Peter (*Petrus*), a high priest in Buda and a former notary of King Bela III.[40] This is now considered the most probable hypothesis about the identity of the anonymous notary.

A Summary of the Gesta Hungarorum

In the first sentence of the prologue, the author refers to himself—*P. dictus magister ac quondam bone memorie gloriosissimi Bele regis Hungariae notarius . . .* [and] then writes about his schools where he became fond of the history of Troy and Greece as well as the works of Dares Phrygius, works that prompted him to write "the genealogy of the Hungarian Kings and noblemen" and describe their wandering from Scythia to Hungary. The first chapter gives the description of Scythia,[41] largely taken verbatim from *Exordia Scythica* [whose author took it] from a work by Justinus. In the second chapter the author explains that the name *Hungari* [came] from the place name of *Hunguar* (Ungvar). The third to sixth chapters relate the election in Scythia of Álmos as a leader. The seventh through eleventh chapters describe the wandering of the Hungarians from Scythia to Pannonia.[42] According to the author, the Hungarians crossed the Volga (Ethyl, the old Hungarian name) and the province of Suzdal (*in Rusciam, que Susudal dicitur*) and arrived at the town of Kiev (*ad civitatem Kyeu*) where seven Cuman leaders (*VII duces Cumanorum*) and their peoples joined the Hungarians; and the Russian leaders (*duces Ruthenorum*) committed themselves to pay an annual tribute of 10,000 Marks. From there, they marched to the town of Vlagyimir (*ad civitatem Lodomer*) and then to Galicia (*in Galiciam*). The chiefs of Vlagyimir and Galicia opened the gates of their towns to the Hungarians, honored their leader Álmos with a very precious gift, and asked the Hungarians to move on to Pannonia, describing the country and its habitants. The twelfth and the thirteenth chapters relate the crossing of the Carpathian Mountains (*per silvam Houos*) and the occupation of Ungvár; the fourteenth through eighteenth chapters describe the occupation of the region between the Tisza River and the Tátra Mountains (*mons Turtur*); and the nineteenth through twenty-third chapters concern the military operations against Menumorout, who reigned over the Chazars (*populus Cozar*) in a country situated between the Tisza and Maros rivers. Chapters twenty-four through twenty-seven, inserted later, interrupt this narrative to describe the occupation of Transylvania where the Vlach leader Gelou reigned (*dux Blacorum*). Chapters twenty-eight and twenty-nine return to the military occupation of the territory between the Tisza and Nyitra rivers, most of which was ruled by the Czech leader Zubur with a small part under the Bulgarian Salan, a vassal of Byzantium. The occupation of Salan's province between the Danube and Tisza rivers is covered in chapters thirty-eight through forty-one, while the forty-second and forty-third narrate the conquest of Dalmatia, Croatia, and the area around Zagreb. In chapters forty-four and forty-five the country of Glad between the Maros and Danube rivers is conquered, and a military expedition is made in the Balkans. Chapters forty-six through fifty-two deal with the conquest of Pannonia, which until then was dominated by the Romans, as well as the conclusion of the military campaign against Menumorout. Chapters fifty-three through fifty-six are taken partly from the annals of Regino and describe the "wandering" military expeditions in the West during the time of Crown Prince Zulta. The fifty-seventh and last chapter describes the establishment of Hungary's frontiers and settlement of foreign peoples there in the tenth century.[43]

The author of the *Gesta* rejected the oral tradition, declaring in the preface: "It would be unfortunate for the noble Hungarian people to hear about their origins and some of their heroic deeds from the false tales of peasants or from the chattering songs of the minstrels. The Hungarian people will now hear the truth from reliable written descriptions and with a clear interpretation of the historical works, as is proper for noblemen."[44] One of these historical writings, *De excidio Troiae historia* by Dares Phrygius, was mentioned in the preface and was the author's model. He took several passages verbatim from this text as well as from another work by the same author, *Gesta Alexandri Magni*. He also borrowed several sections from the annals of Abbot Regino (d. 915). Most of chapter 1 (*De Scythia*) is taken from *Exordia Scythica*, a seventh century text based on the work of Justinus (second century). Some expressions were borrowed from the Bible and others from *Etymologiarum libri* by Isidorus Hispalensis and *Rationes dictanti prosaice* by Hugo Bononiensis. The anonymous Notary also used, as previously mentioned, the first early Hungarian chronicle, the *Gesta Ungarorum*, written at the turn of the twelfth century and known today only from later modified versions. This narrative is no longer considered to have been his main source, as had been thought earlier.[45] Similarities in style indicate that the Notary was well acquainted with the romantic Gesta literature that became fashionable in Western Europe, especially in England and France, in the twelfth century.

The Passages of the Gesta that Refer to Eastern Hungary and Transylvania

From chapter 11:

> The territory between the Tisza and the Igyfon Forest toward Transylvania and from the Morus[16] (Maros) River to the Zomus (Szamos) River was occupied by Duke Morout (Marót), whose grandson was called Mén-Marót by the Hungarians because he had several wives.[47] This territory was inhabited by a people called Cozar (Kozár).

From chapter 19:

> The Hungarian leader, Árpád, sends messengers to Menumorout in Bihar Castle and asks him to cede the territory between the Zomus (Szamos) River and the Mezes (Meszes) Mountains.

From chapter 20:

> Menumorout refuses, referring to his lord, the Byzantine Emperor, who supports him. Árpád therefore attacks and occupies his country. From that day on, all the places on which chief Álmos and his son Árpád had walked with their noblemen were owned by their descendants and are owned by them until this day [p. 99].[48]

From chapter 21:

> Szabolcs and Tas then went to the castle of Zotmar (Szatmár). They won a victory after three days of siege and battle. On the fourth day, they entered the castle and bound all of Menumorout's warriors that they found there and put them into dreadful dungeons, taking the sons of the inhabitants as hostages. They left the castle full of warriors, and they themselves departed for the Mezes (Meszes) Gate (*ad portas Mezesinas*) [pp. 99–100].

From chapter 22: The Nyr (Nyír):

Tétény and his son Horka riding through the area of the Nyr (Nyír), subdued a large number of people in the region between the forests of the Nyír and the Umosoer (Omsóér). In this way they reached Zyloc (Zilah); and no one attacked them, because Duke Menumorout and his people did not dare fight them but had started to guard the Cris (Körös) River. Then Tétény and his son Horka departed from Zilah and reached the region of the Meszes (*in partes Mezesinas*), where they met with Szabolcs and Tas. They were very glad to see each other again and prepared a feast, at which each of them boasted of his victory. In the morning, Szabolcs, Tas, and Tétény held a council and decided that the frontier of their country would be at the Meszes Gate. Thus, the inhabitants of the area built, upon orders, gates of stone, and erected, from felled trees, great boundary-dams at the frontier of the country [p. 100].

In chapters 51 and 52:

The story is told once again but in a somewhat different way: When Menumorout was attacked by the Hungarians, he fled from his Bihar Castle to the forests. The castle was occupied after 13 days of siege. Menumorout sent messengers to Árpád to tell him that he, Menumorout, who had earlier declined "with a Bulgarian heart" (*bulgarico corde*) to yield any part of his territory, now offered Árpád the whole country plus his daughter in marriage to Árpád's son, Zolta. Árpád accepted this and ordered that "Menumorout have the Castle of Bihar" [p. 126]. Menumorout died two years later without a son, leaving his country to his son-in-law, Zolta.

About Duke Glad and his territory (From chapter 11):

Finally, with the help of the Cumans, the territory between the Maros River and the Castle of Orsova was occupied, by a duke named Glad (Galád), who came from the Castle of Vidin. His descendent was Ohtum (Ajtony) who much later, in the time of King St. Stephen, was killed by Sunad (Csanád), the son of Dobuca (Doboka), the cousin of the king, because he had defied him in many ways. In exchange for Csanád's help, the king gave him a wife and the Castle of Ajtony with all its dependencies, according to the custom of good lords of providing gifts to their faithful followers. To this day the castle bears Csanád's name [pp. 89–90].

From chapter 44:

[The Hungarians] wanted to send an army against Duke Glad (Galád), who ruled over the territory between the Morus (Maros) River and the

tunc nimiam audita ... ... Gelu uiam est.
bonitate tre ille mifit legatof fuof ad ducem arpad ut
s licentiam daret ulf filuaf eundi s gelou ducem pug
nare. Dux li arpad unto sfiho uolumtatem tulucum lau
dauit. et ei licentiam ulf filuas eundi of gelou pugna
re ceffit. Hoc dum tulucum audiuiffet a legato. ipita
ut fe cu fuis militib. et dimiffis ibi fociis fuis egreffus
e. ulf filuas uerfuf orientem of gelou ducem blacop.
Gelou u dux ulf filuanus audiens aduentum el. congregauit
exercitum fuum et cepit uelociffimo curfu equare ducam ei
ut eum p portas mezefinas phiberet. Sed tulucum uno
die filuam pntfiens ad fluuium almas puenut. Tunc utq;
exercit ad muice puenerunt medio fluuio intiacente. Dux
uero gelou uolebat qd ibi eof phiberet cu fagitarius fuis.

Chapter 26 of Anonymus *Gesta Hungarorum*; from the facsimile edition
by Magyar Helikon, Budapest, 1975. - The original is found in the National
Széchényi Library, Budapest, under Cod. Lat. Medii Aevi 403.

English translation of the Latin text:

Tuhutum, having been informed of the good quality of the territory
(*Tuhutum audita bonitate terre illae*) sent messengers to duke Arpad and
asked for permission to go beyond the forests (*ultra siluas eundi*) to fight
duke Gelou. And duke Arpad held a council and favoured the intention of
Tuhutum and permitted for him to go beyond the forests (*ultra siluas
eundi*) and fight Gelou. When Tuhutum heard this from his messengers he
prepared himself together with his warriors and leaving his comrades
behind, he headed towards the east beyond the forests (*ultra siluas*)
against Gelou the blac duke. Gelou duke from (the territory) beyond the
forest (*Gelou dux ultra siluanus*) hearing his arrival, gathered his army
(*congregavit exercitum suum*) rode in a hurry to meet him and stop him
at the Mezes gates (*portas mezesinas*). But Tuhutum passed the forest in
one day and reached the river Almas (*fluvium almas*). The two armies
were there separated only by the river. Duke Gelou wanted, however, to
stop the Hungarians with his warriors armed with arrows in that place.

militib(us) suis c(on)donaui(n)t. D(um) eni(m) dix(isset) ali(u)d reg(n)i loc(u)m p(ro) m(i)
se(m) unu(m) (in) galicia habuisset. Tunc dix(it) galicie co(mi)t(i)q(ue) (con)soci(is)
sui(s) q(uod) fili(i) in (ob)sides positi erant sic alni(ri)u(m) ducem er suos
nobiles rogare ceperunt. ut ult(er)i(us) h(on)or(is) uersus occidentem
in t(er)ram pannonie descenderent. Dicebant eni(m) eis sic. q(uod) t(er)ra
illa nimis bona esset et ibi (con)fluerent nobilissimi fontes q(uod)
no(m)ia hec esse(n)t ut sup(ra) d(ic)tum(est). danubi(us). tyscia. Uag. oporis(us). c(ri)s(us)
temi(s). et ce(ter)i. q(uod) etiam p(ri)mo fuisset t(er)ra athile regis. Et mort(u)o
o illo p(re)occupassent romani principes t(er)ram pannonie usq(ue) ad
danubium. ii colloc(ass)ent pastores suos. Terra u(ero) que iacet
int(er) thisciam et danubiu(m) p(re)occupauisset s(ibi) Keani magni dux
bulgarie auus salani duci(s) usq(ue) ad (con)finiu(m) ruthenor(um) et
polonor(um). et fecisset ibi habitare sclauos et bulgaros.
Terram u(ero) que e(st) int(er) thisciam et siluam igfon. que iacet
ad erdeueln. a fluuio morus usq(ue) ad flumiu(m) zom(us). p(re)occu
pauisset s(ibi) dux morouc. cui(us) nepos di(ctus) e(st) ab hungaris me
numorout. eo q(uod) plures habebat amicas. et t(er)ram illam
habitarent gentes cozar. qui dicun(tur). Terram u(ero) que e(st)
a fluuio mors usq(ue) ad castrum v(r)scia. p(re)occupauissent
q(ui)dam dux no(m)e glad de bundyn castro egress(us) adiutorio cu
manor(um) ex cui(us) p(ro)genie ohtum fuit nat(us). que postea longo
post temp(or)e s(anc)ti regis stephani. Gunad fili(us) dobuca nepos re

Castle of Horom (Haram). . . . They stayed two weeks in the area of Böge, until they subdued all the population of that territory from the Maros River to the Temes (Temes) River, and took the peoples' sons as hostages. They then marched their army toward the Temes River and pitched camp at the Föveny ferry. When they tried to pass the Temes River, the duke of that country came against them. It was Glad (Galád), whose descendant is Ahtum (Ajtony), with a great army of cavalry and infantry, as well as with Cuman, Bulgarian, and Blach support (*adiutorio*). On the following day, the Hungarians defeated the enemy, killing many of them. In this battle, two Cumanian dukes and three Bulgarian leaders [kenez] died (*duo dyces cumanos et tres kenezi bulgaros*). The enemy duke, Glad, fled; but his army was dissolved as wax is by fire. After this triumph, Szovárd, Kadocsa, and Vajta went toward the Bulgarian frontier and pitched camp near the Panyóca River. As we said above, Duke Glad, fearful of the Hungarians, fled seeking refuge in the Castle of Keue (Keve). On the third day, Szovárd and Kadocsa, together with Vajta, who was the ancestor of the Baracska family, organized their army and laid siege to the Castle of Keve. When Glad, the leader of the enemy camp, saw this, he sent messengers seeking peace and surrendered the castle and gave gifts. From there, the victors went to the Castle of Orsova and occupied it, spending one month there [pp. 117–118].

Chapter 24: With regard to the territory beyond the forest:

Tuhutum, the father of Horca, found out from the inhabitants about the high quality of the territory beyond the forest (*bonitatem terre ultra siluane*), where some Vlach (named) Gelou ruled (*ubi gelou quidam blacus dominium tenebat*). Tuhutum was a smart man and began to long for the territory beyond the forest, to win it if possible for himself and his descendants with the kind help of his lord Arpad. In time this came to pass, and the territory beyond the forest (*terram ultra siluanam*) was held by the descendents of Tuhutum until the time of St. Stephen and, indeed, would have continued to be possessed by them if Gyla the Younger with his two sons, Buia and Bucna, had been willing to adopt the Christian faith and had not always acted against the will of the saint-king, as will be described later (p. 101).

From chapter 25–27:

The Hungarian leader Tétény sent a spy beyond the forest to report on the country he found there; it was rich in salt and gold and had many good rivers. "The inhabitants of that country are the most unworthy in the whole world. Because they are Vlachs and Slavs[49]". . . they have no other weapons than bows and arrows . . . "and also because the Cumans and the Pechenegs cause great damage to them" [p. 102]. "A fierce battle started, in which the soldiers of Gelou were defeated and many of them were killed or taken prisoner. When their leader Gelou saw this, he prepared, together with a few of his people, to flee in order to save his life. While fleeing in haste toward his castle near the Zomus (Szamos) River, however, he was pursued by warriors of Tétény and killed at the Copus (Kapus) River. When the inhabitants of the country saw the death of their lord, they wanted to make peace and chose Tétény, the father of Horka, as their leader. They confirmed their loyalty by an oath at a place named Esculeu (Esküllő); and from that day on, the place was called Esküllő, because they had sworn an oath there.[50] Tétény ruled that country in peace and good fortune, and his descendants kept it until the time of King St. Stephen. Tétény's son was Horka; Horka's sons were Gyula and Zombor. Gyula had two daughters: one was named Karold, the other Sarolt. Sarolt was the mother of King St. Stephen. Zombor's son was Gyula the Younger, the father of Bolya and Bonyha. In Gyula's time St. Stephen subdued the country beyond the forests. He bound Gyula and brought him to Hungary where kept him captive for the rest of his life, because he was proud of his faith and refused to become a Christian and did many other things against the will of King St. Stephen, even though he was related to [Stephen's] mother"[p. 103].

It must be pointed out that the anonymous notary of King Bela III, who wrote much later than the Russian compilers, had a very limited knowledge indeed about the Carpathian Basin. Written 300 years after the Hungarian conquest, Anonymus's narratives are, in many respects, of very questionable historical value, which not only has been noted by Hungarian scholars but is generally acknowledged in the international literature.[51] Anonymus was neither an eyewitness to nor a participant in the historical events that he described in the *Gesta Hungarorum*, and his sources did not include contemporary eyewitness accounts regarding the course of the Hungarian conquest. Instead, the observations of a Western chronicler, Regino, and the *Gesta Ungarorum* served as secondary sources. Two important events, for example, recorded by contemporary sources and related to military actions, were not mentioned at all by Anonymus: in 896 Emperor Arnulf appointed Braslav to defend Pannonia; and in 907 the Hungarians defeated the Bavarian army at Bretslavspurc, today Bratislava (Pozsony) in Slovakia. There are, however, a few correct elements in the narrative, such as most of the place names and the fact that the Hungarians conducted military raids in Western Europe and the Balkans, especially in the first half of the tenth century. The details Anonymus gave about these battles were not compatible with descriptions from other sources, and place names often were used merely to tell a story about someone of the same name who died at the place. The Hungarian leader Botond, for example, was mentioned in Byzantine sources in connection with raid against Byzantium in 958, while Anonymus placed him in the first years of the tenth century; and Lél and Bulcsu were killed, according to some sources,[52] in 955 at Augsburg, not in 913, after the Hungarian defeat at the Inn River, as Anonymus thought.

The Gesta did make mention of some historical figures who really existed, such as Prince Ahtum (Ajtony), who lived in the region of the lower Maros and Küküllő rivers, and Gyula (Djila or Djula) [the name means commander-in-chief], an Hungarian leader in southern Transylvania at the beginning of the eleventh century.[53] Ajtony (whose origin has not yet been clarified) was the lord of Marosvár [Latin: Morisena] Castle and adopted the Byzantine Christian religion in Vidin.[54]. On the other hand, contemporary records mention some twenty rulers and significant historical figures who played an important political role in the history of the ninth century; Anonymus is unacquainted with any of them.[55] Anonymus's biographical data about members of the Árpád dynasty are also fictional.[56] The individual who reworked the Hungarian Chronicle (Magyar Krónika) in the thirteenth century recorded, for instance, the settlement of the Huns in the present-day territory of Hungary as the first Hungarian conquest. The rest of the names found in the Gesta in connection with south-eastern Hungary were apparently not the names of real persons but were figures created by Anonymus for the purpose of his narrative.

At the end of the twelfth century, when the Gesta was written, King Emerich (1196–1204) was making many royal land grants to a new, foreign aristocracy.[57] King Bela's anonymous notary wrote his narrative also with the aim of defending the positions and rights of the landowners who had inherited their estates from the time of the conquest and the following century.

The notary took up the tradition about the fight between King St. Stephen and several powerful local Hungarian leaders, who resisted central rule and ofteri also Christianity. Their names were in many cases still borne by their descendants, the landowners of the notary's own time. They also knew about the castles and areas possessed by their ancestors but did not know what peoples their ancestors had had to fight with or the details of the conquest. Anonymus wrote a narrative to demonstrate the courage of the landowners' ancestors, and for this he needed fearless leaders whom he simply invented.

While the Hungarians were living north of the Black Sea, the Chozars and the Székelys joined them and followed them to the Carpathian Basin. These peoples then were settled in the region of

Nyitra (Slovakian Nitra) and Bihar, and their territories were ruled by the princes of the Árpád dynasty.[58] Furthermore, the *Gesta* noted that Zulta, the son of Árpád, received the territory of the Chozars, the Bihar region; but the name of Zulta's ancestor, defeated in the narrative by the Hungarians, was invented by the anonymous notary on the basis of the names Menrot and Morot, found in the Hungarian Chronicle of the eleventh century. Morot, according to this chronicle, was the leader the Hungarians met in Pannonia. This story was based on the tradition that Moravia, a country in the northwestern Carpathian Basin, was attacked by the Hungarians at the time of the conquest;[59] Marót is the old Hungarian designation for the Moravians. The notary did not, however, know about Moravia and placed the country of the invented leader in the region of Bihar because of the villages of Marót and Marótlaka.

King Saint Stephen (King from between 970 and 975 to 1038), who Christianized Hungary, subdued the Hungarian chief Gyula in Transylvania in 1002 and Ahtum (Ajtony) in the Banat several years later. Gyula and Ajtony, as mentioned previously, were known by Anonymus; but he constructed the names of their unknown ancestors whom the Hungarians defeated in the *Gesta* from place names in the areas in question: Glad, of Bulgarian origin from Galad (1332–1337: Galad; 1462: Galadmonostora), today Gilad, in the Banat; and Gelou (name of Turkish origin) from the name of the village Gyalu where, according to the *Gesta*, this imaginary leader was killed.[60].

The anonymous notary was very fond of inventing etymologies: there are twenty-one in the *Gesta Hungarorum*;[61] and they are often connected with an event described in the story, such as the death of the prince of the Czechs, Zubur. According to Anonymus, Zubur was killed on a mountain that was thereafter called Zubur (Zobor). There had, however, been a monastery on that mountain since the ninth century whose Slavic name [zɪborɪ] (*cf.*, modern Czech, Slovak, and Polish zbor) must have been connected with the name of the mountain.

It is important to note that also in the thirteenth century chronicle of Simon de Kéza (Kézai Simon), as in the *Gesta Ungarorum*, fictional battles, historical events, and people were often associated with place names. In his writings about the history of the Huns, Simon de Kéza first referred to Romans, Langobards, and Germans in Pannonia; but later, in his reports dealing with the period just before the Hungarian conquest, he wrote (probably under the influence of Anonymus) about Slavs (*Sclavis*), Greeks (*Graecis*), Germans (*Teutonicis*), Bulgarians (*Messianis*), and Vlachs (*Ulahis*) in Pannonia. It is well known that

Kézai did not differentiate between the *Romani* and *Teutonici* (Alamanni, Germanici).

Ethnical Criteria in the Gesta Hungarorum and the Russian Primary Chronicle with Special Reference to "Romans" (Romani) and "Blachii" (Vlachi or Voloch)

The first medieval chronicler to mention the name "Voloch" (Voloh) north of the Danube was the twelfth century anonymous Russian monk, who wrote the *Russian Primary Chronicle*. The first to use the form "Blachi" was Hungarian King Bela III's anonymous notary who wrote the *Gesta Hungarorum* at the end of the twelfth century. It has repeatedly been demonstrated that neither chronicle, even if it gives valuable data about the ethnic relationships in the ninth and tenth centuries, can be accepted as historical proof, especially 800 years after it was written. It is, moreover, also impossible to conclude, on the basis of the texts of the anonymous notary and the Russian chronicler, that there was a Romanian population in Transylvania or in the Banat at the time of the Hungarian conquest. In the first place, the anonymous notary did not use the word "Romanians," as Romanian historians maintain, but rather "Blachii," the ethnic significance of which will be discussed.

The population of the Bihar area was, according to *Gesta*, Chazar; Duke Menumorout who ruled there said about himself that he had "a Bulgarian heart." As already noted, his name was most probably constructed from the old Hungarian *morva* or *Marót*, the name for the Moravians. Another of the notary's inventions was in his description of the peoples found by the Hungarians upon their arrival in the Carpathian Basin. Contemporary sources recorded the presence of six different peoples: Avars, Danubian Slovenes, Moravians, Bavarian Franks, Bulgarians, and Gepidae.[62] Anonymus mentioned *Sclauii* (which probably corresponds to the Slovenes), *Bulgarii* (Bulgarians), and *Blachii*; and spoke of Romans, Czechs (Boemy),[63] Greeks, Chazars, and Cumans. At the beginning of the tenth century, however, the Czechs had no contact with the Hungarians,[64] nor were such contacts developed until the eleventh and the twelfth centuries. They were quite intensive at the time of Anonymus. The Turkic-speaking Cumans, called Polovtsy by the Russians, lived in the time of the Hungarian conquest on the Pontic Steppe north of the Black Sea. They migrated westward in about 1050 and reached the plains east and south of the Carpathians (present-day Moldavia and Muntenia) in the second half of the twelfth century. From then until the mid-thirteenth century, these areas, which had belonged before to the Pechenegs, were called

Cumania. The Cumans helped the brothers Peter and Asên create the second Bulgarian Empire (1186–1393), fighting against Byzantium only a few years before Anonymus wrote his narrative. It is not surprising that a scribe rewriting a chronicle or translating foreign texts would change the ethnic names. It is documented that the conquering Hungarians fought the Bulgars in Transylvania, but it is not impossible to assume that Anonymus substituted or confused the Bulgars with the Vlachs. In the days of Anonymus the Vlachs were indeed in Transylvania while the Bulgars were no longer there.

As is known, there were Bulgars on the east side of the Tisza River at the time of the Hungarian conquest; and it is known that they fought the Magyars, although the extent of the fighting is unknown.[65] There is documentary evidence that the troops of the Danubian Bulgar King Simeon (reigned from 890 to 927) included, in addition to Greeks, Balkan Vlachs who fought against the Hungarian conquerors. This was recorded 300 years later by the anonymous notary who knew of this from oral traditions. The name Bulgar at that time encompassed the mixture of Bulgars, Slavs, Vlachs, and other groups that populated the Bulgarian state. The pertinent literature in English refers only to the Franks and the Pannonian Bulgars, who occupied the territory of modern Hungary after the end of the Avar domination (about 800) and at the time of the Hungarian conquest.

The designation "Voloh" (Volochi) appears three times in the *Russian Primary Chronicle*.[66] The early Slavic literature on the subject considered the "Volohs" of the *Russian Primary Chronicle* to be Celts or Roman legionaries from Dacia; the early Hungarian writings interpreted the name "Voloh" to be a reference mainly to the Romans but also to the Bulgarians, Romanians, and Getae. According to the Russian scholar A. Sahmatov, the term "Vlach" or "Voloch" is used by the Slavs to mean Roman, not just Italian.[67] According to the Hungarian scholar Mátyás Gyóni, the "Volochs" of the *Russian Primary Chronicle* were Franks,[68] a theory that is supported by the Slovene, D. Trstenjak, and by most Hungarian researchers.[69] Romanian historians, however, consider the "Volochs" to have been Romanians; this opinion is shared by Moldavian-born V. D. Koroljuk. After exhaustive research, the Hungarian Gyula Kristó determined that the most plausible historical explanation was that the "Volohs" of the *Russian Primary Chronicle* were a New Latin-speaking people of Western Europe, certainly the French, that is, the Franks of the ninth century.

The wide range of theories indicates the difficulties involved in identifying the "Volohs" of the *Russian Primary Chronicle*, a subject that will continue to spark controversy for a long time to come. It is, in fact, questionable whether an authoritative answer can be found owing to the inaccuracies, confused statements, and inventions of the medieval chroniclers. Ethnic names are used loosely in medieval sources and do not reveal a people's identity or history. The name Vlach, for example, is sometimes but not always used to indicate Romanian ethnic identity. Correct conclusions can only be reached with the help of philology and a careful study of the causes of historical events.

It is interesting to quote the opinion of the Romanian scholar and main proponent of the theory of Roman continuity north of the Danube, Constantin Daicoviciu: "I am convinced that the disputed passage from the pseudo-Nestor chronicle refers, in fact, to the Volochii of Pannonia [and not Transylvania], which [therefore] reveals a different situation."[70]

In the *Gesta Hungarorum* the anonymous notary referred to "Romans" (*Romani*) in three different periods:

1. Before the fifth century, that is, until Attila drove them out and began his reign in Pannonia;
2. From the fifth through the tenth centuries. As Álmos, the chief of the Hungarians, left Scythia, he was told by the Russian leaders that Pannonia was inhabited by Slavs, Bulgarians, and Blachs, and by shepherds of the Romans (*Sclaui, Bulgarii at Blachii ac pastores Romanorum*);
3. In Anonymus's own time. In connection with the pastures of the Romans, he wrote: "One could say in all fairness that Pannonia is the pasture land of the Romans, because right now the Romans are pasturing [their herds] from the goods [territory] of Hungary."

Contemporary Hungarian and, to some extent, international scholars consider that the designation "Roman" before the fifth century in Pannonia referred without doubt to the ancient Romans.[71] There are, however, sharply differing opinions about the identity of the "Romans" in Pannonia from the fifth through the tenth centuries. It is highly likely that the anonymous notary believed that the Romans of this period were, in fact, ancient Romans who had returned to Pannonia after the death of Attila. The anonymous notary's imagination doubtless played a role here, however, since the Hungarians found no Romans when they entered Pannonia.

The designation "Vlach" is referred by Anonymus in the *Gesta Hungarorum* as *Blacus* (plural *Blachii, Blasii, Blacorum*) and is associated with three events:

1. On the way to the Carpathian Basin the Hungarians were told by the Russian leaders that "Pannonia is inhabited by Slavs, Bulgarians, and Blachs, and by shepherds of the Romans";
2. A "Blach" by the name of Gelou was a ruler in Transylvania;
3. The conquering Hungarians went to battle with Glad (Galad, the ruler of the area between the Maros River and the lower Danube), who was "supported by the Cumans, Bulgarians, and Blachs."

An Analysis of the Treatment of the Gesta Hungarorum as an Historical Source by Modern Romanian Historians

During the last decades, Romanian historiographers have produced several surveys analyzing the text of the anonymous notary of King Bela III. Here, however, our discussion is limited to the interpretations from only a few Romanian historical works. The Romanians' main historical argument for the theory that their ancestors lived in Transylvania before the arrival of the Hungarians is the *Gesta Hungarorum* of Anonymus, supported by the chronicle of Simon de Kéza written about 1283.[72] The Romanian historians generally see in Anonymus's "Romani" the ancestors of the Romanians north of the Danube. A detailed analysis of the modern Romanian interpretation of Anonymus's *Gesta Hungarorum* will follow.

In *Istoria românilor* (1975) Constantin C. Giurescu refuted the assumption that mention of Vlachs in Transylvania in the early tenth century was only a transposition of circumstances of Anonymus's own time into the past. He explained this opinion by referring to the fact that Anonymus did not write in the *Gesta* about Saxons in Transylvania in the tenth century, in spite of their presence there in his own time. This comment, however, creates a serious chronological inconsistency: the settlement of the Germans in Transylvania, as is well known, was organized by the Hungarian King, started in the mid-twelfth century, and was in progress when Anonymus wrote his chronicle. Obviously, he could not have described the Saxons as having lived in Transylvania three centuries earlier. Giurescu tried to prove that even the Hungarian historian Bálint Hóman considered the narrative of the anonymous notary as a reliable source and that its mention of Vlachs in Transylvania at the beginning of the tenth century was supported by the *Russian Primary Chronicle*, which wrote about "Volohs ans Slavs" whom the Hungarians encountered in the Carpathian Basin.[73]

With regard to Homan's opinion about the reliability of the anonymous notary, one should consult the whole text[74] from which Giurescu only quotes a few words: "The *perfect elaboration* of the history of the Hungarian conquest *from the geographical and strategic points of view* proves the advanced nature of his *critical spirit,* his *systematic thinking* and *solid knowledge.*[75] It was, in fact, his independent criticism that caused his errors, the most characteristic of which was his inclination for ethnographical anachronisms. All thinking medieval authors were, in their descriptions of past ethnographical, political, and social situations and constitutions, influenced by the ethnographical, political, and social situations and the constitution of their own time, except when they relied upon contemporary written sources. Anonymus, too, fell into this error, explaining events and facts of "once upon a time" by transposing the situation of his own period into the past. He saw Cumans in the people of Ed and Edömen, because of the fact that Cumans were living in Ruthenia in his time. He identified the shepherds living in western Hungary under Frankish rule and the Pannonian Vlachs, called "Roman shepherds" by the eleventh century *Gesta* and "Danubian Volochs" by the eleventh century Russian chronicle, with the Vlach shepherds. He referred to the Moravian prince of the Slovenes in the region of Zobor as a Czech. He constructed the document about the oath of the Hungarians (*vérszerződés*), according to the custom of the contemporary royal court."

The comparison of Giurescu's quotations with the original text shows that the support he claimed from Hungarian historiography was quite spurious, that his argument with Hungarian historians about Anonymus's credibility was untenable, and that he considered this narrative of great importance, since he resorted to the most unscholarly methods to try to preserve its credibility.

Ironically, current Romanian historians often question the reliability of Anonymus and the other medieval sources they so often cite, when these sources do not support the desired conclusions. It is maintained, for example, that the reports of the Byzantine chronicler Kekaumenos are not reliable sources,[76] that Eutropius's writings about the evacuation from Dacia are not accurate, and that early written sources are in general scarce, incomplete, and at times contradictory.[77]

On the other hand, Romanian historians have drawn numerous conclusions from the *Gesta Hungarorum* that are not warranted by the text itself, before one even questions the author's credibility. All these conclusions are notable for their methodical deficiencies: there is an almost total absence of any rigorous, scholarly examination of the sources; instead of objective, linguistic arguments, they use unsubstantiated and arbitrary statements; and facts are taken out of context to defend preconceived theories.

Although it is asserted that Anonymus mentioned "three Romanian or Romanian-Slavic countries" called "voivodships,"[78] in only one of them were Romanians (Vlachs) actually mentioned. The *Gesta* clearly stated that the country of Menumorout was inhabited by Chozars (a Turkic people), with no mention whatsoever of Vlachs. The territory between the Maros River and Haram Castle was said to have been ruled by Glad, who came from Vidin; but the ethnic character of his people was not specified. Glad's army was described as "a great army of cavalry and infantry" supported by Cumans, Bulgarians, and Vlachs. Nothing in this text, however, would indicate that Vlachs were living in that territory; on the contrary, one may infer that the supporting troops came from abroad. The whole description, of course, bears all the marks of having been written at the end of the twelfth century, the time of the revolt of Bulgarian nobles in Byzantium in 1185 under the brothers Peter or Kalopetros (usually called Theodor) and Asên.[79] This revolt led to the foundation of the independent Second Bulgarian Empire (which lasted from 1186 to 1393) and was strongly supported by the Cumanians, who at that time lived north of the Danube and on the Pontic Steppes, and by the Vlachs of the Balkan Peninsula. It is noteworthy that at the end of the twelfth and beginning of the thirteenth centuries the Byzantine chroniclers reported an alliance of the Vlachs and Cumanians on the Balkan Peninsula against the Byzantine Empire and also mentioned Latin refugees in Pannonia (Hungary). Certainly, these reports were still fresh in Anonymus's mind and were obviously the inspiration for his narrative. The text of the anonymous notary thus mentioned the Vlachs as living in Transylvania in the areas southeast of the Meszes Mountains.

It is asserted that Anonymus claimed "the mass of the Hungarian tribes was forced to retreat mostly to Pannonia." This is not, however, found in the text; nor does it follow from it. Most of the time, Anonymus described successful offensive attacks, in which the ancestors of his contemporary Hungarian lords fought bravely and, in several cases, won the estates owned by these lords. Another example of warranted conclusions was the assumption of some "representative authority" in the territory of Gelou, on grounds of resistance to the Hungarians and because Tuhutum had "reached an agreement" with the population, "strengthened by an oath."

So far, two types of methodological mistakes in the above-mentioned treatises have been discussed: taking most of Anonymus's statements as confirmed facts and drawing conclusions, even from nonexistent statements, about the presence of Romanians in eastern and south-eastern Hungary in the tenth century. To these may be added the Romanian historiographers' erroneous assumption of the existence in that period of Romanian polities in other parts of Transylvania. All these errors have been exaggerated even more by Ştefan Pascu,[80] whose reasoning is reminiscent of the eighteenth century Transylvanian School, whose works were admittedly produced for use in a political struggle. Considering the scarcity of materials from the ninth through the twelfth centuries, it is clear that Pascu's work was of necessity based largely on hypotheses, supported by the *Gesta Hungarorum* and archaeological finds. Like many of his contemporaries in Romania, Pascu adapts his research to support an ideology. His analyses of the ethnic makeup of the population of Transylvania have been influenced by the theory of Romanism and continuity. He draws many conclusions from the narrative of Anonymus, describing (albeit with frequent reservations such as "possibly," "probably," or "one may presuppose") a Romanian Transylvania even to the smallest valleys. He enumerated more than 80 so-called "village communities"[81] that allegedly existed in the ninth and tenth centuries. The borders of the land ruled by Gelou were not described by Anonymus, but Pascu assumed that the northeastern frontiers might have been situated at the Meseş (Meszes) Mountains, because Gelou tried to oppose the Hungarians there. (Repeated attempts to locate the fortress of Gelou, prince of Vlachs and Slavs, in Gilău [Gyalu], Dăbîca [Doboka], and Cluj-Mănăştur [Kolozsmonostor, all in Cluj County] have been fruitless.) The unfamiliar reader would believe that in the period between the tenth and fourteenth centuries in Transylvania there was a continuous existence of Romanian villages, lead by dukes, such as Glad, Menumorout, Gelou, Negru Vodă, Dragoş, and Bogdan.[82] It is known, however, that Negru Vodă (or Radu Negru) was a figure in popular traditions in Fogaras (Făgăraş) County and is said to have been lived there in the thirteenth century,[83] while Dragoş and Bogdan were Romanian leaders (with names of Slavic origin) in Máramaros (Maramureş) in the mid-fourteenth century; Glad (Galád), as previously mentioned, was of Bulgarian origin in the vicinity of Temes (Timiş), where several localities in the Middle Ages already bore the name Galád and where even today there is a village called Gilád.[84] Two of the other names, Gelou and Menumorout, as stated above, were created by Anonymus; and the two others, Ahtum (Ajtony) and Gyla (Gyula), were Hungarian leaders (the name Gyula is of Turkish origin and that of Ahtum has not yet been clarified).

With respect to the castles mentioned by Anonymus and cited by Pascu (Bihar, Szatmár, Orsova, Haram, Keve, and Doboka), it has been proven that no wood-earthen fortifications were built in Transylvania between 650 and 950 and those built after that period were Hungarian.[85]

It is even strange that Pascu did not discuss the question of Anonymus's credibility inasmuch as he questioned his reliability elsewhere. He pointed out, for instance, that Anonymus confused the Pechenegs with the Cumans "because, when he wrote his *Gesta*, the Cumans were the dominant people on the Danube."[86] Moreover, Anonymus wrote about the *cnezes* of the Bulgarians, "but the Bulgarians never had cnezes."[87] Pascu also mentioned the medieval writers' habit of creating personal names out of existing place names[88] to be used for legendary figures in narratives, and he questioned the assertion of Anonymus (as well as of Simon Kézai) that the Székelys originated from the Huns.[89] These doubts alone would seem to warrant a thorough analysis of the *Gesta* before he would base so many assumptions on it.

One Romanian historiographer recently made an interesting analysis about those passages in the *Gesta Hungarorum* that probably refer to Romance populations: *pascua Romanorum, pastores Romanorum, Blachi,* and *Blasi.*[90] Based on rich references to both old and more recent literature, the author of the survey makes a long argument which is, however, not convincing and shows serious defects. He claims that starting in the second half of the nineteenth century political considerations prompted the severe criticism of Anonymus as an historical source.[91] On the other hand, however, the author himself had asserted that the idea of continuity became a basic political argument for the national movement of Romanians in Transylvania beginning at the end of the eighteenth century.[92] Under these circumstances, the narrative of Anonymus, considered as "one of the basic proofs in favor of continuity,"[93] must also have been regarded by the Romanian historiographers as an argument in a political struggle rather than a topic of objective historical investigation.

According to the current Romanian historiography, one may presume from the explanations given by Anonymus that there was a tradition in the eleventh to fourteenth centuries that the Romanians were the oldest population of Transylvania. This view, however, confronts its proponents with a dangerous corollary: if Romanian historians accept this conclusion from Anonymus's text, they must also accept Anonymus's statement that the Székelys were the successors of Attila, that is, the Huns, and that the Székelys were already on the territory before the arrival of the Hungarians.

Anonymus's *Gesta Hungarorum,* as already discussed, was an example of the romantic descriptions that became fashionable in Europe during the twelfth century. To glorify the Hungarians, the ancestors of the author's contemporary landholders, the ancient Hungarian nobility, are presented mainly in fierce battles with their victories over their enemies securing their lands. It would, therefore, not be unlikely that Anonymus, in search of enemies and not being familiar with the real ethnic situation of the Carpathian Basin three centuries before his own times, placed the Vlachs there for reasons of expedience.

There are several medieval texts in which "Romans," "shepherds of the Romans," and *Blachi* are mentioned as living in Pannonia[94] (and in several Balkan provinces). In the Middle Ages the designation "Blach" (Vlach) was not, like "Vlach" is today, a specific reference to the ancestors of the present-day Romanians. The Germanic tribes, for example, designated both the Celts and Romans as "Walh" (Vlachs), just as the Rhaeto-Romanic and Italian-speaking peoples were called "Walchen" by the Germans until modern times. From "Walach" came the Slavic name for the Romans, Vlach (plural Blasi, Vlasi; Russian Voloch), which was used by the Bohemians, Poles, and Slovenes until modern times to describe the Italians. The inhabitants of the Dalmatian cities and islands still use the Slavic Vlah for all the farmers and shepherds on the mainland, while in Croatia Vlach is used to describe a member of the Eastern Orthodox Church.

When the thirteenth century Hungarian chronicler Simon de Kéza refers to the "Blachs" who remained in Pannonia during the Hunnish domination, this cannot mean Romanians in the present sense of the word, because in the fifth century, the period of the Hunnish domination in Pannonia, one can only speak about Romans. The development of the Romance languages had scarcely started in that century. If the tradition has any real substance, it can only be interpreted as referring to a "Romanized population." Such populations are known to have existed in the Balkans, in Raetia, Noricum, and Pannonia even after the collapse of the Roman Empire.

It must be emphasized that in all these texts, the territory in which the Romanized population is described is always Pannonia and several Balkan provinces but never Dacia.[95] Anonymus also mentions only Pannonia and not Dacia in connection with a former Roman population. When writing about Transylvania, he merely mentions *"Blasi et Sclavi"* and *"quidam Blacus"* but does not connect these Vlachs with a Roman population. The tradition about Hungary (Pannonia) being the former "pastures of the Romans" is also mentioned in the Hungarian chronicles of the thirteenth and fourteenth centuries.[96]

According to certain Hungarian historians,[97] the Vlach and *Blacus* (Blak, Blacii) were two different peoples: the Vlachs were the ancestors of the Romanians, while the Blaks were a Turkic people from the Trans-Ural territory who probably lived at one time in symbiosis with the Onoguric Bulgars, with whom they shared a common culture. They eventually reached Transylvania, perhaps even together with the Onoguric Bulgarians, where they became assimilated with the Székelys.[98] Anonymus, as previously indicated, mentioned the Blaks twice in connection with the Bulgarians and once in connection with the Slavs. The plural of *Blacus* appears as both *Blachi* and *Blacci* (Blaks, as Blacki).[99] The first reference to the Blaks as *Blachi, Blaci,* or *Blacci* was in 1222 in the Hungarian charters: *terra Blacorum* was said to be in the area of Fogaras (Făgăraş).[100] Information is provided also by Simon Kézai on the Blaks as Blackis. A charter of Pope Honorius III mentions in 1222 *terra Blacorum,*[101] the area that the Blachi had occupied with the Pechenegs and that was under Bulgarian sovereignty at that time.

Place Names Mentioned by Anonymus in Transylvania and the Banat

If one were to assume, as contemporary Romanian historiographers do, that the territory between the Meszes Mountains and the sources of the Szamos River was inhabited by Romanians and Slavs in the ninth century and that the Hungarians systematically subdued them, toward the eleventh century, one would expect that the Hungarians would have borrowed place names from Romanian as is normal in such cases. While the place names are among the reliable elements of the *Gesta Hungarorum,* they do not reflect the situation in the tenth century but are taken rather from the time of Anonymus at the end of the twelfth century. Anonymus mentioned the names of three villages, six rivers, and a mountain in northwestern Transylvania and in the Banat. It would be reasonable to expect at least some of these names to be of Romanian origin, if the population of the area had really been Romanian before the Hungarian conquest. What, then, is the origin of these names?

Meszes Gate: from Hungarian *mész* "limestone," a common name for mountains; it was borrowed by the Romanian language as *Meseş.*
Almás River: from Hungarian *alma* "apple" + *s,* "something with apples"; borrowed by Romanian as *Almaş.*
Körös (Criş) River: the old Hungarian name *Kris* mentioned at the first time in 950 and later changed to Kërës, Körös; the Romanian name Criş was borrowed from Hungarian.
Morus (Maros) River: the Hungarian-Latin *Morisius, Morus, Mors, Maros* is attested for the twelfth to thirteenth century and was most probably adopted from the Slavic *Morisъ.*[102] The Romanian *Mureş* may be derived from the medieval Hungarian form *Maros.*

Zomus (Szamos) River: ancient names: Latin, *Samus*; Hungarian, *Szamos*; and Romanian, *Someş*. The Romanian form is not directly inherited from Latin because Latin *s* did not change to Romanian *ş*. The ancient river name *Zomus* was transferred to Hungarian most probably by the Slavs and to Romanian either by Hungarians or Slavs.

Temes River: the old Hungarian form *Timis* was replaced in the thirteenth century by *Temes*. The Romanian form *Timiş(ul)* was borrowed from the old Hungarian form.

Kapus River: from *kapu* "gate, door" + *s* "something with doors", borrowed by Romanian: *Căpuş* (*a* without stress changes to *ă* in Romanian borrowings from Hungarian).

Zyloc village: modern Hungarian *Zilah*. The origin of this name has not yet been established. It may derive from Slavic (*cf.*, the Ukrainian personal name *Zel'ak*).[103]

Esculeu (Eskütlő) village: from old Hungarian *es* + *küllő* "old" + "swallow"; German *Schwalbendorf*. The Romanian form is *Aşchileu*, evidently borrowed from Hungarian. There is another village with this name in the district of *Élesd (Aleşd)*, west of Nagyvárad (Oradea).

Gyalu village: from the Hungarian personal name *Gyeló, Gyaló*, documented in 1246 as *Golou*.[104] There are several villages with this name in other parts of Hungary. The Romanian *Gilău* is borrowed from Hungarian and is not a personal name in Romanian.

As already noted, nothing about these place names would indicate Romanian presence in that area at the time of the Hungarian conquest. On the contrary, the Romanians borrowed all the village names and nearly all of the river names from the Hungarians. Moreover, two of these names have sound patterns in Romanian that give some indication as to the period in which they were borrowed by the Romanians: *Căpuş* and *Zalău*. (The time of borrowing is, in this case, identical with the appearance of the first Romanians in the area.) In the *Gesta* the modern *Kapus* River is written *Copus*. In Hungarian, the vowel *o* changed to *a* during the twelfth to thirteenth century; by the mid-fourteenth century, this change was almost general. Since Hungarian *o* is generally preserved in Romanian borrowings from Hungarian but the Hungarian *a* changes (if unstressed) to *ă*, the form *Căpuş* must have derived from Hungarian *Kapus* after the *o>a* change or, in other words, after the thirteenth to fourteenth centuries.[105] The Romanian *Zalău* from Hungarian *Zilah* is also a later borrowing; in the *Gesta*, at the end of the twelfth century, this name ended in a consonant (*Zyloc*). In Romanian borrowings from Hungarian, *-k* was preserved: Hungarian *Széplak*>Romanian *Săplac*. At the time of borrowing, the consonant had already disappeared from the end of this name.

The place names that appear in the *Gesta* suggest that in the anonymous notary's time, northwestern Transylvania was inhabited by Hungarians and that the Romanians appeared there no earlier than in the thirteenth century. The number of place names in the *Gesta* is, of course, far too low to draw a definitive conclusion. A detailed survey of the problem of Transylvanian place names is given in chapter IV (Geographical names).

THE HUMANISTS

The Latinity of the Romanians

The Byzantine chronicles that mentioned the Vlachs were not generally known in Europe. Only beginning with the Humanist era (fourteenth to sixteenth centuries) and initially in connection with the defense of the Christian World against the Mohammedan Turks was more information spread about the Vlachs, who lived both north and south of the Danube in that era. Toward the end of the fourteenth century, the Turks expanded northward on the Balkan Peninsula; and the European powers, often under the leadership of the Pope, organized resistance against them. A lively diplomatic interchange resulted; and several of the high priests, diplomats, and statesmen that traveled to the Balkan Peninsula, the territory in immediate danger, later described their experiences. The introduction of printing in the late fifteenth century widened the distribution of their writings. One of the first of these travelers was Archbishop Ioannes de Sultanyeh, who described in 1404 the country of the Serbs and the Bulgarians and the population living in the same areas: *Ipsi ideo jactant se esse Romanos et patet in linguam quia ipsi locuntur quasi Romani.*[106] There is also a vague reference to a certain Roman emperor who once colonized the area. These references were all to the Vlachs south of the Danube; but Sultanyeh also described "Volaquia" defining its frontiers to the east, as "the great sea"; to the south, Constantinople; to the west, Albania; and to the north, "*Russiam sive Litfaniam*" ["Russia or Lithuania"]. The author thus knew about the Vlachs living south of the Danube as well as about those on the Wallachian Plains, but he was unable to correctly define these territories. When this treatise was written in 1404 there were already two Romanian principalities, Ţara Românească (Wallachia) and Moldavia, with a considerable population within their frontiers, although there were a great number of Vlachs still lilving in the central and southern part of the Balkans.

Many similar descriptions followed in the fifteenth century. The struggle against the Turks made it necessary to study the geography and the populations of the Balkan Peninsula, thus turning people's interest to the realities of their own time and own national history. The spirit of free inquiry following the Renaissance also changed the approach of scholars to the origins of contemporary peoples and their languages. In the same period, reaction was slowly emerging against the dominant scholastic way of thinking: While explanations had previously been sought on the basis of mythical personalities, the new approach was much more scientific. This new ideological and cultural movement of the fourteenth through the sixteenth centuries, which sought to draw on the spiritual traditions of classical times, was Humanism, a term derived from Cicero's *Humanitas*, meaning civilization as opposed to barbarism. A certain tendency toward nationalism often played a role. The Humanists claimed, for instance, the Illyrian was a Slavic language in order to explain the South Slavic (or Croatian) character of the area that had been populated by the Illyrians. The Humanists sought to return to the real values, to the best original Latin and Greek authors; and they regarded the literature of classical antiquity as the source of all "civilized" values and considered it their duty to analyze these texts critically. At the same time, interest also increased in research of modern languages, and many grammars were written.

It is obvious that the adherents of the Humanistic [classical] ideas were extremely interested in everything left by the great classical cultures: not only material vestiges, but perhaps even more in their living vestiges, such as peoples and languages with Latin origins. This explains the enthusiasm with which many Humanists described and commented on the discovery of the Romanian language as a descendant of Latin. For the Italians it must have been of particular interest.

The first Italian Humanist to write about the Roman origin of the Romanians was Poggio Bracciolini (1380–1459).[107] This author himself did not travel in areas inhabited by Vlachs but most probably received his information from other Italian travelers. He wrote about a colony "left by Trajan," "so they say," thus implying the continuous presence of the Vlachs in those areas since the time of Trajan. He did not give the details of this assumed continuity and resistance "among many barbarian peoples";[108] he merely quoted others.

The most important scholar to contribute insights about the Roman origin of the Romanians was Aeneas Sylvius Piccolomini (1405–1464), who was Pope Pius II for the last six years of his life. Interested in geography (his *Asia* was read by Christopher Columbus) and having written a history in a truly critical spirit,[109] Piccolomini tried to convince the European powers of the necessity of fighting against the Turks; and his preoccupation with this conflict led to interest in the Balkan Peninsula, which was directly threatened at that time by the expanding Turkish Empire. From Dominican and Franciscan missionaries, he received information about Southeastern Europe, thus also about the Vlachs. He could not, however, evade the etymologizing fervor of his time and took up the idea of *Vlachus* originating from a Roman general named *Flaccus*.[110] Piccolomini had probably read about the *Flaccus>Vlachus* etymology, which had been mentioned before by others including Ansbertus, the chronicler of the third Crusade.[111] It was characteristic of the Humanist period to try to explain the origins of nations and their languages by means of historical personalities and events. Flaccus, for example, was now considered to be the ancient father of the Vlachs (cf, Italus, Francus, Germanicus, Britannicus). The writings of Piccolomini were widely read and respected; his passage about Flaccus was still being quoted as late as the eighteenth century by many historians and geographers.[112]

The Athenian historian Laonikos Chalcocondylas wrote a contemporary history whose central theme was the growing power of the Turks and the fall of the Byzantine Empire. He mentioned the Vlachs, referring to those living north of the Danube as Dacians and those in the south as Vlachs. The designation "Dacians" is explained by the preference of Byzantine authors for the archaic.[113] Chalcocondylas knew that the Vlachs on the Balkan Peninsula and those north of the Danube, in Wallachia, were of common origin.[114]

Since the authors of the Renaissance aspired to the highest values of antique civilization, they also adopted the Greeks' view that language is a people's most relevant feature. They also reflected on the way the Romance population of the Vlachs had come to the areas of Southeastern Europe. One explanation was that they descended from general Flaccus, as described by Ovid (43 B.C. to 18 A.D.), but not all authors took such explanations for granted. Chalcocondylas, for example, showed signs of a more developed critical sense and stated that he had neither heard anything worthy of note about this question nor could comment on it.[115] This attitude suggests that there was no generally known popular tradition in the fifteenth century about how the Romanians had come to their lands.

Of all the Humanist authors, Antonio Bonfini (c. 1427–1502) wrote the most about the Romanians and their Roman origin. Living from 1486 to 1502 in the Hungarian royal court, he had a particular reason to occupy himself with the problem: the Hungarian King Matthias (Mátyás, 1443–1490) was partly of Vlach origin. Authors in the court of Matthias developed the theory that the king was of Roman origin, a descendant of a Roman named Valerius Volusus. Bonfini knew that the language of the Vlachs had a Latin character; and he also knew about the history of the Roman Empire, Trajan's wars with the Dacians, and the final occupation of Dacia.

Transylvanian German (Saxon) Historians of the Seventeenth to Eighteenth Centuries on the Origin of the Romanians

The scholar who had most influence on the Romanian chroniclers of the seventeenth century was a Transylvanian German with a Humanist education, Lorenz Töppelt (Laurentius Toppeltinus, 1641–1670), whose chief work, *Origines et occasus Transsylvanorum*, appeared in Lyon (Lugduni) in 1667. Widely known throughout Europe, it was the main source of the Moldavian chronicler Miron Costin and was also used by other Moldavian chroniclers. Toppeltinus, carefully studying the literature about the peoples of Transylvania, affirmed 1) the Roman origin of the Romanians (on the basis of their language, which he knew well), and 2) their continuity in Dacia. He does not seem to have considered the background of this assumption, although he was probably aware of the absence of historical mention about a Romanic population north of the Danube for about 900 years. That he was not purely scientific when affirming the Romanic origin and continuity of the Vlachs north of the Danube is shown by the fact that he consciously falsified an important source to suit his own views. The Roman chronicler Flavius Vopiscus wrote about Emperor Aurelian: *provinciam trans Danubium Daciam a Trajano constitutam, sublato exercitu et Provincialibus, reliquit.* When quoting this passage, Toppeltinus omitted the conjunction "*et*," altering the meaning of the sentence to say that Aurelian removed the army and left Dacia to the population. [116]

This distortion of a document by an otherwise erudite scholar is quite incomprehensible. It may have originated in his desire to prove the Dacian origin of the Transylvanian Germans, which was a popular thesis among their scholars of the seventeenth century. (It stems from the attempts of most European peoples of that time to show their antiquity.) The Transylvanian German scholars were anxious to prove that the Romanians were of purely Roman origin and had nothing to do with the Dacians, in order to affirm that the Dacians were their ancestors.

Another Transylvanian German historian, Johannes Tröster[117] (died 1670), endeavored to maintain that the name *Walache* (its equivalent in the Transylvanian German dialect was Blôch) derived from *Gallen* or *Wallen*, the etymology for the German word *Wellen* ("waves"). He argued that this could be explained by the fact that the Vlachs settled in the vicinity of the waves of the Danube. The dialectal word *Blôch*, Tröster said, derived from the Swedish *bölja*, meaning "billow, wave".

This exemplifies the fantastic etymologies characteristic of the period. Tröster, however, knew the Romanian language; and he put this knowledge to good use in his work. He was, in fact, the first Transylvanian German scholar to use Romanian words and expressions in his arguments to prove the Roman character of the language. In addition to their language, Tröster considered that the Romanians exhibited typically Roman traits in their customs, dress, dances, popular beliefs, and everyday life. He did not accept the derivation of Vlachus from the name of the Roman general Flaccus, because the general never passed the Danube to the territory north of the river.[118] The Transylvanian scholars of the Humanist tradition were typical of this period in general, but to a much lesser extent they also described what they knew from their own experiences.

The ideas of Toppeltinus (the Dacian origin of the Transylvanian Germans and the Latinity and continuity of the Romanians in Dacia) were taken up by several younger Transylvanian German scholars. George Haner (1672–1740), for example, considered that the Hungarian kings had not brought Germans to Transylvania but had only converted them from their Gothic Arianism to Roman Catholicism. Toppeltinus's influence on the chroniclers of Moldavia and Muntenia in the seventeenth and eighteenth centuries was of great historical significance.

The writings of the seventeenth century Transylvanian Germans (Saxons) about the area's ancient history caused a major sensation among the German-speaking peoples. An Austrian scholar of Swiss origin, Franz Joseph Sulzer,[119] contested the theory of Daco-Roman continuity, as did the Transylvanian Saxon Joseph Karl Eder,[120] the most important historian of his time. Johann Christian Engel, Michael Ballmann, and Carol Schuller, as well as the Hungarian Martin Bolla, joined in the opposition to the theory.

Sulzer argued that the lack of linguistic elements in Romanian from the period of the people's migration, which, after all, lasted seven hundred years, disproved the theory of continuity. Eder even went so far as to oppose the arguments pleading for equal rights that the Transylvanian Romanians had made in their petition (*Supplex Libellus Valachorum*) to Austrian Emperor Leopold II. The debate over Daco-Roman continuity north of the Danube was initially a matter between the Germans (Transylvanian Saxons) and the Romanians, reaching its heights in the eighteenth century. It was hundred years before Robert Roesler developed his theory, based on the assumptions of Sulzer, about Romanian ethnogenesis south of the Danube.[121]

As early as in the sixteenth century German Humanists had developed a theory about a Geto-Gothic origin of the Transylvanian Saxons, and this was expanded upon in the seventeenth century by the Transylvanian Saxons themselves.[122] This concept that the Transylvanian Germans were the descendants of the Getae and Goths continued until the eighteenth century.

THE MOLDAVIAN AND WALLACHIAN CHRONICLERS

The Origins and Development of the Idea of Roman Continuity North of the Danube

Grigore Ureche (c. 1590–1647) was the first chronicler of Romanian nationality to describe the Roman origin of the Romanians.[123] Born to a family of boyars (nobles), he studied in Poland, where he became acquainted with Humanist literature. He was above all interested in his own country, Moldavia, whose history he described in his chief work, *Letopisețul Țării Moldovei până la Aron Vodă (1359–1594)*, written between 1642 and 1647.[124] Ureche discussed at length the origin of the name Moldova and described, on the basis of an old Moldavian chronicle written by an unknown author before 1504, the founding of the Moldavian state by boyars from Máramaros (Maramureș). He occupied himself with the origin of the Moldavians but was also obliged to discuss the origins of the Romanians, whose unity he considered as fact, based on their common language. His considerable objectivity is shown also by his following statement: "Also our language is composed of many languages and our speech is mixed with that of our neighbours who are living around us, although we originate from Rome." Later historiographers, who selected material according to its usefulness in a political struggle, cut short (distorted) this statement quoting only the last words: "we originate from Rome" (*"de la Rîm ne tragem"*). This selective quotation did an injustice to Ureche, whose views about the Romanian language were more realistic and based on his own knowledge and did not try to conceal the many non-Latin elements of Romanian. Ureche knew from his Humanist sources about the Latin character of the Romanian language but did not consider this to be of the same importance as did later Romanian chroniclers.

Miron Costin (1633–1691), who continued Ureche's work, also came from a family of boyars. His father was forced to emigrate to Poland, where Costin spent the first 18 years of his life. His sources were the Polish and Hungarian Humanists, as well as Transylvanian German scholars, the most significant of whom was Toppeltinus, whose *Origines et occasus Transsylvanorum* he translated. It was here that Costin read about the Roman origin of the Vlachs and about Emperor Trajan, which was certainly a great revelation to him.[125] According to modern Romanian historians, Toppeltinus's work was Costin's most important source. Costin himself referred to authors from Hungary "who knew about the colonists of Trajan and wrote about them."[126]

Involved in the political struggles of his time, Costin was the first Moldavian politician to exploit the idea of a Roman origin as a political argument.[127] His most significant achievement was, however, the creation of the basis of a Romanian national consciousness, through the development of the following theories: The Romanian language and, consequently, the Romanian people were of Latin (Roman) origin; they were of purely Roman origin, without admixture from other peoples; and they were the descendants of Emperor Trajan's soldiers and colonists and had been living in the former province of Dacia Traiana ever since the time of Trajan.

Costin did not reflect much on the details and implications of the theory of continuous existence of the Romans in Dacia but considered this, as had his sources, a matter of fact that did not need to be proven. He knew, of course, very little about the real historical circumstances; he did not, for example, even have a correct idea about the extent of Dacia Trajana. Costin believed, as he had read in his sources, that the former Roman province north of the Danube was situated between the Dniester River and the Black Sea to the east, the Danube to the south, Pannonia (*i.e.*, Hungary) and Moravia to the west, and Podolia in Poland to the north.

The ideas initiated in the Romanian Principalities by Grigore Ureche and Miron Costin were best expressed by Dimitrie Cantemir (1673–1723).[128] Voivod of Moldavia in 1693 and in 1710 and 1711, he spent his last years in Russia as an emigrant (1711–1723). Cantemir was a famous European scholar and wrote several works, mostly historical and philosophical but also about religion, politics, and the arts. Two of Cantemir's works were of the utmost importance to the development of Romanian national consciousness: *Descriptio antiqui et hodierni status Moldaviae* (1719) and *Hronicul vechimei româno-moldo-vlahilor* (1719–1722),[129] based on the narratives of the Byzantine historian Niketas Choniates. The *Descriptio* was written for the Academy of Sciences in Berlin, of which the author became a member in 1714. In this work, Cantemir defended the theory that the Romanians originated from the Dacians and the Romans. He described the Moldavia of his own time, in which several different ethnic groups were living: Besides Moldavians, there are Greeks, Albanians, Serbians,

Bulgarians, Poles, Cozaks (Cazaci), Russians, Hungarians, Germans, Armenians, Jews, and the prolific Gypsies.[130]

One wonders why Cantemir, in contrast to his main source, Toppeltinus, defended the theory of the mixed Dacian and Roman origin of the Romanians. In any case, he changed his mind in his following work, *Hronicul*, in which he declared that the Romanians were of purely Roman origin, because the Dacians had disappeared from Dacia. The Romanian national sentiment was much stronger in *Hronicul* than in *Descriptio*.

Cantemir did not say anything new; his merit was that he adopted the ideas of Costin and gave them a more firm and concise expression. It is interesting that this reputed scholar sensed the danger of criticism by foreign scholars because of nationalist bias: "we [must] avoid arousing enmity among our neighbors, from becoming ridiculous, and to [keep them from] considering [that we] have been maddened by the love of our Fatherland and say[ing] that we have transgressed the frontiers of historical credibility."[131]

Cantemir also questioned why there was no historical mention of a Roman or Romanian population north of the Danube for about 900 years before the twelfth century, when the first Vlachs were described in Moldavia. His explanation reflected his deep conviction about Roman continuity in Dacia: he simply stated that events had not been recorded.[132] Evidently for the same reason and because of his lack of knowledge of basic historical facts, he believed that there had been a single Romanian state from the time of Trajan until 1274, when it was divided by the migrations of Radu Negru and Dragoş from Fogaras and Máramaros, respectively. Cantemir even explained the existence of Vlachs on the Balkan Peninsula south of the Danube by Trajan's colonization. Cantemir also described the Vlachs' crossing the Danube toward the north following their defeat by the Bulgarians and Latins (Romans) in 1236.

The Muntenian Chroniclers

The oldest Muntenian chronicle, attributed to Stoica Ludescu, preserved a very significant popular tradition among the Romanians that was, however, ignored or dismissed by later historians:[133] "They belonged to the Romanians who originated from the Romans and went to the north. Crossing the waters of the Danube, some settled at Turnu Severin; others, along the waters of the Olt, the Mureş, and the Tisza; and still others in Hungary, reaching as far as Maramureş.

Those who settled at Turnu Severin extended along the foot of the mountains to the waters of the Olt, [and] others wandered downward along the Danube, and thus all places having been filled by them, they came as far as the borders of Nicopolis."[134] Therefore, there was a tradition among the Romanian people in the sixteenth century about a migration of their ancestors toward the North, most of which took place three to four centuries earlier. Although this does not in itself prove the migration, as no popular belief can prove anything in history, it is important to point out its existence. It is unfortunate that so much effort has been spent searching for evidence of the Romanian popular tradition about a Latin origin, while the tradition about the northward migrations from Bulgaria has been neglected.[135]

With Constantin Cantacuzino (c. 1640–1714) historiography in Wallachia (the present-day Muntenia) reached the level of that in Moldavia. Cantacuzino studied at Adrianopol, Constantinople, and Padua. He knew the chronicles of Ureche and Costin. In *Istoria Țării Românești 1290–1690 (Letopisețul Cantacuzinesc)*[136] he described the origin of the Romanians and their history up to the time of the Huns (the fourth century A.D.). His chief source was Toppeltinus; but he also used the works of Bonfinius, Carion, István Szamosközy, Aenas Sylvius Piccolomini, and others.

Cantacuzino followed his predecessors, with regard to the Roman origin of the Romanians and their continuous presence in Dacia Traiana. In contrast to Cantacuzino, however, Radu Popescu contested the continued presence of Romanians in Dacia Traiana in *Istoriile domnilor Țării Românești* (written between 1718 and 1729).

A general survey of seventeenth century Moldavian and Muntenian chroniclers shows that they relied largely upon the writings of Humanist scholars,[137] especially Toppeltinus, the Transylvanian German historiographer from Mediasch (Medgyes). From these scholars, the chroniclers of the Romanian Principalities took over the idea of the Roman origin of the Romanians and of their unity and continued existence in the former province of Dacia Traiana. One would expect that if there had indeed been a popular tradition among the Romanians about their Roman origin and about their continuity in Dacia (that is, a strong awareness of linguistic or ethnic ties), as claimed by modern Romanian historiographers,[138] these seventeenth century chroniclers would have recorded it. This is, however, not the case. The popular traditions or records from the older chronicles they mention tell us about the migration of some boyars from Transylvania (Máramaros and Fogaras) to Moldavia and Muntenia in the thirteenth and fourteenth centuries, respectively. There was also a tradition about the migration of Romanians northward across the Danube.

The Moldavian and Muntenian chroniclers followed their sources, the Humanist authors, also insofar as they were not particularly interested in religion. The Humanists wrote very little about religious problems, the history of the Church, and similar subjects. Although adherence to the Orthodox Church had been, since ancient times, the most important link among all Romanians, the Moldavian and Wallachian chroniclers paid little attention to it in their histories.[139]

The importance of the early chroniclers is that they laid the foundations of Romanian national sentiment, without, however, a political aim in their works: The Latin origin of the Romanian language; the Roman origin of the Romanians, and even the consciousness of geographical and historical unity. The national sentiments remained on the level of popular traditions. These works had no immediate effect; they were unknown except to a very restricted circle of educated boyars in Moldavia and Wallachia. At the end of the eighteenth century the panorthodox awareness of the high-ranking clergy in the Danubian Principalities was stronger than their consciousness of linguistic or ethnic ties. The Latin origin of the Romanians was of no interest to the Orthodox Russians with whom Cantemir allied himself against the Turks, since their cultural relations were directed to Byzantine Orthodoxy. Quite different circumstances and a different political situation were needed for the ideas of Latinity and continuity to be taken up and used in actual politics, which happened in Transylvania in the eighteenth century.

THE ROOTS OF THE ROMANIAN NATIONAL AWAKENING

At the turn of the seventeenth century the social order of Transylvania was a feudal one, with the Hungarian nobles, the Székelys (Szekler), and the Germans (Saxons) constituting three "nations," mostly in the social and political senses of the word. Those Hungarians, Székelys, and Saxons who did not belong to the nobility were outside the privileged classes, as were the Romanian peasants, most of whom were serfs and did not make up a "nation" but were simply "tolerated." The official classification of the Transylvanian Romanians as "tolerated" was first codified in Transylvanian civil law in the *Approbatae Constitutiones Regni Transsylvaniae et Partium Hungariae eidem adnexae.* This collection of laws was approved by the Diet of Nagyvárad[140] in 1653 and was expanded in 1669 in the *Compilatae Constitutiones,* which also contained other resolutions of the diets from 1654 to 1669.

Suppression was social rather than national; the Romanians had the opportunity to enter the nobility. Until that era or somewhat later, they looked upon nobility as the best way to rise socially; and when they became noblemen, many of them also converted to Catholicism or Protestantism and merged into the Hungarian nobility. This situation resulted in the almost total lack of a Romanian noble class in Transylvania. Attempts made by Protestants during the sixteenth century to convert the Orthodox Romanians of Transylvania were largely unsuccessful. Their chief cultural institution was the Orthodox Church. There was no Romanian intellectual class in Transylvania in that period; indeed, with the exception of Brassó (Braşov), there were no permanent Romanian schools until the end of the seventeenth century. Parish priests received their education in monasteries or from their fathers and many of them could read but not write. They often worked together with their parishioners in the fields in order to support themselves.[141] This situation had a decisive influence upon the Romanian national movement throughout the eighteenth and nineteenth centuries. Generations of intellectuals were priests or the sons of priests.[142]

The three constitutional "nations" of Transylvania with their established rights were the major obstacle to Vienna's attempts to extend its power. It was not a problem of constitutional, administrative, or social jurisdiction but rather of religion. It is relevant to note that a large share of the Hungarians and the Székelys were Protestant (Reformed [Calvinist] and Unitarian), and the Germans were chiefly Lutheran. The Protestant Churches held considerable power. Throughout most of the eighteenth century the Hapsburgs used more or less violent methods to further Catholicism and drive back the Protestant Churches, which were the leading social element in Transylvania. The Hapsburgs, in their attempts to strengthen absolute central control over local government, felt that it was necessary to increase the power of the Catholic Church, believing, as they did, that the people should adhere to the same religion as the ruler (*"cuius regio eius religio"*). In a drive that could be called a "late Counter Reformation," the Protestant Churches were attacked in different ways with the aim of decreasing their influence and membership. The biggest gains for Catholicism could be made, however, by converting the Orthodox Romanians. Vienna hoped, on the one hand, to increase its power in this way at the expense of the other nations, especially the Hungarians, and, on the other hand, to make the Romanians their allies in the struggle against those in power. The large Romanian population in Transylvania was an important political factor for Vienna's centralist policies. The Romanians in Transylvania at the end of the seventeenth century accounted for about 40 percent of the total population. They increased during the next century, mainly because of the immigration of large numbers of Romanian peasants from the neighboring Romanian principalities of Moldavia and Muntenia (Wallachia), where they were exploited and suppressed by the Greek Phanariots[143] and the Romanian landlords.

The union between one faction of the Orthodox Church in Transylvania and Rome (the Uniate Church) was carried out in 1697 and 1698 by Bishop Teofil and Atanasie Anghel and 38 chief priests.[144] This was part of the Hapsburg dynasty's nationality policy of using the Romanians to increase its own power. The Romanian clergy were promised the same rights as those enjoyed by the Catholic clergy; and they hoped to improve their social and political situation, which was certainly the main reason for their accepting the union. The Orthodox peasants scarcely took notice of the change; but the Orthodox leader, Metropolitan Teofil of Gyulafehérvár (Alba Iulia), insisted that the Uniate clergy "be no longer merely tolerated but rather received as sons of the Fatherland."[145]

This was the Transylvanian Romanians' first political move,[146] several decades before the theory of the Roman origin of the Romanians was discovered by the Romanian intellectuals who appeared during the first half of the eighteenth century. The national movement of the Romanians in Transylvania did not begin with the belief in their Roman origin or in their continuity north of the Danube but was rather a part or a consequence of the union of the Orthodox Church and Rome, supported by Vienna and Rome (*Sacra Congregatio de Propaganda Fide*). The union with the Roman Catholic Church was, therefore, of utmost significance in making at least the leading stratum of Transylvanian Romanians aware of their supposed Roman origin.

In 1691 Emperor Leopold promulgated the First Leopoldine Diploma (*Diploma Leopoldinum*) which, in accordance with earlier promises, granted Uniate priests the same status as the Roman Catholic clergy and exempted them from compulsory labor and tithes to the landlord. In 1701 the so-called Second Leopoldine Diploma was issued in which the emperor ruled that all Romanians that accepted the union would be regarded as belonging to the Catholic Church and would no longer be merely "tolerated" ("*tolerati*") but would have all the rights of the other nations (Article 3). Although this was not put into practice, the Diploma's existence was of great significance, because it provided a legal basis for the Romanian national movement and for those struggling for the rights of the Romanians during the eighteenth century, especially Bishop Inochentie Micu-Klein (also Clain).

The union did not cause the Romanians to abandon their ancient Orthodox faith, which had, after all, supported national unity; nor did the emperor keep all his promises about the rights and status of Uniate priests. The most significant effect of this act was the opportunities it gave a large and ever increasing number of Romanian youngsters to receive a higher education.[147] Romanian schools were established, Balázsfalva (Blaj) became the spiritual center for Transylvanian Romanians, and at this time the first beginnings of a distinctly Romanian cultural life appeared.[148] Many Romanians were able to study at Hungarian middle schools and universities. Bishop Atanasie, Bishop Ioan Inochentie Micu-Klein, Gheorghe Şincai, Petru Maior, and many other representatives of the Romanian intellectual movement of the eighteenth century studied at Transylvanian Hungarian Jesuit and Protestant colleges in Kolozsvár, Gyulafehérvár, and other cities.[149] Many of them continued their studies at the universities of Nagyszombat (the present-day Slovakian Trnava) and Vienna, as well as in several Italian cities. At these schools, the Romanians learned Latin, which was, of course, a prerequisite for understanding the Humanist writings about the Latin origin of their own language.

The ideology that characterized Vienna's policy through most of the second part of the eighteenth century is generally called *Josephinism*:[150] a political-philosophical ideology and stateman's policy which, in the contradictory ethnic, social, and cultural conditions of Southeastern Europe, aimed at the creation of a centralized, authoritarian state in which the outdated social orders (*Stände*) would be abolished, thus contributing indirectly to the social evolution of those people of the monarchy who adhered to the Orthodox religion.[151]

One of the factors that contributed substantially to the rise of the Romanian population of Transylvania was the organization of the frontier guards (1762 to 1851).[152] Those Romanian peasants who were organized in these guards were exempted from their duties to the landlord, and they were given land and weapons. The Romanian villages were incorporated into the militarized border zone, which made possible the creation of a school system and the training of teachers. The Romanian officers of the border guards instilled in the villagers for the first time a sense of national identity. The organization of the border guards is therefore considered the first act of emancipation of the Romanians of Transylvania.[153] It was also the aim of the Viennese court to favor the non-noble groups and the socially underprivileged stratum of people in the territory of St. Stephen's crown and, in this way, to weaken the Hungarian feudalistic nobility and hasten the creation of the enlightened and centralized authoritarian state.[154]

In the 1760s, the *Tabulae continuae* were organized in Transylvania. These were courts before which even the peasant serfs had the right to petition. Moreover, complaints were allowed to be sent directly to Vienna, without going through the local administration.

Josephinism was not a nationalist ideology; on the contrary, the notion of "nation" had no place in its system. It may seem paradoxical that the reforms brought about by the domination of this ideology in Southeastern Europe contributed substantially to the emergence of nationalism. For the Romanians, the importance of Josephinism lay in the psychological effect it had of giving the Romanians a feeling of national identity (1744–1762), which found expression in the petition *Supplex Libellus Valachorum* of 1791–1792. In this petition they called for recognition of the historical primacy and continuity of the Romanians in Transylvania.[155] In 1792 the theory of the so-called Daco-Roman continuity was first propagated in the schools and by the Church; and in 1850 the Latin alphabet replaced the Cyrillic.[156]

The Development of the Theory of Continuity as a Political Tool

As previously stated, the national demands of the Transylvanian Romanians found strong support in the confessional motivated policies of the Hapsburg rulers as well as from a small part of the Uniate clergy. It should be mentioned that only a small group of priests, educators, and nobility—not the Romanian population in general—supported the movement for a national identity.

Ioan Inochentie Micu-Klein (1692–1768), a bishop from 1729 to 1744, was one of the important leaders of the new movement and a promoter of the Romanian demands for equal social and political rights. He was born near Nagyszeben (Sibiu/Hermannstadt), to a family of free peasants and studied at the Hungarian Jesuit gymnasium in Kolozsvár and at Nagyszombat University.

Bishop Micu-Klein based his legal claims on the Second Leopoldine Diploma. Initially, linguistic and cultural demands were voiced; they were followed by demands for national recognition and autonomy. Micu-Klein tried to convince his fellow Romanians that the best way to obtain equal rights with the other "nations" of Transylvania was to accept the union. At first, he fought mainly for the rights of the clergy, but later he extended his struggle to comprise all Romanians. In his conception, the continuity and priority of the Romanians in Transylvania was the most effective argument for his struggle. This idea was presumably strengthened by the reading of Dimitrie Cantemir's chronicle, a manuscript he bought in Vienna from a merchant who had brought it from St. Petersburg.[157] In about 1730 the manuscript of Dimitrie Cantemir (*Hronicul vechimei româno-moldo vlachilor*) as well as Costin's work became the foundation of the Romanian clergy's new view of history.[158]

As previously mentioned, in 1791 a petition was sent to Emperor Leopold II (1747–1792), the *Supplex Libellus Valachorum*,[159] which attempted to justify the Romanian national movement in Transylvania and the demands for social and political reforms. The Supplex was the first manifestation of Romanian national consciousness and the new historical ideology to be supported by Vienna, although it was only one of the results of the political movement in the 1780s. Its authors were a group of intellectuals of the Romanian clergy in Transylvania and the main figures of the so-called Transylvanian School, as well as other supporters in Vienna. One of the chief compilers was Josif Méhesy, the secretary of the Hungarian-Transylvanian court-chancellery. In contrast to the arguments used by Bishop Inochenţie Klein, the authors now had the opportunity to apply a new historical source, published in 1746, the *Gesta Hungarorum* of the anonymous notary of King Bela III. Referring to a few documents from the fourteenth and fifteenth centuries, it was argued that the Romanians at that time had had fully equal rights with other nations and that it was merely the "injustice of the times"[160] that deprived the people of them. Thus, they did not demand new rights but only asked for the reinstating of the ancient ones that they had before 1437. They alleged that the remarks about the Romanians only being tolerated or "admitted only for the public good" were not part of the law but had been inserted by compilers. The most important argument drawn from the present situation was the reference to the large numbers of the Romanians in Transylvania.[161] This was also used to gain support in Vienna. The idea of Daco-Roman continuity, which originated from the Humanist authors and the Moldavian and Muntenian chroniclers, was developed and expanded further by the proponents of the "Transylvanian School," who supported it by historical, linguistic, and ethnic arguments.

The Transylvanian School (Şcoala Ardeleană)

As previously noted, the national awakening began at the beginning of the eighteenth century as a general movement throughout Central Europe and aroused the interests of the Transylvanian Romanian intellectuals. The Latin origin of their language increased their national consciousness, and the so-called "Daco-Roman" theory became the focal point of their ideology. As a result of the Enlightenment, religion was replaced by the nation, as a leading concept in Europe; but this was not possible for the Romanians, who lacked a developed national culture. The Transylvanian School came into being under the influence of this new interest in history.

The most important leaders of this group, which consisted of Uniate priests, were Samuil Micu-Klein (also Clain, 1745–1806), Gheorghe Şincai (1754–1816), and Petru Maior (1756–1812).[162] They studied mostly at Hungarian schools in Transylvania and received their university education in Vienna and Rome. Samuil Micu-Klein, the son of a Uniate chief priest (protopope), one of the leaders of the Transylvanian School, was born near Hermannstadt (Nagyszeben/ Sibiu) in 1745. In 1762 he entered the Order of Saint Basil in Balázsfalva (Blaj) and spent six years at the Pazmaneum Institute in Vienna. At that time the ideas of the Enlightenment dominated the institute, and the influence of the Jesuits was decreasing. It was significant for a Romanian from Transylvania, while in Vienna, to hear the idea propagated of a national Church, as opposed to the doctrine of an all-powerful universal Catholic Church.

Micu-Klein spoke several languages and possessed a vast knowledge of historical works and records. One of his chief interests was the Romanian language; and in cooperation with Gheorghe Şincai he wrote the first Romanian grammar in the Latin alphabet: Elementa linguae daco-romanae sive valachicae (Vienna 1780). He also introduced his own etymological system of transcribing the sounds of Romanian into the Roman alphabet. The greatest preoccupation of Micu-Klein was with the history of the Romanian people, which he did not study for its own sake but in order to present historical arguments in favor of Romanian demands for equality with the three Transylvanian nations.[163] In his historical work written in Latin, De ortu, progressu, conversione Valachorum episcopis item archiepiscopis et metropolitis eorum (1774), Micu-Klein described the history of the Christian Church, as he saw it, in the territory of former Dacia Traiana. He affirmed that the Church, as well as the Romanians, had existed there without interruption since the time of Trajan.

Micu-Klein dealt with the origins and the history of the Romanians in several works: Historia daco-romanorum sive valachorum; Istoria şi lucrurile şi întîmplările românilor; Istoria românilor cu întrebări şi răspunsuri, and others.[164] The last work was written in the form of a catechism. The content of Micu-Klein's works is largely similar to that of other writers of the Transylvanian School; and like other leaders of the movement as well as later generations of Romanian historians, his purpose was to provide arguments in a political struggle, which consequently bound him to the theory of the Romanians' Roman character and their continuity in Dacia Traiana. He considered continuity an axiom that could not be questioned. As early as in the mid-1730s Bishop Micu-Klein used the ideas about the continuity of Moldavian Romanians and Vlachs, which had been formulated in good faith by the Moldavian chronicler Dimitrie Cantemir, as arguments in his political struggle with the ruling class.[165] As the theory of continuity became increasingly more remote from the requirements of scholarship the exploitation thereof for special purposes becomes ever more apparent.[166]

Although their Romance language was the main reason for considering the Romanians to be descendants of the Romans, historians with Humanistic traditions had already endeavored to find elements in Romanian folklore, customs, and habits that could have been of Roman origin. Micu-Klein claimed that many Romanian customs had been handed down from one generation to the next since the days of Dacia Traiana. He also believed in a theory that dates from the Humanist scholars and still appears in Romanian historical works: that the existence of certain words of Latin origin in the language of the Vlachs proved that they were acquainted with the meanings of the words as early as in Roman times and have continued to use them ever since *in Dacia.* He argued that such Romanian words as *biserică* ("church", from Latin *basilica*), *duminecă* ("Sunday) from Latin *dies dominica*), and *crăciun* ("Christmas" from Latin *creatio*)[167] proves that Christianity had existed in Dacia from its earliest time.

It is remarkable how many scholars have unquestioningly followed this way of reasoning, apparently ignoring the fact that people have always migrated to new territories, taking their language with them. This error is even more glaring because the members of the Transylvanian School were well aware that the Latin language had also been taken to Dacia by Roman soldiers, officials, and colonists in the second century A.D.

Gheorghe Şincai was born in Marosvásárhely (Tîrgu Mureş). He studied in his home town, the Jesuit Academy in Kolozsvár, and in Beszterce (Bistriţa), and then for several years in Rome, where he collected a vast number of books and manuscripts about the history of the Romanians. He also spent several years in Vienna together with Samuil Micu-Klein. In 1784, Şincai left the Church, and in 1804 he became proofreader of Romanian books for the University of Buda's press in Hungary. He spent his last years at the home of the Hungarian noble family Daniel Wass, in Cege (Ţaga).

Şincai's most celebrated work is *Hronica românilor şi a mai multor neamuri*, published posthumously (despite Maior's attempt to suppress it) in 1853, in which he wrote that the Vlachs lived not only north but also south of the Danube.[168]

Petru Maior was born in Marosvásárhely as the son of an Uniate chief priest of that town, and his three older brothers were also priests. He attended schools in his native town and in Kolozsvár and then joined the Balázsfalva (Blaj) monastery of the Holy Trinity and received a scholarship to Rome in 1774. In 1779 Maior studied canon law in Vienna and in 1780 became professor of logic and metaphysics in Balázsfalva. Like Şincai, he was appointed "censor et corrector valachicus" at the University press of Buda in 1809.

Maior's works were mainly historical and religious. The first, called *Procanon*, was a sharp criticism of the doctrine of Papal supremacy. He wrote his chief work, *Istoria pentru începutul românilor în Dacia*[169] in only a few years in Buda. First published in 1812 (a second edition in 1834), this work had an enormous impact upon several generations of Romanians, both laymen and historians. Maior's writings and especially his *Istoria* have become the Gospel of the younger generation[170] and still has a significant influence upon Romanian scholars; and its theses are generally recognized as valid, even today.[171]

Undoubtedly, Petru Maior's works are indispensable for a study of the development of modern Romanian historical thought. A brief description of his chief work will be given here, with most of the titles of his chapters and sections translated. Besides this survey of the whole work, certain parts will be discussed in some detail, with the purpose of giving an idea about the author's methods and the contents of his chief work.

Istoria pentru începutul românilor în Dacia contains 15 chapters, 1 through 11 dealing with the Romanians north of the Danube and 12 through 15 with those south of the Danube. Chapter I discussed the conquest of Dacia by the Romans: the Roman-Dacian wars before Trajan; Trajan's first Dacian war; Trajan's second Dacian war; the Roman extermination of the Dacians; the Roman colonization of Dacia; Maior claims that the Romans sent by Trajan to settle Dacia did not marry Dacian women. Chapter II covers the Romans in Dacia after the death of Emperor Trajan. (Special sections deal with the eras of the different emperors.) Chapter III describes the withdrawal of the Romans back across the Danube from Dacia during the reign of Aurelian. Ancient authors are quoted with regard to the Romans' withdrawal from Dacia. Maior points out that it would have been impossible for all the Romans to have left Dacia for Moesia in the time of Aurelian; and, in fact, most of them did not leave. He also quotes and analyzes the writings of Flavius Vopiscus, Rufus, and Eutropius about the Romans' crossing of the Danube. Chapter IV discusses the assumed Romans of Dacia from the time of Aurelian until the appearance of the Hungarians in the Carpathian Basin. Maior affirms that the Romans of Dacia were dominated consecutively by the Goths, the Huns, the Gepidae, and the Avars, but the Romanians (*românii*) remained in Dacia even after the time of Aurelian as a distinct population [*neam osebit*]. Chapter V deals with the appearance of the Hungarians in Transylvania and Pannonia. Maior asserts that the Notary of King Bela had excessive sympathy for the Hungarians. In chapter VI, the situation of the Romanians in Transylvania from the beginning of Tuhutum's rule is discussed as well as the eras of Tuhutum and King St. Stephen and the period after St. Stephen's death. Chapter VII covers the empires of Menumorout and Glad and their territories, according to Bela's Notary; the peoples in Pannonia at the time the Hungarians reached there; and the first and second Hungarian wars against Menumorout, who, it is alleged, was Romanian. Maior also claims that Glad, the duke of the Banat, was not Bulgarian. Sections 7 and 8 of Chapter VII deal with the Székelys (Szekler) and the Germans (Transylvanian Saxons), respectively. Chapter VIII makes the claim that the name of the Romans in Dacia was changed into *rumani, romîni,* and *rumuni,* and into *vlahi* and *valáhi.* Chapter IX discusses the origin of the names of some other peoples among whom the Romanians lived. Chapter X discusses and refutes the opinion of the Austrian scholar Joseph Sulzer that the Romanians came to Dacia across the Danube in the thirteenth century. Chapter XI refutes the claim by the Transylvanian Saxon scholar, Johann Christian Engel, that the Romanians came to Dacia across the Danube in the ninth century. Chapter XII deals with the history of the Romanians living beyond the Danube from the time of Aurelian to the coming of the Bulgarians to Moesia. Chapter XIII recounts the history of the Romanians beyond the Danube from the time the Bulgarians arrived in Moesia until the reign of the Greek Emperor Isaac II Anghelos (also Isaak II Angelos). Chapter XIV covers the history of the Romanians living beyond the Danube in the time of Emperor Isaac II Anghelos. Chapter XV analyzes the situation of the Romanians beyond the Danube after Isaac II Anghelos.

As previously stated, the Transylvanian Romanians found it urgently necessary in the eighteenth century to find proofs to justify their claims to social and political equality with the other peoples of Transylvania. Those rights had been denied to them and, from a legal standpoint, the Romanians did not constitute a "nation." This was due, on the one hand, to the feudal system and, on the other, to the cultural gap that separated the Romanians from the other Transylvanian peoples. In order to match the arguments of the other Transylvanian peoples, the Romanians had to put forth the same kinds of claims as their adversaries. Nothing could have been more suitable than to postulate their existence in Transylvania long before the Hungarians and the Germans entered the country, that is, the theory of their continued existence there since the time of Trajan.

The ideas of the Latinist movement (Transylvanian School) became successful tools in the political and national struggle and would be used for more than a century. The purpose of the authors was to demonstrate with their writings the legitimacy of the Romanians' claims, to enable the masses to understand their own interests, and, to a lesser degree, to contribute to the development of writing history. Polemical needs most often dictated the quality of arguments and the carefulness of research.[172] The political situation required a premise that could convince Romanians in different countries of their unity. This unity, determined by a common language of Roman origin, was strengthened by the theory of continuity in Dacia.[173] The fact that the authors' chief concerns were political ("to awaken, at all cost, the Romanian nation")[174] and ideological had, of course, a negative effect on the objectivity of their works. These works often arrive at conclusions that did not correspond to reality.[175]

With respect to the problems connected with the origin of the Romanians, Maior constructed a system of more or less plausible arguments, which led to the conclusion that because of the great hostility between the Roman conquerors and the Dacians, all Dacians fled the country. Maior maintained this because of the fierceness of Dacian opposition to the Romans and because of the Romans' custom of destroying their enemies (pp. 7–8).[176] Maior also purported that if any Dacian women remained in Dacia, the Romans did not marry them, because the wrath against the Romans there was nourished not only among the Dacian men but also among their women (p. 17).

Maior's Theories About the Presence of a Roman Population in Dacia After 275 A.D.

Maior, studying the historical sources, made a great effort to bridge over the gap between the abandonment of Trajan's Dacia by the Romans in 275 A.D. and the appearance of the Hungarians in the Carpathian Basin, a period nearly devoid of any reliable historical records. Beginning with the records concerning the Goths, Maior maintained that Dacia was reconquered by Constantine the Great (about 306–337), although, as is known, in Constantine's times merely a few bridgeheads and towns along the northern shore of the lower Danube, as well as the southern part of Oltenia, were under the domination of the Eastern Roman Empire.[177]

Maior discussed the Hunnish domination of Dacia and referred to reports by Priscus, a fifth century Byzantine historian who visited King Attila in his court and described his experiences. Someone named Zerhon Maurusius had amused the guests by mixing Hunnish, Gothic, and Ausonian words in his speech; and someone else at the table had spoken to Priscus in Latin (p. 65). From this report, Maior drew conclusions characteristic of his way of reasoning that the Huns knew the Latin and Gothic languages. Moreover, Maior quoted Otrococius, who "says that what Priscus called the language of the Ausonians was the Romanian language. It follows, therefore, that Attila and his lords knew Romanian." In Maior's view, "It is not surprizing that Attila and the other Huns knew Romanian, inasmuch as Attila and almost all the other Huns in that period were born and grew up in Dacia among Romanians. It also follows that in those times, a multitude of Romanians lived in Dacia and that there were many more Romanians than barbarians. . . . This is the case today in Transylvania, where the Romanians outnumber the Hungarians and the Saxons, who usually know the Romanian language, while there are very few Romanians who speak Hungarian and it is very surprising to find a Romanian who speaks the language of the Saxons." (pp 65–66)

Maior only wrote a few lines about the Gepidae and the Avars, who lived for several centuries in the Carpathian Basin. In 568 A.D. the Avars drove the Longobards out of Pannonia: All Avars no doubt, left Dacia, when they moved to Pannonia, because it was the custom of the barbarian peoples to live some time in a country and then, when they moved, for all to leave (p. 71). In Dacia, therefore, "only the Romans were left." (p. 71)

In the last section of the same chapter, Maior again took up the question of Roman continuity in Dacia, in answer to Johann Christian Engel, who claimed in *Apendicea* that even if a number of Romans had remained in Dacia Traiana after 275 A.D., it would be difficult to believe that they could have preserved their Latin identity and resisted assimilation with those numerous other peoples who were living there, while mixing with them.

Transylvania in the Tenth Century in Maior's Work

In chapter V Maior described at length the situation in Transylvania at the time of the Hungarian conquest (pp. 82–128) based almost entirely on the *Gesta Hungarorum* by King Bela's Notary. He considered most of the statements found in the *Gesta* to be reliable except that the writer had a special sympathy for the Hungarians and always described them as the victors.[178] Except for minor points, Maior took the *Gesta Hungarorum* very seriously, using it as the basis of hypothetical, detailed descriptions about the Romanians he assumed were living in Transylvania at that time.

According to the *Gesta*, assumed Maior, the "Vlachs and the Slavs" elected the Hungarian chief Tuhutum as their leader similar to the election of the Hungarian leaders Álmos and Árpád. It was only when King Stephen (later canonized) subdued Gyula at the beginning of the eleventh century that the Romanians in Transylvania lost their independence. Furthermore, Maior inferred that the Romanians had received the Hungarians in Transylvania of their own will (p. 129), with the purpose of getting help in defending the country against outside attacks. He also claimed that the followers of Menumorout were Romanians despite the Notary's text, which said they were Chazars (p. 143).

There can now be little doubt that most of Maior's conclusions were mere imaginatory. He was also not above altering texts or deliberately misinterpreting them. Maior's nationalism necessarily led him to extremes and, like the other representatives of the Transylvanian School, he was intolerant of all those in disagreement with the glorious descriptions of the Romanian people.

As previously stated, the seventeenth century Moldavian and Muntenian chroniclers did not occupy themselves seriously with the problem of the absence of historical records about a Roman population north of the Danube after 275 A.D. They simply assumed, on the basis of their Humanist sources, that the Romanians had developed in the former province of Dacia Traiana. To them this was the most logical explanation. Maior, however, studied several historical records in search of references to Romans or Romanians. Finding none, he claimed that certain other peoples referred to were actually Romanians. Several of Maior's errors have been refuted by modern Romanian historians, although there is no consistent, critical analysis of his entire text. Many of his assertions are defended even now, and his *Istoria* is still considered by some as an important historical treatise.

THE ROMANTIC WRITING OF HISTORY

The Rise of Modern Nationalism in Europe

The Enlightenment of the eighteenth century, which was initially rooted in Humanism, decisively changed the way of interpreting history: the nation became the focus of interest. At the beginning of the nineteenth century or, indeed, even in the last decades of the eighteenth century, the idea developed throughout Europe that the concept of the nation could only be defined by its history. Historiography, therefore, became a very important source of national consciousness, as did language, culture, and popular traditions. The notions of "chronological primacy," "historical rights," and "nation" became essential elements of writing history. During this period, which became known as the age of Romanticism, the medieval myths of previous times were abandoned, historical theses revised, and fabrications exposed. At the same time, however, a new concept was created in the search for a justification for national continuity. The main emphasis of nineteenth century Romanticism was on nationalism, which developed as means of filling the need for an emotional and ethical ideology based on such principles as "the unity of a people" and "national independence." The excesses of national fervor in the historical writings inevitably led to the rise of modern nationalism. Throughout Europe in the eighteenth and nineteenth centuries these trends in historiography prepared the way for national integration. Although the Romantics abandoned the medieval view of history, they turned to the legacy of national myths as a source of legitimacy for "national rights." It is therefore not surprising that "historical mythology" was revived: a writer with a vivid imagination could put together a glorious history outshining that of his adversaries. That was the best way for the peoples of Europe to become modern nations, that is, a group of people, usually speaking the same language and sharing a basic concept about their identity, origins, and place in history.

The later a nation established itself, the greater its emphasis on history, as can be seen in Central and Eastern Europe, where a whole new psychological situation was created at a relatively late date by the expulsion of the Turks. Nationalism, which had already declined in Western Europe, became a major movement in the East. Out of Romantic ideology grew the various forms of nationalism, which became increasing complicated and emotional in proportion to the number of ethnic groups involved. Not only the conflicts between the Western and Eastern (Byzantine) cultures but also those among the various ethnic groups created an almost unbridgeable gap. In contrast to the countries of Western Europe, the nationality question in the East was and has remained to the present a serious problem.

While in Western Europe nations had already been established as political units because of their linguistic and national unity, in Central Europe the creation of national states (Serbia, Romania, and Poland) was the primary task. The political factors involved in achieving this end made it necessary to maintain a nationalistic ideology. Ideas came to the fore that had long ceased to be of importance in Western Europe.

Romanian Nationalism

The first signs of Romanian nationalism appeared with the revolution of the Romanian Principalities under Tudor Vladimirescu in 1821, as a reaction to centuries of Turkish domination and to suppression and exploitation by the Phanariots.[179] Later, liberation from Russia and the union of the two principalities played an important role.[180] Nationalism in the principalities therefore lacked the elements of a Latin origin and a basic unity of Romanians that were central points of nationalism in Transylvania and had arisen from the Church union and the writings of the Transylvanian School in the eighteenth century. Another difference between Transylvania and the principalities is the fact that in Wallachia and Moldavia the main supporters of nationalism were the boyars, the upper aristocracy, while in Transylvania it was a small group of intellectuals. The boyars sought more freedom and through the influence of French ideas brought the Balkans into closer contact with Western Europe. Fundamental difference, not the least with regard to their views about social problems, continued to arise between the nationalist movements in Transylvania and in the Romanian Principalities.[181] The history of the Transylvanian Romanians in the eighteenth and first half of the nineteenth centuries clearly shows that their political aim was to obtain equal rights. The claim of modern Romanian historians that the revolts during this time (Horea, Cloşca, and Crişan, for example) were of both a social and a nationalist nature is clearly absurd. They were, in fact, strictly antifeudal and not patriotic movements. It is true, however, that from the middle of the nineteenth century nationalist-Romantic ideas served the cause of nationalist movements. In the second and third decades of the nineteenth century Romanian nationalism became a more popular phenomenon. The national movement in Wallachia took up from Romanian refugees the idea of Latinity and the claim that Romanians were the descendants of the Dacians and the Romans. While the idea of Daco-Roman continuity was not the direct source of Romanian nationalism, it had a strong influence and later became a determining factor in the development of the movement insofar as it gave it an ideological basis. In this way the irredentist ideas of the Transylvanian Romanians and the efforts to unite all territories inhabited by ethnic Romanians found support in the Romanian Principalities by the end of the nineteenth century.[182]

It can be concluded that from its very beginnings Romanian nationalism had a political character. Its ideology contains pronounced medieval aspects insofar as it uses "ancient origin" and the "ancient occupation of territory" as the source of so-called historical rights. Early historical and ethnogenetical suppositions became the fundamental support for modern Romanian consciousness.[183] This ideology has also acted as a kind of psychological compensation for the failures of national development and as a justification for the country's rights to the territories gained after World War I: Transylvania, Bessarabia, the Bucovina, the Banat, and Dobrudja.

The Beginnings of Modern Romanian Historiography

Romanian historiography dates back to the seventeenth and eighteenth centuries, the time of the Moldavian and Wallachian chronicles. Modern concepts in Romanian historiography became apparent at the end of the eighteenth century and in the first decades of the nineteenth century after the publication of works by the Transylvanian School and the systematization of the archives in the Romanian Principalities. Shortly thereafter, an intense period of writing history began, in the favorable climate after the union of the two principalities (1859). Bogdan Petriceicu Hasdeu (1838–1907) examined many historical documents and published critiques of them, and Ion Bogdan prepared a translation and critical edition of the Slav chronicles. The first compilation of Romanian history was written in this period by Alexandru D. Xenopol (1847–1920). The nationalistic ideology of the century in Europe required historical works that reflected a people's glorious past, a characteristic that is also present in Xenopol's works.

There was a reaction against this nationalist-romantic way of writing history toward the end of the nineteenth century.[184] Ion Bogdan, for example, defying the nationalistic sentiments, pointed out the weaknesses of past Romanian leaders as well as the foreign influences exerted on the Romanians by their neighbors. These authors did not, however, write syntheses. They realized that there had not been sufficient preparatory work, and for this reason their influence on Romanian historiography is not significant.

During the decades before the First World War and for a time after, Nicolae Iorga (1871–1940), a man of great imagination and enormous productivity, was Romania's chief historian. Several of his works were published in West European languages and had a lasting influence on European public opinion. During the time of Iorga, nationalistic ideology was predominant in Romanian historiography.[185]

As previously stated, the Romanian language, like historiography in the nineteenth century, became a source of national consciousness. There were sufficient data about the Romanian language by the end of the nineteenth century for some far-reaching conclusions to be made, and it is no coincidence that the most significant departure from the traditional ideology of national sentiments came in the field of linguistics. With new information about the Romanian Balkan dialects, Italian dialects, Albanian, and South Slavic languages, only a qualified scholar was needed to establish the origin of the Romanian language. This scholar was Ovid Densusianu (1873–1938), who, in addition to his great knowledge and ability to synthetize, also refused to be influenced by public opinion. These were the first signs of the differences of opinion between the historians and linguists that exist to this day.

Densusianu's *Histoire de la langue roumaine* (1901), the first scientific history of the Romanian language, was a revelation.[186] In the introduction to this work, the author gave a concise review of the state of research on the history of Romanian and pointed out the difficulties in writing a synthesis. One of these difficulties was the scarcity of preparatory work; and the other main obstacle, encountered by everyone who wanted to make an objective, scientific analysis, was the prevailing nationalistic bias, because of which the most extravagant theories had been proposed and defended with an ardor, that only could hinder scholarship.[187] Stating that acceptance of the Latin origin of the Romanian language had nothing to do with where it was formed, Densusianu pointed out that the question of continuity north of the Danube had above all a political significance and that political considerations had heated up the debates about this problem.[188] Densusianu noted that Bogdan Petriceicu Hasdeu, had also created hypotheses without a sound basis. Hasdeu had assumed, for example, the Dacian origin of a series of Romanian words and combined his theory with his ability to debate to make them sound convincing, often stating mere assumptions as fact.

It is obvious that in such an atmosphere, Densusianu could not hope to be understood and appreciated. In the preface, he stated that his work was meant for scholars with open minds, mostly foreign students of Romance languages, because "in several aspects our opinions differ from those current in Romania."[189] He noted that the "way in which we describe the formation of the Romanian language is not, in fact, what would satisfy the sensitivities of our fellow countrymen."[190] He warned his fellow Romanians to abandon outdated theories.[191]

With this work, the main problem of the origin of the Romanian language was clarified. This language contains vestiges from the time its speakers lived within the Roman Empire, in close contact with Italy and the Latin-speaking world. These characteristics appeared in Late Latin during the fourth through the seventh centuries A.D., thus, at a time when Dacia Traiana no longer belonged to the empire. The South Slavic influence shows signs of having reached the Romanians south of the Danube, indicating that they also lived there from the seventh to the twelfth centuries. These theories, well documented and presented in Densusianu's monumental work (the 1975 edition is 859 pages), also paved the way for historians, showing that the origins of the Romanian language were to be sought in the central parts of the Balkan Peninsula, south of the Danube and the Sava River.[192]

The Period Between the Two World Wars

After World War I ethnic Romanians were united into a unitary state. Obviously, this fulfillment of national goals must have had a great effect on the nationalist movement and ideology as well as on the writing of history. The younger generation of historians, however, was positively influenced by the new situation in that it endeavored to consider the national past in an objective manner. A similar goal was also set in the periodical *Revista Istorică Română*, which was founded in 1931 and edited by Constantin C. Giurescu, Gheorghe Brătianu, and Petre P. Panaitescu. First of all, Nicolae Iorga was criticized. In a brief survey published in several languages, Giurescu, after analyzing Iorga's work, came to the conclusion that Iorga had often made unsubstantiated statements, presented presuppositions as facts, had not taken the opinions of others into consideration, and had drawn unwarranted conclusions from isolated data.[193] Giurescu also pointed out the influence of foreign peoples on Romanian history, mentioning, among Western influences, also that of the Hungarians. The works produced by these young historians were based more on solid data than those by Iorga, although they did not abandon a certain national prejudice. This period did not, however, last long.

Traditional Romanian nationalism, supported by the Orthodox Church's domination over the spiritual life, encouraged an intolerant attitude toward non-Romanians as early as in the nineteenth century. An extremely nationalistic attitude appeared, especially among the Romanian middle classes and intellectuals at an early stage. Alexandru C. Cuza, a professor of political science at Iași University, preached anti-Semitism at the beginning of this century. He founded the National Democratic Party in 1909, adopting the swastica as its symbol. In the 1920s and 1930s Fascist ideas were being spread in Eastern Europe. Since these ideas originated in nationalism, the traditions of Romanian nationalism made them very easy to accept. The chief hallmark of the Romanian Fascist movement was the Romanian Legionary or Iron

Guard movement[194] started between 1920 and 1923 as a student organization, first in Iaşi, then in Czernowitz, Bucharest, and in Cluj (Kolozsvár) in Transylvania. Its leaders were Corneliu Zelea (Zelinsky) Codreanu (1899–1938) and Ion Mota. The first expression of this movement rooted in "Romanianism," a religious-mystical nationalism, is to be found in Codreanu's organization, the "Association of Christian Students," established in Iaşi in 1922. In 1923 Codreanu and Alexandru C. Cuza formed the right-wing, anti-Semitic, political party, the League of National Christian Defense (*Liga Apărării Naţionale Creştine*). In 1927 the first independent political organization of Codreanu's movement, the "Legion of the Archangel Michael" (*Legiunea Arhanghelului Mihail*), was established. Its meetings were proceded by Orthodox religious services, primarily because the Orthodox clergy were among the strongest supporters of Codreanu's movement. The activist political unit of this organization, with its nationalistic political program, was the *Garda de Fier* (Iron Guard). Its name was adopted in 1930. It was banned in 1933 by the government of Ion G. Duca but was soon re-established as a formal political party, headed by Codreanu, under the name of *Totul Pentru Ţară* (All for the Fatherland). Outlawed again by the royal dictatorship in 1938, the Iron Guard finally came to power in September 1940 with the establishment of the "National Legionary State," a fascist military dictatorship led jointly by General Ion Antonescu and Horia Sima, the head of the Guard. The Iron Guard, however, was liquidated by Antonescu in 1941 following an unsuccessful rebellion by the legionaries; and many of its leaders were executed.[195] In that manner they shared the fate of Corneliu Zelea Codreanu and his closest associates, who had themselves been executed in November 1938 on orders of King Carol II.

The Iron Guard was a typical populist, national fascist organization—ritualistic, Christian-Orthodox, idealistic and romantic in character, antidemocratic and anti-Western, aiming at the moral regeneration of the nation and directed against domestic corruption and foreign influence, with the "personal dedication and sacrifice . . . [of] young fanatics ready to kill and be killed."[196] Later, however, the Iron guard became a terrorist, racist, anti-Semitic, and antiminority (at first anti-Hungarian) mass movement. Its members were primarily of peasant origin and included numerous young intellectuals. In 1937 the total membership was at least 200,000 and probably significantly higher.[197] In the elections of 1937 the Iron Guard received 500,000 votes.[198]

The magazine *Gîndirea*, edited by Nichifor Crainic and published in Cluj from 1921 to 1940, was considered the spiritual guide of Romanian nationalism after 1920. With its two main ideas, the return to historical tradition (the legacy of the Church) and service to the Romanian people, it continued to some extent the traditions of the periodical *Semănătorul*.[199] Toward the end of the 1930s *Gîndirea* adopted the fascist ideology.

THE DOMINATION OF MARXIST IDEOLOGY

The Period After the Second World War

It is a well-known fact that changes in political systems must be evaluated in the light of the historiography of a particular period. After the occupation of Romania by the Soviet Army in the autumn of 1944, the country was gradually transformed into a socialist state. Instead of nationalism, proletarian internationalism was proclaimed. The leaders of the nationalistic movements and a part of the upper middle class either fled the country during the war or were imprisoned. It took several years to indoctrinate historians to the point that they were able to follow the new ideas; those who had been most active during the so-called "bourgeois" period were not allowed to publish their works in the first years of socialism. In this way, important historians of the interwar period, such as Nicolae Iorga, Petre P. Panaitescu, Constantin C. Giurescu, Aurelian Sacerdoțeanu, Ion Moga, and others, were silenced. Interest at that time was directed predominantly toward the immediate past. In a 1952 textbook of Romanian history, for example, the creation of the first Romanian social organizations in the fourteenth century was given only seven lines.[200] Similarly, the problem of the origins of the Romanian language and people was scarcely mentioned in historical treatises.

With the introduction of historical materialism, the Marxist dogmatic-schematic writing of history was initiated, reaching its peak in the Russocentric "Roller-Period" (1947–1954).[201] According to an official decision in 1954 (during the period of "Russification"), the letter â was completely dropped and was replaced by î. In 1963 some of the orthographic changes were revoked: The word România and all its cognates were again written with â.[202] The dogmatic theses of Soviet historiography were uncritically adopted by all the countries of Eastern Europe except Yugoslavia. Historical writings had a conceptional and methodical orientation that gave predominance to politics and ideology. Marxist clichés, platitudes, and methodological deficiencies gained the ascendary. Traditional nationalism was displaced by internationalism, which, however, was not devoid of definite national characteristics.

The dogmatic interpretation of history, introduced from abroad and imposed on Romania more or less artificially, had no real chance of changing the minds of historians and politicians. In *Istoria Republicii Populare Române*,[203] "bourgeoise historians," foreign as well as Romanian, were criticized; but instead of refuting errors and unfounded theories that had resulted from hypothesizing without material evidence, the criticism was aimed mainly at those who denied the theory of continuity. The official view, even then, was that a Romanized population had occupied Dacia Traiana and remained there through the centuries of the peoples' migration.[204]

Historical materialism and internationalism also provided an opportunity to establish cooperation in the field of historical research with neighboring countries. Such cooperation had been almost nonexistent during the "bourgeois" era; no real progress took place, however, in this area under socialism either. Until about 1960 the significance in Romanian history of the Slavs, especially of Russia, was stressed. In *Istoria României* (especially the first volume), for example, the role played by the ancient Slavs in the development of the "Daco-Romans" was considered very significant. It was necessary, for example, during the "Russification" of the Stalinist period to demonstrate the existence of Slavs in Transylvania through archaeological finds; "they had to be found."[205]

The Re-evaluation of Nationalism

As previously mentioned, the ideas of internationalism and historic materialism were not rooted in Romania; and the vigorous traditions of nationalism were revived through "de-Russification" after the withdrawal of Soviet troops from Romania (1958), a political and ideological turning point. Until the mid-1960s, a process was introduced in which the Romanian leaders abandoned internationalism step by step and changed to a national form (characteristic of the "bourgeois" era) of communism. This was partly a reaction to pressure from the Soviet Union and was also aimed at gaining some public support for the leadership.[206] Chauvinism, anti-Semitism, anti-Russian and anti-Hungarian attitudes, and excessive patriotism were integral parts of the new nationalism and were perhaps as important as social and economic reform.[207]

As a consequence of this new orientation, nationalism received increasing importance in the writing of history, and historians of the "bourgeois" period were increasingly given the opportunity of publishing their works. The first significant deviation from the ideology of the 1950s and from the influence of Soviet historiography came in the second volume (1962) of *Istoria României*. While the Moldavian Duke Stephen the Great (Ștefan cel Mare, 1457–1504), for example, was described in 1955 as a ruthless exploiter of the masses and his familial and political contacts with Kiev and Moscow were stressed, in volume II he was called a great defender of the freedom of Moldavia.[208] In the new volume, the Wallachian Prince, Michael the Brave (Mihail Viteazul, 1593–1601), was described as a hero who succeeded for the first time in uniting "the three Romanian countries"; and the peasant revolt in Transylvania (1599–1600) was said to have been strongly marked by Romanian discontent and solidarity with Romanians living outside the Carpathian region.[209] This exaggeration of the achievements of "heroic" historical figures, based on false analogies, has become characteristic of current Romanian historical writing. Michael the Brave, for example, is represented as having created the forerunner of Greater Romania by having "for the first time united all Romanian lands," even though the modern concept of the nation was unknown to him. The third volume of *Istoria României* (1963 and 1964) appeared shortly before the abrupt change in relations between the Romanian and Soviet Communist Parties in 1964. The worsening relations were accompanied by a change in ideology sharp enough to warrant the immediate publication of a new "third volume." There were not many changes; but they were of significance insofar as they put the emphasis on Romanian leaders and Romanians in general, rather than on the role of non-Romanians, particularly Russians.

A significant turning point in the writing of Romanian history occurred in 1965. A campaign was begun to reinterpret the national history; and the encouragement given to historians went far beyond that in any other East European country. The nineteenth century historical traditions were reformulated as a national mythology and a legitimator of historical rights. The concepts of "national" and "progressive" became central to a system in which the "national" took precedence in every case over Marxist-Leninist ideology. Everything that was labeled "national" and "progressive" was positive, and what was negative was antinational and antiprogressive; the national aspect gained equal significance with class considerations. Some parts of the texts are often kept unchanged, some are changed, biased, or falsificated, and others—such as significant data—are deliberately omitted to obtain the desired historical picture.[210]

History and Ideology

Since the mid-1960s the glorification of national history has been used to give the government some degree of legitimacy in the face of the country's external and serious domestic problems: in external politics to justify historically the possession of territories gained after World War I, and domestically to gain popular support for the regime's current policies and at the same time draw attention away from the country's internal problems. By historical rights is meant the claim to the territory that comprises present-day Romania as derived from the historical continuity of the Romanians.

Party and state leader Nicolae Ceaușescu proposed theses and leitmotifs about the evolution of history and is committed to establishing communist Romania as the crowning point in the historical continuity of Romanian state and national history starting from the legendary Dacian King Burebista, who was supposed to have created the first centralized and independent Dacian state more than two millenia ago,[211] and extending to himself. In the process, a good deal of "continuity" has been invented, which has been all the easier to do inasmuch as historical materialism had freely permitted historical revisions on the basis of contemporary dogmas and political opportunism. In this manner historiography becomes ever more remote from scientific requirements and performs a triple function: as executor of the irrefutable official line decreed by the Party; an instrument for deepening a sense of national identity; and a tool for persuading foreign readers unacquainted with the historic facts. This concept of history, characterized by militant ideological and political motivations and a schematical form in which myth and reality are confused, is obviously, like any other dogmatic synthesis, not in conformity with realities.

Characteristic of the contemporary Romanian historiographical orientation is the revival of nationalism, which survived uninterrupted from the nineteenth century through interwar bourgeois nationalism to 1947. In the last two decades there has been a shifting of emphasis of historical themes. The patriotic and nationalist aspects have gained precedence over Marxist ideology, although in certain works nationalist and dogmatic Marxist ideas are still closely linked.[212] Thematic emphasis has been put on the ethnogenesis of the Romanians,[213] national unity (the unification of all ethnic Romanians into a unitary state), national independence, and demonstrations of patriotism (that is, a right-wing nationalism under the guise of "socialist patriotism"). The theories of Daco-Roman continuity and Romanity were stressed more strongly than before World War II. Works with these themes account for an overwhelmingly large share of all the historical works and monographs published in Romania. Political commitment is of greater importance than even scholarly considerations.[214]

Not only historiography, but also other related disciplines, such as linguistics, archaeology, anthropology, historical statistics, demography, and ethnography, are promoted. Three years of Romanian history have been compulsory in the elementary schools since 1977; and university departments require a survey of Romanian history and recommend Latin, in view of the Latin roots and "Daco-Roman" continuity. The extent to which historiography has grown in importance can be seen in the increasing rehabilitation of previously outlawed "bourgeois" historians, such as Constantin C. Giurescu, Constantin Daicoviciu, Petre P. Panaitescu, and others, whose sharply nationalist interpretation of history can again be of use. Even many respected scholars are not without a commitment to militant Marxism or national subjectivity.[215]

After the 11th Congress of the Romanian Communist Party, held from November 24 to 27, 1974, Romanian historiography assumed a specific and Party-dictated political function. Historical facts and events of several centuries earlier, of the medieval and early modern periods, are interpreted through the prism of contemporary ideologies. It is evident that the dual insistence on the ideas of the nation and of ideology, which is so prevalent in historiography, does violence to theoretical and methodological principles. In summary, it is fair to say that during the 1970s Romanian historical writing lent itself to more and more exaggerated statements and hypotheses, which were presented as irrefutable facts, albeit unsupported by demonstrable evidence. Positions incompatible with official theses were unacceptable. Romanian historiography had to promote the people's instruction according to nationalistic and Marxist interpretations. Indicative of these trends was the subordination of historical research to the Party's "Section for Culture and Propaganda." The increasing publication of historical works in foreign languages is designed to intensify Romanian propaganda abroad.[216]

Historical writing has focused on the history of Transylvania with a view to proving Romania's historical rights to that territory. In an ideological speech about Transylvania made to historians, the head of the Party and State, Nicolae Ceauşescu, postulated that the Daco-Roman origins and continuity of the Romanian people in Transylvania would become the fundamental premise of all ideological, theoretical, and political-educational activities.[217] Political considerations require that the emphasis be put on the Dacian component of "Daco-Roman" and that the lands of the "Thraco-Dacians" constantly be expanded in order to legitimize the possession of Romania's present territories.[218]

Omissions, truncations, and falsifications are the most relevant features of historical writings on Transylvania. Above all, Transylvania, which belonged to Hungary until 1918, is regarded as a former Romanian principality just as Moldavia and Wallachia are. The history of Transylvania is, therefore, presented strictly as an integral part of Romanian national history. Neither the determining role of Hungary nor the significant contribution of the Transylvanian Saxons to the history of Transylvania is taken into account; instead, the centuries-long national and social struggles of the Romanian people for independence, which are represented as irresistible, legitimate, and progressive, are presented.[219] National unity is presumed *a priori* and is the preconceived basis of false analogies, myths, hypotheses, and historical facts deliberately taken out of context.

The union of Transylvania with the old kingdom is depicted as a fundamental preconception, interpreted as a natural historical evolution. At the same time, in direct contradiction to reality, it is claimed that a significant proportion of the Hungarians of Transylvania favored the union.[220] The desire to justify historical rights from a nationalistic standpoint is achieved at the expense of scholarship.[221]

The peasant uprisings in Transylvania, such as the common rebellion of Hungarians and Romanians of 1437, is described as purely Romanian and, as such, a link in the chain of uprisings for national independence. The concepts of "class struggle" and "nationality" are fused into one. The history of the peoples' settlements and ethnic development of Transylvania is subject to like interpretations. Contrary to international usage, old Hungarian and German place names, as well as the names of historical figures, have been changed into Romanian without any reference to the original language. Party chief Nicolae Ceauşescu declared at the Second International Thracian Congress, held in Bucharest in September 1976, that "we are dealing with an idea."

II

ARCHAEOLOGY

Methodological Problems

The nineteenth-century Romantics believed that all manifestations of a people or a nation were part of a great whole and that one could consequently draw conclusions about the whole from its parts, about the material and spiritual culture and even linguistic aspects. It was believed that a well-defined area of common material remains always indicated a special, uniform population or tribe. Great uncertainty prevails therefore with regard to the circumstances under which conclusions about migrations of people have been drawn; it is unclear whether a change in the material culture or, conversely, a continued presence of material remains in a certain area always indicates a respective change or continuity of the same population.

Great skepticism is needed in trying to answer such questions, particularly because archaeological finds do not always provide a reliable means of ethnical identification. A "uniform" archaeological area, for example, has too often been defined on the basis of insufficient analysis and interpretation of all the remains. Moreover, a really uniform material culture does not necessarily indicate an ethnically uniform population. It may be explained as easily by the existence of commerce.[1] The continuous presence of material remains in the same place does not in itself prove that the population did not change, since different peoples might use the same place, favorable for human settlement, near the estuary of a river, along an important road. A newly arrived people can, of course, also use the huts or the houses of the former inhabitants. It is also possible that the archaeological materials of two ethnically different groups coincide. Not taking such considerations into account, it has been assumed, for example, that the culture of the later Bronze Age in Northern Europe showed an ethnically uniform population and that this was Ancient Germanic.[2]

In conclusion it can be stated that it is methodologically erroneous to attempt the classification of material culture on the basis of ethnicity or language rather than on that of the prevailing culture. Archaeological data can only establish linguistic and ethnic continuity when the ancestral population lived for a long period of time on the same territory and when no alien peoples intermingled with it. It is thus imperative to separate archaeological material and its evaluation from historical and ethnic interpretations.

Archaeological finds do make it possible in certain cases to arrive at conclusions about a social organization of ancient peoples. There are cases in which such conclusions have been corroborated by other sources, especially chronicles. In the region of the Elbe River and east of it, for example, the amount of material remains increases and rich tombs appear during the first century A.D., indicating the emergence of a powerful ruling class. In the same period, the material remains from the territory further to the west, between the Rhine and Leine rivers, do not show signs of a more pronounced social differentiation. These finds agree well with the literary sources: Roman authors wrote about kings in the eastern area, while they mention exclusively chieftains in the area between the Rhine and Leine.[3] Considering the material remains and the literary sources, a likely conclusion can be drawn about the political situation: in the east, notable Germanic tribal unions or polities were being organized during the first century A.D., while this was not the case farther to the west.

With regard to the language of the people who left a certain material culture, there are, of course, major problems to determine the ethnicity: it is clearly illogical to ask the name of the maker, what language he spoke, or to what race he belonged—only historical and anthropological evidence can provide those answers.

The Significance of Archaeology in Current Romanian Historiography

It is now official policy in Romania for archaeology to play a leading and, indeed, disproportionate role in research dealing with Romanian history in ancient times and in the early Middle Ages.[4] In *Istoria Romîniei*,[5] of archaeology, history, and linguistics, for example, archaeology is discussed first and at greatest length. Constantin Daicoviciu claimed in 1966 that a monograph by the archaeologist Dumitru Protase[6] gave absolute proof of Roman continuity north of the Danube. The view of many historians about the continued existence of a Roman population north of the Danube was "verified and confirmed by the concrete and indisputable data of archaeology." In the last decades innumerable publications have tried to emphasize the same view.[7] It is interesting to note that an irreconcilable difference of opinion on the ethnogenesis of the Romanian people separates Romanian archaeologists and linguists. Suffice it to cite, for instance, the views of the prestigious linguist Ion I. Russu who stated that "the results of linguistics, by the historical comparative study of the Romanian language, appear more exact and conclusive" than archaeological finds, whose conclusions are not able to throw too much light on the origin of the Romanians. Linguistic evidence "is particularly important and instructive, especially because other available documentary sources are incomplete and deficient."[8]

The assumption in current Romanian historiography is that the material remains from the second and third centuries found on the territory of contemporary Romania indicate that the autochthonous population, that is, the Dacians, were Romanized culturally to a high degree and, therefore, that they had also adopted the Latin language;[9] these "Daco-Romans" were allegedly the ancestors of present-day Romanians.

There are a number of very serious problems with this theory that have not been pointed out sufficiently in international historical literature. To begin with, the basic catchword of the theory, "Daco-Roman," cannot be considered a scientific term, since it has several different meanings: it is used to designate Romanized Dacians as well as colonists living in Roman Dacia and non Romanized Dacians.[10]

All too often, there is a remarkable lack of critical spirit in the interpretation of the material finds. It is rarely asked, for example, which characteristics in the material culture might be accepted as criteria of Romanization as opposed to the simple Roman influence found in most areas of Europe during the first centuries A.D. Another feature of Romanian historical treatises is the lack of any serious research aimed at correlating data about an assumed Romanized population in Romania with those found in the corresponding periods south of the Danube, in the former Roman provinces of Moesia Inferior and Superior, Dacia Ripensis and Mediterranea, Pannonia Inferior and Dardania, territories included by authoritative Romanian treatises on history and linguistics within the territory of the ethnogenesis of the Romanian language and people.[11] The unlikelihood that Romanian was formed over this extremely large territory makes it imperative to find correlations in language and culture. In other words, if one believes that material remains can explain the origin of the Romanian language, one should look for such remains in all the territories in which the early development of this language is assumed. Finally, some important conclusions were drawn from more recent archaeological excavations without taking into account certain characteristic features of the Romanian language.

The possibility of Romanization north of the Danube should not be dismissed. To find evidence of this is, however, of little value, particularly because ancient literature offers comparatively little information about the remote Dacia, so far away from Rome and Greece. The problem is the degree of Romanization, that is, the extent to which people living there adopted Roman culture and the number of such people. In other words, to what extent should one accept archaeological evidence to support the hypothesis that a significant Roman population (culturally Romanized Dacians) existed north of the Danube in the mid-third century A.D.

The new concept of early Romanization throughout the entire territory of contemporary Romania is defended almost exclusively by references to the material remains unearthed in those territories. It has even been suggested that archaeological research could entirely replace history and linguistics in the study of Romanian ethnogenesis.[12]

Conclusion

It must be noted that in Romanian territories the archaeological legacy is to a major extent insufficiently differentiated to allow exact ethnic determinations on the basis of typological characteristics. In spite of considerable efforts and promising results, archaeological research has not freed itself of contradictions, erroneous conclusions, and speculation. We are faced with an overvaluation of the extant material culture, based only on examination of one area without consideration of the entire European-Asiatic complex or of facts derived from other disciplines, especially linguistics. The scientific evaluation of individual cultures can only be made through the study of the culture prevailing throughout the area of its dissemination. It is not possible, for example, to reach conclusions regarding chronology and, above all, ethnicity on the basis of archaeological excavations without comparing them with those in neighboring countries. Chronological evaluations of archaeological remains require comparisons with findings of previous as well as later centuries which, on Romanian lands in general and in Transylvania in particular, are very difficult to make. Both the periods that separate as well as (those that) bind for the definition of archaeological remains are missing: the periods separating individual cultures can be as long as several hundred years so that forced attempts to bridge these gaps produce hypothetical and unscientific conclusions.

The Roman Cultural Influence
on the non-Romanic Peoples of Europe:
Roman Imports in Barbaricum

It is important to distinguish between the Roman remains, on the one hand, and objects of Roman style or production that could have been left by Romans as well as non-Romans, on the other. There are ruins of stone buildings, baths, amphitheaters, roads, and aquaducts throughout the Roman Empire. From such monumental traces it can be inferred that the people who made them were Romans (at least partially) and that they therefore spoke Latin. In these areas are also found Roman earthenware and other objects of everyday use—small statuettes, weapons, coins, and other things. Such objects, however, are easy to transport and are found in abundance beyond the frontiers of the empire. They in themselves are not, therefore, proof of the ethnic character of the people who left them behind.

For many centuries, the European frontiers of the Roman Empire were the Rhine and Danube rivers,[13] but exploratory and punitive expeditions into Barbaricum (barbarian lands)[14] were not infrequent. These expeditions, as well as temporary occupation of some areas have also produced important traces. Part of free Germania was occupied for some years at the beginning of the first century A.D.; parts of the present-day Romanian provinces of Muntenia and southern Moldavia, from 106 to 117 A.D.; southern Oltenia and Muntenia up to the Furrow of Novac and possibly also certain southern areas of the Banat for some decades in the fourth century; and other areas were occupied as well. Roman forts (*castra*) were found up to 100 km beyond the border of the empire, east of the Rhine in the contemporary Benelux countries, and north of the Danube in modern Austria and Romania. In Austria four forts were situated on the

Danube and another four at distances of up to 70 kilometers from the river. Roman settlements were also found in Slovakia and Austria, the majority close to the Danube in the north, although one was situated in Slovakia on the Hron River (Garam) about 50 kilometers from the Danube. Stones with Roman inscriptions have been found in the Netherlands, Austria, and Slovakia; on the map of the German archaeologist Hans Jürgens Eggers, a total of eight are shown in Barbaricum.[15]

Roman remains in the barbarian lands, however, more often were a result of commerce or left by returning soldiers. After the occupation of Gaul (Gallia) and the territory between the Alps and the Danube (Noricum) by the Romans, direct contact was established in the first century B.C. between the empire and the free Germanic peoples. This and flourishing industries in several Roman towns created conditions favorable for trade between the Romans and other European peoples. The degree of commerce with the Roman Empire and Roman influence upon style and customs in Barbaricum could be measured by analyzing remains of Roman origin or style. The materials found in cemeteries reflect funerary customs; but in settlements, everyday objects such as earthenware, are usually found in plenty. The amount of imported material found correlates to the population of the settlement in that period. Increased amounts of Roman products may be found in a specific area during certain periods. There were many Roman imports, for example, in the early imperial period in Bohemia and in Denmark, which may be explained by the existence of powerful societies (in the case of Bohemia the Marcomann kingdom).

The imported material is of different kinds: earthenware, bronze and glass vessels, jewelry, weapons, statuettes, and other items, as well as many coins. Two kinds of commerce can be recognized: short-distance commerce over an area within about 100 km of the frontiers; and the export of products to places as distant as present-day Russia and western Siberia and the middle parts of Sweden and Norway. Long-distance commerce used particular routes and usually started from certain Roman cities. As rich finds of Roman earthenware, especially of *terra sigillata* type,[16] relatively near to Roman frontiers have shown, short-distance trade with such products was very intense, although not uniformly distributed in Germania. Brooches and other small objects are also found frequently in these areas.

In certain cases, imported Roman products could give some indication of the political or ethnical situation. The greater variation of such products in the late imperial period, for example, reflects the increasing organization of the Germanic tribes and the development of more potent tribal unions. The Roman brooches found throughout

Germania up to the frontier with the Finnish-Ugrian peoples in the Baltic probably also indicate an ethnic frontier, inasmuch as the Finnish-Ugrians did not wear brooches. An even more interesting conclusion can be drawn from the distribution of bronze buckets of the Hemmoor type, which were used in the Roman Empire and also exported to Germania. They were found in different sites: in Germania, finds come predominantly from cemeteries, while south of the *limes*, they are found in former settlements or buried in the earth, obviously with the aim of finding them again. If the frontier between the Roman Empire and free Germania were not known, it could thus be ascertained with considerable accuracy by the way in which these buckets are treated.[17]

The Roman Influence on Culture

Most important, of course, was the intense cultural influence the Roman civilization had on the peoples of Europe. In some areas, stone houses were built on the Roman pattern, new weapons were introduced, and Roman styles of clothing were adopted. Since Romanian archaeologists use Roman characteristics in the material culture, especially in the earthenware, to support their theory of Roman continuity north of the Danube, the impact of Roman culture on non-Roman peoples of Europe should be pointed out. In examining the arguments in support of a Romanized population, this strong and widespread influence must be taken into account.

Greek and Roman art influenced that of the Germanic peoples beginning in the first century A.D., replacing the Celtic influence, which had previously been dominant. The initial effect was restricted to certain areas and was quite weak. An early characteristic was the filigree work, which spread during the first century A.D. from the Greek towns along the Black Sea and the lower Danube to large areas of Germania. The Roman influence on the Germanic peoples, that is, a group of works in which Old Germanic and provincial Roman elements are mixed, can be seen at this early stage, especially in the remains excavated from marshes in Schleswig-Holstein and in Denmark. These were probably produced partly in the Roman province of Lower Germania, in the region of the lower Rhine, and partly in the adjacent areas of free Germania.[18]

In the third century A.D. there appears in free Germania a type of sheet metal fibulae in the shape of animals, made after the animal motifs found on Roman *terra sigillata*. Another type of fibulae, made of silver, found in rich third century tombs in free Germania shows the stylistic influence of Roman provincial fibulae but developed further by the Old Germanic smiths, who made use of the antique techniques of filigree, granulation, and gold-covering.[19] A total of 13 figurines, in the shape of cattle, probably made after provincial Roman statuettes, were found in free Germania. They were most probably attributed a magical effect. All the pictures (mostly of animals) on vessels and fibulae made in the second to fourth centuries by Old Germanic craftsmen show a clear Roman influence.[20]

The Old Germanic potters began to use the meander-motifs found on Roman cloth.[21] Many different kinds of vessels of glass, bronze, and *terra sigillata* were taken as models for a series of indigenous pottery forms. There were even connections between Roman workshops of pottery and workshops in Barbaricum, for example, in Pannonia, on the one hand, and in the valley of the Vistula River, on the other.[22]

The Roman influence was so intense that it affected even the funeral customs: in the rich tombs of chieftains, a Roman vessel (of bronze, glass, or earthenware) was almost always included. In a number of tombs, coins were also interred, according to an ancient Greco-Roman tradition.[23]

The territories south of the Sudetes and the Carpathian Mountains show in several respects a more intense influence from Roman civilization than those lying north of these mountains. Consequently, in the southern area, Roman vessels were used extensively, even in everyday life, while the population living north of these mountains owned far fewer of them but often put them in the tombs. This is shown by the analysis of finds from settlements and cemeteries.[24] Also, the number of Roman fibulae is much higher in the southern area: out of a total of 600 found between the Danube and the Baltic Sea, the majority were found in Bohemia and Slovakia.[25] These are attributed to the lively contacts between the Romans and the Marcomanns and the Quadi, respectively.

In the territory between Pannonia and Dacia Traiana, several trade routes existed, for example, that between Aquincum and Porolissum. As also in free Germania, Roman products from the first four centuries A.D. were found in the Great Hungarian Plain. The records of the finds of the numerous pieces of *terra sigillata* have not yet been completely published. After the abandonment of Dacia, several peoples of Dacian origin appeared in the plains, among whom were also potters. They produced earthenware similar to that found at Cristeşti-Mureş (Maroskeresztúr, Mureş County).[26] The number of fibulae found in the Hungarian Plain is comparable to that from the areas north of Pannonia. The majority of these are sheet metal fibulae and knee-fibulae brought to this area during the late second and early third centuries. The commerce between the Sarmatians and the empire was predominantly of a local character (with Pannonia and Dacia). In

Sarmatian tombs many bronze mirrors have been found. The number of bronze statuettes is less than that found in Germania. Roman glass was found in 21 places. In Pannonia, Sarmatian earthenware was found, which could be explained by commerce and also by the settlement of Sarmatians in the province in the fourth century. After 322 A.D., the Sarmatians had an agreement with the Roman Empire, which can explain the construction of fortifications: a Roman tower at Hatvan-Gombospuszta and a camp at Felsőgöd-Bócsa[27] (both in Hungary).

The Circulation of Roman Coins in Barbaricum

The study of the presence and distribution of Roman coins could make valuable contributions to historical research, if certain methodological principles are followed. It is, for instance, not sufficient to consider generally the total number of coins found in a certain area; coins found in settlements or tombs, isolated or in hoards must be evaluated separately, since coins in different sites have different meanings. An important aspect is, of course, also the metal of which the coins are made: bronze, copper, silver, gold. A few hoards usually do not have much significance; but in increasing numbers, they indicate wars, invasions, and periods of unrest. In the territory of free Germania, it was possible to compare the presence of accumulations of hoards with data given by literary sources. Whenever reports exist for the time and territory in question, the findings confirmed this.[28] Coins appear in tombs, of course, only in areas where it was customary to put them there. Isolated coins could indicate trade routes. It should also be pointed out that the varying degrees of excavations cannot accurately reflect the number of actual remains in different territories.

In free Germania, Roman coins from the time of the Republic to the sixth century have been found without any significant hiatus. The Swedish archaeologist Sture Bolin, in 1926, knew of 2,500 sites with 401 hoards (114 were described in detail) and a total of 50,000 or more coins.[29] In Central Europe, coins have been found in all inhabited areas. The density of finds varies, however. Areas with large numbers of coins include Friesland, certain areas along the Rhine River, the region around the Elbe River, and the estuary of the Oder and Vistula rivers. In contrast, in the territory west of the confluence of the Morava and Danube, the number of Roman coins is low, evidently because of the low population in that frontier area.[30]

With regard to the presence of Roman coins in tombs, there is a sharp dividing line made by the Passarge River in Prussia: west of the river no coins were placed in the tombs, while to the east they are common.[31]

There are a number of places where coins were accumulated over long periods of time. Roman coins were thrown into a well in Bohemia, for example, from Celtic times until about 400 A.D.; and settlements in Friesland show a similar pattern.[32] The continuation of the same tradition, however, does not necessarily indicate the persistence of the same population.

The number of Roman coins found in the territories of Europe that never belonged to the Roman Empire varies with the different periods and the different territories.

1. From the late first century B.C. to the early second century A.D. the circulation of coins was sparse.
2. From the early second century A.D. to the first third of the third century the number of find sites increases threefold over the earlier period. This was the time of the most intense circulation of coins.
3. From the second third of the third century to the early fourth century a general decrease of the circulation of coins is found, especially in Poland and in Sarmatia but less pronounced in Austria and north of the Danube in present-day Czechoslovakia.
4. From the early fourth century to about 360 A.D. the number of bronze and gold coins increased, especially south of the Sudetes and the Carpathian Mountains.
5. From about 360 A.D. to the sixth century masses of *solidi* were brought especially to Pomerania. The circulation of Roman coins ends in Poland and in northern Austria in the first half of the fifth century and in all regions north of the Danube in the sixth century.[33]

The Role of Roman Coins in Free Germania and Other Territories Outside the Roman Empire

An important question is whether the people living in Barbaricum used the Roman coins as a means of payment; in other words, did these coins in Barbaricum have the function of money? There is apparently general agreement about the situation in the areas along the Roman frontier: there, Roman coins were used regularly as means of payment for goods.[34] In areas at some distance from the Roman frontier, for example, in inner Germania, the situation varied with the different areas and periods. Probably, in most instances, the Roman coins had a function as money in these areas also, although the degree of this function varied. Most of the coins were indeed found in the same state and in a chronology similar to that in the empire.[35]

In order to answer the question about the degree of this function in the different areas of free Germania, a statistical analysis of the following aspects was undertaken: 1. the structure according to which the finds appear; 2. the metal, that is, the proportion of bronze, silver and gold coins; 3. the number of Roman coins found in an area of 1,000 square kilometers. On the basis of these data, five different regions could be determined: 1. the territory of Austria north of the Danube and western Slovakia, where the coins were employed as money to a very high degree;[36] 2. Bohemia and Moravia, where this function was intense; 3. Silesia, where this function was at a medium level; 4. eastern Slovakia, Poland, and Pomerania where the coins served as money to a lesser degree; and 5. Masuria, with the lowest degree for this purpose. The differences were mainly connected with the distance of the region in question from the Danube, its relations to the main routes and also with the level of socio-economic development.

In general, Roman coins have been found in every inhabited territory. The number of isolated finds of coins is very high in regions that were centers of commerce: for example, the isles of the Baltic Sea during the first centuries A.D. It has also been shown that the coins found on Gotland (Sweden), for instance, became worn on this island.

Another question of importance is the metal of the coins. One of the chief arguments in favor of a Romanized population in the fourth century north of the Danube is the circulation of bronze coins, which, it is argued, were used by a population accustomed to commerce with money, rather than by the Old Germanic populations, who appreciated the coins mostly for their intrinsic value. Bronze coins, however, were extensively used in several parts of Europe outside the Roman Empire, that is, by non-Roman populations. Consequently, finds in northern Austria and in Slovakia show a similar distribution with regard to the metal as those found in the Roman provinces of Noricum and Pannonia: they contain more bronze than silver coins. In Bohemia and in Moravia, there also are many bronze coins, although the number of silver coins is slightly higher. In Poland, with the exception of Masuria, silver coins are in the majority.[37] Bronze coins were also accumulated in hoards. In this respect, there is a certain difference within free Germania. The almost worthless copper coins from the period after 250 A.D. appear sparsely in the central parts of Germania, while they are numerous in the countries along the Roman frontier. Many hoards of such coins from the second half of the third century were found in the region of the Rhine. Later, in

Roman Provinces in Southeastern Europe From 106 to 275 A.D.

the fourth century, the areas north of the Danube are richest in hoards of this type.[38]

Roman coins were also found in the plains between Pannonia and Dacia, from the second century A.D. in more significant numbers. In that century, denarii predominate (225 pieces compared with 28 bronze coins and one of gold). In the third century, the proportion is 25 denarii, 61 bronze and 12 gold. In the fourth century, bronze coins are most common among the finds: there are 262 of them, compared with 3 denarii and 24 gold coins.[39] In this territory, Roman coins of bronze or silver were found at 227 sites. The coins show signs of having been used for a considerable time. The finds suggest that the tribes living in those plains, for example, the Sarmatians, used Roman coins as money.[40]

THE QUESTION OF ROMANIZATION NORTH OF THE DANUBE

Dacia

The territory which stretched, during the first millennium B.C., from the lower Danube to the river Dniester was named Dacia by its inhabitants, the Dacians. Several tribes, related to the Thracians, were united by the Dacian King Burebista (Burvista, Burobostes) 70–44 B.C. and, again, in 80 A.D. by Decebal. It is impossible, however, to consider in either case that a valid, unified Dacian state organization existed.

As the Dacians became a threat to the Roman Empire they were defeated in two wars, in 101 A.D. and 105–106 A.D., by Trajan. Their central settlement of Transylvania with the capital Sarmizegethusa, became a Roman province known as Dacia Traiana, which was to be an outpost of the Roman Empire against the barbarians. Dacia Traiana was divided into two parts: Dacia Superior and Dacia Inferior (118–119 A.D.). Outside the province, in the northern and eastern frontiers, lived the "free Dacians." The military occupation forces consisted of two legions, one of which, at the end of 110 A.D., was withdrawn but later replaced.

As is known, the wars brought considerable losses to the Dacian men; part of the local population was deported or fled. It is also known that during the age of Trajan, and also during that of his successors, there was a significant colonization by foreign peoples from all over the Roman Empire.[41] The largest landholdings were appropriated by foreign colonizers. Likewise, the majority of the urban population—the actual Romanizing force—consisted of the upper strata of foreign colonizers: Syrians, Greeks, and others. It is difficult to conceive that under these circumstances, in about 170 years, any effective Romanization could have taken place.[42]

The central area of urbanization and colonization was in the mineral-rich western part of the province where, for that matter, the capital Sarmizegethusa (modern name Grădişte/Várhegy), known as Ulpia Traiana in Roman times, was located. The town was somewhat to the west of the old Dacian capital of Sarmizegethusa and was inhabited, *inter alia*, by soldiers of the wars of conquest. Close to the military camps were built *canabae*, whose inhabitants were primarily soldiers' dependents and businessmen.

As a result of threats from barbarians, a new legion was transferred from Moesia to Dacia (Potaissa, Turda) in 167–168 A.D.; and Dacia was administratively redivided into Dacia Porolissensis in the north, Dacia Apulensis in the south, and Dacia Malvensis in the territory of contemporary Oltenia. The first two incorporated the territory of the former Dacia Superior.

Around 230 the number of barbarian attacks on the Roman frontiers, particularly by the Goths, increased. As a consequence, from 242 to 244, the region to the east of the Olt River was abandoned and the border relocated on the river. It is possible that a partial evacuation of the province occurred as early as 260, in the age of Emperor Gallienus. This evacuation would have encompassed the eastern part of Transylvania, and it is to be assumed that at that time the Goths were already in this territory. No findings from the military camps of this area attest to the utilization of the camps after 250 A.D.[43]

In 271, Emperor Aurelian finally ordered the evacuation of Dacia.[44] After the evacuation the lower Danube became once again the northern frontier of the Roman Empire. A total evacuation of Dacia, as reported by Eutropius, would hardly have been possible. It must be assumed, even in the absence of evidence, that a part of the local population remained in Dacia. However, the army, the entire administrative machinery, and with them also the business people, landholders, and aristocracy—in other words those whose interests were related to the Roman Empire, those who were the actual instruments of Romanization and who could have been the disseminators of the Latin language—left the province.

Concurrently with the evacuation of Dacia two new provinces, to the south of the Danube, were created for the evacuated population: Dacia Ripensis (part of Moesia Superior in the valley of the Timok) and Dacia Mediterranea (part of Dardania, the present-day eastern Serbia and western Bulgaria) with the principal fortresses of Naissus (Niš) and Serdica (modern Sofia).

Provinces of the Roman Empire in Southeastern Europe
After the Abandonment of Dacia Traiana in 275 A.D.

Eutropius's and Vopiscus's accounts of the total evacuation of Dacia are generally questioned by Romanian historians,[45] although there are also divergent opinions. Vladimir Iliescu, for example, agreed with Eutropius's narratives that Dacia was totally evacuated.[46] In his later study, however, Iliescu changed his opinion and, based on Jordanes' accounts,[47] assumed that only the Roman legions were transferred to Moesia.[48] It is to be assumed that not only were the legions transferred to Moesia but that a mass-evacuation of Dacia by Emperor Aurelian had taken place.[49]

Roman Influence Before 106 A.D.

The Greek towns that flourished along the shores of the Black Sea during the first millenium B.C. certainly exerted a significant influence, probably mainly through commercial contacts, upon the peoples living on the plains to the west, and north, just as the Roman Empire later would profoundly influence all the peoples of Europe, including those north of the Danube. The great importance of this fact was recognized by earlier Romanian historians; Vasile Pârvan, for example, asserted that the Romanization of the Dacians had been prepared for a millenium before the Roman conquest of Dacia.[50] This idea has been elaborated a great deal in current Romanian historiography; and some treatises now refer not only to preparation but to actual Romanization, beginning when the Romans reached the line of the Danube at the time of Emperors Augustus and Tiberius and continuing after the withdrawal of the Roman authorities in 271 or 272 A.D.[51] This is considered to be substantiated by the fact that the Roman army supervised the lowlands of present-day Muntenia already before the conquest of Dacia.[52] From the first century B.C. on, Dacia was an important market of Rome. Merchants from the empire wandered through the country with products from Italy and Dalmatia. Roman coins were forged in Dacia. Fugitive craftsmen from the empire were engaged at the courts of Dacian kings and noblemen; and there were even deserters from the Roman army, "all of whom were bearers of the Latin language." Furthermore, King Decebal of Dacia (87 to 106 A.D.) as a Roman ally received financial aid and advisors for his army, whose contribution to the spread of Roman civilization and the Latin language could not have been without significance.

An inscription in the Roman alphabet has been found on a Dacian clay vessel, *Decebalus per Scorilo*, which has been interpreted as either "Decebal, the son of Scorilo," or with *per* as a preposition.[53] Greek and Roman letters, engraved in stone, on pieces of earthenware, and on objects of various kinds have been found at a number of sites.[54]

Dio Cassius (150–235 A.D.) mentioned that people allied with King Decebal had sent a message written in the Latin alphabet to Trajan in 101 A.D. Some 50,000 Dacians during the reign of Augustus (63 B.C. to 14 A.D.) and 100,000 "Transdanubians" during the rule of Nero (37 to 68 A.D.) were settled south of the Danube.

Some of the circumstances mentioned above certainly contributed to rapprochement between Dacians and other barbarian peoples and the Romans. Commerce with the empire may have introduced a number of Latin words into the language of the peoples north of the Danube as it did in most other European languages. Advisors and craftsmen could also have contributed to the spread of Latin words to Dacian. A very few Dacians probably even knew the Greek or the Latin alphabet and could write, but this could not be true of more than just those at the top levels of society.[55] Several other circumstances cited as evidence, such as military raids and supervision by populations serving the empire, cannot be considered factors of Romanization. The idea of a proper Romanization before the conquest has been also refuted by some Romanian scholars.[56]

**The Degree of Romanization
in Dacia Traiana from 106 to 275 A.D.
The Definition of Romanization and the Problem in Dacia**

Romanization must be studied as a process of acculturation, based on the military and political domination of Rome.[57] Such a process can result in assimilation or fusion or syncretism (partial adoption of the model); the model can also, of course, be totally rejected. In the case of assimilation, a non-Roman population living in the Roman Empire would adopt entirely the Roman material, social, and spiritual way of life. The first stage is the adoption of Roman material culture and economic life, followed by social, political, and spiritual assimilation.[58] The process of Romanization reaches its highest degree only when the Latin language is adopted.[59] The intensity of the process can only be studied by analyzing data referring to the Roman period of the territory in question.[60]

With respect to Romanization, primary consideration must be given to its social and political aspects. The bearers of Romanization in the Roman provinces were the two dominant social strata: the urban aristocracy and the army, both closely tied to the interests of the Roman Empire. It is, however, not known to what extent they themselves were Romanized and/or what the extent was of their contacts with the lower strata of the local population. In any event, any possible further contacts were interrupted as soon as the leading strata—as in Dacia's case—left the land. Moreover, the Roman legions and auxiliary troops incorporated a large number of foreign, primarily eastern, elements; and there was an even greater share of them in Dacia than, for example, in Pannonia. To Trajan's Dacia came not only Greek businessmen and artisans but also miners. Moreover, Thracians emigrated to Moesia Inferior and Dacia. Under the circumstances, not only did the Latin-speaking part of the population decrease but the language of the local population also disappeared since there were no independent institutions or state organization that could have preserved the language.

The ancestors of the Romanians were a Latin-speaking people, most probably an ancient Southeastern European population, which adopted the Latin language. If and how much they adopted the Roman material, social, and spiritual way of life is not reliably known; hypotheses with regard to such a heritage are vague and of dubious value. The only thing we reliably know about the Romanian people's ancestors is that they spoke a language of Latin structure. The adoption of Latin can, therefore, not be regarded only as "the highest degree" of Romanization but the *sine qua non* of it; and beyond the Roman character of the ancient material remains, the real question is: Under what circumstances (in what territory, surrounded by which peoples) could the adoption of Latin take place?

There are neither historical records nor other evidence from Dacia Traiana about the degree of Romanization, that is, about the extent to which Latin was used by the inhabitants. This should be stated clearly at the beginning. Conclusions have been deduced largely from analogies with other provinces and from archaeological finds. There are records, for example, about a large number of colonists from the entire Roman Empire, about the army units stationed in the province, and about the number of towns; some 3,000 inscriptions have been found. The Roman domination lasted for about 165 to 169 years, that is, the Roman rule collapsed in Dacia earlier than in other Roman provinces. On the basis of these data, one must conclude that the possibility of Romanization existed in Dacia Traiana, insofar as there were opportunities for the spread of Roman culture and the Latin language among the non-Roman colonists and among the Dacians who possibly lived there. Beyond this general statement, there is a dearth of solid information. Many important questions remain unanswered: what, for example, was the exact proportion of Latin-speaking people among the entire population; to what extent did their number increase in the course of time; and what was the geographical and social distribution of those speaking Latin. Furthermore, the sources of information about the spread of the Latin language through the empire is all based on Roman sources, which prevented an accurate determination of the language of the inhabitants. Since making inscriptions was a Roman custom, they indicate only the presence of people who knew Latin but reveal almost nothing about the number of people who spoke other languages.[61] From the situation in other Roman provinces we can deduce that the people who spoke Latin lived mainly in towns and were Roman functionaries or from the leading social groups.[62] Based on the Balkan Peninsula, Noricum, northern Gallia, Dardania, northern Africa, and several other territories, it is known that many native languages persisted stubbornly for long periods of time. In Africa, for example, or in Noricum as well as in Pannonia, Roman domination lasted almost twice as long as in Dacia and there were many more towns; but in spite of this, only some of the inhabitants adopted the Latin language. In several areas of this territory, people kept their original mother tongue, and a significant part of the indigenous population was only partially Romanized.[63] Similar situations are reported from other provinces.[64]

Romanization affected primarily the lower territories such as Dalmatia and the southern part of the lower Danube, and intensive Romanization occurred only in places where there were larger settlements. In Dalmatia, for example, outstanding conditions existed for Roman continuity but only until the Ostrogothic-Byzantine war of 536.[65] The invasions during the period of the peoples' migrations had devastating consequences here. Despite the exposed location of Noricum Mediterraneum, today's Slovenia, in Roman times, for example, in the three most important Roman towns of Emona, Celeia, and Poetovio, most of the Roman vestiges disappeared by the end of the fourth century and only a few elements reveal the continuity of settlements in the fifth and perhaps even into the sixth centuries.[66] Necropolises reveal Gothic and Longobardian development although continuity in the seventh century cannot be demonstrated; in other words, there is no direct connection with the Slavs.

In Pannonia, for example, the continuing existence of provincial Romans, that is, the remnants of their culture, can be discerned archaeologically, albeit with difficulty, even in the sixth century. This, however, must not be equated with Romanity and total Latinity. Therefore, it is difficult to assume that the Romanization developed differently in Dacia than in other Roman provinces. In mountainous areas like Transylvania conditions were less favorable for rapid Romanization. After the Roman occupation of Dacia the remaining population lived mainly in the rural areas, largely in mountainous regions where Romanization hardly occur. On the other hand, in areas where there was not a high degree of Romanization, the place names of the autochthonous population should remain. Not a single Dacian place name, however, survived north of the Danube.

Roman domination of Transylvania can be determined both territorially and chronologically. Recent archaeological excavations in eastern Transylvania, for example, reveal that in this area, Roman garrisons left earlier, in fact, as early as in the middle of the third century during the reign of Gallienus.[67] In the same area, only an insignificant number of inscriptions were found. It is a well-known fact that in areas with military camps but no towns there was no Romanization - and this was the case in eastern Transylvania.

Archaeological remnants may give the answer to the following questions of crucial importance for the problem of Romanization: 1) was there a significant Dacian population in the Roman province - for example, are there a number of Dacian settlements that continue after the conquest; did Dacians live in the towns and in what proportions? - and 2) does the material culture found in originally Dacian settlements show any evidence of a progressive adoption of Roman material culture, - an evolution similar to what is known from the western provinces, - beginning in the early second century A.D. and concluding in the mid-third century? If the answer to these questions is affirmative, one may seriously consider the possibility that this population also adopted the Latin language. In the absence of such evidence, however, the language change seems unlikely.

Towns and Rural Settlements in Dacia Traiana

Of all the provinces of the Roman Empire, Dacia Traiana had the lowest number of cities: 11 or 12 towns are known to have existed, of which the more significant were Sarmizegethusa, with an estimated population of 15,000 to 20,000; Apulum and Ampeium in the area of the gold mines in the Apuseni Mountains (Erdélyi Szigethegység); Potaissa or Potavissa; Porolissum; Tibiscum; and, in southern Oltenia, Romula, Drobeta, and Dierna, of which the two last were on the shores of the lower Danube. In addition to these names, the names of a number of urban centers were preserved, such as Alburnus Maior, Vicus Pirustarum, Germisara, Blandiana, Micia, Brucla, Aquae, Salinae.[68] In contrast to other provinces, where several settlements of the subdued local populations were left autonomous (for example, as *civitas stipendiaria*) no such settlement is known in Dacia Traiana.[69]

Roman culture was essentially urban; and it was in the towns where Romanization first began, when the leaders of the conquered populations in Gallia, Iberia, and elsewhere adopted the Roman culture and the Latin language. What, then, was the situation in Dacia? Did Dacians live in the new Roman towns and in what proportios were they there? There are very few hard facts with which to answer such questions.

Inscriptions and written records provide no information about Dacians in towns since these were predominantly made by colonists of foreign origin. D. Protase, in his monograph about Roman Dacia expresses his *belief* that there must have been Dacians in the Roman towns: ..."beyond doubt, the autochthonous elements from the rural areas of the province were assimilated in the Roman towns to a substantial but not yet known degree" (D. Protase, *Autohtonii in Dacia*, 1980, p. 85.) However, he is forced to state that "it is known and acknowledged since a long time that the Dacians subdued by the Romans lived predominantly in the rural areas of the province" (p. 35); and his final conclusion is: ..."in contrast to Italy and the western provinces, where some urban centres of the autochthons continued to develop into genuine Roman towns, in Dacia, the more significant settlements of the indigenous population ceased to exist with the Roman conquest. All the towns of Trajan's province were created during the Roman domination from civilian and military settlements and of the old Dacian localities only the names were borrowed: Sarmizegetusa, Apulum, Potaissa, Napoca, Porolissum, Drobeta, Dierna, etc. In Dacia, one can not speak about a Daco-Roman urbanistic evolution. The towns, with the exception of the Greek towns in the region of the Black Sea, appeared in Dacia with the Roman domination and disappeared as such after the abolishment of this domination..." (Protase, 1980, *op. cit.*, p 251-252).

Dacian Settlements After the Conquest
The Number of Dacians in Dacia Romana

After the conquest of Dacia in 106 A.D., "part of the autochthonous population"[70] was transferred from their villages to other territories within the province, because of the control and also for economic reasons (that is, good arable land was given to the colonists). This is the hypothetical explanation of the fact that only a few settlements and no cemeteries continued to exist after the conquest. Most of the settlements and all cemeteries of the Roman era were established after 106 A.D.[71] The new settlements in which the existence of Dacians is assumed were situated in rural areas far from the towns; the nearest one, that discovered at Obreja (Obrázsa, Alba County), was 25 kilometers from Apulum.[72] If one accepts the assumption, then one must conclude that the Dacian population that survived the wars and the conquest was almost entirely displaced. Fundamental changes in the situation of this population are indicated also by the fact that all the Dacian forts and large settlements ceased to exist at the time of the conquest.[73] As may be seen from archaeological excavations, the population of the Dacian settlements were moved, during the wars and in the following years, from the politically and strategically affected areas to insignificant territories.[74] That part of the Dacian material culture that was the most developed also disappeared from the country.[75] High-quality Dacian earthenware is almost non-existent in the provincial era, and the old Dacian village communities were abolished.[76] Many Dacians were transferred from the province to Rome and other areas of the empire, mostly as slaves and soldiers.[77]

All these changes must have caused a significant decrease in the number of Dacians and fundamental transformations in Dacian society in general. In the past, many Romanian historians concluded on the basis of historical records that the persistence of a Dacian population in the Roman province of Dacia Traiana was questionable. According to the current official Romanian concept, however, Dacians lived in the province and were numerous in the rural areas.

Dacian personal names found in inscriptions are often cited to demonstrate that Dacians lived in the province. A breakdown of this in the inscriptions found in Dacia Traiana according to origin is as follows:[78]

Roman:	more than 2,200 (70–75%)
"Graeco-Oriental":	about 420 (16%)
Illyrian:	124 (4%)
Celtic:	74 (3%)
"Thraco-Dacian":	64 (below 3%)
Northwest African, Egyptian, others:	(over 1%)

The share of Thracian or Dacian personal names is thus insignificant, and some of them may even have belonged to colonists from the Balkan Peninsula. According to the Hungarian scholar András Kerényi, there are 2,600 personal names found in inscriptions in Dacia, of which 1,860 are of Latin-Italian origin, 355 Greek, 184 western Balkan and Celtic, and 67 Oriental; furthermore, 66 names are in very bad condition, and 17 are unclassified. There are only 51 Dacian or Thracian names.[79] On the other hand, it is not possible to determine to what extent Dacians used Roman names. It is also reasonable to assume that, because of socioeconomic conditions, only a small number of Dacians made inscriptions. In any case, however, these names do not suggest a significant, numerous Dacian population.

The number of military units formed by Dacians (*alae*, *cohortes*, *numeri*) or, more correctly, designated as *Dacicus* in inscriptions and military diplomas,[80] is estimated at 12 and the total number of soldiers at 8,000 to 9,000.[81] It is claimed that this indicates the existence of a "large autochthonous population"; but it is a very dubious under-taking to try to infer the number of the Dacians living in Dacia Traiana from the number of military units designated "*Dacicus.*" Immediately after the conquest, such units were possibly composed mainly of Dacians; but later the names of the army units did not always indicate their ethnic composition. From the fourth decade of the second century A.D., the auxiliary units were regularly filled by soldiers from the territory in which they served; and their national character disappeared.[82] If Dacians were living in the province of Dacia Traiana, Dacian men could have been recruited in the auxiliary units serving there, but the auxiliary units called "*Dacicus*" serving in other provinces (Moesia, Pannonia, Britannia, and so forth) were certainly composed not only of Dacians. Moreover, 12 units, even if composed exclusively of Dacians, cannot be considered a high number. In 1934, the Romanian scholar Constantin Daicoviciu was, in fact, of the opinion that it was "extremely low."[83]

About 100 hoards of Roman coins are known to have been buried in the territory of Dacia Traiana during the Roman domination; 16 of them show a composition that suggests that their accumulation began before the conquest and continued after it. Several of them contain large numbers of coins from the Roman Republic.[84] They were found in Oltenia along the Olt and Danube rivers, in southwestern Transylvania, and in the valley of the middle course of the Mureș (Maros) River.[85] The large number of republican denarii found in Dacia must be traced to the slave trade of the free Dacians with the Romans.[86]

There are also Roman coins from the time of Emperor Hadrian (117–138 A.D.) with the picture of a woman symbolizing Dacia holding an eagle in one hand and a curved sword (*falx Dacica*) in the other. The appearance of this ancient Dacian weapon on a Roman coin "must be interpreted as a sign that the autochthons were being taken up in the Roman auxiliary troops."[87] From the time of Emperor Antoninus Pius (138–161) there is a coin on which Dacia holds the Roman banner and the Dacian sword, which, according to the official view of current Romanian historiography "expresses the Roman concept about the integration of the local population into the Roman Empire and constitutes an important element in the problem of continuity."[88]

It is possible that the accumulation of these 16 hoards began before the Roman conquest in the territory of Dacia. We do not know how many of them were taken from their Dacian owners by Roman soldiers or colonists after the conquest. Nothing indicates that they were buried by members of the family whose ancestors once began to collect them: they were found isolated, without any connection to a settlement; and the vessels or fragments of vessels in which they were found give no such indication either. These hoards could perhaps contribute to the evidence that Dacians were living in Roman Dacia; but since this was not questioned here, their significance in this analysis is limited. They are not helpful in the investigation of the possible number of Dacians living in the province. One must conclude that the available data are not sufficient to determine the approximate number of Dacians in Roman Dacia.

The Rural Settlements in Dacia Traiana

Material remains of earthenware, farming equipment, and other tools and the remains of buildings with mortar, from the period between 106 and 275 A.D. have been found at about 400 sites in the former province of Trajan's Dacia. Excluding sites in which the remains indicate towns, military stations, and baths, it is estimated that there were about 300 civilian settlements.[89] Most of these were inhabited by a peasant and pastoral population; a smaller number of these villages were inhabited mainly by workers in the salt and gold mines; and in a few villages, pottery workshops existed. At about 40 sites remains of what could have been villages (*villae rusticae* and *suburbanae*) have been found. This important type of Roman agricultural unit never became as significant in Dacia Traiana as in other provinces. The villages were called *pagi* or *vici*; *pagi* are known only on the territory that belonged to Sarmizegethusa.[90] Micia (modern Veţel) was such a *pagus*, developed from the civilian settlement (*canabae*) established in the vicinity of an important fort. Its population consisted of veterans and Roman citizens.[91] In a large number of settlements, rich finds of Roman buildings, aqueducts, and other typically Roman features are found, while others are poor and do not contain similar discoveries. The former type of villages is generally attributed to the colonists, while the Dacians are sought among the poorer ones.

The assumption of the presence of Dacians is based primarily on finds of earthenware of the primitive Dacian type in association with Roman provincial earthenware. On this basis, there were 58 rural settlements that, according to Dumitru Protase, could be attributed to the local Dacian population or in which they can be found in certain proportions.[92] These settlements were not fortified; they occupied areas of eight to ten hectares. None of them ever developed into a town.[93]

The Dacian earthenware does not include all the pre-Roman forms but only a few of them. After the conquest, the Dacian earthenware of superior quality, produced on a wheel, disappeared completely, obviously because of the disappearance of the Dacian pottery workshops. No more Dacian bowls, large jars, or fruit dishes were produced. The earthenware was made by hand and consisted of a few primitive kinds of vessels. Dumitru Protase is of the opinion that the Dacian cup with the features typical of the preceding period, the pot of approximately a sac-like or bitronconic shape, different small mugs with a handle, and other indigenous forms of vessels must have existed, but their reconstruction is not always possible from the few and disparate fragments that have been preserved.[94] The ornamentation is also simplified, although the main motifs are preserved: the woven, alveolated, or incised belt; round prominences; incisions or alveoli on the rim of the vessel; and the simple line or the wave-line. The usual alveolated belt over the middle of the vessel is replaced by a simple streak in relief, and often no ornamentation is used at all.[95] A serious difficulty in the study of this pottery is the fact that it is generally not possible to determine the age of the vessels with any reasonable accuracy. In many cases it cannot even be proved whether a vessel was produced in the period before or after the conquest,[96] and those that are assumed to have been made in the time of the province are generally dated merely as "second or third century."[97]

It must be noted that this kind of earthenware is practically the only material attributed to Dacians living at these sites. Its quantity is low: only about 10 percent of all earthenware found in these settlements belongs to this category. Roman earthenware dominates the picture both qualitatively and quantitatively. Present everywhere, it consists of bowls, different kinds of pots, cans, lids, and other patterns of Roman provincial style. Some pieces imitate the *terra sigillata*[98] type. Besides pottery, of course, other objects specific to Roman culture, such as hand mills made in specialized workshops, fibulae, jewels, and coins, have also been found. A very important finding is that Roman style earthenware appears in the settlements from the first decade after the Roman conquest, without any period of transition and without showing any connection with the Dacian type.[99] In many cases these sites were insufficiently investigated; and the available descriptions are consequently vague, without exact data about relevant details, such as the stratigraphic situation. Often, further investigations will reportedly be needed in order to clarify the chronology or the ethnic attribution of the site in question.

On the basis of the estimated degree of accuracy of the descriptions, an attempt will be made to classify roughly these sites in two main groups. There are settlements in which the material was found in archaeological strata or at least in the remains of dwelling places (huts). In other cases, the finds were made on the surface, in fields or in vegetable gardens. In the latter, the original association of Dacian earthenware with that of the Romans is uncertain. According to a generous estimate, 39 sites could be included in the first group and 19 in the second. This does not mean, however, that data about the 39 settlements are satisfactory. There are also in this group too many incomplete investigations, a lack of systematic excavations, and unproven assumptions. The settlement Sic (Szék, Cluj County), for example, is said to be probably Dacian, dating to the Roman period, and seems to continue to the beginning of the fourth century; at Vulcan (Vulkán, Braşov County), and at Cernatul de Jos (Alsócsernáton, Covasna County),[100] a pre-Roman Dacian village seems to continue its existence during the Roman period. At Archiud (Mezőerked, Bistriţa County) a 40 to 90 cm thick stratum of archaeological remains were found; in its middle appear, mixed, all the material remains from the third to the fourth century and from the eleventh to the twelfth century, and it is not possible to establish between them a strict stratigraphic succession.[101] The archaeologist Mihail Macrea dated the beginning of this settlement in the years after the Roman retreat, while Protase believes that it began in the final stage of Roman rule.[102] At Boarta (Mihályfalva, Sibiu County) poor fragments of Dacian ceramics were found; at Curciu (Küküllőkörös, Sibiu County) the inhabitants seem to have been autochthons; Ocniţa (Mezőakna, Bistriţa County), on the basis of the finds, could have a "Daco-Roman" symbiosis. At many sites, "future investigations" are considered necessary for an adequate appreciation of the situation, such as the villages in the first group: Cernatul de Jos, Feldioara (Földvár, Braşov County), Micoşlaca (Miklóslaka, Alba County), Rădeşti, former Tîmpăhaza-Ujfalău (Tompaháza-Szászújfalu, Alba County); in the second group: Ciumbrud (Csombord, Alba County), Ciunga (Csongva, Alba County), Matei (Szászmáté, Bistriţa County), Rîşnov (Barcarozsnyó, Braşov County), Şieu-Odorhei (Sajóudvarhely, Bistriţa County), Sînmihai de Cîmpie (Mezőszentmihály, Bistriţa County), Viişoara Mică (Dolj County).

Since the publication of Protase's monograph in 1966, in which 30 settlements were mentioned as showing Roman-Dacian symbiosis, another 28 settlements have been found with similar characteristics. While this can be considered a large quantity, there has not been much progress qualitatively. The relationship between the settlements in which the finds were made in strata or at least within huts is the same (in 1966, 20 to 10; after 1966, 19 to 9), and the number of those in which future investigations are considered necessary is also similar. Thus, the scanty evidence that could be provided by the association of small amounts of earthenware of the Dacian type with the Roman provincial earthenware in a number of rural settlements of Dacia Traiana is further weakened by the fact that the primary material has been unsatisfactorily investigated. Furthermore, it should be noted that the evaluation of archaeological findings in contemporary Romania is solely designed to demonstrate the continuation of the autochthonous provincial population. Only to a limited extent, if any, is there any attention paid to the achievements of other researchers.

Most of the settlements above mentioned are not ancient Dacian villages but were created after the Roman conquest of Dacia. Only a few of them reveal some evidence of existence in pre-Roman times. More or less reliable signs of this are described at Roşia, Sibiu-Guşteriţa (Szenterzsébet), Slimnîc Şarba-Stempen (Szelindek), Şura Mică (Kiscsűr), and Copşa Mică (Kiskapus), all in Sibiu County. At two sites, Cernatul de Jos and Vulcan, material remains indicate a pre-Roman Dacian settlement whose continuation in the Roman period is uncertain.

In a monograph, Ioan Glodariu gives some details of interest regarding southern Transylvania.[103] It appears that all the Dacian villages in Făgăraş (Fogaras) were abandoned after the conquest of Dacia, and some of them were destroyed. From these findings it has been concluded that the population from this area was transferred to other areas, possibly to the north of the Olt River. The Romans built fortifications along the Olt, and settlements during the Roman domination existed only north of the river. Most of these were newly created after the conquest; but some of them, such as that Şarba-Stempen, thought to be one of the largest villages of southern Transylvania during the Roman domination, existed also in the pre-Roman era. The settlement dates to the time between the second century B.C. and the mid-third century A.D.

A very important aspect to investigate is the period of time during which these villages could have existed. Under the circumstances given, with many uncertain and insufficient data, it is not, of course, possible to establish this more accurately. Meaningful conclusions may, however, be drawn from rough data, indicating whether a village was inhabited before, during, or after the Roman domination or in any two or all of these periods.

One of the main characteristics of a local, indigenous population must be that they stayed in their villages for a longer time; in this case, one would expect that while the villages of the Roman colonists (and also their towns) would be emptied of their Roman population, those of the autochthonous population would be less affected by the Roman retreat. In other words, one would expect to see at least some degree of continuity on the village level. There are, of course, no general rules for such situations; but it would be peculiar, if, say, half or at least a third of these villages would not have continued their existence after the Roman retreat from the province.

After the Roman conquest and the defeat of the Dacians in 106 A.D., there was a significant discontinuity of the Dacian rural settlements. This has been explained by the regulations of the Roman state, aiming at better possibilities of supervising the Dacians as well as giving valuable farming land to the colonists. A similar, or even greater, discontinuity is, however, observed at the time of the Roman retreat from Dacia. All these settlements showed signs of decline already during the first half of the third century, and most of them end their existence in the second half of that century. Romanian researchers attribute this fact mainly to the political-military situation in the north-Danubian zone of the empire, in Dacia.[104]

Of 30 rural settlements in which a Roman-Dacian symbiosis was assumed in 1966, 3 showed some evidence of continuing existence after the second half of the third century A.D. Since 1966 an additional 28 settlements have been discovered in which such a symbiosis is assumed, and only one of them continues after 275 A.D. Thus, of a total of 58 settlements, only 4 (7%) continued to be inhabited after the Roman withdrawal. Far below even the modest expectation of a third of all settlements, this is an insignificant share and also a negligible absolute number. (See Table I) It is noteworthy that in the material known up to 1966 about 30 villages, only 3 show signs of continuity after 275 A.D. and that those discovered and published from 1966 to 1980 (1 out of 28 villages suggests signs of continuity after 275 A.D.) do not offer very bright prospects toward proving the presupposed continuity in the post-Roman period in Dacia Traiana. (See Table II)

It appears from the table that less than 20% of all civilian settlements contained primitive earthenware of the Dacian type. The great majority of these settlements (more than 90%) were in existence in a period restricted to the Roman domination in Dacia.

Rural Farms (villae rusticae)

As with rural life in Dacia Traiana in general, our knowledge of farming is extremely limited.[105] The farms (villae rusticae) were important units of Roman agriculture in most provinces. In Roman Dacia, however, they never reached the size and the significance they had in other provinces.[106] The number of such farming units is difficult to establish; remains of small buildings, a wall, and other remains,

TABLE I
Settlements in Dacia Traiana in which the presence of Dacians is claimed
and which continued to exist after the Roman retreat from the province

Found at present-day village:	Existed:	Notes:
Archiud Erked Bistriţa County	end of Roman era or shortly after to end of fourth cent.	excavations in 1961 and 1963. Free Dacians settling after 275?
Mugeni Bögöz Harghita County	end of Roman era to fourth cent.	excavations in 1961 and 1962
Şura Mică Kiscsűr Sibiu County	second century B.C. to fourth century	excavations from 1976 to 1979
Obreja Obrázsa Alba C., Slimnic	mid-second cent. A.D. to about 370 A.D.	excavations from 1961 to 1966 and 1969 to 1973

Source: Dumitru Protase, *Problema continuităţii în Dacia în lumina arheologiei şi numismaticii* [The Question of Continuity in Dacia in the Light of Archaeology and Numismatics], Bucharest: 1966, and Dumitru Protase, *Autohtonii în Dacia*, vol. I, *Dacia romană*, vol. I, (Bucharest: 1980), p. 83.

could have belonged to a single farming family and do not necessarily indicate a real *villa rustica*. So far, 10 *villae rusticae* have been excavated, another five were probably *villae suburbanae*, and about 25 are presumed to exist on the basis of finds from the surface but have not been confirmed by excavations.[107] There are, at present, intense investigations underway to determine whether Dacians were among the workers on these farms. This has not been established, nor is there any record of a Dacian owner extant. The same assumption, as in the case of the civilian settlements in general, has been made also in this connection: The presence of Dacians, according to Protase, is considered to be indicated by Dacian cups (*ceasca dacică*) and a few fragments of other vessels, made by hand from a paste of inferior quality which, judged by their form and ornamentation, could be assigned to the category of primitive earthenware of local, Dacian origin.[108] It is doubtful that this assumption is correct, a doubt shared elsewhere by Protase himself, who concluded his description of the rural farms with the remark that future investigations are necessary in order to establish if, to what extent, and when one may speak about the existence of a significant number of Dacians on the Roman farms.[109] It has been assumed that the local population lived pre-

TABLE II

Data about the civilian settlements in Dacia Traiana 106-275 A.D. in which the presence of Dacians is claimed

Total number of civilian settlements in Dacia (estimated)	Known in 1966	Added between 1966 and 1980	Total	
		300	300	
Pre-Roman settlements, probably continued in first half of second century	1ᶜ	1ᵛ	2	
Considered as existing in the Roman period and Dacian inhabitants assumed	29	27	56	< 20% of all civ. settl.
Existing in the pre-Roman period and under the Roman domination	1	4	5ˣ	9%
Founded after the Roman conquest	28	23	51	91%
Continued existence after the Roman retreat	3	1	4ˣ	7%
Life of settlement ended with Roman retreat	26	26	52	93%
Existing in the pre-Roman, Roman, and post-Roman periods	—	1	1ˢ	1.7%

Source: Dumitru Protase, *Problema continuității în Dacia în lumina arheologiei și numismaticii*, (Bucharest: 1966), and *Autohtonii în Dacia*, vol. I, *Dacia romana*, (Bucharest: 1980).
(c = Cernatul de Jos, v = Vulcan, x = including Şura Mică, ş = Şura Mică).

dominantly in areas in which no *villae rusticae* existed, for example, in eastern Transylvania.[110]

Almost all of these farms are limited to the period of Roman domination. In 1966 Protase expressed his opinion that excavations should be carried out in the surroundings of the *villae rusticae* to search for a possible continued presence of workers after the Roman withdrawal. In his monograph of 1966 he noted that at most two such farms (at Iernut and possibly at Răhău) showed some signs that this might be the case. In 1979, the archaeologist Kurt Horedt mentioned the possibility that Rǎhǎu (Rohó) and Cicǎu (Csákó) showed signs of continuity after 275 A.D.[111] In his monograph of 1980 Protase did not give any new data about this question.

Cemeteries and Funeral Rites

The Dacians cremated their dead; inhumation was practiced to a very small extent. Most frequently in the pre-Roman period, as well as later, through the fourth century, tombs consisted of an urn placed in a simple cavity of varying shapes and sizes. So far, about 300 such tombs are known. The next most frequent and simplest method was to place the remains of the burned bones in a simple cavity, without the use of an urn. The urns varied in shape and in quality, the simplest having been hand-made. In the present-day Romanian province of Dobrudja, dominated for centuries by the Greeks, and to a lesser extent in other transcarpathian areas, Greek amphorae were also used. The cavities were most often round or slightly oval when urns were used and rectangular in the absence of urns. In all these cases, the bodies were cremated in an *ustrinum* at a different place from that of the burial.

The other kinds of funeral rites appear almost exclusively in the transcarpathian territory, predominantly in Dobrudja and southern Moldavia. Cremation in the place of burial was frequently practiced by the Thracians, south of the Danube. One of the methods is with an oven; two such tombs are known, at Poieneşti and Zimnicea (in Vaslui and Teleorman Counties, respectively) dating to the fourth to third centuries B.C. Another is the typical Graeco-Roman form of the plane tomb without an urn, with a burn cavity of an alveolar shape. This form is found only in Istria, from the fourth century B.C. until the Roman period. Finally, there are barrow graves of Graeco-Thracian origin in Dobrudja and in southern Moldavia, and at two places in Transylvania, Şimleul Silvaniei (Szilágysomlyó, Sălaj County) and Viscri (Szászfehéregyháza, Weisskirch, Braşov County). Such tombs were probably made for tribal leaders and were not used by the Dacians in the second and third centuries A.D. Objects found in these tombs are quite poor and include clothing accessories, jewelry, knives, and similar objects, as well as earthenware. Coins were not placed in the tombs.[112]

Of importance is the relation of these funeral customs and rites to those of other peoples living in Southeastern Europe. The barrow grave form, as well as tombs with an urn, for example, was very frequent south of the Danube, among the Illyrians, as well as among the Old Germanic peoples.[113] It is noteworthy that the most common funeral custom among the Dacians was also practiced extensively by several groups in other Roman provinces during the second and third centuries A.D. The provincial Roman cemetery found at Bad Reichenhall, in Bavaria, offers a good example of the composition of such burial spots: of the 307 tombs, the majority use an urn; there are also cavities without an urn, urns in stone boxes, such boxes without an urn, the burning of the bodies at the place of burial, and tombs with a recess.[114]

A total of 12 cemeteries and tombs from Roman Dacia attributed to a Dacian population have been presented in a monograph by Dumitru Protase.[115] Existing data about several sites, however, are too inadequate and can be used only to a very limited extent. Either the material was investigated long ago and the descriptions left by nineteenth century authors show considerable deficiencies, or decisive data are lacking because of insufficient investigations or because of the destruction of significant parts of the material. At Sighişoara (Segesvár, Schässburg, Mureş County) and at Sebeş (Szászsebes, Alba County) remains of tombs dated to the Roman period were discovered more than hundred years ago and the descriptions are from 1861 and 1876, respectively. They are, of course, not of the quality required today; thus, the report on the finds at Sebeş is, according to Protase, summary and not very clear,[116] lacking such important details as data about the shape of the cavities. Of importance is the fact that the cavities are said to have been burned, a funeral custom unusual among the Dacians but common south of the Danube. At Sighişoara the primitive earthenware is said to have been entirely destroyed, and it is not known whether there were any ornamentations on the fragments of vessels. An unusual circumstance was the presence in this tomb of 112 Roman coins (denarii from the first century B.C. to 157 A.D.) which—in Protase's view—is a unique occurrence in Dacia.[117] At three other sites, the observations are quite recent and no detailed investigations have yet been carried out. At Apele Vii and at Leu (Dolj County), remains of tombs, probably of the same type as those found at Locusteni, were found in 1972 and "are to be systematically investigated by archaeological excavations."[118] At Spahii (Gorj County), remains from a cemetery dating to the second century A.D. were found in 1974; they included Dacian but no Roman earthenware. More detailed archaeological excavations have not yet been made.[119] At Iacobeni (Mezőszentjakab, Cluj County), 4 kilometers from the cemetery at Soporu de Cîmpie (Mezőszopor, Cluj County), while clearing the soil in 1961 to plant grape vines, workers found about 15 tombs. Unfortunately, all the material was destroyed with the exception of four urns, which are of the red Roman type and of high quality, possibly made at Cristeşti (Maroskeresztúr, Mureş County) and similar to those found at Soporu de Cîmpie, Lechinţa de Mureş (Maroslekence, Mureş County), Obreja, and other places. In an attempt to carry out systematic excavations in the same year, it was not possible to find any material at these sites; One cannot make precise conclusions about the funeral rites and rituals, the ethnic character of the people buried here, the size, and an exact date of the cemeteries.[120] At Şpălnaca (Ispánlaka, Alba County), 15 tombs were excavated in 1976 and 1979. They were in very poor condition: The urns and other vessels are, in general, of Roman origin. On the site of the cemetery, Dacian fragments were also found.[121] Obviously, under such circumstances, it is not possible to decide the relationship of the Dacian fragments to the Roman material. From the cemetery at Lechinţa de Mureş, three tombs were already known before the First World War, and further investigations in 1951 and 1957 have uncovered another five. Of these eight tombs, six were of the cremation type. The urns were of the red Roman provincial style, made of a high quality paste. The objects found there were also of the Roman provincial type; no Dacian earthenware was found in the cemetery. The assumption that in spite of this it belonged to the autochthonous population is based upon general considerations, such as similarities of the details of cremation with those found at Soporu de Cîmpie and Obreja, or the vicinity of the settlement found at this village in which autochthons are assumed. They may or may not be correct. Similar general considerations or assumptions are based on the premise that the rest of these above-mentioned seven cemeteries are Dacian.

More satisfactory descriptions are extant about the cemeteries excavated at the present-day villages of Locusteni (Dolj County), Cinciş (Csolnakos, Hunedoara County), Obreja, and Soporu de Cîmpie.

Locusteni. Excavated with the settlements, from 1969 to 1975 a total of 290 graves are described, of which 215 are of the cremation type and 37 contained bodies (mostly of children) interred without cremation. Of the cremation tombs, 167 contain an urn with a cover, and 48 lack an urn, having a simple unburned cavity. As is the case at Soporu de Cîmpie, the tombs were marked by stones on the surface. The earthenware found here is, like that in the nearby settlement, of both the Roman and the primitive, hand-made Dacian types. Objects are quite scarce and include fibulae of the Roman type, small Roman vessels, and silver filigree jewelry. The cemetery of Locusteni is dated to the second half of the second century A.D. and the first half of the third century.[122]

Cinciş (Csolnakos, Hunedoara County). Excavated in 1961 and 1962, it was also described in Protase's monograph 1966. Seventeen cremation tombs and one inhumation were found here, the last with a sarcophagus made of Roman bricks. Remains of a *villa rustica* were found 200 meters from this cemetery. Four of the graves are places in a mausoleum with walls of stone and mortar. These four graves are richer in objects than those placed outside and are thought to have belonged to the Roman owners of the *villa rustica*, while eight tombs outside this construction, poorer in objects, could be attributed to the autochthonous Dacian element.[123] Primitive Dacian earthenware was found in nine tombs, all outside of the mausoleum. The tombs were of the Roman provincial type, with a burned cavity, and usually built in an east-west direction. Most of them were covered by a small hillock of earth and surrounded by a stone-ring of three to six meters in diameter. A big stone was often placed above the cavity. The objects found in this cemetery were all of the Roman provincial type: rushlights, pearls, grey vessels, four coins, four fibulae, and knives. The fragments of primitive pottery were either without ornamentation or were ornamented by alveolated or striated bands. The fibulae and the rushlights date this cemetery to the period of Roman domination.

Obreja (Obrázsa, Alba County). Most of the material in this rather big cemetery is also of Roman style. The tombs are predominantly of the cremation type (236), and in about half of the cases an urn was used. Most of the cavities are round or slightly oval. Of 165 urns of the Roman provincial type, 38 are red, of superior quality; 7 are blackish-grey, also of superior quality, while 120 are of rough Roman earthenware. Primitive hand-made earthenware was found in a much lesser quantity. Because of the coarse paste and the poor firing, these pieces are difficult to reconstruct; and their shapes cannot always be determined.[124] They are ornamented by incised belts, buttons, ornamentation used by the Dacians in the pre-Roman times but much simplified. A total of 12 such pieces, or 7.3% of all earthenware in this cemetery, were found. The Dacian cup does not appear here. An interesting and unique phenomenon is an urn of the Roman provincial type, decorated by an incised belt in the Dacian manner. Two bronze coins from the second century A.D. were found in these tombs, apparently used as oboli of Charon according to the ancient Graeco-Roman custom, and one lachrimatory (*lacrimarium*), presumably another indication of Roman funeral customs. These phenomena can be explained either by admitting that in the Dacian community which lived at this site, Roman colonists were also living or that the local Dacians had adopted some funeral customs from the provincial Roman types.[125]

Many of the archaeological findings of Obreja must be attributed to the Carps, such as the Carpic fibulae, the silver jewelry, and the types of ceramics and fibulae's form, which are the same or similar to those found in Soporu de Cîmpie.[126]

Soporu de Cîmpie (Mezőszopor, Cluj County).[127] Excavated in 1955 and 1961, this is one of the largest of the cemeteries attributed by most Romanian historians to the Dacians in Roman Dacia. Out of a total of 189 tombs, 168 (89%) are of the cremation type and 21 (11%) of the inhumation type. Most of the graves contain an urn, in 136 cases placed in an usual cavity, in 3 cases in a stone box, and in another 2 cases covered by a platform of tombstones. A lesser number (27) are tombs without an urn, consisting of a simple cavity, round or oval, and small; some of these too are covered by a platform of gravestones. In all cases, the burning of the body was carried out in a place different from that of the burial. Among the Roman urns, there are high quality red ones made on a potter's wheel; grey-brownish urns of inferior quality; and hand-made, blackish-grey urns of rough paste, with Dacian ornaments. In three cases, the urn was covered by a Dacian cup. The 21 inhumation graves contain mostly the remains of bones of children below seven years of age. At least six of these contained Roman provincial pottery, while Dacian vessels (shards) were found in only one.

Earthenware was found in 167 tombs. Out of these, fragments or entire vessels of both Roman and Dacian type were found in 45,[128] or 27% of all tombs in which earthenware was found. In another 17 tombs, only pottery of the Dacian type was found. Of all earthenware pieces in the cemetery, 90% are of the Roman provincial type, and the rest are considered Dacian. The objects are all of Roman provincial origin. The fibulae are of four different types, all of which were used in several other Roman provinces too.

There are few available data that can be used to establish the age of the remains in Soporu de Cîmpie. The earliest objects from this cemetery are two fibulae with nodules on their arch and coins from the time of Trajan through that of the Emperor Antoninus Pius (138–161 A.D.)[129] The fibulae were in use during the first century and the first half of the second century A.D. in Germania, Pannonia, north of the Black Sea, and, for example, in the Lipitza culture. They are not present in the Carpic sites, since these were settled after this type of fibula had disappeared from use. These objects date the beginning of the cemetery to the mid-second century. Of those 14 fibulae that can be dated, 11 are from the third and only 3 from the second century A.D.[130] Materials whose age could be determined with some accuracy, such as coins, fibulae, pendants, and some other jewelry, were found in 25 of the 95 tombs that contained objects. Of these 25 tombs, 9 contained objects dating to the second and 16 to the third century. It seems that more burials took place in the third than in the second century, but the number of tombs from which conclusions can be drawn is too low (about a fourth of the tombs that contained some objects and only 13% of all tombs in the cemetery) for reliable conclusions. Of the 62 tombs with Dacian pottery, only 13 contained material that could be dated; in 6 of these, the objects indicate the second and in 7, the third century.[131] One must conclude that the material is not sufficiently representative for reliable conclusions.

With regard to the last use of this cemetery, one can set it at the beginning of the fourth century on the basis of a pendant with rhomboid plaques, of a type that has been dated to the early fourth century.[132] This is questioned by Protase, who notes that the pendant found in tomb no. 1 is similar to some found in a settlement of potters at Zofipole, near Craiova, dated to the period between 200 and 400 A.D.[133] It should be noted that the rhomboid plaques are to be found also among the Carps.

The fibula with an inverted foot was in use from the end of the second to the fifth century A.D. in a vast territory of the Roman Empire as well as in Barbaricum.[134] The remains of four huts built over pits have been discovered in which there were ceramics and fibulae similar to those found in the cemetery of Kisszombat (Hungary).

The above-mentioned objects do not exclude nor do they prove a continued use of the cemetery at Soporu de Cîmpie after the Roman retreat from Dacia. It is not an ancient Dacian cemetery, already in use in pre-Roman Dacia, but was begun several decades after the conquest and fell into disuse most probably with the end of Roman domination. Later a Gepidic settlement appeared here.

In examining the excavations at Soporu de Cîmpie, Kurt Horedt concluded[135] that the cemetery can be divided in three parts, corresponding to three periods of time: Phase one, the northwestern part, is characterized by the predominance of Dacian vessels and a generally poor inventory; in phase 2a, urns of a greyish-brown color dominate and a Carpic silver ornament appears; and in phase 2b, Roman influence increases with the appearance of red toilet-powder, ball-formed urns, and imitations of sarcophagi (boxes of stone). Only in this phase were old coins from the second century placed into the tombs.[136] Such a division is, however, poorly corroborated by reality. There are indeed more Dacian vessels in the northwestern part of the cemetery than in the southeastern part where three stone boxes were found, and most of the coins are found in the southern part; but there is a significant overlapping in most respects.[137] Moreover, most of the inhumation tombs situated in the northwestern part contain chiefly Roman material; only one of 21 contains fragments of Dacian vessels.

There are two different opinions among archaeologists about the people who once used this cemetery: In 1962 Kurt Horedt expressed his theory of a Carpic colonization, maintained also by Mihail Macrea,[138] while Dumitru Protase assumes they were Dacians living under Roman rule. This controversy underlines the great difficulties in arriving at reliable conclusions on the basis of the scarce historical records and the available archaeological material.

The migration of the Carps primarily encompasses the area from the rim of the eastern Carpathians to the heart of Moldavia. After the abandonment of the province of Dacia Traiana, the Carps moved into Transylvania, although in the years 245 to 247 Dacia was threatened by Carpic incursions. Carpic archaeological remnants have been found in various places in Transylvania (Ilişua-Uriu, Alsóilva-Felőr, Bistriţa County, Obreja, Sebeş, Mediaş.) and the ceramics thus found are difficult to differentiate from Dacian earthenware.[139]

About thirty hoards of coins found in Transylvania date from the time of the Carpic incursions and were obviously buried because of the attacks.[140] Most probably, the inscription made by an inhabitant of Apulum, a *Carpis liberatus*,[141] also refers to this event. In Horedt's view,[142] Carps taken as prisoners of war in those years were settled at several places in Transylvania, in the vicinity of military centers: at Soporu de Cîmpie, 20 kilometers from Potaissa, where a Roman legion was stationed; at Obreja, near Apulum at Fărcaşele, Locusteni; and Reşca, near to the military center of Dacia Malvensis-Romula (in present-day Oltenia). This hypothesis is mainly based upon the finds of several objects considered specific to the Carps; these include a piece of granulated, filigree-ornamented silver jewelry of which about 100 pieces were found in Moldavia (Carpic Poieneşti culture of the mid-third century), and safety pin with a long feather-cylinder. Horedt therefore believes that the cemetery belonged to the Carps and was begun in the first half of the third century A.D. On the basis of the older coins and Dacian ceramics erroneously taken to date the cemetery, it was assumed that the use of the cemetery began in the second century and belongs to the indigenous Dacians. However, there is a chronological gap of more than one hundred years between the Roman conquest of Dacia and the beginning of the cemeteries during which the Dacians of the first group were not in any way influenced by the Romans.[143]

The settlement of free Dacians in the Roman province of Dacia must also be postulated, since there are no historical records about the relations between these tribes and the Romans. According to Dio

Cassius, Sabianus, the governor of Dacia in 180 A.D., "has also subdued 12,000 Dacians living in the vicinity [of Dacia], who have been driven away from their ancient homeland, and was ready to help the others, promising them land in our Dacia."[144] Although this record suggests a colonization of free Dacians, it offers no proof of it, since it is not known whether Sabianus kept his promise. It must be pointed out that the immigration of free Dacians from the areas northwest and west of the territory of the former province after the Roman withdrawal is well established and unquestioned. Archaeological remains show that free Dacians settled after 275 A.D. at Cipău (Maroscsapó, Mureş County), at Archiud, and most probably also at Soporu de Cîmpie.

Dumitru Protase emphasizes that the material culture of the free Dacians is not yet sufficiently known. The following finds were connected with the presence of Carps in Dacia Traiana: Grey amphorae and fruit dishes made on a wheel; pearls, earrings of silver, and filigree jewelry; small, columbine-shaped, iron pendants; mirrors of the Sarmatian type, made of white metal; certain forms of bronze fibulae, dating to the end of the second century; and similarities in the funeral customs.[145] The objects appear in relatively small numbers. Although elements more or less characteristic of the Carps have been found at 21 places in Transylvania and Oltenia, it is not certain that Carps really settled in all these sites. Especially jewelry and fibulae can easily pass from one area to another; and it cannot be excluded that such filigree jewelry and fibulae were produced in provincial Roman workshops.[146] If one accepts as the most reliable evidence of the Carps only earthenware and the find of several objects specific to them, a colonization of Carps in the mid-third century A.D. in the Roman province of Dacia, is possible at Bezid (Bözöd, Harghita County), Mediaş (Medgyes, Sibiu County), Sebeş, Cristian (Keresz-ténysziget, Sibiu County), Mereşti (Homoródalmás, Harghita County), Şopteriu (Septér, Bistriţa County) and, possibly, Govora-Sat.[147]

The problem has not been concluded, but the settlement of free Dacians and Carps in Dacia after the Roman retreat can be considered as proved; their settlement at several places already in the mid-third century is likely. An even earlier colonization of Carps is not documented but is not entirely to be excluded. In any case, it is unlikely that the inhabitants of Obreja or Locusteni or those buried at Soporu de Cîmpie would have been exclusively Carps or free Dacians coming in the second half of the second century.

The presence of the primitive Dacian-type earthenware in the settlement and cemeteries and the practice of cremation are practically the only solid evidence for the existence of Dacians at these sites. The amount of this type of earthenware is, however, very low (10%

of all earthenware in the sites), the majority being Roman provincial. It is not known whether the primitive earthenware was produced in the province or not; it is, in any case, practically identical to that found among the free Dacians in the same period. The Roman provincial earthenware is present from the beginning at all these sites, and no changes related to time were indicated in this respect.

Already these circumstances raise the question of whether the earthenware and the practice of cremation are really as significant as has been assumed. At some places, there are practices that would be unusual for the Dacians. At Sighişoara, for example, a large number of coins were found in the cemetery, something that is not encountered in the rest of the cemeteries. In connection with the discovery of coins, however, it must be noted that in order to make a case for Roman continuity, coins of the fourth century were deceptively included in the excavations. At Sighişoara contemporary excavations have revealed seven different phases of settlements ranging from the third to the eighth or ninth centuries. The remains indicate not only a Germanic population (pitchers with spouts) but also an as yet deliberately unnamed population group.

At Cinciş and Sebeş, the cavities were burned, contrary to Dacian custom (the Romans used predominantly inhumation). These burned cavities appear from the beginning of the cemeteries insofar as this can be determined. This would sooner suggest a group of people that had the funeral custom in question at the time they colonized the sites rather than Dacians adopting a non-Dacian funeral custom.

A difficult problem for the theory about significant numbers of Dacians in Dacia Traiana is the absence of any evidence of the old Dacian gods. In Italia, Hispania, Gallia, Germania, and Britannia, for example, strong evidence exists to indicate that under the Romans, the indigenous gods were worshipped for a long period of time under different forms and under their earlier names.[148]

All these facts taken together suggest a non-Dacian population. Dacia was populated "from the whole Roman world" (Eutropius), and this statement is corroborated by the inscriptions, the indications of many different religions. There were Thracians, Illyrians, Greeks, Orientals, and others. On the other hand, very few people came to Dacia from Italy. It is noteworthy that until the mid-1970s, the peoples that left the remains of settlements and cemeteries at Caşolţ (Hermány, Sibiu County), Calbor (Kálbor, Braşov County), and Ighiu (Magyarigen, Alba County) were considered by Romanian archaeologists to be autochthonous ("Daco-Roman").[149] This interpretation, however, was changed a few years later. The character of the barrow graves in question was no longer demonstrable as Dacian; instead it could be attributed to colonists from Pannonia, Noricum, and Illyria (Dalmatia).[150] It can be assumed that after the fourth century vestiges of Dacians are no more ascertainable. The risk exists, moreover, that cemeteries or settlements, in which the archaeological material known today is not as specific, have not been correctly attributed but have been erroneously assigned to the Dacians.

It is also possible that the material at the sites in question is insufficient to determine the real origin of the inhabitants; obviously the Dacian hypothesis is not by far the only possibility and, in fact, not even the most likely. It has been admitted that the material remains of Roman culture could have been left by Roman colonists,[150a] in which case, the assumption of Dacians living there is not necessary.

If one accepts the reasoning that the Dacians living in Roman Dacia adopted Roman culture and then the Latin language and had been Romanized by the time the Romans left the province around 275 A.D., Dacian elements among the remains of such a population would decrease successively and be replaced by Roman material.[151] As it appears from the description of the cemeteries there are no signs to indicate such gradual changes. It is, however, even more important to investigate whether the non-Roman population at Soporu de Cîmpie and at the other places where Dacians are assumed to have been living in Roman Dacia adopted Roman culture as a whole, in an organic way, which could indicate the emergence of a new, specific culture in which both the ancient Dacian and the new Roman elements are combined.

Relating to the adoption of funeral rites, there are, of course, major problems with regard to the assumed Romanized population and those of the non-Roman population in Dacia Traiana. In the cemetery at Soporu de Cîmpie five Roman coins from the period from 112 to 182 A.D. were found (two of them in urns) and probably were placed in the tombs for payment of the oboli of Charon, an ancient Graeco-Roman custom. It is assumed that the people living here had adopted this custom in the second century A.D. from the Roman colonists. From the whole territory of Dacia Traiana, about 20 such cases are known, which would be a consequence of the Graeco-Roman cultural-religious influence.[152] This "cultural-religious influence" is seen, however, also among peoples who did not adopt the Latin language, for example, in eastern Prussia, east of the Passarge River[153] and, in fact, also among the Carps in Moldavia.[154] The latest date of the coins found in the cemetery at Soporu de Cîmpie is 182 A.D., and it is assumed that they "date burials made in the second century A.D."[155] They were extremely worn, however, and could have been placed in the tombs much later than their date of issue. Still, if this were a general adoption of a Roman funeral custom by Dacians living in the province, it is very peculiar that not a single coin from the third century was put into the tombs, in spite of the considerable number of Roman coins circulating in the province in the first half of that century. Moreover, the low number (five in a total of 189 tombs) of oboli of Charon far from indicates a generally adopted or widespread custom.

Although frequent in the Roman world, burned cavities in the form of a trough did not belong to the funeral customs of the Dacians in the pre-Roman era.[156] Such tombs were not found at Soporu de Cîmpie but exist at two sites in Transylvania: at Cinciş and at Sebeş. This is said to prove that the Dacians adopted this custom from the Roman colonists and used it in the interior of the province.[157] At Cinciş, this may have happened in 8 tombs and at Sebeş, in several tombs, described quite deficiently in 1876. Besides the low number of such finds, the fact that all tombs at these two places have a burned cavity while no such tombs exist in other cemeteries attributed to Dacians fits badly with a progressive adoption of funeral customs.

Roman Influence on Primitive (Dacian) Earthenware

At Soporu de Cîmpie, two urns were found that could be Dacian imitations of Roman earthenware forms: In tomb no. 89 fragments were found of a Dacian urn made by hand of a blackish paste and poorly fired.[158] The urn in tomb no. 185 was improvised from the lower part of a Dacian pot of brick-red and beige color, made on a wheel of crude paste, and without ornamentation, which could be as also the case of the urn from tomb no. 89, an imitation of an urn of Roman shape by Dacian village potters, but this time made on a wheel.[159] Two vessels can be mentioned in this context at Şarba-Stempen: The shape of a vessel decorated by Dacian ornamentation (bands in relief) and the rim of another Dacian vessel imitate Roman forms. Shards of these vessels were found among other fragments in a hut dated to the third century A.D.[160]

The only reference to a possible increase of Roman provincial material is from Şura Mică, but without any more detailed data.[161] These and a few similar examples suggest, at most, single imitations of the Roman earthenware, very frequently found in most European countries in the period in question.[162]

Adoption of Dacian forms in the provincial Roman pottery made in Roman Dacia is assumed but not demonstrated. In other provinces, for example, in the Balkan Peninsula and along the Rhine River, the influence of local earthenware upon the Roman provincial forms can be proved extensively.[163]

The Roman influence upon the primitive, probably Dacian, earthenware found at a number of sites from the time of the province is thus insignificant. The Dacian earthenware shows only small changes in the period in question, is quite uniform and preserves generally, within and outside the province, its traditions from the local Latène period,[164] from which it developed;[165] and insofar as there were changes, they consisted of a decrease in the number of shapes and the simplification of ornamentation. The primitive Dacian earthenware, made crudely by hand, lacking any counterpart in the Roman provincial earthenware, persisted in the rural areas of the province throughout the time of Roman domination.[166] A consequence of the persistence of the traditional forms is the similarity of the Dacian earthenware throughout all the Roman period. It is not possible to decide, on the basis of the earthenware's characteristics, whether it is from the second or third century.[167] If the people who used this kind of earthenware in the province were colonists from another Roman province, all this is of little significance. If they were Dacians, however, the earthenware used throughout the Roman domination hardly fits with the hypothesis of their Romanization. The replacement of their own, ancient culture, including their native tongue, by that of the Romans would obviously imply an enormous change. It is difficult to imagine that it would have left their earthenware affected to such a small degree that the differences are insignificant when compared with the earthenware of the free Dacians and that it is not possible to demonstrate a clear difference between early (second century) and later (third century) forms.

The Inscriptions of the Roman Period in Trajan's Dacia

After a closer analysis of the archaeological complex in the former Roman province, it should be noted that the preserved inscriptions speak more against than for a rapid assimilation of the Dacians. The approximately 3,000 inscriptions from Trajan's Dacia are remarkable for the short period of Roman domination but are less so for two territories that were subject to a more extended occupation by the Romans and for which territories a better case for intensive Romanization can be made: About 7,500 inscriptions were found in Dalmatia and 3.500 in Pannonia Superior.[168] However, less than 3% of the personal names found on the inscriptions in Trajan's Dacia are Dacian (or Thraco-Dacian), some of which belonged to colonists from the Balkan Thracian language area.[169]

The closer the Roman border, the larger is the number of

inscriptions; the largest number is to be found in the Dobrudja (more than two hundred) and, after that, in Oltenia and in the Banat. The fewest are encountered in Transylvania[170] and then in the western part where the earlier Roman settlements occurred. In eastern Transylvania, in the marginally Romanized areas, only some 100 to 150 inscriptions are to be found.

THE FOURTH CENTURY A.D. IN TRANSYLVANIA

There are no written records about the conquest of Dacia.[171] The withdrawal of Aurelianus's legions is also difficult to date precisely. It could have occurred in 268 A.D. but also as late as 275 A.D.[172] Whether part of the population of Dacia Traiana remained in place after the Roman retreat has been a much debated question. Eutropius's statement that Emperor Aurelian removed the Roman population from Dacia Traiana[173] and settled them south of the Danube[174] may or may not be true. There is not much point in continuing this debate, however, because we are now able to analyse archaeological material (remains of settlements and tombs, earthenware, coins, and so forth) advanced in support of the hypothesis of a Roman or Romanized population in Transylvania in the fourth century. The material remains of non-Roman peoples in Transylvania in the centuries after the Roman retreat have been known long, but new data about them have been discovered in recent decades. The problems could be formulated as follows: 1. how reliable are the arguments in favor of the Roman character of a part of the population; and 2. assuming that Romans were living there in the fourth century, what was their situation, their share of the total population; and 3. what influence from the non-Romans could reasonably be expected to be found under the given circumstances?

The material remains dated to the fourth century in Transylvania (the greater part of which was a significant share of Dacia Traiana) were recently described by Kurt Horedt,[175] who distinguishes three principal areas: 1. the western part of Transylvania, the area of the former Roman towns of Sarmizegethusa, Apulum, Potaissa, Napoca, and Porolissum, characterized by Roman finds, and a western group of rural settlements in which a "Daco-Roman" population is assumed to have been living; 2. the Sîntana de Mureş (Marosszentanna) culture in the Transylvanian Basin (Mezőség, Cîmpia Transilvaniei) and the adjacent areas (north-central Transylvania), which can be identified with the western Goths' settlements, and 3. the people of Sfîntu Gheorghe (Sepsiszentgyörgy) in eastern Transylvania with a Dacian, Roman, and Germanic (Gothic) mixed culture. To these must be added groups of free (non-Romanized) Dacians who migrated to the former province during the second half of the third century. The boundaries between these areas are not clear-cut, and there is a considerable overlapping among them.

The Former Roman Towns

The third quarter of the third century marked the twilight of Roman life in Transylvania, and certain phenomena characteristic of the period of the peoples' migrations now come into evidence. Following the abandonment of the province of Dacia, Roman urban life shows a picture of a total extinction. No Roman town names survived in Transylvania in contrast to Noricum Mediterraneum (contemporary Slovenia), for example. This argues against Roman continuity in Transylvania. Although a few towns are located on Roman foundations, it is not possible to ascertain a continuing existence of the population; an ethnic gap exists.[176] The ancient name of Porolissum, for example, was changed in the early Middle Ages to the Slavic Moigrad. Objects such as gems, earthenware, lamps, fibulae, and coins are imported goods of the late Roman period. Remains of buildings and other signs of construction the former Roman towns in Transylvania in the post-Roman period are very few and mostly tombs, of which a total of 90 are described by Horedt; all show the rite of inhumation.[177] They were made of bricks (70%) or stone (29%), and there is one made simply in the earth. The stone sarcophagi were constructed mostly of reused pieces, and it is questionable whether new sarcophagi were constructed after the Roman retreat.[178]

An essential but quite difficult problem is a reliable estimate of the period in which the different tombs were built. In several cases, such as the tombs found in the former Roman baths (*thermae*) in Apulum, the situation in the former town gives an indication. Objects found in the tombs could also be helpful, such as coins, bracelets, fibulae, and so forth, while the form of the tomb is less relevant. A layer of chalk in the bottom is considered an early Christian custom; it is found in 12 tombs from 4 towns. A short review of the situation in the former Roman towns in Transylvania—Sarmizegethusa, Apulum, Potaissa, Napoca, and Porolissum—will be given here, mainly on the basis of Horedt's monograph from 1982.

At Sarmizegethusa, near to the territory of the former Roman capital of the province of Dacia Traiana, simple fireplaces, a canal, and a wall (the last to be mentioned in the *Aedes Augustalium*)[179] were constructed, showing that the area was also inhabited after the Roman retreat by a poor and numerically very much reduced population.[180] The amphitheater was blocked by gravel, which is thought to indicate that it had been used for defense. On the basis of a hoard of Roman coins that end in the reign of Emperor Valentinian I (364–375) or of Emperor Valens, it is considered that all this was done during the second half of the fourth century. A total of eight isolated Roman coins from the time after 275 A.D. have been found in the territory of former Sarmizegethusa; in addition, a hoard with reportedly 69 coins was also described from the area. There are three tombs that probably date from the fourth century A.D.; all are made of bricks. One, discovered near the amphitheater in 1935, is in an east-west direction and has a thick layer of chalk on the bottom. A glazed-bronze vessel with a handle indicates its late construction. Another tomb was found in the area of the cemetery and the third one on the grounds of a suburban villa 150 meters from the walls of the town. Eleven rushlights found in the territory of Sarmizegethusa were dated to the third century or the beginning of the fourth.[181] It might be added here that after the fourth century no archaeological findings are ascertainable for the two following centuries; only a seventh century fibula of the Sarmizegethusa type, presumably from a Slavic cremation tomb, is known.[182]

At Alba Iulia (Gyulafehérvár) on the site of the ancient Apulum, the center of Dacia and a legionary town, southeast of the eighteenth century tower, several remains of buildings, Roman baths, and pagan churches from the Roman period were unearthed between 1899 and 1915. The excavations showed that tombs had been laid down between them in a later period. The Hungarian archaeologist, Béla Cserni, excavated 56 tombs of the inhumation funeral rite from 1902 to 1908, approximately half of which are probably late Roman with the rest belonging to the Bijelo-Brdo culture. Two tombs can be dated more reliably to the fourth century by coins, another two by their contents of late Roman bracelets; and a fifth, made of bricks and attached to the wall of the Roman building unearthed here, is also considered late Roman.[183] In 1970 and 1971 some tombs that are probably late Roman were discovered at a place called Podei, in the Roman cemetery of Apulum. They were made of bricks and oriented roughly in a west-east or northwest-southeast direction. Stone monuments were reused in the construction of two of them, and three others had a layer of chalk on their bottom.[184] A rushlight found in the baths shows a cross on its bottom[185] and belongs to the objects of a Christian character from the fourth century. A total of 14 probably late[186] rushlights were found in this town, of which two have a Christian cross. A total of 45 isolated coins from the period of Diocletian to that of Gratianus were found here.

No remains of habitation from the fourth century were found in the area of the former Roman town of Potaissa (present-day Turda, Torda), one of the chief military stations of the Roman army in Dacia Traiana. Only coins from the fourth century, 15 with the place of discovery known and another 19 without (but reportedly "found in Turda") suggest that the area was inhabited in the fourth century.

Here, as in Sarmizegethusa and Apulum, the main finds are tombs. South of the Arieş (Aranyos) River, a large area of cemeteries is found. Some of the tombs here are consdiered to be late Roman. Of those discovered in 1894 and 1895, two were laid southwest by northeast, the bottom of another was covered by a thick layer of chalk, and a third had a flat cover.[187] From 1951 to 1957 several tombs were discovered between Valea Sîndului and the Arieş, on a hill named Şuia. Four of them, constructed of bricks, were oriented from west to east or southwest to northeast. Two of them were empty, and one was trapezoidal in shape.[188] A tomb discovered in 1964 on the northern shore of the Arieş was constructed of bricks, contained a silver onion-button fibula, and could be dated to 300 A.D. at the earliest.[189] In 1937 the stone sarcophagus of a child was found among other tombs east of the site of the former Roman garrison. It was made of a reused piece. Another sarcophagus of a child was trapezoidal. In 1969 5 tombs were discovered 150 meters from this site. One of them, oriented east by northeast to west by southwest and built in the shape of a trapezoid, contained bits of chalk at the head and feet of the body. In another, a silver fibula of the onion-button type, dated to the mid-third century, and a coin from the era of Emperor Commodus (180–192 A.D.) were found. A gem with the picture of the "Good Shepherd" and with the Christian inscription IXOYC was found "in Turda," but the exact spot of the find is not known; it belongs to the objects of Christian character from the fourth century.

In the area of the former capital of Dacia Porolissensis, Napoca (present-day Cluj, Kolozsvár), no traces of buildings made after the Roman domination have been found; only tombs can probably dated to the beginning of the fourth century. A three-meter thick stratum of debris between the Roman town and the present ground level may contribute to the lack of such finds. On the territory of the former town of Napoca, a hoard containing seven coins from the time immediately after the Roman retreat was found. Around the city, for example, in present-day Mănăştur (Kolozsmonostor), a total of 26 isolated coins have been reported, most of them during the last decade.

Around 1885 three sarcophagi made of reused tombstones were discovered on the present-day Ştefan cel Mare (formerly Hunyadi)

Square, somewhat to the northeast of Petőfi Street, where three sarcophagi were found in 1914. In one of these, there were two late Roman earrings. On the same site in 1927 a sarcophagus worked from an antique memorial-stone (*cippus*), dated somewhere from the second through the third century A.D., reused and excavated to serve as a box of a pagan sarcophagus, was discovered. Christian symbols were added to the inscription; the tomb also contained four needles. A fourth tomb was a sarcophagus made of brick, and from the same site there is also a stone sarcophagus with a cover made of an Aedicula wall.[190] Not far from this site, in Kogălniceanu (Farkas) Street, a stone sarcophagus covered by a reused Aedicula Wall was discovered, in 1974. Southeast of Roman Napoca, in Plugarilor Street, five tombs were found in 1933 and another 32 between 1972 and 1976. Of these, 28 were oriented in a west-east direction, and some of them had a layer of chalk on the bottom. There were nine stone sarcophagi and 22 tombs constructed of brick. Older monuments were reused in at least six cases. No objects were found in these tombs, because all had been plundered.[191]

Finds dating to the fourth century are scarce in the area of Moigrad (Mojgrád, antique Porolissum), near Zalău (Zilah). As is the case with the other former Roman towns, no later settlement was built here, nor have thorough excavations been done here.[192] The remains of a Benedictine monastery from the twelfth century, also mentioned in documents, were excavated in 1914. Near this building, 17 tombs (6 sarcophagi, 11 without sarcophagi) laid down later, were found, of which six were made of brick. Several Romanian archaeologists have considered these tombs to be remains of "Daco-Romans."[193] Also the Romanian archaeologist Dumitru Protase considered that, on basis of the brick construction, these tombs can be dated to the post-Roman period.[194] Horedt rejects this interpretation and considers that these tombs were medieval.[195]

The Roman coins found at Moigrad (Porolissum) dated from the time of Emperor Constantine the Great to that of Valens. A number of objects of Christian character from several centuries were also found here; from the fourth century there is the bottom of a dish with a Chrismon (signs of Christian letters) and a votive inscription engraved on its inner side, "*Ego . . . vius vot(um) p (osui),*" as well as a tree and a pigeon. (As shown by István Bóna, *Erdély története*, Budapest, 1986, vol. I, p. 564, this is most probably a forgery.) Another find from Moigrad is considered possibly of Christian origin: a fragment of a clay vessel, on which the formula *Utere Felix* was engraved.[195a] The inscription *Utere Felix* can be traced back to the last years of the province of Dacia Traiana (Horedt). Following the abandonment of the province, inscriptions were no longer used.

Cemeteries in Rural Areas

No significant continuity from the Roman epoch and after in the cemeteries found in Transylvania can be demonstrated. Even those nine cemeteries attributed by Horedt (1982, p. 96) to "Daco-Romans" were founded after 275 A.D. Moreover, while inhumation is the only funeral rite known to have been practiced in the former Roman towns, the cemeteries in rural areas show inhumation and cremation in approximately the same proportion. There is no geographical correlation either: in Suatu (Magyarszovát, Cluj County), not far from Napoca, we find inhumation; but in the two cemeteries nearest to former Roman towns (Baciu/Bács, near Napoca and Soporu de Cîmpie near Potaissa), cremation was practiced. The funeral rites are, however, of very great significance in the study of ethnic characteristics; and nine cemeteries are not, with regard to the general scarcity of finds, too low a number. In any case, the cemeteries attributed to a Roman population in Transylvania during the fourth century A.D. do not strengthen the argument for a western Roman area in Transylvania.

The Western Group of Settlements

Horedt assumed in 1982 sixteen settlements in western Transylvania to have been inhabited by a Roman population. Only one of these (near Iernut) continued from the Roman epoch, all the others were founded after the Roman state abandoned the province. This lack of continuity calls for even greater evidence that the population in these newly founded villages were Romans. It is therefore necessary to scrutinize these criteria. Many different ideas have been advanced: Horedt's hypothesis in his monograph from 1982 is only one of them.

Roman coins and fibulae with an inverted foot, found in the western settlements, also appear in the eastern settlements of Transylvania, which are attributed to a non-Roman population (see below).[196] Horedt argues, however, that in the western settlements, there are two kinds of late Roman finds that appear only there: onion-shaped fibulae and twin-rowed combs. These became more general in the following centuries in the row-graves but also existed in the Roman period. An analysis of the lists of finds in Horedt's monograph shows, however, that the fibulae are found in only two sites, at Obreja and documented indirectly by a find from a tomb at Tîrnăvioara (Kisekemező, Alba County). They are, moreover, not exclusive in the group called "western" but also appear at two sites in the southeastern corner of Transylvania: Two were found at Comolău (Komolló, Covasna County), a settlement attributed to the eastern group, and one somewhat to the south of this site, at Hălmeag (Halmágy, Brașov County).[197] Twin-rowed combs were found at three sites: Aiud-Rădești (Szászújfalu, Alba County), Cluj-Mănăștur, and Țaga (Cege, Cluj County).[198] The basis of classification is therefore inadequate, with only five of the sixteen settlements in this group showing the distinguishing features and then not even exclusively.

Earthenware, one of the most reliable indicators of differences between populations, cannot be used to distinguish a possible Roman from a non-Roman population in Transylvania. To be able to analyze the pottery in the post-Roman period, it would be necessary to have a good knowledge of the earthenware from the time of the province as well as in the period immediately following the abandonment of the province, especially with regard to possible Dacian and Roman elements. Such knowledge is not, however, extant.[199] The progressive barbarization of the earthenware, parallel to the general decline of Roman culture and civilization in Dacia Traiana as early as the mid-third century, has been noted earlier.[200] It will probably never be possible to establish the features of post-Roman pottery in Transylvania and to distinguish it from that produced during the Roman period.[201]

The continued production of Roman earthenware in the post-Roman period is questionable; it "may, in any case, be assumed."[202] The grey earthenware, which contains sand and was also available earlier, increased and eventually replaced the red pottery.[203] At the same time, the grey earthenware changed, becoming better fired and getting a glazed surface. This phenomenon was not, however, restricted to the territory of former Dacia Traiana but can be observed over a much larger area, such as in the valley of the Tisza River among the Sarmatians and in the Černjachov culture to the east.[204]

A total of 27 rushlights were found in Transylvania, but it is uncertain whether they are from the time of the province or later. They were found predominantly in the territories of the former Roman towns, one of them in Mercheaşa (Mirkvásár, Braşov County), near Braşov. Since no molds have been found in Transylvania, they must have been imported from the empire. It has been assumed that they were produced in the fourth century, but their forms and motifs of decoration do not contain decisive characteristics that would indicate their production in the period after Aurelian.[205]

Finds of a Christian character are cited to strengthen the assumed Roman features of the former towns in the fourth century, and bronze coins found in Transylvania are considered to be connected with a Roman population.[206] These finds will be analyzed separately. The silver and gold coins belonged predominantly to the Goths and, later, to other populations; these people used bronze coins as well, as is clearly shown by the fact that the area in which bronze coins were found in Transylvania is not restricted to the western, assumed Roman, settlements and towns but covers practically the whole province.[207] The use of such coins in Transylvania by the Goths and by the

people of the so-called Sfîntu Gheorghe culture invalidate the assumption that bronze coins must be connected with a Roman population.

Non-Roman Settlements and Tombs in Transylvania
from the Mid-Third to End of the Fourth Century
The So-called Sfîntu Gheorghe (Eastern) Group of Settlements

In the valleys of the upper Olt and the Rîul Negru (Feketeügy)
rivers, in a well-defined area in southeastern Transylvania, a special
culture is found.[208] Because the first finds of this kind of culture were
made between 1882 and 1891 at Sepsiszentgyörgy (Sfîntu Gheorghe),
these settlements are called today the Sfîntu Gheorghe group. There
are about 22 settlements of this kind; and the cemetery no. 1 at
Bratei most probably also belongs to this culture. It is characterized
by Dacian, Carpic, Roman, and Gothic remains. The Dacian influence
manifests itself in simple forms of hand-made pottery, somewhat
similar to that produced by the Dacians in pre-Roman times, and the
hand-made, handless conic cup with a dotted circle on the lower rim
characteristic of the Sfîntu Gheorghe culture. Red earthenware made
on a wheel shows Roman influence, and the grey pieces made on a
wheel include forms that could also be derived from Roman forms.[209]
The ruffle-finished vessel very frequent in the Roman military settlements at the time of Roman rule is found in most of the settlements
of the Sfîntu Gheorghe culture.

An interesting phenomenon in eastern Transylvania, which cannot
be overlooked, is the early appearance of the Černjachov culture. As
mentioned previously, Roman influence was strongest in western
Transylvania, while in eastern Transylvania Romanization was very
weak if not altogether absent. Rather a Dacian substratum is to be
recognized here. After the gradual disappearance of Dacian elements,
however, the components of the Černjachov culture made a very early
appearance. As previously stated, after the fourth century the Dacian
element is no longer archaeologically ascertainable. Excavations made
at Sfîntu Gheorghe, Reci (Réty), Cernatul (Csernáton, Covasna County),
and Bezid brought forth several objects characteristic of the Černjachov
culture. The later phase of this culture in Transylvania was designated
by the name Sîntana de Mureş. Both cultures, that of Sfîntu Gheorghe
as well as the Černjachov culture, are characterized by the shiny grey
pottery, the decoration by surface-glazing, and the large number of
dishes. Some forms, such as cans with a withdrawn opening and the
can from Tîrgu Secuiesc (Kézdivásárhely), described by the Romanian
archaeologist Vasile Pârvan in 1926,[210] originate directly from the

Černjachov culture. The single-rowed combs with a special worked middle handle appear in the Černjachov culture but not among the remains of the Dacians or the Carps. Because of the many elements from the Sîntana de Mureş culture, these 22 settlements in the southeast have been thought to belong to that culture. They show, however, a pronounced Dacian influence; and their funeral rite was cremation, while the Sîntana de Mureş people predominantly used inhumation.[211] Whether the differences really are decisive is difficult to tell.

The Cemetery from the Fourth and Fifth Centuries A.D. at Bratei

Since 1959, at Bratei (Baráthely, Sibiu County), on the shore of the Tîrnava Mare (Nagykükülő) River, several settlements and cemeteries have been excavated, which cover a time span from the third and second centuries B.C. (Celtic tombs) to the thirteenth century A.D. (Pecheneg settlements). The excavations reveal elements characteristic of different peoples, among which one may distinguish Romans, Germanic tribes, Slavs, Avars, and medieval inhabitants of Transylvania. A significant part of the cemetery was destroyed for a sand-pit before it could be studied (Ligia Bârzu, 1973, p. 9). A severe shortcoming of the description of this cemetery is that it does not indicate in which tomb each of the objects was found; therefore, a horizontal-stratigraphic investigation is not possible (Horedt, 1982, pp. 97–98).

A total of 348 tombs have been excavated, with all showing cremation. Most of them are quite shallow, 1.2 to 1.5 meters long, and 40 to 60 centimeters wide. The majority of the tombs (270, or 77.5%) show a red color on the bottom and sides, the effect of fire. This effect of fire and the oval shape of the tombs is explained by the burning of the body over the pit. Similar circumstances are known from several areas in modern times (New Guinea, Japan.), where this type of cremation is practiced. The signs of fire have no ethnic significance as had been believed earlier.[212]

The vessels found in the cemetery are of four different kinds. There is hand-made earthenware of the Dacian type in almost every tomb. It is characterized by pots with carved margins. There are three conical dishes with handles, without a row of spots. The third kind of the earthenware, fired red with a ruffle-finish is found in almost every tomb. There are seven glass fragments from vessels probably imported from Pannonia or from the region along the lower Danube. There are also amphora, which are found in the Carpic tombs in Moldavia. Another kind of earthenware (six vessels) is fine, grey, with surface-glazed ornamentation. These, as well as the large number of dishes and probably also the cans with the trefoil-leaf opening, are characteristic of the Černjachov-Sîntana de Mureş culture. The rest of the objects found in cemetery no. 1 at Bratei also include many pieces that belong to the Sîntana de Mureş culture,[213] including different kinds of glass cups. Three bone combs with a single-row and rounded handles were found here.

All this is very similar to the situation in the Sfîntu Gheorghe culture. When considering the differences, one should be aware of the fact that the comparison is made between objects placed in tombs (Bratei) and those found among the remains of settlements (Sfîntu Gheorghe).[214] This could explain the more frequent appearance of amphoras at Bratei (the custom could have been to place them in tombs). In spite of the many analogies with the Sîntana de Mureş culture, Horedt does not believe that the cemetery at Bratei belonged to this culture, the decisive difference being cremation at Bratei, while the Goths in Transylvania used inhumation (with the exception of those at Lechinţa de Mureş). It seems impossible today to determine whether this view is correct, but it is clear that the Roman influence in this cemetery is not more pronounced than may be expected in that period in Southeastern Europe and, in any case, is only one of several influences.

The archaeological complex of the Bratei cemetery is designated as the Bratei culture by Romanian archaeologists, even though one cannot speak of an independent culture in this instance. Rather, it is a fabrication based on hypotheses by several contemporary Romanian archaeologists influenced primarily by Ion Nestor and Eugenia Zaharia.[215] In 1973 both archaeologists proposed that the Bratei culture be called "Roman" (cultura romanică). Suzana Dolinescu-Ferche used the same designation for the remains found at Dulceanca in 1974.

One of the cemeteries, designated no. 1, from the second half of the fourth and the early fifth centuries, has been called "Daco-Roman" by the Romanian archaeologist Ligia Bârzu. The author of the most exhaustive monograph on this cemetery[216] defends this hypothesis, but the arguments advanced for this theory are not convincing.[217] Such reasoning is common in many writings defending the theory of a Romanic population in post-Roman Dacia Traiana: A single letter on a piece of earthenware, for example, is called a "linguistic document." Another argument in favor of Romanization is the mere fact that the funeral rites found in this cemetery were not typically Dacian. From the presentation given in the monograph mentioned above, it is clear that these customs were not typically Roman either.[218]

There are also Romanian archaeologists who do not believe in the "Daco-Roman" character of the Bratei people. According to Gheorghe Diaconu, for example, the funeral rites at Bratei cannot be attributed to the autochthonous component in Transylvania,[219] and the majority of the material finds there have analogues in the Sîntana de Mureş culture. Kurt Horedt believes that the cemetery in question was left by the representatives of the Sfîntu Gheorghe culture, who wandered to the site along the Tîrnava Mare River from southeastern Transylvania.[219a]

In summary, it can be concluded that the cemetery of Bratei reveals, in the first place, elements of the period of the peoples' migration and is an example of a continuity of settlement and is, at the same time, illustrative of ethnic discontinuity in Transylvania. The archaeological findings do not reveal a new, specific culture that was the product of Roman and Dacian components. In the fifth century Roman cultural influence is quite weak and diminishes further. Artifacts of a Romanic population are claimed to exist in Germanic row-tombs as is the case in Western Europe; this, however, does not mean that the same assumptions also can be made with respect to Slavic cremation tombs. Written sources of the fifth to sixth centuries as well as the archaeological complex of this period attests only Germanic peoples.

The Černjachov-Sîntana de Mureş Culture

The area of dissemination of the Černjachov-Sîntana de Mureş culture is bordered on the east by the steppe of the left bank of the Dnieper and on the west by the Olt River and mid-Transylvania as far as Volhynia; on the south by the Danube and the Pontic Steppes. Its chronological limits are probably between 270 and 380 A.D. - On the basis of examination of burial sites, the German archaeologist Volker Bierbrauer places the late phases of this culture in the second half of the fourth century and sees a link between it and the Eastern Germanic tribes of the fifth century.[221] Most suitable for chronological determination of the Černjachov-Sîntana de Mureş culture are the large necropolises of Gavrilowka, Kosanowo (Ukraine), Sîntana de Mureş (Marosszentanna), Tîrgşor, and Independenţa (Romania). The earliest phases of this culture are characterized by graves laid from north to south (Târgşor, Kosanowo) while in later phases most graves are already laid from west to east by an increasing number of graves devoid of enclosures. As the number of tombs without enclosures increases during the later phase of the Černjachov-Sîntana de Mureş culture, components of the earlier East Germanic archaeological remains are observable, such as richly endowed women's graves, combs with high handles, and thin fibulae with semicircular handles.[222] The spread of the number of richly filled women's tombs is limited to the period of Hunnic rule, that is, shortly after the culture's end, and reaches from Lower Austria to the Hungarian Plain. The hoards found in Şimleul Silvaniei, Pietroasa, and Apahida in Romania provide a similar picture.[223]

The Černjachov-Sîntana de Mureş culture is not exclusively Gothic, except Transylvania, but representative of all the peoples who lived between the Dnieper and the Western Carpathians in the fourth century.

The Černjachov culture penetrated Transylvania only at a later stage of its evolution when their Gothic carriers moved into Transylvania in the second half of the fourth century through the Eastern Carpathians under Hunnic pressure. The name Sîntana de Mureş (Marosszentanna) culture is derived from the burial grounds of the same name, the largest of its kind, in Transylvania and represents a later stage of the Černjachov culture.[224] Nevertheless, it is possible to distinguish an earlier from a later phase even here.[225] In 1903 77 tombs were excavated. Unfortunately, the middle, and probably oldest part of the cemetery, was destroyed for a sandpit before it could be studied.' The principal characteristics of the Sîntana de Mureş culture are the burial of bodies (inhumation) and the remains belonging to early East Germanic finds, such as single-rowed combs with straight rather than semicircular handles but with a bell-shaped middle section, as well as the predominance of fibulae with an inverted foot and semicircular headplates, metal clasps, and belt buckles with stamped fittings.[226] Similar material remains (of the Goths) were also found at Tîrgu Mureş (Marosvásárhely), Cluj, Ocna Mureş (Marosújvár, Alba County), Ocniţa (Mezőakna), and Pălatca (Magyarpalatka, Cluj County). The increased absence of enclosures and the west to east rather than north to south orientation of tombs would indicate a later origin for the burial grounds of Sîntana de Mureş and attest to the expansion of Arian Christianity among the Goths in the second half of the fourth century.[227] The silver- and wire-framed fibula is specific to Lechința, Pălatca, and Valea Strîmbă (Tekerőpatak, Harghita County).

The earthenware of the Sîntana de Mureș culture is known from both the older and later settlements and tombs. It is of a good quality, well fired, without air bubbles, and includes ball-formed pots and various dishes and jars. This kind of earthenware is quite uniform and characteristic of a large area from the Dnieper River to the Apuseni Mountains (Erdélyi szigethegység) in Transylvania. About 10 cemeteries belonging to this culture are known in the Transylvanian Basin.[228]

In Transylvania the only cemetery of this type in which cremation was practiced is that found at Lechința de Mureș. Some of the Romanian archaeologists believed that it belonged to the "Daco-Romans," on the basis of the cremation and the Roman provincial type urn;[229] but cremation is usual in the Černjachov culture, and other objects in this tomb belong to the Sîntana de Mureș culture.[230]

More recently, several sites have been described that show characteristics of the Sîntana de Mureș culture but also contain foreign elements, one of the most important of which is influence from the north: Wooden buckets and iron axes, frequent finds in the territory between the Northern Carpathian Mountains and the Baltic Sea were found at Ciumbrud, Ocnița, and Fîntînele (Újős, Bistrița County). In the cemetery found at the brick factory in Tîrgu Mureș, three grey jars and a glass cup show Roman influence.

A number of tombs could have been left by Sarmatians. In the tomb from 30 decembrie (Unió) Street in Cluj, the skeleton was laid down in a sitting position, a Sarmatian custom; and among the objects, several pieces were found that are not usual in the Sîntana de Mureș culture, as well as a Sarmatian mirror and a jadeite bracelet of unknown origin. Which people really left these tombs cannot at present be established. A Sarmatian mirror may, for example, have been used by others than the Sarmatians, while a skeleton in the sitting position is perhaps more likely to have belonged to a Sarmatian community.

Free (non-Romanized) Dacians from the west settled in the former province. The earthenware in three tombs of the cremation type at Cipău (Maroscsapó, Mureș County) reveals Sarmatian influences; and only the funeral rite of cremation indicates that it was left by Dacians, because the Sarmatians used only inhumation.

The Sarmatians, known also as Sauromathians, were related to the Scythians and, like them, were nomads roaming between the Ural Mountains and the Volga River and spoke an Iranian language.[231]

Like the Jaziges,[232] Roxolans, Alans, and Aorsians, the Sarmatians during their centuries-long rule exerted a significant influence over the culture of the peoples of the Pontic Steppes. They lived in the area along the Volga from the seventh to the third century B.C. and then moved west. In their western migration the Sarmatians subdued the Scythians of the Black Sea and reached the Danube and, later, also the territory of modern Hungary. They settled for hundreds of years on the edge of the Roman Empire. During the period of Roman rule in Dacia they occupied the plain between the Tisza River and Transylvania. In the third and fourth centures A.D. their rule was terminated by the Goths and Huns. It is not impossible to assume that Sarmatian tribes were included among the Kuvrat Bulgars in the Carpathian Basin, who, however, were later assimilated with the Hungarians.

The presence of another population in post-Roman Dacia Traiana is more questionable. Horedt defends the hypothesis that Carps settled at several places in the province as early as in the third century,[233] but this is not generally accepted and the material evidence is not very strong in favor of a real settlement of Carps. Here, too, the problem is to distinguish between material influence of one culture on another in a part of Europe where such influences are very complicated and the effective presence of people who were the bearers of the material finds in question. The objects of Carpic origin are considered by those who do not believe that Carps settled in large numbers in Transylvania to be imported material.[234]

A search for signs of inhabitation and activity on the sites of different types of Roman villages from the period of the province gives poor results. Villages whose inhabitants occupied themselves with different trades were frequent in other Roman provinces but are not known in Dacia Traiana. Such villages existed at some places also in Barbaricum, such as along the upper Tisza River, where villages with earthen vessels were quite numerous. From Dacia Traiana, however, only Cluj-Mănăștur, Mugeni, and Sfîntu Gheorghe, near the location called "Epresteto," where ovens of Roman construction were preserved and possibly used during the fourth century, may be mentioned in this connection. Whether the production of earthenware continued at Cristești after 275 A.D. is similarly uncertain; reliable proof has not been presented.[235] Of about 40 (established and assumed) farms from the time of the province, only 2 were possibly inhabited in the fourth century.[236] At only three of the thirty-seven Roman military camps it is assumed that settlements were possibly occupied in the fourth century; in two cases this assumption is made only on the basis of fragments of earthenware possibly dating to the fourth century, and at one, Comolău, there are more intense signs of use by the Sfîntu Gheorghe people. Following the abandonment of the province, the military camps fell into disuse and were no longer inhabited. From the seventh to the eleventh century, prior to the Hungarian period, no forts existed in Transylvania. In the former civilian settlements around Roman military camps (*canabae*), no traces of life have been found in the post-Roman period. In the surroundings of about a third of these, however, coins from the fourth century were found, as well as fibula in one, and a ring in another; and at Sărățeni (Sóvárad, Mureș County) two tombs of cremation were found in the former Roman garrison. A fifth category of settlements would be those built on high mountains. The existence of such a settlement was assumed at Tîrnăvioara, but the buildings in question were more likely erected much later, in the Middle Ages. At Cetatea de Baltă (Küküllővár, Alba County), as well, the construction of a tower shows the characteristics of buildings from the Middle Ages; but because the pottery fragments found here are Dacian or Roman, it is assumed to have been built earlier.[237]

The Roman Coins from 275 to 395 A.D. Found in Transylvania

In 1958 45 places were known in Transylvania in which Roman coins from the period between 275 and 395 A.D. had been found. In the following decades, many new finds have been described; and in 1982 Horedt could report 814 coins from 85 places.[238] Unfortunately, much of this material is of limited value, because many cases, especially the older finds, were poorly described and documented. The calculated results reflect only approximately the characteristics and the changes of circulation and are not mathematically exact values, since basic data about them are often uncertain.[239] Even such data as the kind of metal, the exact place of discovery, and the total number of coins originally found in the hoard are often lacking.

The distribution of the coins could contribute to our knowledge of the ways and the intensity of commerce and similar questions. More than half of the coins whose origin can be established were produced in the three Roman towns of Siscia (93 coins), Sirmium (44 coins), and Aquileia (13 coins), suggesting that most of the commerce with the empire in the fourth century went through the Mureș River valley and further through the valleys of the Tisza and Sava rivers.[240] Large numbers of coins were found along the Roman border, showing that commerce was most intense in those areas. This was also the case, of course, in the rest of Europe, with the highest numbers of Roman coins along the entire course of the Danube and the Rhine. In the Banat, for example, more than 40,000 Roman coins (mostly in hoards) have been discovered, and in Oltenia, 15,161, including 10,000 at Celei and Craiova.[241] In Transylvania, at some distance from the empire, the number of finds is much lower (814), the ratio of Transylvania to Oltenia (without Celei and Craiova) to the Banat being 1:5:50.[242] Of those 814 isolated coins found in Transylvania, 648 (79.6%) are made of bronze, 157 (19.3%) of silver, and 9 (1.1%) of gold. Between 275 and 305 A.D., there are only 1.4 coins for each year; between 305 and 364 A.D., 9.08; and between 364 and 395, 3.54 coins a year. Thus, the circulation of Roman coins was very low during the decades after the Roman retreat from Dacia and increased considerably during the time of Emperor Constantine the Great.[243]

An Analysis of the Ethnic Significance Attributed to the Roman Coins

The circulation of Roman coins in the territory of present-day Romania is considered by Romanian archaeologists and historians as an argument of primary significance,[244] proving a Roman continuity in Dacia. This function is attributed to single finds of coins, as well as to certain hoards. Already, the very fact that Roman coins continued to be used after the Roman retreat from Dacia—from the end of the third century A.D. to the beginning of the fifth century—is considered to imply a Romanized population living there.[245] A somewhat more specific argument is that many bronze coins were found in the territory in question and that these must have been used by the autochthonous population and to a lesser extent by the Goths, "who did not appreciate so much the coins as such, but rather the precious metal they contained."[246] But there are also different opinions that reject the theory. The archaeologist Kurt Horedt, for example, believes that bronze coins in general could be attributed with more probability to the Roman population, since they had value as money but only a small intrinsic value. This statement, however, should not be generalized, because the bronze coins from Cipău (Maroscsapó, Mureş County) belonged to free Dacians who migrated to the territory.[247]

An up-to-date summary of the main arguments for ethnic continuity in post-Aurelian Dacia Traiana as compared to the territories inhabited by the Sarmatians (Cf., D. Gabler in *Römer und Germanen in Mitteleuropa*, Berlin 1975, p. 98.) is formulated by the archaeologist Nicolae Gudea criticizing I. I. Russu.[248] Gudea refers to D. Gabler's map no. 5, showing the find-sites of gold coins in Barbaricum east from

Pannonia from the first to fourth centuries A.D. Gabler remarks that the situation is not yet sufficiently known; the single findings from this territory have not yet been comprehensively published. According to Gabler, a total number of 42 gold coins (aurei and solidi) have been found in 41 places. Of these 24 were from the fourth century A.D. The number of denarii from the same century is only 3. In Transylvania 9 gold coins and 157 of silver were found from the period between 275 and 395 A.D. - These data, in spite of Gudea's assertion (Gudea, 1983, *op. cit.*, p. 909), can not "demonstrate the ethnic character of the population of the former province (of Dacia Traiana) and the characteristic features of its life."

Finds of Single Coins

The extent to which the coins were used in commerce varied with the different territories and periods. By analyzing the finds it is now possible to determine to what extent the coins had the function of money in a certain area. The main factor that determined this was the intensity of commerce; the ethnic situation is irrelevant. North of the Black Sea, bronze coins were found with increasing frequency from the Crimea toward the west. In the fourth century A.D. the regions north of the entire course of the Danube, just beyond the Roman border, are richest in hoards consisting of copper and bronze coins of low value.[249] The number of single finds of bronze coins from the same century found so far in the plains west of Dacia (in the present-day Hungarian Plain) is 262 (compared with only 24 aurei and solidi and 3 denarii). All of the 227 find-sites of silver and bronze coins from the first to fourth centuries are located in this territory.[250] In several areas of free Germania a typically provincial Roman structure of the circulation of coins is found. In such territories as Bohemia and Slovakia, the coins were used as money to a very high degree, reflecting the general situation in the empire. The provincial circulation is thus not unique and not specific to the area of former Dacia Traiana.

The situation in the territory of former Dacia Traiana in that century can be studied from the maps supplied by Protase,[251] Preda,[252] and Horedt.[253] Corresponding to the general rule, the greatest numbers of bronze coins were found along the Danube: in Oltenia; and in the Banat, between the Timiş and Mureş rivers, where the Sarmatian Jaziges were living, which shows that this non-Roman population used bronze coins intensively.[254] In Transylvania proper a far smaller number were discovered in the valleys of the Someş, Mureş, the two

Tîrnave, and the Olt rivers. The distribution of these finds in Tran-sylvania does not indicate any clear-cut concentration in a special territory. Bronze coins were found in the northwest, north of the Crișul Repede (Sebes-Körös) River, in an area of free Dacians. The find at Cipău has already been mentioned; and also in southeastern Transylvania, in the valley of the Olt River, many bronze coins were found. That was most probably the area of the non-Roman population called the Sfîntu Gheorghe people in the fourth century.[255] The non-Romanized Dacians living in other parts of the territories north of the Danube used Roman coins of bronze at least up to the end of the fourth century. There are finds of Roman bronze coins in Moldavia, on the plains of Muntenia, in Crișana, and in the area of Transylvania that was not occupied by the Romans.[256]

The Hoards of Coins

Six hoards of Roman coins found at Hunedoara (Vajdahunyad, Alba County), Nireș (Nyires, Cluj County), Vîlcan (Vulkán, a mountain pass), Borlova (Caraș-Severin County), Orșova, and Reghin (Szász-régen, Mureș County), containing Roman coins from the first two and a half centuries A.D. and, after a hiatus, a few coins from the fourth century, have been considered by the archaeologist Mihail Macrea to indicate the presence of "Daco-Romans" after the retreat of Aurelian.[257] Protase later developed this hypothesis further and in his monograph from 1966 considered the hoards found at Hunedoara, Vîlcan, Reghin, Nireș, Orșova, and Borlova to belong to a "Daco-Roman population."[258] Constantin Preda (1975) agreed with this theory in principle but with reservations, one of his objections being the long interruptions in the process of accumulation.[259] Preda would not take into account here the hoard of Orșova, "situated in a zone that was reconquered by the Romans."[260] Those 50 coins found in the surroundings of Reghin, are, however, also questioned by Protase, and should be eliminated from the discussion, because it is not even sure whether they really were found together, that is, whether they really were originally from a hoard. Thus, only four hoards remain, of which three contain denarii and only one consists of bronze coins (see Table III). This is insignificant historically both as an absolute number and with regard to the total number (23) of hoards reported in Transylvania and dated to the fourth century A.D.

Horedt discussed the possible historical conclusion that could be drawn from the hoards of coins found in post-Roman Dacia. Of the 23 hoards buried in Transylvania during the post-Roman period, 15 contained bronze coins. Of these 15, 7 also contained coins from the period before Aurelian; 3 (those found at Hunedoara, Nireş, and Laslea/Szászszentlászló, Sibiu County) contained predominantly such coins and are therefore attributed to "Daco-Romans." The other four (Bistriţa, Bran-Poarta, Gherla, and Vîlcan) contained predominantly post-Aurelian coins; in these cases,"ethnic attribution is impossible.[261] There are also hoards with all coins from the post-Aurelian period (Anieş/Dombhát, Bistriţa County, Cipău, Cluj, Cluj-Someşeni/Kolozsvár-Szamosfalva, Fizeş/Füzesd, Hunedoara County, Gilău/Gyalu, Cluj County, and Sarmizegethusa), which have no connection with the period of the province.[262]

The hoards of silver and gold coins are not considered to be connected with "Daco-Romans." Only silver is contained in the hoards found at Sibiu (Nagyszeben) and at Ungurei (Gergelyfalva, Hunedoara County) and silver and gold in those found at Valea Strîmbă (Tekerőpatak, Harghita County) with predominantly pre-Aurelian coins. A hoard of silver at Valea Strîmbă is a remnant of Gothic material culture buried, in all likelihood, in the second half of the fourth century, probably before the invasion of the Huns. As at Firtuşu and Vădaş (Vadasd, Mureş County), only gold coins were found at Borsec (Borszék, Harghita County), from the end of the fourth century; but these were buried later than the fourth century. The hoard of gold coins at Korond-Firtosváralja (Firtuşu) was found in 1831 and could be from Gepidic-Avar times; however, it could also be attributed to the Kutrigurs. The find consisted of 237, or possibly more than 300, gold coins, of which the latest were from the times of Heraclius and Heraclius Constantinus (around 625). The burying of the treasure and the death or flight of its owner is dated at approximately the year 630.[263] The treasure of Şimleu Silvaniei (Szilágysomlyó, Sălaj County), discovered in 1797, was in all likelihood hidden by the Huns advancing from the Eastern Carpathians. The gold bars found at Crasna (Kraszna, Sălaj County) and at Feldioara (Földvár, Braşov County) are considered to have been subsidies paid by the Roman Empire to the Goths. No fewer than 19 of these hoards (except perhaps that of Firtuşu) have their latest coins dating from the time between 350 and 395 A.D. and were probably buried because of the Hunnish invasion.

About one-fourth of the hoards discussed here were buried in mountain passes and are therefore considered to have belonged to migratory populations. In Horedt's view, if one takes into account all criteria (the kind of metal, the composition of the hoard, the time span during which it was accumulated, and the place where it was found), the following hoards could be attributed to the indigenous Roman population: Cluj, Cluj-Someşeni, Gherla (Szamosújvár, Cluj County), Hunedoara, Laslea, and Nireş.[264] Of these, only the last three hoards fulfill the criteria used earlier by Macrea, Protase, and Preda in attributing hoards of coins to "Daco-Romans": they contain bronze coins, made predominantly in the pre-Aurelian period. The accumulation of the largest part of the hoards during the Roman period was considered the fact that could connect the owners with people who had lived in the province earlier. It is therefore questionable whether the hoard found at Gherla (with predominantly post-Aurelian coins) and especially those found at Cluj and Cluj-Someşeni; with exclusively post-Aurelian coins, should be put in this group. As is known, the treasure excavated at Cluj-Someşeni, not far from Apahida, in 1962 belongs to the Gepidae; parallel finds of this sort were also discovered in several places in Hungary, as well as in the treasure-trove at Apahida (Cluj County).

The study of the hoards also indicates that bronze coins were used and frequently accumulated by non-Romans: At least three hoards attributed with certainty to non-Roman populations (Bran-Poarta, Vîlcan Pass, and Cipău) contain predominantly or exclusively bronze coins. (See Table III)

The population of Dacia Traiana buried their money, as shown by a considerable number of hoards from the last decade of the third century, when the Carps invaded the province.[265] No hoards were found, however, from the time the empire abandoned Dacia, two or three decades later.[266] This is quite unusual if one believes that a large number of people remained in the province, since these people (as was the case around 245 A.D.) would have had every reason to expect plundering in connection with the intrusion of barbarians after the Roman withdrawal. The low intensity of circulation of coins in the period in question (caused by the economic crisis in the empire) would not prevent this, since hoards usually contain money accumulated over longer periods of time.

After the end of the fourth century, the circulation of Roman coins in the former province decreased significantly, with the exception of gold coins, whose number increased. Only eleven isolated bronze coins have been found in Transylvania from the time between the end of the fourth century and 450 A.D., and in the Banat, even fewer. This could be explained by the Hunnish invasion and, as has been previously mentioned, the economic crisis of the empire; in Roman provinces, as well as in Moesia Superior, for example, a sharp decrease in the circulation of coins is recorded in that era.[267]

TABLE III
Data on Six Hoards of Fourth Century Roman Coins Allegedly of "Daco-Roman" Origin

Place of discovery	Year	Number of coins	Hiatus in the period of:	Metal
Hunedoara	1905	1,138	Gallienus (253-260) and Constans (320-350) A.D.	Denarii, 3 small pieces of copper, 21 impossible to determine
Nireş	1953	About 150, of which 30 are still known	Severus Alexander (222-235) and Constantine II (337-361 A.D.)	Denarii, 1 bronze coin from the time of Constantine II
Vîlcan Pass	1869	35 bronze coins from Tiberius to Iulianus	Philip the Arab (244-249) and Maximius Daza (305-313 A.D.)	All of bronze
Borlova	1885	Several hundred	Philip the Arab (244-249) and Constantine II (337-361 A.D.)	All of silver
Orşova, on the northern shore of the Danube	1895-1896	About 50, possibly from a hoard	Composition unknown	Unknown
The surroundings of Reghin	1859	33 coins, probably from a hoard	Philip the Arab (244-249) and Maximius Herculius (268-305)	Not given by Protase, 1966

Source: Dumitru Protase, *Problema continuității în Dacia în lumina arheologiei şi numismaticii*, (Bucharest: 1966); Constantin Preda, Circulația monedelor romane postaureliene în Dacia, *Studii şi cercetări de istorie veche şi arheologie*, 26, no. 4 (Bucharest: 1975). The lack of coins from the period between the mid-third and the early fourth century can be explained by the scarcity of commerce with the empire in that period. As one can see from the table, the data available about these hoards are not sufficient for reliable studies. In two cases it is not even known whether the coins described were initially really found in a hoard. The circulation of Roman coins ceased in the fifth century. The coins may no longer have had a monetary value but merely an intrinsic value as metal. The richly endowed graves are Germanic.

Conclusion

With regard to the circulation of coins in the post-Aurelian period, it can be said in conclusion that because of the economic and political situation, the circulation of Roman coins had already markedly declined by the middle of the third century. In the time of Gratianus (375–383), and at the latest during the rule of Theodosius I (379–395), the circulation of bronze coins ceases.[268] Late third and fourth century Roman coins are known from over 80 sites in Transylvania; 80 percent of these coins were bronze. During the ensuing four centuries the circulation of coins in former Dacia Traiana, if it did not come to a complete halt, continued to dwindle and thus became insignificant in comparison to other finds. Thus, it would be an exaggeration to speak of an "uninterrupted continuity" in the circulation of Roman coins. The notion of coin circulation can be used only reservedly with respect to the times of the Germanic peoples, that is, during the people's migration period. In this period gold coins belonging to the Germanic people were found; however, they had no exchange value as they were hoarded for the intrinsic value of the gold. In addition to the solidii there were also bronze coins, about 11.5 percent, which must have served as money or means of payment.[269] Of a total of 87 coins found in 33 places, 77 are solidii. Indications of the stock of coins during the period from 395 to 641 are given by Horedt;[270] additional data provided by Constantin Preda were used.[271] The majority of coin finds consist of individual pieces, and only at six places could hoards be assumed to have existed: Dobra, Firtos, Hida (Hidalmás, Sălaj County), Şeica Mică (Kisselyk, Sibiu County), "Transylvania," and Sîngeorgiu de Cîmpie (Mezőszentgyörgy, Mureş County).[272]

The coins of the first half of the seventh century still belong to the times of the Germanic peoples; the last coin of Constantine III (641) marks the end of this period.[273] No coins from the next two hundred years have been found in Transylvania. The period of coin usage ended in Transylvania earlier than in other parts of the Carpathian Basin where the circulation of coins ended only with Constantine IV Pogonatus (668–685).[274] Only at the end of the ninth century is the existence of a solidus of Basilios I (869–870) recorded in Transylvania.[275] Actual circulation of coins began anew, however, during the reign of Stephen I, when Hungarian coins were minted.

With respect to the ethnic significance of the coins, one should not demand too much of them since they cannot, because of their function as a means of payment, unequivocally be attributed from the ethnic point of view.[276]

Christianity in Transylvania in the 4th - 7th Centuries: A Critical Analysis of Its Alleged Significance for Romanian Ethnogenesis

Since Vasile Pârvan published his work *Contribuţii epigrafice la istoria creştinismului daco-roman* (Epigraphic contributions to the history of Daco-Roman Christianity) in 1911, much has been written in Romania about early Christianity in the region of the lower Danube.[277]

It is essential to define more precisely the territory to be examined. The Danube was the frontier of the Roman Empire for many centuries, and the history of the territory south of the river (including Scythia Minor, present-day Dobrudja) was very different from that north of the Danube. Such terms as "the region of the lower Danube" or "the Carpatho-Danubian-Pontic territory" used in current Romanian historiography as equivalents to present-day Romania blur the difference that existed between the different territories of present-day Romania— Dobrugea, Moldova, Muntenia, Oltenia, Transylvania—also with regard to early Christianity. Especially misleading are terms such as "Daco-Scythian Christianity" used by Eugen Lozovan.[278] He makes an attempt to prove that as early as the first millennium A.D. the two territories together with the other areas of present-day Romania were a unitary territory, to which Christianity provided "moral cohesion."[279] Christianity, it is claimed, contributed significantly to the preservation of the Latin language in this territory. These ideas are based on a faulty historical perspective with the author projecting the present situation and contemporary borders into the past.

It has been claimed that Christianity presupposes a Latin-speaking population and thus proves the existence of "Daco-Romans" in the territory and that it strengthened this Latin-speaking element. The arguments supporting this idea have varied. In *Istoria României* (1960), for example, the following arguments are presented: 1. In the fourth century, north of the Danube, Christian objects appear only in the area of former Dacia Traiana, which strengthens the conviction that they belonged to the Roman population; 2. In Transylvania, no objects of Christian character have been found among the material remains of the Goths, who, therefore, in contrast to the "Daco-Romans," do not seem to have been Christianized; and 3. Christianity in the fourth century north of the Danube is of the Latin character, because the objects were imported from the territory south of the Danube, the best analogues being found in the Danubian provinces of Latin Illyricum, in neighboring Pannonia, and farther away in Italy. In general, this is, as has been noted, also the economic and commerical orientation of Dacia in the fourth century.[280]

It was, however, considered necessary to support the arguments based on archaeological finds by other disputes. Even more than in the type of the archaeological objects, the Latin character of the primitive Christianity of the Daco-Romans allegedly appears clearly in the Latin origin of the words preserved in the Romanian language for the basic notions of the Christian faith: for example, *crux* (cruce), *domine deo* (dumnezeu). In this treatise on Romanian history from 1960, the Christianity of the "Daco-Romans" is described as a faith spread from man to man, by direct contacts with the people of the empire, not by missionaries. The authors refer in this connection to the modest character of the archaeological finds and to the religious words of Latin origin, which mainly denote the basic ideas of Christianity.

In 1966 Dumitru Protase listed the objects of Christian character that were known at that time. For Transylvania, he described about 10 objects dating to the fourth and fifth centuries and emphasized that most of them had been discovered in places that had been towns or rural settlements during the Roman period and, moreover, were situated mainly in the central and southwestern part of inside-Carpathic Dacia (the mostly Romanized areas). On the other hand, no such objects were known from Gothic sites. Protase concluded that the objects of Christian character can be seen as a testimony to support the theory of the existence in "masses of the Romanic population in Dacia after Aurelian."[281] Since the appearance of Protase's monograph, the situation has changed considerably. Many new objects of Christian character have been found, also in areas other than the territory of Dacia Traiana (in Muntenia, Moldavia) and, within that territory, also among the material remains of the Goths (the Sîntana de Mureş culture). At the same time, the official theory has also changed: from continuity only in the territory of former Dacia Traiana, as asserted earlier, to "Daco-Roman" continuity in all areas of present-day Romania.

An informative description of the situation in Transylvania is given by Kurt Horedt,[282] with references to more important earlier literature. The author presents the finds critically, distinguishing clearly between objects that, with some degree of certainty, could be considered Christian and those that are not unequivocally Christian. He also gives a map showing objects of a Christian character found in Transylvania, dated separately according to century, from the third to the seventh century. Although Horedt adheres in this treatise to the theory that the finds of Christian character are connected with a Roman population north of the Danube, he does not emphasize this thesis.

Mircea Rusu, supporting the theory of Roman continuity north of the Danube, argues that the objects of Christian character were found mainly in places where Roman towns or forts (*castra*) were once situated and must therefore be connected with a Roman population that continued to live there. There is only one group of finds that Rusu calls "proof": the inscriptions.[283]

The Geographical Distribution of Christian Finds in Romania

Mircea Rusu gives a list of the objects of Christian character from the third through the eighth centuries found on the territory of present-day Romania. The total number of sites, according to this list, is 117. Rusu does not, however, distinguish between proven and questionable Christian objects. As shown by the list, Christian objects dated to the third through the eighth centuries were found in 53 places in Transylvania, of which 7 are situated in or near a former Roman town and 5 near a *castrum*.[284]

The largest number of Christian objects and, what is more significant, the great majority of the churches were found in Dobrugea (former Scythia Minor). Ruins of a total of 36 churches have been found at 18 different localities.[285] No such finds have been made in Transylvania, although it has been assumed that a Liber-Pater-Bel-Tempel at Moigrad may have been transformed into a Christian basilica.[286]

In Transylvania 13 possible and 7 certain Christian objects were found and dated to the fourth century in 1982.[287] Four of the latter group were discovered in the territories of former Roman towns— Alba Iulia (Apulum), Turda (Potaissa), Cluj (Napoca), and Moigrad (Porolissum)—and three in other places: Biertan (Berethalom, Sibiu County), Pălatca (Magyarpalatka), and "Transylvania," that is, one from an unknown site. It should be noted that Alba Iulia, Turda, and Cluj are quite large towns, which increases the chances of archaeological finds being made and reported to scientists. Of the 13 questionable Christian objects 7 can be considered to have been found on the place of former Roman towns or important settlements: Sarmizegethusa, Alba Iulia (Apulum), Vețel (Micia), 2 pieces at Turda (Potaissa), and 2 pieces at Moigrad (Porolissum). One was discovered at Bologa, the site of a Roman *castrum*; and the other 5 objects are from other places: Cristești, Pălatca, Feisa (Alba County), Mercheașa, and "Transylvania" (possibly Zlatna).[288] The connection of these objects with a former Roman settlement or a Roman population is thus very hypothetical even for the fourth century.

The situation in Transylvania was quite different in the fifth century from that in the fourth. Objects of Christian character dated to this century have been found only at Apahida and Cluj-Someșeni. These were made in Byzantium and appear not in a Roman but in a Germanic context from the time of the peoples' migration.[289] Objects of Christian character dated to the sixth century have been discovered in the southeastern corner of Transylvania and in the northwest. This was the period of expansion of the Eastern Roman Empire under Emperor Justinian, when the territory up to the lower Danube was reconquered. The region thus came under the influence of Byzantium, which reinforced Christianity; the inscriptions were now written in Greek. In Transylvania 14 Christian objects dated to the seventh century were found at two late-Germanic cemeteries on the middle course of the Mureş River (at Noşlac/Marosnagylak, Alba County, and Unirea-Vereşmort/Felvinc-Marosveresmart, Alba County).[290]

Rusu mentions 14 casting molds used for the fabrication of crosses or other metal ornaments. Most of them were discovered outside of the former province of Dacia Traiana.[291] This emphasizes the conclusion about the accidental character of such sites, that is, that the Christian objects are not related to the situation in the Roman period or to a Roman population.

The Inscriptions

Given the great difference in early Christian vestiges from Dobrugea (former Scythia Minor) and from Transylvania (a large part of which was Dacia Traiana), a scholarly analysis must consider these territories separately. Here, the inscriptions found in Transylvania will be discussed in some detail. Rusu's list (1984) of third to eighth century Christian vestiges found in Romania contains the following Latin and Greek inscriptions discovered in the territory of Transylvania:

Biertan: Donarium with the inscription: "*Ego Zenovius votum posui*," made in the fourth century in northern Italy, most probably in Aquileia.

Veţel (Vecel, Hunedoara County): An arch of one silver fibula transformed into a ring with the inscription: "*Quartine vivas*." Possibly Christian, according to Horedt, 1982.

Bologa (Sebesvár, Cluj County): Silver ring with the inscription: *UT(ere) F(elix)*. Christian character questionable, according to Horedt, 1982.

Moigrad: Vase with the inscription: "*Utere Felix*." Christian character questionable, according to Horedt, 1982.

Turda: Gold ring with the inscription: "*Utere Felix*." Christian character questionable, according to Horedt, 1982.

Apahida: Ring decorated with a cross and the inscription: OMHARIUS; ring with the monogram: *MARC(us)*.

Cluj: A Roman *cippus* reused as a sarcophagus; a cross was scratched later over the Greek letters *alfa* and *omega* is questionable according to Horedt, 1982.

Micăsasa (Sibiu County): Vase with a cross and inscription.

Orşova: Two gold plates (gnostic) with inscriptions; a gem with an inscription.

Sînnicolau Mare: Several vases of gold with inscriptions in Greek, Turkish with Greek letters, and Runic script.

Tîrgu Secuiesc: Amfora with a Christian inscription in Greek.

Poian (Kézdipolyán, Covasna County): Vase with a Christian inscription in Greek.

The Donarium Found at Biertan

Since this piece occupies a special place among the early Christian vestiges in Transylvania, it will be discussed in some detail.

In 1775 an *ex voto* with the inscription *EGO ZENOVIUS VOTUM POSUI* (I, Zenovius, have placed [this] present)[292] and a bronze chrismon disc with the monogram of Christ (*crux monogrammatica*) [of the Greek pattern, but used throughout the Christian world in the fourth century], originally probably part of a chandelier, was found in southern Transylvania.[293] The size of the inscription is 32.5 x 12.6 - 13.2 centimeters and the diameter of the disc is 23.7 centimeters. It was found under a felled oak-tree near a large spring in a valley about six kilometers south of Biertan (Berethalom, Sibiu County). In 1958 and 1976 attempts were made in vain to find remains of an ancient settlement in the area.[294] These pieces were found in the Bruckenthal Museum in Sibiu (Hermannstadt, Nagyszeben) by Kurt Horedt and published in 1941.[295]

Similar pieces have been found at Bonyhád (Hungary), Poetovio (modern Ptuj), Emona (modern Ljubljana, Slovenia), and Aquileia (Italy). These finds can show the trade routes between Italy and Transylvania that corroborate the evidence of the Roman coins.

According to the current view in Romania, this *ex voto* was probably given by a missionary to a Christian community. The Latin text indicates, according to this interpretation, that Latin-speaking people lived in the area of present-day Biertan.[296] There are, however, serious difficulties with this interpretation and, in any case, other alternatives. With regard to the assumption of a Christian missionary, this is not impossible, although the records are vague and give no information about the areas in which they might have worked. - More important: the *ex voto* was found outside the western Transylvanian area where a Latin-speaking population is assumed to have been living in the fourth century: twelve kilometers from Bratei, the site of a non-Roman population from the fourth century, and fifteen kilometers from Mediaş, where a fourth century site with remains of the Sîntana de Mureş culture was found. In his original publication, Horedt believed that the *Donarium* could have belonged to the Goths.[297] This was also the opinion of the Hungarian scholar András Alföldi.[298] In his later work, however, Horedt changed his opinion and attributed the *Donarium* to a Romanized group.

Another major difficulty with this find is that it is not connected with an archaeological site (for example, remains of a church or at least a dwelling place). It may originally have been in a wooden chapel, but this is very hypothetical. Produced in the fourth century probably in Aquileia, it is not known whether it was transported to the area near Biertan in the same century or later. If this occurred in the fourth century, it is still uncertain under what circumstances it reached the place. Commercial contacts with the empire existed, and a chandelier once dedicated to a Christian community living in a quite different territory could have been imported by people who did not understand the writing it contained. Even the most recent Romanian interpretation does not preclude the possibility that the *Donarium* of Biertan is imported.[299] Soldiers serving in the Roman army might have brought with them similar object from, for example, plundered churches, that may later have been found in distant places in Europe. Even if the object had been given to a Christian community, the Latin inscription of the *Donarium* does not necessarily imply that it was destined for a Latin-speaking population. Possession of an object, in those days, did not necessarily imply ideological identification with it. It is not impossible that Christians whose priests also knew Latin lived in the region of Biertan in the fourth century. But an object with a Latin inscription does not prove that the population living there also understood Latin. The inscription EGO ZENOVIVS VOTVM POSVI on the tabula ansata was prepared in the same place as the Chrismon - in Sirmium or in Aquileia, for the person who originally ordered it, and its connection with Dacia is not greater than that of the bronze vessels buried together with it.[300]

Inscriptions written in the Greek language were found at three places, according to the list above. The others, eight inscriptions in addition to that on the *Donarium*, were in Latin. They are claimed to be proof of the existence of a plentiful "Daco-Roman" population in Transylvania who "spoke popular Latin."[301] These objects—vases, fibulae, rings, gold plates, and other items—were, however, not made in Transylvania but were imported there from the Roman Empire; they do not tell us anything about the language of the population in that territory. A possible increase in the number of such objects in the future will not change this situation.

The Written Records About Christianity

There are a considerable number of records about Christians, bishops, persecutions, and so forth, north of the Danube in the centuries after the Roman retreat from Dacia. Those mentioned by Rusu (1984) will be briefly summarized here.

In the third century, Christian martyrs are mentioned in Scythia Minor (Halmyrs). In the fourth century, there are records about the Goths living in the plains of Muntenia; and several bishops are mentioned by name: Ulfila, Goddas, Sava the Goth. Bishop Teofil of Gothia took part in the Sinod of Nicea (Nikaia) in 325 A.D. There are numerous north-Danubian priests and martyrs, such as Sansalas, Batuses, and Versas.

Epiphanios, in his work entitled "Against Those 80 Heresies," written from 374 to 377 A.D., described the persecution of the Christians north of the Danube and told how they fled to the empire.[302] In 381 A.D. the Sinod in Constantinople stated that Terentius was Bishop of Scythia. Bishop Theotimos of Tomis "carried on a lively missionary activity north of the Danube, trying also to convert the Huns." In 399 A.D. the Patriarch Ioannes Hrisostomus of Constantinople asked Leontios, the Bishop of Ancyre, to send him people who could be missionaries among the Huns. For Scythia Minor, with some interruptions, the names of many bishops are preserved up to the eighth century. In 392 A.D. Socrate the Scholastic described Selenas, the Bishop of the Arian Goths north of the Danube, who was Goth on his father's side and Frigian on the maternal side and preached in both Gothic and Frigian. The Ostrogothic King asked the Patriarch Ioannes Hrisostomus in 404 A.D. to ordain Moduarius (Moduhari) a bishop. Sozomenos mentions Sigisharius, who was Bishop of the Arian Visigoths of Alarich in 409 A.D. In 438 A.D. "Marcus, the Bishop of the Novatiens in Scythia" was mentioned. In the *Edict of Justinian,* it is reported that "*limitanei* (soldier-farmers) had settled along the northern frontiers of the Eastern Roman Empire, in the territories beyond the Danube (Ister), in order to guard those frontiers."[303] In the mid-sixth century mention is made of the Gepidic Bishop Thrasaric, who fled to Constantinople after the defeat of the Gepidae by the Avars in 568 A.D.

To summarize the available records: 1. Early Christianity is richly documented in Scythia Minor (present-day Dobrudja), where ruins of eight churches are found. 2. Concrete data (the names of several bishops, martyrs, persecutions) about early Christians north of the Danube refer mainly to the Goths and the Gepidae, although other populations, such as the Huns, are also reported to have been exposed to missionary activity. 3. There is not a single record about any Latin-speaking population north of the Danube in these centuries. This is not, of course, as has been pointed out many times, sufficient evidence to exclude the possibility that some Latin-speaking people may have lived there, especially in the fourth century. It is not, however, very probable that Roman authors, who clearly distinguished between different populations—Goths, Gepidae, Sarmatians, Huns, Avars, and so on—and were interested in the fate of Christians, themselves being Christians, would not have mentioned the presence of a large, Latin-speaking, Christian population living outside of the empire in the fourth and subsequent centuries.

Conclusions

A great deal has been published by Romanian archaeologists and historians with the aim of proving the presence of a Roman population in the former province of Dacia Traiana in the post-Aurelian period (fourth century A.D.). The current official view is that such a population existed. In general, the studies that deal with this problem conclude with the statement that certain material remains must be connected with a Roman population that remained in the province after 275 A.D.; but the general situation of such people, their possible relations with the other populations living in that territory in the same period, and similar problems are not adequately discussed.

An exception, to some extent, is Kurt Horedt's monograph, published in 1982, about Transylvania in the post-Roman period, in which the material remains dating from the fourth century (more exactly, from about 275 to the end of the fourth century) are described. As it clearly appears from the preceding analysis, it is quite difficult in many cases to know what remains were produced in the post-Roman period. It is often impossible to be sure that a certain find is really from the fourth century and was not left over from the Roman period. Besides the difficulties with the dating in many cases, it is often questionable whether the finds we know really represent the original situation, since most of the tombs have been plundered and are thus poor in objects. Moreover, objects of Roman style or even Roman products are found among the material vestiges of practically all contemporary European populations and do not necessarily suggest that the people who once used them were Romans or spoke Latin. Sarcophagi made of reused tombstones or other monuments could perhaps be connected with Romans; they might have been Christian, although the objects of Christian character found in the former Roman towns add little to the evidence that would be needed to ascertain a Roman population. Christianity in the fourth century was not a specifically Roman movement but embraced many different peoples. The objects chosen to distinguish the rural settlements from others are neither universally present in the Roman sites, nor are they found exclusively there. The earthenware found in the settlements and the cemeteries is not helpful: The late Roman earthenware can scarcely be distinguished from that produced at the time of the province.[304] Finds from tombs and from settlements whose age is reliably established are very rare so far, and their post-Roman character is stated by intuition rather than evidence.[305] If one compares the funeral rites of the towns with those found in the rural settlements in which Romans are assumed to have been living, one finds a discrepancy. The number of neither the towns nor the rural cemeteries is, of course, very high, which makes a meaningful comparison difficult.

With regard to the existence of a Roman population in Transylvania in the fourth century, there are, therefore, only possibilities, conjectures, and theories but no cogent proof. Some of the material remains and circumstances advanced in favor of the theory are even contradictory and certainly are not decisive for the problem of continuity.

Not much is known about economic life in the former Roman towns in Dacia Traiana. It is not even certain whether the kilns working during the Roman era remained in use. In any case, there is nothing in the material remains to indicate large numbers of people in these places; and also the total number of towns is low (11, perhaps 12). Moreover, after the Hunnish invasion toward the end of the fourth century, the Dacian towns were entirely depopulated. Even these few towns, however, are situated along a line that goes in a roughly northerly direction from Sarmizegethusa across a heterogenous territory to Porolissum. Instead of forming a unity in a geographically uniform area, as the Transylvanian Basin would be, for example, they are separated from one another by mountains and valleys and not insignificant distances.

The former Roman towns of Apulum, Napoca, and Potaissa were situated in the vicinity of the large area of the Sîntana de Mureş culture in the Transylvanian Basin; Porolissum was in the north, in the immediate vicinity of the free Dacians. The rural settlements also assumed to have been inhabited by Roman peasant farmers were situated among settlements of non-Roman populations: In the area between the Mureş River and the Tîrnava Mare valley there are about 12 assumed Roman sites and about 15 sites that certainly belonged to non-Roman populations who immigrated to the area beginning in the second half of the third century. This area must therefore be considered, even if one accepts the existence of Romans in certain settlements, ethnically mixed. Toward the north, in the northern part of the Transylvanian Basin, the proportion of sites is rather in favor of certainly non-Roman peoples. On the whole, most of the Transylvanian Basin was characterized in the fourth century by a very distinct culture: the Sîntana de Mureş culture, mainly representing the Goths. In the southeastern corner of Transylvania and in the valleys of the upper Olt and the Rîul Negru River (Feketeügy), there was again a compact area of non-Romans, the bearers of the Sfîntu Gheorghe culture.

The situation of the Romans in the former towns and in the western group of settlements would have been analogous to that of the Roman peasants in the former provinces of Noricum and Raetia in the century after the retreat of the Roman administration from those provinces. Names of such peasants are extant. Isolated from the masses of Latin-speaking people, these Roman peasants assimilated eventually into the surrounding Germanic population. Assimilation is thus the most probable fate of a Roman population assumed to have been living in Transylvania in the fourth century. If, however, an assumed Roman population would have survived, preserving their language, then they necessarily were exposed to a very intense foreign influence. Their continuous contacts in the given geographical situation with the Goths, the free Dacians, the bearers of the Sfîntu Gheorghe culture, to mention only the most obvious non-Roman elements, would inevitably have led to a mixing—socially, culturally, and linguistically—of the different populations. The Romanian language shows no traces of such a foreign influence from this early period. It does not contain any elements from the fourth through the sixth centuries that could not be explained by the ancestors of the Romanians living within the greater area of Latin-speaking peoples. It shows, on the contrary, a purely Latin structure (with Slavic elements from a later, well-defined time) and contains all the innovations and usages that appeared in the period in question (the fourth through the sixth centuries A.D.) in the idiom of the Roman populations in the Balkan Peninsula and in parts of Italy.

THE FIFTH TO THE SEVENTH CENTURIES IN TRANSYLVANIA

The Old Germanic Peoples

After the withdrawal of the Romans from Dacia Traiana, in the post-Aurelian period, the historical and ethnic picture of the former Roman province was radically changed. These changes were caused primarily by invasions of the Huns from the east that scattered the Germanic population (the Goths and the Gepidae) in Eastern Europe and destroyed all vestiges of Roman urban life north of the Danube. Contacts with the Eastern Roman Empire decreased; and money-based commerce declined and was replaced by barter trade; coinage had already ceased in Dacia Traiana by 225.

There are numerous written accounts about the history of Germanic tribes in the period of the peoples' migration. The presence of a Germanic population in Transylvania, most probably Ostrogoths, can be attested from the fourth century. Written sources of the fifth and sixth centuries refer only to Germanic peoples in that territory, and archaeological findings of that period have a Germanic character. A two-centuries-long period, from 378 to 568, marked by Eastern Germanic influence along the middle course of the Danube, has left behind extremely significant archaeological remnants whose importance, however, is deliberately played down in contemporary Romanian historical works.

The following six gold treasure-troves of the period of the peoples' migration are known to exist in the Carpathian area:

1. Pietroasa, on the south side of the Carpathians in Muntenia;
2. and 3. The two treasure-troves of Şimleu Silvaniei (Szilágy-somlyó, Sălaj County), in northwestern Transylvania;
4. The grave of Prince Omharius (Apahida I) near Cluj;
5. The second princely grave of Apahida; and
6. The treasure-trove of Cluj-Someşeni.[308]

These all reflect the cultural horizon of the fifth century and are most likely attributable to the Ostrogoths. Germanic elements pertinent to Ostrogoths and Visigoths cannot, however, be easily differentiated. The Visigoth graves ceased to exist between 376 and 381 as a consequence of the advance of the Huns into Southeastern Europe.

Characteristic of the Gothic period are fibulae, belt buckles, combs, pearl necklaces, pendants of Roman origin, and spindles with clay heads located in the graves of women.

The richly-endowed graves of a Germanic (most probably Ostrogothic [Gepidic]) princely residence at Apahida (Cluj County) may be traced to the Sîntana de Mureş culture at the beginning of the third quarter of the fifth century.[309] Three princely graves were discovered at Apahida in 1889, 1968, and 1978 and have been designated respectively as Apahida I, Apahida II, and Apahida III. It is assumed that such sumptuous funerary provisions originated at the time of Attila's empire, around 490, since the Germanic peoples were particularly influenced by the gold opulence of the Hunnic Empire. Small fibulae and Ostrogothic fibulae of Transylvania are characteristic of this early stage of the Merovingian period.

Fourth century Gothic and sixth century Gepidic remains have been found in the cemetery of Tîrgu Mureş. In the Mureş valley, in the cemeteries of Ciumbrud, Ocna Mureş, Gorneşti (Gernyeszeg), and Alba Iulia, remnants of a Gothic material culture, such as pearls, fibulae, ornamental combs, and vessels, have appeared. In the Tîrnava River valleys, in places such as Bezid, Odorheiu Secuiesc (Székelyudvarhely) and Porumbenii Mici-Galáttető (Kisgalambfalva, both in Harghita County), remnants of Gothic settlements have been discovered. Gothic settlements occurred most probably also in Bratei. One of the most important settlement areas of the Visigoths was in the basin of Covasna (Kovászna-Háromszék) and in Ţara Bîrsei (Barcaság). Their most important settlement has been uncovered at Sfîntu Gheorghe.[310]

The Goths

The Goths were a Germanic tribe whose original home was on the Baltic Sea and on the banks of the Vistula River.[311] At the beginning of the third century A.D. the Ostrogoths (Eastern Goths) reached the Black Sea; and by the middle of that century they split from the Visigoths (Western Goths) who advanced toward the lower Danube and wrested Dacia from the Romans (271). The territory, which earlier had been called Dacia, now became Gothia: the Gothic Empire (from 271 to 385 A.D.). In the fourth century the Goths founded a large empire extending from the Don to the mouth of the Danube.

The date of the Goths' appearance in Transylvania has been variously given.[312] The Germanic period in this territory had already begun in the second half of the second century; *de facto*, however, Romania's present-day territory was subject to the influence of the

Germanic peoples from the fourth to the seventh century. This conclusion is reached through archaeological and historical data.

The Ostrogoths, overrun by the Huns, moved their settlements into northwestern Transylvania and toward Pannonia. Archaeological remains related to them may be found until 471 A.D. One part of the Ostrogoths migrated south of the Danube. The Getae, south of the Danube, in Moesia, had been called Goths from the second until the fourth century A.D. In the year 488 the Ostrogoths moved into Italy because of the Gepidae penetration into Transylvania. Chris-.tianity, mostly in the form of Arianism or Audnism, was spread among the Goths as early as the beginning of the fourth century.

The Gepidae

There are no written sources about the early history of the Old Germanic people, the Gepidae.[313] They migrated together with other Germanic tribes, with the Goths, Bastarns, Eruls, Vandals, and Longobards, in the middle of the second century A.D. from the shores of the Baltic Sea and Vistula River toward the Black Sea and partially penetrated the Carpathian Basin.[314] They spoke the same or a similar language as the Goths.

The Gepidae are first mentioned in written records at the same time as the Goths, in the second half of the 250s, when they attacked Dacia. In the second half of the third century, about 269, they settled in the northeastern part of the Carpathian Basin, in the region of the upper course of the Tisza and Someş rivers. In the year 290, after the withdrawal of the Romans from Dacia, the Gepidae sought to conquer this territory by warring against the Ostrogoths, who were living there. They were, however, defeated. They continued to settle in the mountainous region of the Northern Carpathians (Tisza region), although certain groups had lived in the area occupied by the Sarmatians, in the region between the Criş, Tisza, and Mureş rivers, since the last quarter of the fourth century. Their characteristic ceramics with surface-glazed ornamentations and the bronze fibula with an inverted foot are to be found in this territory.

The Gepidae were among the main allies of the Huns and were under Hunnic rule for a half century. After Attila's death, the Gepidae in alliance with other peoples attacked the Huns and defeated them at the Nedao River, in Pannonia, in 454. After conquering most of Pannonia, the Gepidae ruled for a century over the eastern part of the Carpathian Basin, including Transylvania as far as the estuary of the Olt River. From 454 to 567 this territory was called Gepidia.

In the first years of their dominance, the Gepidae settled in the valleys of the greater Transylvanian rivers; and, according to written sources,[315] their military power reached from the lower Danube to the mouth of the Olt River. Beginning with the sixth century, however, the center of the Gepidic settlements was established in the Transylvanian Basin (Mezőség, Cîmpia Transilvaniei) and its surroundings, primarily the regions of the Someşul Mic (Kis Szamos) and Mureş (Maros) rivers.

The presence of the Gepidae in the Carpatho-Danubian area in the sixth century is mentioned in several records. During the reign of Justinian (527–565) they conquered Dacia Ripensis. Theophylaktos Simokatta reported three Gepidic villages in the Banat in connection with a Byzantine military raid in the year 601.[316] In the year 626 Gepidae were also reported to be fighting in the army of the Avars at the siege of Constantinople. The capital of the Gepidic kingdom was moved to Sirmium (modern Mitrovica, Yugoslavia) around 560.

Following the settlement of the Avars in the Carpathian Basin and the defeat of the Gepidae in 567, the predominance of the Germanic peoples in the Carpathian Basin, that of the Gepidae in the Tisza region as well as in Transylvania, came to an end: The Longobards and Gepidae, as well as Romans from Raetia and Noricum and the Sarmatians, moved to Italy. Archaeological and written sources show that splinter groups of Longobards were located in the western parts of contemporary Hungary. Late Germanic groups still existed on the eastern bank of the Tisza at the beginning of the seventh century, but there was no continuity of settlements with the previous Gepidae.[317]

To this day some 21 settlements of the Germanic period have been discovered in Transylvania.[318] In addition, there are some 54 sites with cemeteries.[319] The material culture, of which the Old Germanic population was the main component, is called Černjachov-Sîntana de Mureş. During the Merovingian period (500–567) several settlements of Gepidae were established in Transylvania, especially in the Mureş region and in the northern area of the Transylvanian Basin. Gepidic material remains are also found in the eastern parts of the Great Hungarian Plain (Alföld).

Moreşti-Podei (Malomfalva-Podej, Mureş County) is a typical settlement from the period of the peoples' migration, that is, of the Transylvanian-Merovingian culture.[320] The settlement started at about the turn of the fifth to the sixth century and ended with the collapse of the Gepidic Empire (567). Similar cemeteries are also known to have existed in the Hungarian Plain. The excavations made from 1951 to 1956 uncovered 81 graves. Although there are many archaeological strata at Moreşti, there are few remains that can be used to date the levels chronologically. During the peoples' migration period the principle remains in Transylvania are of a Germanic population. Evidence of the Gepidaes' presence may still be found in the burial fields of Morești: Twin-rowed combs with five buttons ornamented with a headplate; fibulae with five buttons, ornamented with headplate and a rhomboid foot; and pearl jewelry attached to the head were found here; analogous objects were found also in the Gepid-inhabited Tisza region.

The red ceramics of the late Roman times were replaced in the period of the Germanic peoples (sixth century) by the grey high-fired earthenware made of a sandy material. Some was made on a potter's wheel and some by hand, the latter becoming increasingly more common. Ornamentation considered as being specific to the migration includes wave motifs, surface-glazing,[321] and impressed designs. A decisive change in the production and form of the fibulae occurred around the middle of the fifth century: Sheet metal fibulae were no longer made and were replaced by small cast fibulae. Somewhat later, larger fibulae with spiral ornamentations and clasps were used for clothing (Căpușul Mare [Magyarkapus, Cluj County], Fîntînele, Morești, Țaga). Small fibulae and those with spiral ornamentations do not appear in the first half of the sixth century.

Earthen fortifications of the sixth century, as well as houses erected above the ground level and square-shaped pit-huts, served primarily economic purposes, and were typical of those used by the Germanic tribes (Gepidae) in the first millenium A.D. in all the areas they inhabited. The row-graves of the Merovingian period began in the second half of the fifth century. The placing of armor and weapons in men's graves, according to East Germanic custom, was characteristic of Gepidic tombs. Men and women were buried separately.

The Roman remains at Morești give only a partial picture of the settlement of this area in Roman times, although in the second and third centuries it was the most important settled region in Transylvania; and no evidence exists to connect these remains with those of the later periods.[322]

The cemetery of Band (Mezőbánd, Mureș County) is part of the largest Gepidic remains in Transylvania. The cemetery of Noșlac with its 125 graves belongs to this group. Other Gepidic tombs are found in Cipău, Sighișoara, Ocnița, and Ciurgo (Csurgó, Cluj County). In Țaga a more elaborate woman's grave was uncovered.[323] In contrast to those on the Hungarian Plain, the continuity of use of the cemeteries of Noșlac, Unirea-Vereșmort, Band, and Bratei 3 has been verified.[324] All are located outside the areas of Avar sovereignty.

Gepidic graves of the earlier period, in the second half of the fifth century, appear in several locations in the Transylvanian Basin (Lechinţa de Mureș), as well as in the Tîrnava valley (Mediaș, Odorheiu

Secuiesc) with their characteristic Gepidic silver and gold earrings with buttons. The gold-covered fibulae and ornamented earrings found in Şeica Mică (Kisselyk, Sibiu County) in 1856 belong to the oldest Gepidic finds in the Carpathian Basin. Similar finds were discovered in Tîrnava (Nagyekemező, Sibiu County), Sighişoara, Cîlnic (Kelnek), and Cluj.[325] In Noşlac Gepidic remnants of the Avar period were found. Arrowheads characteristic of the Germanic peoples were found in Cipău, Lechinţa de Mureş, Moreşti, and Ocniţa.

After 567 the Gepidic burial grounds ceased to exist, which may be explained either by the ousting of the Gepidae or by the plundering of the graves. The continued presence of the Gepidae during the Avar period, however, is unquestionable: Gepidic remnants can be archaeologically determined until 670, as eastern equestrian nomadic elements are to be found in Gepidic graves.[326] Late Germanic finds are Gepidic; however, there is no continuity of settlement in Transylvania between the Gepidae of the sixth century and the Late Germanic peoples of the first half of the seventh century. It is also possible that the Gepidae were moved or displaced by the Avars.

Since the most significant ethnic element in post-Roman Dacia Traiana was the Germanic tribes, discovery of evidence of a Romanic population among them would be of great significance. In current Romanian historiography the presence of a Romanic element in the settlements of the Old Germanic populations is generally considered an established fact and is said to be "illustrated in the predominantly Gothic archaeological complex of the Černjachov-Sîntana de Mureş culture by Geto-Dacian pottery and by some rituals."[327] A symbiosis of the Romans with the Gepidae is now assumed to have led to the assimilation of this Germanic population into the autochthons and "can no longer be identified in the archaeological material from the territory of Romania."[328]

In several earlier works published in Romania, the archaeologist Kurt Horedt has argued that certain objects found in Gepidic tombs suggest a Romanic population.[329] It has been maintained that no Gepidae dwelling places have been discovered so far on the Hungarian Plain;[330] in Transylvania, the Gepidic houses at Moreşti and Band may thus have been built "perhaps with a Roman influence."[331] The settlements in question clearly reveal characteristics of an Old Germanic people, with buildings on the surface surrounded by huts for weaving and for the preparation of meat. The earthenware, the characteristic fibulae, and the graves also indicate a Germanic people.

In a recent article published in West Germany, however, Horedt mentioned the difficulties of proving the presence of a Romanic population in the Merovingian period[332] and pointed out that several investigations had furnished no decisive proof of a Roman population in that period.[333] Late Roman influences can no longer be detected in the sixth century Gepidic tombs.

With regard to the Gepidae living together with a Romanic population, the very generalized arguments amount to mere speculation. It is nevertheless possible that remnants of a Roman population could have been survived in Transylvania until the sixth or seventh century; this, however, cannot be proven through archaeological evidence and, in any case, cannot involve remnants of a Romanized Dacian population. Vestiges of Romans could, at best, be found in Germanic row graves but not in Slavic cremation tombs as has been assumed in several Romanian studies. This alternative is untenable as the Romans could not have practiced inhumation and shortly thereafter cremation. The change in funerary rites and the general use of cremation since the seventh century, as evidence of a comprehensive Slavization, provide the most serious archaeological objections to the assumption of late Roman continuity in Transylvania.[334] Archaeological and historical data converge in this instance.

In reference to the objects found among Gepidic material remains considered as being specific to the Romanized population in the former Roman province of Dacia, it should be noted that the Roman influence in this period was very pronounced throughout Europe; this fact certainly does not presuppose Romans living among the Goths. Furthermore, it is not possible to determine the exact dating or the designation of the archaeological finds, particularly those of objects of daily usage of the Roman population at the end of the fourth century and later. The assumption that the hairpins are an indication of a Romanized population is groundless, inasmuch as they are also found in the graves of the Gepidae. Fibulae with an inverted foot, such as those found at Moreşti, should also not be offered as evidence, since they are common throughout the Balkan Peninsula and between the Danube and the Carpathian Mountains, and are also to be found, albeit to a lesser extent, in the Gepidic tombs.[335] Furthermore, Celts could also have been the bearers of wheel-turned pottery (such as that from pre-Roman Dacia) and fibulae. Iron brooches and hairpins of the Roman bronze style, for example, of which a few have been found in Transylvania, have been also found in third to fourth century Sarmatian tombs in the region of the Tisza River and among fourth and fifth century Germanic material remains from the same area (the Hungarian Plain).[336] They also appeared in Longobard tombs in Pannonia, Bohemia, and Italy, as well as among the remains of the Bajuwars, the Franks, and other Germanic peoples. It was, in other words, a common and widespread object of ornamentation in Merovingian times; it was not, however, characteristic of Roman tombs from the territory of the Roman Empire.

Cube-shaped earrings found in Gepidic tombs in Transylvania were claimed to be of local Roman origin.[337] They are indeed of Roman style and characteristic of the fourth to fifth centuries, but it is a misinterpretation to consider them as indications of a local Roman element in Transylvania. They belong, instead, to a large group of objects made after Roman patterns in barbarian Europe and are also found in parts of Germany, Austria, Bohemia, on the Hungarian Plain, in northern Moldavia, and in regions as remote as the Crimea.[338]

The grey, fourth-century earthenware of the Hungarian Plain often suggests a Sarmatian origin. Furthermore, wheel-made pottery in the shape of a pear or a bag is characteristic of mounted nomads in sixth and seventh centuries. Several kinds of pottery from the Carpathian Basin—the vessels of stamped ceramics and pottery with surface-glazed ornamentation—are typical of the peoples' migration period and therefore from a Germanic population. Excavations carried out in the last few years in Hungary have shown houses of the same type as both those described in Moreşti and Cipău and those with two or six poles, at Tiszafüred, Battonya (Hungary), and Eperjes (Slovakia).[339] To this one must add the fact that the number of graves and remains of settlements that could be ascribed to the Dacians in Transylvania is very low in comparison with the large volume of Celtic remains.[340] There are only a few Dacian remains of settlements, for example, in southeastern Transylvania; after the fourth century, however, the presence of Dacians in Transylvania is no longer demonstrable.

The existence of Old Germanic elements in the Romanian language has been assumed by several scholars, including the German Ernst Gamillscheg, Günter Reichenkron, and the Romanian Constantin Diculescu. Their etymologies do not, however, meet scientific requirements and belong, in fact, to the realm of fantasy. Quoting the reputed Romanian linguist, Alexandru Rosetti, "one may say that none of the proposed etymologies stands up to critical analysis. Those few words for which no other etymology than the Germanic one has yet been proposed have small chances of belonging to this group of words."[341]

It is claimed that a Romanic population was living in the valleys of Transylvania and in the Transylvanian Basin in symbiosis with the Goths and Gepidae. In the same settlement or cemetery, material remains of a Romanic population are asserted to have been found, together with material left by the Germanic peoples. If this is correct, then the two kinds of people were living in the closest possible symbiosis for several centuries. The gist of the old question is, therefore, whether such a close symbiosis would be possible without having any effect on the language of the assumed Romanic population. If a Romanic population had coinhabited with and been subject to the rule of Germanic peoples in Trajan's Dacia for 300 years (275–567), the Romanian language would have to have acquired Germanic loan words just as traces of Gothic, Frankish, Burgundian, and Longobardic are to be found in the vocabulary of the Italian, Gallic, and Iberian languages. This problem will be discussed in the chapter dealing with the history of the Romanian language.

THE HUNS

A catastrophic period in Southeast Europe began with the appearance of the Huns and Avars. As a consequence of the Hunnic invasion at the turn of the fourth century, ties with the Roman Empire come to an end and Byzantium sought to recover the lost western territories. Historically, this occurrence has been regarded as a catastrophe for Southeastern Europe. The arrival of the Huns coincides with the beginning of the early Middle Ages.

The Huns were of Scythian descent and, like the Turks, were probably of a common Turanian-Turkic origin from Inner- and Middle Asia. The first significant Hunnic invasion on the lower Danube was recorded in 395. The plain between the lower Danube and the Southern Carpathians—present-day Muntenia—became the principal settlement area of the Huns at the turn of the fourth century. After 420 to 430 A.D. remains of the Huns east and south of the Carpathians disappear because of their movement westward. Their vestiges in the transcarpathian territories can be verified in Buhăieni (Iași County), Dulceanca (Teleorman County), Gherăseni (Buzău County), and Concești (Botoșani County).

In 422 the Huns entered the Carpathian Basin. They chased the Goths from the Sea of Azov into Dacia; and later they themselves moved toward Dacia, for instance, against the Agathirs who inhabited the Carpathians. By 425 the empire of the Huns under Attila (433–

453), was established on the plain between the Tisza, Mureş, and Criş rivers (the present-day Hungarian Plain). During the later 430s the empire stretched as far as the Rhine. After Attila's death in 453, the empire disintegrated; and in 454 it collapsed following the defeat of the Huns by the Gepidae on the Nedao River.[342] Contemporary records of the dismemberment of the Hunnic Empire are scarce.

Following the collapse of the Hunnic Empire, the Gepidae and Ostrogoths were the dominant powers in the Carpathian Basin. The Gepidae occupied all of Dacia, that is, the territory between the Tisza and Danube, the Olt, and Carpathians, until the end of the fifth century. The Ostrogoths acquired Pannonia. Between the Danube and Tisza lived the Sarmatians and the Skirs. The history of the Carpatho-Danubian area between 454 and 473 was determined primarily by Ostrogothic warfare.[343]

The archaeological remnants of the Huns have been primarily of concern to Hungarian and German archaeologists.[344] Characteristic of Hunnic art are the gold diadems recovered from numerous graves of women. The barbarian cemeteries on the Hungarian Plain to the south of the Criş River ceased to exist after the settlement of the Huns in the Carpathian Basin.

CEMETERIES IN TRANSYLVANIA FROM THE SIXTH TO NINTH CENTURIES

The Avars

As mentioned previously, the archaeological configuration of Transylvania, with its rows of burial graves, bears the stamp of Germanic peoples. In the second half of the seventh century the row-cemeteries of the Germanic peoples came to an end and the first Avar row-cemeteries appeared in the Carpathian Basin:[345] in Transylvania along the middle course of the Mureş and Arieş rivers and in the eastern part of the Hungarian Plain along the Tisza River.[346]

The origin of the Avars is still obscure. They might have been partly Mongol, but their language was apparently Altaic. They were part of the Inner Asiatic peoples and probably stemmed from two ethnic groups. They have been traced by archaeologists to Inner Asia and to neighboring territories.[347] The Avars advance toward Europe, under pressure from the Turks, began after they lost sovereignty over the Onoguric Empire, in the Pontic Steppe, of the Bulgarian Khan Kuvrat. Toward the end of 557 they crossed the Volga and appeared in northern Caucasia. In 562 they reached the lower Danube under the leadership of Khan Bajan. In 567, following their victory over the

Gepidae and the collapse of the Gepidic Empire, the Avars moved into Transylvania and eastern Pannonia. In 568 the Avars occupied the entire plain of modern Hungary, including Pannonia, and established the Avar Empire, which assumed the role previously held by the Huns as the dominant power in Central Europe. The settlement of the Avars imposed profound ethnic and cultural changes in the Carpathian Basin, which following the Avar conquest ceased to be an area of Germanic interests. During their rule of 230 years the Avars developed new political and economic structures as well as new means of communication.

According to earlier historical views, the Avar Empire was destroyed by the Frankish King and Emperor Charlemagne and his son Pepin, with the help of the Bulgar Krum (803–814). Recent research has shown, however, that the collapse of the Avar Empire was also a result of internal discord. In the absence of evidence of the Avars' leaving the Carpathian Basin, it is fair to assume that they were assimilated into the Hungarian state, which appeared toward the end of the ninth century. The latest research indicates that east of the Danube, in the territories not occupied by Franks, the Avars retained their ethnic identity, language, and culture until the arrival of the Magyars.[348] Their territorial-political organization in this area was, however, destroyed by the Bulgarian Krum.

The remnants of Avar culture in the Carpathian Basin have not yet been explored; nevertheless, the few relics of their material culture that have been found, such as bronze castings and ornamented belt buckles, bear testimony to the Avars' highly developed culture. With the arrival of the Avars, weapons are to be found more frequently in burial grounds. The use of molded metal objects is characteristic of early Avar finds and is most probably attributable to the Kutrigurs. The dissemination area of Avar culture stretches from southern Vojvodina (Yugoslavia) as far as Transylvania, southern Slovakia, and Austria, south of Vienna.

As previously mentioned, in 567 the Avar conquest was completed. The belt buckles of this period are an important cultural characteristic. At the same time contacts developed between Byzantium and the Avar Empire. The chronology of the middle Avar period, from the last quarter of the seventh century to the beginning of the eighth century, has been established. The chronology of the late Avar period is still a subject of controversy: It is dated between the middle and end of the eighth century to the turn of the ninth century, presumably into the early ninth century; and it is characterized by cast bronze work. Equestrian nomadic objects, besides sheet metal artifacts, are limited to stirrups and snaffles.

The Avars' presence in Transylvania can be attested through archaeological evidence to having been on the middle course of the Mureş River in Gîmbaş (Marosgombás, Alba County), Noşlac, Unirea-Vereşmort, Aiud (Nagyenyed, Cluj County), Teiuş (Tövis, Alba County), Cicău (Csákó, Alba County), Band, Cipău, Moreşti, Lopadea Nouă (Magyarlapád, Alba County), Aiudul de Sus (Felenyed, Alba County), Măgina (Muzsnaháza) and Heria (Hari, both Alba County). There are remnants of the Avar culture in Transylvania in the Arieş River valley in Moldoveneşti (Várfalva, Cluj County), Corneşti (Sövényfalva, Cluj County), Cîmpia Turzii (Aranyosgyéres, Cluj County), and Turda, as well as in Corund (Korond, Harghita County), Dumbrăveni Erzsébetváros, Sibiu County), Nuşfalău (Szilágynagyfalu, Sălaj County), Someşeni, and Ocna Sibiului (Vizakna, Sibiu County). The pendant of an Avar cast iron filigree from the eighth or ninth century was found in Dăbîca (Doboka, Cluj County). Contemporary Avar cast iron artifacts are also known from the cemeteries of Nuşfalău and Someşeni and were still used by the Gepidae after the Avar period, as late as 630. In Noşlac Gepidic remnants of the Avar period and a belt buckle used by equestrian nomads at the beginning of the seventh century were found.

As mentioned previously, the furnishing of the late Transylvanian burial grounds (Band, Noşlac, Unirea-Vereşmort) do not necessarily reveal continuity from the Gepidae of the sixth century and the late Germanic people of the seventh century. All the cemeteries mentioned are analogous to those on the western edge of the Avar Empire, such as the ones at Környe (Hungary) in the transdanubian area. One of the most important Avar khan tombs has been excavated at Kunbábony, Hungary. In the second quarter of the seventh century today's southern Slovakia was incorporated into the Avar Empire. Equestrian nomadic graves have been found in this region.

Avar grave groups, with the characteristic equestrian nomadic material culture, appear around 670 in the Mureş valley in Transylvania, as new ethnic groups, presumably Onogur Bulgars, settled in the Avar Empire. Consequently, the ethnic structure of the late Avars is altered through the appearance of this new element whose culture is closely related to that found in the treasure-laden tombs of the Ukraine. The equestrian nomadic peoples' working of cast bronze ceases with the destruction of the Avar Empire at the end of the eighth century.

With the first Avar wave several tribes moved westward, primarily Slavic groups such as Antes, Volhynians, and Sorbs. The early Avar-Slavic symbiosis is set chronologically between 630 and 700. Slavic settlements were originally separate from the Avar; however, in Avar cemeteries of the seventh century Slavic elements appear (Bratei 2 is, for instance, the heretofore largest known late Avar-Slavic cemetery in Transylvania). In the eighth century it is almost impossible to differentiate between Avar and Slavic material culture, for instance in ceramics.

On the basis of archaeological finds it is possible to establish the presence of the Avars in the Mureş and Tîrnava valleys of Transylvania in the eighth century. The continuing existence of the late Avars, in contrast to the account of the Russian Primary Chronicle, is assumed by Hungarian researchers. Proof of this continuity are Avar cemeteries of the tenth century.[349] At the beginning of the ninth century the Avars abandoned their graves, after which the Slavic components become more and more evident. Slavic cemeteries with Avar remnants are in Someşeni, Dăbîca, Căuaş (Érkávás, Sălaj County), and Nuşfalău (Szilágynagyfalu, Sălaj County).

THE APPEARANCE OF THE SLAVS IN THE CARPATHIAN BASIN

The period between the seventh and tenth centuries in the Carpathian Basin is marked by two decisive events: the settlement of the Slavs and the arrival of the Magyars. As is known, the original home of the Slavs stretched over a considerable area of the East European plain, between the lower Vistula and Niemen to the north and the Carpathian Mountains to the south and from the middle Dnieper and Pripet in the east to the Oder and Elbe in the west.[350] This corresponds approximately to the written sources, especially those of the sixth century historian Jordanes.[351] Further data regarding the Slavs, particularly for the sixth century, are provided by Procopius.[352] Jordanes distinguishes among three groups of Slavs: the Venedi, the Sclavini, and the Antes. After the sixth century all Slavs called themselves *Sloven* (plural Slovenes) which was transcribed in Latin as *Sclavus* or *Sclavinus* (plural Sclavi, Sclavini) and which the Greeks identified as *Sklavenoi* or *Sklavoi*. The Southern Russian Slavs, who lived in the area stretching from the Moldavian Carpathians and the mouth of the Danube to the Crimea, were designated as Antes or Antai by Byzantine writers. Jordanes places the location of the Antes between the Dnieper and Dniester. The *Sclavini* were the Balkan Slavs while the Antes were part of the community of Eastern Slavs later known as Russians.

Written records regarding the first phase of the Slavic conquest are not always reliable. The first wave of Slavs reached the Danube toward the end of the fifth century; they were already mentioned in written sources at the beginning of the sixth century as living on the lower Danube. With the arrival of the Avars in the Carpatho-Danubian area, Slavic attacks tend to diminish; however, regular Slavic attacks against the Balkan provinces occurred even before the arrival of the Avars, during the last years of the rule of Emperor Justinus I (518–527). During the reign of Justinian, in the years 530 to 531, Slavic incursions across the lower Danube became increasingly more frequent. In 550, with the help of the Gepidae, Slavic peoples penetrated into most of the Balkan Peninsula; in 623 an independent Slavic dominion was established north of the Danube, and the northern, frontier of the Byzantine Empire collapsed. Between 610 and 641 the Slavs occupied all of the northern and central regions of the Balkan Peninsula, from the Alps to the Black Sea and from the Adriatic to the Aegean Sea. The territory stretching from the Haemus (Balkan) Mountains to the Adriatic was known as Slavinia and was incorporated into the Bulgarian kingdom in the late seventh century.

The Slavs found in the mountainous central parts of the Balkan Peninsula the ancestors of the Vlachs, as shown by numerous geographical names[353] of Rumanian origin, such as Durmitor (2528 m) and Visator, the two highest peaks in Montenegro; cf. Du Nay, 1977, *op. cit.*, pp. 26-27: a list and map with 35 names of villages of Romanian origin, including the Romanian appellatives from which they are formed (list and map after S.Dragomir: *Vlahii în nordul peninsulei Balcanice în evul mediu*, 1959). There are also appellatives of Romanian origin in certain Serbian dialects.

The Slavic penetration south of the Danube was completed in the seventh century; their conquest of the Balkan Peninsula, with the exception of Greece, was essentially accomplished. As a result, new ethnic relations arose in Southeastern Europe. In the ninth century, for example, even Thracia was called Slavinia; the rural areas were Slavic but the towns Greek. Concurrently with the Slavic advance to the Danube and the Balkan Peninsula, western Slavs were moving toward the Elbe by way of the Oder.

During the second half of the fifth century eastern Slavic peoples probably occupied the Gepid-inhabited parts of Transylvania, even though the earliest Slavic archaeological finds reveal no connection with the pre-568 Gepidic culture. According to recent archaeological research in Slovakia, it seems that the Slavs made their appearance in the Carpathian Basin, coming through various mountain passes, as early as in the sixth century. It is a fact, however, that the earliest reliable extant Slavic (eastern Slavic) remains are to be found in Transylvania, that is, in eastern Transylvania in the Trei Scaune (Háromszék-Kovászna) Basin, in the valleys of the Olt and Tîrnava rivers, and can be dated to the period stretching from the sixth to the ninth and tenth centuries. Eastern Slavic peoples, the Antes, penetrated eastern Transylvania with the Avars in the second half of the sixth century. This is indicated by the existence of Slavic place names (Borosnyó, Kovászna, Zágon, Csernáton, Lisznyó, Szacsva, Doboly, Esztelnek, Gelence, and others), hand-made ceramics of the Prague type, cast bronze fibulae, and cremation graves from the second half of the seventh century. After the Antes, western Slavic peoples also settled there. Larger and smaller rivers have retained their Slavic names to our time. In general, it may be assumed that Slavs lived in Transylvania from as early as the seventh century (Band, Moreşti). Their presence there can be shown to have lasted until the twelfth and, to some extent, the thirteenth century.

The second Slavic wave reached the Carpathian Basin in the seventh and eighth centuries. There, they settled primarily in the middle sectors of the river valleys. An ever greater Slavic wave displaced the Avars, who still inhabited the Carpathian Basin in the seventh century; as a consequence, following the collapse of the Avar Empire, the Slavs became the most numerous inhabitants of the Basin. At the beginning of the seventh century the Slavs who inhabited the Alpine region rebelled against the Avar Empire, and between 630 and 640 the Slavs who inhabited Dalmatia freed themselves from Avar rule.

In the years of transition from the sixth to seventh centuries more Slavic peoples appeared in the valleys of the Northern Carpathians and in the region of the Morava and upper Tisza rivers as well as in northern Transylvania. These were the White Croats, related to the Poles, who lived side-by-side with the later Avars. Their presence is still mentioned in the tenth century. With the Hungarian conquerors other splinter groups of eastern Slavs from the region of the Dniester and Bug rivers reached the Carpathian Basin. It is assumed that they lived side-by-side with the Hungarians for an extended period of time. Toponymic and archaeological remnants such as place names and characteristic funeral mounds (tumulus) of eastern Slavs may still be seen in the region of Sălaj and in the valleys of the Someş (Szamos), Kraszna, and Berettyó rivers, especially in Şimleu Silvaniei and Szeged. One of their citadels was built on the ruins of ancient Porolissum and another in Ziligrad (Sóvár), in proximity of Doboka (Dăbîca).

On the eve of the Hungarian conquest the so-called Danubian Slovenes and Moravians lived west of the Danube; Bulgaro-Slavs in the larger but sparsely inhabited eastern half of the Carpathian Basin; and, as previously mentioned, the so-called White Croats in the valleys of the Northern Carpathians. The Slavic-Hungarian symbiosis lasted some 150 years; part of the Christian terminology of the Hungarian language was introduced by slavic-speaking Western missionaries in

Hungary in the tenth century. Yet, the Magyars had almost certainly come into close contact with Slavonic Christianity before their migration to Central Europe.[354]

One of the most important historical events marking the end of Antiquity and the beginning of the Middle Ages is the advance of the Slavs. Their arrival in the Southeastern European area caused a decisive alteration of the ethnic, linguistic-cultural, and historical configuration. In the seventh and eighth centuries the whole of the Balkan Peninsula, except Greece, was Slavized. The ancient geographic nomenclature used in the Balkan Peninsula was replaced by a new set of names that have generally survived until now. With the Slavic occupation, Latin ceased to be the official language on the Balkan Peninsula. In contrast to Western patterns, in the eastern part of the Carpathian Basin (in Transylvania) no pre-Slavic place names have been preserved. No ancient, pre-Slavic population survived: Late Germanic peoples or remnants of Avars disappeared, that is, assimilated into Slavdom in the seventh century.[356]

The archaeological landscape was changed altogether. The Slavs replaced inhumation by cremation and the specific burial custom, the widow's sacrifice, characteristic of earlier Slavic tombs, was introduced. The archaeological remnants of their culture reveal a close relationship to the so-called Saltovo culture of Russia. The Slavs' conversion to Christianity was the work of Byzantium; the Serbs adopted Christianity between 867 and 874.[357]

As indicated by place- and river names of Slavic origin, the Hungarians found a Slavic population when they populated several parts of Transylvania beginning with the tenth century. But Slavs were living there also later, because the Saxons, who started to colonize certain areas beginning with the mid-twelfth century, borrowed many geographical names from them. This Slavic population disappeared after the twelfth century, being assimilated into the Hungarian, and, in some parts of southern Transylvania, into the Romanian population (see below, chapter IV).

Archaeological Remnants of the Slavs in Transylvania

As mentioned above, at the turn of the sixth to seventh century the period of the Germanic peoples came to an end in Transylvania; and the Slavic period began. Nevertheless, until the last quarter of the seventh century, late Germanic, Avar (nomadic equestrian), and Slavic elements converged. The archaeological excavations of Transylvania reveal a continuity of settlements in the 6th and 7th centuries, that is, between the Old Germanic and Slavic and, in part also, the Avar cultures. The discontinuation of row graves marks the disappearance of late Germanic population. In juxtaposition, the appearance of cremation funerals since the seventh century signals the arrival of the Slavs. During the sixth and seventh centuries the Slavs borrowed much from the Roman culture, particularly in the fields of technology, earthenware, jewelry, and house-building. The most salient archaeological characteristics of Slavic culture in its earliest stages are the hand-made earthenware, cremation burial, and square pithouses. Square and horseshoe-shaped stone fireplaces are of Slavic origin. Slavic ceramics are characterized by hand-made or wheel-made kiln-fired earthenware, with circular or waved ornamentation. A grey paste (clay) is the identifying characteristic of early Slavic ceramics. The list of places where this kind of ceramics was found in Transylvania has been established by Horedt as follows: Sighişoara, Bezid, Cipău, Sfîntu Gheorghe, Sălaşuri (Székelyszállás, Mureş County), Cernat, Comana de Jos (Alsókomána, Braşov County), and Poian.[358] The earliest Slavic ceramics are difficult to distinguish from those of the Černjachov culture.

Starting with the seventh century the first Slavic cremation cemeteries, frequently with Avar remnants, are found in Transylvania. The largest Slavic urn cemetery in the Carpathian Basin is cemetery no. 2 of Bratei, on the southern bank of the Tîrnava River. At the same time it is the only cemetery that reveals an Avar-Slavic symbiosis.[359] According to archaeological findings the cemetery of Bratei 2 was put into use at the earliest at the beginning of the eighth century, in the Avar period. Some of the urns should be attributed to the post-Avar period, to the so-called Mediaş group. No connection with the cremation cemetery of Bratei 1 of the third-fourth centuries can be assumed.[360]

Six funeral groups can be distinguished in Transylvania: Mediaş, Gîmbaş, Nuşfalău, Blandiana (originally Cîrna/Maroskarna, Alba County), Ciumbrud, and Cluj. They were named after the places where they were first known to have existed.[361] The Mediaş group through its Slavic characteristics is defined as Slavic. Nevertheless, as mentioned previously, late Germanic, Avar (nomadic equestrian), and Slavic elements converge. Chronologically they are set in the first half of the seventh century. The first of these tombs was excavated in 1960. In Berghin (Berve, Alba County) 360 graves were uncovered from 1976 to 1979; and in 1980 another 151 tombs were excavated.[362] Also in eastern and southern Transylvania some earlier finds of this group appeared. This type of tomb is also found in Czechoslovakia, Poland, and in the area of the Balkan-Danube culture, as well as in the area of the Slavs as the result of their wanderings toward the west and the south;[363] the urns show Slavic characteristics in their shape, technique, and ornamentation.[364] These tombs, such as those at Bratei, Boarta, Bistriţa, and Berghin (Alba County), and also in other areas of Romania, were the predominant type for about two centuries: from the early seventh to the late ninth century. One exception is along the middle course of the Mureş River and the eastern part of the Tisza River plain where tombs of Avar equestrians are frequent.

In about half of the places, a small number (about 9%) of the bodies were buried without cremation. There are several explanations for these inhumation tombs,[365] which could be connected with religious rituals and social, or ethnic circumstances. Most of the bodies were buried with the head towards the east, contrary to the Christian funeral rites; the lower classes may have been buried in this way. The presence of such objects as a Byzantine clasp or a knife of iron in such tombs suggests, however, that even rich and powerful people were buried in this way. With regard to the ethnic character of these tombs, cremation replaces the inhumation cemeteries of the row-graves in Transylvania and is connected with the arrival of the Slavs. Furthermore, there are also biological differences between people: At Ocna Sibiului, for example, 63% of the children were buried by inhumation although some adults were also not cremated. Chronological factors also played a certain role: Inhumation replaced cremation in the ninth century, but there were inhumation tombs as early as in the seventh century.

Most of the objects found in the cremation tombs were destroyed by fire; in about 20% of these graves, bones of animals, mostly sheep, birds, and goats, were also found. The most common objects are knives, generally in a very poor condition. At Tîrnava a Byzantine clasp from the second half of the seventh century was found. Bone fragments with an ornamentation of plant motifs, probably found at Ocna Sibiului, are from the seventh to eighth centuries and belong to the Avar culture. Similar remains have been found at Alattyán, Sopronkőhida (Hungary), and Havelberg (East Germany). The fibulae are of the Slavic type; one was found at Săcuieni, for example and has been classified as belonging to group I c of Slavic fibulae in the shape of a bow.[366] A bronze clasp of the Byzantine type of the seventh century was found at Tîrnava.[367] A similar piece is known from Keszthely, and another identical piece was found in the Avar cemeteries at Szentes-Kaján (both Hungary).

The graves of the Gîmbaş group are ascribed to the equestrian nomadic population. The chronological connection between the Slavic burial grounds and the Avar is revealed by an equestrian tomb of this group. The burial ground of Bratei is certainly Slavic, and the assumption that it may be connected with branches of Romanic peoples is incorrect.

The group of graves at Blandiana (defined as Blandiana A), which is located some 20 kilometers from Alba Iulia on the Mureş, is placed chronologically in the South Slavic (Bulgarian) period of the ninth century, the time of the arrival of the Hungarians. The place and field names which are to be found in the region, Bulgarian (Slavic) in origin, attest to this. The dissemination area of this culture reaches the lower Danube, to the former Bulgarian Empire of the ninth and tenth centuries. The territory in which this culture (also known as Balkan-Carpathian culture) originated is located to the south of the Danube on the Balkan Peninsula. The culture penetrated from the West and not from the Southern Carpathian passes into Transylvania, as is archaeologically demonstrable (Blandiana A group around Alba Iulia).[368] In conclusion, Horedt states that these typically Slavic tombs were predominant in Transylvania for two centuries, from 650 to 850.[369]

The Extension of the Theory of Romanization to Territories Beyond Roman Dacia

Several current Romanian historical works and surveys of the last decade have assumed that the early Romanization had been extended to all the territories of contemporary Romania, that is, even to those territories that never belonged to the Roman Empire.[370] The absence of any convincing evidence suggests that these arguments are the product of the current political imagination. It has been postulated that the tribes living in central and northern Moldavia (for example, the Carps), being neighbours to Dacia and Moesia, also adopted some forms of Roman civilization because of their contact with Roman culture;[371] historians speak about workshops east of the Carpathians in which Roman artisans produced glass of good quality and about buildings of Roman style, both of which are signs of Roman life in the fourth century. Another phenomenon referred to is the appearance of bronze coins, since "it is known that bronze coins were used in commerce only by the Roman population and never by the barbarians."[372] Other historians have expressed the opinion that the transcarpathian territories were increasingly Romanized from the fourth to the sixth centuries, as shown by ovens for the production of iron, pottery, and other objects, as well as by houses of the Roman type. The survival of the Romanized population is explained by reference to their assumed superior culture and "the extensive and continual process of Romanization."[373]

The Assumed Romanization in Muntenia

In a work published in 1974 a Romanian historian argued that the presence of a Romanized population ("Daco-Romans") in Muntenia in the fourth to seventh centuries had been "indisputably proved in the numerous settlements and cemeteries."[374] The following historical circumstances are said to have contributed to the Romanization of Muntenia: The territory belonged for some years in the early second century to Moesia Inferior; and in 112 and 113 A.D., a Roman army unit (the *Cohors I Hispanorum veterana*) was stationed there. In the same period, the Romans erected a number of fortifications in several parts of Muntenia and southern Moldavia. Some of these have been excavated, including those at Drajna de Sus, at Mălăieşti, Tîrgşor, and Pietroasele (near Buzău).[375] After the death of Emperor Trajan in 117 A.D., the Sarmatians attacked Moesia Inferior and Dacia; they subsequently settled at several places in Muntenia. The new emperor, Hadrian, was advised to give up the Dacian province but did not follow this advice. He abandoned, however, all the towers in the interior of Muntenia and southern Moldavia; and the Roman border was drawn along the lower Danube and not far from the Olt River. The merchants traveling through Muntenia from the towns along the Black Sea toward the central areas of Dacia are also often mentioned as having contributed to Romanization.

During the time of Emperor Constantine the Great (306–337), the Byzantine Empire expanded. The area of the present-day Romanian provinces, Muntenia and Oltenia up to the furrow of Novac (*Brazda lui Novac*), was occupied for some time.[376] The invasion of the Huns put an end to this period. In the sixth century, the Byzantine Empire expanded northward again and reconquered the northern areas of the Balkan Peninsula up to the lower Danube. A number of towers were built along the northern shore of the river (at Litterata, Dierna, and Turnu Măgurele); the ruins of the last two towers still exist. Romanian historians attribute great importance to this period of time, as well as to a record (the *Novella of Justinian*) that gives some hints about the circumstances along the lower Danube.[377] It must be emphasized, however, that immediately after the death of the Byzantine ruler Maurikios (602) the Romans lost all contacts with the middle Danube.

The chief arguments for an early Romanization of Muntenia, however, are archaeological. Earthenware dating to the second and third centuries A.D. shows Roman provincial characteristics, and most of the metal objects are of Roman origin. This is the case, for example, in a settlement dating from the second half of the second century to the beginning of the fourth century at Mătăsaru, in western Muntenia (fifty kilometers from the *limes Trans-Alutanus*), where excavations began in 1962; the techniques of making earthenware found here are "of the type found in the settlements of Roman Dacia."[378] Further excavations at the same site in 1977 resulted in the find of two fragments of vessels on which Roman letters were engraved after firing: *RAT* or *BAT* and *NVS*. At two other places in Muntenia, within 25 kilometers from the Roman frontier, fragments of vessels with Roman letters were found in the woods and fields, without any connection to a dwelling place or tomb. At Curcani, the upper part of a bowl bearing the letters *MITIS* was found; since similar reliefs are known from the earthenware of the Militari-Chilia culture, the vessel is thought to have been made in Muntenia.[379] At Socetu in 1968 the bottom of a vessel was found with the inscription *AVRELI(V)S SILVAN(V?)S FECIT PATELAM BONAM*, which was incized before firing; the vessel is probably from the third century. Available information does not make it clear whether the vessel was imported from the Roman Empire or produced locally.[380]

One of the first archaeologists to write about an allegedly Romanic material culture in sixth century Muntenia was Suzana Dolinescu-Ferche, who, with Petre Roman, described the findings: "The huts belonged to a rural settlement without fortifications on the left bank of the Olt River. The major part of the settlement was destroyed. The huts were rectangular, with rounded corners, about 2.5 by 3.0 meters, sunken in the soil at most by 0.4 to 0.5 meters. The floors were not covered with clay; no pits of poles, steps, or benches were found. The oven was made by digging in the yellow soil and had an oval shape."[381]

Based on a detailed analysis of earthenware at Ipoteşti stress is placed on the characteristics that emphasize a Dacian and provincial Roman origin, with reference to the techniques, the prevailing types, and the forms that show similarities to the autochthonous types, [as well as] the types of huts, and ovens, that may also be seen among the free Dacians in the third century A.D. In southwest Muntenia, the discoveries of the Ipoteşti and Olteni types also include a large quantity of earthenware of the Roman provincial tradition. Furthermore, it has been maintained that in the fifth and sixth centuries, the types of earthenware derived from the Dacian and provincial Roman forms changed (a change brought about by the economic, ethnic, historical, and social circumstances in the territories north of the Danube), and as a consequence of these changes a new cultural picture of a rural population developed over a large area, categorized as a Romanic culture [*o cultură romanică*] of rural character.

The Assumed Romanization in Moldavia

According to the second century Greek astronomer and geographer Ptolemy (Ptolemaeus), the area between the Siret and Dniester rivers was inhabited in the second century A.D. by Sarmatians, Carps, and a Celtic population (Britolagai).[382] These eastern parts of Moldavia were dependent on Moesia Inferior.[383] Bastarnae were living in the northern part of the province and Costoboci (Kostobokoi) and Carps in the west.[384] The Costoboci and the Carps are considered to have belonged to the Dacians.

Since Romanian historians consider the Carps to be one of the group from which the Romanian people originated, it is necessary to examine some of their main characteristics. Historical records about them are extant from the mid-second century A.D. until 381 A.D. Most of what is known about them, however, is based on archaeological excavations. On the basis of these findings, it can be concluded that the Carpic material culture was a continuation of the Dacian La Tène culture but was greatly influenced by the Sarmatians and the Romans and, to a lesser degree, by the Celts and Germanic peoples. They probably lived in Moldavia between the Eastern Carpathians and the Siret River beginning in the second century A.D.; later, they spread eastward, to the Prut River and even beyond it. The Costoboci lived in northern Moldavia until about 170 A.D., after which the Carps expanded to that area. At certain sites (Poiana Dulceşti, Lutărie, Tirpeşti)[385] there is a continuity between the late Dacian settlements and the early Carpic ones. The first level of settlements ends in many sites at the end of the second century A.D. Turbulent events at the end of that century are indicated by 23 hoards of Roman coins (denarii), which end with the reign of Commodus (180–192 A.D.), found in the former territory of the Carps. These hoards were usually connected with an attack of the Goths; but it is more probable that the attackers were Romans.[386] At some sites, there is continuity between the first and the second level of settlements (at Varniţă and at Silişte, for example).

During most of the third century, the Carps made occasional incursions into the Roman Empire. The first known attack occurred in 214 A.D.; the most violent one, a veritable war, was fought from 245 to 247. Emperor Philip the Arab himself was in Dacia on this occasion with the Praetorian guards (cohors praetoria), and army units were brought to Dacia from the Rhine area. Many of the inhabitants of Roman Dacia probably left the province because of this attack, although Romanian historians endeavor to maintain that it did not imply the end of Roman domination in Dacia.[387]

The Carpic culture ends in the last decade of the third century A.D. Records describe the wars with Rome from 295 to 297 and affirm that at this occasion, *Carporum natio translata omnis in nostrum solum* or *Carporum gens universa in Romania se tradidit.*[388] A large number but not all of this population had certainly settled by this time in the Roman Empire, south of the Danube. This is shown in records about fights with the Romans from 306 to 311 and 313 to 319. According to an inscription discovered in Mauritania and dated to 319 A.D., Emperor Constantin the Great was called "Carpicus Maximus." As late as in 381, the Carps, together with the Huns, were still attacking the empire. The Carpic culture was, in any case, replaced at the beginning of the fourth century by the Černjachov-Sîntana de Mureş culture. Carpic elements were discovered among the remains of this culture. Whether this indicates the existence of Carps or only the perpetuation of certain cultural characteristics is not known.

The earthenware of the Carps is thought to have originated from the Dacian La Tène but reveals many influences from other peoples. Wheel-made vessels are more frequent (about 60% in the settlements and up to 90% in the cemeteries). From this type of vessels, about 75% were grey and the rest red; in the later phases of the Carpic culture, the number of the grey forms increased.[389] Several circumstances indicate that the red pottery in these sites was produced by the Carps and not imported from the Roman Empire. The Dacian cup is frequently found in the settlements, where it was used as a rushlight; Roman rushlights are not found in these settlements. In the cemeteries, the Dacian cup was used as a censer. One typical decoration was a belt in alveolate relief,[390] typical of Dacian vessels; but the Carps used many other types of ornamentation.

The Roman influence upon Carpic earthenware was considerable. For example, with one exception, all amphorae show a more or less intense Roman influence. The autochthonous potters changed the pointed bottom and the narrow rim, characteristic features of the Roman amphora, and created a new, specifically Carpic type.[391] Many other types of vessels and their covers are similar to Roman earthenware in certain details.[392] The Sarmatian influence upon Carpic culture was significant. Coming from the east, the Sarmatians migrated to the areas west of the Prut River in the first decades of the first century A.D. and lived together with the Costoboci and the Carps, especially at the end of the second and the first half of the third centuries. From this population no settlements are known, only cemeteries. In 1973 37 Sarmatian cemeteries were known in Moldavia; they are mostly situated on the plains and are generally quite small, containing from 2 to 13 tombs, rarely more. From the Sarmatians the Carps borrowed several types of pearls, the characteristic mirrors, and other objects. At the beginning, finished products were borrowed, but later some Sarmatian objects were also produced by the Carps.[393] These include vessels with zoomorphic covers and protuberances. In their turn, the Sarmatians adopted the Carpic art of making earthenware on a wheel; certain vessels of a Daco-Carpic type appear frequently in the Sarmatian tombs even in the territory east of the Prut River (in the present-day Moldavian Socialist Republic). The Roman influence is seen in the earthenware, jewelry, and different objects, but especially fibulae. Among the imported products, the most frequent was the amphora. Both trade and the payment of subsidies by the Romans could have contributed to the influx of Roman earthenware to Moldavia. All imports came from Moesia Inferior (not from Dacia).

The number of isolated Roman coins found in the Carpic sites is not very high. Of a total of 55 coins, 35 were of silver, 18 of bronze, 1 of copper, and 1 unknown. Only 12 were from the third, and the others from the second century.[394] Of these 55 coins, 7 were found in tombs: 1 in an urn from the cemetery at Poieneşti, 1 silver and 4 bronze coins in the same cemetery; and the last, a silver coin, is from a cemetery at Dochia.[395] The largest single group (23) of a total of 74 hoards, ends with the reign of Emperor Commodus (180–192 A.D.); 29 hoards have been dispersed or are unpublished.

Material remains of Roman style up to the third century A.D. in Moldavia have been found at Barboşi (Vaslui County), a village about 17 kilometers from Galaţi, on the shore of the Siret River, a few kilometers north of the Danube. As previously mentioned, an important military camp existed there in the second and third centuries A.D. Only Roman material remains have been found in the ruins of the Roman fortification; but in the civil settlement west of it, "the Dacian material accounts for a significant proportion."[396] Besides Roman material, the main types of Dacian earthenware and some variants frequently used by the Carps and the Sarmatians were found there.[397] It is, however, often difficult to differentiate between the Dacian earthenware made on a wheel and that made by other groups; for one thing, the grey paste used in making it was used by several peoples. About 5–15% of the earthenware considered Dacian was made on the wheel. Some of the vessels show a Roman influence in the paste as well as in some forms; others are similar to Sarmatian vessels.[398] The inscriptions found at Barboşi contain Greek and Latin names, as well as names originating from Asia Minor. The majority of the graffiti is in Greek. A large number of amphorae of different kinds and origin (from the shores of the Aegean Sea), lamps, fibulae, Roman bronze coins, and other objects widely used in the Roman

Empire were found around the fortification at Barboşi. Besides Greek and Roman objects of religious cults, statues and reliefs of the Thracian and Danubian equestrian gods, as well as a number of Oriental gods, have also been found at Barboşi. The myth of the Danubian equestrian god is considered to have been of Dacian origin; it was, however, widespread, and a total of 220 representations are known today. Even more widespread was the Thracian equestrian god, of which about 2,000 were known in 1971 in Southeast and Central Europe. Traces of the Christian faith are quite uncertain and, at best, rare. Only four ancient Christian objects have been found from the time in question at Barboşi. There were no traces of cults from Asia Minor nor of any Germanic cults.

At several places in Moldavia, as also in other areas of Romania (and, of course, many areas of Europe in general), a certain continuous presence of human dwelling was shown from the third century A.D. during the rest of the first millenium. The stratigraphic analysis made at Dodeşti (Vaslui County), for example, indicates a succession of levels from the third to the tenth century; there is a hut dated to the sixth or seventh century, half of which is covered by a dwelling built in the eighth or ninth century; and at one meter distance from this, there is a third hut, dated to the tenth or eleventh century.[399] At Costişa-Manoaia, a settlement continues from the third to the first half of the sixth century. The level dated to the fifth century in this last mentioned site is superposed on that of the Sîntana de Mureş culture, from the end of the fourth century.[400] This is the case in several other places, for example, at Botoşana, where two levels were built upon a Sîntana de Mureş type of settlement.

With regard to dwelling places, the most common pit house is rectangular and 40 centimeters deep. A much less common form is of 80 to 110 centimeters deep and from 2.8 by 3.2 meters to 3.0 by 3.5 meters in size. Surface huts are rarely found, probably because they were of a seasonal character; made of woven twigs cemented together with clay, they were easily destroyed. The hearths are made of clay, are oval or circular, and are three to five centimeters thick, which is uncommon. Similar hearths of the same period have also been found in Slavic areas (Soviet Union and Poland). Stone ovens are frequently found in the dwelling places of the sixth to seventh centuries. They consist of an oval or circular hearth surrounded by a wall made of pebbles cemented together by earth. They are usually either one meter square with one side open or horse-shoe shaped with a size of 80 by 60 centimeters. Ovens of clay have been found in all settlements. They are cirular with a clay vault[401] and were probably used both for bread baking and firing pottery. Special kilns have not yet been found. In some of the ovens, clay cylinders similar to those of the ovens of the Ipoteşti-Cîndeşti and Dridu cultures have been found. Pits for storing grain and other products are cylindrical or sac-shaped; most of them were empty.

Tombs from the period between the mid-fifth and the mid-seventh centuries are very rare.[402] It is difficult to determine the age of those tombs that do not contain any objects. There are the following tombs from this period: 1. An inhumation tomb with the body lying from northwest to southeast. A fibula dates this tomb to the second half of the fifth century. 2. Two inhumation tombs, one in a south by north direction and containing two bronze bracelets dating to the fifth to seventh centuries, and the other from west by northwest to east by southeast. 3. An inhumation tomb containing a bronze clasp of Byzantine origin, from the sixth or seventh century and two or three others, with a Byzantine bronze clasp of the Sucidava type from the same period in one of them.[403] From these few finds it is not possible to determine much about funeral rites. In most of the tombs the bodies were placed in a direction different from that in Christian cemeteries (east to west).

Metal objects, such as different kinds of knives, have been found in almost all dwelling places. In many sites there were also iron axes of the sixth and seventh centuries, usual in the Danubian regions, as well as arrows, hooks, chain loops, clasps, and so forth. Two fragments of an iron sickle, an iron ploughshare, a bell, and a tinder box have also been discovered at these sites. Objects of bone include knife handles, chain loops, a double comb (from the sixth century) and a cut stone awl. There are also casting moulds. Fusaiols (a weight used in spinning, usually made of clay) are found in almost all settlements.

Most of the jewels and ornaments were imported from the Byzantine towns along the southern shore of the lower Danube: fibulae of Byzantine type, "attributed especially to the Romanic population,"[404] earrings, and a small, fragmentary ring with an incised eagle, a Byzantine motif; several clasps of the Sucidava and Siracuza types from the sixth to seventh centuries; and bronze bracelets. A clasp found at Botoşana is a late imitation of an Old Germanic clasp from the fifth century.

A few Byzantine coins from the sixth century have been discovered at nine places, but only two from the seventh century. Three hoards containing Byzantine coins from the first half of the fifth to the first half of the sixth century were found in southern Moldavia (two in Galaţi County and one in Bacău County), and contain 28, 26, and 30 coins, respectively.[405]

Earthenware made on a fast wheel is mostly grey and includes a vessel of Roman style that was also adopted by the Černjachov-Sîntana de Mureș culture. In Moldavia it was used between the mid-fifth and the mid-sixth centuries and is quite uncommon. The other type of earthenware made on a fast wheel, a kind of a can, is found even more rarely. Earthenware made on a slow wheel was made from two kinds of paste, one consisting of sand and gravel and the other also containing pounded fragments. These pieces are unusual. They are of a russet-brown color with grey spots and are mostly of low quality, with irregular surfaces. This type of vessel is from 15 to 20 centimeters high and is ornamented, beginning in the fifth to sixth centuries, with a simple line, and from the sixth to seventh centuries with horizontal or wave-like lines. In the sixth to seventh centuries, this type became more frequent. Hand-made pottery is found most frequently. The paste used for these pieces almost always contains pounded fragments. Most of these pieces are carelessly made, and the firing is incomplete and not uniform. Their color is predominantly russet-brown, sometimes with brownish-grey tones. The surface shows irregularities, and the vessels are often deformed. A small vessel of 15 to 25 centimeters in height is encountered often and is found at almost all the settlements. It is similar to certain Dacian vessels from the preceding period. A medium-sized vessel (height 20–25 centimeters) is rare before the eighth century. Medium-sized tureens (20 centimeters high) are found in the shape of a truncated cone, ornamented by cuts or small notches; they are unusual; and small ornamented cylindric mugs (8–10 centimeters high,) are very rare. Round pans or patens from 15 to 20 centimeters high, made to the greatest extent carelessly, are found from the mid-sixth century to the end of the tenth century. From the imported pottery only fragments have been found so far of Byzantine amphorae made of a fine paste, of yellow or reddish color, and ornamented by wide grooves or dense horizontal streaks. They are similar to those found in the settlements of the Ipotești-Cîndești culture, as well as in the Roman (Byzantine) towns along the lower Danube. One bronze pot from the Byzantine Empire was found in 1968 at Horgești-Bacău.

The Material Remains at Costișa-Botoșana

At several places in Moldavia, such as Costișa-Manoaia, Botoșana, Dodești, Bacău, and Davideni, a stratum is superposed on the level of the period after the Hunnish domination up to the mid-sixth century (the arrival of the Slavs). This stratum contains material remains of the Costișa-Botoșana group. From the second half of the fifth century onward, all forms of pottery became simpler. Moreover, those made on the fast wheel decreased in frequency and in the sixth century, were almost entirely replaced by pottery made on the slow wheel or by hand. In the sixth and seventh centuries, most of the pottery was made by hand.[406] From the remains of the material culture, such as the technique and shape of some hand-made vessels; the preservation (although modified in some way) of some older, Roman forms in the form of the vessels made on a wheel, even if the changes in the techniques are obviously retrogressions; the use of almost the same tools and some of the ornaments; and the preservation of the type of dwelling place, one can conclude that these elements indicate contacts with the late Roman style and illustrate at the same time the local roots (in this case Dacian) of the civilization of Moldavia in the fifth to sixth centuries.[407]

It has been maintained that the "multiple parallels" between the material culture of the fifth to seventh centuries in Moldavia and the contemporary remains from southeastern Transylvania (the Bratei-Mediaş culture) show that in that period, there was a relatively uniform cultural evolution of "Daco-Roman" character in a considerably large territory.[408] According to this view, the Costişa-Botoşana culture would be a variant of the Bratei-Mediaş culture. The differences between the two could be explained by the presence in both of them of Dacians, Romanized to different degrees. The unity of these civilizations is explained in the current Romanian historiography by the multiple and continuous influences of the Roman and Romano-Byzantine civilizations, which had had a much larger role in the East-Carpathian regions of Romania than was thought earlier.[409]

The Hypothesis of the "Daco-Roman"–Slav Symbiosis in the Fifth to Seventh Centuries in Moldavia

The earliest Slavic vestiges in the western Ukraine (from the fifth and sixth centuries) were found northeast of Moldavia. Most of the Slavs came to the territory of Romania from that area. Several groups of Slavs migrated to Moldavia from the north, along the Siret River; and another group came from the area east of the Prut River and continued toward the plains of Muntenia.

The first unquestionably Slavic vestiges in Moldavia were discovered in 1953 at Suceava-Şipot. During the first decade of the excavations, a series of remains were, according to the archaeologist Dan Gheorghe Teodor, erroneously attributed to the Slavs or other migratory people but belonged in reality to the "autochthonous population." The single periods were chronologically determined by comparison with Slavic material in adjacent territories, the stratigraphical situation of the individual discoveries, and by objects such as coins and ornaments: fibulae digitatae, brackets of the Martinovka type or from Byzantium, clasps, and Byzantine fibulae.

The early Slavs lived in shallow pit houses with a rectangular shape and slightly rounded corners. In some of them, cavities were found in and halfway between the corners; these were made for the poles supporting the roof. In one of the corners was situated an oval hearth, surrounded by pebbles or gritty stone, held together by yellow, pounded earth. The objects found in Slavic sites in Moldavia were also found in the areas east of the province (in Russia). They include pocket knives, tinder boxes of iron, different kinds of arrows, awls made of bone, grind stones, and simple hand mills. The most important ornaments are the characteristically Slavic fibulae digitatae, found also at Pastirsk (Russia).[410] A fragment of a bracket of the Martinovka type and the semicircular bronze fibulae (fibulae with handles) of the seventh century, which are scattered all over Southeastern Europe as far as the Peloponnesus, also belong to the early Slavic objects. Most of these objects were found, however, without any connection to a known archaeological site. This is indicative of the scope of Slavic trade relations.[411]

The early Slavic earthenware is hand-made from a primitive paste containing pounded fragments. It was fired ununiformly and probably in the ovens found in the dwelling places or at any rate in open ovens. The surface of the vessels is therefore usually reddish-brown. It is carelessly made; the vessels are of an irregular shape and asymmetrical. During the seventh century, there were some changes in the pottery, which has been attributed to the influence on the Slavs of the "autochthonous population."[412] The Korčak, Penkovka, and Koločin types of Slavic earthenware from the sixth to seventh centuries are found in Moldavia and the western Ukraine and are all often found in the same settlement. The Koločin group reveals Baltic influences. Different types of vessels also have their counterparts in the Slavic areas to the east, in the Soviet Union; one example is a vessel with a long body and very short rim, which is characteristic of the archaic Slavic Korčak-Zhitomir group of the western Ukraine. Similar vessels also exist in some settlements of the Ipoteşti-Cîndeşti-Ciurelu culture (at Bucharest and at Sărata-Monteoru), on the Danube plains, and in a few places in southeastern Transylvania (Poian and Cernatul). It should be noted that the Slavs of the Przeworsk culture and the West-Ukrainian groups migrated toward the southwest in approximately the same period. Elements of the Przeworsk culture have been discovered not only in Moldavia but also on the plains along the lower Danube (at Strălucești and at Militari), as well as on the Balkan Peninsula, south of the Danube.

To the Penkovka Slavic group[413] belong a vessel of an approximately bitronconic shape (truncated at both ends), also found in Muntenia but not in Transylvania, and another vessel of similar shape, with a tapering rim. A very common type in Moldavia, it is also found at Ciurelu and Dulceanca in Muntenia. A very rare vessel with a large opening and straight rim belongs (according to its shape) to the Koločin type of Slavic pottery. At Suceava-Șipot, Botoșani and Cucorăni, decoration typical of the Koločin group were also found on fragments of earthenware: small incised circles, broken lines in the shape of "worms," simple belts in relief beneath the rim.

The Romanian archaeologist Dan Gheorghe Teodor believes that the Suceava-Șipot culture (or "aspect") reveals Slavic material remains from the Ukraine, reminders of the Przeworsk culture but showing the "autochthonous Romanic element in the majority."[414] This is based on the claim that "the autochthonous vessels of Roman style were in the majority."[415]

In Teodor's opinion, during the seventh century the Slavic material culture underwent important changes through contacts with "the superior culture of the autochthons." The assimilation of the Slavs was, according to this view, very rapid after 602 A.D., when the Byzantine Empire was forced to retreat from the Danubian frontiers.'[416] Teodor concludes that the tools used by the Slavs were inferior to those of the "autochthons." The Old Slav population that migrated to Moldavia had only "poorly developed, extensive and periodic agriculture."[417]

Conclusions

On the basis of some commonly known historical facts, the following observations can be made in reference to the assumed Romanization of the transcarpathian territories in Romania. The extent of Roman civilization in these territories is difficult to define, and the spread of the Latin language is only a probability. Because of the presence of Carps, Sarmatians, Goths, and other migratory peoples, it is not possible to reach definitive conclusions regarding ethnicity and language on the basis of archaeological findings. To secure a more precise picture of the assumed Romanization of the transcarpathian territories, especially of Moldavia, it is necessary to investigate more closely historical records, particularly those regarding ethnic and archaeological considerations pertinent to this territory. However, few historical records are available.

To designate a Romanic population in Moldavia in the sixth century A.D. as "the autochthonous Romanic elements"[418] would make sense only in relation to the Slavs. It is, moreover, most unappropriate to refer to Romans in an area north of the Danube, which never was a Roman province, as "autochthons." Generalized terms such as "local," "indigenous," or "autochthonous" are used loosely and do not give a clear picture as to what group is actually autochthonous or indigenous. As is known, after the great uprising of the Dacians the Roman occupied areas of southern Moldavia and Muntenia were abandoned. The designation "autochthon" or "local" which means "original," "indigenous" inhabitants explains little in the "Daco-Roman" context and is imprecise and dispensable. Even more important is the fact that this vague term, as it is used currently, makes it more difficult to gain a clear picture of the different peoples that lived in the territory of contemporary Romania during the first centuries A.D. But who is an autochthon or indigen? Even if one uses the term "Dacian" or "Daco-Roman," it is not certain that this has anything to do with Romanians. If one accepts the free Dacians and the Carps to be "autochthons," the major difference between them and any Latin-speaking population—the fact that they spoke different languages—is blurred. The fact that these non-Latin groups migrated to Dacia in the very period when a Latin-speaking group there is assumed to have become independent from Roman domination cannot have contributed to a "revitalization of the Daco-Roman synthesis." The Romanian language, which in its pre-Slavic elements is (almost) entirely Latin, presupposes, if it developed from Latin spoken in Dacia Traiana, that the large majority of the population there spoke Latin as a mother tongue at the end of the third century A.D. Without a majority, Romanian would contain a significant amount of non-Latin elements, a mixed language would have developed, or there would have been no Romance language at all. If Latin-speaking people did exist there, the immigration of free, non-Romanized Dacians and Carps would have decreased their proportion of the population. Talk of a revitalization of the "Daco-Romans" only obscures this fact.

The confusion over the basic terms of "Daco-Roman" continuity is increased even more by the ambiguous use of "Daco-Roman." This term was said to apply to Romanized as well as non-Romanized Dacians. It is a very serious deficiency that this term is used in entirely different senses: It may designate Dacians who speak their own language and also colonists living in Roman Dacia who were not Dacians and not even necessarily Romans. The Romanian archaeologist D. Protase stated that the term "Daco-Roman", without a qualification, is equivocal, since it is used by Romanian historians today to mean several different things. If one says "a Daco-Roman settlement" and does not know the ethnicity of the population living there, one must think of four or five possibilities: a settlement of local Dacians in the period and area of Roman Dacia; a settlement of Roman colonists in Dacia; a settlement in which a mixed population of local Dacians and Roman colonists lived; a settlement inhabited by Romanized Dacians from the post-Aurelian era; or a settlement of Romanized Dacians and Roman colonists from the same period.[419]

With respect to the alleged Romanization in Moldavia, it is relevant to note that in the second and third centuries A.D., a Roman military camp existed at Barboşi, at the southern border of present-day Moldavia. Adjacent to this camp, in the civilian settlement, remains of Dacian (Carpic) and Sarmatian earthenware were also found; and the presence there of these two ethnic groups is thus possible. Otherwise, there are no typically Roman complexes in the territory of Moldavia.[420] Thus, the Romanization of Moldavia is frequently concocted from hypotheses. There is no proof that Latin was spoken in either Muntenia or Moldavia. Many Romanian historians admit that is difficult to determine the extent of Roman civilization in the above-mentioned territories and that the spread of the Latin language can only be presumed. In his valuable monograph about the Carps, Gheorghe Bichir stated clearly that the Carps were not Romanized in the third century.[421] Even Sanie admits that in Moldavia, remnants of Roman material culture were found, but in most of that territory, the spread of the Latin language is not certain (although, according to Sanie, probable).[422]

The Sarmatians and Carps living in Moldavia in the second and third centuries A.D. were enemies of the Romans most of the time. In spite of the presence of Roman goods, they were not Romanized, just as the rest of the European populations (the barbarians) were not Romanized but still to a great extent used objects imported from the empire, which they also tried to imitate. In addition to gold or silver coins or other precious objects, objects of everyday use were imported into territories to the north of the Danube. Imitations (imitatio imperii) of Roman costumes are also to be found.[423] That does not mean that the users of these objects were either Romans or Romanized people. All over Europe, the areas near the Roman border are rich in such remains. Particular caution is therefore necessary when drawing conclusions about the ethnic significance of such cultural effects. As is known, in the fourth century the territory of Moldavia (like most of Muntenia and part of Transylvania) was occupied by the Černjachov-Sîntana de Mureş culture, which ethnically was mainly, as previously mentioned, Old Germanic, influenced by Roman culture, as well as by Dacians, Carps, and Sarmatians. The continued existence of certain

Roman and Dacian characteristics in the material culture of the area is natural and does not presuppose the existence of Romans or Dacians (Carps).

Remains from the fifth to seventh centuries in Moldavia are scarce, often primitive, and monotonous, showing few distinguishing characteristics. With regard to earthenware, there are vessels resembling Dacian forms and certain Roman elements, although "in some way modified."[424] During the fifth and sixth centuries, the techniques become more primitive, with the share of wheel-made vessels decreasing; and in the seventh century, all earthenware was made by hand. Imported earthenware and other products from the Byzantine Empire indicate trade with the inhabitants of Moldavia. Obviously, then, the material culture shows Byzantine elements, but this does not presuppose any Romanizing effect upon the inhabitants or the furthering the Latin language.

In the settlements where both Slavs and "autochthons" allegedly lived, it is not possible to differentiate between the objects belonging to the two groups.[425] The number of graves attributed to the allegedly "autochthonous" population is, at least so far, very low. Most of them do not show Christian funeral rites. The important domain of funeral rites can therefore not be used in investigating the ethnic question in Moldavia during this period.

What contemporary Romanian scholars claim to be evidence of a Roman population is in reality the effect of cultural interplay among neighboring peoples. Although the primitive Dacian earthenware is not very characteristic, which means that its similarities to other primitive earthenware do not necessarily indicate a direct relationship, such relationship certainly existed in many cases. The Sarmatians used and imitated the Dacian earthenware extensively, and Dacian influence can also be seen in the Černjachov-Sîntana de Mureş culture. Roman vessels were frequently imitated by all these peoples (Dacians, Carps, Sarmatians, Goths). Archaeological finds such as fibulae, clasps, and Christian objects of the Byzantine Empire do not offer evidence of a Romanic population, since such findings are also characteristic of the Gepidae. The simple hearth found in the dwelling places from the fifth to seventh centuries and attributed to the "autochthons" is also known at Slavic sites in Russia and Poland.[426] When talking about a unitary evolution of the material culture over a large territory (that of modern Romania) during the first millenium A.D., Romanian scholars use special aspects of culture—the Roman influences—as their point of departure. Considering this the principal characteristic and given its presence throughout the territory of Romania, they spontaneously see a unitary picture. They overlook, however, the fact that a similar or in many cases even stronger Roman influence can be also seen beyond the frontiers of present-day Romania, in many European territories in which there can be no question of a Romanic population.

With respect to the alleged "Daco-Roman" (Romanian) - Slav symbiosis in the fifth to seventh century in Moldavia,[427] it should be noted that, according to the linguistic development, the Slavic influence upon Romanian is of a much later date. If, before the twelfth century, a Romanic population had lived in Moldavia together with the Slavs in the same settlement for 3 centuries, this would have resulted in the transfer of some elements from the Slavic dialect spoken by these Slavs to the Romanian spoken in Moldavia. This is not the case. The Moldavian sub-dialect of Northern Romanian contains all the Slavic elements of Bulgarian origin existing also in the other sub-dialects. It also contains Ukrainian elements; but these do not show ancient characteristics. They are all, without exception, from the period after the twelfth century when the Ukrainian loan words started to penetrate into the Romanian language in the northeastern part of the country.[428] Romanian archaeologists also claim now that no purely Slavic settlements or typical Slavic cemeteries have been discovered so far in Romania; everywhere, remains of the "autochthons" are found. The "autochthonous population" is also said to have been in the majority in Moldavia all the time and to have assimilated the Slavs as early as the ninth century, about three centuries after their first migration to the territory of Moldavia.[429]

If all this were historically sound—the Slavs coming to the villages of a sedentary Romanic population, which exists in every settlement of the country and always remains in the majority there, and the Slavs, living on a lower cultural level and assimilating to the Romanic population after three centuries—then ideal circumstances would have existed for the preservation of Romanic place names. Moreover, the situation would have been very unfavorable for the creation of Slavic place and river names.

Before turning to the question of place names in Moldavia, it should be pointed out that the situation described above did exist for some period of time on the Balkan Peninsula. In several areas there, the Slavs found a Roman population living on a higher cultural level than the newcomers and at the beginning also in the majority. As a consequence of this historical situation, the Slavs migrating to the Balkans borrowed a large number of place names from Latin. This is true not only about names of important towns, such as Naissus > Niš, Scupi > Skopje, Ulpiana > Lipljan, or river names, such as Almus > Lom, Margus > Morava, Timacus > Timok, but also about the names of insignificant villages, islands, mountains, and so forth. These include, the Slovenian Cedad and the Serbian Cavtat (from Latin *civitatem*); Serbian Poljud (from Latin *paludem*); Kimp (from Latin *campus*); Kosljun (from Latin *castellione*); Silba, the name of an isle (from Latin *silva*); Sutomore (from *Sancta Maria*); and Sutlovrec (from *Sanctus Laurentius*);[430] or Vrčin (from Latin *Orcinum*, a church of the goddess Orcea existed there); Vrsar (from Latin *Ursaria*; *cf.*, Italian Orsera); Grocka (from Latin *Gratiana*); Boleč (from Latin *Bolentium*);[431] and many others, which have survived to the present.[432]

In Moldavia, the opposite true, as is the case in other areas of present-day Romania. Not a single Latin place name has survived, while the entire territory abounds with place and river names of Slavic origin, including the very name of the province: *Moldova*, archaic Moldua, Mulduva; *mold* (*molid*, "spruce fir" *cf.*, Bulgarian *molika*)[433] + the Slavic suffix *-ov*, *-ova*.

According to an earlier concept, the assimilation of the Slavs occurred in Moldavia during the eleventh to twelfth centuries, when "new ancient Romanian elements" were added to the population.[434] As Romanian history was rewritten in the 1960s and nationalist-patriotic elements came to the forefront of historical writing, this concept was also altered. The new interpretation affirmed that the ethnic assimilation had reached its final stage by the eighth century.[435] Similar statements are made about other Romanian territories.[436]

The Romanian language shows a different picture, however. On the basis of a series of characteristics of the sound pattern of the majority of the South Slavic elements, Romanian linguists agree that the most intensive South Slavic influence was exerted upon Northern Romanian from the tenth to the twelfth and early thirteenth centuries. According to this view, the Slavic influence began in the ninth or tenth century; it was during this time that the elements (lexical, phonetical, syntactical, and morphological) that are most widespread entered the Romanian language, some of them appearing even in the south-Danubian dialects.[437] Thus, the period of the most intense South Slavic influence on the Northern Romanian language, established by linguistic criteria, began almost two centuries after the date recently given by archaeologists and historians as the end of the Slavic influence upon the Romanian population. Consequently, the people to which the Slavs were assimilated in the eighth and ninth centuries, if they existed at all, could not have been the ancestors of the Romanians. In other words, if the Slavs north of the Danube had been assimilated by the ninth century and had disappeared, those Slavs who exerted the very intense South Slavic influence upon Romanian must have been living, together with the Romanians, in a territory different from that north of the Danube.

With regard to the problems connected with Romanization in Muntenia, one must note that not much is known of any activities except military of the Roman, and later, the Byzantine Empire in this area. Roman fortifications were built there and garrisons stationed from 105 to 117 A.D.; the southern part was occupied in the fourth century (during the reign of Constantine the Great); bridgeheads were created and some army units stationed north of the Danube in the sixth century. These were short episodes in the history of Muntenia. Military activity in an inimical area is otherwise not likely to exert cultural effects.

The *Novella of Justinian* from the sixth century A.D., to strengthen the frontier of the Byzantine Empire, attest to Emperor Justinian's interest in the plains north of the Lower Danube. It is known that Justinian tried to restore the Roman Empire in the sixth century but his efforts were only perfunctory.[438] Any further attempt was finally frustrated in the seventh century by the advance of the Moslems into the Mediterranean area. Immediately after the death of the Byzantine ruler Maurikios (602), the Romans lost all contacts with the middle Danube. Rome's control over the abandoned province of Dacia virtually ceased after the withdrawal of Aurelian's legions. For this reason another Dacia was established in this period south of the Danube. From the fourth century until the beginning of the fifth century there are no reports of crossing the Danube. During the fourth through the sixth centuries, especially after the dismemberment of the Hunnic Empire, a certain "barbarization" of the lower Danube occurred (through Ostrogoths, Visigoths, Sarmatians, and Bastarns), and the Romanized population declined. Finally, it must be noted that the significance of Justinian's work, already begun during the reign of Anastasius, in fortifying the Danubian *limes* is overestimated.

The archaeological evidence for a Romanic population in Muntenia from the fourth century A.D. onward is based on elements of Roman provincial traditions, mainly in the manufacture of earthenware and partly in the dwelling places, as well as the presence of imported products from the empire.

Theories About the Material Culture in the First Millenium in the Territory of Romania

It is noteworthy that during the last decade more than 20 cultures and their variants have been suggested as inhabitants of the territory of present-day Romania in the first millenium A.D.[439] The practice of regarding peoples who left material remains of Roman style and used Roman objects and coins as a Romanized population has quite logically led to the recent revised views of the cultures in question. A detailed analysis of these cultures shows, however, that the officially-formulated theories are untenable. The way of classifying historical times into periods, which reflects the current trends of Romanian historiography, stubbornly disregards all evidence that does not support Romanian historical claims based on the uninterrupted presence of the Romanian people on the territory claimed to be Romanian at the end of World War I.

In 1979 it was suggested that concepts about the material cultures of the period from the second to the tenth centuries be revised. According to this view, from the second through the fourth centuries, one single culture developed on the territory of Romania, the "Daco-Roman" culture, which was comprised of numerous cultural groups. At the turn of the fourth century, a new culture called the Romanic culture emerged, developing further in the fifth through the seventh centuries.[440] The Romanic culture was influenced by foreign peoples that migrated to or lived temporarily in the territory of Romania during the fifth to seventh centuries A.D.[441] Gheorghe Diaconu is of the opinion that for the third period (from the eighth to the tenth or eleventh centuries) "the specialists use inappropriate terms: As is known, the culture of the ancient Romanian population from the eighth to the tenth centuries is designated by the terms Dridu, Bucov, Blandiana, Carpatho-Danubian, Carpatho-Balkanic, Hlincea, Dodeşti, and so forth."[442] Considering the fact that more than 20 archaeological cultures appear for the period from the second to the tenth centuries and that this number is increasing each year, Diaconu proposed abandoning these terms and designating the period from the eighth to the tenth centuries as ancient Romanian culture (*cultura veche românească*).[443]

An analysis of the proposed changes shows that the new concept is not based on any significantly new evidence but rather on deductions made about objects of a Roman style, as is the case in many writings referring to the period in question. It must be pointed out that the material culture in the territory of contemporary Romania in the centuries after the abandonment of Dacia Traiana by the Romans is not peculiar to a Roman population. This also applies to the Ipoteşti-Cîndeşti-Ciurelu culture, the Dridu culture, and others, which recently have been assumed to contain elements of a Romanic population. These cultures did not even cover a uniform territory but extended to different areas of Romania from the outside, which is not in accordance with the assumption that they represented a single population: the ancestors of the Romanians.

On the basis of some commonly known facts, in reference to the Dridu and the Ipoteşti-Cîndeşti culture, the following observations can be made. The so-called Dridu culture has been placed chronologically between the eighth and the eleventh centuries. It was originally a Slavo-Bulgarian, that is a Balkan-Danubian, culture. According to the compendium *Istoria României*,[444] the Dridu culture was not indigenous to the territory of Romania, since its material remains are "more numerous and better represented on the territory of Bulgaria, where this culture was also formed." The material remains of this culture were found also outside Bulgaria in the regions of the Prut and Dniester rivers in the Soviet Union. The concept of certain Romanian scholars that the Dridu culture is a Romanian culture or, rather, a provincial Byzantine-Romanian culture,[445] has been contradicted even by certain Romanian archaeologists. In Petru Diaconu's view, for instance, the Dridu culture cannot provide well-grounded arguments for supporting theories on Romanian ethnogenesis, since finds of the Dridu type, as heretofore assumed, did not substantiate assertions concerning Romanian ethnicity.[446] Constantin Daicoviciu, one of the most outstanding representatives of Romanian historiography after World War II, considered that the Dridu, or Balkan-Danubian, culture originated from Bulgaria and was created by a Slavic population.[447] This concept was refuted after Daicoviciu's death in 1973, and the official theory now is that the Dridu culture was the culture of the Romanians.

The so-called Ipoteşti-Cîndeşti-Ciurelu culture, like the Bratei culture, is a pure fabrication by contemporary Romanian archaeologists. This culture is chronologically placed in the sixth and seventh centuries; and the area of its dissemination is given as Muntenia, Moldavia, and southern Transylvania. As in the case of all new cultures, the proponents of the Ipoteşti-Cîndeşti-Ciurelu culture attempt to bridge a time gap between the late Germanic population and the arrival of the Slavs but are unable to produce any evidence, archaeological or otherwise, for the continuation of a romanized population in Dacia Traiana.

THE CARPATHIAN BASIN IN THE NINTH TO ELEVENTH CENTURIES

The Hungarian Conquest

The events of the ninth and tenth centuries had a decisive influence on the historic and ethnic configuration of the Carpatho-Danubian area that has persisted to some degree to our own time. In the ninth century the empire of the Avars collapsed, and the Frankish Empire established itself. Byzantium and Rome continued to exert significant influence in this area, while Greater Moravia and the empire of the Danubian Bulgars were important political factors. Finally, the Hungarian conquest (*Landnahme*) occurred in 895. In that age three powers exercised direct influence in the Carpathian Basin: To wit, Pannonia, as far as the Danube frontier, was under the suzerainty of the Frankish Empire; to the north Greater Moravia was dominant; and most of the eastern part of the Basin was under Bulgarian rule.

After the collapse of the empire of the Avars the numerical majority of the population of the Carpathian Basin was of Slavic origin, that is, Moravians, Sloveno-Karantas, and Bulgarian Slavs. Several settlement areas developed in accordance with the dates of the appearance and settlement of the Slavic peoples. On the basis of surviving place names, linguistic remnants, and known historic sources, it is possible to determine that "Danubian-Slovenes" lived to the west of the Danube and Bulgaro-Slavs to the east of the river, including in Transylvania. Toward the middle of the ninth century mention is made of remnants of the Gepidae who were later assimilated by the Slavs. Descendants of Romans and Huns driven from this area by Gepidae and Lombards were not to be found, since they left the Carpathian Basin during the initial phase of the nomadic peoples' migration.

As previously mentioned, the Hungarian conquest of 895 was one of the factors that had a decisive influence on the history of the Carpathian Basin. In the tenth century the Carolingian Empire (751–987) collapsed, and German influence was stopped through the appearance of the Hungarians. A further consequence was the separation of the Northern and Southern Slavs. Under the leadership of their ruler Árpád, the Magyars moved westward and northwestward from their last home (*Etelköz*), west of the Dnieper, and occupied the territory east of the Danube. A few of the tribes crossed the Carpathian passes and occupied Transylvania and the upper Tisza region. Historians have until now failed to agree on the chronology of the territorial acquisition of Transylvania by the conquering Hungarians. According to the majority (Hungarians and others), the Hungarians began to populate Transylvania from the west in several stages, starting from the ninth century; and by the tenth or eleventh century at the latest, the Hungarian settlements had reached the Eastern and Southern Carpathians. These data have been established by historical records as well as by the study of the geographical names of the area. It is, however, most probable that during the first phase of the conquest, at the turn of the ninth to the tenth century, the Magyars first penetrated Transylvania through the East Carpathian passes. This is indicated by archaeological remnants and place names, as well as by the oldest Magyar oral traditions and the earliest written source of the eleventh century chronicle, Gesta Ungarorum. Following the Hungarian conquest there were changes in place names, as the majority of the place names of the ninth century, mostly of Slavic origin, disappeared.

Transylvanian conditions in the ninth and tenth century are mentioned in frequently contradictory medieval chronicles and in scarce records. According to evidence derived from surviving place names, ethnic groups of Bulgaro-Slavs and Bulgar-Turks, which were assimilated by the Hungarians by the twelfth century, lived in Transylvania. Before the Hungarian conquest, the territory to the north of the Mureş River was inhabited by an eastern Slavic population, while south of the Mureş line, the region of salt- and goldmines was settled by Bulgars. The specific areas inhabited by Slavic peoples can be determined through excavations of Slavic cemeteries of the ninth, tenth, and eleventh centuries.

Numerous Pecheneg (Patzinaks, Latin Bissenus) formations and fewer groups of Uzes appeared in the Danubian-Carpathian area about the ninth century. The Pechenegs, a nomadic Turkic people, appeared originally in the Inner Asian steppes between 750 and 850 and occupied the steppe areas of southern Russia; later, under Tatar pressure, they fled westward. They were part of the western Turkic empire and lived on both sides of the Dnieper. In the ninth century they occupied Moldavia and Wallachia as far as the lower Danube, and in 1043 they crossed the Danube. Their movement toward Hungary followed in the tenth and eleventh centuries, following the collapse of their empire. They undertook a raid against Hungary in 1068, but their forces were largely destroyed in the vicinity of Sajósárvár (Şirioara). Afterward, the Pechenegs joined the Hungarians. In the twelfth and thirteenth centuries they lived in Transylvania and were used by the Hungarians as border guards; however, except for localities bearing their names, there are no traces of their existence.

The Uzes, also a Turkic nomadic people from the south Russian steppes, shared a common origin with the Pechenegs. Like the Pechenegs before them, they were chased by the Cumans from the south Russian steppes; and in 1064 they invaded the Balkan Peninsula by way of Bulgaria, Thrace, Macedonia, and Greece. Decimated by war and disease some of them moved to the north of the Danube as far as Transylvania, while others moved into Byzantium. A few places in southeastern Transylvania, in areas inhabited by Székelys, still bear their name.

The Cumans became separated from the Mongol-related community of peoples and established their independence between the fifth and seventh centuries A.D. By 1050 they inhabited a territory in Eastern Europe to the east of the Carpathian Mountains. Around 1080 they reached the lower Danube and the Carpathians; and later they occupied Moldavia and present-day Muntenia, which, until the end of the twelfth century, was known as Cumania. They settled in the thirteenth century to some extent in Hungary and were assimilated by the Hungarians. The Cumans played an important role in the medieval history of the Balkan Peninsula.

A generally reliable source for the history of Eastern Europe in the ninth and tenth centuries is to be found in the *De administrando imperio*, the work of the Byzantine Emperor Constantine VII Porphyrogenitus (905–959).[448] Like the Byzantine chroniclers, Constantine often confused or misidentified the names of contemporary peoples. For instance, he identified as "Turks" all the peoples who inhabited the Carpathian Basin during the ninth and tenth centuries.

Aside from the Byzantine sources, there are Muslim historical narratives, the reliability of which, however, appears to be questionable. The so-called Bavarian Geography giving a description of the lands north of the Danube, which depicts the situation in Eastern and Central Europe around the middle of the ninth century, mentioned several peoples such as the Moravians, Khazars, Ruses, Onogurs, Ungari, and Danubian Bulgars; but no mention was made of a Romanic population.

The Bulgars

The Bulgars emerged as a group of nomadic tribes composed of Ogurs (or Onogurs) and to some extent also of Huns and other Turkic peoples who lived in the second half of the fifth century (about 463 A.D.) in the Hunnic federation in the southern Russian Pontic Steppes.[449] The first written mention of the Proto-Bulgars (called Bulgari by an anonymous chronicler) is recorded in the first half of the fourth century when they were overrun by the Huns. Also known as Kutrigurs or Turanian Bulgars, they were part of the western Turkic-Altaic-speaking peoples. The name "Bulgar" is interpreted as "semi-nomadic mixed people." They were under Avar rule for a while.

Groups of Onogurs, also called Bulgarians, moved with the Avars into the Carpathian Basin and formed a considerable part of the Avar army.[450] The founder of their empire, Khan Kuvrat (Kovrat, Kobrat) succeeded in freeing himself from Avar rule sometime between 630 and 635 and established the Onoguric Kingdom—the "Old Great

Bulgaria"—which was a major military power stretching from the Caucasus (Kuban River) to the west as far as the Don. The Byzantine Empire supported Kuvrat's Onoguric Kingdom politically and economically. Around 750 several Onogur-Bulgarian ethnic groups migrated to the middle Volga; these were the Volga Bulgars.

Great Bulgaria collapsed after Kuvrat's death (642) under pressure from the westward-moving western Turkic tribe, the Khazars. Some of the Bulgarian tribes submitted to the Khazars. Others moved westward under the leadership of Kuvrat's son Asparuch (Isperich, Isperikh); and sometime between 660 and 670 they reached the mouth of the Danube, an area encompassing the southern part of Bessarabia, part of the Wallachian Plain, all of Dobrudja, and the province of Lower Moesia (679). Kuvrat's fourth son, Kuber, moved with his people and entourage into the Avar Empire in Pannonia and accepted Avar rule. The arrival of the Bulgars in Pannonia (Pannonian Bulgars) is mentioned in historical sources.

A considerable group of Bulgars moved to the Danube, and in 679 the Proto-Bulgarian conquest took place. Asparuch was the founder of modern Bulgaria (680–681) south of the Danube, which also included the Roman province of Moesia Inferior. (These were the Danubian Bulgars). In this Bulgarian state the name Bulgars was used for various ethnic groups such as Bulgars, Slavs, Vlachs, and others. In alliance with the different Slavic tribes, the Danubian Bulgars founded two successive kingdoms in the Balkan Peninsula, from 681 to 1018 and from 1186 to 1396, respectively. Their conversion to Christianity occurred in 865.

Together with Byzantium, the Bulgars were the most powerful nation between the Danube and Haemus (Balkan) Mountains after 679. They had called themselves Bulgars only from the time of Simeon (888–927), even though they were referred to as Bulgars as early as 482 in Latin, Greek, and Armenian sources.

After the destruction of the Avar Empire (796) by Charlemagne (771–814) and his son Pepin, the Bulgars, under the leadership of their Khan Krum (803–814), moved into the valley of the Tisza. During the battles that took place between 827 and 831 Khan Omurtag (814–831) annexed the eastern part of modern Hungary, the ancient Dacia (modern Transylvania), which adjoined the Frankish Empire (on the Tisza River). We are dealing here with the so-called Pannonian Bulgars whose territory, at the time of the Hungarian conquest of this area, reached as far as the Carpathian Mountains. Their resistance against the conquering Hungarians in Transylvania and on the Mureş (Maros) River was short lived.

The presence of the Bulgarians in Transylvania in the ninth century can be ascertained not only through written records[451] but also through archaeological remnants and from surviving place names. The jewelry of the ninth and tenth centuries in Ciumbrud, for example, reveals a close relationship to objects found in Bulgaria. It is known that the salt mines in the Mureş valley were held by the Bulgars and that on the middle course of that river, in Cîrna-Blandiana B (Maroskarna, Alba County) and in Ciumbrud, Bulgarian graves of the ninth century were found, which contained earthenware and jewelry of a kind that had counterparts only in Bulgaria south of the Danube. The above-mentioned cemeteries reveal a Bulgaro-Turkic rather than a Bulgaro-Slav connection.[452] It may be assumed that the carriers of the culture of the cemetery of Cîrna-Blandiana B are the people who moved from the south to the north of the Danube. According to archaeological evidence, the Bulgarian Empire settled peoples from the south to the lower Danube, in the second half of the ninth century, in the territory adjoining the middle part of the Mureş River. The sources provide no data on the ethnic composition of this population; it is known, however, that the population of the Bulgarian Empire at that time consisted of several different Slavic tribes. The locality of Zeligrad (Sóvár) in Transylvania, in the vicinity of Blandiana and Zlatna (Zalatna), the Bulgarian Zlatica (the Gold Town) also attests to one-time Bulgarian rule.

In 809 Krum conquered Serdica (modern Sofia), which up to that time had belonged to the Byzantine Empire. The inhabitants of towns and villages were carried away into Bulgarian territories on the other side of the Danube, which were regarded as the borderlands of the Bulgarian Empire. During the military campaign, which lasted until the beginning of the tenth century, Krum expanded his rule from northern Thrace to the Carpathian Mountains and from the lower Sava to the Dniester, including the territories east of the Tisza River.

The Byzantine Empire, in time, exerted increasingly greater influence over the Bulgarian territories with the result that the Bulgarians fought their oppressors, (in 1040 and 1041 and 1072 and 1073), for instance. The Byzantinization of Bulgaria and Macedonia continued in the eleventh and twelfth centuries, so that part of Macedonia fell under Byzantine suzerainty. Concurrently, attacks against the Bulgars were launched by the Magyars, who had settled in the Carpathian Basin.

From the ninth to the eleventh century the Proto-Bulgarians (Turkic Bulgarians) were absorbed into the larger Slavic population and took over the language and culture of the Slavs. In 1018 the Bulgarian landholdings were entirely conquered by the Byzantines. Following the collapse of Bulgaria, the Danube again became the northern border of the Byzantine Empire after its earlier abandonment under pressure of the Pechenegs and Uzes.

Following an uprising in 1186, in which Cumans and Vlachs also participated, the Bulgarians, led by the brothers Asén and Peter of Cumanian origin, regained their independence. The Second Bulgarian Empire (1186–1396) was established, comprising initially the territory between the Haemus (Balkan) Mountains and the Danube. During the fourteenth century, as the Bulgarian state became divided into 3 parts, it fell under Turkish rule (1393–1396). As a result of the Russo-Turkish war of 1877 and 1878, Bulgaria again regained its independence.[453]

The Theory of the Dual Hungarian Conquest
The Onogur Bulgars

As mentioned previously, the Hungarian conquest of 895 A.D. marks a historic turning point in the Carpathian Basin.[454] No other interpretation is possible. Only details discovered by subsequent research are subject to discussion. It is also known that the conquerors knew the Carpathian Basin before the conquest, since about 862. It is also known, as previously mentioned, that after the death of the founder of the Onoguric kingdoms, Khan Kuvrat (642), the Turkic-Bulgarian community was subdivided among his five sons in the southern Russian steppes and that his fourth son Kuber moved into Pannonia in 670 A.D. Except for archaeological data and information about Kuber there are no historical records. It is certain, however, that around 670, following the establishment of the empire of the Khazars, splinter groups of Onogur Bulgars made their appearance in the Carpathian Basin. Archaeological findings can be traced as far as eastern Asia as well as to the middle Volga and Kama rivers. There also, on the basis of linguistic, anthropo-geographic data, must be found the original homeland of the Magyars (that is, Hungarians).[455]

Hungarian archaeologists have assumed that a Hungarian conquest could have taken place as early as 670 A.D.[456] According to the proponents of this theory of dual conquest there were early Hungarians who came to the Carpathian Basin, or rather into the lands comprising the later Hungarian Empire in 670 and spoke Hungarian even then. The history of Kuvrat's son, Kuber, who in those years settled with his people, the Onogurs, in Pannonia may readily be related to this scenario.[457] It is known that before the conquest the Magyars lived in the Bulgar federation within the Khazar Empire.

Archaeological evidence would indicate that we are dealing with two peoples different in origin who, however, coexisted side by side:

one, wearers of belts cast in bronze bearing Byzantine tendril ornamentations (during the Avar period, after 568) and the others, with belts bearing griffin ornaments (during the Avar period, after 670). The latter moved in with the peoples already present of the Carpathian Basin.

It may be assumed that Ugric-Hungarian groups came into the Carpathian Basin with the first Avar waves around 568 or, perhaps, even as early as the fifth century with the Proto-Bulgars. The proponents of the theory of dual conquest, however, claim that the peoples who arrived in 670 were undoubtedly Ugric-Hungarians whose material civilization continued to exist also in the ninth and tenth centuries.

Other archaeologists, however, suggest that the proponents of the dual conquest theory ignore the methodological fundamental laws of archaeology. In their view the culture of griffin and tendril ornamentation could only have existed in the eighth to the beginning of the ninth centuries and not in the seventh century. Therefore, neither the carriers of that civilization nor their material civilization could have survived into the ninth to tenth centuries. Furthermore, the gap between the late-Avar culture and that of the conquering Hungarians is too great: In the ninth century the gap between the character of the late Avar and the conquerors' grave structure is so marked that still it cannot be closed.[458] A noteworthy but still now unique example is the cemetery of Sopronkőhida in Hungary.[459]

It would be premature, on the basis of archaeological research to date, to opt for the so-called dual Hungarian conquest. Chronological problems exist, especially with respect to the tying together the late Avar and the conquerors' graves. Recent excavations would tend to confirm the continuation of the late Avars, that is, of the semi-nomadic Onogur-Turkic Bulgars who joined the Avars in the seventh century, until the conquest. A village from Avar times that corresponds to villages of the time of the conquest was excavated, for instance, at Dunapentele (Hungary).[460] Graves of the late Avar period have been uncovered in several settlements of the conquerors of the tenth century;[461] some 60 graves were excavated.[462]

That various groups of peoples lived together in the Avar Empire is historically demonstrable. Also established is the general appellation of all nomadic peoples of the East as Scythians and Huns in Byzantine literature. One may, therefore, not exclude the hypothesis that Hungarian-speaking ethnic groups in the company of westward moving groups of peoples could have penetrated the Carpathian Basin even before the Hungarian conquest. One may further assume that the original Turco-Bulgarians (Kuvrat-Bulgars) and the early-Magyarized

Székelys settled in the Carpathian Basin as early as the middle of the seventh century. However, whether they in fact spoke Hungarian cannot be determined from materials related to post-conquest place names. On the other hand, it is known that the Finno-Ugric-speaking Magyars and the Bulgaro-Turkic groups like the Onogurs and Kutrigurs did live in some sort of symbiosis for centuries before the Hungarian conquest. Richly endowed princely graves[463] at Bócsa, Kunbábony, Átokháza (Hungary) and jewels from the graves of Ozora-Tótipuszta (Hungary), as well as the treasure of Nagyszentmiklós (Sînnicolau Mare) and the Runic script, represent an archaeological connection to the Onogur Bulgars, that is, to the presumed ancestors of the Székelys. Furthermore, the jewelry of Ozora-Tótipuszta shows a remarkable resemblance to the Onogur Bulgarian finds excavated in Maloje Perescepina, Kelegerskije Hutora, and Zascepilovka (Soviet Union).

The Onogur Bulgars are mentioned for the first time in written sources during the first half of the fourth century.[464] It can be assumed that Onogur Bulgars wandered into the Carpathian Basin as early as in 567 and played a certain role in the multiethnic Avar Empire. Following their expulsion in about 631, they moved westward to Pannonia. After the defeat of the Avars, the Onogurs moved—probably with another splinter group of the Bulgars, the Kutrigurs—from Pannonia to Transylvania, which was incorporated into the Bulgarian State.

The Székelys (Szeklers)

There are several hypotheses regarding the origin of the Székelys (Szeklers), one of the oldest branches of the Hungarians, none of which, however, is satisfactory.[465] According to the Hunnic Chronicle of Simon de Kéza (Kézai Simon), the Székelys lived in the region of the Csigla field (*campus Chigla*) prior to the arrival of the Hungarians. The word "Csigla" (Chigla) is of Turkic origin. The anonymous Notary of Bela III refers to the Székelys as *Siculi, Sicli, Sycli* and identifies them as descendants of the Huns who were to be found in the Carpathian Basin at the time of the Hungarian conquest. In all probability the Székelys belong to the Turkic-Bulgaro ethnic group (Kuvrat-Bulgars) of the *sekils, siki, eskils, eszekel* ("of noble origin") of the middle Volga region. From their earlier inhabitation, from the Caucasus, the Székelys moved with the Huns or with the Avars into the Carpathian Basin. According to another assumption, the Székelys had joined the Hungarians in the Hungarians' earlier homeland, Etelköz. There are also assumptions that the Székelys had joined the

Kuvrat-Bulgars and moved into the Carpathian Basin as early as the middle of the seventh century. According to this assumption the name Székely is of Onogur origin.

It is known that the Székelys moved from the trans-Danubian region (western Hungary) into middle-Transylvania during the age of the Árpáds and from there were resettled, as defenders of the eastern frontier of the empire of the Árpáds, to their present area of inhabitation in southeastern Transylvania. There are some 700,000 Székelys nowadays. Their material culture was identical to that of the Hungarians in the eleventh and twelfth centuries. The Székelys preserved their Runic script, (*rovásírás*) of which sixteen characters have been borrowed from the Turkish Runic script, until modern times.

The Treasure of Nagyszentmiklós

The treasure of Nagyszentmiklós (Sînnicolau Mare, Timiş County) is one of the most significant archaeological finds from the early Middle Ages in the Carpathian Basin. Discovered in 1799, it is currently located in the Kunsthistorisches Museum in Vienna.[466] The treasure comprises 23 golden objects: drinking-vessels, pots, cups, and jugs. The ninth cup is inscribed in Runic letters; an additional 12 vessels also contain Runic markings. The others are inscribed with Greek capital letters.

It has not yet been determined with any degree of certainty when and where the treasure was assembled or who ordered it and what the meaning of the Runic and Greek inscriptions may be. The Sassanide character of the objects, however, may be readily recognized. They are characteristic of the convergence of the Iranian and Middle-South Asian cultures of the steppe. The use of Greek letters in the Turkic-Bulgarian Runic script is indicative of Byzantine influences, since the Old Bulgarian letters, taken over by the Greek alphabet, are identical to the Greek ones. When taking all these factors into account, according to the German archaeologist Kurt Horedt, we are dealing with Sassanide and Byzantine influences that can be traced to Kuvrat's Turkic-Bulgarian Empire in southern Russia of the seventh century.

Recent Hungarian research places the treasure of Nagyszentmiklós (Sînnicolau Mare) as part of the late Avar cultural domain in the seventh to eighth centuries. According to this concept, the treasure cannot be related to Bulgarian art of the eighth or ninth centuries, to Bulgarian-Byzantine art, to Byzantine artworks, or even to Hungarian goldsmith art of the ninth to tenth centuries.[467] The question, then, is who in fact were the late Avars; that is, what peoples are supposed to comprise the concept of "late Avars?" Even under the post-sixth century classification of "Avar," several different peoples may be included. It is necessary to note that the early alphabet of the Hungarians, the so-called Székely-Hungarian Runic script (*rovásírás*), belongs to the Turkic Runic writing used by the peoples of the Central-Asian Turkic-Khazar Empire, which in the fifth century stretched from eastern Asia to the Black Sea.

As is known, the ancestors of the Hungarians lived in their original home under Turkic-Khazar rule[468] together with the Onogur Bulgars and that Kuvrat's fifth son, Kuber, as mentioned previously, moved to Pannonia where he submitted to the Avars in the second half of the seventh century. Thus, the possibility may not be excluded—in fact, it is most likely—that part of the Magyars who lived in Kuvrat's empire, today's Székelys, the presumed successors of the Kuber Turkic-Bulgars, moved into the territory of contemporary Hungary during the second half of the seventh century and still used their original alphabet in Runic script at that time. Moreover, it is also probable that the treasure of Nagyszentmiklós may be traced back to the Onogur Bulgars, whose successors were the Székelys. The inscriptions in Runic script are related to the Runic inscriptions used in the empire of the Khazars. Furthermore, the structure of the Székely Runic script shows a near relation to that of the drinking ware contained in the treasure of Nagyszentmiklós. The cross on the three Greek-inscribed cups means that those who ordered them were Christians.

As far as the Byzantine influence on the peoples of the Pontic Steppes—including the pre-Magyars—is concerned, several different points of view have been expressed by historians. There is every reason to believe that the Magyars, who once lived between the Don and the Caucasus, were in touch with the Byzantine centers in the Crimea (Pontic Steppes) as early as the sixth century and that Greek missionaries had attempted to convert them to Christianity.[469] In the first half of the sixth century the Crimean Huns were already in contact with the Christian Church in Constantinople; and by the seventh century Christian, Jewish, and Moslem missionaries had begun their activities among the peoples of the southern Russian steppe. Here, it is also best to mention the ethnic continuity in this area, which is related to the subsequent Iranians (Sarmatians, Alans, Scythians) and, later the Turkic-Mongol peoples, the Huns, Bulgars, Avars, Turks, Pechenegs, Uzes, Cumans, and Tatars.

With regard to the gold treasure of Nagyszentmiklós, it can most likely be traced to the seventh century.[470] The bent golden drinking horn was the symbol of the high status of the leaders of the equestrian nomads, such as Onogur Bulgars, Avars, and others, who ruled over the Pontic Steppes and the Carpathian Basin in the seventh and eighth centuries. The same drinking horns as those of Nagyszentmiklós were also found in the archaeological remains of the Onogur Bulgars, the one-time rulers of the Pontic Steppes, in Malaja Perescepina (Ukraine).[471]

The Turkic Runic script, related to the Hebraic, Greek, Latin, and Arab ones, is derived from the Aramic and was disseminated in the interior of Asia by the Iranian tribal groups of the Sogdians. The western Turks introduced the script into western Asia. The script, as used by the Hungarians, was known later as the Székely Runic script (*székely rovásírás*) and was preserved and used in several localities in Székely inhabited territories until the sixteenth century. The old Runic script, however, which is found primarily on wood, has not survived. One of the most important remains of the Székely-Hungarian Runic script is the so-called Nikolsburg (Mikulovo, Czechoslovakia) Alphabet, consisting of 46 letters, which constitutes the foundation of early Székely-Hungarian Runic writing. Also known is the alphabet of Marsigli, of 1690, which is preserved in the library of the University of Bologna.

The Székely-Hungarian Runic script consists of 20 letters; 16 of which are of Turkic origin and 4 derived from the Greek alphabet, of which 2 resemble the Glagolitic (Old Bulgarian) script. It is written from right to left. The Turkic alphabet was deciphered by the Danish linguist V. Thomsen in 1893. It is clear from the account above, that the treasure of Nagyszentmiklós could be Old Bulgarian or Avar-Magyar; the exact determination will be made only when the script is deciphered.

The treasure of an Avar khan found at Vrap (Albania) is analogous to that of Nagyszentmiklós. Vrap is located some 25 kilometers south of Tirana. The treasure was discovered in 1901 and contained 5.6 kilograms of gold and 1.5 kilograms of silver. Through the cast tendrils and griffin ornaments the finding can be identified as one falling within the framework of the Avar culture of the last decades of the seventh century.

The Bijelo Brdo Culture
Early Archaeological Remnants of the
Hungarians in the Carpathian Basin

The Bijelo Brdo culture derives its name from the village Bijelo Brdo, located in the vicinity of the town Eszék (Osijek, Croatia) and can be dated between the second half of the tenth century and the beginning of the twelfth.[472] Before the end of the last century some 200 common people's row-cemeteries were excavated in that village; the dead were laid in their graves with hairpins with S-form tails. The most recent Hungarian investigations question whether any ethnic significance can be attached to these hairpins.

The Bijelo Brdo culture appears to have been expanding in the Carpathian Basin after the second half of the tenth century. At the beginning of the twentieth century cemeteries of the Bijelo Brdo type were excavated in Transylvania at Vajdahunyad (Hunedoara) and Várfalva (Moldovenești, *castrum* Turda), as well as in Moldavia (Costișa-Botoșana); identical tombs were found throughout Hungary during the age of the Árpáds, and similar types are encountered throughout Eastern Europe. For a long time this culture was attributed to the Slavs. Although its Slavic character (Croatian, Slovenian, Serbian, Slovakian) is evident during the early stages of this culture, in its later stages it is regarded as Hungarian.

Characteristics of this culture are wood and earthen fortifications which were hitherto unknown. Archaeologically the Bijelo Brdo culture in Transylvania can be shown to have existed in Lopadea Nouă (Magyarlapád, Alba County), Dăbîca (Doboka, Cluj County), Morești-Citfalău (Malomfalva-Csittfalva, Mureș County), Șirioara (Sajósárvár, Bistrița County), Moldovenești (Várfalva, Cluj County), Cîlnic (Kelnek), and Zăbala (Zabola, Covasna County). The existence of the Bijelo Brdo culture is also revealed by the excavations carried out in Alba Iulia.

The seven graves, dating to the first half of the tenth century, that were uncovered in 1911 in Kolozsvár (Cluj) in Zápolya Street reveal equestrian nomadic Hungarian characteristics (swords, arrowheads). Women's jewelry has its counterparts in Blandiana and Tokaj (Hungary).[473] Early Hungarian equestrian finds mostly from the twelfth century were uncovered in Transylvania in Deva, Marosgombás (Gîmbaș), Kolozsmonostor (Cluj-Mănăștur), Székelykeresztúr (Cristuru Seciuesc), Csapószentgyörgy, Malomfalva-Csittfalva (Morești-Citfalău), Kozárvár (Cuzdrioara), Doboka (Dăbîca), Várfalva (Moldovenești), Marosvásárhely (Tîrgu Mureș), Marosszentgyörgy (Sîngheorghiu de Mureș), Magyarlapád (Lopadea Nouă), and Felvinc-Marosveresmart (Unirea-Vereșmort). The first evidence of the presence of the Székelys in their actual location, in southeastern Transylvania, is the burial ground of Zabola (Zăbala) from the first half of the twelfth century, where 192 tombs were uncovered.[474]

Fortifications of the Tenth to Twelfth Centuries in Transylvania. Doboka

The citadel of Doboka (Dăbîca), in the vicinity of the Someș (Szamos) River, is one of the large fortifications that were built as part of the Hungarian defense and county systems after 950.[475] Three additional great fortifications were built in Transylvania: Várfalva (Moldoveneşti near Turda, *castrum* Torda, Cluj County), from the second half of the tenth century to the twelfth century; Kolozsmonostor (Cluj-Mănăştur), from the second half of the twelfth century; and Fogaras (Făgăraş), from the twelfth century (not yet excavated). Smaller fortifications were in Kozárvár (Cuzdrioara, Cluj County), from the eleventh century, to the east of the confluence of the Someşul Mare and Someşul Mic (Kis-Szamos and Nagy-Szamos) rivers; in Malomfalva (Moreşti), from the tenth century; and in Sajósárvár (Şirioara), from the second half of the eleventh century. Romanian archaeologists also include Dedrad (Mureş County), Chinari (annexed to Sîntana de Mureş), and Moigrad (Sălaj County), among these smaller fortifications.

The introduction of wood and earthen fortresses into Transylvania began only in the tenth century during the rule of Prince Géza (?– 997). The construction of earthen fortresses, well known in Eastern Europe, had been undertaken by Hungarians already in their ancestral homeland in the region of the Volga and Kama rivers. The very Hungarian word *vár* (fortress) penetrated into the Hungarian language through the Iranians with whom the pre-Magyars lived as neighbors for more than a thousand years. The utilization of earthen fortresses represents, in Eastern Europe, the *gorodisce culture*, from the Russian word *gorodisce* meaning earthen fortress. It cannot be assumed, therefore, that earthen fortifications were to be found in Transylvania as early as the ninth century; they were built later, in the age of Hungarian territorial expansion, and are Hungarian and not Romanian-Slavic as had been assumed by a few archaeologists. Attempts were made also to claim that the development of fortresses at Doboka (Dăbîca) and also at Kolozsmonostor (Cluj-Mănăştur) occurred in earlier times, before the arrival of the Hungarians, and to assign them to the Vlach chieftain Gelou.[476] It has been proven, however, that no earthen fortifications were built in Transylvania between 650 and 950;[477] after that period they are Hungarian. The archaeological data derived from the fortresses refutes a pre-Magyar or non-Magyar origin.[478]

The excavations that started in 1975 in Voronezh (USSR) relate to the ninth century *Saltovo-Majazkoi* culture, which is related to the pre-Magyar. A stone fortress with Runic inscriptions was uncovered which proves that the Magyars built not only earthen but also stone fortresses in the territories of their early settlement.

So far as the dating of the structural components of the citadel of Doboka is concerned, Romanian scholars assumed that the first layer of the citadel dates back to the ninth and tenth centuries and, as such, can be designated as Slavic-Romanian.[479] According to Romanian archaeologists, the bell-shaped pendants found along the lower (I-II) layers, as well as the findings of Darufalva (Drassburg), are Moravian products of the ninth century; or, at least, they underwent Moravian influences. This view has, nevertheless, been shown to be untenable. The numerous similar finds of treasures and jewel show that we are not dealing with a "pagan tomb" and that the treasure of Darufalva (Drassburg) can be classified with regard to age and character with the Byzantine or Russian adornments (silver earrings, Kiev) of the eleventh century. The silver of Darufalva-Doboka has no counterparts in Czech or Moravian territories of the ninth to eleventh centuries. On the other hand, some 26 finds of the Bijelo Brdo culture (primarily silver earrings, silver chains, gold-plated bell-shaped silver buttons) were brought to light, among other places, in the cemeteries of Szolnok-Repülőtér and Szob-Koliba (Hungary), as well as in Poland, Russia, Denmark, Bulgaria, and Sweden and offer proof for dating the treasure of Darufalva-Doboka to the tenth and eleventh centuries.[480] Moreover, the spores, arrowheads, flints, and in more recent periods (after 1050) a bracelet and (in the age of King Kálmán I, 1068–1116) parts of crosses, coins, and ceramics, all of which were found in the second to fourth layers of Doboka, are characteristic of the Árpád era. The finds, according to historical sources, do not antedate the end of the tenth or the beginning of the eleventh centuries.

The name Doboka is not of Slavic origin and is not derived through the evolution of the Old Slavic form *glambokъ*.[481] It is, rather, ascribable to the name of the Hungarian conqueror Doboka. The excavations have demonstrated beyond any doubt that the citadel of Doboka was built in three or four periods in the age of Árpád. The first of these was in the second half of the tenth century; the second, from 1025 to 1050; the third occurred at the turn of the eleventh and twelfth centuries during the rule of the Hungarian King Kálmán (coin dated 1100); and the fourth during the first half of the thirteenth century.

Concurrently with the wood and earthen fortresses of the tenth to twelfth centuries, ecclesiastical stone buildings were also constructed. In various places in Transylvania stone churches were also constructed next to wooden churches in the Árpád period at Doboka, Moreşti-Citfalău, Almaş (Sălaj County), Moldoveneşti, Peteni (Petőfalva, Covasna County), and Streisîngeorg iu (Sztrigyszentgyörgy, Hunedoara County). More than 20 churches from the Árpád period have been discovered, of which 5 or 6 are of stone.[482]

III

LINGUISTICS

THE ROMANIAN LANGUAGE

The Testimony of Language

The theory of Roman continuity north of the Danube emerged as a result of the discovery that Romanian, spoken in a territory that was once a Roman province (Dacia Traiana), is a Romance language. The early proponents of this theory (the 18th century Transylvanian School) were chiefly concerned with a political struggle, but at that time the lack of sufficient data and scientific methods of investigation made it impossible adequately to analyze the origins of Romanian. With the accumulation of such data and better methods, it was again the facts of language that carried the problem further: the discovery of the ancient characteristics of Romanian and their relationship with several Balkan languages challenged the theory of continuity in the former Roman province of Dacia.

As mentioned previously, the material culture showing Roman provincial influence—Roman patterns in pottery and other products, the circulation of Roman coins, and similar phenomena—does not prove the existence of a Latin-speaking population. Such phenomena can be observed in wide areas of Europe and to a comparable degree as in the former Dacia, since all the non-Roman peoples were strongly influenced by Roman culture and civilization during the period in question.

In contrast to the data provided by history and archaeology, the facts of language are specific. The Romanian language, with its ancient elements inherited from a pre-Roman population, as well as from those who spoke Late Latin, is the link between the speakers of present-day Romanian and their forebears. Consequently, knowing the antiquity of a certain linguistic phenomenon that exists both in Romanian and in one of these idioms (for example, a Late Latin lexical element), it can be postulated that the ancestors of the Romanians must have been living under circumstances that permitted the incorporation of that element into their language. One or a few elements are not sufficient, of course; and in many cases difficulties arise about details; but this principle, if used judiciously and consistently, could give the most reliable results in resolving the difficult problem of the origins of Romanian. More concretely, the problem can be formulated as follows: is the theory that the ancestors of the Romanians lived outside the Roman Empire, beginning at the end of the third century A.D., compatible with the facts of the Romanian language?

There are several types of linguistic phenomena to be investigated in this connection. In this chapter, two of the most important will be presented: 1. the Latin elements (the vestiges in modern Romanian of a territorial variant of vulgar Latin, namely East Latin), as well as the vestiges of the Late Latin period, and 2. the pre-Latin elements (in other words, the vestiges from the substratum). This analysis will show the close relationship of the Romanian language with several idioms spoken in the central parts of the Balkan Peninsula. Considering them in the context of the historical situation in Southeastern Europe between the end of the third century A.D. and around 600 A.D. (or somewhat later), conclusions can be drawn about the territory in which the ancestors of the Romanians were then living.

Romanian scholars have produced several theories about the Romanian language that will be treated in the second part of this chapter; but since no really critical analysis of the problem has been permitted in Romania for several decades, these theories have not been exposed to normal critical scrutiny. The resulting gap cannot be compensated for by foreign studies, which are never as comprehensive or systematic as one would wish. The present analysis will point to the great need for international contributions to resolve these problems and will also suggest that political pressure on the Romanian scientific community has created a conflict between the officially desired conclusions and those based on facts.

It is well known that opinions differ among Romanian linguists and archaeologists on the subject of Romanian ethnogenesis. Linguistic research has brought more accurate and conclusive results, given the nature of that discipline. While in the past, linguists such as Alexandru Philippide and Ovid Densusianu could express their views freely, any deviation from the official line at this time is severely criticized. Such is the case with Ion I. Russu's *Etnogeneza românilor* [The Ethnogenesis of the Romanians], which has been criticized by the archaeologist Nicolae Gudea.[1] Russu may justifiably be criticized, among other things, for the fact that he considers too many words of unknown etymology to be of substratum origin and in a significant number of cases such an origin is dubious. Many of Russu's proposed Indo-European etymologies for the substratum words are uncertain and not accepted by most linguists.[2] Russu presents, however, a vast spectrum of material (partly incorporating his own earlier investigations into this monograph) and presents an interesting discussion of the relevant problems.

Russu's point of departure is that the only really specific element of documentary value about the early history of the Romanians is the Romanian language. Archaeological finds including those reported recently, are not able to throw too much light on the origin of the Romanians:[3] "We are still far from a reliable and evidenced, or at least probable, conclusion generally accepted by scholars. From the sparse records of the ancient chroniclers and from the often inconclusive archaeological remains, it never will be possible to know exactly what the extreme political-military act of official evacuation consisted of and what remained Roman in the old Carpathian province".[4]

In Gudea's opinion, Russu assigned too much significance to the autochthonous words—the presence of the substratum elements—which show a very close relationship with Albanian, that is, with a language spoken in a territory different from Dacia Traiana. In criticizing Russu, Gudea stated that "the way in which Russu conceives the contribution of the autochthon stratum of words [in reality, of the autochthonous population] in the process of ethnogenesis, an isolated and even unhistorical way, is another exaggeration and, because of the lack of connection with history, leaves the hypothesis open that the Romanian language and people may have been formed anywhere in the Balkans."[5] The archaeologist Gudea, in contrast to the linguist Russu, attributes great significance to archaeology; but he does not use the occasion to discuss the fact that linguistical and archaeological research give such different results.

In his monograph, Russu defends the hypothesis, as do most contemporary Romanian linguists, that the Romanian language and people were formed in a large territory both north and south of the Danube. This may be considered a compromise between the demands of the official concept and the conclusion suggested by the analysis of the Romanian language (in this case, the pre-Roman elements). This compromise is, however, quite fragile.

Another contemporary Romanian linguist considers Russu's *Etnogeneza românilor* to be a synthetic introduction into Romanian historiography, accepting Russu's historical concept that only the Romanian language may give concrete information about the ethnogenesis.[6]

Another illustration of the conceptual differences about Romanian ethnogenesis between archaeologists and historians, on the one hand,

and linguists, on the other, is given in a monograph by Iancu Fischer.[7] The author of this study, dealing with Romanization and its manifestations, considers, not without reservations, the official doctrine on the origins of the Romanians. Even when he states that the adoption of the Latin language must have been paralleled by an adoption of the Roman way of life, he continues that such an affirmation is by itself vague and refers to notions that are not only difficult to define but also impossible to investigate with scientific exactness. Fischer does not fully accept as immutable the conclusions reached by archaeologists adhering to the current official views on continuity. In his opinion, the elements of material culture may cross the borders of states and could, in ancient times, be adopted by non-Romanized populations.[8] A material object cannot give any information about the language of its user (or producer); and it is also a fact that the material (and spiritual) aspects of a culture are more easily spread than a language and consequently, the adoption of elements of Roman civilization would not presuppose a change as profound as linguistic Romanization. Archaeological vestiges may be used only as partial evidence in elucidating certain aspects of the process of Romanization.[9]

Language Community: A General Consideration

The characteristics of Balkan Latin that have survived are to be found mainly in Romanian, but also in the extinct Dalmatian language, the Latin elements of Albanian, New Greek, and to a certain extent in the Southern Slavic languages. A significant differentiation in languages occurred in the Balkan Peninsula. Through their specific characteristics, the Balkan languages constitute a "language community."[10] The term "language community" was first used by N.S. Trubetzky.[11] In the linguistic sense, G. Weigand considers Albanian, Romanian, and Bulgarian characteristic of Balkan languages, while Serbian, Greek, and Turkish are regarded as Balkan languages only in the geographic sense, because they are used on the Balkan Peninsula. The Bulgarian linguist Vladimir Georgiev places the Balkan languages in the following sequence: Romanian, Bulgarian, Albanian, and Greek. According to the German linguist Georg Renatus Solta, the true Balkan languages are Romanian (with its dialects), and Bulgarian; according to other researchers, also New Greek belongs to the Balkan languages.[12] The Romanian linguist Alexandru Rosetti agrees about the Balkan ties of the Romanian language. In Rosetti's view, the so-called Balkanisms may be traced to common substratum influences. This interpretation is also supported by other linguists including Ion I. Russu who, however, is otherwise opposed to the notion of Balkan linguistics.

According to Vladimir Georgiev, the substratum and adstratum influences on Balkan languages are not necessarily decisive but rather represent a "multiple convergence."[13] To support these views he points out, for instance, the post-position of the article—characteristic of Bulgarian, Macedonian, Romanian, and Albanian. The Romanian linguist Emil Petrovici believes that the Balkan characteristics of the Romanian sound system are due to Slavic influences.

One of the common phenomena of the Balkan language is the change from the unpronounced *a* to *ă* (Romanian and Bulgarian) and *ë* (Albanian). Rhotacism, that is, the transformation of the inter-vowel "l" into "r", is the result of the original, neighboring locations of Albanians and Romanians.[14]

The Apennino-Balkan Group of Romance Languages
The Descendants of East Latin

The first division of the Romance languages was made by F. Diez (1882). He distinguished an eastern group (Romanian and Italian), a southwestern group (Spanish and Portuguese), and a northwestern one (French and Provençal). His criteria, besides linguistic aspects, were literary, geographical, and political. The Italian linguist M. Bartoli, who described Dalmatian, which was not yet known by Diez, developed this division further, adding the criterion of the substratum. Bartoli places Middle and Southern Italian, Dalmatian, and Romanian, as well as the Latin elements found in Albanian, New Greek, and the Slavic languages of the Balkan Peninsula, in the eastern Apennino-Balkan group; and the rest of the Romance languages in another group called Pireneo-Alpino.[15] Later, the frontier between the western and eastern Romance language areas was established with a line drawn from La Spezia to Rimini. The territory of Italy south of this line is considered to belong to the eastern group.[16] This designation is used also by Rosetti, who believes that Romanian belongs to the Apennino-Balkan group together with Dalmatian, Albanian, and the central and southern Italian dialects (Abruzzian and Puglian).[17]

From these languages, as well from the Latin elements of the South Slavic languages and of New Greek, a variant of Latin spoken in the eastern provinces may be reconstructed; this can be called East Latin. The frontier is, of course, only approximate, the division not absolute, since the real situation is complicated both from the chronological and from the territorial points of view. Sardinian, for instance, often shows correspondences with the East Latin idioms, and there also are many cognates between northern Italian dialects and Romanian. On the other hand, Dalmatian also showed similarities to the western group.

In 1960 a monograph was published about the Latin language spoken "in the Danubian provinces of the Roman Empire."[18] It contains a study of the inscriptions and of the literary texts from the first six centuries A.D. found in Noricum, Pannonia Superior and Inferior, Dalmatia, Moesia Superior and Inferior, and Dacia Traiana (in the last-mentioned province only between the years 106 and about 260 A.D.). The population of this area of about 600,000 square kilometers is estimated to have been about three million during the Roman period. The inscriptions provide only limited information about the Latin idiom spoken in these provinces, since usage was in many cases inconsistent, final development often occurring very late.

As mentioned previously, Rome conquered part of the southern Balkan Peninsula in 168 B.C. and Illyria in 167 B.C. Dalmatia followed in 156 and 155 B.C.; Pannonia, from 12 to 9 A.D., and northwest of the Balkans, Noricum and Raetia, in 15 A.D. Moesia was created at approximately the same time; in 86 A.D., it was divided into Moesia Superior and Inferior. At the official division of the Roman Empire in 395 A.D. into eastern and western parts, Dalmatia remained with the western part and Preavalitana (Montenegro and northern Albania) went to the eastern part. The frontier between the two territories went from the gulf of Cattaro to the area west of Belgrade. Since most of Dalmatia was in the sphere of influence of Rome for almost another one-and-a-half centuries (in 535 A.D. it was conquered by Byzantium), it was able to take part in several linguistic developments that did not affect the rest of East Latin.[19] The Balkan provinces belonged to the empire until the end of the sixth century.

Roman life in this territory, south of the Danube, is well documented; and the Roman population was numerous, as indicated by a large number of roman towns: 24 in Dalmatia, 28 in Moesia Inferior, 13 in Moesia Superior, and 31 in Pannonia. Beginning with the fourth century, the organization of the Christian Church was intensive: the ruins of 45 buildings of religious character from the third to the sixth centuries inclusive have been found in the Balkan provinces, excluding Dalmatia. From the same territory, at least 57 bishops, all with Latin names, are known, beginning in the third century.[20] The official language of the Byzantine Empire was, until the early seventh century, Latin and was then replaced by Greek. The records of the fifth ecumenical council in Constantinople (553 A.D.) were written in Latin. The epigraphic material found in the Southeastern European provinces (a total of about 21,000 inscriptions) shows a Latin similar to that used in documents in the western parts of the Roman Empire, and the same is true about the texts of writers from the Balkan provinces.[21] The inscriptions were made, however, predominantly by a small number of educated people near the top of social hierarchy; the texts were written by leaders of the Church, mostly for the masses, "who probably understood them without much difficulty."[22]

Until the sixth century the eastern part of the Roman Empire (Eastromania) was characterized by a definite degree of uniformity. After that, ties with Romanized peoples were broken. There is no doubt that the process of Romanization was brought to an end by the arrival of the Slavs around the year 600 A.D.; but as late as in the eighth century, Romania was the name of the Eastern Roman Empire and used by the Slavs and Latins in Thracia, Macedonia, and the Thessalian coastal regions.

In the former province of Dacia Traiana, which belonged to the empire for only about 165 years, no remains of religious buildings have been found, no written texts are known, and the 11 or 12 towns that existed during the Roman period had disappeared entirely by the second half of the fourth century at the latest. Of the more than 21,000 inscriptions found in the Southeastern European provinces, almost 3,000 came from Dacia. In spite of this apparently high number, this material does not provide information about the Latin spoken in the north-Danubian province. According to Haralambie Mihăescu, these inscriptions reflect a *lingua franca*, a Latin used by the Roman administration and the army. This is because those who ordered the inscriptions in Dacia Traiana belonged prevalently to these organizations. They rarely reflect the sincerity and speech of the simple citizen or the slave. Therefore, we lack any evidence that the Latin language of Dacia was different from the common Latin spoken in the other provinces of the Roman Empire. On the contrary, those almost 3,000 inscriptions from Dacia illustrate, in general, characteristics of language that appear in similar documents from the entire territory of the Roman Empire.[23] It may be added that the differentiation of Latin in the time that these inscriptions were made (106 to 260 A.D.) was probably relatively slight; more significant regional differences developed in the centuries that followed.

Danubian Latin

The review of the sources of East Latin shows that all data about its main differentiating characteristics derive from the territory south of the Danube, with the exception of the Romanian language, which today is spoken both north and south of the river.

The designation "Danubian Latin" is used by Romanian scholars[24] to describe "succinctly the Latin idiom on which the Romanian language is based. The description will focus on the main differentiating characteristics of this territorial variant of the Latin language limited to both shores (Dacia and Moesia) of the Danube."[25]

The term "Danubian Latin" is not exempt from criticism. According to Iancu Fischer," we are dealing here with an hypothetical Danubian Latin, which may be nothing more than the Latinized reflection of the Romance data we possess. In other words, we consider that there was a Danubian Latin whose only descendant is Romanian, because we describe it on the basis of the characteristics of Romanian."[26] The risk would be avoided, argues Fischer, if we are able to define the chronological limits of our investigation (that is, of the Latin idiom from which Romanian developed), and to give the stages of evolution of each linguistic fact. Such a method would result in the establishment of really Latin phenomena (thus, from the period before the 8th–9th centuries) and of "a dialectal variant that will not be the creation of our fantasy or of faulty reasoning."

In this way, however, only the chronological problem can be solved. The question of the area in which this Latin idiom once was spoken is not answered; and in assuming that "Danubian Latin" was once also spoken in Dacia Traiana, because it was the ancestor of the Romanian language, spoken today mainly north of the Danube, one risks the circular reasoning that Romanian originates from the territory of former Dacia Traiana, because Danubian Latin was spoken there.

The term Danubian Latin is also inadequate because it could be applied to the provinces of Moesia Superior and Inferior and to Pannonia but not to the areas where most of the descendants of this Latin idiom were and are spoken: Dalmatian, the central and southern Italian dialects, and the Latin elements of Albanian and the South Slavic languages. (It is not known whether the speech of the Romans who were living in Dacia from 106 to 275 A.D. showed any regional peculiarities. There is no evidence to assume a special Latin idiom for the provinces of Moesia).

The Characteristics of East Latin
Phonology

Vowels: The reduction of Latin *ŭ* to *o*, characteristic of the Western idioms, did not take place in the East: Lat. *crŭcem* > Northern Romanian *cruce*, Albanian *kryqe* (as opposed to Italian *croce*, French *croix*); Lat. *pŭlverem*, Dalmatian *pulvro*, Romanian *pulbere*, Albanian *plluhur* (cf., Italian *polvere*).[27] Another conservative trait in the East was the preservation of *ō* without diphthongation to *uo*, as occurred in Western Romance languages. Mihăescu remarks that *uo* in the place of *o* is also absent from the inscriptions found in Pannonia, Moesia Superior, and Dacia.[28]

The diphthong *au* was, in stressed syllables, preserved in Dalmatian, Friulian, Sicilian, Provençal, Catalan, and Romanian, for example, Lat. *aur* > Vegliotic (one of the Dalmatian dialects) *yaur*, Old Provençal *aur*, Romanian *aur*, but French *or*; Lat. *taurus*, Friulian *taur*, Old Catalan *taur*, Romanian *taur*, but Spanish *toro*. If the following syllable contained a *u*, the diphthong *au* was reduced to *a*: Lat. *auscultare* > Italian *ascoltare*, Old French *ascouter*, Rom. *asculta*; Lat. *augustus* > Italian *agosto*, Spanish and Portuguese *agosto*, Rom. dialectal *agust*. This phenomenon occurred in most of the Romance idioms, but in Romanian, it is also found in certain cases if the syllable is not followed by a *u*: Lat. *repausare* > Rom. (through *răpăsa) *răposa*; Lat. *plausare* > Rom. *plăsa*. In Albanian, this is the rule: Lat. *aurum* > Alb. *ar*, Lat. *aut* > Alb. *a*, Lat. *paucum* > Alb. *pak*.[29]

Consonants: Here also are many instances of conservation as opposed to innovations in the West. The intervocalic voiceless occlusives (*p*, *t*, *k*) of Latin (with the exception of *k* before *e*, *i*) show, in the Western Romance idioms, a tendency toward sonorization. In the southern Italian dialects, in Dalmatian, partially in Sardinian, and also in Romanian, they were preserved: Lat. *ripa* > Dalmatian *raipa*, Sicilian *ripa*, N. Romanian *rîpă*; Lat. *capistrum*, *rota*, *pecorarius* > Italian *capestro*, *rota*, *pecoraio*, N. Rom. *căpăstru*, *roată*, *păcurar*, as opposed to Spanish *cabestro*, *rueda*, Portuguese *pegureio*, respectively.[30] The situation is similar with the occlusives before *r*, *l* (except *cl*): Lat. *capra* > Ital. *capra*, N. Rom. *capră*, but Spanish *cabra*, Lat. *petra* > Ital. *pietra*, N. Rom. *piatră*, but Spanish *piedra*, Lat. *lacrima* > Ital. *lacrima*, N. Rom. *lacrimă*, but Spanish *lágrima*.[31]

Latin *-ct-* changed in East Latin to *-pt-* or *-ft-*, and Lat. *-cs-* to *-ps-* or *-fs-*. The labial treatment of Latin *-ct-* is characteristic of the Balkan Peninsula.[32] (It has been explained by a possible Thracian influence, but it also appears in certain Greek dialects as well as in Macedonian.) With regard to Latin *-cs-*, it changed in all Romance languages to *s* or, if followed by *i*, to *š*: Rom. *măsea* from Lat. *maxilla* and *ieși*, from Lat. *exire*. In Romanian, however, there are several words in which *cs* changed to *-ps-*: Lat. *coxa* > N. Rom. *coapsă*, Lat. *fraxinus* > Arumanian *frapsin*, Lat. *toxicum* > N. Rom. *toapsec*. This phenomenon has its counterpart in Albanian: Lat. *coxa* > Alb. *kofshë* (also *koshë*), Lat. *metaxa* > Alb. *mëndafshë* (also *mëndafsh*, *mëndash*).[33]

The final *s* was preserved in the West, while it disappeared in Italian and Romanian. Latin *nos*, *minus*, *cantas* > Sardinian *nos*, *minus*, *cantas*, French *nos*, *moins*, *chantes*, Spanish and Portuguese *nos*, *menos*, *cantas*, but Italian *noi*, *meno*, *canti*, N. Romanian *noi*, *cînți*.[34] The final *-i* was not simply added, since it also appears in words in which it is not the inflectional ending of the plural (Lat. *post* - pos > N. Rom.

poi), but must be explained by the substitution of one sound for another.[35] This change was very late, beyond doubt after the sixth century,[36] although it may be an independent reflection in Italian and Romanian of some older trends.[37] (In view of the numerous correspondences between Italian and Romanian, it seems at least as likely that also this phenomenon is an example of the close relationships between these two idioms.)

Late Latin had probably, at least in monosyllabic words, an extra vowel, (usually an -*e*) after -*r*, -*l*. This was preserved in Sardinian, Italian, and Romanian: Lat. *cor, fel, mel, sal* > Sardinian *koro, fele, mele, sale*, Italian *cuore, fiele, miele, sale*, N. Rom. *fiere, miere, sare*.[38] Latin -*gn*- corresponds in many of the Romance languages to a guttural or palatalized nasal occlusive: Lat. *agnellus* > French *agneau*, Italian *agnello*, Friulian *añel*, etc. In Romanian, Lat. -*gn*- changed to -*mn*-: Lat. *lignum* > N. Rom. *lemn*, Lat. *cognatus* > N. Rom. *cumnat*, Lat. *signum* > N. Rom. *semn*. This labial treatment is also found in southern Italian dialects: Lat. *agnum* > *aunu*. The area of this pronunciation in Italy was formerly much larger than it is today.[39] Latin *cl* > *ch*: Lat. *clavis* > Italian *chiave*, Rom. *cheie* (as opposed to French *clé*); Lat. *Sclavus* > Arum. *scl'eau*, N. Rom. *şchiau*.

There are also a few particular features of *morphology and syntax*, such as the plural of the nouns in the third declension in -*i*: Italian *monti*, Rom. *munţi*. Some changes characteristic of East Latin also appeared in the conjugation; in the first conjugation, the type *izo/ amus* was spread in Moesia, in certain Rhaeto-Romanic dialects, partly in southern Italy, and is present also in Romanian. The construction of the future by the auxiliary verb corresponding to Latin *vol o* "I will" is found in Romanian, partly in Dalmatian, and in the Tosc dialect of Albanian, as well as in other Balkan languages.[40]

Lexical elements: More than 100 Latin words exist exclusively in Romanian, for example Lat. *adjutorium* > N. Rom. *ajutor, blanditia* > *blîndeţe, lingula* > *lingură*.[41] There are Latin words that appear exclusively in Romanian and Dalmatian, and another, larger group, found only in Romanian and Albanian, such as Lat. *densus* > N. Rom. *des*, Dalmatian *dais*; Lat. *cerebrum* > N. Rom. *creier* "brain," Albanian *krie* "head"; Lat. *imperator* > N. Rom. *împărat*, Alb. *mbret* "king." All these words must have existed in East Latin.

The Latin words that did not exist in East Latin are more difficult to determine. Beginning with Romanian, one may state that the number of Latin words found in most of the Romance idioms but not in Romanian is high. Of all Romance languages, it is, in fact, Romanian that has the fewest Latin lexical elements.[42] There are 214 such words, of which 129 are nouns, 26 adjectives, 5 adverbs, 13 numbers, 38 verbs, and 3 particles.[43] These words are largely grouped in certain semantic areas, and it is characteristic that the Latin terms regarding urban life are among them. There are, for example, 11 marine terms, 12 connected with farming, 8 terms of commerce, and 8 of civilization, as well as many important everyday words, such as *amo* "I love," *corpus* "body," *dexter* "right," *hortus* "garden," *laboro* "I work," *nego* "I deny," *pauper* "poor," *sapio* "I know," *semper* "always," *uia* "way." The lack of these words in present-day Romanian does not, of course, prove their lack in East Latin as well. It is not plausible that the Latin terms of commerce and urban life in general were lacking in the speech of the Romans living in the numerous Roman towns of the Balkan Peninsula. An attempt to determine which of these words really were absent in East Latin was made in *Istoria limbii române* (ILR).[44] One of the criteria was whether the word in question was, in Romanian, replaced by another Latin word or by a foreign borrowing; and the other, the situation in the Romanian language of the family of the words that disappeared.

The frequent use of certain suffixes is characteristic of East Latin: *ex* (*de ex*), *extra*, *cf.*, Ital. *scapeta*, N. Rom. *scăpăta* "to set down, to decline," Ital. *stravecchio* "old," N. Rom. *străvechi* "ancient"; *in*: Sicilian dialectal *intiniriri* "to rejuvenate," N. Rom. *întineri*.

The lack of a large number of urban terms suggests that the population's way of life was a rural one. This is also indicated by the *changes of meaning* of a number of Latin words, many of which are shared by Romanian and Albanian. There are, for example, N. Rom. *pădure*, Alb. *püli* "forest," from Lat. *palus* (genitive *paludis*), Vulgar Lat. *padule* "marsh"; N. Rom. *şes*, Alb. *shesh* "lowland," from Lat. *sessum* (*sedere* "to sit"). Other examples of changes of meaning shared by Romanian and Albanian are words of everyday use, such as N. Rom. *cuvînt* "word," *cuvînta* "to say, to utter, to speak," Alb. *kuvendoj* "I discuss," from Lat. *conventus* "district court, session, agreement"; N. Rom. *cui* "nail," Alb. *kuj*, with the same sense, from Lat. *cuneus* "wedge." The largest semantic group among these words concerns the pastoral way of life, that is, they are Latin words whose sense was adapted to the conditions of this life: Lat. *meridies* "middle day" > N. Rom. *meriză* "place where the cattle rests at midday"; *animalia* "animals" > N. Rom. *nămaie* "small cattle"; *coccineus* "scarlet red" > N. Rom. dialectal (Oltenia): *coasin* "sheep with reddish spots on its head."

There are several groups of words (and other elements of language) shared by Romanian, Italian, Sardinian, and Corsican; by Romanian and the dialect of Calabria; by Romanian and the southern Italian dialects; by Romanian and Sardinian.[45] An interesting group among these lexical elements is that of thirty pastoral and peasant words shared by Romanian and the southern Italian dialects. Rosetti considers that these correspondences cannot be explained by simple coincidence but attributes them to the colonization of Dacia Traiana during the roman period by colonists from Dalmatia, who introduced the idioms spoken in Apulia to Dacia.[46] This is a possibility that cannot, in certain cases, be excluded; but it must be remembered that correspondences between Romanian and the idioms from the area in question exist also from the period after 275 A.D., when Dacia Traiana no longer belonged to the empire and such colonization was no longer possible.

Late Latin

The problem of the unity or diversity of the Latin language is a much debated question. Since the texts were in general written in a language that the writer or author considered correct, the speech of the common people was not directly preserved in them. One might say that most of the East Latin characteristics belong to post-classical Latin (from about 14 A.D. to around 200 A.D.) or Late Latin (after 200 A.D.).[47] Many elements of the popular or vulgar speech (*sermo urbanus, rusticus, plebeius, vulgaris*) were preserved in Latin grammars, whose authors tried to combat the "erroneous" forms, giving examples of the "mistakes" along with forms considered correct at the time. One of the most useful of these is the *Appendix Probi*, from the late sixth or the seventh century,[48] with 277 "incorrect" forms. Latin glossaries also give lists of Latin words, explaining them by terms generally known at the time. Such is the *Glosses of Reichenau*, written in northern France in the eighth century. Other sources of popular speech are inscriptions (often with "incorrect" forms), technical texts, and laws; the Christian authors, who used a language that was understood by the people, contributed much in this respect. From the sixth century on, historical treatises give valuable information about contemporary Latin.[49]

Late Latin forms can also be deduced from the Romance languages. In general, if a characteristic is found in all or most of these or in a geographically ascertainable group of them, it is considered to have existed in Late Vulgar Latin; there are, however, many exceptions to this rule.

Changes in language occur usually successively, over considerable lengths of time, and not necessarily simultaneously through the entire territory where the idiom is spoken. In Latin most of the innovations began in Rome and spread later throughout the whole territory of the empire. It is often difficult to determine the earliest date of a particular feature. An innovation that became general in a certain century may have had much earlier precursors. Then there is also the possibility that different Romance languages changed independently in the same direction on the basis of a similar structure. It is, however, improbable that usages that were considered wrong as late as in the fifth to seventh centuries A.D. would have already existed before 275 A.D. The great majority of changes that lead from Latin to the Romance languages probably occurred after that year, that is, after the Roman retreat from Dacia Traiana.

Assuming that the speakers of the Latin idiom from which Romanian developed lived outside the Roman Empire after 275 A.D., one would expect considerable differences between Romanian and the rest of the Romance languages with regard to the Late Latin developments. A comparison from this point of view of Romanian with the other idioms of the Apennino-Balkan group and also with the rest of the Romance languages is therefore indispensable.

The Changes of Late Latin Continued in Romanian
Phonology

Vowels: Stressed short Latin *e* was diphthongized, according to the grammars, in the fifth century A.D. The language of the ancestors of the Romanians took part in this change, as shown by Arumanian *a(i)eri*, from classical Latin *heri*, "yesterday," N. Romanian *fier*, from Lat. *ferrum*. This change in late Latin should not be confused with the pronunciation with an *i* of initial *e/iel*, for *el*, which became the rule in N. Rom. (but not in Arumanian) after the eleventh century as a result of the symbiosis with South Slavs.

Latin *malum* "apple" had had a phonetic variant *melum*. This form became general in Late Latin and resulted in Italian *melo*, Rom. *măr* (both of which presuppose Latin *melum*).

Latin unstressed *i* was confused with *e*: Lat. *vicinus*, Spanish *vecino*, Provençal *vezin*, Rom. *vecin*; Lat. *civitatem*, Rom. *cetate*. Latin *silvaticus* (from *silva* "forest") had a popular variant: *salvaticus*. This variant is the basis of Italian *salvatico*, Friulian *salvadi*, French *sauvage*, and Rom. *sălbatec*.[50]

Consonants: *c* + *e*, *i* > *č*. - In the texts written in the western parts of the empire, some examples of this change are found as early as in the fifth century A.D.; but on the Balkan Peninsula, it is not found even in the sixth century.[51] Other indications of its late date are a number of German place names transferred from Latin during the fifth to sixth centuries: Lat. *Celio Monte* (in 470 A.D.) > German

Kellmünz, Lat. *Celeusum* (6th century) > German *Kelsbach.* Also German *Keller* (Old Germanic *kelari*) and Old Germanic *kista,* from Latin *cellarium* and *cista,* respectively, presuppose a *k* in the Latin words pronounced in the fifth century, when they were transferred to Old Germanic.[52]

In Arumanian, Lat. *c* + *e, i* corresponds to *ţ,* in N. Rom., to *č.*[53] Dalmatian had *č* before *i* but preserved *k* before *e.*

Lat. *t* + *e, i* and *d* + *e, i* were assibilated after the sixth century: Lat. *terra* > N. Rom. *ţară* "land"; Lat. *teneo* > N. Rom. *ţin* "I hold"; Lat. *decem* > Arum. *dzate,* N. Rum. *zece* "ten"; Lat. *deus* > Arum. *dzău,* N. Rom. *zeu* "god". The assibilation of Lat. *d* + *e, i,* followed by a vowel started as early as the second century[54] (Lat. *medius* > N. Rom. *miez* "the midst").

Intervocalic *v* disappeared in certain situations: *Appendix Probi* writes: "*rivus non rius,*" and *v* changed in certain cases to *b*: Appendix *Probi: "alveus non albeus."* Both innovations appear in several Romance languages: Late Latin *rius* > N. Rom. *rîu,* and Late Latin *albeus* > N. Rom. *albie.* The case of intervocalic *b* is similar: Lat. *caballus* > N. Rom. *cal,* Lat. *vivus* > N. Rom. *viu;* and in some instances *-br-* disappeared too: Lat. *fabrum* > N. Rom. *faur.*

Intervocalic *b,* pronounced as present-day English *w,* followed by *u* changed to *g*: Lat. *nebula* > N. Rom. *negură,* Lat. *rubus* > N. Rom. *rug,* Italian *rogo.* The *w* > *g* change after *a, o* and *u* is attested to in Late Latin texts.

Before *a,* Lat. *kʷ* changed to *k* in the West; in East Latin and in Sardinian, only in the following words:

Latin:	Romanian:	Vegliote:	Sardinian:	Old Italian:	Friulian:
qualis	*care*	*kal*	*kale*	—	—
quam	*ca*	—	*ca*	*ca*	—
quando	*cînd*	*cand*	*kando*	—	*cand*
quantus	*cît*	*kont*	*kantu*	—	—

This is explained by the hypothesis that these words were drawn into the sphere of the Latin pronouns *quid* > N. Rom. *ce, quem* > N. Rom. *cine.*[55] In all other instances, Latin *kʷ* developed in Romanian to *p,* in Sardinian to *b*: Lat. *aqua* > Sardinian *abba,* Rom. *apă.* In this respect, the Latin elements in Albanian are different from Romanian: Lat. *quattuor* > Alb. *katrë,* Lat. *quadragesima* > Alb. *kreshmë* (as opposed to N. Rom. *patru* and *păresimi,* respectively.)[56]

Morphology: The flexion of the noun shows the syncretisms of Late Latin, in the same way as in all the other Romance languages: the genitive merged with the dative and the accusative with the ablative. The three genders are preserved in a way that may be deduced from the late texts and from the other Romance languages: "The tendency of grouping the inanimate objects as neutrals, the plural neutral in -*a* and -*ora*, the accord of the neutral nouns in the plural with the feminine form of the adjective."[57]

Since all the idioms that came from Common Romanian have the definite article, this must have existed in Common Romanian. The form *illorum*, genitive until the seventh century and after that period also dative, gives a more exact date: " . . . the definite article appears in Common Romanian after the seventh century, when positive signs of the reorganization of the flexion of the nouns are observed."[58]

Also the verbal flexion corresponds to the late patterns.[59] The Romanian compound perfect (*habere* + past participle) "came from constructions in which *habere* indicated possession and received the value of the perfect not earlier than after the fourth century."[60] For example: *promissum enim habemus . . . nihil sine eius consilio agere* "we have promised . . . not to undertake anything without his knowledge," in the text of Gregorius Turonensis, Gallia, from the years 538 to 594 A.D.; *Matheum quem ante te ibi missum habui* "Matheus whom I have sent there before you," in *Acta Andreae et Matthiae apud anthropophagos*, Italia, sixth to eighth centuries A.D.[61] *Cf.*, the Romanian compound perfect: Arum. *mi-amᵘ dúsi-m-pizári* "I went to the town" (" I have been in the town"), N. Rom. *m-am dus la oraş* "id." The auxiliary used here is, in Arum., *amᵘ, ai̯, ari; avémᵘ, avéţⁱ, au*,[62] and in N. Rom., grammaticized, *am, ai, a; am, aţi, au*, from Lat. *habeo* "I have."

Lexicology: A series of new expressions appeared during the Late Latin period. A large group consists of terms used and partly created by the Christian Church.[63] This process was going on beginning in the first centuries A.D., although it became most intense during the fourth century. *Basilica* with the sense of "church," for example, is attested to beginning in the fourth century.[64] A term of Byzantine origin, it is found in Dalmatian (*basalka*), Albanian (*bjeske*), and Romanian (*biserică*): in the Western Romance languages, *ecclesia*, with the original sense of "community of the Christians" was continued: *basilica* is preserved probably in some place names and in the Engadin dialect (*baselgia*). Most of the basic Romanian terms of the Christian faith are of Latin origin: Lat. *angelus* > Rom. *înger* "angel," Lat. *baptizo* > Rom. *boteza* "to baptize, to name," Lat. *paganus* Rom. *păgîn* "heathen." It is sometimes asserted that missionaries from the empire were active in Dacia during the fourth century and that they could have taught these terms to the "Daco-Romans" living there.[65]

This is not *a priori* impossible, although there are only vague reports about early Christian missionaries north of the lower Danube.

It is not necessary, however, to assume missionaries north of the Danube to explain the presence of this group of words in the Romanian language. The general rule is that the Late Latin innovations in lexicology (as in the other branches of language) appear also in Romanian. The *Glosses of Reichenau*, written in Gallia in the eighth century, contains several words in use during the Late Latin period and different from the classical forms. These are found also in Romanian. The following examples are given by Iancu Fischer:[66]

Classical Latin	Eighth Century	French	Romanian
femur	*coxa*	*cuisse*	*coapsă*
seuit	*seminavit* (perfect tense)	*semer*	*semăna*
emit	*comparavit* (perfect tense)	*acheter* (from Lat. *accaptare*; descendents of *compar- are* are found in southern Gallia)	*cumpăra*
flare	*suflare*	*souffler*	*sufla*
concidit	*taliauit*	*tailler*	*tăia*
iecore	*ficato*	*foie*	*ficat*
catulus	*cateilus*	*chael*	*cățel*
uocaui	*clamui* (perfect tense)	*appeler,* (from Lat. *appellare*	*chema*
detegere	*discooperire*	*découvrir*	*descoperi*
fissura	*crepatura*	possibly Old French *creveure*	*crăpătură*

This text also contains characteristics specific to Gallia, among them some transferred from Old Germanic. For example, instead of classical Latin *dem* "that I give," in the eighth century Gallia used *donem*, from which French *donner* derived, while Romanian has *da*; similarly, classical Latin *opilio*, eighth century Gallia (. . .) *berbicarius*, from which French *berger* derived, while Romanian has *păcurar*, from Latin *pecorarius*.

Appendix Probi lists many "erroneous" forms, giving what in the sixth to seventh centuries was considered correct by the grammaticians. The parallelism between Romanian and the rest of the Romance languages is evident also here:[67]

Classical Latin, considered as correct by grammaticians of the sixth century:	Latin spoken by the people in the sixth century:	Romanian
uetulus	*ueclus*	*vechi*
tristis	*tristus*	*trist*
auris	*oricla*	*ureche*

palumbes	*palumbus*	*porumb*
oculus	*oclus*	*ochi*
socrus	*socra*	*soacră*
uiridis	*uirdis*	*verde*

In *Itinerarium Egeriae*, written in about the year 400 A.D., probably in northwestern Spain, the verb "to eat" is expressed by *manduco* and the words *edo* and *comedo* do not appear. Spanish preserved, however, *comedo*, while *manduco* was preserved in Italian and in Romanian (*mangiare* and *mânca*, respectively). The verb *plicare* was, in the classical texts, used in the sense of "to bend, to curve"; in this text from 400 A.D. it means "to go toward." This sense was preserved in Portuguese, Spanish, and also Romanian (*chegar, llegar* and *pleca*, respectively).

In the Late Latin period, short words were increasingly replaced by longer ones, which were felt to be more distinct: for example, instead of classical Latin *aes* "metal, copper," one said *aeramen*, from which Italian *rame*, Northern Romanian *aramă* "copper." The original Romanian word for the Slavs (Northern Romanian *șchiau*, Arumanian *scl'eau*) derives from the Late Latin name given to the Sloven branch of the Slavic peoples: *Sclavus* (or *Sclavinus*), attested to beginning with the sixth century.[68] This word is found also in Albanian: *shqua* "Bulgarian" (plur. *shque*). The correspondence with Albanian is in this case revealing also because the Romanians' ancestors, if they had lived north of the Danube in the sixth to seventh centuries, would have met other groups of Slavs than the Slovenes and would hardly have borrowed a designation used on the Balkan Peninsula to name them.

During the Late Latin period, several Latin words changed their meaning. Reliable data about the century in which the change occurred are extant, for example, about *hostis* "enemy." This sense changed, beginning with the sixth century to "army." Romanian *oaste*, Spanish *hueste* and Portuguese *hoste* continue this sense.[69] Latin *necare* "to kill" received, also during the sixth century, a narrower sense: "to choke, suffocate, stifle," gradually developing the sense of "to drown," continued by French *noyer* and Romanian *îneca*.

Late Latin Characteristics Not Found in Romanian

It is evident that Romanian is based on Late (Vulgar) Latin like the other Romance languages and to the same degree. This applies to the entire structure of language as well as to particularities of minor significance. This was concisely stated by ILR, II, 1969 (p. 15–16): "The partial systems that constitute its [of the Romanian language] grammatical structure continue without any interruption the original Latin systems, almost all of the linguistic changes that occurred between the fifth and the eighth century being found in one form or another in Late Danubian Latin."[70] (Here "Late Danubian Latin" stands for the idiom spoken by the ancestors of the Romanians).

The reason why a discussion of the exceptions to this rule is necessary is that Romanian linguists have repeatedly mentioned the isolation of Dacia in the third century A.D., which would explain the lack of some Late Latin innovations in the Romanian language:"From the third century onwards, Rome in fact no longer possessed the strength to impose its lexical innovations upon the remote and more autonomous provinces, such as Dacia. A series of words, known through the occidental Romance languages, do not penetrate into Dacia: *aviaticus, carruca, (ex)tutare, sugia,* and others."[71] A number of terms could not have penetrated into Dacia because they spread at a late period of time.[72]

The examples given are, however, neither significant nor numerous. All that Rosetti mentions in this context are those four lexical elements above. Mihăescu presents somewhat more; all of his examples will be presented and analyzed in the following:

1. The expression *in se* "together, in the same time" (*cf.,* Italian insieme) appears in Gallia, Italia, Dalmatia, Pannonia Inferior, and Moesia Inferior beginning with the third century: "very probably, it was a late innovation that did not circulate in Dacia."

2. Two words of Old Germanic origin appeared in the documents after the third century and do not exist in Romanian: *brutis* "bride" and *sculca* "military guard."

3. Some lexical elements appear only in Dalmatia and in Noricum: *anna* "mother, nurse," *socerio* "brother-in-law," *sponsa* "spouse" (instead of *marita* or *mulier*).

4. The word *mansio* "building, post station" remained unfamiliar north of the Danube, "because Dacia was situated outside of the large trade and military routes that connected Constantinople and Asia Minor with Italia and Gallia."

5. The propagation of *e* in words such as *espiritus, esponsa* (*cf.,* French *esprit, épouse*) did not go farther than Dalmatia.

6. The suffix *-ment(e),* originating from western Romania in the fifth century, "remained on the surface and could not penetrate into the masses in the Danubian provinces."

Some of even these few features represent differences between the Balkan Romance idioms (including Romanian) and the Western Romance languages: *anna, socerio,* and *sponsa,* as well as *e* in such words as *espiritus* appeared in the Balkans only in Dalmatia; and the suffix *-ment(e)* is absent from all Balkan Romance idioms. The word *brutis,* of Old Germanic origin, exists only in Rhaeto-Romanic *(brut)* and French *(bru).*[73] The absence of numerous lexical elements does not have much importance here; every Romance language shows the absence of several words that exist in the other Romance idioms. Moreover, the Latin words that are lacking in Romanian are grouped in specific semantic groups, which suggests that they disappeared for social reasons rather than isolation from the rest of the Romance idioms.

The Relationship of the Territory of Former Dacia Traiana to the Roman Provinces South of the Danube During the Late Latin Period

The relationship between the former province of Dacia Traiana and the Roman provinces south of the Danube in the Late Latin period is an important, if not decisive, factor in the question of the territorial evolution of the Romanian language. First of all, it is necessary to clarify whether the relationship between the former province of Dacia Traiana and the Roman Empire, specifically to the Romanized regions south of the Danube, was retained even after the abandonment of the province and, if so, to what extent. Furthermore, it is needful to prove which specific linguistic differentiations occurred in the Late Latin in general, that is, in the period from the third to the sixth century.

The historical circumstances argue in favor of the presumption that no large-scale communication among peoples was possible between the area of former Dacia Traiana and the Roman Empire across the Danube, as had been the case earlier when the province belonged to the empire.

Changes in the political situation much less radical than detachment from the Roman Empire resulted in the development of regional differences in the Latin language. The division of the empire in 395 A.D. into two halves is considered to have caused a divergent development of the Balkan Romance idioms from the language spoken in the West[74]; both halves were Roman states and had relations with each other quite different from those that prevailed between the empire and Barbaricum in the third century. The territory of the former Dacian province was, after 275 A.D., separated from the empire by the Danubian frontier, which was guarded by the Roman army. Communication with the empire was not entirely disrupted; Christianity, for example, was spread during the fourth century among the Goths living north of the Danube. Also, as in the case of most other European areas, trade contacts have been attested to by archaeological finds. Roman merchants probably traveled through the territory to distant places, but such activity had no significant effect upon the language of the masses. Local trade involved more people and also those living in Barbaricum, who were allowed to visit certain market places. This occurred under strict military supervision, not only for the security of the empire but also in order that the different customs regulations be enforced.[75] Such markets were permitted at only a few places; in 369 A.D., for example, there were only two along the entire Gothic frontier.[76] Even if more market places were permitted in the period when the frontier became weaker and trade increased, it is obvious that the contacts were restricted both to a very small proportion of the population and to the Roman market places along the (Danubian) border. Under these circumstances, no significant movement of peoples across the Danubian *limes* was possible, at least during the first centuries after the abandonment of Dacia by the empire. The occupation by the eastern empire of certain areas in southern Muntenia and Oltenia and possibly also of the southern Banat for some decades in the fourth century cannot be considered as having promoted communication on a large-scale between the Latin-speaking inhabitants of the south and the populations living north of the Danube.

Consequently, if a Roman population remained in Dacia Traiana after the retreat of the Roman army and administration in 275 A.D., its Latin language could no longer have developed in the same way that it did earlier, in close contact with speakers of Latin in the Balkan Peninsula and in Italy. If there was such a language, it must have eventually disappeared, its speakers having been assimilated to the surrounding Goths, free (non-Romanized) Dacians, Gepidae, and the other populations known to have been living there after the Roman era; nothing will probably ever be known about it. But the ancestors of the Romanians, whose language contains all the Late Latin characteristics, must have been in close contact with the speakers of Late Latin, and thus can not have been living north of the Danube in the epoch of Late Latin (the 4th - 8th centuries A.D.).

Conclusion

Romanian is a Romance language that contains, to the same degree as the other Romance languages, all the characteristics of Late Latin, that is, the changes that appeared in Latin during the third to seventh centuries. It also shows the peculiar characteristics of East Latin, that is, correspondences with the southern Italian dialects, Dalmatian, and the Latin elements of Albanian and Serbo-Croatian. This implies that the ancestors of the Romanians lived in close contact with the speakers of East Latin not only at the beginning of the Late Latin period (from around 200 A.D. to 275 A.D.) but also during the following centuries, probably up to the eighth century. An analysis of the historical records and the archaeological findings from the period shows that such contacts did not exist between the empire and the inhabitants of the territory of former Dacia Traiana, which was separated from the Roman world by the Danubian frontier. The assertions of Romanian scholars that after the Roman withdrawal Dacia could not have remained entirely isolated from the Romanized areas south of the Danube until the end of the sixth century and that there were religious contacts through the intermediacy of Byzantium[77] is sheer hypothesis.[78] Other circumstances, such as trade contacts and the occupation by the empire of some areas north of the Danube for short periods of time, do not suggest contacts of any linguistic significance. Consequently, the ancestors of the Romanians could not have been living, in the Late Latin period, in the territories north of the Danube; but they did belong to the Roman population living in the Balkan Peninsula.

THE PROBLEM OF THE ETHNO-LINGUISTIC SUBSTRATUM

Ancient Indo-European Elements in Romanian

Pre-Roman remnants in Romanian have been analyzed by several linguists, and many bold hypotheses have been advanced at the expense of scientific evidence.[79] A number of Romanian words may derive from Indo-European roots. Romanian *rezema* "to lean, to rest," for example, could derive from Indo-European *reg'* "right; to straighten, to raise helping,"[80] which developed into *re(d)zem, ra(d)zem,* in a satem language. The same Indo-European root is at the basis of Latin *regem, regimen,* and of Celtic *rig-;* but Romanian *rezema* cannot have derived from these languages because of the *(d)z.* Ion I. Russu gives 166 such Indo-European roots which, with more or less probability, could, on the basis of Romanian words, be of pre-Latin origin:[81] Indo-European *bhas-k* "band, bundle, handle," romanian *bască* "wool" (*cf.,* Albanian *bashkë,* id.); Indo-European *bhol* "steam, smell," Romanian *boare* "breath of wind"; Indo-European *dereu(o)* "branch, tree," Romanian dialect *druete* "wood" (*cf.,* Albanian *dru,* "id."); *ster* "sterile," Romanian *sterp* "sterile, lifeless."

These lexical elements probably originate from a pre-Latin language, the substratum of Romanian. This language contains, however, substratum elements in other areas as well: phonetics, morphology, and syntax. The criteria for deciding the substratum origin of any element of an unknown etymology are given by Cicerone Poghirc[82] and summarized in English by André Du Nay.[83] Ideally, elements of Ancient Romanian (or Common Romanian), before the development of the dialects, should be used. One of the main criteria for establishing the substratum origin of any element of language is its existence in Albanian. Poghirc maintains, however, that other Indo-European languages, including the old Balkan languages, must also be taken into consideration and, above all, the remains, even if questionable and uncertain, of Daco-Moesian, which have been almost totally neglected until now. Reference to Indo-European roots is not sufficient; words actually existing in one Indo-European language or another must be sought and the entire Romanian word explained.

The elements most probably from the substratum are: in *phonetics*, the phonemes /ă/ and /h/ and the *kt* > *pt* (Albanian *ft*) change; and in *morphology*, the definite article and the particle -*ne* of the accusative of the personal pronoun (the neuter gender in Romanian also probably has some connection with the substratum). About 10 to 13 suffixes probably originate from the substratum, of which -*esc* is very common. It is found in Thracian (-*isko*) with the same value as in Romanian and in Albanian (Alb. -*ish*); in Latin, this suffix appeared in words borrowed from Greek or Thracian. This problem will be discussed in some more detail below, in connection with the elements that Romanian shares with Albanian, including the important group of lexical elements from the substratum.

The pre-Roman Languages of Southeastern Europe

The few remains that have been preserved from the ancient languages spoken in Southeastern Europe before (and, for a considerable period of time, also during) the Roman conquest are not sufficient to determine even their basic characteristics. Thus, it is nearly impossible to set up a linguistic schema for this area. No sentences remained, and we therefore know almost nothing about their grammar. What we do know is a number of lexical elements, most of them without any known meaning, and something about the sound patterns, based on these lexical elements. In the period in question the main languages, after Greek, were Illyrian (in the west) and Thracian (in the east). In smaller, but not insignificant, areas Paeionian, Dardanian, and Scythian (in the northeast) were spoken. Getae and Dacians are mentioned mainly north of the Danube, but their languages and their relations to the Thracians and the Illyrians are not clear. Some scholars also assume that there was a "Daco-Moesian" language. Among the remains of all these languages of the Indo-European family, there are certainly also pre-Indo-European elements. This complex problem can only be summarized briefly here.[84] For Romanian, the essential question is the possible dissemination area in which its substratum-language was spoken. An attempt will therefore be made to analyze the linguistic material from this viewpoint. Since the substratum of Romanian shows very close connections to present-day Albanian, the question of the ancient territories of this population will be investigated too.

Illyrian is generally considered to have been a separate language, spoken in the northwestern parts of the Balkan Peninsula (mainly the south Dalmatian coast and surroundings). About 300 place names, 600 personal names, 80 ethnic names (names of tribes), and 20 names of gods, all found in Greek and Roman texts, are attributed to Illyrian. This, in itself, would represent considerable material; but etymologies have been proposed for only about 10% of these lexical elements, of which 50 to 60 at most are acceptable or certain.[85] Most of the Indo-European sounds seem to have been preserved in Illyrian, as shown by these lexical elements. In general, Illyrian has been considered a satem language;[86] but the division centum/satem is, according to several more recent investigations, not applicable to this language, in which both developments appear. Illyrian and also Thracian are considered to have been spoken in the territory between the centum and the satem areas.[87] According to this view, Albanian shows a similar situation with regard to the phenomena in question. The frontier between Illyrian and Thracian went across Dardania and reached the Danube approximately at present-day Belgrade, but several areas were mixed Illyrian and Thracian. The relationship between these two ancient idioms is quite obscure and has been given various interpretations by different scholars.

Pacionian was spoken south of Dardania (north of present-day Thessaloniki). According to some scholars (Tomaschek, Jokl, Kretschmer), this language belonged to Illyrian; others (Detschew) believe it was similar to Thracian or was a completely separate language (like the Bulgarian linguist I. Duridanov).

Dardanian, spoken mainly in the valley of the Vardar River in the ancient province of Dardania (the region of present-day Niš and Skoplje), is also of unknown origin. Among the ancient authors, Strabon of Amascia[88] considered its speakers to be Illyrians while Polybios[89] said they were not. According to the Bulgarian scholar

Dimităr Dečev, this population was related to the Thracians but had been subdued at some time by the Illyrians. They also can represent an even older Balkan population. Another Bulgarian scholar, Ivan Duridanov, defined them as "Daco-Moesians." The name Dardania could have derived from Albanian *dardhë* "pear tree," and several place names there also seem to originate from Albanian (or from an ancient language but mediated to the Slavs by Albanians).

Thracian. The areas of dissemination of the Thracian language extended into the southeastern part of the Balkan Peninsula, reaching as far as north of the Danube and encompassing contemporary Bulgaria and parts of Greece and Turkey. The disappearance of this language occurred approximately in the middle of the sixth century A.D.; south of the Haemus (Balkan) Mountains it was Helenized and north of there Romanized. It is generally felt that Thracian belonged to the Indo-European languages and consequently must be investigated in this context on the basis of historical linguistic comparisons.

According to the Romanian linguist Ion I. Russu, for instance, the remains of the Geto-Dacian language are fewer in number than the remains of the language of the Southern Thracians. The names of medicinal plants as well as personal and place names present special regional nuances; but the words (or names) with a clear or very probable etymology show that it is possible that only a dialectal differentiation was present between the Geto-Dacians and the Thracians south of the Danube and the Haemus Mountains.[90] In accordance with this view Ion I. Russu discusses the characteristics of "Thraco-Dacian," not differentiating between Thracian and Dacian. It must be stated, however, that most of the material preserved is clearly Thracian (originating from the Balkan Peninsula south of the Danube); the Dacian material is restricted to a few words. Russu's presentation can be summarized as follows.

The "Thraco-Dacian" Linguistic Data

Distinguished scholars, such as Wilhelm Tomaschek, Dimităr Dečev, Vladimir Beševliev, and, more recently, Vladimir Georgiev, Ion I. Russu, and I. Duridanov, have devoted their attention to the Thracian language. It is well known that the Thracians descended from various tribes and only few remnants of their language, in the form of inscriptions, glosses, given names, and place and ethnic names, have survived; even these remnants are sharply contested. From the standpoint of Balkan linguistics, it is first necessary to determine to what extent the Dacians and Getae may be subsumed under the Thracians.

Since no texts but only fragmentary lexical elements have been preserved in this language, virtually nothing is known about Thracian grammar.[91] In Greek texts, 70 to 80 glosses have been found that could be attributed to this language. Only a few of these have a known meaning, and therefore they are not very helpful in the study of language. The main Thracian linguistic data consists of names: There are about 1,190 personal names (890 simple and 300 compound) and 910 place names (700 simple and 210 compound).[92]

Simple names are, for example, Bendis, Bithus, or Abro-zes, Dria-zis, the last two mentioned with suffixes. Compound names are Aulu-centus, Dece-balus, Epta-tralis. In contrast to Illyrian, in which compound names were rare, about one-fourth of the Thracian proper names are compound. The first element is often an adjective, for example, Germi-sara "warm water (source)", Diu-zenus "born from a god."

The endings of the place names in Thracia proper are mainly - *berga, -bria, -burd, -cella, -diza, -pani, -para, -zura*. In the territories north of the Danube, as well as on parts of the Balkan Peninsula, for example Dardania, Dacia Mediterranea, Little Scythia, Lower Moesia, and Thrace proper, the following endings predominate: *-dava, -dina, -sara, -stur*.

On the basis of these glosses, an attempt has been made, to reconstruct *the phonetic features of Thracian*, which Russu summarized as follows:

Vowels: a, e, o are largely preserved; as well as u, (in a few cases given as y). The diphthongs ai, ei (?), oi, au, eu were preserved.

Consonants: u͎ > v (or, in some cases, b). The voiceless occlusives k, p, t and the voiced ones, g, b, d, are preserved; "a consonant shift (*Lautverschiebung*) in Thracian does not appear probable."[92a] Indo-European bh, dh, gh lose their aspiration: b, d, g. The palatal occlusives k', g'(h) are represented by the post-dental spirants s and z (a satem phenomenon); a similar phenomenon is the delabialization of the labiovelars ku͎ and gu͎(h): k, g; the liquids are preserved, as well as m and n; s is preserved in all positions. The group sr is interposed with a t: Strymon, Istros.

Russu's conclusion is that most of the sounds of Indo-European were preserved in Thracian, according to the rules of a satem idiom of the East-European group. Other scholars believe that the centum/satem distinction cannot be applied to Thracian, this language, together with Illyrian, being in an intermediary zone. Thracian seems to have been related to Illyrian and also to Balto-Slavic and to Indo-Iranian. Even less is known about Dacian than about Thracian: The elements preserved from the Dacian language are few and often uncertain with regard to their form and meaning. They are words, proper names (place names, personal names, names of ethnic groups, names of gods), and inscriptions (with uncertain interpretations).[93] A few semantically similar words, however, cannot be designated as Dacian.

With respect to the supposed Dacian names of plants, the linguist C. Váczy stated that the 35 names of plants contained in various versions of Dioscorides Pedanios and those 10 names of plants given by Pseudo-Apuleius could be considered to be of "probable" Dacian origin; but an even partial reconstruction of the language of the Dacians presents a major difficulty and would be extremely dubious.[94]

The name of the Dacians, Δακοι, Δᾶοι, (*Dakoi, Dakai*) is not explained. The Greek *daoi* (wolf) or the Phrygian word *daos* (wolf) may be connected with it (*dhāukos*, Georgiev), but other etymologies have been proposed too.[95]

Similarly little is known about the origin of the ethnic name "Getae." (*gᵘet* "to speak, to talk" ? , *ghend-, *ghed - "to grasp"?).[96] P. Kretschmer believed that the Getae were a Thracian stratum of common people with a Scythian ruling class. They were referred to in Greek texts by names of an Iranian type, such as Massagetai and Taurogetai.[97] Dacian personal names are extant, but their sense is unknown, and they are not helpful in the study of language.[98] The Dacian morphology, most important for the investigation of this language, is nearly unknown.[99]

With regard to the language spoken by the Getae, there is a single record by the Greek geographer Strabon of Amascia (60 B.C.–20 A.D.), who stated that "the Getae spoke the same language as the Dacians."[100] This assertion is, however, no longer generally accepted:"The affirmation made by Strabon (VII,3,10) that the Dacians spoke the same language as the Getae, who had the same language as the Thracians, (VII,3,13), should not be given more credence than the assertions of Italian travelers in the Romanian countries in the sixteenth century, who believed that Romanian was a dialect of Italian".[101] The Bulgarian scholar D. Simenov also argued that Dacian and Getian were two different languages.[102] With the lack of sufficient data, this question cannot be clarified.

The existence of a "Daco-Moesian" language has been assumed by the Bulgarian epigraphist and linguist Vladimir Georgiev,[103] who believed that the speakers of this idiom migrated from the territories north of the Danube to the areas of the Roman provinces of Dardania, Dacia Mediterranea, and Dacia Ripensis as early as during the second millenium B.C. This population was, according to Georgiev, the ancestors of the Albanians and their language the substratum of Romanian. This migration is, of course, difficult to substantiate; and the linguistic arguments proposed by Georgiev in favor of a "Daco-Moesian" language, compared with Thracian, are vague and unconvincing.[104]

This does not, however apply to the idea that the language of the ancestors of the Albanians was the substratum of Romanian; this may be investigated by comparing the two languages.

Thracian and Dacian

Russu's opinion that Thracian and Dacian ("Geto-Dacian") were dialects of the same language is based on very weak evidence. Russu seems to be aware of this when he says that it is possible that this was so. The frontier between Thracian in the south and "Geto-Dacian" is also given only approximately (the lower Danube? The Haemus Mountains?)[105] The identity (or very close relationship) of these idioms is not generally accepted. On the basis of a comparison of what is known about the phonetical characteristics of the ancient Southeastern European languages (after V. Georgiev), *Istoria limbii române* (1969) considers that Illyrian, Thracian, and Dacian were separate languages:[106]

Ind.-Eur.	Dacian	Alb.	Thrac.	Illyr.	Phryg.	Arm.	Maced.	Greek
o	a	a	a	o,a	o	o	o	o
n̥	a(n?)	ën,un	un		un	an	a	a(n)
r̥	ri	ir,ri	ur		ur	ar	ar	ar,ra
		(ur)						
Tenues (Surde)	T	T	TA	T	TA	TA	T	T
Mediae (Sonore)	M	M	T	M	T	T	M	M
k′	s	s(p̃)	s(p̃)	k(s?)	s	s	k	k
kȗ̯	k(p?)	k	kh	k	kh	kh	p	kȗ̯

It must be emphasized that this table comprises only a few phonetical elements, that is, it is not exhaustive even with regard to the sounds and does not contain anything about other areas of language. Nevertheless, it seems reasonable to assume that the above-mentioned languages were distinct from one another. In the conditions of Southeastern Europe at that time, with many tribes living without any large and stable political organization in a vast and geographically heterogenous territory, it is not probable that a uniform language would have been spoken throughout any large area. Today six major languages (and other idioms with smaller communities of speakers) are spoken in that territory. The ethnic diversity of the Balkan Peninsula was certainly not less in pre-historic times than it is in the modern times.[107]

The Problem of the Dacian Elements in Romanian

One of the basic problems of the history of the Romanian language is that of the special idiom spoken by the ancestors of the Romanians before their Romanization. One approach to analyzing this problem is that used by the German linguist Günter Reichenkron. Departing from the belief that the pre-Latin elements of Romanian were necessarily derived from Dacian, Reichenkron constructed various theories that connected more than one hundred Romanian words of unknown origin with assumed Dacian lexical elements. Reichenkron also assumed a consonant shift from Indo-European to Dacian (bh > b, dh > d, g > k, b > p, and d > t). A typical example of these etymologies is the following scheme:[108]

Dacian *barðo* is, however, not attested to in any source and is also unnecessary; Romanian *barză* could as well derive from Indo-European *bhərəg* via prehistoric Albanian *barðo*. Deleting one of the assumptions in Reichenkron's scheme, it should be written as follows:

Ind.-Eur. *bhərəg*⟶prehistoric Albanian *barðo*⟶ Alb. bardhë barth
                                                        Rom. barză
                                                        Rom. bárd + (-áș/oș)

The vague etymologies of the German linguist Günter Reichenkron have been refuted by most scholars (Georgiev, Hubschmid, Russu, and Rosetti). Although Reichenkron's ability to investigate the substratum may be recognized, it is difficult to go along with him in the details; and, with regard to the hypotheses on morphology, it is not convincing. The way in which Reichenkron uses the declared principles in his etymologies, as well as the great majority of his examples, is unlikely and unacceptable, because they ignore Romanian etymological laws, in the first place, as well as the phonetic laws of Romanian and of Thraco-Dacian.[108a] Of those 130 Romanian words for which Reichenkron proposed a Dacian etymology, only four (*leagăn, melc, viscol,* and *băiat*) are accepted by Russu as "Thraco-Dacian" (not Dacian, thus not giving any indication of an origin north of the Danube).[109]

A Comparison of the pre-Roman Lexical Elements in Romanian with Thracian and Dacian Words

A basic question is whether those more than 100 pre-Latin words in Romanian (or any of them) appear in an ancient Southeastern European language and, if so, in which language? The possibilities of finding an answer are strongly restricted by the limited number words with a known meaning in Illyrian, Thracian, and Dacian. Moreover, the ancient lexical elements are preserved in texts written not by native speakers but mainly by Greek and Roman authors and in many cases are probably not quite correct. An analysis of the Thracian lexical data[110] gives seven words for which there exists a Romanian word from the substratum:

Thracian:		*Romanian:*
Buzo-, cozeil	"male goat"	ţap
-centus, poris	"child"	copil
Gordion, -gordum	town name in Phrygia	gard "fence, enclosure, pilework"
-maros, -mērula	"big"	mare
-para, -vissos	"hamlet, small village"	cătun
priadila	"tendril, stem"	curpen
Rome-	"joy"	bucurie

Only two of these seven Romanian substratum words show a similarity with the Thracian word *mare,* "big," and *gard,* "fence, enclosure, pilework." Romanian *mare* has been connected with one part of such compound personal names as Βηριμαρος, Καρσιμαρος. It could derive from Indo-European **mero-,* moro-, "big, stately"; *cf.,* for example, Old High German **mār* in names such as Volkmār, Hlodomār.[111] Romanian *gard* has been connected with names of towns: Gordion, Manegordum. The sense of these names is not known, however; and it therefore cannot be determined whether *"gord"* really has something to do with Romanian *gard.* Romanian *gard* could derive from Indo-European **gerdh,* "to knit, to enclose"; it also exists in Albanian *gardh,* "fence, enclosure."

Istoria limbii romăne lists 35 words "for which a substratum etymology is probable or at least possible" and that have been "connected with words known in Daco-Moesian or other ancient Balkan languages."[112] Of these, 11 refer to Thracian words and 2 to Dacian ones; in one case, similar words are found in both.

Romanian *argea:* "room (made in earth)," Thracian αργιλος, "mouse"; Albanian *ragal,* "hut," Old Macedonian άργελλα, "id."
baltă: "swamp, marsh," Thracian toponym *Di-baltum,* "two marshes" (near Burgas, Bulgaria). Albanian *baltë,* "mud, swamp."

buză: "lip," Thracian *Byzas, Byzos,* Dacian *Beusas;* also Illyrian *Buzos, Buzetius;* Byzantion "town on the shore." Albanian *buzë,* "lip." *drum*: "road," Thracian 'Aνά ζραιμος, translated as "nine roads"; Greek δρόμος, Albanian *dhrom,* "id." *mal*: "shore, bank, edge." Thracian toponym *Malua,* Dacia Maluensis, translated to Dacia Ripensis, also Illyrian *Malontum, Dimallum,* cf., Alb. *Dimale,* "two mountains." The ancient Albanian form is reconstructed as **mol-no;* modern Alb. *mal,* "mountain," Romanian *mal,* "bank, mountain."
(Northern *măldac, maldac* Rom. dialectal): "bunch of hay," Thracian μανζάκης, "id." Modern Greek μανζακης, "bundle of osier willow" is considered to be a loan from Thracian.
mînz: "foal," Thracian *Mezenai,* (the surname of the Thracian knight) and a reconstructed Thracian stem **mel(d)z-* "to milk." Albanian (Tosc dialect) *mës, mëzi,* (Gheg dialect), *mâz, maz,* fem. *mëzë.*
murg: "dark," Thracian toponym Mυργίςκη and name of a tribe Mόργητες. Indo-European *mer(ə)g,*"to become dark," Albanian *murk, murgu,* "dark."
rămf rîmf, rimf, remf: (only in Northern Romanian, Transylvania) "Aristolochia clematitis," German "Osterluzei." Thracian ρομφαία, "lance." Transylvanian Saxon *Rimf(ərt)* "Tanacetum vulgare," German "Rainfarn."
scai: "thistle," *Cirsium lanceolatum,* Thracian σκάλμη, μάχαιρα Θρακία, Greek σκόλυμος, "artichoke, Cynara scolymus." Albanian *halë,* "chip, sliver," *hele,* "lance."
şiroadă: "tub, vat," *şirimpîu,* "canal." Thracian σῖρος, σεῖρος, "cavity in which cereals were laid down," probably of Thracian origin. Armenian *širim,* "cavity, tomb."

In most of these cases, the connection of the Romanian word with the Thracian one is questionable and is only one of several etymologies that have been proposed. Frequently, the meaning of the Thracian word is unknown (place names); but even if it is known and fits or may in some way be connected with the sense of the Romanian word, it is no proof of connection. Northern Romanian *rămf, rîmf, remf, rimpf* "Aristolochia clematitis," German *Osterluzei,* for example, has been connected with Thracian ρομφαία, "lance." The semantic explanation seemed obvious: the leaves of this plant are lanceshaped (Hasdeu). This Romanian word appears only in Northern Romanian, however; and even there, it is dialectal and found in Transylvania. Therefore, the etymology from Transylvanian Saxon *Rimf(ərt)* is by far more probable, as is recognized also by Poghirc.[113]

Among elements that are more likely to have derived from Thracian, one should mention the suffix *-isko*, which has the same value as Romanian *-esc* (and Albanian *-ish*), with the adverbial variant *-eşte* (Alb. *-isht*). In Greek the suffix does not have the same value as in Romanian; in Latin, it appears in words derived from Greek or Thracian. With regard to Dacian, the Romanian linguist Cicerone Poghirc lists three words:

buză: "lip," Dacian, Beusas;
druete: "wood," Dacian toponym, Drobeta;
mic: "small, little," Dacian toponym, Micia (Veţel on the Mureş River), ethnic name Micenses, personal name Miccos, Miccas, Greek dialectal μίκκός.

The connection in these cases is purely conjectural, since the Dacian lexical elements are all place names whose meanings are not known. Besides these words, four appellatives (names of plants) found in the treatise of Dioscorides were compared with Romanian words: *riborasta*, "Filzkette, Maskenblume," with the variants *ribobasta, peripobasta, peripomasta*. This word has been connected with Northern Romanian *hrústur(e)* (pl. *brusturi*), (Arumanian *brostu, broştu, brustir, bruşluiă, bruştirusescu, broştur, brustur, brústură*), "common burdock, *Arctium Lappa*." Albanian *brushtullë* "id."; *guoleta* "*Lithospermum arvense*," with Romanian *gorun* (variants *gorón, gorîn, gurún*), "species of oak"; *mozula, mızela*, "thyme, *Thymus vulgaris*, savory, bean tressel *Satureia hortensis*," was compared with Northern Romanian *mazăre* (mazere, mazîne) Arumanian *mádzăre, madzîre* "pea, *Pisum sativum*." Albanian *modhullë* "id"; *pro-diarna* "Nieswurz, *Veratrum nigrum*" with Romanian *zîrnă* "black nightshade, *Solanum nigrum*."
It must be emphasized again that any connection between these Romanian words and the Dacian names is hypothetical and only one of several proposed etymologies. *Dicţionarul explicativ al limbii române*,[114] considers *gorun* and *zîrnă* to be of Slavic origin (from Bulgarian and Serbo-Croatian *gorun* and from Slavic *zrüno* "grain, seed");[115] with regard to *mazăre*, it refers to Albanian *modhullë* and considers *brusture* to be of unknown etymology. In Russu's opinion, "the connection of *brusture* with the Dacian medicinal plant *riborasta* is difficult to accept phonetically and is not very probable."[116] The identification of the Indo-European root **guel* is problematic in the Dacian word *guoleta*; one would in Dacian expect **gul-, *gol-*.[117] In the case of *mazăre*: "Thraco-Dacian *mozula* (*mizela* Dioscorides) meaning wild thyme (*Thymus serpyllum*), is semantically inadequate";[118]

and Russu considers the etymology of Romanian *mazăre* unknown. At present "only the identity" of Romanian *mazăre* and Albanian *modhullë* are certain; the fourth word in this list, *zîrnă*, is not discussed by Russu.

After the conclusion of this analysis, it must be noted that there is not a single Romanian word that can be reliably demonstrated as originating from Dacian[119] or from Thracian, although some suffixes could originate from Thracian. The Romanian linguist Ovid Densusianu pointed out this fact: "Romanian phonetics or lexicology do not show any characteristic that would be found among the elements that are preserved from the Dacian language."[120]

Why "Thraco-Dacian"?

In view of the fact that Northern Romanian is generally called in the Romanian historiography "Daco-Romanian," a term that suggests a Dacian origin of the Romanian language, it is important to establish the absence of any certain Dacian element in Romanian. There is, however, no proven Thracian or Illyrian element in this idiom either; and the theory that the ancestors of the Romanians were Thracians or "Thraco-Dacians" is pure hypothesis. Russu expressed this as follows: ..."the Thracian language had not (as far as we know today) any exclusive phonetic feature, existing only in our autochthonous words and entirely unknown in other Indo-European languages; the Thraco-Dacian language of the satem type had the same phonetic system as had Illyrian and had very many common elements with other languages of the satem type (Iranian, Baltic languages, Slavic). If we had, therefore, data indicating that the ethnic-social basis of the territory of Romanization in Moesia, Dacia, etc., was Illyrian, Iranian, or Balto-Slavic, one could admit the possibility of such an origin for the autochthonous Romanian words..."[121]

Russu asserts that the archaeological findings can never solve the problem of the substratum: such material, "in spite of its increasing abundance, will always, on the whole, remain of dubious or contestable ethnological significance."[122] Instead, he proposes that an analysis of the Romanian language should be used to appreciate correctly the value of the pre-Roman linguistic and ethnic elements.[123] But in his opinion it will be necessary to use (even if only as an hypothesis and in order to simplify the terms) the notion "Thraco-Dacian" (or "Thraco'Illyrian?") to designate the pre-Latin (autochthonous) Romanian words.[124]

It is obvious that problems of language, in this case the origin of the pre-Latin lexical elements of Romanian, can ultimately be solved only by linguistic methods; data and conclusions furnished by this discipline should be decisive. Neither historical sources nor the archaeological material give any conclusive proof. Supposing that the lexical elements in Romanian were "Thraco-Dacian" (or "Thraco-Geto-Dacian, Thraco-Illyrian") implies that the ancient language was spoken in a vast territory of the Balkan Peninsula north of Greece as well as in the region north of the lower Danube. The term "Dacian" points especially to Transylvania. - As was shown above, however, there is nothing among the linguistic data that would indicate a north-Danubian origin of the Romanian language. Consequently, the term "Thraco-Dacian" is misleading and should not be used, even "as an hypothesis and in orther to simplify the terms."

The Origin of Albanian

Two main suggestions have been proposed for the ancient language that was the forerunner of present-day Albanian: Illyrian and Thracian. The opinion that Albanian is a continuation of Thracian and that the Albanians lived during the Roman period (and immediately before it) mostly in Dardania, east of contemporary Albania, was mainly defended by Alexandru Rosetti, Dimităr Dečev, Henrik Barić, Ivan Popović, and Gustav Weigand.[125] The Bulgarian scholar Vladimir Georgiev argues that most data indicate that Albanian developed mainly on a Thracian ethnic basis, in a region east of Albania.[126] Albanian scholars, especially the Albanologist Eqrem Çabej, have more recently emphasized the circumstances that support the theory of autochthoneity in Albania.[127] According to this view, Albanian would be the continuation of Illyrian. In Russu's opinion, the historical phonetics of the Albanian language as a satem type could be in accordance with the Illyrian as well as the Thracian [which are] both the same type, satem.[128]

It is quite likely that the peoples described by Greek authors as Illyrians and Thracians were a result of ethnic mixings, superpositions of heterogenous elements.[129] The frontier between them went through the towns Scupi (modern Skoplje) and Ulpiana; Dardania was divided between these two major areas. It was, however, not as clear-cut as a line drawn on a map would suggest. Thracian place names, for example, appear in Illyrian (for example, Thermidava, in the vicinity of Scodra [Skodër], Quimedava, in Dardania).[130] Several tribes are mentioned as being Illyrians in one source and Thracians in another (for example, the Triballes, the Tralles, the Istres, and the Daorses).[131] The people living in Dardania in ancient times were also described differently by different scholars: Strabon and Appianos of Alexandria considered them to be an Illyrian tribe, while Polybios distinguished them from the Illyrians.[132]

It is therefore not surprising that at least the possibility of both Illyrian and Thracian elements have been demonstrated in the Albanian language. The etymologies are not, however, completely reliable for either Thracian or Illyrian: Everything is based on linguistic or ethnologic material, which frequently is doubtful.[133] The Bulgarian scholar Vladimir Georgiev defends the theory that Albanian derives from "Daco-Moesian" once spoken in Dardania and in parts of Macedonia and Moesia Superior. He argues that the sound changes from Indo-European to modern Albanian (for example Indo-European *e* > Albanian *je*; Ind.-Eur. *ā* > Alb. *o*) can also be demonstrated in "Daco-Moesian."[134] The linguistic data on which this hypothesis is based is scanty, and the examples are taken from the heterogenous and vast literature of the ancient era. The spelling of the ancient non-Greek and non-Latin names is often dubious. These etymologies are thus uncertain.

The lack of any decisive connection between Albanian and the remaining fragments of Thracian and Illyrian could be partly explained by the scarcity of documentary material; such connections may or may not exist. Albanian could, however, have derived from an ancient language (for example, a dialect of Illyrian or Thracian, or an idiom quite different from both) that simply remained unnoticed by the Greek and Roman scholars. This is, in fact, plausible with regard to the social situation of the population: they were a peasant population, predominantly pastoralists practicing transhumance. Living in the region of the high mountains, they and their small villages were scarcely a center of interest for Greek and Roman authors.

The problem of the territory in which the ancestors of the Albanians were living before and during the Roman period on the Balkan Peninsula has also been intensely debated. Albanians on the territory of present-day Albania were first mentioned in the twelfth century. Therefore, only an analysis of place names and of the Albanian language itself can give some indication of the origins. Attempts have been made to find place names of Albanian origin or showing a sound pattern characteristic of Albanian in Albania and in other areas of the Balkan Peninsula. Frequently, the difficulties are great and the problem cannot be settled. The name of the Serbian town Niš (Nish), for example, could have developed from Latin Naissus, with a typically Albanian hypheresis (especially usual in Latin loans: *cf.* Albanian *pyll* "forest," from **pëyll*, Popular Latin *pa[d]ule*) and the *s* > *sh* change, similarly regular in Albanian. The German scholar Gottfried Schramm argues on the other hand [135] that the *i* in this name is a strong indication against this explanation (and the *š* may be an ancient phenomenon, common in place names and river names in Southeastern Europe).

Most of the place names in Albania are of Slavic origin, and most of the names known from ancient times do not show an Albanian sound pattern. According to Ivan Popović, in clear cases the Slavic mediation is certain and is not impossible in any case, while the same cannot be said about Albanian sound patterns.[136] The name of the town Durrës, for example, must be a loan from Slavic, since Latin *ki* in Dyrrachium would have resulted in Albanian **q*, while in Slavic, this sound regularly developed to *č*. When such words were transferred to Albanian, this *č* changed, to modern Albanian *s*. There are, however, many geographical names in Albanian for which an Albanian origin or mediation seems probable: Lesh, in northern Albania, from Latin Lissus shows an Albanian evolution (*cf.* Latin *spissus* "dense" > Alb. *shpesh*) or the mountain name Shar, along and east of the northeastern frontier of Albania (Šár Planina), from Shkárdos, Shkardon, with the sound change *sk* > *sh*. The names of some rivers in Albania can be of Albanian origin, such as Bunë (earlier Buenë), which could be compared to Albanian *buenë, bujenë, boenë* "inundation."[137]

Most of the place names with an Albanian sound pattern, however, seem to be found east of present-day Albania, in the ancient province of Dardania and in adjacent territories. The name of this province has been connected with the Albanian appellative *dardhë* "pear tree," and *dardh-an* "peasant," originally "producer of pears."[138] There are the names of the town Štip, from Astibos, with the typically Albanian elision of *a-* and *s* > *sh*; Štiponje, from Stiponion, also *s* > *sh*; of the mountains of Šar Planina in the northwest (partly in Albania); Oxrid from Αυχνίς, with *n* > *r* after a velar consonant.

The Albanian language also gives some indication about the ancient regions of the Albanians: the oldest stratum of Greek loan-words in Albanian, for example, shows an ancient Greek sound pattern: Albanian (the Gheg [northern] dialect): *mokën(ë)*, (Toskë); *mokërë* "millstone," from Greek μήχανη with *k* for Greek χ (which later, in the Byzantine era, changed to *h*); or *bretëkë* "frog," from Greek βρώταχος, also *k* and not *h* for Greek χ.[139]

The Austrian scholar Norbert Jokl summarized the criteria that determine the areas of the Albanians in the pre-Roman and Roman era on the Balkans as follows: 1. an area of contacts between Illyrian and Thracian; 2. an area that came under Roman influence relatively early; 3. an area in the vicinity of the ancient areas of the Romanians; and 4. an area under some Greek influence.[140] Since the third area refers to the very problem discussed here, it should not be considered; but areas one, two, and four can apply to the ancient province of Dardania.

The conclusion about the ancient territories of the Albanians can be recapitulated as follows: the prevalently pastoral population, whose ancient Balkan language is continued by modern Albanian, lived immediately before and during the Roman domination on the Balkan Peninsula east of present-day Albania, in Dardania, in parts of Macedonia, and probably also in parts of present-day Albania, although this last mentioned area is contested by several scholars (Ivan Popović, Gottfried Schramm, not to mention earlier writers on the subject who considered that only the area east of contemporary Albania that comes into question, in modern geographical terms, is southern Serbia and northern Macedonia).[141] For the problem of Romanian, the question of the autochthoneity of the Albanians in their present-day country is not very important. It is essential, however, that the central areas of the ancient Albanians were in Dardania, that is, in the region of the Vardar River; and the limits of their areas in that time, while not known exactly, cannot have been very far from the frontiers of that province. Nothing suggests, for example, that the ancient Albanians were also living in northern Serbia and northern Bulgaria. Ancient Albanian was thus a language of the central areas of the Balkan Peninsula, about which designations such as an idiom of the "Carpatho-Danubian region" cannot be applied.

The Relationship of the Substratum of Romanian to Albanian

Albanian, next to Greek, is the oldest language spoken today in the Balkans. It belongs to the Indo-European group but is not genetically related to any of the modern languages spoken in Southeastern Europe. The majority of the ancient, pre-Latin elements of Romanian, however, have their counterparts if Albanian. Evidently, these two languages have had a common substratum. Romanian and Albanian are more closely related than either of them is with Dalmatian.

Romanian-Albanian concordances are found in all areas of language: phonology and syntax, as well as lexical elements and phraseology.

Phonetics and Phonology

Romanian contains a vowel *ă*, and Albanian has this vowel too (written *ë*). In both languages, it developed, along with other sounds, from unstressed Latin *a*, from *a* in front of a nasal, and in certain conditions from any other Latin vowel. The opposition a : ë is found in the category of determination (Albanian *vajzë* "[a] girl," *vajza* "the girl," Romanian *fată* "[a] girl," *fata* "the girl"), and in gender. The phonemization of *ă* developed under almost identical conditions in Romanian and Albanian.[142] In a later development, the Albanian *ë* underwent more change than the corresponding Romanian vowel. This is one of the circumstances supporting the idea that modern Albanian is a continuation of the language that possessed the vowel *ë* while the ancestors of the Romanians abandoned this language (becoming totally Romanized), preserving only some elements of it, such as the vowel *ă*. In its new surroundings, this vowel could be considered a borrowed sound.[143]

Latin *-ct-* shows similar changes in Romanian and Albanian. In the Romance languages, this consonant group evolved toward an open syllable: Latin *lacte-*, Romanian *lapte*, Italian *latte*, French *lait*. Albanian and Romanian reached the first stage of this development: Latin *lucta* > Albanian *luftë*, Romanian *luftă* (Arumanian), *luptă* (Northern Romanian). Latin *-lv-*, *-rv-* developed into Albanian and Romanian *-lb-*, *-rb-* : Latin *servire* > Albanian *shërbenj*, Romanian *şerb*.

These phonetical characteristics of Albanian and Romanian originate most probably from an ancient pre-Latin language, which, through almost total Romanization, developed into Romanian and through partial Romanization resulted in Albanian. Compared with the common elements in the fields of syntax, vocabulary, and phraseology, these phonetical concordances would seem less impressive. There is, nevertheless, a basic phonetical similarity between these languages, which they share with the other typical Balkan languages: The basis of articulation is very similar or almost identical; a Bulgarian, for example, easily learns Romanian, Albanian, or Greek and can speak these languages almost without any foreign accent.[144]

Morphology and Syntax

In both Albanian and Romanian, the definite article is enclitic. They also have a proclitic article. How the postpositional article developed and in what way it evolved has not been definitively established. One explanation is that the article of the noun evolved from a proclitic article of the adjective. Another opinion is based mainly on the fact that the postpositional article is stable and always has the same function, in contrast to the proclitic article. According to E. Çabej, this suggests that the postpositional article existed first and the proclitic article developed from that.[145] The postpositional article most probably existed in Proto-Albanian.[146]

The close connections between Albanian and Romanian can clearly be seen from an analysis of the use of the article: these two languages coincide in the use of this element of speech to the smallest details of its syntactical position, which contradicts the assumption of a spontaneous evolution in each of the two languages.[147] Many circumstances indicate that the Romanian constructions, which are to such a great extent similar to the Albanian ones, cannot be explained without them.[148]

It is significant that the postpositional article also appears in Bulgarian (and the Macedonian dialect) but not in Serbo-Croatian: It is a Balkan phenomenon, which did not reach the Serbo-Croatian language.[149] The particle *-ne* of the accusative of the personal pronoun (Romanian *mine, tine* "me," "you") appears in both Albanian and Romanian and is considered to have derived from Proto-Albanian.[150] Of 13 Romanian *suffixes* that are probably of pre-Latin origin, 6 are also found in Albanian (for example, the relevant suffix *-esc, -eşte*).

The pre-Latin Lexical Elements in the Romanian Language

A difficult problem is to establish which of the several thousand Romanian words with an unknown etymology originate from the pre-Latin substratum of the language. Definite conclusions do not appear to be possible at present, as evidenced by the large number of proposed etymologies and the widely divergent opinions among scholars who have studied the problem. Some investigators consider that not a single word could be attributed with certainty to the substratum; others believe that all Romanian words of unknown or uncertain etymology derive from it (10 to 15 percent of the entire Romanian word stock). Between these extreme views, the proposed figures vary: about 85 [words], according to Bogdan Petriceicu Hasdeu and Alexandru Rosetti; about 160, according to Ion I. Russu (72 also existing in Albanian, 90 only in Romanian); 30, according to Vladimir Georgiev.[151] In reference to Ariton Vraciu's statement, "the etymologies proposed until now for the elements attributed to the substratum are mostly inadequate."[152]

One of the basic questions in this context is the proportion of words from the ethnolinguistic substratum that Romanian has in common with Albanian. It must be stated from the beginning that these common words are not loans from one of the languages to the other but chiefly derive from a common source, an ancient language once spoken in Southeastern Europe. As regards those of the assumed substratum words that do not exist in Albanian, I.I. Russu stated: "these do not make out a distinct group, deriving from another source than those which Romanian shares with Albanian, with which they in fact constitute a single pre-Roman, autochthonous lexical block." [153] This is very dubious indeed, because there are significant differences between these two groups from the semantic viewpoint, as will be shown below (see Table II, p. 240 and pp. 241-245).

Given the long period of time of separate development, one should, of course, not expect that all substratum words of Rumanian are also found in Albanian.

Another problem is the distribution of substratum words among the Romanian dialects. About 50 of those assumed by Russu to have originated from the substratum are found only in Northern Romanian, which has been thought to indicate "the greater resistence of the autochthonous population to Romanization north of the Danube" (compared with the Balkan Peninsula).

First of all, one may examine the present-day (or, in several cases, Northern Romanian from the seventeenth century) form of the Romanian words. On the other end of the time scale, there are ancient Indo-European stems that have been established by reconstruction from modern Indo-European languages, from Sanskrit, Old Iranian, Balto-Slavic, Old Germanic, Celtic, Latin, and Greek, languages.[154] Connections between the Romanian word and the reconstructed Indo-European stems are then decided on the basis of formal and semantic criteria. This means that there are five to six millenia between the reconstructed ancient Indo-European stems and the present-day Romanian words, an extremely long period of time, which only contributes to the uncertainty and precarious nature of the procedure.[155] The existence of words preserved from Thracian or other ancient Balkan languages could shorten this long period significantly; but, as was shown above, not a single Romanian word can reliably be connected with any such lexical element. Russu also admits that this method is uncertain;[156] and any attempt to explain the origin of the Daco-Getae, Thracian, Illyrian, (and others) or to search for connection between them and Indo-European is more or less hypothetical.[157]

An example of this method will be given here (the proposed derivation of the Romanian verb *răbda* "to endure, to bear, to tolerate"): (This word) belongs to Indo-European *orbho-, robh-* "lacking some-

thing, worn out, tortured, miserable," from which derived the Latin
orbus "without sight," Greek όρφανός "without parents," German
Arbeit "work," Slavic *robu* (*robie*); Romanian *răbda* is part of this
etymological group, without the possibility of being a Latin, Greek,
Slavic, or German word, originating from a language in which *bh*
changed to *b*, *o* possibly to a; its morphological structure (the derivation
with *-d-*) is specific and ancient.[158] Russu gives a thorough analysis
of the words assumed to originate from the substratum of Romanian,
including all of the more significant etymologies proposed in the
literature and a critical discussion of each problem.[159] The conclusion
with regard to the pre-Latin origin of the word in question, may be
correct in several cases but in others, not.

Scholars are in general skeptical about the etymologies proposed
by Russu. Cicerone Poghirc, using the criteria for considering a word
of substratum origin, does not agree with Russu, giving only 125
Romanian words for which the origin from the substratum is probable
or at least possible, of which about 100 are also found in Albanian.
These words are divided into three groups: 1. Romanian words that
have been connected with lexical elements from Daco-Moesian or
other ancient Balkan languages; 2. words that Romanian shares with
Albanian; and 3. substratum words deduced from a comparison with
other Indo-European languages.[160] It is, however, questionable whether
the words in this third group really come from the substratum - it seems
more probable that most of them have a different origin. *Istoria limbii
române*, 1978, p. 72, mentions 19 words which according to Russu,
originate from the substratum - (*băga, băiat, brînză, burtă, butuc, cîrlan,
creț, doină, genună, melc, mişca, morman, muşca, nițel, prunc, răbda,
şoric, țăruş, zer*) - but of which *Dicționarul Explicativ al Limbii
Române* (DEX,1975) states: "of unknown etymology".[161]
Also *Istoria limbii române*, 1978, states that some of the words given by
Russu in *Elemente autohtone* ... as originating from the substratum could
be explained from Latin. [162] In Vraciu's opinion, the vocabulary statistics
of Russu must be reconsidered, many words are attributed arbitrarily to
the pre-Roman substratum of Romanian.[163]   (See list, p. 231-238.)

The Semantic Aspect

Discussing the semantic aspect of these words, (see Tables I and
II) according to Russu the specifically Romanian nature of the autochthonous words also appears from an observation of the groups
of terms existing in both Romanian and Albanian, of which many
denote plants, animals, natural phenomena; half of them refer to the
human body, one in five refers to the age of man (*moş*), two in five
denote psychological states (*bucur-, mărat*).[164] Those groups that are
not found in Albanian are words denoting psychological states, diseases

A List of Northern Romanian and Arumanian Words Probably or Possibly
Originating from the Substratum
(On the basis of ILR, 1969, vol. II and Russu, 1981)

A. MAN:

a) Parts and organs of the human body:

Words existing also in Albanian:

buză	"lip; rim, edge"
ceafă	"nape"
ciuf, ciof	"tuft (of hair), crest (of birds)"
grumaz	"neck; nape; back; throat, windpipe"
şale	"loins, small of the back"
bumbărează	"coccyx"
rînză	"stomach", (dial.: gizzard);

Words not inexisting in Albanian:

beregată	"throat, gullet, windpipe"
burtă	"belly, stomach";

b) Physiological functions, disease:

Also in Albanian:

—

Not in Albanian:

(a se) uita	"to look"
urdoare	"bleariness"
vătăma	"to hurt, to injure";

c) Psychological features, emotional states:

Also in Albanian:

mărat	"poor, miserable"
(a se) bucura	"to gladden, to please";

Not in Albanian:

răbda	"to suffer, to endure, to tolerate"
gudura	"to fawn (upon), to cajole"
dezmierda	"to caress, to fondle, to please, to flatter"
mădări	(obsolete & regional) "to deride, to scoff at"
întărîta	"to excite, to irritate; to incite, to stimulate"
aprig	"fiery, ardent; harsh";

d) Age, family relations:

copil	"child, infant" (Alb. kopil' may be a loan from Romanian, Russu, 1981, p. 295)
ghiuj	"gaffer, old fogy"
moş	"old man; forefather"
spîrc	"beardless; boy, child";

Not in Albanian:

băiat	"boy"
mire	"bridegroom"
prunc	"baby, infant in arms";

B. CLOTHING, FOOTWEAR:

Also in Albanian:

brîu	"girdle, belt"
căpută	"foot; toe (of shoe), a low boot";

Not in Albanian:

baier	"thread; band, strap, string"
mununā	"wreath (as a decoration for a girl's head")"
pînză	"linen, cloth";

C. DWELLING PLACE, HOUSEKEEPING:

Also in Albanian:

argea	"room (made in the earth)"
cătun	"small village"
colibă	"cabin, hut, hovel"
vatră	"hearth, fireplace; house, dwelling"
gard	"fence, enclosure";

Not in Albanian:

bordeiu	"cottage, cabin, hut, shelter"
leagăn	"cradle"
ţărînă	"field under cultivation"
zestre	"dowry";

D. TOOLS AND OBJECTS OF SPECIAL USE:

Also in Albanian:

burduf	"skin" (a primitive leather bag made out of the hide of oxen, sheep, or a bladder; cheese, flour, water, oil are usually kept in it); "bellows", "package bag"
grapă	"harrow"
gresie	"grindstone"
zgardă	"dog collar"
mătură	"broom";

Not in Albanian:

custură	"blade (of scythe or other tools)"
caier	"flax, tress, hemp bundle; tuft of hair"
dop	"cork, plug"
cîrlig	"hook; fishing line"

undrea	"knitting needle; clavicle"
razem	"prop, support, stay"
cărîmb	"top (of a boot)";

E. FORM, QUANTITY AND QUALITY OF MATTER:

Also in Albanian:

abure	"steam, vapor; breeze"
druete	(dial., Oltenia) "wood"
fărîmă	"small piece, morsel, fragment; bit"
gardină	"chime"
grunz	"lump, clod"
scrum	"ash";

Not in Albanian:

droaie	"multitude, crowd, swarm"
lespede	"plate, slab, flagstone, gravestone"
morman	"pile"
şir	"row, line"
niţel	"a little"
steregie	"soot";

F. NATURE, FORM, AND GEOGRAPHICAL FEATURES:

Also in Albanian:

baltă	"marsh, moor"
bară	"swampy ground"
bîlc	"swamp, bog, narrow and swampy valley in the mountains"
groapă	"pit, hollow, cavity"
ciucă	"peak"
mal	"lakeside, coast, beach, bank"
măgură	"hill"
pîriu, pîrău	"brook";

Not in Albanian:

gruiu	(regional) "hill top; hill slope"
genune	"abyss, chasm; deep"
stîncă	"rock";

G. NATURAL PHENOMENA:

Also in Albanian:

amurg	"twilight, afterglow"
spuză	"burning ash; eczema"

Not in Albanian:

| boare | "breath of wind" |

viscol	"snowstorm"
adiia	"to blow (a breeze); to whisper, to touch lightly";

H. PLANTS:

Also in Albanian:

brad	"fir tree (*Abies alba*)"
brusture	"common bur(dock) (*Arctiun Lappa*)"
bunget	"(thick' old forest, thicket; covert"
coacăză	"black currant"
copac	"tree"
ciump, ciomp	"knot in wood, stump"
curpăn, curpen	"tendril; stem; certain species of Clematis"
ghimp(e)	"thorn"
leurdă	"wild garlic"
mazăre	"pea (*Pisum sativum*)"
mărar	"dill (seed), (*Anethum graveolus*)"
mugur(e)	"bud, burgeon; small excrescence; (fig.:) offspring"
spînz, spînt	"hellebore"
păstaie	"pod"
buc	"beech (*Fagus*)";

Not in Albanian:

brîndușă	"colchicum"
butuc, butură	"stump of tree, log; tree trunk"
măceș	"wild rose (*Rosa canina*)"
strugure	"bunch of grapes"
gorun	"common oak (*Quercus pedunculata*)"
scai	"thistle (*Cirsium lanceolatum*)"
zîrnă	"black nightshade (*Solanum nigrum*)"
măldac	"hay stacks";

I. ANIMALS (see also shepherd words):

Also in Albanian:

barză	"stork"
cioară	"crow (*Corvus*); rook (*Corvus frugileus*)"
cioc	"beak; rostrum"
ghinoaie	"woodpecker (*Picus*)"
gușă	"coop, maw, gizzard (of birds); goiter, wen"
măgar	"ass, (*Equus asinus*)"
mînz	"foal"
murg	"dark-bay horse"
mușcoi, mîșcoi	"mule"
năpîrcă	"(common) adder, viper (*Pelias berus*)"

rață	"duck (*Anas*)"
șopîrlă	"lizard (*Lacerta*)";
Not in Albanian:	
melc	"snail"
ghiară	"claw"
necheza	"to neigh"
șoric(i)	"skin of bacon, rind";

J. SHEPHERD WORDS:

Also in Albanian:

baci	"shepherd in charge of a sheepfold" (Alb. *batsë, baç* from Rom.? Russu, 1981, p. 253.
balegă	"dung, manure"
bască	"sheep's wool"
bîr	interjection used by the shepherd to drive the sheep
boreasă	"(young) woman"
căciulă	a cap made of sheepskin or the fur of other animals
cursă	"trap, snare, pitfall"
căpușă	"sheep louse (*Melophagus ovinus*)"
ciut, șut	"hornless, poll; single-horned"
fluier(ă)	"little whistle pipe, shepherd's flute"
daș	"lamb of the house"
gălbează, călbează	"sheep pox; liverworts (*Hepaticae*)"
ghioagă	"club, cudgel"
strepede	"cheese maggot"
strungă	"sheepfold"
știră	"sterile"
țap	"male goat"
țarc	"fold, pen"
urdă	"soft cow's cheese" (Alb. *urdha* from Rum.? Capidan, Dacoromania II, Cluj, p. 470)
viezure, viezune, viezine	"common badger (*Meles taxus or vulgaris*)"
vătuiu	"one-year-old kid; one-year-old lamb; whelp of a hare"
țeapă	"stake, point of a pile";
Not in Albanian:	
brînză	"cheese" (*cf.*, however, Alb. *brëndësa*; ILR 1969 II p. 354)
cață	"sheep hook"
mărcat (Arum.)	"curdled milk"
cîrlan	"one-year-old lamb; horse (up to three years old)"

străghiată	"curdled milk"
zară	"buttermilk" (etymologically related to zăr; also has similar in meaning)
zăr	"the yellowish-green liquid that remains after milk", "coagulated into cheese" (connection possible with Alb. dra, Russu, 1981, p. 421);

K. ADJECTIVES:

Also in Albanian:

băl, bălaş	"fair, blonde"
hameş	"gluttonous"
murg	"dark-bay"
creț	"curly; wrinkled"
mărat	"poor; miserable"
sarbăd	"sour";

Not in Albanian:

mare	"big"
mic	"small"
mieru	"blue"
muşat (regional)	"beautiful"
tare	"strong";

L. ADVERBS:

Also in Albanian:

abeş	(dial., in the Banat "really, in fact")
aş(i)	"not at all, by no means"
gata	"ready, finished"
pururea	"always";

Not in Albanian:

—

M. VERBS:

Also in Albanian:

ciupi	"to steal"
lehăi	"to chatter"
scăpăra	"to strike; to throw; to sparkle; to lighten"
cruța	"to spare; to forgive"
curma	"to interrupt, to break off; to stop; to break"
dărîma	"to demolish; to break down; to level"
scula	"to wake; to rise"
zgîria	"to scratch";

Not in Albanian:

| acăța, agăța | "to hang up, to suspend; to hook up; to accost; to seize" |

(a)darari	"to make; to construct; to give life"
anina	"to hang up, to hook; to accost, to waylay"
arunca	"to throw"
băga	"to put (into/in)"
cotropi	"to invade, to conquer"
deretica	"to clean a room, to tidy up;" (in 17th century: "to take, to lift" Russu, 1981, p. 307)
desbăra	"to break someone of (a habit); to wean (someone from)"
încurca	"to tangle; to confound, to mix up"
înghina	"to join, to unite; to combine; to connect"
îngurzi	"to fold; to pleat"
întîmpina	"to meet; to greet; to find"
întîmpla (16th century: tîmpla)	"to happen, to occur"
lepăda	"to let fall; to throw; to lose; to leave"
mişca	"to move"
muşca	"to bite"
păstra	"to keep, to preserve"
rădica (ridica, ar/i/dica)	"to raise, to lift"
scurma	"to scratch, to scrape"
urca	"to mount, to ascend; to increase"
urdina	"to go frequently, to visit; to have diarrhea"
zburda, sburda	"to sport, to frolic, to frisk about"
zgîrma, zgrîma, sgrîma (Arum.)	"to scratch, to scrape"

The following verbs are variants of verbs mentioned above or derive from nouns mentioned above:

descăţa - cf. acăţa; descurca - cf. încurca; desghina - cf. înghina; deşela - cf. şale; îndopa - cf. dop; înşira - cf. şir; rezema - cf. razem

N. ABSTRACT NOTIONS:

Also in Albanian:

lete	"free time"

Not in Albanian:

modru	"means, possibility";

O. POPULAR MYTHOLOGY:

Also in Albanian:

balä, balaur	"dragon; monster";

Not in Albanian:

—

Words whose origin from the substratum is considered questionable by Russu:

(None of these also exists in Albanian.)

A. *Man: physiological functions, disease:*

ameți	"to drug, to anaesthetize, to stupefy"
întrema	"to recover"
leșina	"to faint"
urcior	"jug, pitcher; eyesore";

C. *Dwelling place, housekeeping:*

burlan   "pipe, tube; pin, prop";

D. *Tools and objects of special use:*

țăruș   "pile, stake; peg, wooden plug";

E. *Form, quantity and quality of matter:*

țărină   "dust; earth; ground";

F. *Nature, surface features and phenomena:*

noian   "multitude; sea; immensity, vastness; abyss";

I. *Animals:*

buiestru	"ambling, ambling pace"
strănut, stărnut	"(horse) with a white spot on the snout";

J. *Shepherd words:*

stînă   "sheepfold, pen" (probably from Old Slavic *stanŭ* (ILR, 1969, II, p. 356; according to Russu, 1981, p. 389, a Slavic origin is as possible as an origin from the substratum);

M. *Verbs:*

însăila, înseila   "to tack, to stitch; to improvise; to imagine"

TABLE I
The semantic distribution of Romanian lexical elements probably or possibly
originating from the substratum

Semantic spheres	Also in Albanian		Not in Albanian		Total
A. Man: parts of the human body	7	6.4%	2	2.3%	9
physiological functions, diseases:	—		3	3.4%	3
psychological traits, emotional states:	2	1.8%	6	6.8%	8
age, family relations:	4*	3.6%	3	3.4%	7
B. Clothes, footwear:	2	1.8%	3	3.4%	5
C. Dwelling place, housekeeping:	5	4.6%	4	4.5%	9
D. Tools and objects of special use:	5	4.6%	7	8.0%	12
E. Form, quantity, and quality of matter:	6	5.5%	6	6.8%	12
F. Form and geographical features:	8	7.2%	3	3.4%	11
G. Natural phenomena:	2	1.8%	3	3.4%	5
H. Plants:	15	13.6%	8	9.1%	23
I. Animals (cf., also shepherd words):	12	10.9%	4	4.5%	16
J. Shepherd words:	22**	20.0%	7***	8.0%	29
K. Adjectives:	6	5.5%	5	5.7%	11
L. Adverbs:	4	3.6%	—		4
M. Verbs:	8	7.2%	23	26.1%	31
N. Abstract notions:	1	0.9%	1	1.1%	2
O. Popular mythology:	1	0.9%	—		1
Total:	110	99.9%	88	99.9%	198

Source: Ion I. Russu, *Etnogeneza românilor*, 1981, pp. 244-245 and C. Poghirc,
in ILR, vol. I, 1969, pp. 327-356 [the list of words considered autochthonous].
The semantic categories are those used by Russu, to which "abstract notions"
and "popular mythology" were added.
*One of the Alb. words (*kopil'*) may be a loan from Romanian.
** Two of the Albanian words (*batsë and urdhë*) may be loans from
Romanian.
*** Three of these words (*brînză, zară and zăr*) may have counterparts
in Albanian.

TABLE II
The semantic distribution of a total of 198 Romanian words probably or possibly originating from the substratum on the basis of Table I in which the absolute figures are given

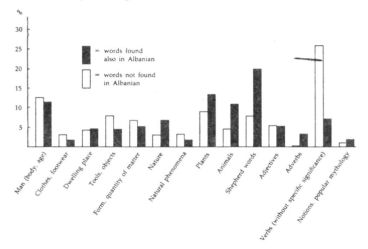

The difference from the semantic viewpoint between words that also exist in Albanian and those that are not known in that language is shown. This is a word stock of the most elementary notions of human life, notions connected with the primitive dwelling place etc. The two groups compared contain largely similar numbers of this kind of words. To this comes, however, a group of words of special interest for a pastoral population: in the first place phenomena met in everyday life by shepherds in high mountains. The number of these words is much higher in the group of words that also exist in Albanian. In contrast, the group of words that do not exist in Albanian contains many more verbs without a specific significance. The differences are too large to be coincidental.

and features of the body, and many tools. If the terms of general significance for shepherds are common (*baciu? ţarc, strungă, bască,* as well as the names of the domestic animals), the terms for milk products are exclusively Romanian: *străghiată, mărcat, brînză, zăr, zară, urdă.*[165] Russu also notes that only a small number of the more than 40 verbs assumed by him to originate from the substratum also exist in Albanian. Thus, also Russu noted the striking difference from the semantic point of view between those lexical elements that Romanian shares with Albanian and those which only exist in Romanian. He did not, however, draw any conclusion from this fact, but expressed the view that "it is perhaps accidental" (*Etnogeneza românilor*, 1981, p. 132). He continued this sentence as follows: ..."the semantic grouping and the meaning of these words do not plead at all for the thesis of a more close linguistic psychological, and socio-ethnic community of the Romanians with the Skipetars, for the pretended 'Albanian-Romanian symbiosis' during the Middle Ages".[166]

A list of the semantic distribution of the substratum words in Romanian can only be approximate. Many etymologies are uncertain, and no one is able to say exactly which words really originate from the substratum. The lexical elements also found in Albanian are relatively easy to classify; in most cases, the sound pattern of the word suggests its origin from a common, ancient language. There are, however, a few cases in which a borrowing can be discussed: *baciu,* according to Russu, Albanian *batsë* "shepherd in charge of a sheepfold," could either be inherited or "a loan from Romanian";[167] *copil* "child" corresponding to Albanian *kopil', kopil* "young boy, servant" (the Tosc dialect of the Albanian), *bastard* (the Gheg dialect of the Albanian) could be similarly a loan from Romanian or inherited;[168] *mistreţ* "wild boar," Albanian *mistrets;* the connection (of Romanian *mistreţ*) with Albanian *mistrets* is not at all clear;[169] Albanian *urdhë* "soft cow cheese" may be borrowed from Romanian *urdă,* according to C. Poghirc.[170] Words not existing in Albanian could be assumed to derive from a certain, reconstructed Indo-European stem, but it may only be a question of probability. In the following list the words proposed by Russu as well as many of those given by Poghirc are presented on the basis of *Istoria limbii române* (1969). From this last source, several words were omitted, mostly those that are not presented in Russu's list, especially in cases in which the connection with the proposed Proto-Indo-European seems poorly documented. The total number of words arrived at this way is really high, but it should be noted that these words have been assumed to derive from the substratum of Romanian by competent scholars; the probability of the derivation   varies.

Another problem is the semantic grouping. While *baciu* "shepherd in charge of a sheepfold" is a typical shepherd word, *ţap* "male goat" belongs to the group of animals, although it denotes an animal of great importance to shepherds. The word *zgardă* "dog collar" could be used by a peasant farmer population as well as by a pastoral population; *căciulă* "fur cap" is an item of clothing but one typically used by shepherds. The names of animals that appear here denote mainly animals existing in a pastoral society or wild animals. In his listing of the semantic groups, Russu classifies all animal names in a special group, but in the text (p. 132) he considers them, together with such words as *baciu* "shepherd in charge of a sheepfold," *strungă* "sheepfold," *ţarc* "fold, pen" as of general significance to shepherds. The semantic groups used by Russu[171] will be used here with slight modifications.

A Comparison of Two Groups of Words: Those with and Those Without an Albanian Counterpart

Of a total of 209 (+11?)[172] lexical elements possibly originating from the substratum, 113 have also an Albanian equivalent while 96 (+11?) exist only in Romanian (half of them only in the Northern Romanian dialect). There is a clear difference with regard to the semantic areas presented by these two groups: of those 113 words also existing in Albanian, 22 (19.5%) are specific shepherd words and another 36 denote things and notions of special importance to a pastoral population: names of animals, plants, and natural phenomena, with all of which shepherds usually have everyday contact. The total number of lexical elements of special importance to the pastoral way of life is 58 (51.3% of the entire group). There are only 9 verbs (8%) of importance to all human beings and societies, without being specific to any special type of society.

On the other hand, the group of 96 (+11) words not found in Albanian contains only 8 specifically pastoral words[173] and another 15 (+3?) of special importance to pastoral way of life, making up a total of 23 (+3?), corresponding to 24% (27%?). The number of verbs without special significance is much higher in this group: 37 (+4?), corresponding to 38.5% (38.3%?) and the largest semantic group among these words. The proportion of words of special importance to pastoral life among words also existing in Albanian is thus more than twice that in the other group which, on the other hand, contains many more verbs of general significance (38% compared with 8%).

The Lexical Elements of Importance for a Pastoral Population

Of the 80 (+4?) lexical elements assumed to originate from the substratum of Romanian that are of primary importance to a pastoral population (specific shepherd words, names of animals, plants, and natural phenomena), the majority (at least 58 [72%]) also exist in Albanian. In contrast, verbs of no specific significance appear only in a small number in Albanian (10 out of 47 [+4?], that is, 20%).

As mentioned above, no exact figures can be given about the semantic distribution of the substratum words. The differences discussed here between the two groups (Albanian and non-Albanian), however, are also recognized by Russu (see above). - Russu is also right when he states that these words "do not suggest an Albanian-Romanian symbiosis during the Middle Ages," since most of them are not loan-words.

A Comparison of Two Groups of Words:
Those Found in Northern Romanian Only and Those
Also Existing in at Least One of the Southern Dialects

According to a list, Russu assumes a total of 169 Romanian words to be of substratum origin, of which he considers 12 as questionable, listing them with a question mark.[174] In the following analysis, the numbers of words considered by Russu as certain will be given first and the questionable words thereafter in parentheses. Of a total of 169 words in this list, three are not found in Northern Romanian (one exists only in Meglenitic and two only in Arumanian). Since the problem discussed here is a possible difference between Northern Romanian and the southern Romanian dialects, those not found in Northern Romanian are not taken into account. There are thus 166 words (169 minus 3) or 154, plus 12 with a question mark.

The Presence of the Words in Albanian

Of 107 (+1?) lexical elements found in Northern Romanian and in at least one southern dialect, 62, or 58%, also exist in Albanian. Of the 48 (+11?) words that exist only in the Northern Romanian, only 16, or 33.3% (27.1%?), are also found in Albanian.

The Presence of Words Found in Albanian and
Also in the Southern Dialects

Of the words that are also found in Albanian (a total of 78), one finds that the great majority (62 or 79.5%) also exist in at least one of the southern dialects, only 20.5% being restricted to Northern Romanian.

The Semantic Spheres

There are 32 (+11?) Romanian words that are assumed to have originated from the substratum but exist exclusively in Northern

Romanian (also lacking in Albanian). The largest semantic group among these words is that of verbs of general significance to all human beings, which make up about a third of the group: 11 (+4?). There are only three specific shepherd words (one of which is *zară*, possibly connected with Albanian) and 10 (+2?) that are of special significance to a pastoral way of life. The rest of the lexical elements are spread throughout all semantic spheres.

The etymologies of these lexical elements remain obscure. Russu collected all the more significant suggestions from the literature and gives a critical discussion of each.[175] It appears clear from this presentation that most of the proposed etymologies are uncertain, even unlikely; and not a single one could be considered correct beyond doubt. Russu tries to connect these words with Indo-European stems: in some cases, the connection seems plausible; in others, there are difficulties with the sound pattern and/or with the meaning. Many of these words could have an Indo-European origin, but we have no criteria whatsoever for deciding which language or languages were the direct source. The possibility of non-Indo-European words,[176] as well as of borrowings from such languages as Gypsy, for example, should also be considered. The distribution of the etymologies of these 32 words given by *Dicţionarul explicativ al limbii române*, 1975, is as follows: from Latin, 9; from Albanian, 3; from Slavic, 2; from Hungarian, 1; unknown, 16; and 1 of the words is not mentioned.

There must, of course, also be some difference among Albanian, Northern Romanian, and the different southern dialects with regard to this group of words, as there are differences in every area of the word stock. It would be illogical to believe that all these idioms have preserved exactly the same lexical elements from the substratum that they once shared. For this reason and with the uncertain origin of these few lexical elements assumed by Russu to derive from the substratum of Romanian (an assumption not accepted by several Romanian scholars), no conclusion about the Romanian language can be drawn from this group of lexical elements.

As mentioned previously, there is a correlation between words that 1. denote things and notions of specific importance to pastoral population; 2. also exist in Albanian; and 3. are found both in Northern Romanian and in at least one of the southern dialects. The other correlation found for the assumed substratum words of Romanian is that between verbs 1. of a general significance to all human beings and societies, without being connected to any specific activity or way of life; 2. of which only a few exist also in Albanian, and 3. which are mainly found in the Northern Romanian dialect. (All words for which the substratum origin is considered uncertain even by Russu belong to those not found in Albanian [a total of 12], and 11 of them are found only in Northern Romanian).

It is unlikely that the relationship discussed here would be accidental, since the differences, especially between the words of significance to shepherds (most of them existing also in Albanian) and the verbs of unspecific character (only a small number of them being found in Albanian), are too large to be coincidental. A likely explanation of the findings is that at least a majority of the words whose group shows the first correlation really originate from the substratum, while a significant number of those that show the second correlation are in reality not substratum words but derive from some other sources. (See Table II)

Theories Based on the Distribution of the Assumed Substratum Words Among the Romanian Dialects

The Romanian scholar Theodor Capidan[177] advanced a theory to explain why the number of words assumed to derive from the substratum is much higher in Northern Romanian than in the southern dialects (so far as these have been investigated). Capidan assumed that the Northern Romanians had preserved more words from the substratum, because they were living in closer contact with the Albanians than were the speakers of the other dialects. This explanation implies, however, that the words in question are loans from Albanian, which is not tenable. Another, still current, theory is that the pre-Latin language was more vigorous north of the Danube and resisted Romanization with more success. This view was recently expressed by Russu in *Etnogeneza românilor*, 1981.[178] This could be explained, in Russu's opinion, by the circumstances that Dacia Traiana was conquered a century later and abandoned much earlier than Moesia; the "Geto-Dacian element" north of the Danube was more conservative and resisted Romanization for a longer period; and the position of Carpathian Dacians was more peripheral than that of the Romans living in the Balkan Peninsula, having more intense and more prolonged contacts with the Thraco-Dacian groups outside the frontiers of Dacia.

It must be noted that Russu only mentions this as a possibility, not as a concrete theory. The difference in this respect between Northern Romanian and the southern dialects is not established, since no one knows with any certainty which words derive from the substratum and because the word stock of the southern dialects is not very well known. Since, however, this view sometimes appears in writings about Romanian ethnogenesis, it may be conducive to discuss it briefly.

TABLE III
Substratum lexical elements assumed by Russu found only in Northern Romanian

A. MAN:	
physiological functions:	*a se uita* "to look"
psychological traits,	*aprig* "ardent; harsh"
affective states:	*întărîta* "to irritate; to incite; to stimulate"
	mădări (regional and obsolete) "to deride, to scoff at"
age, family relations:	*băiat* "boy"
	mire "bridegroom";
C. DWELLING PLACE:	*bordeiu* "hut";
D. TOOLS AND OBJECTS OF SPECIAL USE:	*carîmb* "top of a boot, leg of a boot";
E. FORM, QUANTITY AND QUALITY OF MATTER:	*droaie* "multitude, crowd, swarm"
	lespede "plate, slab, flagstone; gravestone"
	morman "heap, pile";
F. NATURE, FORM AND GEOGRAPHICAL FEATURE:	*genune* "abyss, chasm; deep"
	noian "multitude; sea; immensity; vastness";
G. NATURAL PHENOMENA:	*viscol* "snowstorm";
H. PLANTS:	*butuc* "stump of tree, log, tree trunk"
	gorun "common oak (*Quercus pedunculata*)"
	strugure "bunch of grapes";
I. ANIMALS:	*ghiară* "claw"
	şoric "skin, rind; bark";
J. SHEPHERD WORDS:	*cîrlan* "one-year-old lamb; horse (up to three years old)"
	caţă "sheep hook"
	zară "buttermilk";
L. ADVERBS:	*niţel* "a little";
M. VERBS:	*anina* "to hang up, to hook; to accost"
	cotropi "to invade, to conquer"
	deretica "to clean a room, to tidy up" (in 17th century: "to take, to lift")
	îndemna "to urge, to stimulate, to goad"
	îngurzi "to pleat, to fold"
	întîmpina "to meet, to greet, to find"
	întîmpla "to happen, to occur"
	urca "to mount, to ascend, to increase";
ABSTRACT NOTIONS:	*modru* "mode, means, possibility".

The real question is the presence of these words in Common Romanian, that is, the idiom spoken by the Romanians before the development of the dialects. With the lack of any written document, Common Romanian must be reconstructed from the present-day Romanian dialects. In general, any ancient element in these dialects could be considered to have existed in Common Romanian; and this is most probably also true of the lexical elements. According to Russu's view, it could assumed that most (if not all) of the autochthonous words existed in the Carpatho-Balkan idiom, having been lost during the Middle Ages from the Arumanian, Meglenitic, and Istro-Rumanian dialects.[179] Citing *Istoria limbii române*, it must be assumed that the words that are lacking in Arumanian or in the other dialects have disappeared, and what is more interesting, that some of them were replaced by Albanian (or by Greek, in the case of Arumanian) elements.[180]

Assuming that all these words once existed in Common Romanian, the whole problem is solved and the theory about a "more vigorous substratum in the north" becomes unnecessary. The number of these words, about 50, is, however, perhaps too high to be explained in this way, even adding the possibility that some of the words exist in reality in one or another of the southern dialects but are unknown, not having been recorded by the investigators. It is this reasoning that prompted the elaboration of new theories about this question.

Considering the facts given above, it is likely that many of the discussed words do not derive from the substratum of Romanian: the majority of these lexical elements belong to those that do not exist in Albanian and denote notions of general significance for all human beings and societies (in contrast to those words which mainly denote things of special importance for a pastoral population and also exist in Albanian).

It is true that Trajan's Dacia was under Roman rule for a much shorter time (about 169 years) than were the provinces south of the Danube, (about 600 years) and that Dacia was a peripheral province. The great difference in history must have had its consequences on Romance languages developing in the two areas (if such languages existed). During the period of Late Latin, when numerous innovations and popular constructions came into use, the area of former Roman Dacia was divided from the Latin-speaking population in the Roman Empire by the Roman frontier. Even without "more conservatism and more prolonged resistance against Romanization" shown by the autochthonous population, this situation would have led to a Romance language substantially different from one that could develop on the Balkan Peninsula during the period of Late Latin. This difference would not be restricted to the substratum words only but would also affect substratum elements in other areas of language and, most significantly, also the Latin elements of Northern Romanian. Such an effect is, however, not discernible.

Conclusions

The Romanian words originating from the substratum that do not exist in Albanian are probably much fewer than are assumed by Russu (about 90). The same can also be said of the substratum words found only in Northern Romanian and lacking in Arumanian, Meglenitic, and Istro-Rumanian. Any theory assuming a stronger substratum north of the Danube is unacceptable of this fact, not to mention the other difficulties.

Most of those Romanian words that are most likely to have derived from the substratum exist also in Albanian and in several Romanian dialects. The major semantic areas in this group of ancient lexical elements are those of special importance to a pastoral population. The pre-Latin linguistic material, existing in all areas of language, is of basic significance to the history of the Romanian language. It is shared to a great extent by Albanian, which suggests that the pre-Roman substratum of Romanian was the language spoken by the ancestors of the Albanians or an idiom very closely related to their language. Albanian is thus the direct continuation of this ancient idiom. The large proportion of words of primary importance to a pastoral population among the lexical elements from the substratum indicates that the people in question practiced a pastoral or transhumant way of life. During the centuries of Roman domination in the Balkan Peninsula, the population speaking this idiom was exposed to a prolonged Latin influence. Part of them borrowed a number of Latin elements but largely preserved the original language. Another part was entirely Romanized, preserving only several ancient elements (the most significant examples of which were given above). This last mentioned part of the ancient pastoral population developed into the Romanians.[181]

It has not been determined whether the ancient, pre-Roman language was similar to Illyrian, Thracian, a mixture of these two, or some other idiom; it has also been called Daco-Moesian. This much debated problem is not, however, decisive for the question of the substratum of Romanian, since this must have been Proto-Albanian. The territories of the ancient Albanians are known: they were living in southern Serbia, northern Macedonia, and some adjacent areas. In those same areas the ancestors of the Romanians also once lived. Pastoral terminology demonstrates that the Romanization of the Albanians antedates that of the Romanians.

Albanian-Romanian Contacts in the Late Latin Period

Besides the substratum elements, there are also relevant correspondences between Albanian and Romanian with regard to the Latin elements.[182] There are, of course, also differences, mostly from an archaic period. Albanian has preserved numerous archaic Latin elements, borrowed during the first one or two centuries B.C., most of which have no counterpart in Romanian. This fact could shed light on the ancient territories of the Albanians through an analysis of place names and the Albanian language. The ancestors of the Romanians may also have used these Latin elements but lost them later in the course of total Romanization; but it is just as possible that their situation was somewhat different from that of the Albanians at that time.

Most of the Latin influence on Albanian, however, was exerted later, during the first centuries A.D. These elements show conspicuous similarities to corresponding elements in Romanian: Latin words only found in these languages, parallel changes of meaning, and so forth. These will be discussed below ("The Correspondences Between the Latin Elements of Albanian and Romanian.")

Common Romanian. The Early Slavic Influence

The elements in common with Albanian (the substratum elements and the similarities in the Latin influence) are, with some variation, extant in all Romanian dialects. They can be explained by the existence of the ancient Romanians in southern Serbia and northern Macedonia; nothing suggests that this population also lived north of the Danube. Some other phenomena in the Romanian language also attest to this.

The characteristics of Common Romanian or Ancient Romanian (*română comună, străromână*) were established by an analysis of the present-day dialects: Northern Romanian with Istro-Rumanian, and Arumanian with Meglenitic.[183] This common language existed through the tenth century A.D. This fact is not compatible with the idea that Romanian is the descendant of the entire Latin-speaking population that once lived on the Balkan Peninsula. That population was exposed to the Slavic invasion and conquest, which divided its formerly large areas into smaller territories during the seventh century at the latest. The language of the Vlachs was not affected by this but continued its own development for another three or four centuries without any significant dialectal differentiation. The only effect that the Slavic occupation of the Balkan Peninsula had on this idiom was a relatively weak Slavic influence. Living mainly as a pastoral population in the mountains of Serbia and Macedonia, this population also avoided assimilation to the Slavs, in contrast to the rest of the Romanized populations with the exception of those on the coast of Dalmatia. The habitat of the pastoral population was relatively isolated, the farmer peasant Slavs having preferred, for a long time, the lower mountains, the valleys, and the plains. This situation also made it possible for the Albanians to preserve their own language and identity.

A characteristic feature of all Romanian dialects is the similarity of the oldest Slavic influences. This would hardly have been possible if the ancestors of the Romanians had lived not only in Serbia and Macedonia but also north of the Danube, in Carpathian Dacia. All Romanian dialects contain a group of the same 70-odd words of Slavic origin, of a sound pattern characteristic of Slavic in the period before the tenth century. These words obviously existed in Common Romanian.[184] These lexical elements are not only found in all dialects; they also show some quite specific features, that is, changes compared with Slavic: there are, for example, several words formed from the Latin prefix in- and a Slavic loan-word such as Latin *in* + Slavic *vrtěti* "to turn, to twist, to wind" which resulted in a Common Romanian word from which there are today the Arumanian *anvîrtésc* "to whirl, to spin; to dance; to wield"; or Latin *in* + Slavic *plesti* "to plait, to braid": Arumanian *mpletesc*, Meglenit *amplites* and Norhern Romanian *împletesc* "knit, weave." Changes of meaning also occurred when Slavic words were transferred to Common Romanian: Slavic *koža* "skin" resulted in Arumanian and Northern Romanian *coajă* "shell, crust, rind," Slavic *loviti* "to hunt, to seize" was borrowed by Common Romanian in the sense "strike" (Northern Romanian *a lovi* "to strike, to beat; to hit; to attack; to hurt").[185]

These loans must originate from a special contact in a certain period and in a specific territory, indicating that the speakers of Common Romanian belonged to a homogenous community of people. It is most unlikely that their territory comprised, in addition to the central parts of the Balkan Peninsula, the plains north of the lower Danube and the territory within and east of the Carpathian Mountains.

The Development of the Dialects

It may be suggested that the uniformity of this language until the 10th century can be explained by the pastoral way of life of its speakers.[186] This may partly be true, but since dialects *did* develop later, it is probable that a more important reason was that they were living in a quite small area. After the tenth century, dialects developed in a territory not larger than Serbia (the distance between the Aromanians and the southern part of the area with place names of Northern Romanian origin still existing in the Slavic toponymy is less than 150 km.) What conclusions may be drawn from the unitary character of the Romanian language (even today, there are only dialectal differences between the different areas) seen against the history of the region in question?

If Northern Romanian would be the continuation of Latin spoken in Dacia Traiana, it would have developed largely independently from Aromanian and Meglenoromanian on the Balkan peninsula from the end of the third century A.D. onwards. Common Romanian could not have been unitary in these circumstances, and in more than 1700 years without everyday contacts between the speakers of Northern Romanian and Aromanian, the two idioms would have diverged toward mutual unintelligibility, as shown, for example, by the case of Italian and French.

The dialectal differentiation of Common Romanian began in the tenth to eleventh century, following the emigration of the Romanians to the north, and resulted in two main dialects, each with one subdialect: Arumanian with Meglenitic and Northern Romanian with Istro-Romanian. The fact that Arumanian has no Hungarian loan-words indicates that the separation must have occurred prior to the tenth century.[187] Obviously, the cause of the diverging development must have been that contact between different groups of speakers was lost or weakened. Under the circumstances of the tenth through twelfth centuries this must have been caused by migration of groups of speakers in different directions. In this way, a southern area of Arumanian was created in the region today divided by the Yugoslav-Greek frontier and a northern one of Northern Romanian in Serbia, Montenegro, and eastern Bulgaria, where place names with the Northern Romanian sound pattern still exist in the Slavic toponymy. The Vlachs were first recorded in these areas in a report in 976 A.D., which mentioned them as being between Lake Prispa and Kastoria in northern Greece. At the beginning of the eleventh century, Byzantine sources recorded Vlachs "throughout Bulgaria." The Byzantine chronicler Kekaumenos described the Vlachs as living in Greece in the second half of the eleventh century.

The Northern Romanian dialect shows a very strong South Slavic (Bulgarian) influence from the sound pattern of Bulgarian in the eleventh through thirteenth centuries. The Bulgarian lexical elements transferred to Northern Romanian in that period are often terms dealing with social and state organization as well as with religion and Church hierarchy. In Arumanian the Slavic influence from that period is much weaker. Consequently, after the disruption of contacts between the speakers of Arumanian and Northern Romanian, the former continued what was essentially their earlier way of life, relatively isolated from the Slavs, while the Northern Romanians changed their social situation to a considerable degree, taking part in the social life of the Bulgarian population. With this stage, the reconstruction of the main historical events can be corroborated by more detailed historical records; these tell us that strong groups of Vlachs living in Bulgaria took part in the organization of the Second Bulgarian Empire in 1186 A.D.

THE ROMANIAN LINGUISTIC LITERATURE

Contemporary Romanian historiographers consider the theory of the Romanian ethnogenesis mainly north of the Danube as axiomatic. Many examples have been given above to illustrate the effect of this fixation on the treatment of problems connected with the origin of Romanian in historical and archaeological works. The study of the Romanian language is also, however, of major significance to the problem. Historically, the discipline of linguistics determined that the speakers of early Romanians must have lived within the Roman Empire and in close contact with Italy for many centuries after the abandonment of Dacia Traiana by Rome in 275 A.D. With respect to the problems connected with the ethnogenesis of the Romanians, the Romanian linguistic literature contain more reliable data than most historical and archaeological works. *Istoria limbii române*[188] or *Istoria limbii române*,[189] for example, gives a very good picture of the Romanian language; and many other works and articles published in linguistic periodicals in Romania offer valuable information. Unfortunately, however, not even these publications are immune to influence from official policy. Because of the scarcity of materials, the problem of the origin of Romanian is hard to determine; and with regard to many details, one must be content with more or less plausible hypotheses. Debates and discussions, with the presentation of widely different ideas, are necessary and could lead to the clarification of problems. The opposite is achieved, however, by the systematic use of statements lacking any material evidence, by "solving" linguistic questions mostly or exclusively by means of archaeological finds, and by reaching conclusions that are in contradiction to the facts or to other conclusions presented in the same work. The subjective and one-sided treatment of the problems and the failure to draw logical conclusions from established facts also exacerbate the situation.

Correspondences Between the Latin Elements
of Albanian and Romanian

One of the most important tools available to explicate the early history of the Romanian language is the study of its connections with Albanian. Numerous treatises have been written with the aim of diminishing their importance, since they obviously point to the early Romanians' prolonged presence in the central parts of the Balkan Peninsula.

Haralambie Mihăescu claimed the oldest Latin influence on Albanian showed that the ancestors of the Albanians were exposed to the Latin language as early as the beginning of the second century B.C., in contrast to Romanian, which lacks most of these ancient elements. Mihăescu discussed a total of 545 words of Latin origin, giving them the following classifications: 1. words in wide circulation, preserved in Albanian (with their original meanings), Romanian, and in the Western Romance languages (a total of 270); 2. words that are lacking in the Romanian language but have left traces in the Western Romance languages (a total of 151); 3. words preserved only in Albanian and Romanian (a total of 39); and 4. words found only in Albanian (85).

This classification is misleading. A large share of the words in Mihăescu's first group do not belong there, as can be seen in a comparison of Mihăescu's classification with the data on the Pan-Romanic words in *Istoria limbii române*.[190] The following are the words beginning with the letter "a" in Mihăescu's first group that are not found in the *Istoria limbii române*'s list:[191]

Latin:	Albanian:	Romanian:	Meaning:
armissarius	harmëshuar	armăsar	stallion
aeramen	rrem, rremb	aramă	copper
aestimare	çmonj "appreciate"	pietre nestimate	precious stones
amita	emtë, ëmtë	mătuşă amita +	aunt
		suffix - uşă	
angustus	i ngushtë	îngust	narrow
arena	rërë	arina (Old N. Rom.	sand
		and Arum.)	
*ascla (assula)	ashkë, ashqe	aşchie	chip, sliver
avunculus	unq	unchi	uncle
axungia	ashung	osînsă (N. Rom.)	lard

There are 21 words beginning with "a" in the first group; take away these 9, which are not Pan-Romanic words, and almost half of Mihăescu's examples are shown to be misclassified. Far from being in "wide circulation," most of the 270 words of Latin origin and shared by Albanian and Romanian are characteristic of these languages and appear at most in one or two dialects in Italy, Sardinia, and France. (Among those beginning with "a," Mihăescu remarks only about one [armăsar] that it also appears in a central Sardinian dialect [armissarius]). It also appears from these examples that the sound pattern of these words is in many cases similar or identical and expressly specific to Albanian and Romanian:

Latin:	Albanian:	Romanian:	Meaning:
cogitare	kuitonj	cugeta	to think, to reflect
cognatus, -a	kunat, -ë	cumnat, -ă	brother-in-law
*stancus	i shtënk "one-eyed, one-sided; bad"	sting	left
*strambus	shtrëmp	strimb	crooked, curved

Mihăescu also included the Latin *cuneus* in the group of words in "wide circulation," in spite of the fact that this word means "wedge" and only Albanian *kuj* and Romanian *cui* have the sense of "nail." The case is the same with Latin *hora* "hour." In Albanian and Romanian, this word is used in the sense of "time": Albanian *hërë*, Romanian *oară: de două ori* "twice," *de multe ori* "many times." The only example of this sense besides Albanian and Romanian is found in the Venetian dialect (*doi ora* "twice").[192] In Mihăescu's first and largest group of words of Latin origin in Albanian and Romanian, many specific Balkan-Latin elements are hidden, or classified there with a particular purpose, to deprive them of their significance.[193]

Mihăescu admitted that only 39 words belonged exclusively to Albanian and Romanian; but he did not allow even these to indicate a close relationship between the two languages, saying that 19 of the 39 words "were used widely." They are found in ancient sources. They could have developed "independently in Albanian and Romanian." This group omits, for example: Albanian *krushk*, Romanian *cuscru* "father of a son-in-law," from Latin *cónsocer*, although all other Romance languages, including Dalmatian, derive this word from *consócer*; Albanian *mbret*, Romanian *împărat* "emperor," the only popular surviving form of Latin *imperator*; and Latin *pacare* "to reconcile," which changed its meaning in the Western Romance languages to "pay" (*cf.*, Italian *pagare*, French *payer*), with only Albanian and Romanian having preserved the original Latin sense of this word: Albanian *pagonj*, Romanian *împăca* "to reconcile."

Another 12 of the 39 words did not prove any similarity between Albanian and Romanian, according to Mihăescu, because "they show either important morphological or semantic differences or analogies with the Western Romance languages."[194] This group includes, for example, Albanian *pyll*, Romanian *pădure* "forest," from Latin *pal-*

ude(m), padule(m) "marsh." The sens of "forest" is found exclusively
in Albanian and Romanian and appeared in this sense in records
from Italy in the sixth or seventh century. Latin *draco* "dragon"
appears in Albanian and Romanian in the sense of "devil" (Albanian
dreq, Romanian *drac*), as it does in a southern French dialect (*drac*),
which shows that one can find single examples in different Romance
idioms and dialects for many of the Albanian-Romanian isoglosses.
This is natural, since they all are Latin words. The point is that
Albanian and Romanian not only share isolated elements but whole
series of words, in most cases of a peculiar sound pattern, distinct
from those found in the rest of the Romance languages. Moreover,
and most significant, common changes of meaning are frequent.[195]

A third group in these 39 words consists of words from the
Byzantine culture. The existence of such words supports the characteristic of the East Latin idiom. In several cases, the exact derivation
of a word cannot be established; but its appearance in Albanian and
Romanian is, nevertheless, significant: Independently from the etymology of Romanian *codru* "forest, mountain" (and also "big piece of
bread"), the word cannot be separated from Albanian *kodrë, kodër*
(with the same meaning).[196] Mihăescu's third group contains 151 words
found in Albanian and in the Western Romance languages but not
in Romanian, which can be explained by the fact that Albanian
contains many Latin words borrowed during the first two centuries
B.C. and that Albanian and Romanian history was not the same in
later periods. Furthermore, the lack of a Latin word in a Romance
idiom does not prove that the word did not exist at an earlier time.
Many of the words in this group are represented in Romanian by
Slavic loan-words. Therefore, only when one Latin word in one of
the languages is represented by another in the other language may
it be regarded as a certain difference.

The fourth group is 85 words of Latin origin that survived only
in Albanian. What was said about the third group also applies to
the fourth. Indeed, all Romance languages and idioms influenced by
Latin contain several words do not appear in the rest of the Romance
languages. It is therefore evident that the Latin elements of Albanian
and Romanian are also closely related.[197]

The "Carpatho-Balkan Territory" as the Assumed Area
of the Origin of the Romanian Language

In a linguistic textbook published in Romania, it has been stated
that the theory of an exclusively north-Danubian origin of Romanian
is no longer tenable: it could not be proved from the scientific viewpoint,

since the existence of the dialects south of the Danube (Arumanian, Meglenorumanian, and Istro-Rumanian) do not support this hypothesis.[198] According to authoritative Romanian historians and linguists (*e.g.*, Ştefan Pascu and Alexandru Rosetti), an extremely large territory, both north and south of the lower Danube, was inhabited in ancient times by the ancestors of the present day Romanians.[199] This large territory is often called the "Carpatho-Danubian area," [200] a designation unknown in ancient historical records. It is approximately 460.000 km^2 large, and extends from Moldavia through Transylvania and Wallachia to Serbia and Macedonia. It is heterogenous from both the geographical and the historical viewpoints.

In works on the history of the Romanian people and language, it would be suitable to treat the entire area, both south and north of the lower Danube. One should, in fact, consider the area south of the Danube more important, because it is not only much larger than the Roman province north of the Danube (about 200,000km^2 compared with about 80,000 km^2) but was under Roman rule for six centuries compared to only 169 years for Dacia Traiana. This cannot be without significance for the development of a Romance language. It is, therefore, surprising to find that modern Romanian historiographers are interested mainly in the area north of the Danube, limiting most of their investigations to the present area of Romania. As was shown in the chapter on archaeology, several excavations are being carried out with the aim of finding early vestiges of Romanians there.

Romanian linguists have studied the Romanian dialects in the central parts of the Balkan Peninsula (including the Northern Romanian dialect) and have collected data of great significance,[201] which have been presented in recent works, such as that by Alexandru Rosetti and the two volumes of *Istoria limbii române*. The results of these works have not, however, been used sufficiently in historical research in current Romania, which, as was previously stated, persistently concentrates on the territory of present-day Romania. A recent review of the development of Romanian linguistics[202] demonstrated this error. According to this treatise,"the Latin culture began to vanish in Dacia at the beginning of the third century after the withdrawal of the Romans (271 A.D.), while the language spoken in that time remained in direct contact with Western Latinity for about three or four centuries. The Daco-Roman population consisting mainly of poor people continued to exist after 271 A.D. but in double isolation—geographical and cultural (the cultural relationships with Western Romance-speaking peoples resumed only two hundred years ago)."[203] The presumption

that the language of the "Daco-Romans" remained in direct contact
with Western Latinity for about three or four centuries (after the
abandonment of the province of Dacia Traiana), while these same
"Daco-Romans" were isolated from Western Latinity both geographically and culturally, is a contradiction of fundamental significance.
The evidence of early Romanian's development in close contact with
the Western Romance languages (northern Italian dialects) and in the
central Balkan Peninsula with Albanian and South Slavic is often
mentioned in contemporary Romanian linguistic literature; but the
available conclusions are ignored or denied, with reference be made,
instead, to archaeological data.[204]

Ion I. Russu admitted that the sound pattern of the pre-Latin
elements of the Romanian language was not specific to Dacian,
Thracian, or Illyrian. He was, however, supposed to demonstrate the
validity of the theory of continuity and therefore elaborated a hypothesis based on historical and archaeological data, independent
from any linguistic considerations. He departs from the present
territories of the Romanians and from the territory in Southeastern
Europe that was once under Roman rule.[205] In his view, it was
admitted as early as in the mid-nineteenth century that only Dalmatia,
northern Thracia, Moesia, and Carpathian Dacia could be considered
as the area of formation of the Romanian language.[206] Russu uses
compound terms such as "Thraco-Dacian" to designate the pre-Latin
(autochthonous) elements of Romanian. He states clearly that he uses
these terms .."only as an hypothesis and in order to simplify the terms"
(Russu, *Etnogeneza...*, 1981, p, 114).

There is strong evidence to doubt Russu's method that is outside
of linguistic research. Investigations carried out on this field indicate
a very close relationship between autochthonous elements of Romanian
and Albanian language. Nevertheless, Russu prefers not to use the
term "Albanian" or "Proto-Albanian" because of an alleged "general
consensus" about the formation of Romanian.

Iancu Fischer admitted that the Romanian language contained all
the changes that appeared in Late Latin from the fourth through the
sixth centuries.[207] It may be concluded, therefore, that Romanian
developed from Late Latin, which was spoken within the Roman
Empire in the fourth through sixth centuries when the former province
of Dacia Traiana was no longer part of that empire.

This problem of central importance for the history of the Romanian
language is generally avoided in surveys and works published in
contemporary Romania. All conclusions contradicting the theory of
continuity are omitted, and the facts that are not in agreement with
the theory are presented only fragmentarily. For example, a number

of sound changes in Late Latin are mentioned but without any indication of the fact that a large number of them appeared after the third century A.D. It is, of course, difficult to determine exactly the period of change in pronunciation or usage of grammar, and such changes are usually gradual. Several alterations becoming general in Late Latin could have started earlier, during the second or third centuries. The construction of the perfect tense with the verb *habeo*, for example, already appeared in the third to fourth centuries; but many others, such as the palatalization of Latin *k* in front of *e, i* (for example *cellar, vicia*); the assibilation of Latin *t* + *e, i* : Latin *terra* > Romanian *ţară*; the development of the syncretism of the genetive + dative; the characteristic patterns of declension of the verb in the modern Romance languages; and many other characteristics began in the period when the territories north of the Danube no longer belonged to the Roman Empire. All these Latin changes affected the language of the ancestors of the Romanians, since, as is also shown above, they all are present in the Romanian language.

An important problem of the South Slavic influence on Northern Romanian is its late character, the majority of the South Slavic (Bulgarian) elements in this language showing the sound pattern of Bulgarian in the eleventh to thirteenth centuries.[208] In that era, the Slavs north of the Danube did not, in contrast to the Bulgarian Empire, constitute a state and had no ecclesiastical institutions. This is one of the reasons for rejecting the theory of continuity north of the Danube. By formulating four theoretical possibilities, Ion Coteanu assumed that the late date of the strongest Slavic influence on Northern Romanian did not intimate that the ancestors of the Romanians were living south of the Danube. He considers that the contacts between the Slavs and the assumed Roman population north of the Danube were different from those existing between the Slavs and the Byzantines in the Balkan Peninsula. The four possibilities are that 1. Dacia was entirely uninhabited when the Slavs began to populate it. This hypothesis cannot be accepted, Coteanu continues, since the ancient names of rivers were preserved, which presupposes a local population from whom the Slavs could learn those names. The most significant statement in this passage is that these names show a Slavic sound pattern (*"pronunţate după manieră slavă"*).[209] 2. Only non-Romanized Dacians lived in Dacia at the time of Slavic colonization. In that case, either the Dacians would have been assimilated to the Slavs or the other way around. "Since none of these theoretical possibilities occurred in reality, this hypothesis too is baseless."[210] 3. In Dacia, only a small number of a Romanic population remained. In that case, "since in a certain period of time, *terra Blacorum* is mentioned in

Dacia,"[211] it must be concluded that this scarce population, showing a great vitality, had Romanized at least a part of the Slavs and all Dacians. 4. Finally, there is the theory of Daco-Roman continuity, which assumes that Romanians were living in several "lands" (*țări*) in the tenth century, when the Hungarians began to populate Transylvania.

These four theoretical possibilities do not, at any rate, clarify the issue. Hypothesis 1 is absurd; no serious scholar supports it. Hypothesis 2 corresponds in principle best to reality, but this is obscured by faulty formulation. It is surprising that Coteanu does not mention at least the Gepidae, a people known to have been living in several areas of former Dacia in the sixth century and who must has been the largest population when the Slavs arrived; Dacians no longer existed in significant numbers, if at all.[212] The Slavs consequently needed neither a Roman population nor Dacians in order to learn the ancient names of the rivers. The result was a Slavic population, from whom the Romanians later borrowed a vast number of geographical names, including those of the great rivers. Coteanu's statement that "none of these results has been produced" is based on the situation in a much later period, when Romanians already lived north of the Danube. The reasoning in 3 is also erroneous. Coteanu evades the fact that the Vlachs are not mentioned in Transylvania before the thirteenth century by using the vague formulation "in a certain period of time." That period is irrelevant in this context, since this mention of Vlachs does not prove that the Slavs found a Romanic population in Dacia some 600 years earlier. Finally, hypothesis 4, as it appears also from this text, is not supported by any evidence.

Discussing the question of the substratum of Romanian and its connection with Albanian, C. Poghirc does not exclude the possibility that "the substratum of the Romanian language is the language from which also modern Albanian derives" [213] Since the ancient Albanians lived in parts of present-day Albania and in areas to the east, this also implies the possibility that Romanian originated from the central parts of the Balkan Peninsula. Poghirc could not question the validity of continuity in Dacia Traiana; and such implications were therefore not discussed.

In the comments written to Ovid Densusianu's *Histoire de la langue roumaine* (1975 edition), it is admitted generally by Slavists that the Slavic language that influenced early Romanian was spoken south of the Danube (Old Church Slavonic).[214] These temporary admissions as well as the ambiguity of many texts indicate the tension felt by

Romanian linguists between objective research and the requirements of imposed official ideology.

About the Relationship of Latin to Gothic and
Its Assumed Relevance to the Romanian Language

Several Romanian lexical elements are assumed to have originated from Old Germanic. None of these etymologies has, however, proved valid; and Romanian linguists now believe that there are no Old Germanic elements in Romanian with the exception of a small number of words borrowed from Old Germanic by the East Latin spoken on the Balkan Peninsula.[215] Nevertheless, certain authors still return to the subject with new hypotheses. According to one assumption, the linguistic exchanges between Latin and Gothic occurred to the greatest extent in Dacia Traiana, between the middle of the third century A.D. and the end of the fourth century. The symbiosis between the two populations there resulted in the borrowing of Latin elements by Gothic of any period as well as in a Gothic influence on the Latin spoken in the area, the vestiges of which can be found in modern Romanian.[216]

In a critical analysis of this theory the difficult problem of the Latin influence on the Old Germanic languages must be viewed in its entirety, that is, without focusing or restricting attention solely to Dacia and to the third and fourth centuries. There are two main problems: The Latin influence on Gothic and its alleged significance for the history of Romanian, and the alleged Gothic influence on the Latin from which Romanian developed. The main difficulty here is the scarcity of data. The most important source about the language spoken by the Goths is the Bible translated by the Gothic Bishop Wulfila (or Ulfila) in the years 340 to 350 A.D.; data from later periods are very scarce. Wulfila wrote, no doubt, in a Gothic that was intelligible to his fellow countrymen; but his text also contains learned elements such as loan-translations of such words as *misericordia* "dispensation" or *conscientia* "conscience" that were not known earlier by the pagan population of Goths and were most probably created by Wulfila. Another problem, in many cases, is the fact that it is often hard or even impossible to determine whether a certain word was taken from Latin or from Greek. The Goths had also close contacts with the Greek population; and many loan-words exist, in several cases with the same sound pattern, in Greek as well. On the other hand, the sound pattern of several words gives an indication about the period of borrowing. It is also well known that the Goths had extensive trade contacts with the Roman Empire beginning in the first century

A.D. and that in the fourth century some of them were settled as *foederati*[217] in the Roman Empire, in Moesia. Beginning in the third century the Goths made frequent raids and expeditions from their settlements north of the lower Danube into the Roman Empire, reaching Asia Minor and the Greek islands. They thus came into contact not only with Roman civilization but also with Greek and various Oriental civilizations.

In the first two centuries A.D., while the Goths were living along the Vistula, several Latin lexical elements were transferred to their language.[218] Western Europe was under Roman rule, and Old Germanic-speaking peoples were living beyond the frontiers. The non-Roman populations of Europe used and often imitated the products of the superior Roman civilization. Roman merchants traveled throughout Europe, and members of the Old Germanic communities lived in the Roman Empire for varying periods of time as soldiers or political representatives of their tribes. The Italian linguist Vittoria Corazza mentions 26 words that most probably were transferred from Latin to Gothic during the first two centuries A.D., when the Goths lived along the Vistula. Early borrowing is suggested in these cases by several criteria: Latin sounds that later changed were preserved in *wein* (< Latin *uinum*; with the preservation of the semivowel *u*), *kapillon* (< Latin *capillus* "hair"; *i* preserved, later borrowings show *e*); *kaisar* (< Latin *Caesar*; the diphtong preserved). The loss of the final vowel is considered an indication of early borrowing; Latin *lucerna* > Gothic *lukarn*, *pondo* > *pund*, *mensa* > *mes*. Several words (*asilus*, *ana-kumbjan*, *murikreitus*, for example) show signs of having been very well assimilated into the Gothic language. Groups of semantically related words are likely to have been borrowed in the same period; for example, *wein* "wine," *akeit* "vinegar," *alew* "oil"; or the words related to eating habits: *ana-kumbjan* "to sit down to dinner," *kubitus* "group of people dining together," *mes* "dish," table, wine-press." The fact that a word exists in several modern Germanic languages also suggests an early borrowing by Old Germanic (in any case, a borrowing not restricted to the Goths or to a specific territory): *wein*, compare, for example, English "wine"; *pund*, cf., English "pound"; *katils*, cf., German "Kessel"; *asilus*, cf., German "Esel"; *kaupo*, cf., German "kaufen." The following Latin words were most probably borrowed by Gothic during the first and second centuries A.D. when the Goths were living along the Vistula:[219]

kaupon	to trade
pund	pound
wein	wine

ake/i/t	vinegar
alew	oil
lukarn	oil lamp
aurkjus, aurkeis	pot
katils, katilus	vessel
asilus	ass
sakkus	sackcloth
faskja, faski	bandage
aurtigards	kitchen garden
anakumbjan	to sit down to dinner
kubitus	group of people dining together
mes	dish, wine-press, table
kapillon	to cut one's hair
paurpura, paurpaura	purple
sulja	sandal
marikreitus	pearl
nardus	spikenard
sigljan	to seal
sigljo	seal
kaisar	emperor, Caesar
Agustus	Augustus
Ruma	Rome
Rumoneis	Romans
kreks	Greek

From the viewpoint of semantics, most of these words are connected with everyday life, first of all with fashion (5 words), followed by food, eating habits, and domestic objects. Two words denote Southern European products; another two are related to commerce; and five are foreign names (for example, *Ruma* "Rome") adapted by Gothic. According to Corazza, only 17 lexical elements were borrowed during the third century. This number itself can hardly be decisive; many words of Latin origin may have existed at the time without having been used by Wulfila. It is also necessary to analyse the semantic groups to which these words belong, since this aspect may be of more significance.

The following Latin words were most probably borrowed by the Goths in the third century A.D.

assarjus	a bronze coin
drakma	drachma
unkja	a measure of land
arka	bag, ark

balsan	ointment
militon	to serve in the army
anno	soldiers' pay
intrusgjan	to graft
saur	Syrian
skaurpjo	scorpion
spaikulatur	watchman
karkara	prison
plapja	street
maimbrana	parchment
barbarus	barbarian
saban	shroud
ulbandus	camel

Vittorio Corazza believed that the contacts between the Goths and the Romans were closer than in earlier periods: such words as *assarjus, drakma, unkja,* and *arka* indicate that the Goths continued to have trade with the Romans; such words presuppose deeper contacts than those that existed along the Vistula. The penetration of the words of a military character is explained by the fact that Gothic soldiers fought as mercenaries in the Roman legions. Beginning in the middle of the second century, the barbarians made up the most important part of the Roman army.[220]

It is, however, difficult to see any significant difference between this list and the lexical elements transferred to Gothic during the previous period. Evidence of deeper contacts is, in any case, limited, despite the fact that it would be expected because of the increased number of Gothic soldiers serving in the Roman army in the third century. There are two words connected to the Roman monetary system: *drakma* "drachma" (a Greek coin, also widely used by the Romans), and *assarjus* (a bronze coin of low value)—such loan-words are usually indicative of commerce; there are also *unkja* "a measure of land" and *arka* "bag." Such borrowings are few and not even unique to the third century (*pund* "pound," thus, a unit of measure, had already been transferred to Gothic in the first two centuries A.D.). Moreover, *unkja* was not an isolated word in Dacia but was borrowed by most Old Germanic populatios: *cf.,* Old High German *unze,* Old Icelandic *unzia,* Danish *unse,* modern English *ounce.* With regard to the rest of these words, *balsan* was probably (according to Corazza) borrowed by Gothic merchants somewhere in the region north of the Black Sea and *ulbandus* "camel" in Asia Minor; *saur* "Syrian" could have been borrowed anywhere in Europe after Syria became a Roman province in 62 B.C. and Syrian merchants traveled throughout the continent. *Skaurpjo* "scorpion" and *saban*, a linen cloth made at Saban, a locality near Bagdad, are also more likely to have been borrowed elsewhere than in Dacia, as are the three military terms (*militon*, "to serve in the army," *anno* "soldiers pay," and *spaikulatur* "watchman"), which were probably introduced into Gothic by soldiers returning from service in the Roman army. It should also be remembered that none of the Latin words from which these 17 Gothic loans originate exists in the Romanian language, not even *platea*, of Greek origin, which was widespread in the Roman world and appears in the major Romance languages as Italian *piazza*, French *place*, and Spanish *plaza*.

The following borrowings from Latin were most probably transferred to Gothic in the fourth century:

aurali	handkerchief
kintus	a small coin
mota	taxes, the place where taxes are collected
Naubaimbair	November
puggs	bag
sinap or *sinapis*	mustard

To this must be added the fact that Wulfila's text contains several loan-translations of Latin words:

armahairts	Lat. *misericors*	dispensational
armahairtei	*misericordia*	dispensation
gudhus	*domus dei*	temple
haiþno	*paganus*	pagan
hundfaþs	*centurio*	centurion
miþwissei	*conscientia*	conscience
skillings	*clypeus, clipeolus*	shield

Of these *haiþno* may be a very old, Proto-Germanic loan-translation from Latin (although there are other etymologies too, none of which implies Dacia). With regard to *skillings*, in the third century, *clypeus, clipeolus*, was the popular name of an imperial Roman coin in the region of the Rhine River. (Latin *clypeus* "shield," Gothic *skildus* "shield"). Also, *hundfaþs* may be an ancient loan-translation from Latin (but could also originate from Greek). The rest of these loan-translations are learned constructions, most of them having been made by Bishop Wulfila.[221] In the Gothic language the number of loan-translations from Greek is much higher than those from Latin.[222]

The borrowings from Latin dating from the fourth century are too few to warrant any historical conclusions (they also belong to a variety of semantic categories). Obviously, our knowledge of the Latin borrowings by Gothic, at least from the third century A.D. and later, is extremely limited. At any rate, the linguistic material does not indicate anything about the territories in which the Gothic population was living during those centuries, and assumptions about Dacia being the main territory of borrowings lacks any evidence.[223]

This is also the case with possible Latin influence on the grammar of the Gothic language, including the Latin prefix *dis-* and the suffix *-arius*. Such cases in themselves never indicate a certain geographical area; they are significant only in determining the extent of the Latin influence on Gothic. It is claimed that Latin influenced the following grammatical elements in Gothic: the analytical past continuous and past passive; the present perfect; the accusative with the infinitive; and the accusative with the participle. This would be of great significance, since "the grammatical system of a language yields only to very high pressure from another language."[224] Not all of these phenomena were, however, with certainty borrowed from Latin (an Indo-European origin comes into question as well); and, more important, given the close and lengthy contacts between the Romans and the Old Germanic peoples, it is not surprising that the language of the latter was quite deeply influenced by Latin.

The Alleged Gothic Influence on the Romanian Language

The Romanian linguist Ştefănescu-Drăgăneşti claimed that Romanian was the first Romance language to be influenced by Old Germanic. Without giving any evidence, he wrote about many Romanian words of Gothic origin, giving, however, only five examples: *a găti* "to prepare"; *iubit* "beloved"; *leac* "remedy, medicine"; *lăutar* "singer"; and *isteţ* "shrewd, cunning." He added that most of these borrowings were considered to be of Slavic origin, because they occurred in Slavic, too, which borrowed them, in its turn, from Germanic.[225] Standard Romanian monographs on the history of the Romanian language,[226] however, consider the Slavic origin of these lexical elements to be firmly established. (With regard to *a găti*, this could also be a pre-Latin substratum word or a Slavic one borrowed by Albanian and from Albanian by Romanian).

The Romanian grammatical structures that Ştefănescu-Drăgăneşti believes were borrowed from Gothic are in reality Balkanisms: the analytical future with the auxiliary *a voi* "will" is found not only in all Germanic languages and in Romanian but also in Greek, Bulgarian, dialectally in Serbo-Croatian, and in the southern (Tosc) dialect of Albanian. The analytical future with *a avea* "to have" (not meaning "must"): *am să fiu* "I shall be" appears not only in Romanian but also in Bulgarian, Byzantine Greek, and the Tosc dialect of Albanian. In Old Romanian texts *a avea* also appears with the infinitive: *n'am a te lăsa* "I shall not let you," a perfect counterpart of Albanian *kam + me +* infinitive. The definite article in postposition is also a typical Balkan characteristic of Romanian that occurs in Albanian and Bulgarian as well. As the Albanian scholar, Eqrem Çabej,[227] pointed out, Romanian shows a concordance with Albanian in the use of the definite article in the smallest details of its syntactical position.

In conclusion, the Latin influence on the Gothic language was already strong in the first two centuries A.D., when the Goths were living along the Vistula. In the third and fourth centuries, the Goths were spread over a large area, from the Don River to Moesia, also including Dacia Traiana. The Latin loan-words from this time can be explained mainly by continuing trade contacts with the Romans, Gothic soldiers' serving in the Roman army, and military expeditions to the Balkan Peninsula and Asia Minor. The Latin influence on Gothic was exerted over several centuries and in a great territory, of which Dacia was only a small part. Of the 17 words probably borrowed during the third century, none suggests any connection with circumstances in Dacia; and none of the Latin words from which they derive exists in Romanian.

The assumption of a Gothic influence on the Romanian language is based on false etymologies and imaginary relationship of grammatical phenomena. The lexical elements assumed to derive from Gothic are mostly of Slavic origin, and the Romanian grammatical elements believed to be of Gothic origin are in reality a part of the many Balkanisms in the Romanian language and also are found in Albanian, Bulgarian, and other Balkan languages. There is nothing to support the idea that the Goths living north of the Danube in the third and fourth centuries would have had any influence on the speech of the ancestors of the Romanians. The assumed Old Germanic elements of the Romanian language are propagated mainly with the aim of defending the theory of continuity. Therefore, most of the proposed explanations are chosen in order to support a preconceived theory.

Assumptions often came to be accepted as more or less established facts, even by foreign scholars. Vittoria Corazza, for example, remarks that the Gothic domination over Dacia left interesting vestiges in some Romanian geographical names, such as Goteşti, Munte Gotului (correctly: Muntele Gotului or Muntele Gotul, cf. Iordan, 1952, *op. cit.*, p. 230), Pârăul Gotului, and the personal names Gotes, Manea (from Gothic *manna* 'man'), and Goma, Guma, from Gothic *guma* 'man', from which the place names Gomeşti, Gumeşti were created. Corazza refers to *Romania Germanica* of Ernst Gamillscheg.[228]

A detailed study of each individual element made by several Romanian scholars has shown that none of the Old Germanic etymologies (including those referring to place names) can be accepted. A study of these etymologies may, however, throw some light on the method by which such hypotheses are made plausible. There is first the historical basis: "Goths were once living in Dacia." There are also less rational ideas: Why would these names of different Germanic tribes have been preserved in France but not in Dacia?[229] With regard to the historical basis, one must remember that the Goths disappeared from Dacia at the end of the fourth century (and the Gepidae, in the seventh century). More important, no identifiable traces of these Old Germanic cultures are to be found in the popular traditions of any people now living north of the lower Danube. There is no historical tradition preserved in the folklore of the Romanian people about the ancient period of the formation of Romanian.[230] Because of these considerations, the scholar is forced to seek other, alternative explanations for these assumed Old Germanic names. In doing so, the phonetic laws of the Romanian language must be considered.

Romanian geographical names containing *Got-* are based mainly on personal names. Romanian, Slavic (Bulgarian), and Hungarian personal names come into question: Gotea could derive from the Romanian personal name Grigore-Gore, which in the speech of children is pronounced Gote.[231] The Romanian linguist Iorgu Iordan discusses an exhaustive list of geographical names of this kind: Muntele Gotului (Alba County), Pârâul Gotului (Alba), Goţi and Pârâul Goţilor (Sibiu County), Goţa (Slatina, Argeş County), Goţul (Pâşcani, Iaşi County), Gotca (Vaslui County), Gotea (Mihăileşti, near Bucharest), Goteşti (Murgeni, Bîrlad County), Goteşul (Cislău, Buzău County), and Gotgoaia (Iaşi County).[232] In explaining names, with a *t* (not those with a *ţ*), Iordan refers to the theory of the Hungarian scholar István Kniezsa, who derived these names from the personal name Got (Goth, Gót) existing in Slavic and in Hungarian and probably a diminutive of Gotthard, Gottlieb, and similar names. The geographical names of this type found in Muntenia and Moldavia (and perhaps also in Transylvania) may, also according to Iordan, be based on the Bulgarian personal name Goto or Gota, the diminutive of Georgi. This Bulgarian name was borrowed by the Romanians in the form Gotea, from which developed Goteş, Goteşti. Alexandru Philippide proposed an explanation related to *gotcă*, the Romanian name for a mountain hen. In Romanian, *got-* could have existed as the name of a bird, and this *got-* may be the basis of geographical names containing *Got-*.[233] The names with *ţ* (Goţ-) derive from the Romanian word *goţa*, monster, with which children are frightened when they are crying: *"Taci, că vine Go/a/ţa!"* (Don't cry, or Go/a/ţa will come). Iordan also adds, that if Goţa is the feminine of Goţul and this the name of the Goths, then it would contain the diphtong *oa* (with *a*, or, in the form without the definite article, *ă*, in the following syllable).[234]

Scholars who have critically analyzed the etymologies of Romanian lexical elements assumed to be of Old Germanic origin have also examined the personal names advanced in this connection and refuted these etymologies, in most cases concluding that the name derives from Slavic.[235] An example of this is Manea which was borrowed from the Bulgarian Manjo.[236] The Gothic language therefore does not contain any element that would suggest a symbiosis of Goths with a Latin-speaking population in the area of former Dacia Traiana; nor do the Romanian language and toponymy show any influence from Gothic.

With regard to the question of whether the Gothic language indicates anything about the neighbors of the Goths in former Dacia, there are only hypotheses. Gottfried Schramm has advanced the hypothesis of an *a > o* change in the barbarian languages of Southeastern Europe during the first two or three centuries A.D. The Gothic word *aikklēsjō*, which ultimately originates from Greek or Latin (*cf.*, Latin *ecclesia*), could have been borrowed from such a barbarian language.[237] Because of chronological considerations, those barbarians were probably living in a mountainous territory, possibly in Dacia Traiana. If this hypothesis were to prove correct, this would add another non-Roman population to the Goths, among whom Christianity was spreading north of the Danube as early as in the third or fourth century. It must be emphasized, however, that is only an hypothesis.

The Inherited Latin Words in Romanian

The study of the Latin vocabulary inherited by the Romance languages gives interesting insights into cultural history. In the Western Romance idioms, many terms connected with urban life have been preserved, indicating that at least some of the speakers of these languages lived in towns and practised trades already known by the Romans throughout the centuries. Romanian, however, did not preserve the Latin terms for urban life. The Romanian *oraş* "town" is of Hungarian origin; *drum* "road" derives from Greek *dromos*; *cale* "way," although a Latin word, originally meant the way used by transhumant flocks of sheep.[238] Latin *pavimentum* "floor" changed its meaning to "earth" in Romanian (*pămînt*). This suggests that the speakers of the

Romance language from which Romanian developed were, at least over a considerable period of time, a rural rather than urban people. Furthermore, the terminology of Latin origin of the most important agricultural plants (wheat, barley, rye, millet, and flax) and farming tools (plough [*aratru*], sickle, pitchfork, axe, and others) and farming activities (to plough, to sow, to sift) proves that the Romanian people practised farming without interruption.[239]

The Romanian language originates from one area of Roman colonization, whose southern frontiers in the Balkan Peninsula were established by Jireček and Skok.[240] South of this line, mostly Greek was spoken. The Vlach shepherds in their wanderings, however, reached areas south of the Jireček line in an early period. From the eighth century, there were Vlachs living in Greece, south of the Jireček line; and from the end of the tenth century onwards, groups of Vlachs were reported in almost all areas of the Balkan Peninsula. As the two main dialects of Romanian, each with a sub-dialect (Arumanian, with Meglenitic, and Northern Romanian [spoken north of the Danube] with Istro-Rumanian) developed, the language was disseminated by the wanderings of its speakers. The inherited Latin elements were spread with the language. No one has suggested that Arumanian, for example, originated in the area where its speakers are now living, simply because it contains several ancient, inherited Latin elements.

It is therefore strange that theories similar to this have been advanced about the Vlachs living north of the Danube. There is, for example, a group of hypotheses that connect the presence of certain physical remains (huts, objects of everyday use, such as pottery and open hearths) found in present day Romania with the corresponding words in the Romanian language.[241] The terms of Latin origin connected with agriculture and pastoral life are considered to indicate that the ancestors of the Romanians were peasants and pastoralists (not town-dwellers) in Dacia.[242] The words *sat* "village" and *cetate* "fortress" are also often given to prove the presence of the Romanians' ancestors in the former Roman province of Dacia Traiana after the retreat of the Romans.[243] Some Latin words, which changed their original meaning in Romanian (*e.g.*, Latin *veteranus* "soldier who served his term" > Romanian *bătrîn* "old"), were also thought to be connected with Dacia Traiana. The German linguist, Günter Reichenkron, for example, claimed this indicated that veterans of the Roman army settled in the province north of the Danube and that this is still testified to in our day by such Romanian words as *bătrîn* < *veteranus*, *bărbat* < *barbatus*, *mire* "bridegroom" < *miles* as well as the somewhat rough expression *fată* < *foetus* and, according to Tiktin, perhaps *copil* "child."[244]

In the same way, the religious terms of Latin origin have been connected with objects of Christian use found in former Dacia Traiana: oil lamps (*lucernae*), stamps for the fabrication of crosses, Byzantine amphoras on which a cross and the letters Alfa and Omega were painted, all dating from the fourth through to sixth centuries.[245] *Istoria României. Compendiu* went even further, claiming that Illyrian Christianity played an important role in the preservation of the Latin language in the Carpathian Mountains, because, beginning in the fourth century, missionaries spread Christianity in the Latin language, not only south but also north of the Danube. In this way one can explain the basic terminology of Daco-Roman Christianity, which is of Latin origin: *biserică* (*basilica*); *dumnezeu* (combination of *dominus* and *deus*, "Lord and God"); *lege* "law" in the sense of faith (*legem*); *cruce* (*crucem*) "cross."[246]

Haralambie Mihăescu, describing the dissemination of the Christian faith in the Latin language on the Balkan Peninsula beginning in the third century, asserted that in the fourth century, Christianity was generally accepted and reached Dacia north of the Danube; the word *quadragesima*, from which the Romanian word *păresemi* developed, is known, with a Christian sense, from that period. In Mihăescu's opinion, the Christian religion spread from the ecclesiastical centers south of the Danube to the populations north of the river; and this fact explains the preservation in the Romanian language of Christian terminology of Latin origin.[247]

There are several other hypotheses based on false premises. It must be noted that inherited Latin words do not indicate anything about the territory in which the ancestors of the Romanians were living. These words only show that the population from the time of Romanization onward, used the objects and at least knew religious concepts denoted by them. Such knowledge is totally independent of a people's territory. Physical remains connected with the rural way of life as well as objects of a Christian nature, have been also unearthed in many other territories, such as southern Poland and Slovakia, which had a Vlach pastoral population for several centuries; but no one would argue that these finds proved that the Vlachs had always lived there.

Such words as *zână*, *zănateci*, and *Sînziana* do not indicate that the cult of Diana survived the Romanization of Dacia. The word *sat* and the change of *pavimentum* to mean "earth" (*pămînt*) are connected with the rural way of life of the speakers of Romanian but tell us nothing about the territory in which they had lived earlier in their history. The basic Christian terms in the Romanian language only show that the ancestors of the Romanians were Christianized during the Roman period, which could have occurred on the Balkan Peninsula as well. Indeed, as even Reichenkron has remarked, these terms must have been adopted by the ancestors of the Romanians in an area in which the Latin language dominated.[248] The Christian Church was widely established beginning at the time of Constantine the Great (fourth century) when Dacia Traiana no longer belonged to the empire and would not have been affected.

The conditions for the development of basic religious terms in the Romanian language were really favorable in Dardania, the central part of the Balkan Peninsula. According to historical records as well as archaeological finds (ruins of several churches), this province was the center of religious life for a large part of the Balkan Peninsula for about three centuries. With regard to the cult of Diana (or Artemis), for instance, it is assumed that this cult survived the Romanization of Dacia and that Northern Romanian *sînziana* derives from the Latin Holy Diana "of Sarmizegethusa." It is also claimed that a religious and linguistic continuity was assured by the fact that the process of transformation took place in a rural milieu. This is probably true, but there is nothing to suggest that the process of transformation occurred in Dacia Traiana and that the cult of Diana was more widespread or more intense there than in other parts of the Roman Empire. The cult of the goddess Diana was widespread throughout the Roman Empire. It is clear that "les monographies soulignent à l'envi la diffusion du culte d'Artemis-Diane au Sud du Danube, en Pannonie, sur la côte Adriatique, en Norique."[249] Diana appears in antique place names in Africa and Syria, as well as on the Balkan Peninsula (*cf.,* ad Dianam in Epirus, mentioned in the Peuteringian Tables, and Ζάνες, given by Procopios). Today, in the Balkans there are Dzîna and Zona (probably from Arumanian *dzînă* "fairy"). North of the Danube, however, there are no such vestiges. In addition to Romanian, the name Diana is preserved in several Romance languages, as well as in Albanian: "Les langues roumaine et albanaise ont gardé le nom de la déesse avec la signification de 'fée': *zână, zanë.*"[250] Romanian folk traditions connected with the wild flower *Gallium verum* (Romanian *sînziana*) were even taken over by the Slavs living in the Balkan Peninsula.[251] There is nothing to imply that this cult survived the Romanization of Dacia and that the religious and linguistic continuity of this cult refers to that territory. On the contrary, all evidence is found in the Balkan Peninsula and other parts of the former Roman Empire. The ancestors of the Romanians inherited this cult in the central part of the Balkan Peninsula, where they also inherited their Romance language, and took it with them in their wanderings: the Northern Romanians north of the Danube and the Arumanians south of the Jireček-line.

The word *sat*, from Latin *fossatum*, reveals a borrowing south of the Danube: Its sound pattern does not agree with an inherited Latin word, because Latin *o* did not disappear in Romanian in this position. The disappearance of *o* occurred most probably in Albanian, *cf.*, Albanian *fsat* "village" (from Latin *fossatum*). As late as in the sixteenth century, *fsat* was recorded in the Northern Romanian territory. This word is thus probably an Albanian loan-word in Romanian. The meaning "village" is found only in Albanian and Romanian.

Another example is Romanian *bătrîn* "old" from Latin *veteranus* "soldier who has served his term" (classical Latin) or "old" (Vulgar Latin) in several texts, *veteranus* = *antiquus vel vetustus* (*cf.*, Vegliotic *vetrum*, Friulian *vedran*).[252] Obviously, veterans settled all over the Roman Empire and the change of the sense occurred in Late Latin.

The derivation of the Romanian word *mire* "bridegroom" from Latin *miles* "soldier" is considered dubious.[253] Rosetti mentions two possibilities: 1. a loan-translation on the pattern of Serbo-Croatian *vojno*, *vojino* "husband," from *voinu* "soldier" (the original sense of this Serbo-Croatian word would have been "courageous"); 2. an evolution of sense in the liturgical language (the young bridegrooms form an "army").[254]

Romanian *bărbat* "man, male, husband, manly, manful, virile" is of Byzantine origin (βαρβᾶτος) and meant "man" in contrast to eunuch.[255] None of these words mentioned above contains any element connected with Dacia Traiana; but they all show characteristics that point toward South, the vicinity of Albanian and Byzantine Greek, as well as the area in which Late Latin was spoken.

THE THEORY OF "CORE REGIONS" (KERNGEBIETE) OF THE ROMANIAN LANGUAGE

Some historians advance the hypothesis that certain peculiarities of speech of the Romanians living in the region of the Apuseni Mountains (Erdélyi-szigethegység) indicated that Romanian had been spoken there uninterruptedly since the Roman period (106–275 A.D.)[256] and even after the abandonment of Dacia Traiana.[257] Departing from the observation of Bartoli, according to the Romanian scholar Sextil Puşcariu, there was a correlation between the geographical position and the age of a linguistic phenomenon.[258] Puşcariu concentrated on the area of the Apuseni Mountains (northwestern Transylvania), disregarding the fact that the words in question are found in a much

TABLE IV
Romanian dialectal words cited by Sextil Puşcariu to support his *Kerngebiet* theory: the words, their Latin origin, and their meaning

Romanian dialectal word	From Latin	Meaning
ai	alium	garlic
arină, anină	arena	sand
ceteră	cithera	violin
cotătoare	Rom. căuta, dialect.: cota	mirror (căuta: to seek)
cuminecătură	communicare	eucharist, the sacrament
curechiu	coliclu, dimin. of caulis	cabbage
cute	cos, cotem	whetstone
june	juvenem	youth, young boy
moare	mūria	sauerkraut brine
nea	nix, nivem	snow
păcurar	pecorarius	shepherd
pedestru	pedester	poor man (only the sense specific for the region)
Sâmedru	Sanctus Demetrius	
Sînicoară	Sanctus Nicolaus	

larger area than those mountains. In his view, the Roman settlements were most dense in this region and, consequently, Romanization most intense. "A comparison of Giurescu's map[259] with our map, [Puşcariu continued], the words *aiu, pedestru, nea, păcurar, june,* and *cuminecătură* made it clear that the Romans extended from western Transylvania partly toward the west (where we find the words *ceteră* and *cotătoare* preserved), and toward the northwest, including all the territory north of the Mureş River and reaching towards the east in Moldavia and Bessarabia up to the Prut River and even beyond it, a process that may be followed historically and that is reflected in its final stage by linguistic maps such as those for *moare, curechiu,* and *cute.*"[260]

Three of the words mentioned in Table IV and Table V—*moare, curechiu,* and *cute*—induced Puşcariu to construct another hypothesis. In Muntenia the corresponding words are *zeamă de varză* (*zeamă* is of Greek origin), *varză* (from Latin *viridia-virdia*) and *gresie* (from

TABLE V
Romanian dialectal words cited by Sextil Puşcariu to support his *Kerngebiet* theory

Romanian dialectal word:	Found in area of:				Arumanian:	Corresponding word in Muntenia:	Origin:
	Banat,	Transylvania, Maramureş,	Moldavia,	Bessarabia			
ai	+	+ (excl. SE)	—	—	al'um	usturoi	("ai usturoi", from Lat. ustulare, Slavic pattern)
arină, anină	—	(central+ northern)	—	(part of)	arină	nisip	Bulg. nasip
ceteră	—	(centr.+NW)	+	—	—	vioară	Lat. uiola
cotătoare	—	(western)	—	—	—	oglindă	Slavic
cuminecătură	+	(part of)	—	—	cuminicătură	grijanie and other	Slavic words
curechiu	+	+ (excl. SE)	+	+	—	varză	Lat. virdia
cute	+	+ (excl. SE)	+	+	—	gresie	Alb. gërresë
june	+	+ (SW)	—	—	ğone	tînăr, flăcău	Lat. tenerus, Slavic chlakü
moare	+	+ (excl. SE)	+	+	moare	zeamă	from Greek
nea	+	+ (western)	—	—	neauă	zăpadă	Slavic
păcurar	+	+ (excl. S)	—	—	picurar	cioban	Turkish
pedestru	+	+ (western)	(part of)	+ (part of)	—	(only sense specific)	
Sâmedru	+	+ (excl. SE)	+	+ (north)	(exists in Meglenitic)	Sf. Dumitru	(not inherited Latin name)
Sînicoară	+	+ (NW)	+	—	—	Sf. Neculai	(not inherited Latin name)

The distribution of *moare* and *zeamă* in Romania (1936). North of the departing
line the ancient word of Latin origin, *moare* (< Latin *mūria*) "sauerkraut
brine" is used; south of the line, this word was replaced by a Greek loan
(*zeamă*) (*zeamă de varză* "sauerkraut brine"). (After S. Puşcariu: *Les enseignements
de l'Atlas Linguistique de la Roumanie*, 1936, map No. 12 (ALR-I, 755).

Albanian *gërëse*). On the basis of this difference between Muntenia
and northwestern Romania, Puşcariu assumed a "barrier" of ancient
Latin words between Muntenia and northwestern Transylvania: All
these innovations emanating from the south, in their expansion toward
the west and the north, came up against a relatively powerful wall
behind which the Latin words *curechiu, moare, cute, păcurar, Sânicoară,
Sâmedru,* and *cuminecătură* resisted them; and Puşcariu found on the
same side of this wall such words as *nea, cotătoare,* and *aiu,* instead
of *zăpadă, oglindă,* and *usturoi,* borrowed from the language of the
Slavs north of the Danube.[261]

There are several reasons why these hypotheses cannot be accepted.

1. The most numerous Roman settlements during the Roman era
were probably in western Transylvania, while in other parts of Dacia
Traiana, especially eastern Transylvania, the population was always
mainly non-Roman. Compared with many large areas on the Balkan
Peninsula, however, the Roman settlements in Dacia Traiana were
not particularly dense and, moreover, existed for only 170 years

compared with 600 years or more in the Balkans. In spite of this fact, most Roman settlements in the Balkan Peninsula disappeared within a few centuries after 600 A.D. Consequently, there is no general correlation in Southeastern Europe between dense Roman settlements during the Roman period and a Romanic population today.

2. Puşcariu's argument is illogical even when viewed by itself: The *sine qua non* of his theory would be that a certain area in which more inherited Latin words are used than in other areas coincides reasonably well with a Romanized area during the era of the Roman Empire. Of course, no exact coincidence should be expected; but what we find is rather a lack of any regularity: a large part of Dacia Traiana (the territory west of the *limes Alutanus*, present day Oltenia) is not among the areas in which Puşcariu finds ancient Latin words preserved. Moreover, and more important, all of these words are found in a much larger territory than that referred to by Puşcariu in his conclusion (the area of the Apuseni Mountains). These words are also used in western Romania along the Hungarian frontier, as well as in Maramureş; and most of them also in Moldavia and even in Bessarabia, beyond the Prut River, *i.e.*, in large territories that never belonged to the Roman Empire and consequently never had a Roman population. Puşcariu stated that this distribution was the result of an extension of the Roman population; but if these Latin words could spread over large areas that were not Romanized during the era of the Roman Empire, then their presence in the region of the Apuseni Mountains too may be explained by later expansion.

Puşcariu refers to 12 appellatives and two personal names (names of Saints), of which, however, only about half seem to be found exclusively in the northwestern and northern dialects of Northern Romanian. At least seven of the appellatives also exist in Arumanian:

Northern Romanian dialectal (northwest and north):	Arumanian:	Meaning:
ai	al'u	garlic
arină, anină	arină	sand
cuminecătură	cumnicătură	eucharist
moare	moare	sauerkraut brine
nea	neauă	snow
păcurar	picurar	shepherd
june	ğone	young man
Sâmedru	(exists in Meglenitic)	

Of the rest of these lexical elements, Sânicoară is probably not even an inherited element in Romanian: It has been assumed to have derived from the Latin Sanctus Nicolaus. When Greek Nicoláos was transferred to Latin, however, its accent moved to the long -a-: Nicoláos (as shown by the Old Italian form Nicoláo and modern Italian Niccoló, with the accent on -*lao*, -*lo*). The unstressed -*o*- of Latin changed in Romanian to -*u*-, and so the Latin Nicolaus would thus have become the Romanian *Nicuráu and not Nicoară.[262] Five appellatives remain, of which one has a special meaning in the northwestern dialect, different from the rest of the Northern Romanian territory (*pedestru* "poor man"). Two appellatives have, in other areas, corresponding appellatives also of Latin origin: *ceterā* corresponds to *vioarā* (from Latin *uiola*)[263] and *curechiu* to *varzā* (from Latin *virdia*). In these cases one can hardly speak of the preservation of Latin elements compared with foreign loans. Only two appellatives remain that do not exist in Arumanian and are replaced in Muntenia by foreign loans: *cute*, from Latin *cos, cotem*, is replaced by *gresie*, of Albanian origin; and instead of *cotātoare*, the Muntenian subdialect has *oglindā*, a back-formation from the verb *oglindi*, of Slavic origin.

3. If the ancestors of the present-day Romanians had been living in certain areas of modern Romania since the period of Dacia Traiana, their language would have developed largely independently from the rest of the Roman provinces. (Puşcariu mentions "the isolated Romanians of Dacia Traiana.")[264] The dividing line during this period (largely that of Late Latin) was the Danubian frontier of the Roman Empire. Innovations would thus have easily spread all over the Balkans but with much more difficulty or not at all across the Danube (assuming that a Romance language was spoken there); but if *varzā, gresie*, and *zeamā* once passed the frontiers of the empire (they are found today in Muntenia), what kind of a barrier could prevent them from also spreading to the speakers of Romanian in Transylvania? An analysis of the Romanian language from the viewpoint of the period in which its Latin elements originated shows that most of the new constructions and new lexical elements that appeared in Late Latin (that is, in the speech of Italy from the fourth through the seventh centuries) are, indeed, found in it[265] (including its subdialect spoken in northwestern Transylvania). In other words, there is no difference whatsoever in this respect between the subdialects of Northern Romanian; the differences are of a much later date.

4. Five principles (four areal and one historical) have been established for *linguistic geography*: a) isolated areas (those with fewer contacts, mostly islands, such as Sardinia) and b) lateral areas (in the Roman Empire: Iberia, the Balkans; in Northern Romanian: the

Banat, Crişana, Maramureş, and certain areas in Moldavia and Bessarabia) preserve usually earlier phases of language. c) A phase spread over a larger territory is usually older than the corresponding phase in a smaller area. This principle can only be applied, however, to the Roman Empire *in toto*.[266] d) Areas conquered (and Romanized) later often preserve the earlier phases. (In the Empire, Italy was usually more innovative than the provinces). e) If a phenomenon has two phases of which one is disappearing or has disappeared, this phase is the older one. The Latin *ignis*, "fire," for example, is not found in the Romance languages, all of which preserved the more recent word, *focus*.

It is now generally recognized that these principles are to be understood only as general tendencies. "All of them are full of exceptions and contradictions,"[267] and the opposite (especially of principles [c] and [d]) often occur. More important in the context of the *Kerngebiet* theory is that these principles at best can only give some indication of the relative chronology of changes in language.[268] They are not helpful in determining the absolute age of linguistic phenomena. One linguistic phase may indeed be earlier than another, but this does not indicate that it has existed in the area in question ever since the time of the Roman Empire. It is also needful to take into account the continuous change of language. Most Romance languages, for example, preserve the Latin *caballus* instead of *equus*, "horse." One could conclude from this that *equus* or *equa* survived only in lateral areas: Spanish *yegua*, Romanian *iapă* (< Latin *equa*, both with the sense of "mare"). Through ancient texts, however, it is known that the word derived from Latin *equa* was once used throughout the Gallo-Romance territory; Old French *ive* "mare" (from Latin *equa*) was still widely used in the fourteenth century. The areal principles should be examined, therefore, by chronological data.

The most plausible division of the Northern Romanian dialect distinguishes five areas with subdialects: 1. Muntenia, 2. Moldavia, 3. the Banat, 4. Crişana, and 5. Maramureş. Transylvania lacks any particular Romanian subdialect; the Muntenian subdialect extends over southern Transylvania and the Moldavian over northeastern Transylvania. Beyond this division, the Northern Romanian territory can be divided into two, three, or four areas, on the basis of several lexical elements. For example, instead of *ficat*, *varză*, and *năduşeală* in the southern area, there are *mai* (from Hungarian *máj* "liver") *curechiu*, and *sudoare* in the north;[269] or there are three areas: in Muntenia, one says *os* (from Latin *ossum* "bone"), in Moldavia, *ciolan* "animal bone with or without flesh on it" (from Slavic *članŭ*), and Crişana and Maramures, *ciont*, with the same meaning as *ciolan*, from

Hungarian *csont* "bone." For the word meaning "cemetery," for example, four areas can be distinguished: *cimitir* (Muntenia), *ţintirim* (Moldavia), *mormînt* (the Banat), and *temeteu*, from Hungarian *temetö* "cemetery" (Crişana). In Daco-Romanian the same notion can be expressed by one, two, or more words, as a consequence of the meeting within the same linguistic area of some old words with new ones, of some words of primary form (Latin, Slavic) with words created on Romanian territory, of some more or less recent loans from other languages (Hungarian in the west, Ukrainian in the east, Bulgarian in the south).[270]

These facts leave no room for the theory of ancient Roman-Romanian *Kerngebiete*; and Matilda Caragiu Marioţeanu, describing the Romanian dialects and subdialects in detail, does not even mention this theory. The appearance in certain subdialects of the words *nea, arină*, and *ai* is mentioned by this author only as an example of the preservation of some archaic words in lateral areas.[271]

5. In Muntenia Latin words were preserved, words that in other areas were replaced by foreign loans. Some investigators drew the conclusion that the presence of such words indicated that Muntenia (or part of this province) was another ancient Romanian *Kerngebiet*. The arguments were similar to those used by Puşcariu; one as that advanced by Eugen Lozovan is based on Latin words in Muntenia for which foreign loans are used in Transylvania and on geographical names derived from the Slavic name of the Romanians: *codrii Vlăsiei,* and *Vlaşca*. In Muntenia, argued Lozovan, one finds the ancient terms of Latin origin: *celar* "cellar," and *cuptor* "oven, kiln," as well as several words from the substratum of Romanian: *argea* "room made in the earth" and *vatra satului* "the precincts of the village" (*cf.,* Albanian *vatër, vatra* [Tosc dialect] and *votër* [Gheg dialect], "hearth, fireplace, dwelling")." These are modest words, of Latin or of Thracian origin (*argea, vatra*), referring to the settlement of a stable population."[272] Other differences compared with Transylvania are words of Latin origin that were replaced by loans in northwestern Transylvania:[273]

Muntenia:	From Latin:	Northwestern Transylvania:	From:	Meaning:
faţă	facia (Vulgar Latin, from classical Latin facies)	obraz	Old Slavic obrazŭ	face
ficat	ficatum	mai	Hungarian máj	liver
suspin	suspiro	oftez	(cf., Greek áhti)	I sigh
nebun	ne (Slavic ne) +bun (Lat. bonus)	bolînd	Hung. bolond	mad, insane

Moreover, in Muntenia, the iotacized verb-forms (rîz, văz, auz) are used, which in Transylvania and other areas were replaced by analogical forms (rîd, văd, aud). Pointing out that a part of Muntenia is called Vlaşca, indicating the presence of Vlachs there, Lozovan concluded: "To summarize, linguistic geography and toponymy not only do not contradict our theory about the existence of an ancient Danubian zone where a Roman population could survive but can even be used to delineate the frontiers of such a zone."[274] Consequently, the area considered ancient by Puşcariu is now shown to be one in which foreign words have replaced Latin expressions preserved in Muntenia.

6. As shown by the first written texts in Northern Romanian, the speakers of this language in Maramureş and in southeastern Transylvania in the sixteenth century spoke a language much closer to Latin than any present-day Northern Romanian dialect. The so-called rhotacizing texts were translated in the north of Transylvania (Maramureş) beginning with the sixteenth century. One stratum of their language is characterized by the subdialect spoken there and another by that spoken in southeastern Transylvania, from where the copyst came. In these texts there are certain phonetic, morphological, and lexicological characteristics that bring to light a stage of the language closer to the Latin prototype.[275]

Phonetic features: Latin d > dz (a stage between Latin and modern Northern Romanian); the *e* after *r* is preserved: întîniu, spuniu (with a palatalized *n*) instead of the modern Northern Romanian întîi, spui (except in the Banat).

Morphological features: the final *u* was preserved for the nouns of the second declension (Latin -us, -um): domnu, împăratu (today domn, împărat in Northern Romanian, but Arumanian has still final syllabic *u*); the simple perfect of Latin is not entirely abolished: Latin feci— sixteenth century Maramureş, Bucovina, and northern Moldavia: feciu, Latin venemus > venremu (today făcui, venirăm). A form of the conditional inherited from the perfect of the Latin subjunctive, as well as other morphological pecularities, was still in use.

More interesting, however, is the vocabulary, which shows an unsuspected richness of words inherited from Latin, words that have disappeared from circulation in the language today or that perhaps survive as vestiges in some remote region of the country: agru < agrum, "tilled land"; ariră < arenam, "sand"; auă < uvam, "bunch of grapes"; deşidera < desiderare, "to desire, to wish"; fuşte < fustem, "staff, rod, baton"; gerure < gironem, "depth, abyss"; gintu < gentem, "people, family, relative"; ğune < juvenis, "young man"; măritu < maritum, "bridegroom"; a se numără < nominare, "to mention by name, to give a name to"; *păsa* < *passare*, "to go" (today *păsa* < *pensare*, "to weigh on, to press" [now preserved only in such expressions as *nu-mi pasă*]; *urăciure* < *orationem*, "wish, congratulation"; *viptu* < *victus*, "wheat, corn, victuals"; *vărgură* < *virgulum* < *virgo*, "virgin, maiden"; *opu iaste* < *opus est*, "it is necessary, it is needed."[276] To these may be added several words that have preserved the original Latin meaning rather than that of modern Romanian: for example, *codru* (today "forest") with the sense of "mountain"; *fămeaie* (today "woman") with the sense of "family"; *gǔdeț* (today "county") with the sense of "judgment"; *săruta* (today "to kiss") with the sense of "to greet, to salute."[277]

One must note that only a few centuries ago, the subdialect of Northern Romanian (and Northern Romanian in general) spoken in Maramureş and in adjacent areas of Moldavia, that is, in territories in which Roman settlements never existed, was much closer to Latin than any Northern Romanian dialect is today.

7. Returning to present-day Romanian, the most conservative dialect is Arumanian, which shows many archaic characteristics in all areas of language: phonology, morphology, syntax, and lexical elements. "Its archaic features bring Arumanian near to Ancient Romanian (*română comună*)."[278] Many of the archaisms found in present-day Arumanian still existed in the sixteenth century in Northern Romanian. In the following, a short description of the main archaic characteristics of this dialect will be given, based on the presentation by Matilda Caragiu Marioţeanu in *Compendiu de dialectologie română* (1975).

Phonology: The vowel system of the Farserot subdialect of Arumanian is identical to that of Ancient Romanian (*română comună*):

Arumanian has no *i* before an initial *e-*, as Northern Romanian has through Slavic influence: Arum. *eşt*ⁱ, *eşt*ⁱ, N. Rom. *ieşt*ⁱ, "you are." The palatal consonants *l'*, *ń* reappear: Latin *leporem* > Arum. *l'épur*, N. Rom. *iepure*. The vowels are not affected by the character of the vowel in the following syllable: Lat. *pilu(m)* > Ancient Romanian (*română comună*) **peru* Arum. *per*ᵘ, N. Rom. *păr*. The final *-u* of Latin is preserved: Lat. *lupu(s)* > Ancient Rom. **lupu* > Arum. *lup*ᵘ, N. Rom. *lup*. A characteristic feature of Arumanian (as well as of Meglenitic) is the treatment of the Latin velars *c, g* + *e, i*. In N. Rom., these developed to *ĉ, ĝ*; Arum. has *ț, ɖ*: Lat. *cepa* > Arum. *țeápî*, N. Rom. *ceapă*; Lat. *gelu* > Arum. *ɖer*ᵘ, N. Rom. *ger*. - Latin c, - t, followed by io, iu, changed to ĉ, and j + o, u, and d + ió, iú changed to ĝ.

(An innovation of Arumanian is the prothesis of an a before words that begin with a consonant, particularly r, l: Lat. rivus > Arum. ariu̯, (N. Rom. rîu). The palatalization of the labials is general (all labials are affected in all subdialects) and total (there are no intermediary stages).

Morphology: The Latin plural suffix used in the words tata and mamma (tatanis > tatane, mammanis > mammane) is preserved: mumî, "mother"; mumîñ', "mothers." The dative is expressed by analytic means, with the preposition a (Lat. ad), which was also extended to the genitive.

The accusative of the place names is expressed without a preposition, as in Latin: (direction): mi duc" Hrúpişti "I go to Hrupişte," in Northern Romanian: mă duc la Hrupişte; (existence in a place): éscu Sîrúnî di dáu̯î ḑili "I have been in Saloniki for two days"; in Northern Romanian: sînt la Salonic de două zile.[279]

Another archaic feature is the fact that the accusative is expressed without pe (used in N. Rom. in certain cases—an innovation after the sixteenth century). The indefinite article is ună (uní) (< Lat. una): uní casî, uní f̦eatî (N. Rom. Istro-Rumanian have o). Arumanian has preserved Latin viginti "twenty": yñ̆ḡiţ', yíyinţ'.

The verb: (The infinitive does not exist with a verbal value, only the long form, used as a noun.) The simple perfect is, the usual tense of the past in Arumanian, in contrast to Northern Romanian, where it is no longer used in speech (except in subdialects). The conjugation of the verbs shows the following archaisms: the third person plural indicative is etymological: Lat. cantabant > Arum. cînta; we find this in the sixteenth century texts of N. Rom.; present-day N. Rom. has, however, -au. The first and second person plural continue the Latin endings: -m", t": cîntăm", cîntat" (present-day N. Rom. has cîntarăm, cîntarăţi; but in the sixteenth century texts forms similar to Arum. are found.). Like Latin, Arumanian still has the two forms of the simple perfect: "strong" forms, with the stress on the stem, and "weak" forms, stressed on the inflexion. (The strong form also existed in the sixteenth century in N. Rom.) The auxiliary of the compound perfect (perfectul compis) is not grammaticized as in N. Rom.: Arum. am", ai̯, ari, avém", aveţ', au̯ (N. Rom.: am, ai, a, am, aţi au). Arumanian has created a synthetic conditional from the confusion of the Latin prefect conjunctive (-verim) and the anterior future (viitorul anterior): -vero.

Lexical elements: Many lexical elements of Latin origin that have disappeared from the other dialects still exist in Arumanian. M.

Caragiu Marioţeanu gives the following "few examples as an illustration":[280]

Arumanian:	From Latin:	Meaning:
ápiñ	aperio	day is breaking
ávrĭ	aura	freshness, coolness, a light wind
cîrǫári	calor	heat, dog days
cusurín^u	consobrinus	cousin
deápir^u	depilo	I tear my hair
dimîndu	demando	I ask, I inform
fáuĭ	faba	bean
mes^u	mensis	month
nueárcî	noverca	stepmother
cîpríñ	caprina	goat's hair
cîşári	casearia	sheepfold, pen
fîlcári	falcaria	group of related families living
	(*cf.*, falx, falcis	together and led by a "*celnic*"
	"sickle")	
mul^u, múlî	mul(l)us	mule
	(or Ital. mulo?)	
(a)rús^u, (a)rúsî	russus	fair, light (about animals)
picurar^u	pecorarius	shepherd

Several words of Latin origin have, in Arumanian, a sense closer to the original Latin than is the case in N. Romanian; others show a special evolution of meaning (often influenced by the other Balkan languages). *Fumeál'i*, for example, means "family, children," as in Latin (*familia*); (Northern Romanian *femeie*, "woman"). The dialectal sense of *june* (this word is among those referred to by Puşcariu) exists also in Arumanian: *ğoni*, "young boy," although it also has the meaning of "brave" and "bridegroom" (probably developed under Albanian and Serbian influence).

Arumanian has also preserved several Latin adverbs, prepositions, and conjunctions that do not exist in the other Romanian dialects: *iu* "where" (< Latin *ubi*; this word appears in the sixteenth century Northern Romanian texts but exists today only in the region of Crişana (*iuǎ*); *dîndi, didíndi* "there, before" (< Latin *de inde* ± *de*); *lárgu* "far away" (< Latin *largus*); and many others.[281]

If the existence of ancient Latin elements in a Romanian dialect indicates that the speakers of that idiom have been living in their present-day area since the Roman period, then the Arumanians (together with the Meglenitic) would be the most likely candidates for this group. In other words, one could use Puşcariu's own arguments to claim that the present Arumanian territory is an ancient Roman-Romanian *Kerngebiet*, in which the Romance idiom has been spoken uninterruptedly ever since the time of the Roman Empire. The reasoning would in any case be similar to that of Puşcariu for the region of the Apuseni Mountains. As is known, however, the Arumanians migrated to their present territory. Their Romance language could not, therefore, have originated there, far south of the territory influenced by Latin on the Balkan Peninsula, in the region of the Greek language. When migrating there, the ancesstors of the Arumanians took with them, of course, their Romance idiom; that they preserved the Latin elements to a much higher degree than did the Northern Romanians can be explained by their relative isolation in a lateral area but has nothing to do with the territory from which they originated.

Other Proponents of the Kerngebiet Theory

In light of these facts, it is peculiar that the *Kerngebiet* theory, instead of being criticized and rejected at an early stage, was advanced further. The German linguist Ernst Gamillscheg[282] and his disciple, Günter Reichenkron, accepted Puşcariu's theory and cited other linguistic phenomena that they felt would strengthen the hypothesis of ancient Romanian core areas, not only in the region proposed by Puşcariu but also in some areas along the Danube in Muntenia and along the Olt River.

Gamillscheg observed that native speakers in the region of the Apuseni Mountains put a *k* between the consonants *s* and *l* (also in words of Slavic origin): instead of *slab* ("weak"), they say *sklab;* instead of *sloată* ("sleet"), *skloată.* This phenomenon also occurred in Vulgar Latin, for example, *insula > isla > iskla.*

A variant of the diminutive suffix *-culus: -unculus,* was used in Late Latin in certain territories: in northern France, in the Alpine region (Noricum and Raetia), and among "a part of the ancient Romanians." The suffix now common in Northern Romanian originates from Latin *-culus:* for example, Romanian *rinichiu,* from Latin *reniculus,* a diminutive form of *ren* "kidney." In the region of the Apuseni Mountains, however, *rărunchiu* (and *mănunchiu*) forms derived from the suffix *-unculus,* are used. Gamillscheg is of the opinion that from this single circumstance it follows that the Romanian people must have come from at least two *Kerngebiete:* one was situated southward and re-established the connections with the south-Danubian Romanians; and the other was situated within the *renunculus* area, or, if the entire population that used *renunculus* immigrated, was geographically separated from the first named region.[283]

Like Puşcariu, Gamillscheg believed that there were other circumstances to support this theory. He still tried, for example, to find inherited Latin place and river names in the region in question: Abrud, from Latin Abruttus; Ampoi, from Latin Ampeium; Turda, from a hypothetical Dacian Turidava; and the name of the Criş River from ancient Grisia. Moreover, Gamillscheg argued, the majority of the names of mountains were of Romanian origin: of 17 such names mentioned by Gustav Weigand,[284] 13 were Romanian and 4 Hungarian.

The weakness of the theories based on the survival of the diminutive suffix -unculus, the insertion of a k between s and l, and similar isolated phenomena is that certain elements of language are taken out arbitrarily, without regard to the distribution of the subdialects in Transylvania within Northern Romanian. The consonant group skl is not specific to Vulgar Latin but also existed in Greek; and if this phenomenon appeared after the third century A.D. (according to Gamillscheg, it is attested to from the fifth century), one might also ask how it could reach an area outside the frontiers of the Roman Empire? If this phenomenon is connected with that found in some areas of Late Latin, it could indicate that some of the ancestors of the Romanians, living on the Balkan Peninsula within the Roman Empire, had acquired it; being a part of their speech habits, they took it with them in their later migrations. This also applies to the diminutive suffix -unculus.

On a close examination of linguistic facts it appears that Gamillscheg's additional arguments are based on obsolete assumptions. Romanian Abrud cannot have derived directly from the Latin Abruttus, since the Latin -b- disappeared in Romanian; e.g., Latin februa(ris) > Romanian făurar. The Latin Ampeium could not result in Romanian Ampoi, because the Latin a in this position changed to ă > â (cf., Latin campus > Romanian cîmp). *Turidava is pure, unattested conjecture. That the majority of the names of the mountains in this region are of Romanian origin can be explained by the fact that the Apuseni Mountains have been populated since the thirteenth century mainly by a peasant and pastoral Romanian population. The names of the mountains do not date from before the fourteenth century. (The river names of this region, like those of Transylvania in general, are of either Hungarian or Slavic origin).

Largely in agreement with Gamillscheg, Reichenkron[285] distinguished two Kerngebiete of Romanian north of the Danube: the region of the Apuseni Mountains and a strip of territory along the lower Danube, ("the Kerngebiet of Gamillscheg up to Cernavodă") to which Reichenkron added the course of the Olt River. He called this idiom "Geto-Romanisch." A third Romanian Kerngebiet was, in Reichenkron's opinion, in Dardania.

Besides advancing the theory of a Romanian *Kerngebiet* in Muntenia and along the Olt River, Reichenkron tried to find similarities to the phenomena cited by Puşcariu in the rest of the Romance languages. On the basis of the word-pairs *ai* and *nea*, and *usturoi* and *zăpadă*, he believed in an *east-west division*. The use of *rărunchiu, mănunchiu*, as well as that of *curechiu* in the northwest compared with the south, where *rinichiu* and *varză* are found, defines, in his opinion, a *north-south division* as well. This continues, according to Reichenkron, in the Western Romance languages (words derived from *renunculus* are found in Northern France, in Noricum, and in Raetia, while *reniculus* is the basis of words denoting the kidney in the southern area of the Western Romance languages). The east-west division proposed by Reichenkron cannot apply to the Western Romance languages, but Reichenkron believed that it continued in Bulgarian. He referred to the tendency of the end vowels to closeness in the Moldavian subdialect ($e > i, ă > î$). The frontier line between this tendency and other areas of Northern Romanian goes from Czernovitz in the north along the Eastern Carpathians and reaches the Danube at Orlea, continuing toward the south in Bulgaria, since a similar phonetical tendency is found in Bulgarian to the east of this line.

These theories, however, are also based on a few arbitrarily selected linguistic phenomena. As shown above, the Latin image of Transylvania is artificial and does not exist in reality; and the Romanian subdialects do not support the idea of an "east-west division." The phonetical tendency to closeness of the end vowels is a peculiarity of the Moldavian subdialect. One of the bases for the north-south division theory in Northern Romanian is the corresponding word-pair *curechiu* and *varză*; but in the Western Romance languages we find only words that correspond to *curechiu* (derived from Vulgar Latin *coliclus* (< *cauliculus*). The other word, used there to designate "cabbage," has nothing to do with *varză* but is a continuation of the classical Latin *caulis*, which is not preserved in Romanian. The other examp le, the use of the diminutive suffix *-unculus* or *-culus*, does show something like a north-south division in the Western Romance languages; but in Romanian the frontiers of such a division should be sought along the line of the lower Danube, the frontier of the Roman Empire for several centuries after the Roman retreat from Dacia Traiana, if indeed the ancestors of the Romanians had been living in present-day Romania during the time of Late Latin when the use of the diminutive suffixes became widespread. This also applies to the distribution of *curechiu* and *varză*, cited in support of a north-south division and to Northern Romanian in general. If the Romanian language had developed, from the period of Dacia Traiana onwards, both north and south of the

Danube, an important dialectal frontier should go along the Danube, as the consequence of the different historical developments of the territories north and south of the river.

The Kerngebiet Theory and the Romanian Dialects

The hypothesis of ancient Romanian *Kerngebiete* in Dardania, in parts of Muntenia along the Danube and Olt rivers, and in western Transylvania assumes that in those territories Latin and, later, Romanian, have been spoken since the time of the Roman Empire. This situation should have left some traces in the present-day dialects of the Romanian language. Romanian spoken in the central parts of the Balkan Peninsula (in the territory between Skoplje, Niš, and Sofia, that is, in a part of present-day Macedonia) should show some differences in comparison with that spoken in Muntenia, along the Danube; the dialect found in western Transylvania would differ from both. The differences would not necessarily be great; one might also argue that no significant dialectal differences are to be expected because of a decisive influence (certainly exaggerated) from the wanderings of the shepherds which acted as a leveling factor. The wanderings and migrations could have wiped out differences or prevented them from developing.

The real situation, however, is neither a dialectal differentiation according to the assumed *Kerngebiete* nor a more or less uniform language. There are dialects: there is Northern Romanian ("Daco-Romanian") in present-day Romania and south of the Danube in the Timok Valley. During the Middle Ages, the population speaking this dialect occupied a much larger territory of the central Balkan Peninsula. This dense population of Northern Romanians is attested to by written documents (*hrišovs*) of the Serbian kings and monasteries written in the twelfth through the fifteenth century, in which personal names of a Northern Romanian pattern appear. In the central parts of the Balkan Peninsula, the Northern Romanians left their traces in the shape of place names and names of mountains, which still exist in the Serbian and Bulgarian toponymy, especially in the region bordered by the towns of Prizren, Skoplje, Sofia, and Niš, but also north and northwest of this region. The clearly Northern Romanian (not Arumanian) sound pattern of these names is still discernible. Part of this population migrated toward the northwest from the twelfth to the fifteenth century and reached the Istrian Peninsula. The Istro-Rumanians living there today are their descendants; they speak a special dialect, related more to Northern Romanian than to the southern dialects.

The southern dialects of the Romanian language are Arumanian and Meglenitic. The speakers of these dialects are now living on both sides of the Greek-Yugoslav frontier and in parts of Albania and Bulgaria. Since these territories are situated to the south of the ancient frontier between Greek and the Latin languages (the Jireček or the Skok line), their original areas must have been further to the north. To this comes the fact that until the eleventh century, Romanian was essentially a uniform language, with no significant dialectal variation. The reconstruction of this stage of Romanian (*străromână, română comună*, Ancient Romanian) shows, for example, that it was much closer to Latin than the present-day dialects (of which Arumanian is closest to Ancient Romanian) and that the Slavic words borrowed before the eleventh century are the same in all four Romanian dialects.[286] The existence of such a stage fits in badly with assumed *Kerngebiete* a considerable distance from one another.

Dardania and the Origin of Romanian

Reichenkron, like Gamillscheg, recognized the importance of the province of Dardania in the history of Latin on the Balkan Peninsula and in the development of the Romanian language. Reichenkron emphasized that Dardania was intensely Romanized and the cultural center of a large area. In 535 A.D. Emperor Justinian made *Iustiniana Prima* (Scupi, modern Skoplje) the see of the archbishopric, to which belonged the dioceses of Dacia Ripensis and Mediterranea, Moesia Superior, Praevalis, Macedonia Secunda, and the eastern part of Pannonia Inferior.[287] Dardania was also the territory in which the Albanians were living during Roman times on the Balkan Peninsula,[288] and Reichenkron emphasizes the significance of the close and multiple connections between Albanian and Romanian.[289] To all this comes the Latin vocabulary of Christianity in the Romanian language, which the ancestors of the Romanians could only have adopted in a territory in which the Latin language dominated.[290]

On the basis of these circumstances, Reichenkron stated, "it was probably from Dardania that the first expansion of the ancient Romanians [*"Urrumänentum"*], as they have been called since Pușcariu, occurred."[291] With regard to the common lexical elements found in Albanian and in Romanian, Reichenkron considered that only a smaller part of them might be loans: It is more probable that most of the Albanian-Romanian correspondences in the field of the lexical elements developed south of the Danube, in so-called Dardania in the southern part of the Roman province of Moesia Superior, thus, approximately in Yugoslav Macedonia.[292]

The Kerngebiet Theory in Romanian Historiography

Romanian linguists no longer defend the *Kerngebiet* theory. Historians, however, continue to support it. According to Constantin C. Giurescu, for example,"the maps of the *Romanian Linguistic Atlas* (*Atlasul Lingvistic Român*) show the presence of some terms of Latin origin, such as *nea, pedestru,* and *june,* (which are found) only in the western parts of Transylvania, and (are) lacking in the rest of the Carpatho-Danubian area—something that would not be possible if the ancient Romanians had come from the Balkan Peninsula."[293] In the opinion of Ştefan Pascu,"also from the linguistic point of view, the German scholar Gamillscheg has identified a Romance group between Giurgiu and Cernavodă (Muntenia)."[294]

A Romanian scholar living in the West, Vasile Arvinte, refers to the *Kerngebiet* theory as an important proof of Roman continuity north of the Danube. He asserts that recent archaeological excavations "confirm the conclusions of the linguists." The assumed *Kerngebiet* along the lower Danube and in Dobrudja, for example, is said to be confirmed by the Dridu culture, which proves the ancient Romanian element.[295] Eugen Lozovan pointed out the weaknesses of Puşcariu's theory: Puşcariu and his followers have committed two major errors: first, to change from the actual dialectal synchrony (opposition: archaic areas/innovating areas) to diachrony or to an earlier synchrony; secondly, to raise diachrony into a system, because to accept the idea of conservative areas as a more or less exact picture of an earlier phase means to accept the concept of the stability of diachrony, which is absurd.[296]

The Romanian linguist Alexandru Rosetti refutes the theory of ancient Romanian areas based on Latin words that were replaced in other areas. In his opinion, this geographical distribution may have occurred as well in a later period: "a series of other Latin terms that appear in the *Romanian Linguistic Atlas* subvert the proposed Latin image of Transylvania by their presence in Wallachia and Moldavia and prove, by their appearance in regions that were not Romanized, that later linguistic extensions are involved."[297]

The *Kerngebiet* theory no longer seems to be mentioned in Romanian textbooks or linguistic studies. No reference is made to this theory, for example, in the 1969 edition of *Istoria limbii române,*[298] in a recent history of the Romanian language,[299] or in *Studii de dialectologie română.*[300] Matilda Caragiu Marioţeanu gives a detailed and comprehensive analysis of the Romanian dialects and subdialects.[301] It is noteworthy that the author does not mention the *Kerngebiet* theory: the dialectal characteristics taken out from a vast material of linguistic phenomena to support this theory show themselves to be insignificant details, a small share of the examples of linguistic change, and conservatism mostly connected with the situation of lateral areas.

IV

GEOGRAPHICAL NAMES

As was shown above, there is 1) no evidence for the assumption that the Romanian language is the continuation of Latin spoken in the territory which once was Dacia, and 2) there are several circumstances which indicate also the territory from which this language originated, i.e., where the ancestors of the present day Romanians lived before the 12th century.

The question is now: is it possible to determine when, in what period of time, they populated the areas north of the lower Danube, where they are living now?

Theories About Early Romanian Geographical Names

The Romanians were first mentioned in historical records in Moldavia in 1164 and in Transylvania in 1210. This does not, however, exclude the possibility that Romanians (Vlachs) lived in these areas somewhat, or even much, earlier, as is claimed by Romanian historians. Because of the lack of historical evidence, arguments have been based first of all on the geographical names of the territory.

The most promising means of determining the period in which the Romanians arrived in the territories of contemporary Romania has been through studying the geographical names of Slavic origin, because the Slavs lived in almost all areas north of the Danube from the sixth century and because these names are numerous throughout most of Romania. In the transcarpathian territory of the country, Slavic geographical names were usually borrowed directly from Slavic by the Romanian population; there are numerous such names. Within the arch of the Carpathian Mountains, however, this is not the case. Geographical names of Slavic origin are also numerous there; but their sound patterns show that only a few dozen of them were borrowed directly from Slavs. (Most of these names are found in southern and southwestern Transylvania.) Some of the geographical names of Slavic origin contain the reflex of a Slavic nasal vowel. Since the history of these vowels in Slavic is quite well known, these names can give valuable indications about when they were borrowed from Slavic.

Of the numerous theories claiming that the Romanians were in Transylvania first (at least before the Hungarians), the most significant ones are based on the preservation of the Slavic nasal vowel, the fact that Slavic geographical names were borrowed directly by a Romanian population, and the assumption that certain Romanian geographical names were, at an early period, transferred to Hungarian. These theories will be analyzed in the following section at some length. In addition, the assumption of directly inherited Latin place names in Transylvania will be discussed briefly.

The search for evidence to support these theories has frequently been politically motivated. Between the two world wars there was a debate between Romanian and Hungarian scholars over the early settlements of Transylvania. In 1938 the Hungarian Slavist István Kniezsa published his work about the peoples living in Hungary in the eleventh century. In 1944 the Romanian Slavist Emil Petrovici published an article[1] in which his hypotheses were summarized and Kniezsa's work criticized. According to Petrovici, the names of the great rivers in Transylvania "seem to have been passed from generation to generation, from the ancient era to modern times, by the ancestors of the Romanians. This would also be true if the river names that we cited were borrowed by the Romanians from the Slavs, because these Slavs of Dacia must also be considered among the ancestors of the Romanians. Even if there was never a Daco-Roman continuity, there was certainly a Slavo-Romanian one from the seventh century to the present."[2]

In Petrovici's opinion, the Slavo-Romanian symbiosis occurred in the margins of the plains and depressions and in the valleys. The Slavs lived mainly in the villages at the feet of the mountains, while the Romanian population was dispersed in hamlets and isolated settlements, as they are in our time in the mountainous regions. This description is valid, at least for some areas, although not before the twelfth or thirteenth century.

In contrast to the Slavic theory, Romanian scholars also stress the Latin character of Romanian, minimizing or even denying the importance of the Slavic influence. It is in any case essential to differentiate between the Slavs and the Romanians in any study of ancient history. It must be noted here that Petrovici did this in his later publications and that he also changed his opinion about other matters.

The Preservation of the Slavic Nasal Vowels

The nasal vowels that are inherited by Slavic languages from the Proto-Slavic are known. It is also known that the Balkan peoples, as the result of the settlement of the Slavs on the Balkan Peninsula in the seventh century, adopted the earliest Slavic elements including the nasal vowels. The question of nasal vowels, that is, the mutation and disappearance of these vowels from individual Slavic languages, has been and continues to be of concern to linguists. There is, however, as yet no agreement on this subject.

Opinions diverge regarding the dual representation that the Old Slavic ǫ or ọ (the Old Bulgarian sign ѫ is transcribed here as ǫ and not ọ [Reichenkron]), which became -un, -um in Romanian, and -în, -îm through the intermediacy of Serbian or Bulgarian. The dual representation that the Old Slavic ǫ became in Romanian -un, -um and -în, -îm, respectively, was initially based on chronological considerations. While certain Slavists, such as Hermann Tiktin, believe that their origins rest in Old Church Slavonic, the Romanian linguist Ovid Densusianu believes that -un, and -um represent an earlier stage of the Old Bulgarian ǫ while -în, and -îm represent a later stage of the same letter. Moreover, the -în, and -îm occurs concurrently with the convergence of Middle Bulgarian ъm and ъn with Old Bulgarian.[3]

According to the Romanian scholar Theodor Capidan, the Romanian loan-words with -un, and -um reflect a Serbian development.[4] He believes, however, that the representation -în, and -îm indicated loan-words from the Bulgarian. Sextil Puşcariu, Ernst Gamillscheg, Emil Petrovici,[5] and Günter Reichenkron concur in Capidan's opinion,[6] while Alexandru Rosetti rejects it.[7]

In the linguistic development of the Carpatho-Danubian area Bulgarian is the most important language. Old Bulgarian is chronologically closest to the Proto-Slavic; and, therefore, it must be regarded as the isogloss of this extinct language.[8] It is known that alterations of the nasal vowels occurred in remnants of Middle Bulgarian of the twelfth century. Furthermore, it is assumed that the existence of nasal vowels, which constitutes the main criterion for differentiating Old Bulgarian from the remains of Middle Bulgarian, Russian, Old Church Slavonic, and Serbian Church Slavonic is unquestionably important, but not sufficient for definite conclusions. In the case of written Old Bulgarian there are two additional characteristics:

1. The representation of the Proto-Slavic ṭi, kt (before e, i, and ъ) and dị through št, that is, žd;
2. The open character of the Proto-Slavic ě.[9]

The Hungarian scholar István Kniezsa examined the old geographical names in Transylvania and concluded that most of the province was inhabited by Hungarians and Germans (Transylvanian Saxons) when the Romanians arrived in the thirteenth century. He proposed that the presence of a reflex of the Slavic nasal vowel in Hungarian loans from Slavic would indicate that the borrowing occurred during or before the eleventh century, when, as he believed, the nasal vowels lost their nasality in the Slavic languages.[10] Also Petrovici tried to use this assumption for proving a question of history: "the place names of Slavic origin in the Romanian regions of Transylvania, showing the reflexes of the ancient nasal vowels of Slavic in the Romanian form, prove the existence of a Slavo-Romanian symbiosis in the tenth and eleventh centuries.[11] These place names include the following: In Caraş-Severin (Krassó-Szörény) County: Glîmboca (Glimboka, a village), Luncaviţa (Nagylankás, a village and a brook); in Hunedoara (Hunyad) County: Lingina, or Lindina (Lindzsina, today Izvoarele), Pîncota (Pankota, today Hărău), Glîmboceni (a brook); in Mureş (Maros) County: Gîmbuţ (Gombástelke); in Sibiu (Szeben) County: Glîmboaca (Glimboka); in Arad and Bihor (Bihar) Counties: Pîncota (Pankota), and in Cluj (Kolozs) County: Indol (today Indol).[12]

The presence of Glîmboaca southeast of Sibiu (Nagyszeben, Hermannstadt) would prove, according to Petrovici's reasoning in 1944, that Romanians lived in the area before the Hungarians; but, in fact, he enlarged this area to a vast territory, claiming that before the arrival of the Hungarians, the "Slavo-Romanians" were living in the Tîrnava (Küküllő), Ţibin, and Olt River valleys and in the region between these rivers.[13] According to this view, the terra Blacorum mentioned in a document from the early thirteenth century was only the remains of this large "Slavo-Romanian" territory.

Only in Glîmboaca and Glîmboceni is the Slavic nasal preserved. Two of the names (Gîmbuţ and Lingina) given by Petrovici were borrowed by the Romanians from Hungarian, and the origins of three (Indol, Pîncota, and Luncaviţa) are questionable.

Gîmbuţ (Mureş County):

The Romanians borrowed place names from the Hungarians, which the Hungarians in their turn had borrowed from Slavic. The Romanian form may present the group -în, -îm, which renders the Slavic ǫ not directly but through the Hungarian language. Hungarian Gambuc (1303 rivulus, silva, possessio Gumbuch) of the Mureş district (< Slavic Gǫbici) was transferred to Romanian in the form Gîmbuţ.[14]

Lingina (Lindzsina, Hunedoara County, today Izvoarele):

According to Petrovici[15] the local population in Haţeg pronounces Linžina as Ližina, which cannot derive from Slavic lędina, as was supposed earlier. In Slavic borrowings of the Romanian language, the affricate ǧ does not appear. It is found, on the other hand, regularly in borrowings from Hungarian, in place of Hungarian gy (a sound similar to Romanian gh in ghem, gheaţă). There is, for example, megie "limit, frontier," in northwestern Transylvania, from Hungarian mesgye (which in its turn derives from Bulgarian mežda) and megieş, megiaş, "neighbor," from Hungarian *megyés*. Hungarian *gy* is rendered in Romanian by *ğ* also in place names: Hungarian Gyalu > Romanian Gilău, Egyed > Adjud, Gyógy > Geoagiu, Szentegyed > Sîntejude, Gyergyó > Giurgeu, Gyöngy > Giungi.[16] Consequently, *ğ* in Lingina also probably derives from a Hungarian *gy*. Petrovici gives its derivation from Hungarian *lengyen* "Polish" (modern Hungarian lengyel), which appears in documents beginning with the year 1095, as a personal name as well as a place name: Lengen, Lengel, Lengyen; in 1339, Johannes filius Lengyen. (This Hungarian word originates from Old Russian *ledžanŭ* (< Slavic *ledjanŭ*). The name of present-day Lingina appears in documents beginning in 1446, Lensene, Lenczyna, Lyngzyna; later also Lengene. Petrovici concludes that this place name is of Hungarian origin, as are many other place names in the area around Lingina.[17]

Indol: (Indal, Cluj County):
There is no acceptable etymology for this name. It is first mentioned in documents in 1310 as Indol; as Indala in 1311; Indal in 1360; *possessio* Hindal in 1364; Indaal in 1408; kenezius de Indal in 1469; Indally from 1760 to 1762; and Indál, Indal in 1854. Its present-day Romanian name is Deleni.[18] It could be borrowed from Slavic;[19] *jądol* "valley" and the Jândol > Indol change could have taken place in Romanian. As shown by Kniezsa, however, such a change is not specific to Romanian but also occurred in Hungarian: Slavic *joreba* > Hungarian joromba > iromba; Hungarian juhász > johász > ihász.[20] Kniezsa proposed the explanation from Slavic *ino-dol* "another valley" (*cf.*, Polish Ino-pole).[21]

Pîncota (Pankota, Arad County, and a hamlet of the village Hărău in Hunedoara County): called villa Pankotha in 1202 and 1203 and Pankota in 1219. It most probably derives from Slavic personal name Pǫkata. Since place names based on a personal name without a suffix were chiefly created by Hungarians, this name was also most probably given by a Hungarian population.

Luncavița (Nagylankás, Lunkavica, Severin County):
Was known in 1440 as Naghlukavicza, Kyslukavicza; in 1447, Naghlwkawycza, Kislwkawycza; in 1603, Lenkavicza; from 1690 to 1700 as Linkavicza; in 1774, Lukavicza; in 1829, Lungavicza; and in 1840 as Lunkavicza. It is doubtful that this name originally contained a nasal vowel, since up to the seventeenth century it was recorded exclusively in the form "Lukavicza," without an *n*. The present form may have developed in Romanian popular etymology, after *luncă* "waterside, swamp, everglade."

The Rise and Disappearance of the
Nasal Vowels in Slavic

The nasal vowels developed in Common Slavic between the sixth and eighth centuries. There are several pieces of evidence for this, of which two are considered unequivocal: the nasal vowels developed after the change of the clusters $n + j$ into ń, and before the third palatalization of the velars.[22] None of the languages with which the Slavs were in contact in that period had nasal vowels, with the exception of Lettish and Lithuanian, which developed probably them from the Slavic influence.[23]

The loss of the nasal vowels was a protracted process and quite different in the various Slavic languages. At present, such vowels exist only in Polish and in Polabian. According to the Russian scholar George Y. Shevelov, the nasal vowels were lost in Russian, Byelorussian, Ukrainian, Slovak, Czech, and Serbo-Croatian in all probability in the tenth century, that is, antedating the loss of jers; in Slovenian in the eleventh century; and in various dialects of Macedonian and Bulgarian at sometime between the eleventh and the fourteenth centuries.[24] There is evidence of the existence of nasal vowels in Bulgarian (with which Romanian was in contact for many centuries) at least until the early thirteenth century; this is indicated by the presence of -în, -îm in several Romanian borrowings from Bulgarian: un (um) < ǫ (through the eleventh century) as well as în (îm) < ⱅ < ǫ (twelfth century - beginning of the thirteenth century; subsequently, nasalization disappeared in the Bulgarian dialects).[25] There are, however, still Bulgarian dialects today that have preserved the nasal vowel, mainly in northeastern Bulgaria, along the Romanian frontier, but also around Saloniki and Kostur. The Bulgarian dialect spoken until the nineteenth century in Transylvania also had nasal vowels.

As previously mentioned, Petrovici had already stated this in his 1944 article, although only in a footnote and without drawing the logical conclusions: "It is probable that the Slavs who were assimilated into the Hungarians or the Romanians preserved the nasal vowels until their total assimilation. Thus, the Bulgarians in Cergăul Mic, Cergăul Mare, Rusciori, and Bungard (in the districts of Târnava and Sibiu), who settled in Transylvania in the thirteenth century, preserved the Slavic nasal vowels until their complete Romanianization during the nineteenth century."[26]

Petrovici changed his opinion later on, concluding in an article in 1958 that "the preservation of the nasality in the toponyms that appear on chart no. 1 does not give us any indication about the period in which they were borrowed by the Romanians from the Slavs."[27] Consequently, in 1958 Petrovici refuted his earlier theory that the preservation of the Slavic nasal vowel indicated an early borrowing, before the Hungarians' arrival in Transylvania. Petrovici's statement should go on to say that the appearance of reflexes of nasal vowels in certain Romanian or Hungarian geographical names of Slavic origin does not indicate an early borrowing from Slavic (Bulgarian). Theoretically, since the nasal vowels have been preserved in some Bulgarian dialects until the present, such names might have been borrowed quite recently. Since, however, -în (-îm) corresponds to Middle Bulgarian $ă^n$, dated to the period between the end of the eleventh and the early thirteenth century, it must be concluded that the names containing this reflex were borrowed in that period. This is of no significance to the question of Romanian or Hungarian primacy in Transylvania. Most of these geographical names are found outside of Transylvania, in the mountainous regions of Oltenia and Muntenia; and their significance will be discussed below in "Romanian Geographical names of Slavic Origin."

Romanian Geographical Names Borrowed Directly from Slavs

In the transcarpathian territories of Romania, the largest part of the ancient toponymy is of Slavic origin. The sound pattern of these names indicates that the borrowings occurred after the eleventh or twelfth century.[28] Within the arch of the Carpathian Mountains, that is, in Transylvania, the majority of the ancient grographical names are of Hungarian origin with fewer names of Slavic origin. Moreover, a significant difference compared with the transcarpathian territories is that many geographical names of Slavic origin in Transylvania were transferred to Romanian via Hungarian and some even through German; there are only a few dozen that were borrowed by Romanians directly from Slavic. These data reflect that in the course of their settlement in Transylvania, the Romanians found Slavs only in certain areas and by no means throughout the entire province, as was the case in Muntenia and Moldavia.

As in the transcarpathian territory, the situation in Transylvania is complicated by the fact that groups of Slavs settled there for many centuries until recent times. The Ukrainians (Ruthenians), for example, have left place names such as Oroszi, Oroszfalu, Szerdahely, (Reussmarkt, Rusciori; Hungarian *orosz* "Russian" does not appear before the eleventh century). Ukrainian sound pattern were left in the Máramaros (Maramureş), Szolnok-Doboka (Dăbîca), Háromszék (Covasna) Counties, for example in Hruşor which shows the $g > h$

change that occurred in the twelfth century (this village is called Körtvélyes in Hungarian, a translation of the Slavic name, borrowed by Romanian in the form of Curtuiuş) or Herec /vára/ "the tower of/Herec" in Covasna County, from Ruthenian *horec* "hill, little mountain." Bulgarian colonists are known to have settled in Braşov (the district of Şchei, Bolgárszeg) and Ciurgăul Mic (Kiscserged), to which they came from eastern Bulgaria in the thirteenth century.[29] Among the vestiges of Czechs can be mentioned Páncélcseh (> Romanian Panticeu, Cluj County) and Szilágycseh (Cehul Silvaniei, Sălaj County); the village name Horvát (> Romanian Horoat), in 1213 Huruat, preserves the ethnic name of Croatian colonists. Serbians settled in the southwest.

In his 1944 article Petrovici mentioned 25 geographical names that he considered proofs of a Slavo-Romanian symbiosis in Transylvania before the arrival of the Hungarians.[30] It evidently appears from the article, however, that his assertion was not based on any linguistic evidence. In his opinion, it is illogical to assume that the Romanians borrowed the geographical names not from the majority population but from the remainders (already insignificant in the eleventh century) of the conquered Slavic population, reduced to servitude.[31] The Romanians did, in fact, borrow a large number of Hungarian geographical names all over Transylvania, not because of the "prestige of the rulers," as claimed by Petrovici, but simply because people arriving at a new area usually borrow or translate the geographical names found there. Along with the Hungarian names, the Romanians borrowed dozens of geographical names from the Slavs. This indicates that there was a Slavo-Romanian symbiosis in the area, but nothing suggests that this occurred before the arrival of the Hungarians. That borrowings by Romanian from Slavic occurred even in cases when Hungarians lived in the area is shown by the Hungarian geographical names transferred to Romanian by Slavic intermediacy (for example, Hungarian Beseneu [1230], Romanian Beşenova, that is, the Hungarian name with a Slavic suffix).

Romanian Geographical Names in Transylvania Borrowed Directly from Slavs

(The list given by Emil Petrovici according to counties)[32]

Caraş-Severin (Krassó-Szörény) County:
Belareca (Fejérviz), river name, in 1436, Feyerwiz, "white water"; Valea Bistrei (Bisztranagyvölgy), in 1501, Valemare, in 1578, Nagypatak (Slavic *bistra* "rapid"; *nagy+patak* "great+brook").[33]

Hunedoara (Hunyad) County:

Cerna (Cserna), in 1446, *kenez de* Charna, in 1482, *poss.* Charna (Slavic *cerna* "black"); Zlaşti (Zalasd), in 1480, *poss.* Zalosd, *alio nomine* Dobramer.

Alba (Fehér) County:

Bǎlgrad (Gyulafehérvár), the modern Romanian name is Alba Iulia ("the White Tower of Gyula"; "white tower"). In 1097, as *comes* Bellegratae(?), in 1199, *terra Sancti Michaelis*, in 1201, *Jula voiwoda et comes Albe Transilvane*, in 1206, *castrum Albense* (Slavic bělŭ "white"+*gradŭ* "town, tower"); Tîrnava (Küküllő), Mare and Micǎ, river names; Craiova (Királypatak), in 1733, Király-Pataka, in 1750, Krajova (Slavic *kral* "king"); Gîrbova de Jos (Alsóorbó), in 1282, *terra* Vrbo; Gîrbova de Sus (Felsőorbó), in 1505, Oláhorbó. (Slavic *Vrĭbovo); Gîrboviţa (Középorbó), in 1505, Girbovicza, Középorbó (*közép* "middle").

Sibiu (Szeben) County:

Gîrbova (Orbó), in 1291, Wrbow, Slavic *vŏrbovo*, "place with willows"; Cernavoda (Feketeviz, Szecsel), in 1319, Feketewyz, "black + water"; Sibiu (Nagyszeben), between 1192 and 1196 as *prepositus* Cipiniensis, in 1211, *prepositus* Scibiniensis; from the name of the river Slavic *Svibiń, *Sibin, (Slavic *sviba* "cornel"), Romanian Ţibin or Cibin, from German Zibin; Sad (Cód), in 1339 Aquam Zcoth. Originally the name of a brook, it could hardly derive from Slavic *sad* "hamlet"; Hungarian *szád* "opening, entrance" may be more probable (Kniezsa, 1943, pp. 254–255); Slimnic (Szclindek), in 1282, *plebanus de* Stolchunbercht, in 1341, Zelenduk, in 1349, Szelindek; Slavic Slynónikŏ, from *slynónŏ* "famous" (Kniezsa, 1943, p. 255).

Bihor (Bihar) County:

Craiova, Craiva (Bélkirálymező, Krajova), in 1344, *locus* Keralmezei (Slavic *kral'ova* "the king's" [the property of the king]);

Sǎlaj (Szilágy) County:

Cozla (Kecskés), in 1405, *villa olachalis* Kozla; Bozna (Szentpéterfalva), in 1619, Szentpéterfalva, in 1733, Bozna; Ciumǎrna (Csömörlő), in 1460, Chebernye;

Satu Mare (Szatmár) County:

Racova (Rákosterebes), in 1393, *possessio Valahalis* Terebes;

Cluj (Kolozs) County:

Vlaha (Oláhfenes), in 1332, *sacerdos de* Olafenes, in 1733, Blaha (the formation of the Romanian name is not clear: singular form created from plural Vlaši? [Kniezsa, 1943, p. 228]).

Mureş (Maros) County:
Jabeniţa (Görgénysóakna), in 1453, Szebencs, in 1644, Sóakna;

Tîrnava Mare (Nagykükülló) County:
Lovnic (Lemnek), in 1206, *villa* Lewenech (From Slavic *lov* "fishing, hunting," *lovnik* "place for fishing," "place for hunting." From Slavic to German [Leblang] and to Romanian, from German to Hungarian);

Odorheiu (Udvarhely) County:
Vlăhiţa (Szentegyházasfalu), in 1301, as *villa nostra* < *regis* > *Olachalis in medio Siculorum nostrorum de Vduordhel commorancium* (a document of questionable authenticity); in 1406, Oláhfalu, in 1602, Szentegyházas Oláhfalu, in 1808, Oláhfalu, Wlachendorf, Rumun, in 1854, Szentegyház-Oláhfalu (Nagy Oláhfalu), Olafalăul Mare (Suciu, 1968, II, p. 255);

Covasna (Kovászna) County:
Budila (Bodola), in 1294, Budula, 1332 to 1337, Buduli. From the personal name of Slavic origin Budilo, created without any suffix; Dalnic (Dálnok), in 1332 to 1337, Dalnuk, *cf.,* Slavic *dal* "far, distant."
    In most cases, the sound patterns of these names suggest either a parallel Slavic and Hungarian name or a translation of the Slavic name into Hungarian (while the Romanians borrowed it), or a borrowing by the Hungarians directly from Slavic, that is, independently from Romanian.
    Hungarian names translated from Slavic:

Bălgrad	Hung. Fehérvár
Tîrnava	Hung. Küküllő
Cernavoda	Hung. Feketeviz
Belareca (river)	Hung. Feyerwiz
Cozla	Hung. Kecskés
Craiova	Hung. Királymező
Racova	Hung. Rákosterebes

Hungarian names borrowed from Slavic independent of Romanian:

Slavic:	Hungarian:	Romanian:
*Budilo	Bodola	Budila
*Čemerïna	Csömörlő	Ciumărna
*Dalïnikŭ	Dálnok	Dalnic
*Lovïnikŭ	Lemnek	Lovnic
*Lipova	Lippa	Lipova
*Sadŭ (?)	Cód	Sad

*Sibińï	Szeben	Sibiu
*Slivïnikŭ	Szelindek	Slimnic
*Zlaštï (< *Zolt-jï)	Zalasd	Zlaşti
*Žabenica	Szebencs	Jabeniţa

Two settlements have a different name in Hungarian from that in Romanian: Bozna, Hung. Szentpéterfalva and Vlaha, Hung. Oláhfenes. Vlăhiţa in Odorheiu County is not an ancient name, the Romanian name of this village having been Olafalăul Mare until the last century, which is partly a borrowing, partly a translation of the Hungarian name.

Only two of these place names have the same form in both Romanian and Hungarian, but they were essentially the same in Slavic as well: Bistra and Cerna (in the southwest and in Maramureş). These two names could have been borrowed by the Hungarians either from the Slavs or from the Romanians; the sound patterns are no help in deciding the question.

One must conclude that the above names suggest a Slavo-Romanian symbiosis in the areas in question (mainly in southern Transylvania). None of them, however, indicates a borrowing from Romanian in Hungarian, the Hungarian counterparts having forms independent from the Romanian forms or being translations of the Slavic word. (There are cases in which a Hungarian borrowing cannot, on the basis of the sound pattern, be excluded, although not in more than two of the 25 names given by Petrovici.) The direct borrowing by Romanian of Slavic geographical names in Transylvania does not indicate a Slavo-Romanian symbiosis there before the Hungarians but only in a period when Transylvania already had a Hungarian population. Later, in 1964, Petrovici recognized the importance of parallel name-giving and emphasized that this was natural, on the basis of "symbiosis in the past in an area [where there were] several populations."[34]

Romanian Geographical Names Assumed To Be Older Than the Hungarian Toponymy

Another group of geographical names found in Transylvania were asserted to "reveal a Slavic or Romanian form that is older than the Hungarian toponymy, proving a borrowing by the Hungarians from Romanian."[35] These names are: Abrud, Bistriţa, Bogata, Buda, Budila, Câlnic, Cluj, Coca, Cricău, Dobâca, Cristiş, Gârbova, Gherla, Grind, Lomnic, Poiana, Sălicea, Slâmnic, Stana, Straja, Sâncel, and Vineţia.[36] Of these, Budila, Gîrbova, Lovnic (Lomnic), and Slimnic have been discussed above among the geographical names borrowed by Romanians directly from Slavs; Sîncel will be analyzed below. Essential data about the rest follows:

Hunedoara (Hunyad) County:
Câlnic (Kelnek, German Kelling). In 1296, Kelnuk; from Slavic *kalnik* "muddy place" (*kal* "mud"). The Hungarian name derives from German; the Romanian name is also probably from German, although it may have been borrowed directly from Slavic; Grind (Gerend), in 1392, Girid, from South Slavic *gred* (< *grędЪ*).

Alba (Fehér) County:
Abrud (Abrudbánya). In 1271, Obruth. The origin of this name is unknown, but it cannot have been inherited by Romanian directly from Latin (Abruttus), because in that case -*br*- would not have been preserved (*cf.*, Latin *februarius* > Romanian *făurar*). The Hungarian name in the thirteenth century was Obruth; Hungarian *o* changed, during the fourteenth century, to *a*: in 1211, Hoduth, 1355, Hodnog; from 1397 to 1416, Haduth; from 1323 to 1339, Meelpotok; and in 1327, Burustyanuspatak; and appellatives, such as *okol* > *akol*; *nogy* > *nagy*; *bob* > *bab*; *golomb* > *galamb*.[37] In some Romanian place names, borrowed at an early date from Hungarian, this *o* is preserved: Ocoliş, *cf.*, modern Hungarian Aklos. Abrud was borrowed later, probably during or after the fourteenth century. Straja (Öregyháza, Sztrázsa, German Hohenwarte). In 1274, terra Euryghaz; in 1369, Ewreghaz; about 1630, Straza. Cricău (Krakkó, Boroskrakkó) in 1206, villa Karako; in 1291, Crakow; in 1850, Krikou, Krakau.

Făgăraş (Fogaras) County:
Vineţia, Veneţia (Venicze), Veneţia de Jos (Alsóvenicze, German Unterwenitze): in 1235, Venetia or *sacerdos de* Venetis; in 1372, *villa dicta* Venecze; Veneţia de Sus (Felsővenicze, Oberwenitze). This name derives, according to Kniezsa,[38] from the name of the Italian town Venezia (Venice). Such names appear in several places in Hungary: there is Venecia, later Velence in Sáros and Fehér Counties; Italian colonists also left vestiges in Nagyvárad (Oradea), where three suburbs are called Velence, Padova, and Bolonya,[39] and in the name of the village Venter, Romanian Vintiri, in Bihor County from the Italian personal name Ventur (1349:Felwenter);

Satu Mare (Szatmár) County:
Coca: according to Suciu,[40] this is the name of a hamlet of the village Călineşti, in Ţara Oaşului.

Bistriţa-Năsăud (Beszterce-Naszód) County:
Bistriţa (Beszterce, German Bistritz, Nösen): in 1264, *villa* Bistiche; from 1286 to 1289, Byzturche; in 1295, Bezterce, and Byzterce; in 1308, Bystricia.

Cluj (Kolozs) County:
Buda (Bodonkút, Romanian also Buda-Veche, Vechea): in 1315, Buda. This is a personal name of Slavic origin: Buda, Budivoj, Budimir; many settlements have this name in Hungary: Budapest, Budakeszi, Budapuszta, Budajenő. The place name formed from a personal name without a suffix is probably given by Hungarians. Cluj (Kolozsvár, German Klausenburg). This name derives most probably from Slavic *kluž*, which in turn was borrowed from Middle High-German (13th to 14th century) *Klause* "cell, closet": in 1183, Culusiensis *comes* (a questionable document); in 1213, *castrenses de* Clus and *castrum* Clus; in 1275, *villa* Clwsvar; in 1280, Culuswar; in 1348, Clusenburg. Gherla (ancient Gerlahida, modern Szamosújvár, German Armenierstadt, Armenerstadt, Neuschloss): in 1291, Gerlahida; in 1458, Gerlah; in 1552, Wywar; in 1595, Samosuivar; in 1632, Gerla and Szamosújvár. The name derives from the personal name Gerlach of German origin. The new Hungarian name refers to the tower built in this town in the sixteenth century. Dobîca (Doboka): in 1279, *villa castri de* Doboka and *Dobokawarfolua vocata*; in 1290, *possessio seu terra* Doboka. The name derives from the Hungarian personal name Doboka (in the 13th to 14th century: Dobuca). In Baranya County in southern Hungary, there is a Görcsöny-Doboka. Cristiş (Kereszles): in 1288, *villa Cruciferorum de* Torda (Today Romanian Oprişani, it belongs to the town Turda). Poiana (Polyána): in 1291, *terra* Polanteluk; in 1334, Palyan; from Slovakian *pol'ana* "mountain pasture." Sălicea (Szelicse): in 1297, *possessio* Zeleche. The name derives from Slavic *selišče* "hamlet," which is not Bulgarian, because *šč* changed in Bulgarian before the ninth century to *št*. (*cf.*, for example, Ukrainian Horodisce > Romanian Horodişte); the form Sălicea must have been borrowed from Hungarian (Szelicse). Stana (Sztána): in 1288, *terra* Zthana. Iorgu Iordan[41] believed that this name might be related to the name Stînca, which appears in several places in Romania's transcarpathian territories (in Botoşani, Bucureşti, Iaşi, Buzău, Tulcea, and Bacău Counties) and in two cases in Transylvania: Stâncul (Bihor) and Stânceşti (Hunedoara), the last mentioned one deriving from the personal name Stânca.[42] In Transylvania, there are also Dealul Stănişori and Stanuleţ, with a not exactly Romanian sound pattern.[43] István Kniezsa[44] believed that this name derived from the Slavic personal name Stan (Stanislav). In that

case, the name giving was most probably Hungarian, since it is a personal name without a suffix.

Mureş (Maros) County:
Bogata (Marosbogát): in 1211, Bogad; 1291, Marosbogat. This name appears also in Hungary: Nyirbogát, in the northeast, and Bogádmindszent, in Baranya County, in the south.
These names can be divided into several groups:

Hungarian names borrowed by Romanian:

Hung, Abrud/bánya/	> Rom. Abrud
Hung. Krakkó	> Rom. Cricău
Hung. Keresztes	> Rom. Cristiş
Hung. Szelicse	> Rom. Sălicea

Borrowing from Slavic in both Hungarian and Romanian (different forms):

Hung. Beszterce	Rom. Bistriţa
Hung. Marosbogát	Rom. Bogata
Hung. Kolozsvár	Rom. Cluj
Hung. Gerend	Rom. Grind
Hung. Orbó	Rom. Gîrbova
Hung. Lemnek	Rom. Lovnic
Hung. Szelindek	Rom. Slimnic
(similar form):	
Polyána	Poiana

Names created from personal names without a suffix:

Bodonkút	Rom. Buda Veche
Bodola	Rom. Budila
Doboka	Rom. Dobîca
Gerlahida (ancient name;	Gherla
today Szamosújvár)	

The Hungarian name translated from Slavic:

Öregyháza	Straja

The Hungarian name borrowed from German:
German Kelling >   Hung. Kelnek (Rom. Câlnic)

Others and poorly known etymologies:

Hung. Venicze	Rom. Veneţia
Hung. Sztána	Rom. Stana
Hung. Szancsal	Rom. Sîncel
	Rom. Coca

Ion Moga's list[45] contains four place names that the Romanians obviously borrowed from Hungarian (for example, Keresztes > Cristiş). Those created by a persunal name without a suffix probably also belong to this group (for example, Doboka). Eight names were borrowed from the Slavs by Hungarian as well as by Romanian. Only one of these, Poiana, shows a similar form in both languages; this name can, in Hungarian, derive from either Slavic or Romanian. The other 7 names all show different forms in the two languages. Consequently, none of these geographical names proves a Hungarian borrowing from Romanian; and all can be explained either by Romanian borrowing from Hungarian or by independent Romanian and Hungarian borrowing from Slavic.

A Review of the Geographical Names Existing Before 1400 in Hunedoara (Hunyad) County

Caraş-Severin, Hunedoara, Sibiu, and Făgaraş Counties in the south; the highest areas of the Apuseni Mountains and some areas north of there; and Maramureş County have long been considered "the Romanian territories" of Transylvania. They were the earliest areas populated by Romanians (beginning as early as in the thirteenth but mostly in the fourteenth century). In these areas are found most of the Romanian geographical names borrowed directly from Slavic; and the first geographical names of Romanian origin appeared there, in the fourteenth century.

Even in these territories, however, the ancient toponymy contains many names of Hungarian origin. Those geographical names that were known before 1400 and still exist in the Hunedoara County[46] will be analyzed here from the viewpoint of origin. There are 76 of these names (in fact, 78, but in two cases the same name is used for two villages: "upper" and "lower").

Names transferred from Hungarian to Romanian:	43	56.6%
Created parallel in Hungarian and Romanian:	8	10.5%
Names transferred from Romanian to Hungarian:	8	10.5%
From Slavic or Romanian to Hungarian:	4	5.2%
Unknown:	10	13.0%

Three of the names transferred from Romanian to Hungarian are based on Romanian appellatives: Nucşoara (1394, Noxara), *cf.* nucă "nut"; Rîuşor (1377, fluv. Ryusor) "little brook"; and Rîu-Bărbat (1391, Barbadvize), *cf.*, Romanian *bărbat* "man." The rest are Romanian of Slavic origin. There is one name probably transferred to Romanian from German, one parallel Slavic-Hungarian name, and one (Gurasada) with a Romanian (gură "mouth") and a Hungarian (szád "mouth") part, which is thus a tautological name.

Dubious Etymologies. Place Names Assumed To Be Inherited Directly from Latin

It is assumed that the following geographical names found along the lower course of the Tîrnava Mică (Kis-Küküllő) River could prove that Romanians lived in the area before the Hungarians: Sîncel, Valea Borşului, Rotunda (a forest), Hula lu Băşcău, Valea lui Sin, Presaca, and Ohaba.[47]

Sîncel (Szancsal)

"Terra Zonchel" is mentioned for the first time in a document from 1252,[48] which also states that three other villages are found in the vicinity of Zonchel and that they have a church. In 1271 the village is mentioned by the name Zanchalteluky (Hungarian *telek* "ground plot," thus, the ground plot of Zanchal). In 1341 a man named Bazarab de Zanchal is mentioned. This is probably a Pecheneg name; and some years later (1347) the village is called Bezermen-zanchal, "Pecheneg Zanchal." In the same year, Magyar Zanchal, "Hungarian Zanchal," appears in a document. Consequently, according to the testimony of the documents, Pechenegs and Hungarians were living there in the fourteenth century. After its first appearance, Zanchal is often mentioned in the documents in varying forms (Zanchal, Zanczal). A twin village inhabited by Vlachs appears in documents for the first time in 1513, when Oláh Zanchal "Vlach Zanchal" is mentioned. The same document also contains the name Magyarzan-chal.[49] The Romanian name Sîncel, appears in 1854. The origin of this place name is unknown. Nicolae Drăganu proposed the etymology from Latin *sanctus* > **santicellus* > Romanian **sânticel, sînt(u)cel*; or from Latin *summicellus*.[50] V. Frăţilă accepts the second of these. Both hypotheses are, however, unlikely. *Sînt(u)cel* is "a far-fetched form" and neither Latin **summicellus* nor Romanian **sîmcel* is attested to, as was also pointed out by Ioan Pătruţ. Moreover, there are no similar cases anywhere in Romanian territory. Ioan Pătruţ proposes a simpler etymology[51] from the Romanian personal names Simcă, Simca, Simcea, or Sinca, Sincă, Sîncu existing also in Slavic, of which the diminutive would be Simcel or Sincel, respectively.

There are, however, no analogies to such a name; and the usual procedure of creating a place name in Romanian has always been with the use of a suffix (-eşti, -eni, or the masc. plural suffix -i),[52] in contrast to Hungarian, in which personal names are often used unchanged as place names: Hung. Szent Simon > Rom. Simoneşti,

Hung. Szent Domokos > Rom. Dămăcușeni. (It is only in modern times that a number of place names in Romania have been created from personal names without a suffix.)

Valea Borșului

Magyarzanchal is also called Bursiyacobhaza (1347) in documents. Frățilă proposes that this name derives from a Romanian personal name Iacob Borș or Iacob Borșa and is identical with present-day Valea Borșului.[53]

Borș is a difficult case, since this name exists in Slavic (Boriš) as well as in Hungarian (from Turkish *bors* "pepper"). It appears in several parts of Transylvania and Hungary as a place-name as well as a name for rivers. In Hungary, there is, for example, Borsod County; in Transylvania, Kolozs-Borsa.[54] These originate from the Hungarian personal name Bors, which is of Turkish origin. The other part of the name in the document from 1347, Iacob, is a Christian personal name found in most European languages. Its sound pattern is not, however, Romanian. The usual Romanian form is Iacov, attested in Wallachian documents beginning in 1389. Other Romanian forms are Iacovachi, Iacuș, Iacoviță, Iacă. Sometimes Iacobică, Iacobuț and other forms with -b- appear; but "the appearnace of -b- instead of -v- is a result of Roman Catholic influence."[55]

Rotunda

In the area in which this village is situated, there is a forest called Rotunda. A document from 1296 mentions Silva Kerechnuk "round forest" in the same area, and in 1298 Villa Kerechnuk is mentioned. In Frățilă's opinion, it is possible that the old name of the village derives from the name of the forest area called Rotundu, near which the old village was probably situated. In that case, the name of the village in the writings of the Hungarian Chancellery, Silva Kerechnuk, would be a translation of the Romanian name (Pădurea) Rotunda.[56] It is, however, equally possible that the forest and the village were called "round forest" and "round village" (*Kerechnuk*) by the Hungarians and that the Romanians translated the name to Rotunda. Since this village has the Romanian name of Chișcrac[57] (obviously from Hungarian Kiskerék), this is the most probable hypothesis.

Hula lu Bășcău and Valea lui Sin

These villages are mentioned in a document from 1313 under the names Bozkosar and Zyn Potoka, respectively. Frățilă assumes that the Hungarians translated these originally Romanian names. While the appellatives that appear in Hungarian in the documents could be translated, the personal names are not Romanian,[58] which makes Frățilă's hypothesis unlikely.

Presaca de Secaş (Székásgyepü, Székáspreszáka)

This village in Hunedoara County was referred to as Praeszaka in documents as late as 1647. Its German name, Kerschdorf, is mentioned in 1854. The name derives from the Slavic verb *prĕsĕšti*, *prĕsĕko* "to cut, to cut one's way."[59] There are many place names of this type in Romania. The meaning of this word is "a place in the forest with a clearing" and, in Wallachia and Moldavia, a "place outdoors where beehives are placed."[60] In Transylvania the defense system of the Hungarian kingdom was made up of places in the forest that were difficult to penetrate: Hungarian *gyepü*, Romanian (from Slavic) *prisaca*. They thus originate from the period in which the Hungarian Kingdom extended its domination and the Hungarian and Transylvanian German population settled in Transylvania. As the extension of settlement was a gradual process, from the tenth to the twelfth century, place names connected with the frontier defense line (for example, *gyepü*) were created in several areas. The Romanian equivalent of Hungarian *gyepü* appears only in southern Transylvania. There is nothing to indicate that these Romanian place names were created before the twelfth or thirteenth century; and Frățilă concludes "if names such as Presaca and Beşineu had also been created in the period when the Hungarians came to Transylvania, the name of the settlement Ohaba is certainly from the time of the Slavo-Romanian symbiosis.[61]

Ohaba

Another village along the Tîrnava Mică River is called Ohaba (Székásszabadja) [lit.: "the free (village) of Székás"]. It is mentioned in Hungarian documents beginning in 1372 under the name Wyfalw (= modern Hungarian Újfalu): *villa* Wyfalw; Wyfolu (1417), Wyfalu (1418), Wyfaw (1435, 1437), Vijfalu, *census quinquagesimalis da Vyfalw nobilium* (1461). The German name Newdorf (New Village) appears in 1488 and the Romanian Ohaba in 1733.[62]

Frățilă presumed that Romanian Ohaba originates from the time of Slavo-Romanian symbiosis in Transylvania before the arrival of the Hungarians. This is an old hypothesis, which was advanced by Ioan Bogdan and Silviu Dragomir in 1906.[63]

This Romanian place name originates from the Slavic verb *oxabiti sę* "to evade something, to refrain from something,"[64] and refers to the fact that the inhabitants of this village were exempted from taxes. The notion "exempted from taxes" is a typically feudal phenomenon, which implies the existence of obligations to a landlord, the Church, or a state organization. Such obligations appeared in Southeastern Europe during the thirteenth and fourteenth centuries, and the designation Ohaba was first used in Wallachia in Slavonic documents written in the fourteenth century. There are such place names in Oltenia, but most of them (23) are found in the Banat; there are 10 in Hunedoara County and three in Arad County.[65] Colonists from Wallachia settled in these places; and their villages were called Szabadfalu "free village" in Hungarian and Ohaba in Romanian. The Hungarian name Újfalu "New Village" also indicates that the settlement was of recent date (in relation to the period when the document was written). Similar names created in the feudal period are Lehota and Vola in Hungary, which are respectively of Slovakian and Ruthenian origin, and in the Wallachian Principalities, Slobozia, of South Slavic origin and Uric, from Hungarian *örök* "inherited, inheritable, donated estate." Uric is frequently used in Moldavia and also appears in Hunedoara County. It is therefore obvious that Ohaba cannot originate from any time before the fourteenth century.[66]

PLACE NAMES

The Romanian Place Names

According to the meaning of the word it consist of, Iorgu Iordan distinguished four main groups of Romanian place names: 1) geographical, 2) social, 3) historical, and 4) psychological.[67]

1) *Geographical*: Surface formations: *albie* "the lowest part of a valley"; *movilă* "hill"; *capul* "head" (usually a hill, also "the end of something"). A characteristic feature of the place: *lunca* "waterside, river meadow"; *alun, aluna, alunul* "hazel tree"; *boz* "dwarf elder"; *alba* "white"; *neagra* "black"; *sărata* "salty." The position of the place: *dosul* "the back"; *fața* "the face, the front side"; . . . *de Jos* "lower"; . . . *de Sus* "upper."

2) *Social*: Iordan included in this group names of villages based on both personal names—*Augustin, Blaj, Fărcąs,* and *Agnita*—and the names of historical figures given to settlements in the nineteenth and twentieth centuries: *Țepeș Vodă, Dimitrie Cantemir, Traian*.[68] There is a group of names ending in *-falău* "village" (< Hungarian *-falva, falu*): *Petrifalău* (< Hungarian *Péterfalva*), *Ciomafalău* (< Hungarian *Csomafalva*). Several place names indicate ownership or preserve the memory of social institutions (*Slobozie* "free village" of Slavic origin; *Uric* also "free village" but of Hungarian origin) or that of different kinds of servants of the court (*Stolnic* [cf., *stolnic* "High Steward"], *Muftiul* from Turkish "supreme judge"). Other names denote the

occupation of the villages' inhabitants: *bivolari* "buffalo boys," *cărbunari* "coal vendors," and *croitori* "tailors." There are names of religious content such as *biserica* "church," *apatău* (< Hungarian *Apáti, apát* "abbot"), as well as of popular mythology: *balaura* "the dragon," *draca, dracul* "the devil." Certain place names preserve the memory of former settlements: *Odaia* "flat used by the officials of the Turkish state in their journeys across the country"; *Straja* "sentry, guard"; and *Zalhanaua* "slaughter house."

3) *Historical*: Names of different populations preserved in place names: *Arvat, Horovatul* (< Hung. *horvât* "Croatian"), *Bulgari* "Bulgarians"; *Comana* (fem.) "Cumanian"; *Greaca* (fem.) "Greek"; *Iaşi* "Yaziges"; *Jidava* (fem.) "Jew"; *Neamţul* "German"; *Peceneaga* (fem.), *Peceneagul* (masc.) and, in Transylvania, *Beşineu*, "Pecheneg"; *Cuzdrioara* (< Hung. *Kozárvár* "tower of the Cazars"); *Lipovanul* "Russian"; *Ruşi* "Russians"; *Sasa* "Saxon"; *Şcheia* "Bulgarian"; *Sârba* "Serbian"; *Secuia* "Székely"; *Tatarca* "Tatar"; *Tauta, Tăut* "Slovakian"; *Ţiganca* "Gypsy"; and *Unguraş, Ungurei*, "Hungarian." Names of Romanians from different districts: *Bănăţeni* "people from the Banat"; *Munteanul* "man from Muntenia"; *Moldovanul* "man from Moldavia"; *Ungureni* "people coming from /eastern/ Hungary /including Transylvania/ /ethnic Hungarians or Rumanians/"; *Vlaha, Vlaşca* (from the Slavic name of the Romanians), *Româna*. Place names also preserve the memory of certain historic events or objects: *Grădişte* (of Slavic origin) "fortification, tower"; *Luptători* "warriors"; *Orada* (< Hung. *vár*) "tower"; and *Războieni* (cf., *război* "war").

4) *Psychological*: There are place names derived from nicknames: *Grozăvescul, cf., grozav* "terrible, awful"; *Afurisiţi* "those accursed"; and *Risipiţi, cf., risipi* "to scatter, to waste." Some are based on human conditions: *Flămînda* (fem.), cf., *flămînd* "hungry"; *Mămăligari, cf., mămăliga*, "maize porridge"; and *Vai de ei* (approximately) "poor ones." Certain place names are descriptive: *Piciorul Porcului* "the leg of the pig," and *Fără Fund* "bottomless."

The Formal Peculiarities of Romanian Place Names

Phonetics: Spontaneous sound changes: *Ilva* > *Ilua, Oacheş* > *Acheş*. Sound assimilations and dissimilations: *albie* > *Alghia*, Hung. *Egrestő* > Rom. *Agrişteu*. Apocope and syncope: *Altul Cucii* (instead of *înalt-*), Hung. *Magyaró* > Rom. *Măierău*. Prothesis and epenthesis: *găuri* (plur. of *gaură* "hole") becomes *Gavuri*. Analogies: Transylvanian Saxon *Krisbach* (*Krebsbach*) > Rom. *Crizbav*, Hung. *Földvár* > Rom. *Feldioara*. In the process of borrowing the Hungarian and Transylvanian Saxon place names within the Carpathian territory of present-day Romania, many examples of popular etymology, haplology and superurbanism were produced: Hung. *Szatmár* (from a personal name of German origin) > Rom. *Satu Mare* "big village," Hung. *Mondorlak* > Rom. *Mîndruloc* "proud or handsome place," German *Propstdorf* > Rom. *Proştea* (Mare, Mică), *cf.*, Rom. *prost* "stupid, ignorant, bad, poor." Metathesis: *Cărpiniş* > *Căprinişul*; old and dialectal forms; for example, *Ceraşul* for *Cireş*.

Morphology: One finds variant forms of the plural, such as *Baltele* (the plural form of *baltă* "marsh"; today correctly *bălţi*); and an example of an unusual form of the genitive is *Balta Oaiei* instead of *Balta Oii*. Several names appear both in the masculine and the feminine form: *Şomcutul Mic, Şomcuta Mare*, and *Sebeş, Săbişa*.

Word formation: There is a very large number of suffixes by which place names are formed. Feminine forms have the endings *-a, -oaie* or *-oaica*: *Secuia* (in Vaslui district), the feminine form of *Secui* "Székely"; and *Ceauşoaia*, the feminine form of *ceauş* "messenger, chieftain." The most common suffixes in Romanian place names are *-eşti* and *-ani, -eni*. They designate the origin of the inhabitants (coming from a place or belonging to the head of family or to the owner on which the name is based). The suffix *-eşti* is considered to be of Thracian origin; it also exist in Albanian (*cf.*, the Albanian place name *Bukurisht*). The suffix *-ani* (and its variant *-eni*) is of Slavic origin (*čninŭ*). Romanian *Bucureşti* (Bucharest) means "the Bucurescu family"; *Găureni* derives from *gaură* "hole, opening," thus, "people who live in holes or in the vicinity of holes." These suffixes may be used in the study of migrations and colonizations.[69] Another suffix of Slavic origin is *-ăuţi*, from Ukrainian *-ovtsi* today *-ivtsi)*, with approximately the same meaning as that of *-ani*, as in *Rădăuţi*, from the personal name Radu. The meaning of the suffix *-inţ(i)*, of Slavic origin, is also similar to that of *-ani*. In several cases, the Romanian form reproduces the Slavic plural: Romanian *Stremţi*, *cf.*, Slavic * *Srěmītsi* (Serbian *Sremtsi* "people coming from Srem"). This suffix, like *-ăuţi*, indicates the personal origin (not the local one) of the inhabitants.[70] Place names ending in *-ova, -ava* were also created by the use of a Slavic suffix, in most cases by a Slavic population: *Ardeova* from Hungarian *erdő* "forest" + the Slavic suffix *-ova; Craiova, cf.*, Slavic *kral* "king."

A large group of place names all over Romania were created by *diminutive suffixes.* Often, one finds the original form as well as the diminutive not far from each other. In a number of cases the diminutive form was given to the smaller of the two settlements: Blăjel (Kleinblasendorf) near Blaj. Diminutive forms were, however, also created in order to avoid homonymy. The Romanian diminutive, moreover, also has the sense of "similar to" and in geographical names approximately the meaning "in the vicinity of": *Tecucel* is thus a river that flows through the outskirts of *Tecuci*. Then there are, chiefly in Transylvania, "pseudodiminutives," that is, place names ending in -*oara* and -*uş*, such as *Timişoara*, *Feldioara*, and *Adamuş*, which were not originally diminutive forms of place name borrowings from Hungarian: *Temesvár*, *Földvár*, and *Ádámos* (-*oara* thus corresponds in these names to Hungarian -*vár* and -*uş* to Hungarian -*os*).

The suffix -*et* in place names denotes aggregations (mostly of plants, especially trees): *Făget*, cf., *fag* "beech"; *Păltinetul*, cf., *paltin* "sycamore maple." The suffix -*iş* has the same function, and several place names exist with both of these suffixes: along with *Păltinet(ul)*, there is also *Păltiniş*. Because of the phonetical similarity and also the similar sense between Romanian -*iş* and Hungarian -*es*, many Hungarian place names ending in -*es* have -*iş* in Romanian: Hungarian *Örményes* > Romanian *Armeniş*; Hungarian *Kökös* > Romanian *Chichiş*; Hungarian *Kertes* > Romanian *Chertiş*. The suffix -*işte(a)* has a similar function except that the actual presence of the object denoted by the base-word is not necessary: for example, *Arişte* "place where there was a threshing floor." Many of these place names were borrowed from Slavic: *Grădişte*, cf., Slavic *gradište* "fortress"; Bulgarian *gradište* "the place of a former town, fortification, or tower"; *Tîrgovişte*, cf., Slavic *tŭrgovište* "market place."

The suffixes -*ar* and -*aş* (-*ari* and -*aşi* in the plural), form the names of professions [*nomina agentis*]: *strungar* "lathe operator," and *puşcaş* "fusilier, marksman, shot." They often also denote the origin of the inhabitants: *Poienari*, *Baltaşi*. The suffix -*ărie* creates collective nouns and *nomina agentis*: *Bivolăria* (with the definite article) "stable of buffaloes, herd of buffaloes," *Căşeria* "place where cheese was once made."

Syntax: The genitive formed by *de*, which existed once in the Romanian language, is still preserved in several names of small villages: for example, *Păuşeşti de Otăsău*. In certain place names, one finds the genitive with the definite article placed before the noun: *Măgura lui Căţel* "the hill of the whelp" (but the literary form *Măgura Căţelului* is also used); and *Cornul lui Sas*. On the other hand, the postponed definite article could appear, in certain place names based on personal names, which is also an ancient usage: *Drumul Bogdanului* (today one would say *Drumul lui Bogdan*).

A small number of Romanian place names are formed by connecting two nouns. This does not agree with the rules of the Romanian language, and most of these place names were borrowed from other languages. Some of them are tautologies: *Gurasada* (Romanian *gură* "mouth," and in the case of place names "backwater," Hungarian *szád* "mouth, opening"); *Rudabaia, Rudabania* (*cf.*, Slavic *ruda* and Hungarian *bánya*, both with the meaning of "mine"); *-Muráş-Oşorhei* < Hungarian *Marosvásárhely* (today Tîrgu Mureş); *Dicio-Sînmartin* < Hungarian *Dicsőszentmárton*, Hung. *dicső* "glorious," thus properly an adjective, today *Tîrnăveni*.[71] There are also place names formed by combining a noun with an adjective: *Cîmpulung* (*cîmpul* + lung "the long field"). Some place names containing an adjective + a noun are also of foreign origin: *Dobrivîrful* (Slavic) and others in Transylvania of the type *Sîncrai* (< Hungarian *Szentkirály*), which represent the numerous Hungarian names of villages based on the names of Roman Catholic Saints. Examples of place names formed by combining a preposition with a noun are *Sup(t)cetate* (*supt* + *cetate* "under the tower") and (*Dealu)* *Trevăile* (*între* + *văi* "between valleys").[72] There are also combinations of a verb with an adverb or an adjective, such as *Dourme-Răù* "sleep + badly."

Differences Between Northern Romanian Place Names Recorded on the Balkan Peninsula and Those from the Territories North of the Danube

A chronological study of Romanian place names is not available. North of the Danube, only a few Romanian place names were recorded before the fourteenth century. Several such names were, however, preserved in the documents [*hrişovs*] written by Serbian kings between about 1200 and 1450. All these clearly belong to the Northern Romanian dialect. Several of them currently exist, in more or less Slavicized form, in Serbia and Bulgaria.[73] Most of them were formed from geographical or personal names + the definite article: *Piscul, Corbul, Surdul*; with the diminutive suffixes *-şor* or *-el* (*Cernişor, Negrişor, Banişor, Văcărel, Păsărel,* and *Cercel*) or with the suffix *-et* (*Cornet*).

These types of place names are also found north of the Danube, in Muntenia, Moldavia, and Transylvania. There, however, they are in the minority among the large number of place names created by the suffixes *-eşti* and *-eni, -ani*. The first appearances in the documents of these suffixes in place names in Transylvania are the following: *Gureni* (1415); *Petreni* (1425); *Toteşti* (1438); *Luteşti* (1439) in the district of Hátszeg (Haţeg); *Mărgineni* (1437) in Fogaras County; and *Chiuleşti* (1467) in Szolnok-Doboka County. The Romanian population of the central areas of the Balkan Peninsula disappeared during the fifteenth century. Their place names, first recorded in the early thirteenth century, show what is obviously an earlier type of name-giving. This earlier type is characterized by the frequent use of names in the nominative with the definite article. Later, the use of the suffixes -*eşti*, and - *ani*, *eni* became the main way of forming place names. This must have happened in a period in which the connection between the speakers of Romanian north and south of the Danube were severed, because the place names ending in -*eşti* did not spread in the Balkan Peninsula.

A Comparison of Place Names in Transylvania with Those of the Transcarpathian Areas of Romania

Formal Differences

In Muntenia the suffix -*eşti* appears more frequently than it does in Moldavia. There are, for example, about 60 villages with the name Popeşti in Muntenia but only 10 in Moldavia. Moreover, family names ending in -*escu* in the former are more frequent and those ending in -*(e)anu*, in the latter. In Transylvania, these usual Romanian suffixes are found much more rarely and not everywhere. The suffix -*eşti* is most common in the area of the Apuseni Mountains where most Transylvanian names of Romanian origin are also found. This suffix also appears along the border area between Transylvania proper and the Banat. More recently, this characteristic Romanian suffix has been used to create new names, often to replace Hungarian -*falva*, or -*telke*. In northeastern Transylvania, there are place names ending in -*eni*,[74] obviously an influence from neighboring Moldavia.

In Transylvania, intellectuals and, later, officials have created many place names using neologisms, such as the learned expressions *superior* and *inferior*. (In the transcarpathian territory, only their Romanian counterparts *de Sus* and *de Jos* are used almost exclusively). Another example of place names given by learned people is the use of *o* instead of *u* in Nicoleşti, common in Transylvania.[75]

Semantic Features

In the transcarpathian areas of Romania many place names have been created with the appellative *biserică* "church."[76] In Transylvania many fewer names of this kind appear, and they are based on non-Romanian (mostly German) appellatives with the same meaning.[77] A vestige of former frontiers between Transylvania and the Romanian principalities of Muntenia and Moldavia has survived in a number of names such as Carantina, Carantina Veche, Schela ("frontier road not in use, on which grass is growing"), and Vama ("customs").

A reminder of frequent and severe plagues is found in the names Ciumaşi, from *ciumă* "plague." In Transylvania, there are only a few of these, and at least one is a late creation of popular etymology: Ciumani, in Csík (Ciuc) County designed to replace earlier Ciomafalău ("the village of Csoma").[78]

The name Odaia is frequently found in Muntenia and Moldavia but does not appear in Transylvania. It is of Turkish origin and means "flat used by the officials of the Turkish state in their journeys across the country."[79] Several other Turkish terms not found in Transylvania appear in the territory of the former Romanian principalities.

As in all countries there are many place names in Romania that denote plants (especially trees of different kinds) and animals. In Muntenia and Moldavia these appellatives usually derive from Romanian or from Slavic, while in Transylvania the great majority are of Hungarian origin. The appellative *măr* "apple," for instance, appears in 39 place names in the transcarpathian territories but only 7 times in Transylvania,[80] where place names using "apple" are usually formed by Hungarian *alma*.

Pruni "plums" and *Pruniş* "plum wood" appear throughout the country. The Slavic noun *sliva* "plum" is the basis of several place names such as Slimnic (from Slivnic), Slimnul, Slivna, Slivuţa, and Slevnia, all of which (except Slivuţa, in Hunedoara County) are in the transcarpathian areas. In Transylvania (except for the southernmost part), the Romanians borrowed Hungarian *szilva* (from Slavic *sliva*): Silvaş, Silivaş, Silvaşul de Cîmpie, Silvaşul de Jos and Silvaşul de Sus, Silvaşul Român, and Silvaşul Unguresc.[81]

The same is the case with *păr* and Hungarian *körte*; Romanian *fag* and Hungarian *bükk*; Romanian *sălcie* and Hungarian *fűz*; Romanian *mesteacăn* and Hungarian *nyír, nyíres*; Romanian *trestie* (from Slavic) and Hungarian *nád*; Romanian *anin, arin* and Hungarian *éger*; Romanian *râşniţă* and Hungarian *örlő*; and Romanian *coroiu* and Hungarian *karvaly*. On the basis of data from a dictionary of the settlements with Romanian inhabitants within the arch of the Carpathians,[82] Kniezsa drew up statistics on the names of these villages.[83] The Hungarian form of the appellatives mentioned above is used in 69 place names in Transylvania and the Romanian in only 13. In the transcarpathian territories, the Romanian form is used frequently, particularly *păr* (*hruša*), *fag* (*buc*), *sălcie* (*rakita* and *vrúba*), and *mesteacăn* (*brěza*), although the corresponding Slavic appellatives are also common.[84]

Similar differences between the transcarpathian areas and those within the Carpathian regions of Romania are found in the distribution of place names created from the names of peoples that once lived there. *Greaca*[85] and similar place names formed from the Romanian name of the Greeks are frequent in Muntenia and Moldavia but do not appear in Transylvania. The Romanian name for the Germans *neamţ* or *gherman* (recently *german*) and Hungarian *német* have been preserved in many settlements in Romania. In Muntenia and Moldavia these place names are based on Romanian—Neamțul, Nemți, Măgura Nemților, Ghermana, and Ghermănești—while in Transylvania they derive from Hungarian *német* "German" in four cases and *szász* "Transylvanian Saxon" in sixty: Királynémeti > Romanian Crainimăt; Németi > Romanian Nimțiul, later Mințiul (older forms are Nemiti, Nempty, Nempcii, Nemți);[86] Szászváros > Romanian Orăștie; Szász-kézd > Romanian Saschiz; Szászpatak > Romanian Spătac; Szász-lekence > Romanian Lechința; Szászcsűr > Romanian Săsciori; Szász-fehéregyháza > Romanian Viscri (from German Weisskirch—the German and Hungarian names mean "white church"); and Szász-veresmart > Romanian Rotbav (from German Rotbach "red brook," which is also the meaning *veresmart*). In the transcarpathian areas "szász" appears only in southwestern Moldavia, an area once inhabited by Hungarians: Sascut, from Hungarian Szászkút "fountain of the Saxon."

A Turkish people, the Pechenegs, lived from the eleventh through the fourteenth centuries in Hungary and in the territory of present-day Moldavia and Muntenia and imparted their name to several settlements. Most of them were probably created during the period of their occupation; but some may be from a later day, from personal names (Besenyő), or after Pechenegs who owned or inhabited a settlement. Various villages are named *Pecenoge* (after the Slavic form), *Pecenegul* and *Peceneaga* (after the Romanian form), and *Besenyő* (after the Hungarian form), as well as the German equivalent, *Beschen-bach*. Of these Iorgu Iordan mentioned nine Romanian forms (of Slavic origin) in Muntenia and Moldavia and three in the Southern Carpathians near the frontier between Muntenia and Transylvania.[87] In all other parts of Transylvania, only forms of the Hungarian name, *besenyő* appear. Ștefan Pascu lists 14 such villages, including Romanian Beșeneu, Beșineu, Beșînău from Hungarian Besenyő.[88] There is also a village called Beschenbach, a name given by the Transylvanian Saxons; and in two other cases early Saxons lived near the village of "Besenyő," which they named Heidendorf, "village of pagans" in German. The place names related to the Pechenegs are not derived from the Latin name, as it was assumed by Pascu. The Latin name (Bisseni) was only used in the documents, which at that time were all written in the Latin language. The peoples of Transylvania gave the villages in which Pechenegs settled names in their own languages—Besenyő and Beschen—and the Romanians, when they found these names, borrowed them in the forms Beșeneu, Beșineu, Beșinbac.

The Names of Rivers in Romania

The investigation of place and river names requires interdisciplinary work in linguistics, archaeology, and history as well as critical analysis of sources. Individual place and river names must also be considered in the context of the total area of dissemination. It is methodologically untenable to generalize on the basis of individual analyses; that will lead to invalid, or at best to only partially valid conclusions. To attain meaningful results it would be necessary to consider the individual groups comprising the entire dissemination area.

Pre-Slavic place names, antedating the 7th century, are unknown in Transylvania, thus, the oldest place names there are of Slavic origin.

Even pre-Slavic, presumably also pre-Latin names of the large rivers in Transylvania, such as Mureş - Maros - Maris(ia), Someş - Szamos - Samus, and Oltul - Olt - Aluta(s) were transmitted in Slavic form.[89] Consequently, not a single geographical name (place, river, or mountain names) in Romania attests the Roman continuity from the late antiquity to the early Middle Ages.

There are 153 tributaries of the rivers Someş, Criş, Ompoi, Mureş, Olt, Timiş, and Bîrzava that flow through at least two or three villages in the Carpathian Basin on the territory of Romania.[90] They may be broken down according to the origin of the name and number of tributaries:

Tisza	7
Crişul Repede	16
Crişul Negru	6
Crişul Alb	2
Someş	40
Mureş	22
Olt(ul)	23
Timiş	10
Bega	11
Bîrzava	2
lower Danube	14

Of these 38–39, (25.5%) are Slavic; 72 (47.0%), Hungarian; 1 (0.7%), German; 1 (0.7%), Romanian (a name created in a late period); and 41 (26.8%), of unknown origin.

River names of unknown origin

Of the 41 (26.8%) river names of unknown origin, there are 9 cases in which the sound pattern of the Hungarian and Romanian names clearly indicate that the Romanian form originates from Hungarian: for example, Hungarian Visó > Romanian Vişeu; Hungarian Zilah > Romanian Zalău; Hungarian Tőz > Romanian Teuz; and Hungarian Árapatak > Romanian Arpatac. In the remaining cases, the source of the Romanian name cannot be determined with certainty.

None of these names shows a sound pattern indicating a Latin or Romanian origin. Many of them probably derive from Slavic or Hungarian. The southeastern area of Transylvania is one of the regions in which river names of unknown origin are frequent; of a total of 12 tributaries from the south to the Olt River, five (Tatrang/Tîrlung, Zajzon/Zizin, Tömös/Timiş, Barca/Bîrsa (German) Burze, and Porumbák/Porumbac) have names of undetermined origin. Since Pechenegs are known to have lived in that area in the thirteenth and fourteenth centuries, some of these names may be of Turkish origin.

River names of Slavic origin

A total of 39 (25.5%) of the 153 tributaries mentioned above have names of Slavic origin. The distribution of the Slavic names is, however, uneven; a fourth of them are concentrated in a small area (Krassó-Szörény/Caraş-Severin County) in the southwestern corner of Romania. Ten tributaries of the Danube in this area have names of Slavic origin, and all of them were probably transferred to Romanian directly from Slavic: Lisava, Ciclova, Vicinic, Dognacea, Cernoveţ, Prigoru, Oraviţa, Berzasca, Ieşelniţa, and Belareca. Another three Danube tributaries have names of Hungarian origin: Néra, Karas, and Ménes (Romanian Nera, Caraş, and Miniş).

In the rest of the territory within the arch of the Carpathians, there are 29 river names of Slavic origin. In 15 cases, the sound pattern of the Hungarian and Romanian forms makes it possible to determine the language from which the name was borrowed by the Romanians. A direct borrowing from Slavic is shown in 7 cases: Slavic Vŏrbova or Vŏrbovo > Romanian Gârbova (the Slavic word means "willow" and was borrowed by Hungarian in the form Orbó); Slavic Trnava > Romanian Tîrnava (Hungarian Küküllő); Slavic Cernavoda > Romanian Cernavoda "black water" (Hung. Feketeviz); Slavic Sad (from the appellative *sadŏ* "plantation") > Romanian Sad (Hung. Cód, German Zoodt); Slavic *ščiuka* "pike" > Romanian Sciuca (Hung. Csukás); and Slavic *cŏrna* "black" > Romanian Cerna (Hung. Cserna, but in the Middle Ages Feketeér "black brook," preserved today in the name of the village Ficatar). Moraviţa (Hung. Moravica), a tributary of the Berzava in the southwest, must also be considered a direct borrowing, because it is situated in an area where the majority of the Slavic names were borrowed directly by Romanian.

In 8 cases the sound pattern of the Hungarian and Romanian forms indicates that the Romanians did not borrow the names directly from Slavic but via Hungarian: Slavic Jelšava > Hungarian Jolsava (vowel harmony) > Jolsva > Ilsva > Ilosva (*jo* > *i* is usual in Hungarian), from which Romanian Ilişua; Slavic Lȯkȯnica > Hungarian Lekence > Romanian Lechinţa (in the case of direct Romanian borrowing from Slavic, one would expect *Lecniţa); Slavic Trescava > Hungarian Torockó > Romanian Trăscău instead of *Treascava or *Truskava); Slavic Lovȯna or Lovina > Hungarian Lóna (i patak) > Romanian (Pîrîul) Lunei (for example, Romanian Luna instead of * Lomna, as in Slavic Slivnik > Romanian Slimnic, and Slavic Ravna > Romanian Ramna). In the remaining 14 cases, the sound pattern gives no reliable indication about the direct source of the borrowing.

River names of Hungarian origin

Almost half of the tributaries have names of Hungarian origin (a total of 72, or 47%). A few examples are Almás, Nádas, Füzes, Aranyos, Sebes, Ménes, Komlód, Sajó, Kormos, and Vargyas. Romanian borrowed 70 of the Hungarian names, including Almaş, Nădaş, Fizeş, Arieş, Sebeş, and Miniş. One river name is of German origin and was transferred to Hungarian as well as to Romanian: Weidenbach > Hungarian Vidombák, and Romanian Ghimbav. Only a single river name is of Romanian origin: Cornăţel, in the region of Sibiu. This name appeared late in documents; from 1319 to 1555, the village from which this river received its name appears in the forms Hortobagh, Hortobag, Hortobaghfalua, and German Harwasdorf.[91] Kornicsel appeared for the first time in 1733[92] (German Harbach).

The direct source of the Romanian names for the 153 Transylvanian rivers is unknown in 48 (31.4%) of the cases; 87 (56.8%) derive from Hungarian, 17 (11%) from Slavic, and 1 from German. The absence of geographical names of Latin origin north of the lower Danube is often explained by reference to the rural, pastoral life of the "Daco-Roman" population and is thus not considered to contradict the theory of continuity. According to abundant evidence, however, river names are in general borrowed by the new arrivals in a country. The Romans borrowed most of their river names from the peoples they subdued; and in modern times, one can cite the Europeans' large-scale borrowing of Indian river names in the New World. This also shows that the newcomers borrow such names even when they are more numerous and have a more highly developed culture than the indigenous population. In the territory within the arch of the Carpathians a large proportion of the river names used today by the Romanians, Hungarians, and Germans are of Slavic origin. This indicates that the Slavs were living in the territory prior to its present inhabitants. About half the river names are, however, of Hungarian origin; and almost all of these were borrowed by the Romanians. Furthermore, the Romanians borrowed from Hungarian at least eight names of Slavic origin and nine of undetermined origin. At least 56% of all Romanian river names were transferred to Romanian from Hungarian.

Place Names of Slavic Origin in Transylvania
(Hungarian, German, Romanian)

The study of the place names of Slavic origin in all three languages now spoken in Transylvania—Romanian, Hungarian, and German— is indispensable when analyzing the early settlement of these peoples.

Hungarian place names of Slavic origin

These are found mostly along the borderline between mountainous regions and plains; they are rare along the edges of the Transylvanian Basin (Mezőség, Cîmpia Transylvaniei). Most of the Slavic place names are based on appellatives denoting natural phenomena: geographic features, plants, and animals; and a smaller number derive from Slavic personal names. There are also a few names indicating a settlement, such as Szolcsva and Szelicse (in the region of Torda/Turda), from a Slavic appellative meaning "village," or with the Slavic suffix -*an*, as in Kályán (Kolozs/Cluj County). Place names derived from Slavic personal names include Bezdéd, Déda, Dedrád, Dezmér, Gesztrágy, Lecsmér, Miriszló, Naszód, Szopor, Vajola, Vista, Völcsök, and Zovány.[93] Most of these are only names without a suffix, and since the Slavs almost always used a suffix to create place names out of personal names, they were probably formed by Hungarians.[94] A few place names created from Slavic personal names by Slavs (with suffixes) appear in Máramaros (Maramureș)—Bocskó; in the Háromszék (Trei Scaune, now Covasna) County, Papolc, Csernáton; and in Krassó-Szörény (Caraș-Severin) County—Orsova, Radimna, and Mácsova.[95]

There are no reliable chronological criteria in the sound pattern of the Slavic borrowings that would make possible to determine when they were transferred to Hungarian. Some information can, however, be gained by examining the Slavic dialects once spoken in Transylvania. Since several of the Slavic names contain -*grad* (Moigrad, Bălgrad), the Slavic typonymy can hardly have been Russian (in Russian the corresponding form is *gorod*). In the south, the ancient Slavic population was most probably Bulgarian (*cf.*, for instance Bolgárszeg, Romanian

Şchei, in Brassó [Braşov] with parallel Hungarian-Romanian names).
In the southwest there were also Serbians in the Middle Ages. In
the northern areas, however, in the place of Slavic *ě* one finds always
ě or *i* (*e.g.* Hungarian Peleske, old Hungarian Piliske). The Slavs who
left these names were not Bulgarians but, most probably, Western
Slavs.[96]

Different Slavic groups also settled in Transylvania in the later
Middle Ages and thereafter Russians (*cf.*, Hungarian Oroszi, from
Hungarian *orosz* "Russian" + *i* "possessive suffix," German Reussmarkt, Romanian Rusu). There are also place names indicating the
settlement of Czechs and Croatians (*e.g.* Páncélcseh > Romanian
Panticeu, with Romanian borrowing from Hungarian). Hungarian
place names such as Tót and Tótfalu (> Romanian Tăuţi, in early
borrowings and Tot in more recent ones) are frequent but indicate
only Slavs in general (Hungarian *tót* "Slovakian" was the Hungarian
name for the Slavs in the Middle Ages).

In at least five settlements named after different Slavic populations
these settlements were already assimilated to the Hungarians when
the Romanians arrived. This is clearly indicated by the sound pattern
of the Romanian names of these villages: Hungarian Páncélcseh
(Hung. *páncél* "armour" + *cseh* "Czech") > Romanian Panticeu borrowing of the Hungarian name, without any sense in Romanian) in
Cluj (Kolozs) County; and in southern Transylvania, where there are
two villages called in Hungarian Oroszi (Hungarian *orosz* "Russian"
+ suffix -*i*) > Romanian Urusiu and Orăsia, respectively. These
names are borrowings from Hungarian rather than translations of
the Hungarian meanings. Obviously, if the Romanians had found the
original Slavic population in these villages, they would have named
the localities after them (Ruşi or Sîrbi, for example).

Two villages in Transylvania (one each in Hunedoara and in Mureş
Counties) are called in Hungarian Nándor (Lándor), the former
Hungarian name for the Bulgarians which probably disappeared soon
after 1000, when the Bulgarian Empire was subdued by Byzantium.
It is not known whether the two settlements with this name preserve
the memory of Bulgarians found by the Hungarians in the tenth
century or that of later immigrants. The Romanian forms of these
names, however, indicate that when the Romanians arrived in the
area, they did not find Bulgarians there, since they borrowed the
Hungarian name of these villages (Romanian Nandru [Hunedoara
County] and Nandra [Mureş County]). The Romanian name for the
Bulgarians was Şchiau; many villages in Muntenia and Moldavia are
called Şchei.

German (Transylvanian Saxon) place names of Slavic origin

Place names of Slavic origin in Transylvanian Saxon appear in several areas, especially in the region of Bistritz (Beszterce/Bistriţa) and Sächsisch-Regen (Szászrégen/Reghin): Windau, from Slavic Wende; Pospesch (literary German Passbusch), from Slavic Pospech "hurry, haste"; and Billak (*cf., bil* "white"). Among the 242 names of villages in which Transylvanian Saxon dialects were spoken in the twentieth century, 8 were found to be of Slavic origin:[97]

Bistritz, Kleinbistritz	Sl. *bistro* "fast"
Dobring	Sl. *dobre* "good"
Jaad	Sl. *jad* "hell"
	(from which Rom. *iad*)
Kelling	Sl. *kal* "bog"
Kirtsch	Sl. *krz*
Kreweld	Sl. *chrebet* "hill"
Schlatt	Sl. *zoloto* "gold"

That Transylvanian Saxons lived together with Slavs is also indicated by parallel place names such as German Stolzenburg, *cf.,* Slavic *Slyn6nikъ*, from the adjective *slyn6nъ* "famous" (Romanian Slimnic, Sibiu County); and Saxon Stein *cf.,* Slavic Grot "edge" (de Lapide in a document from 1309), the Romanians borrowed the German name Stena and the Hungarians the Slavic Garat.[98]

Romanian Geographical Names of Slavic Origin
The Definition of Geographical Names Borrowed from Slavs

The number of geographical names that are ultimately of Slavic origin is high in many parts of present-day Romania. Discussing early contacts among the different populations that once lived in the country, it is essential to distinguish between the geographical names given by the Slavs and borrowed from them directly by the Romanians and other names of a Slavic pattern.[99] In the latter group there are many geographical names in which a Romanian word of Slavic origin appears: Lunca, Dumbrava, Dumbrăviţa, Izvor, Poiana, Peşteră, Slatina. These were given by Romanians.

Another group of geographical names ultimately of Slavic origin were borrowed by the Romanians from Hungarian. These are found almost exclusively within the Carpathian Mountains (in Transylvania): Slavic *Vrîbovo > Hungarian Orbó (in Satu Mare County) > Romanian Orbău. Slavic *Vrîbovo resulted, when borrowed directly from Slavic, in Romanian Gîrbova (Alba County). Similarly, from Slavic *selišče* "hamlet, small village," Hungarian Szelicse (Cluj County) > Romanian Sălicea; Hungarian Krakkó, of Slavic origin (Alba County) > Romanian Cricău, and Slavic *Gǫbĭcĭ > Hungarian Gambuc (1303: Gambuch),[100] which transferred to Romanian now has the form of Gîmbuţ. There are several river names in this group: Slavic Jelšava > Hungarian Jolsava, later Ilosva > Romanian Ilişua; Slavic Trescava > Hungarian Torockó > Romanian Trăscău. From the viewpoint of contacts between Slavs and Romanians, it is of importance that a Slavic population loaned place names to Romanians as well as Hungarians: Romanian Băcăinţi (Hunedoara County, Orăştie district), Hungarian Bokalyalfalu (in 1278, Bakay); Romanian Covăsinţi (in the region of Arad), in 1333, Couasi; Romanian Cuvin (in the Banat, Lipova district), Hungarian Kövi (Aradkövi); in 1323, possessio [owned by] Kev; Romanian Beşenova (Timiş region), Hungarian Óbesenyő, German Alt-Beschenowa (in 1213, terra castri Boseneu, in 1230, Beseneu).[101] These geographical names are the remnants of a time in which Slavs, Hungarians, and Romanians were living in Transylvania.

Geographical names with a Slavic sound pattern are also found among names given by officials. With regard to the significance of the names in which -în appears, the example given by Petrovici[102] may be mentioned here: There is a small river in Suceava County (northern Moldavia) to which the name Pîriul Dîmboviţei was given. This territory is far from the part of southern Romania where names with -în, -îm are found. The local inhabitants do not use the official name but call the river Apa Rusului.

Geographical names once given by Slavs and borrowed directly from them by the Romanians consist of only the following: names in which a Slavic lexical element not existing in the Romanian language appears and names with a Slavic suffix, which is not used in Romanian. (The question is somewhat complicated by the possibility that place names could have been created using an appellative borrowed from Slavic which later disappeared from Romanian).

The Slavic Elements of the Romanian Language and Romanian Geographical Names of Slavic Origin
The Slavic Elements of the Romanian Language

The oldest Slavic influence reached Romanian (that is, the East Latin idiom from which Romanian later emerged) probably beginning in the sixth or seventh century. In this earliest period, through the eighth century, only a weak influence with a few borrowed words can be demonstrated. The name of a Slavic tribe, slověninŏ (plural slověne) was transferred to Late Latin in the form of Sclavus (or

Sclavinus), plural *Sclavi* (or *Sclavini*). This is attested beginning with
the sixth century. Northern Romanian *şchiau* (plural *şchei*) continues
this (with the characteristic sound change of East Latin: *cl* > *ch*);
Arumanian has *şcl'eau* "servant"; Albanian *shqa* (plural *shqe*) "Bulgarian."[103] There are some words of an ancient sound pattern and
probably of Slavic origin, although these questions have been difficult
to decide definitively. *Mătură* "broom," *sută* "hundred," *stăpîn* "master,
lord, ruler," *stîncă* "rock," are, for example, shown by their sound
pattern to be early borrowings (before the 9th century). The words
smîntînă "(sour) cream," *daltă* "chisel," and *scovardă* "pancake" are
considered to be Slavic and also early, although their sound pattern
from the time before the ninth century may have continued to exist
even later in dialects in lateral areas.[104] In conclusion, there are some
(but remarkably few) Slavic elements transferred to Romanian before
the ninth century.

Most of the Slavic influence on Romanian was exerted from the
ninth through the eleventh centuries, that is, during the last centuries
of Common Romanian, before the development of the dialects, and
shows a Middle-Bulgarian sound pattern. It is therefore from the
period after the metathesis of the liquids, the third palatalization of
the velars, and the disappearance of the *jers* in the weak position.[105]
They do not show *a* for Slavic *o*; *u*, *i* for Slavic *jers* or *u* for Slavic
jery (y).[106] This influence, overwhelmingly Bulgarian, is, in principle, is
found uniformly throughout the Romanian language, that is, in the
entire area of Northern Romanian (including   the territories never
occupied by Bulgarians) and in all or at least in one of the southern
dialects (Arumanian, Meglenitic, and Istro-Rumanian). Moreover, these
lexical elements transferred to Romanian from the ninth through the
eleventh centuries are often also found in other Balkan languages:
"There are isoglosses that comprise Romanian, Bulgarian, Macedonian,
Serbo-Croatian, Albanian, and Greek. These reflect the common
structural features of the Balkan languages."[107]

The Slavic influence on Romanian after the twelfth century shows
a different character. Loan translations made beginning in the thirteenth
century are spread only regionally: Bulgarian words in the south,
Oltenia, Muntenia, and southern Transylvania; those from Ukrainian,
beginning in the thirteenth century but in larger numbers from the
fourteenth and fifteenth centuries, in Moldavia; and Serbian words
in the Banat and adjacent areas, beginning later, in the fifteenth
century.[108]

In Mihăilă's opinion the different distribution of Bulgarian borrowings could be explained by the fact that for a long time Transylvania
had had a political and economic life different from that of Wallachia

and Moldavia; and, in any case, no direct influences could penetrate there from the south. On the other hand, Wallachia's relations with Bulgaria continued and were intense until the occupation of this country by the Turks (fourteenth century); and later the continuous migrations of Bulgarians north of the Danube could have resulted in the transfer to the Romanian language of new words of Bulgarian origin, for example, in the sphere of gardening. A certain influence, Mihăilă continued, could be observed also in the south of Transylvania, a region that had close contacts with Wallachia.[109]

This explanation is far from sufficient and evades the real problem. Not only a subdialect spoken in one area or another but the entire language shows differences between the Slavic influences before and after the twelfth century. This characteristic feature of Romanian must be connected with the early history of its speakers. Assuming that they were living north of the Danube before the Slavs, that is, before the sixth century, a different picture would be expected. The Bulgarian influence on their language would, for example, be mostly restricted to the southern part of the country where Bulgarians were living even before the twelfth century. In Moldavia, at least in the northern part, eastern Slavic elements would be expected from the time before the $g > h$ change and other ancient characteristics. In the Banat, assuming an autochthonous Romanian population, the Serbian influence should be of a much more ancient date than the fifteenth century, since Serbians were living in adjacent areas much earlier.

The Geographical Names of Slavic Origin

Two relevant characteristics of these names will be discussed here: 1) the geographical distribution of names from the different Slavic idioms and 2) their age.

The geographical names of Slavic origin in present-day Romania are of four different types, according to the Slavic idiom from which they originate.[110] Their distribution in the country corresponds roughly to the elements of Slavic origin transferred to Northern Romanian beginning in the thirteenth century.

1. In the northeast, they are of an eastern Slavic type, showing polnoglasia,[111] *h, u, i, (î), -ău (-îu), -ăuţi* in the place of Common Slavic **g, *ǫ, *ě, -*ov, (-ev), *-ovīci*: Dorohoi, Horodnic, Putna, Bilca, Rîşca, Sadău, Başiu, Rădăuţi, instead of **Dorguni, *Gordúniku, *Pǫtína, *Bĕlúka, *Rĕčika, *Sadovú, *Baševú, *Radoívci*.

2. In the south, the place names of Slavic origin show Bulgarian characteristics: *št, žd, 'a (a), -ín, (-îm)* for the Common Slavic clusters **tj, *dj,* and for Common Slavic **ě, *ǫ*: Coşuştea, Medvežde, Breazova

(Brazua), Doftana, Smadoviţa, Dîmboviţa, from Slavic *Košutja, * Medvĕdje, *Berzova, *Degūtĕna, *Smĕdovica, *Dǫbovica.

3. In a smaller area in the west, western South Slavic features are found: *u, e, ģ* for Common Slavic *ǫ, *ļ, *ĕ, *dj*: Muthnuk, Vucova, Belareca, Sagĕvecū, Sagjavīc, from Slavic *Mǫtīnikū, *Vļkova, *Bĕlarĕka, *Sadjavīcī.

4. In a northwestern area (inhabited, however, only partly by Romanians), the Romanian geographical names show the metathesis of the liquids, the preservation of the occlusive character of *g*, and sometimes also the closed pronunciation of *ĕ*: Bălgrad, Moigrad, Zlatna, Craiova, Zagra, Gîmbuţ (Hung. Gambuc), Rişca, (Rîşca), Sici (Hung. Szécs), from Slavic *Bĕlgordū, *Mojīgordū, *Zoltīna, *Korl'evo, *Zagora, *Gǫbīcī, *Rĕčīka, *Sĕčī.[112]

The geographical names of Slavic origin in Romania, in contrast to the borrowings from Slavic found in Romanian, do not show sound characteristics older than Middle Bulgarian. There is, in other words, no geographical name dating to the sixth through the eighth centuries, which would correspond to the words from that period in the Romanian language. Moreover, the geographical names, in contrast to the language, never contain the reflex -un, -um for Slavic ǫ, but exclusively the reflex -în, (-îm):[113]

	-un, -um:	-în, -îm:
Lexical elements:	dumbravă, luncă, scump	gînsac, izbîndi, pîndar
Geographical names:		Dîmbova, Glîmbo(a)ca

With respect to this difference, the first problem that must be examined is the origin of these two reflexes of the Slavic nasal vowel ǫ. It was similar to present-day French õ or, more exactly, to Provençal õ".[114] This vowel changed before the eleventh century to u and, in the following period in Middle Bulgarian, to ă", written in the Cyrillic alphabet ъ .

The two different reflexes (representations) in Romanian have been explained by the hypothesis that -un, -um derived from Serbian and -în, -îm from Bulgarian. This has, however, been shown to be incorrect; and this hypothesis is no longer defended by Romanian linguists. Densusianu, like Philippide (with whom Rosetti, Pătruţ, and Mihăilă agree),[115] as previously mentioned, has explained the different treatment of this sound by chronological circumstances: In an earlier period, the Old Slavic ǫ was rendered in Romanian by -un, -um; later, (in Middle Bulgarian) this vowel changed to ă", which was rendered in Romanian as -în, -îm (More exactly, as ăn; ă developed later to î), for example, Old Slavic *mǫdŭrŭ* > Middle Bulgarian *mănduru* > Romanian *mîndru*.[116] The Slavic nasal vowels were also represented by a vowel + a nasal consonant in the Slavic borrowings of Albanian, Greek, and Hungarian, since no nasal vowel existed in these languages. According to Vladimir Georgiev, the difference shown by Romanian also exists in these languages:

	Romanian:	Albanian:	Greek:	Hungarian:
Slavic ǫ:	-un, -um	-un	-on	-on, -om
Slavic ă:	-în, -îm	-ën	-an	-an, -am[117]

A chronological connection between Romanian and Albanian is considered possible also by Ion Pătruț:[118] in borrowings before the twelfth century, there are, for example, Rom. *luncă*, *dumbravă*, and Albanian *sundoj*<(Slavic *sǫditi*) *-un*, *-um* corresponding to Common Slavic ǫ; and from the following period, for example, Rom. *pîndar* and Albanian *pëndar* (*cf.*, Common Slavic *pǫdarĭ*), *-în* corresponding to Middle Bulgarian *â″*.[119]

through the 11th century:	in the 12th and early 13th century:
Common Slavic ǫ>Rom. -un, -um	Middle Bulgarian ă″>Rom. -în, -îm
Rom. words:	dumbravă, luncă, scump	gînsac, izbîndi, pîndar
Geographical names in Romania:	——	Dîmbova, Glîmbo(a)ca, (In northern Oltenia and Muntenia)

The Discrepancy Between the Geographical Names of Slavic Origin and the Slavic Elements of the Romanian Language

Now to the problem of the difference between Romanian words and geographical names of Slavic origin, the geographical names being clearly of a more recent date than many Slavic borrowings in the Romanian language. An explanation was given by Petrovici, who proposed that earlier the Romanians may also have used *-un*, *-um* in geographical names, thus, they may have had *Dumbova, *Glumboca, but that they adapted their pronunciation to the changes in Slavic. This would have occurred during the time in which the Slavs living north of the Danube were being assimilated to the Romanians and the sound pattern of these names was then preserved in this form (with *-în*, *-îm*).[120]

This is, however, a very unlikely assumption. No example of such a process has been shown from other areas and other languages. On the contrary: The general rule is that elements once borrowed are treated as any other element of the borrowing language, not as parts of the language from which they originate. It is also difficult to understand why a majority population would adapt, without any exception, all the geographical names that their ancestors had used for generations and that they must have considered Romanian, rather than Slavic, to the pronunciation of a decreasing Slavic population, in the course of assimilation.

The Romanian borrowings from Hungarian both appellatives and geographical names, were preserved in their original form, regardless of the subsequent changes in Hungarian; certain early loans from Hungarian have even been used by Hungarian linguists in establishing Old Hungarian (13th to 15th century) sound patterns. The Romanian *tuluaiu, tuloaie* "thief," for example, represents the fourteenth-century Hungarian *tulβoj*. The Hungarian word later evolved to modern Hungarian *tolvaj;*[121] but Romanian *tuluaiu* did not change, accordingly, to **tolvaiu*. In eastern Transylvania, adjacent to Moldavia, there is an area called Csík (Ciuc). Present-day Hungarian has in this name a palatal *i*, which developed from an earlier velar *i*. This velar *i* still existed in Hungarian in the thirteenth century,[122] when the Romanians borrowed it in the form of Ciuc. The Romanian name is still the same, in spite of the change in the Hungarian vowel.

One could counter that in the case of Slavic influence on Romanian, one is dealing with an especially intensive influence exerted in close symbiosis for several centuries and that this circumstance could have led to exceptional results. In spite of this close symbiosis and in spite of the changes in Slavic, however, the Romanian language preserved appellatives with an old sound pattern (for example, all the words with *-un, -um*, despite the change in Middle Bulgarian to *ă"*).

There is a more likely and natural explanation for the appellatives of Slavic origin. As shown above, there is a general agreement that the words of Slavic origin in which *-în, (-îm)* appear were borrowed from Middle Bulgarian, which had *ă"*. The same must have been the case with the geographical names: those in which *-în, -îm* appear were borrowed from Middle Bulgarian, near the end of the eleventh century at the earliest and in the twelfth and early thirteenth centuries.[123]

The area in which such geographical names are found was consequently populated by Romanians during the twelfth and the early thirteenth centuries; and these names appear, in fact, in a well-defined area: the southern incline of the Southern Carpathians. A total of 27 geographical names borrowed from Slavic and containing *-în, -îm* are described by Petrovici in the northern part of Oltenia and Muntenia (Gorj, Vîlcea, Argeş, Dîmboviţa, Prahova, and Buzău Counties; the last one is southern Moldavia).[124] This suggest that the Romanian population arrived in these mountainous areas presumably in the twelfth century and borrowed the Bulgarian geographical names they found there. This mountainous area is connected with the mountains south of the Danube between the Timok and Morava rivers and further to the south with the mountainous central area of the Balkan Peninsula, where several Northern Romanian geographical names existed in the Middle Ages. Many of them are still preserved in the Slavic toponymy; there are still settlements and mountains called "Vlach," for example, Vlaška Planina "Vlach Mountains" near to the town of Pirot. Such names existed as early as in the tenth century,[125] which means that the oldest of them antedate the geographical names mentioned above with -în, -îm in the Southern Carpathians. The pastoral population of the Vlachs living in those areas spread, after the tenth and eleventh centuries, throughout the Balkan Peninsula. In the north the most natural area for them to settle was the continuation beyond the Danube of the mountainous territory of the central and northeastern parts of the Balkans, that is, the southwestern and the Southern Carpathians. Northern Romanians are still living today in the Timok Valley immediately south of the Danube, facing the southwestern Carpathians.

Concerning the historical data, it is known that in the tenth through the twelfth centuries a numerically large Vlach population lived in Bulgaria. In 1020 they were subordinated to the bishop of Ochrida by the Byzantine Emperor; Byzantine documents from that period use the terms "Moesians" or "Vlachs" to designate the inhabitants of Bulgaria. As previously mentioned, the Vlach population played a very active role in the uprising against the Byzantine rule in the second half of the twelfth century. All this does not, however, exclude the possibility that Vlachs also lived north of the Danube in or before that period, as has been pointed out by Romanian historians. The study of the geographical names and the Romanian language, however, greatly decrease the likelihood that this was the case.

Hungarian Geographical Names

Some of the earliest Hungarian place names derive from the names of the Hungarian tribes that occupied the country. These names were preserved only in the writings of the Byzantine Emperor and scholar Constantine Porphyrogenitus, in a text from around 950: Nyék, Megyer, Kürt, Gyarmat, Tarján, Jenő, Kér, and Keszi. They appear as place names in the area around present-day Budapest but also frequently in Bihar (Bihor) County and in the Banat. Kniezsa mentioned 16 such names in those areas.[126] Only three are found in Transylvania proper: Keszü > Romanian Chesău (Kolozs/Cluj County); Jenő > Romanian

The Early Hungarian Place Names

Derivation:	Examples, remarks:
From names of rivers:	Sóspatak, Kőrispatak
From natural phenomena: (plants, animals)	fűz "willow", nyír "birch", bükk "book", erdő "forest", alma "apple", szilva "plum", sólyom "falcon".
From personal names: a) name alone:	Hungarian names of the pre-Christian and the Christian eras; Turkish, Slavic, German names (no Romanian names)
b) name + -i:	Tamási, Pályi, Petri, Kovácsi, (also from names of dignitaries, such as "abbot": Apáti and "bishop": Püspöki,
c) name + -d:	Bánd, Bencéd, Koppánd, (no Romanian names)
d) name + -laka:	Farkaslaka, Zetelaka, (also Széplak, Fellak, Feketelak)
e) name + -falva, -telke, -szállása, -háza	Many names, created mostly in the 13th through the 15th centuries: Péterfalva, Mártonfalva, Györgyfalva; Kendtelke, Gyulatelke. Also Romanian names: Radulfalva, Harnicsháza.
From names of populations: a) name alone:	Tót, Horvát, Káloz, Besenyő (no *Oláh)
b) name + -i:	Németi, Csehi, Horváti, Oroszi (19 such names in Transylvania mentioned by Kniezsa). (No *Lengyeli, *Ráci, *Töröki, * Kuni, *Böszörményi, *Kálozi, *Besenyei, * Oláhi)
c) name + -falva	Tótfalu, Oroszfája, Szászváros, Oláhtelek.
Church, religion: a) names of Saints:	Szentgyörgy, Szentmárton, Szentmihály, Szentmiklós; Roman Catholic Saints only (about 150 such names in Transylvania).
b) Church officials buildings, crusaders, "Angel", "Devil"	Apáti, Püspöki, Veresegyház, Keresztúr, Kolozs-Monostor, Angyalos, Ördöngősfüzes.

Source: I. Kniezsa, "Keletmagyarország helynevei", in *Magyarok és Románok* ["The Place Names of Eastern Hungary," in *Hungarians and Romanians*], ed. J. Deér and L. Gáldi, Vol. I. (Budapest: 1943); Gy. Kristó, "Szempontok korai helyneveink történeti tipológiájához" [Considerations About the Historical Characteristics of the Early Hungarian Place Names], in *Acta Historica*, LV, 1976, pp. 3-99.

TABLE VI
Early place names of Hungarian and Romanian origin within the arch of the Carpathian Mountains of contemporary Romania: settlements existing today

Settlements mentioned in the 13th century	Settlements mentioned between 1301 and 1350	Settlements mentioned before 1400 total
Total 511	820	1757
Names of Hungarian origin 428 (83%)	641 (78%)	1355 (77%)
Names of Romanian origin 3 (0.6%)	36 (4.4%)	76 (4.3%)

Source: István Kniezsa, "Keletmagyarország helynevei" [The Place Names of Eastern Hungary], in *Magyarok és románok* [Hungarians and Romanians], vol. I, ed by J. Deér and L. Gáldi, (Budapest: 1943), p. 158.

Ineu (Szolnok-Doboka/Dăbîca County); and Keszi > Romanian Chiseu (Satu Mare County).

From the end of the eleventh to the middle of the thirteenth centuries, several Hungarian place names were created either alone from personal names and names of different ethnic groups or with the suffixes -*d* and -*i*. An early form of composed place names formed with -*laka*, -*népe*, -*telke*, -*ülése*, -*soka* have been established in the twelfth century, while the form with -*háza*, -*falva*, originate from the thirteenth century (Kniezsa-Bárczi).[127]

The great majority of the early place names (mostly those created before the sixteenth century) within the arch of the Carpathians of present-day Romania are of Hungarian origin. Table VI summarizes the origins of the names of settlements existing today and mentioned in documents before 1400.

The Appearance of Parallel Hungarian and Romanian Place Names

Parallel Hungarian-Romanian place names do not appear before the fourteenth century.[128] In Hunyad (Hunedoara) County (later one of the main Romanian districts), one finds Hungarian Gonoszfalu "evil village" (1360, Gunuzfolu), Romanian Rea "bad"; Malomviz "water of the mill" (1359, Malomwyz), Romanian Râu de mori "river of the mills"; Tamáspatak "river of Thomas" (1341, Tamáspataka),

Romanian Tămăşasa. In the same century the first Romanian place names transferred to Hungarian appeared in Hunyad County: Romanian Râusor (1377, fluv. Ryusor, from Romanian *râu* "river" + diminutive suffix) > Hungarian Rusor; Romanian Nucşoara (1394, Noxara; *cf.*, Romanian *nucă* "walnut") > Hungarian Nuksora. In Szolnok-Doboka (Dăbîca) County, 9 of the 120 place names mentioned for the first time in the fourteenth century were parallel Hungarian-Romanian names: for example, Damunkusfalva, mentioned in 1393, Romanian Dămăcuşeni; Danpataka (1331), Romanian Valeni; Oroszmező "the field of the Russian" (1366, Symisne nunc Wruzmezeu), Romanian Rusu. The incidence of such parallel names subsequently increased; and in the fifteenth century Romanian place names that were transferred to Hungarian also appeared in Szolnok-Doboka County: in 1424 Karbonal was mentioned (today Hungarian Gorbonác), from Romanian Cărbunari "coal vendors," and in 1405, Kocholatfalva from Romanian Cuciulata (derived from Romanian *căciula* "fur cap").[129]

German (Transylvanian Saxon) Place Names

The areas in southern Transylvania in which Germans were settled in the twelfth and early thirteenth centuries were described in several documents as *terra deserta et inhabitata*.[130] Although this could not have been true for the entire territory, the fact that the majority of the place names in the area are of German origin and that there are large areas with such names gives some support to these documents. The two biggest Saxon towns, Hermannstadt and Kronstadt, have German names; other original German names include Agnetheln, Rotbach, Almen, Brenndorf, (Klein- and Gross-) Probstdorf, Reen (*cf*, Regensburg), Reussen, Streitfort, and Weisskirch. These were often borrowed by the Hungarians and the Romanians: for example, Saxon Schorsten, Schorosten > Hungarian Sorostély, Spring, Gespräng > Spring, Burgberg > Borberek (by popular etymology: *bor* "wine," *berek* "riverside coppice, grove") and Romanian Vurpăr; and German Agnetheln > Romanian Agnita; Hochfeld > Fofeldea; Katzendorf > Caţa; Kaltwasser ("cold water") > Calvasăr; (Hungarian Hidegvíz "cold water"); Rotbach > Rotbav; Weisskirch > Viscri; and Ziegenthal > Ţichindeal.

The German place names derive from appellatives that describe local geographical characteristics (mountains, fields, rivers) as in the case of Engenthal, Burgberg, Weidenbach; and social events such as Streitfort. Numerous German place names derive from personal names: Hermannstadt, Petersdorf, Martinsdorf. Over the years many of them changed and today can be recognized as personal names only with difficulty: Brenndorf was formed by popular etymology from an earlier Bringindorf, from the personal name Brink, mentioned in a document from 1396; Neppendorf derives from the personal name Eppo; Etschdorf was mentioned in the documents under several names—Echtorf, villa Arnoldi (> Romanian Iernuțeni), and villa Renuoldi (> Hungarian Radnótfája—and came from the personal name Renuold = Reinhold).[131]

Another group of German place names derived from names of Saints: Sanktgeorgen, Mergeln, Mergenthal, and Mariental (near Agnetheln > Hungarian Szentágota, Romanian Agnita), mentioned from 1332 to 1335 as villa Marie, borrowed by Hungarian Morgonda, and Romanian Merghindeal; and, in the same area, Gürteln in 1336, Gertrudental > Hungarian Gerdály, Romanian Gherdeal.[132]

A list compiled by Thomas Nägler[133] of those villages in which Transylvanian Saxon dialects were spoken in the twentieth century gives some idea about the proportion of German place names: Of 242, 140 (58%) had German names, 16 (6.6%) Hungarian, 8 (3.3%) Slavic, and 78 (32.2%), names of unknown origin.[134]

Among the German settlers from the west were Walloons as well, whose presence is shown by a few place names: in Nagykükültő (Tîrnava Mare) County, for example, there is Wallendorf (in 1231 Villa Latina, in 1396 *possessio* [owned by] Waldorph, from German Wallen-Dorf "Italian village," Romanian earlier Valendorf, and recently renamed to Văleni). There are also an Aldorf in the region of Bistritz (1332 to 1337, Waldorf, from German Wallendorf) and a Galt in the former Nagykükültő County, from Old French *galt* > *gaut* (which derives from Germanic *Wald* "forest"); the Hungarian name of this village, Ugra, is borrowed from Slavic *u -gora "beside a forest, beside a mountain."[135] A parallel Hungarian-Saxon place name is, for example, Szászsebes, German Mühlbach. The two villages Kleinkopisch and Grosskopisch, from Hungarian Kis- and Nagykapus (*cf.*, Hungarian *kapu* "door") along the Nagykükültő (Tîrnava Mare) River indicate former fortifications of the Hungarian kingdom.

There are no early place names borrowed by the Saxons from Romanian.[136] This supports the testimony of the early thirteenth century documents that refer only to the *terra Blacorum*[137] but do not mention any permanent Romanian settlements.

Geographical Names in the Transylvanian Area of the Carpathian Basin in the 12th to 13th Centuries

The earliest stratum of place names and river names in the Transylvanian area of the Carpathian Basin is of Slavic origin (or, in the case of the great rivers, was transferred by the Slavs). In the southern area, the sound characteristics of place names is mainly Bulgarian and, in a small region in the southwest, also Serbian. In the northwest no Bulgarian features are found; and so far as it can be established from the Hungarian loans, the Slavic once spoken there was related to the western group of South Slavic.

These names were borrowed by Hungarian and, in a lesser number, by Romanian and German. Of 511 names of villages mentioned up to the end of the thirteenth century, about one-tenth belong to this category. The great majority of these early names are Hungarian and a smaller share German.[138] In the thirteenth century only three settlements with a name of Romanian origin are recorded. Among the Hungarian place names, there are certain types that were created early, no later than in the thirteenth century: names constructed with the suffixes -*d* and -*i*. Many of the place names formed by a personal name or an ethnic name alone are also early. These Hungarian place names were all borrowed by Romanian; and there is no case of parallel Hungarian-Romanian borrowings similar to the parallel Hungarian-Slovakian place names in present-day Slovakia, in which both the Slovakians and the Hungarians used their own suffixes in creating the names.[139]

As previously mentioned, the oldest stratum of river names in the Transylvanian area of the Carpathian Basin must be that of the Slavic names, borrowed from a Slavic population that was assimilated from the twelfth through the fourteenth centuries (except in the southwest, in Caraş-Severin County). Almost half of the river names are of Hungarian origin. The Romanian population borrowed most of them, together with another 17 river names, of which 8 are of Slavic and 9 of unknown origin. Altogether, 56% of the Romanian river names in the territory in question were with certainty borrowed from Hungarian. Only 11% (17 out of 153) of the river names were transferred to Romanian directly from Slavic; and they are found mainly in southern Transylvania, especially in Caraş-Severin County.

In southern Transylvania, in the region of Hermannstadt (Sibiu) and Kronstadt (Braşov) and in the northeast, around Bistritz (Bistriţa), more than half of the place names are of German origin. Several of these were borrowed by Hungarian and Romanian. There is no German place name among the more ancient stratum of names that have been borrowed from Romanian.

The first Romanian place names appear in southern Transylvania, where most of the direct borrowings from Slavic are also found. Only three are recorded from the thirteenth century, but during the following period such names appear in increasing numbers there as well as in the region of the Apuseni Mountains and in Maramureş. Assuming a Roman continuity north of the Danube, one must ask why there are no ancient Latin names in the Romanian toponymy of small rivers and villages in the mountains, as is the case on the Balkan Peninsula, where several geographical names of this type indicate that the Slavs found a Latin-speaking population in several areas (*cf.*, Ptuj, Sisak, Sitec, Kimp [from Latin *campus*], Poljud [from Latin *paludem*]). It may be argued, however, that inherited Latin geographical names in Romanian are rare (*cf.*, Săruna) even on the Balkan Peninsula and that north of the Danube, no pre-Slavic names were preserved at all.

Geographical names of Latin origin are, however, not the only thing that might be expected if a Romanized (Romanian) population had lived in central Transylvania in the ninth century. The geographical names borrowed from Slavic would show a sound pattern from that time, that is, without the metathesis of the liquids, with -*un*, -*um* in place of the Common Slavic nasal vowel, as is the case with a series of lexical elements of the Romanian language that were borrowed from Slavic. There are no such geographical names whatsoever north of the lower Danube. The only sound pattern in the toponymy borrowed from the Slavs north of the Danube that indicates a certain period of borrowing is the presence of -*în*, -*îm* corresponding to the Slavic nasal vowel. This can be dated to the late eleventh, the twelfth, and the early thirteenth centuries. It is even questionable whether those three village names with -*în*, (-*îm*) on the northern slope of the Southern Carpathians were created in the same era. It seems more probable that they were populated later by Romanians coming from the southern rim of the Carpathians, where similar names were, and still are, common.

The name of Transylvania.

This name is for the first time found in a document from 1075; there is "Ultra siluam" and from 1111, "Mercurius princeps Ultrasiluanus" is mentioned. Later in the same century, "Partes Transsilvanae" appears, and in the documents of the Hungarian kingdom, written in the Latin language, this form is used thereafter. - In the chronicle of Anonymus, the territory is mentioned as *"terra ultra siluam"* or *"terra ultra siluana"* and as *"erdeuelu"* (cf. above, pp. 15 -18). This is the first mentioning of the Hungarian name of the territory, derived from the Hungarian appellative *erdeu* "forest" (Medieval Hungarian *eu* corresponds to modern Hungarian *ő*, thus today *erdő*); and the suffix *elv(e)* "beyond" (an ancient form, but not unknown today, cf. for example *hidelve* "beyond the bridge").

Obviously, the Hungarians, who approached Transylvania mainly from the West, found mountains covered by huge forests in their way, which resulted in this designation.

The Latin names, "Ultrasiluanus", "partes Transsiluanae", are translated from the Hungarian language; the official Romanian "Transilvania" is thus not a popular Romanian name but a borrowing from the Hungarian documents.

The Hungarian name of the territory was translated also to German: in 13th - 14th century documents appear "Überwald", "über Walt" (Ş. Pascu, *Voivodatul Transilvaniei*, 1972, p. 22). The German (Transylvanian Saxon) population has, however, its own designation for Transylvania: *Siebenbürgen*.

The popular Romanian name of the territory is *"Ardeal"*. (The Latin name, "Dacia", did not survive but in antique texts.) The first mentioning in a known document of this name is in the form *"Ardeliu"* in the year 1432 (cf., for example, Pascu, *op. cit.*, vol. I, p. 22). In that century, as well as later, the Romanians borrowed many Hungarian place names; initial Hungarian *e-* was regularly rendered in Romanian by *a-*: Hung. *egres* "gooseberry" - Rom. *agriş*; in place names: Hung. Egyed - Rom. Adjud; Hung. Erked - Rom. Archiud, Hung. Erdőd - Rom. Ardud, Hung. Erdőfalva - Rom. Ardeova, Ardeu, etc. It is obvious that Romanian Ardeal (in the 15th century, Ardeliu) was borrowed from Hungarian Erdély.

NOTES

CHAPTER 1

1. Dimitri Obolensky, *The Byzantine Commonwealth. Eastern Europe 500–1453* (London: 1971), pp. 207–208.

2. On the Thracians the following works provide valuable information: Wilhelm Tomaschek, *Die alten Thraker* I–II (Wien: 1893–94); Dimiter Detschew, *Die thrakischen Sprachreste* (Wien: 1957); J. Wiesner, *Die Thraker. Studien zu einem versunkenen Volk des Balkanraumes* (Stuttgart: 1963); Ion I. Russu, *Die Sprache der Thrako-Daker* (Bucharest: 1969).

3. Among others Robert R. Rösler, *Das vorrömische Dazien*, 1864; *Romänische Studien. Untersuchungen zur älteren Geschichte Romäniens* (Leipzig: 1871). After Rösler, Wilhelm Tomaschek, Franz Miklosich, Gaston Paris, and the Slavonic scholar Kopitar believed that the Romanians originated south of the Danube as, to a certain extent did, the Romanian linguist Ovid Densusianu and recently the German archaeologist Kurt Horedt as well as the German scholar Gottfried Schramm.

4. Abdolonyme Honore J. Ubicini, *Les origines de l'histoire roumaine*, (Paris: 1886), p. 142.

5. Valuable informations on Byzantine sources in: Gyula Moravcsik, *Byzantinoturcica I, II. Die byzantinische Quellen der Geschichte der Turkvölker* (Berlin: 1958); *Die byzantinischen Quellen der ungarischen Geschichte* (Budapest: 1934); *Byzantium and the Magyars* (Amsterdam: 1970).

6. Ioannes Kinnamos, *Historia*, VI, 3, p. 259, quoted by Marin Popescu-Spineni: *România în izvoare geografice şi cartografice* [Romania in the Geographical and Cartographical Sources], (Bucharest: 1978), p. 96. See also, Ioannes Kinnamos (Ioannes Cinnamus), *Epitome rerum ab Ioan et Alexio Comnensis gestarum*, ed. by August Meinecke (Bonn: 1836), Corpus Historiae Byzantinae, vol. 26, 12th century.

7. Kinnamos, *Historia*, VI, 3, p. 259. See further: *Fontes Historiae Daco-Romanae* (Bucharest: 1975), III, p. 239.

8. *Cf., Fontes Historiae Daco-Romanae*, p. 238, note 27.

9. The Greek text and the Romanian translation in: Alexandru Elian, Nicolae-Şerban Tanaşoca, *Izvoarele istoriei României* (Fontes Historiae Daco-Romanae) III, Scriitori Bizantini, sec. XI–XIV, (Bucharest: 1975) pp. 250–251.

337

338   Ethnic Continuity in the Carpatho-Danubian Area

10. Edited by A. Reifferscheid, 2 vols. (Leipzig: 1884); Bernard Leib, 3 vols. (Paris: 1937–45); *Alexiadis libri XV*, vols. I–II (Bonn: 1839–1878).

11. *Historia*, 2 vols. ed. by Johannes Aloys von Dieten (Berlin: 1975). See also C. Neumann, *Griechische Geschichtsschreiber und Geschichtsquellen im 12. Jahrhundert* (Leipzig: 1888); *Fontes Historiae Daco-Romanae*. Izvoarele istoriei României [Sources of the History of Romania], III, Scriitori Bizantini (sec. XI–XIV) ed. by Alexandru Elian and Nicolae-Şerban Tanaşoca (Bucharest: 1975).

12. *Corpus Fontium Historiae Byzantinae XI: 12–13 centuries, Cf.*, Fontes Historiae Daco-Romanae, p. 250, note 21.

13. Year 1970: July 16, 23, 30; August 6, 13, 20, 27; September 28; October 1, 8, 15, 22, 29; November 5, 12, 19; December 3, 12.

14. Constantin Daicoviciu, "Izvoare istorice greşit interpretate" [Misinterpretation of historical sources] in *Tribuna* (Cluj), October 1, 1970.

15. *Ibid.*

16. *Georgius Cedrenus Ioannis Scylitzae ope*, ed. by I. Bekker (Bonn: 1839), 11–12 centuries.

17. Cecaumenus, *Strategicon et incerti scriptoris De officiis regiis libellus*, ed. by B. Vasilevskij and V. Gernsted (St. Petersburg: 1895); new edition (Amsterdam: 1963).

18. *Istoria României* [The History of Romania], ed. Constantin Daicoviciu, vol. I (Bucharest: 1960), p. 798.

19. *Istoria României. Compendiu*, ed. by Miron Constantinescu, Constantin Daicoviciu and Ştefan Pascu (Bucharest: 1969), p. 106.

20. *Istoria României. Compendiu*, third edition, ed. by Ştefan Pascu, p. 88.

21. *Istoria României în date* [A Chronological History of Romania], ed. Constantin C. Giurescu (Bucharest: 1972), p. 60. "Descendants of the Dacians" is emphasized in the original.

22. *România în izvoare geografice şi cartografice*, by M. Popescu-Spineni (Bucharest: 1978), p. 92.

23. An excellent information on the Kekaumenos's *Strategicon* in: Mátyás Gyóni, "L'oeuvre de Kekaumenos, source de l'histoire roumaine" in : *Revue d'Histoire Comparée*, XXIII, année 1945. Nouvelle Série, Tome III, no. 1–4, pp. 96–180.

24. *Fontes Historiae Daco-Romanae* III, 1975, p. 41.

25. *Ibid.*, pp. 149–151.

26. Author of the *De administrando imperio*, as this narrative has been named by modern scholars, a narrative of this emperor addressed to his son Romanós. The *De administrando imperio* is the most valuable Byzantine source about Eastern Europe of the ninth and tenth centuries; it was chiefly devoted to foreign policy of Byzantium in the lands of the Pontic Steppes, north of the Black Sea. Chapter forty-second contains the geographical situation beyond the empire's northern border (*Cf.*, Dimitri Obolensky, *op. cit.*, pp. 182–189). The Greek text of the *De administrando imperio* ed. by Gyula Moravcsik (Budapest: 1949); a new critical edition in English translation by R. J. Jenkins (Dumbarton Oaks: 1967).

27. Gyóni, 1945, p. 165.

28. The passage in question of Dio Cassius's history was not preserved; there are only excerpts by some writers, for example, Mátyás Gyóni, 1945, p. 165.

29. Gyóni, 1945, p. 167.

30. Gyóni, 1945, p. 176.

31. There are no reliable written sources, for example, with regard to the seventh to ninth century history of the territories north of the lower Danube, especially that of Transylvania. It is to mention the Armenian geographer Moses of Chorenatzi of the ninth century and anonymous Ravenna's *Cosmographia*, translated by J. Schnetz (Uppsala: 1951). Both works are, however, no reliable sources.

32. Edited with commentary by D. S. Lichačev; English translation and edition by S. H. Cross and O. P. Sherbowitz-Wetzor (Cambridge, Mass.: 1953). Modern Russian tanslation by D. S. Lichačev and B. A. Romanova, ed. by V. P. Adrianova-Perets, vol. I (Moscow-Leningrad: 1950). *Chronica Nestoris. Textum russico-slovienicum, Versionem latinam glossarium*, ed. by Franz Miklosich, vol. I (Vindabona: 1860). Further sources: *Kievo-pecherski paterik*, ed. by Chiznevski, Slavische Propyläen, 2., 1964.

33. *Fontes Historiae Daco-Romanorum*, Fasciculus VII: *Chronica Nestoris*, ed. Gheorghe Popa-Lisseanu (Bucharest: 1935).

34. Remulus Seisanu, *Rumania* (Bucharest: 1939), p. 38 and 39, quoted by D. Dvoichenko-Markov: The Russian Primary Chronicle and the Vlachs of Eastern Europe, in *Byzantion Revue Internationale des Études Byzantines*, XLIX, 1979 (Bruxelles), p. 177.

35. On the *Gesta Hungarorum* following works provide detailed information: Bálint Hóman, *A Szent László-kori Gesta Ungarorum* (Budapest: 1925); Sándor Domanovszky, *Századok*, 71, 1937, pp. 38–54, 163–184; János Horváth, *Actu Antiqua*, Budapest, 19, 1971, pp. 347–382; György Györffy, *Anonymus Gesta Hungarorumának kora és hitelessége* [The Time and the Authenticity of Anonymus's Gesta Hungarorum], in *Irodalomtörténeti Közlemények*, 1970/1; Gyula Kristó, *Tanulmányok az Árpád-korról* [Studies on the Árpád-age] (Budapest: 1983), pp. 132–190.; a valuable analysis of Anonymus is given by Gyula Kristó in *Magyarország története* [The History of Hungary], (Budapest: 1984), vols. 1. and 2.; György Györffy, *A magyarok elődeiről és a honfoglalásról. Kortársak és krónikások híradásai* [About the Ancestors of the Hungarians and About the Conquest. Reports of Contemporary Writers and Chroniclers], (Budapest: 1975); a critical edition: *Scriptores Rerum Hungaricarum* I, ed. by Imre Szentpétery (Budapest: 1937), pp. 33–117; the Hungarian translation: Dezső Pais, *Magyar Anonymus* [Hungarian Anonymus], (Budapest: 1926); the edition of the Anonymus's text: *Scriptores Rerum Hungaricarum*, vol. I, ed. Emericus Szentpétery (Budapest: 1973), annotations by Dezső Pais. Further literature: Adolf Armbruster, *Romanitatea românilor* (Bucharest: 1972), p. 29; Nicolae Stoicescu, *Continuitatea românilor* (Bucharest: 1980), pp. 187–193.

36. Anonymus, *Gesta Hungarorum*, facsimile edition, translated by Dezső Pais, introduction by György Györffy (Budapest: 1977). A codex text of

Anonymus's Gesta Hungarorum is preserved in the manuscript-collection of the Hungarian National Library Széchényi in Budapest: Cod. Lat. Medii Aevi no. 403.

37. György Györffy, "Anonymus Gesta Hungarorumának kora és hitelessége," *op. cit.*

38. Daniel Cornides, *Vindiciae anonymi Belae regis notarii,* ed. by J. Christian Engel (Budae: 1802).

39. The *Gesta Hungarorum* will henceforth be referred to as the *Gesta.*

40. Györffy, "Anonymus Gesta Hungarorumának kora és hitelessége," *op. cit.,* p. 11.

41. Scythia was located in the southern Russian steppes in the first millenium B.C. and was populated by Iranian nomads.

42. The name of the Transdanubian part of modern Hungary in Roman times.

43. György Györffy, "Anonymus Gesta Hungarorumának kora és hitelessége," *op. cit.,* pp. 1–2.

44. Györffy, *A magyarok elődeiről, op. cit.,* p. 135.

45. Bálint Hóman, *A Szent László-kori Gesta Ungarorum és XII–XIII századi leszármazói. Forrástanulmány* [The Gesta Ungarorum from the Time of Ladislas the Saint and Related Records in the XII–XIII Centuries. A Study of Sources], (Budapest: 1925), *cf.,* Györffy, Anonymus Gesta Hungarorumának, *op. cit.,* 1970, p. 6.

46. When giving the names of rivers and of places, the original Latin spelling of the *Gesta* is used. The corresponding modern forms are given in parenthesis.

47. Hungarian *mén* "stallion."

48. Page numbers in brackets after the passages translated from the text of the anonymous notary refer to the text of the Hungarian translation made by Dezső Pais (*Anonymus - Gesta Hungarorum,* Magyar Helikon, Budapest 1975.

49. "*Habitatores terre illi viliores homines essent toti mundi. Quia essent Blasii et Sclaui . . .*"

50. Hungarian *eskü,* "oath"; an example of the author's naive etymology. This village appears in documents in 1331 (*Eskeleu*) and 1332 (*Sacerdos de Eskulev*). It is composed of *es,* old Hungarian "old" (modern Hungarian *ős*), + *küllő,* "the name of a bird, probably a swallow." The Romanians borrowed the Hungarian name (Aşchileu, which appears in documents in 1733). *Cf.,* I Kniezsa, *Keletmagyarország helynevei,* 1943, p. 225, and C. Suciu, *Dicţionar istoric al localităţilor din Transilvania,* vol. I, 1967, p. 47.

51. Among others, for example, Emanuel Turczynski, *Konfession und Nation. Zur Frühgeschichte der serbischen und rumänischen Nationsbildung* (Düsseldorf: 1976), p. 223, note 156.

52. *Anonymus - Gesta Hungarorum,* a facsimile edition (Budapest: 1975), p. 143.

53. Gyula has been identified by most modern historians with Prince Gylas, mentioned in the Byzantine sources. Gyula Moravcsik identifies him

with Gyla in Transylvania (*Byzantinoturcica*, II, Budapest 1958, p. 115), but in *Byzantium and the Magyars* (Budapest 1970, pp. 55 and 57) he places the tribe of Gylas in the Banat.

54. Gyula, the chief of one of the Magyar (Hungarian) tribal societies of Transylania, went to Constantinople where he was baptised and was raised to the rank of *patricius*. Recent research has shown that the impact of Byzantine Christianity upon Hungary in the eleventh century was far more powerful than was formerly supposed (Dimitri Obolensky, *The Byzantine Commonwealth, Eastern Europe 500–1453*, London, 1971). Under Gyula's political power Christianity took root in the lowlands east of the Tisza River and in Transylvania during the second half of the tenth century. For more details, see Dimitri Obolensky, *op. cit.*, pp. 156–167. Starting in the year 971 Hungary and the Byzantine Empire had a common frontier along the middle Danube and the Sava.

55. *Magyarország története* [The History of Hungary], (Budapest: 1984), I, p. 585.

56. György Györffy, *István király és műve* [King Stephen and his Work], (Budapest: 1977), p. 58.

57. György Györffy, "Honfoglalás előtti népek és országok Anonymus Gesta Hungarorumában" [Preconquest Peoples and Countries in the Gesta Hungarorum of Anonymus], *Ethnographia*, LXXVI, 1965, p. 415.

58. *Ibid.*, p. 432.

59. Constantine Porphyrogenetus, *De administrando imperio*, p. 173, quoted by Györffy, 1965, p. 416.

60. "*iuxta fluvium Copus.*" The Kapus (Căpuș) River flows into the Szamos at the village Gyalu. This village, 16 km west of Kolozsvár (Cluj) is first mentioned in a document 1246 in the form Golou; from 1282 there is the form Gylo and from 1294, Galou (*Cf.*, C. Suciu, *Dicționar istoric al localităților din Transilvania* (Bucharest: 1967), vol. I, p. 261. See also, Zoltán I. Tóth, "Tuhutum és Gelou. Hagyomány és történeti hitelesség Anonymus művében" [Tuhutum and Gelou. Tradition and Authenticity in Anonymus's Work], *Századok* 79–80 (1945–1946), pp. 52–53.

61. Györffy, 1965, *op. cit.*, p. 429.

62. Györffy, "Anonymus Gesta Hungarorumának," 1970, *op. cit.*, p. 8. General considerations in: György Györffy, "Honfoglalás előtti népek," 1965, *op. cit.*

63. Chapters 33 to 37.

64. *Anonymus - Gesta Hungarorum* (Budapest: 1975), p. 114.

65. Steven Runciman, *A History of the First Bulgarian Empire* (London: 1930), p. 150.

66. A recent detailed description on this topic is given by Gyula Kristó in: *Tanulmányok az Árpád-korról* [Studies on the Árpád-age] (Budapest: 1983), pp. 146–147.

67. Kristó, 1983, *op. cot.*, p. 147.

68. Mathias Gyóni, "Les Volochs des Annales primitives de Kiev," *Études Slaves et Roumaines*, Budapest, 1949, pp. 83–92, note 28., quoted by Kristó, 1983, *op. cit.*, p. 502, note 31.

69. Györffy, *Anonymus Gesta Hungarorumának, op. cit.* p. 8., *cf.*, Kristó, 1983, p. 502. note 32.

70. Constantin Daicoviciu, "Corrigenda," in *Acta Musei Napocensis*, X (1973), p. 611 *et. seq.*

71. Gyula Kristó, *Tanulmányok az Árpád-korról, op. cit.*, p. 135. Konrad Schünemann, "Die'Römer' des anonymen Notars," *Ungarische Jahrbücher* 1926, pp. 450–451, *cf.*, Kristó 1983, note 7.

72. The original text, by Simon de Kéza of the thirteenth century was lost at the end of the eighteenth century; thus the original text can only be reconstructed from copies and editions of the eighteenth century. It is not impossible to assume that even the original text contained certain parts copied from other works. Kézai used as one of his sources Anonymus's Chronicle. For more details Sándor Domanovszky, *Kézai Simon mester krónikája* [The Chronicle of Master Kézai Simon], (Budapest: 1906). About the historical view of early legends and chronicles see, Elemér Mályusz, "Krónika problémák" [Problems of Chronicles] in *Századok* [Centuries], Budapest 100 (1966), pp. 714–725.

73. Constantin C. Giurescu, *Istoria românilor* (Bucharest: 1975), p. 101.

74. Bálint Hóman, *A Szent László-kori Gesta Ungarorum*, 1925, *op. cit.*

75. The words in italics are those that Giurescu quoted out of context from Hóman's text (Giurescu, *Istoria românilor*, 1975, p. 154).

76. Adolf Armbruster, *La romanité des roumains. Histoire d'une idée* (Bucharest: 1977), p. 25.

77. Ligia Bârzu, *Continuity of the Romanian People's Material and Spiritual Production in the Territory of Former Dacia* (Bucharest: 1980), pp. 46, 97.

78. *Istoria României. Compendiu.* Miron Constantinescu, Constantin Daicoviciu and Ştefan Pascu eds., (Bucharest: 1974), p. 95.

79. The name is of Cuman origin: princes in Cumania in the 11th century were often named Osên or Asên.

80. *Istoria României. Compendiu*, 1974, p. 95.; Ştefan Pascu, *Voievodatul Transilvaniei*, I–II, (Cluj: 1971 and 1979).

81. Ştefan Pascu, *Voievodatul Transilvaniei, op. cit.*, vol. I, 1971, pp. 33–36.

82. *Ibid.*, p. 36.

83. *Ibid.*

84. *Magyarország története*, I. 1984, *op. cit.*, p. 585.

85. For more detail on Doboka (Dăbîca) see in chapter II.

86. Pascu, 1971, *op. cit.*, p. 57, note 72.

87. *Ibid.*, p. 164.

88. *Ibid.*, p. 86.

89. *Ibid.*, p. 106.

90. "Romani' şi 'Blachi' la Anonymus. Istorie şi ideologie politică" ['Romans' and 'Blachi' in Anonymus's Gesta. History and Political Ideology], Stelian Brezeanu, *Revista de Istorie*, vol. 34, 7/1981, pp. 1313–1340.

91. *Ibid.*, p. 1314.

92. *Ibid.*, p. 1313.

93. *Ibid.*, p. 1314.

94. Among others *Erdély története* [The History of Transylvania], (Budapest: 1986), pp. 241–238.

95. Gyula Kristó, *Tanulmányok az Árpád-korról*, 1983, *op. cit.*, pp. 132–190.

96. The inhabitants of Pannonia were, in ancient times, Illyrians (who were later defeated by the Celts) and Pannonians, after whom this territory was named. During the wars of Roman expansion, between 15 and 8 B.C., in the age of Emperor Augustus, Pannonia became a Roman province. Its territory encompassed parts of modern Hungary, Yugoslavia, and Austria (East Steiermark). Its ultimate frontiers were established during the rule of Emperor Trajan, in 102–107 A.D. The western part became known as Pannonia Superior and the eastern, located on the Danube, as Pannonia Inferior. In the ninth century the frontiers set by Trajan did change nevertheless as the territory to the southwest of the Danube became known as Pannonia Superior while Pannonia Inferior was located between the Drava and Sava rivers.

By the beginning of the fifth century the Romans had abandoned almost all of Pannonia. The Huns, and later the Avars, became rulers of this territory. Following Attila's death and until the Avar invasion the Romans (descendants of the ancient Romans) reoccupied Pannonia as far as the Danube. Written sources, inscriptions, and place names attest the survival of a Romanic population in Pannonia of the fifth to the sixth centuries (For more detail, Endre Tóth, "Zur Geschichte des Nordpannonischen Raumes im 5. und 6. Jahrhundert," in: *Die Völker an der mittleren und unteren Donau im fünften und sechsten Jh*, ed. by Herwig Wolfram and Falko Daim (Vienna: 1980). After the defeat of the Avars, around 800, Pannonia fell under Frankish-Carolingian domination. The Franks and the Bulgars—who ruled the territory east of the Tisza—met one another on that river.

The Christianization of the inhabitants of Pannonia began in 796. The territory south of the Drava fell under the jurisdiction of the Patriarch of Aquileia while Pannonia Superior, as well as Slavic tribes located on the northern Danube frontier, were subordinated to the Archbishopric of Salzburg. Besides Dacia, Pannonia was the second Roman province in the Carpathian Basin. The provinces of Dacia, Pannonia, and Noricum were border areas between Barbaricum and the Roman Empire.

97. György Bodor, "Egy krónikás adat helyes értelmezése" [The Right Interpretation of a Chronicler's Data] in: *Magyar Nyelv* [Hungarian Language], LXXII, 3, (1976), pp. 268–271.

98. *Ibid.* See further, László Rásonyi, *Hidak a Dunán* [Bridges on the Danube], (Budapest: 1981), pp. 52–53.

99. *Scriptores Rerum Hungaricarum*, ed. by Szentpétery: Anonymus 9, 44, and 25.

100. Franz Zimmermann and Carl Werner, *Urkundenbuch zur Geschichte der Deutschen in Siebenbürgen* I, (Hermannstadt: 1892), Urkunde 31, pp. 18–20, and Urkunde 34.

101. *A hun-magyar krónika* [Excerpts from the Hunnish-Hungarian Chronicle of Kézai] in: *Scriptores Rerum Hungaricarum*, ed. Szentpétery, Kézai 21.

102. Gottfried Schramm, *Eroberer und Eingesessene. Geographische Lehn-namen als Zeugen der Geschichte Südosteuropas im ersten Jahrtausend n. Chr.* (Stuttgart: 1981), p. 296.

103. Lajos Kiss, *Földrajzi nevek etimológiai szótára* [Etymological Dictionary of Geographical Names], (Budapest: 1978), p. 720.

104. Zimmermann und Werner, *op. cit.* I, p. 72.

105. Although the first traces of the *o* > *a* change in Hungarian appear in the tenth century, when single examples of *a* are found in the texts, this change first became more general in the thirteenth century. (As shown above, Anonymus used *o*: Copus). *Cf.*, Bárczi, Benkő, Berrár, *A magyar nyelv története* [The History of the Hungarian Language], (Budapest: 1967), p. 151. Stefan Kniezsa, *Die Gewässernamen des östlichen Karpatenbeckens*, (Budapest: 1943), p. 197.

106. Adolf Armbruster, *Romanitatea românilor. Istoria unei idei* (Bucharest: 1972), p. 43. A French publication of this work: La romanité des roumains. Histoire d'une idée (Bucharest: 1977).

107. *Disceptationes convivales*, 1451.

108. Armbruster, 1972, Latin text, p. 47.

109. *The Cambridge Medieval History*, vol. VIII, 1936, p. 773.

110. Armbruster, 1972, *op. cit.*, pp. 48–49.

111. *Ibid.*, p. 50.

112. *Ibid.*, p. 51.

113. *Ibid.*, p. 52.

114. *Ibid.*

115. *Ibid.*, p. 53.

116. *Cf.*, Armbruster, *op. cit.*, p. 180, note 92; Ion Hurdubețiu, *Die Deutschen über die Herkunft der Rumänen*, (Bucharest: 1977), pp. 28–29.

117. *Das Alt- und Neu-Teutsche Dacia. Das ist neue Beschreibung des Landes Siebenbürgen* (Nürnberg: 1666).

118. Armbruster, *op. cit.*, p. 178.

119. *Geschichte des transalpinischen Daziens*, vols. I–II (Vienna: 1781–1782).

120. *Scriptores rerum Transylvanorum*, (Hermannstadt: 1797–1800); *De initiis juribusque primaevis Saxonum Transsilvanorum commentario*, (Viennae: 1792); *Observationes criticae et pragmaticae ad historiam Transsilvaniae* (Cibinii: 1803).

121. Robert Rösler, *Romänische Studien. Untersuchungen zur älteren Geschichte Rumäniens*, (Leipzig: 1871).

122. Valuable information on the Saxon historians and on the Romanian chroniclers in: Adolf Armbruster, *Dacoromano-Saxonica*. Cronicari români despre Sași. Românii in cronica săsească [Romanian Chroniclers on the Saxons. Romanians in the Chronicles of the Saxons], (Bucharest: 1980).

123. Grigore Ureche, *Letopisețul Țării Moldovei* [The Chronicle of Moldavia], ed. by Petre P. Panaitescu (Bucharest: 1955), commentaries 1958; Dumitru Velciu, *Grigore Ureche*, (Bucharest: 1979).

124. Grigore Ureche, *Letopisețul Țării Moldovei*, ed. Liviu Onu, (Bucharest: 1967).

125. Zoltán I. Tóth, "A román nemzettudat kialakulása a moldvai és havasalji krónikairodalomban" [The Development of Romanian National Con-

sciousness in the Moldavian and Wallachian Chronicles], in *A Magyar Tör-ténettudományi Intézet Évkönyve* [The Yearbook of the Hungarian Institute for History], (Budapest: 1942), p. 295.

126. Petre P. Panaitescu, *"O istorie a Ardealului tradusă de Miron Costin"* [A History of Transylvania translated by Miron Costin]. *Ac. Rom. Mem. Sect. Ist. ser. III,* t. XVII, 1936, Mem. 11.232; quoted by Tóth, 1942, p. 295. See further Constantin Giurescu, *"Interpolările și data scrierii De neamul Moldovenilor de Miron Costin."* *Bul. Com. ist. a Rom.* II, 1916, 115; Quoted by Tóth, *op. cit.,* p. 296; Miron Costin, *Opere* [Works], vols. I–II, a critical edition by Petre P. Panaitescu (Bucharest: 1965); Miron Costin, *Opere alese* [Selected Works], ed. Petre P. Panaitescu and Gheorghe Popp (Bucharest: 1966); Miron Costin, *Opere alese* [Selected Works], ed. by Liviu Onu (Bucharest: 1967); Dumitru Velciu, *Miron Costin,* (Bucharest: 1973); Enache Puiu, *Viața și opera lui Miron Costin* [Life and Works of Miron Costin]. To Costin's work joined Ion Neculce, *Letopisețul Țării Moldovei,* 1743; on the subject: Dumitru Velciu, *Ion Neculce* (Bucharest: 1968). It is unfortunate that Giurescu arbitrarily omitted sections of Costin's work, the oldest version of which is in Moscow.

127. *Poema pol.* 88, quoted by Toth, *op. cit.* p. 291.

128. *Dimitrie Cantemir. Viața și opera,* ed. by Petre P. Panaitescu, (Bucharest: 1958).

129. Dimitrie Cantemir, *Descrierea Moldovei (Descriptio Moldaviae),* translated from Latin by Gheorghe Guțu (Bucharest: 1973); Dimitrie Cantemir, *Hronicul vechimei a romano-moldo-vlahilor.* Text ales și stabilit, tabel cronologic, prefață și note de Stela Toma. [The Chronicle About the Ancientness of the romano-moldo-Vlachs. Selected texts, chronological table, preface and notes by Stela Toma], (Bucharest: 1981).

130. Cantemir, *Descrierea Moldovei,* 1973, *op. cit.,* p. 297.

131. Cantemir, *Hronicul vechimei romano-moldo-vlahilor,* p. 9; quoted by Tóth, 1942, *op. cit.,* p. 317, note 1.

132. Tóth, *op. cit.,* p. 320.

133. Constantin C. Giurescu, *Istoria românilor,* 1975, p. 459.

134. *"Istoria Țării Românești de când au descălecat Românii,"* *Magazinu Istoricu* IV, 1847, p. 231, quoted by Tóth, *op. cit.,* p. 309. See also Adolf Armbruster, *La romanité des roumains, op. cit.* p. 217.

135. Attempts were later made to diminish the significance of this record by assuming that it actually referred to an admigration (Dimitrie Onciul, *cf.,* Tóth, *op. cit.* 1942, p. 309).

136. *Istoria Țării Românești, 1290–1690. Letopisețul Cantacuzinesc* [The History of Wallachia, 1290–1690. The Chronicle of Cantacuzino], a critical edition by Constantin Grecescu and Dan Simonescu (Bucharest: 1960); *Istoria Țării Românești în Cronicari munteni* [The History of Wallachia in the Wallachian Chroniclers] ed. by M. Gregorian, I (Bucharest: 1961). *Istoriile domnilor Țării Românești de Radu Popescu vornicul* [Histories of the Princes of Wallachia by Radu Popescu vornicul], ed. by Constantin Grecescu, Eugen Stănescu, Dan Simonescu, and Șerban Papacostea. Introduction and critical edition by Constantin Grecescu (Bucharest: 1963).

137. Contemporary Romanian historiographers erroneously refer to the seventeenth century Romanian chroniclers as "Humanists," although they were, in fact, only involved with Humanistic ideas.

138. Şerban Papacostea, "Der Romanitätsgedanke der Rumänen im Mittelalter," *Dacoromania* I, 1973, pp. 114–123.

139. Tóth, *op. cit.*, 1942, p. 325.

140. The *Diet* was the national assembly and, in contrast to the fourteenth century *Congregatio*, had the power to pass laws.

141. Keith Hitchins, *The Roumanian National Movement in Transylvania, 1780–1849.* (Cambridge: Massachusetts: 1969), pp. 12–13.

142. *Ibid.*, p. 14.

143. The Phanariots were Greek merchant aristocracy and rulers of the Romanian Principalities from the beginning of the eighteenth to the beginning of the nineteenth centuries. They received the name Phanariot from the Fanar-district of Constantinople.

144. The adherents of the Uniate Church claimed that they had officially been designated Greek Catholics in 1773. The Uniates included some of the Ruthenians (Ukrainians), Serbs, and the Transylvanian Romanians who retained the Greek-Orthodox liturgy.

145. Hitchins, *op. cit.*, p. 18.

146. An excellent description in this topic, based to a large extent on original material, is given by Mathias Bernath, *Habsburg und die Anfänge der rumänischen Nationsbildung* (Leiden: 1972). It also contains rich references to older and modern literature. Further literature: Emanuel Turczynski, *Konfession und Nation. Zur Frühgeschichte der serbischen und rumänischen Nationsbildung,* (Düsseldorf: 1976); Radu R. Florescu, "The Uniate Church: Catalyst of Rumanian National Consciousness" in *The Slavonic and East European Review,* XLV, 1967, pp. 324–342; Robert A. Kann, *Das Nationalitätenproblem der Habsburgermonarchie. Geschichte und Ideengehalt der nationalen Bestrebungen vom Vormärz bis zur Auflösung des Reiches im Jahre 1918,* 2 vols. (Graz-Cologne: 1964).

147. Constantin Giurescu, *Istoria românilor* (Bucharest: 1975), pp. 536–537.

148. Mathias Bernath, *op. cit.*, p. 62.

149. *Ibid.*, p. 88.

150. After the enlightened Austrian Emperor Joseph II (1741–1790), the son of the Queen and Archduchess Maria Theresa (1717–1780).

151. Bernath, *op. cit.*, p. 179.

152. There were five units of border guards—three Székely and two Romanian.

153. Bernath, *op. cit.*, p. 181. The Romanians sharply opposed the creation of these frontier guards if it was coupled with pressure to leave their Orthodox religion and turn Uniate. The condition of conversion to Catholicism was eventually given up.

154. Bernath, *op. cit.*, p. 154.

155. *Ibid.*, pp. 220, 224–225. The *Supplex* was contested by the Transylvanian Saxon Joseph Carl Eder and by the Hungarian Martin Bolla.

156. For more detail see Emanuel Turczynski, *Konfession und Nation, op. cit.*

157. David Prodan, *Supplex Libellus Valachorum or the political struggle of the Romanians in Transylvania during the 18th century* (Bucharest; 1971), pp. 137–138.

158. Turczynski, *op. cit.*, p. 118.

159. David Prodan, *Supplex Libellus Valachorum*, 1st edition (Cluj: 1948); 2nd Marxist ed. Bucharest 1967, and the English translation 1971. See also Aurel Rǎduţiu, Ladislau Gyémánt, *Supplex Libellus Valachorum în variantele românești de la Schei* (Cluj-Napoca: 1975).

160. ". . . pristina jura, quae omnibus civibus essentialiter adhaerent quibus saeculo superiori nulla authoritate, sed iniqua duntaxat temporum illorum sorte, ut mox exponetur, expoliata fuit." (*Supplex Libellus Valachorum*, ed. Károly Küllő [Bucharest: 1971] p. 47.)

161. Prodan, *Supplex Libellus Valachorum* (Bucharest: 1971), pp. 19–20.

162. An excellent analysis of the Transylvanian School, with data about its leaders is given by K. Hitchins, *op. cit.*, chapter III. Further literature: Ion Lungu, *Şcoala ardeleană. Mişcarea ideologică naţională iluministă* [The Transylvanian School. An Ideological National Enlightened Movement], (Bucharest: 1978); Mario Ruffini, *La scuola latinista romena (1780–1891). Studio storico-filologico* (Roma: 1941). *Şcoala Ardeleană*, vols I–III, ed. by Florea Fugariu (Bucharest: 1970).

163. Hitchins, *op. cit.*, p. 67, referring to Teodor, "Despre 'Istoria Romînilor,'" 200.

164. *Historia daco-romanorum sive valachorum*, ed. by Aug. Treboniu Laurian in *Foaia pentru minte, inimă şi literatură*, 1862, pp. 81–236, with interruptions; Samuil Micu, *Istoria şi lucrurile şi întîmplările românilor*, 1801–1805 (Fragmentary edition).

165. E. Turczynski, *op. cit.*, pp. 120–121. See also Vasile Netea, "Dimitrie Cantemir precursor al Şcolii Ardelene," in *Viaţa Românească*, 1973, no. 9., pp. 108–112, *cf.*, Nicolae Stoicescu, *Continuitatea românilor* [The Continuity of the Romanians], p. 22, note 45.

166. Nicolae Stoicescu, *The Continuity of the Romanian People*, (Bucharest: 1983), p. 9. See also Stelian Brezeanu, "Romani şi Blachi la Anonymus. Istorie şi ideologie politică" in: *Revista de Istorie*, 1981 (vol.34), pp. 1313–1314.

167. Although not directly but most probably, via Bulgarian *kračun* "Christmas."

168. Hitchins, *op. cit.*, pp. 78–86. See also Gheorghe Şincai, Opere, I–III, ed. Florea Fugariu (Bucharest: 1967, 1969), vol. IV. Bucharest 1973; Mircea Tomus, *Gheorghe Şincai. Viaţa şi Opera*, (Bucharest: 1965).

169. Petru Maior, *Istoria pentru începutul Românilor în Dacia*, [The History on the Origins of the Romanians in Dacia], a critical edition by Florea Fugariu and Manole Neagoe, 1–2 vols. (Bucharest: 1970–71).

170. Sextil Puşcariu, "Părerile lui Petru Maior despre limba română" [The Opinion of Petru Maior About the Romanian Language], in *La centenarul*

348   *Ethnic Continuity in the Carpatho-Danubian Area*

morţii lui Petru Maior. Cuvîntări comemorative (Cluj: 1921), p. 36; quoted in the critical edition, 1970–71, vol. II, p. 287.

171. Alexandru Lăpedatu, "Petru Maior în cadrul vieţii naţionale şi culturale a epocii sale [Petru Maior and his Place in the National and Cultural Life of His Time], in *La centenarul morţii lui Petru Maior. Cuvîntări comemorative* (Cluj: 1921), *op. cit.* p. 288. An interesting analysis in reference to Maior's work, see W. Bahner, *Das Sprach- und Geschichtsbewusstsein in der rumänischen Literatur von 1780–1880*, (Berlin: 1967).

172. Vasile V. Grecu, *Şcoala Ardeleană şi unitatea limbii române literare* [The Transylvanian School and the Unity of the Romanian Literary Language], (Timişoara: 1973) p. 25. See further Vasile Netea, "Dimitrie Cantemir precursor al Şcolii Ardelene," in *Viaţa Românească*, 1973, no. 9., pp. 108–112, *cf.*, Stoicescu, *Continuitatea românilor*, p. 22., note 45.

173. Samuil Micu, *Scurtă cunoştinţă a istorii românilor* [Short Description of the History of the Romanians], p. 163; reproduced in *Şcoala Ardeleană*, critical edition by Florea Fugariu, vol. I (Bucharest: 1970), p. 169.

174. Bogdan Petriceicu Hasdeu, *cf.*, Mihail Macrea, *Contribuţii la istoria lingvisticii şi filologiei româneşti* (Bucharest: 1978), p. 127.

175. *Istoria ştiinţelor în România. Lingvistica*, ed. by Iorgu Iordan, (Bucharest: 1975), p. 18. (in a chapter written by Ion Gheţie).

176. Page numbers in subsequent quotations will refer to Maior, *op. cit.*

177. *Cf.*, for example, Dumitru Tudor, in *Dacoromania*, I, 1973, pp. 149–161.

178. It was "only when they fought against Menumorout at Bihor, he wrote in chapter 81, that 20 Hungarians and 15 Székelys were killed." (p. 85).

179. More detailed by Stephen Fischer-Galati, "Romanian Nationalism," in Peter F. Sugar and Ivo J. Lederer (eds.): *Nationalism in Eastern Europe* (Washington: 1969), p. 375.

180. The Union of Moldavia and Wallachia into a Romanian state in 1859 by the Conference of Paris, given international recognition in the Treaty of Berlin 1878.

181. Fischer-Galati, *op. cit.*, p. 381.

182. The Liga pentru unitatea culturală a tuturor românilor [The League for the Cultural Unity of all Romanians], founded 1890 in Bucharest, had the main task at the very beginning to propagate Daco-Romanism.

183. For an extensive discussion of Romanian nationalism, see John C. Campbell, *French Influence and the Rise of Romanian Nationalism* (Harvard University: 1940); Theodor Schieder, "Das Problem des Nationalismus in Osteuropa," in *Osteuropa und der deutsche Osten*, Series I, book 3 (Cologne: 1965).

184. Dimitrie Onciul, Ion Bogdan, Constantin Giurescu, Radu Rosetti, and others.

185. László Makkai, "Román történetírás a két világháború között," [Romanian Historiography Between the Two World Wars], in *Hitel*, VIII, 1943, Kolozsvár.

186. Iorgu Iordan, in *Lingvistica*, 1975, p. 98, note 11.

187. Ovid Densusianu, *Opere.Lingvistica. Histoire de la langue roumaine*, ed. by B. Cazacu, V. Rusu, and I. Şerb (Bucharest: 1975), p. 12.

188. Densusianu, *op. cit.*, p. 14.

189. *Ibid.*, pp. 5–6.

190. *Ibid.*

191. *Ibid.*, p. 26.

192. Among others, recently: Gottfried Schramm, *Eroberer und Eingesessene. Geographische Lehnnamen als Zeugen der Geschichte Südosteuropas im ersten Jahrtausend n. Chr.*, (Stuttgart: 1981); "Frühe Schicksale der Rumänen" in *Zeitschrift für Balkanologie*, Band XXI/2 (1985) pp. 223–241; Kurt Horedt, *Siebenbürgen im Frühmittelalter* (Bonn: 1986).

193. Constantin C. Giurescu, "O nouă sinteză a trecutului nostru" [A New Synthesis of Our Past], quoted by László Makkai, in *Hitel*, VIII, 1943, p. 578.

194. Corneliu Zelea Codreanu, *Pentru Legionari* [For the Legionaries], (Sibiu: 1936); *Eiserne Garde* (Berlin: 1939); *Mărturii despre Legiune 1927–1967* [Testimonies on the Legionary 1927–1967], (Rio de Janeiro: 1967); Horia Sima, *Histoire du Mouvement Legionaire*, (Rio de Janeiro: 1972); Horia Sima, *Sfârşitul unei domnii sângeroase* [The End of a Bloody Domination], (Madrid: 1977); *Era libertăţii* [The Time of the Liberty], vol. 1. (Madrid: 1982).

195. *Istoria României. Compendiu*, Miron Constantinescu, Constantin Daicoviciu, and Ştefan Pascu (Bucharest: 1969), p. 528.

196. For a detailed discussion, see Zeev Barbu, "Psycho-Historical and Sociological Perspectives on the Iron Guard, the Fascist Movement of Romania" in: *Who were the Fascist. Social Roots of European Fascism*. Ed. by Stein Ugelvik Larsen, Bernt Hagtvet, Jan Petter Myklebust (Bergen-Oslo-Tromsø: 1980), p. 388.

197. Zeev Barbu, *op. cit.*, p. 390.

198. *Ibid.*, p. 392. More detailed treatment of the subject can be found in: *Native Fascism in the Successor States 1918–1945*, ed. by Peter F. Sugar (Santa Barbara: 1971); H. Rogger and E. Weber (eds.), *The European Right* (London: 1967); S. J. Wolf (ed.), *European Fascism* (London: 1967); F. L. Carsten, *The Rise of Fascism* (London: 1967). Modern Romanian historical treatises tend to diminish the significance of nationalism in this period. Constantin Giurescu, for example, characterizes the Iron Guard as simply "the principal exponent of the extreme Right" (Giurescu, 1975, *op. cit.*, p. 732) and *Istoria României. Compendiu*, (ed. by Miron Constantinescu, Constantin Daicoviciu and Ştefan Pascu, 1974) ignores nationalism when describing the ideology of the Iron Guard: "The core of the ideology of the Iron Guard consisted of anti-Communism, obscurantism, anti-Semitism, and religious mysticism" (p. 506).

199. One of the significant nationalistic periodicals in Romania, founded in 1901 by Alexandru Vlahuţă and Gheorghe Coşbuc and having as its most important collaborator Nicolae Iorga.

200. Dionisie Ghermani, "Theorie und Praxis der rumänischen Historiographie der Nachkriegszeit (1948–1978)," in *Südostdeutsches Archiv*, XXI, vol.

1978, pp. 105–117; Ghermani, *Die kommunistische Umdeutung der rumänischen Geschichte unter besonderer Berücksichtigung des Mittelalters* (München: 1967), p. 17.

201. The term is derived from the name of Michael Roller, author of the *History of the Romanian People's Republic* (Bucharest: 1948 and 1952); *Probleme de istorie* [Problems of History], (Bucharest: 1951), and *Scrieri istorice și social-politice* [Historical and Sociopolitical Writings], (Bucharest: 1957). On the "Roller period," see Michael Rura, *Reinterpretation of History as a Method of Furthering Communism in Rumania* (Washington, Georgetown: 1961). In the 1950s, during the time of Russification, Slavic influence became ever stronger; later this aspect markedly diminished.

202. *Guide to Ortography, Orthoepy, and Punctuation* (Bucharest: 1965) pp. 5, 7.

203. See note 201.

204. Ghermani, 1967, *op. cit.*, p. 131, note 503.

205. Kurt Horedt, "Germanen und Romanen in Siebenbürgen. Bemerkungen zu einer Besprechung," in *Zeitschrift für Siebenbürgische Landeskunde*, 6, (77), Heft 2/1983, p. 170.

206. Fischer-Galati, 1969, *op. cit.*, p. 394: Ghermani, *Die kommunistische Umdeutung, op. cit.*, p. 136.

207. Fischer-Galati, 1969, *op. cit.*, 394.

208. Ghermani, "Wandlungen der rumänischen Historiographie im Spiegel der ersten vier Bände der *Istoria Romîniei*," in *Südost-Forschungen*, vol. 26, 1967, p. 356.

209. *Ibid.*, p. 357.

210. Ghermani, "Die Forschungsarbeit der magyarischen Historiker Siebenbürgens nach 1945," in *Ungarn-Jahrbuch* 5 (1973) p. 246. See further Keith Hitchins, *The Roumanian National Movement in Transylvania, 1780–1848*, Harvard Historical Monographs, LXI, 1969, p. 285; Arnold Toynbee, *Constantine Porphyrogenitos and His World*, (London: 1973), p. 457, note 2.

211. *Revista de Istorie*, 32:7, 1979, pp. 1215–1233. A critical analysis is given by Krista Zach, "Von Burebista bis Ceaușescu. Der Mythos von zweitausendjährigen 'unabhängigen Einheitsstaat," in *Wissenschaftlicher Dienst Südosteuropa*, 28 (1979), pp. 200–205. For the political and socioeconomical developments in Romania of the years 80s are provided detailed data in *Romania in the 1980s*, ed. by Daniel N. Nelson (Boulder: 1981).

212. *Istoria Romîniei*, vol. I, ed. by C. Daicoviciu (Bucharest: 1969); *Istoria Romîniei. Compendiu*, (eds.) Miron Constantinescu, Constantin Daicoviciu, and Ștefan Pascu (Bucharest: 1969) 1st edition, 3rd edition 1974.

213. In all historical works and monographs published in Romania since the mid-1960s; this purpose is served by the organization in Romania of international congresses.

214. Lucian Boia, "Angajamentul politic al istoritului," in *Era Socialistă*, LVI (1977) no. 20., pp. 20–24; Ghermani, "Theorie und Praxis," 1978, *op. cit.*, pp. 105–117.

215. For example, *Istoria Romîniei în date*, ed. by Constantin Giurescu (Bucharest: 1972). Not only historians but also fascist politicians of the

interwar period are now being presented in a way that clearly implies a certain degree of rehabilitation. This is done mainly through fiction, as, for example, in the novel *Delirul* (The Frenzy) by Marin Preda (1975), in which General Ion Antonescu, the Fascist dictator of Romania from 1940 to 1944, is described sympathetically as a man who fought for the interests of the Romanian people.

216. *Relations Between the Autochthonous Population and the Migratory Populations on the Territory of Romania.* A collection of studies edited by Miron Constantinescu, Ştefan Pascu, and Petre Diaconu (Bucharest: 1975); Nicolae Stoicescu, *The Continuity of the Romanian People,* (Bucharest: 1983).

217. *Scînteia* [The Spark], daily paper of the Central Committee of the RCP, 2.6.1982.

218. Among others, Iosif Constantin Drăgan, *Noi Tracii. Istoria multimilenară a neamului românesc* [We Thracians. The Multithousand Years-old History of the Romanian People], (Craiova: 1976).

219. Only the most typical works dealing with this theme are listed here: Ştefan Pascu, *Marea adunare naţională de la Alba Iulia: încununarea ideii, tendinţelor şi a luptelor de unitate a poporului român* [The Great Assembly at Alba Iulia: the Crowning of Ideas, of Tendencies and of Fightings for the Unity of the Romanian People], (Cluj: 1968); *Desăvîrşirea unificării statului naţional român. Unirea Transilvaniei cu vechea Românie* [The Accomplishment of the Unification of the Romanian National State. The Union of Transylvania with Old Romania], (Bucharest: 1968); Dinu C. Giurescu, *Illustrierte Geschichte des rumänischen Volkes* (Bucharest: 1982); Ştefan Pascu, *Făurirea statului naţional unitar român, 1918,* (Bucharest: 1983); *Naţiunea română,* ed. by Ştefan Ştefănescu (Bucharest: 1984).

220. *Desăvîrşirea unificării, op. cit.,* p. 435.

221. Ştefan Pascu, *Voievodatul Transilvaniei,* vol. I (Cluj: 1971), vol. II (Cluj-Napoca: 1979). Pascu's historical concept has been contradicted even by certain Romanian scholars, such as, for example, David Prodan.

CHAPTER 2

1. Rolf Hachmann, *Die Goten und Skandinavien,* (Berlin: 1970), p. 201.

2. *Ibid.*

3. *Ibid.,* p. 462.

4. Mircea Babeş, "Arheologia în frontul ştiinţelor istorice" [Archaeology in the Forefront of Historical Sciences], in *Era Socialistă,* 1981, 6, p. 24.

5. *Istoria Rominiei,* C. Daicoviciu, ed., (Bucharest: 1960).

6. Dumitru Protase, *Problema continuităţii în Dacia în lumina arheologiei şi numismaticii* [The Problem of the Continuity in Dacia in the Light of Archaeology and Numismatics], (Bucharest: 1966), to which Daicoviciu wrote the foreword.

7. Mostly in Romanian periodicals of history and archaeology, such as *Studii şi cercetări de istorie veche şi arheologie* (further references will be referred to in the abbreviated form *SCIVA*), [Studies and Investigations of

Ancient History and Archaeology], *Revista de Istorie* [Journal of History], periodicals of the country museums of history, and other publications. A rich and up to date bibliography is given by C. Preda and Florentina Preda: "Contribuția cercetărilor arheologice la cunoașterea istoriei vechi a României" [The Contribution of Archaeological Investigations to the Knowledge of the Ancient History of Romania], *SCIVA*, 7–8, 1980, pp. 1253–1279.

8. Ion I. Russu, *Etnogeneza românilor*, (Bucharest: 1981), p. 155.

9. Dumitru Protase, "Observații asupra așezărilor rurale din Dacia romana și postromana sec. II-VI pînă la venirea slavilor" [Observations of the Rural Settlements in Roman and Post-Roman Dacia in the Second and Sixth Centuries Until the Arrival of the Slavs], *Banatica*, 1, 1971., p. 99.

10. *Cf.* Protase, *Autohtonii în Dacia*, vol. I, Dacia romană (Bucharest: 1980), p. 12., note, and Protase, *Un cimitir dacic din epoca romană la Soporu de Cîmpie*, (Bucharest: 1976), p. 11, note 2.

11. *Cf.*, for example, A. Rosetti, *Istoria limbii române*, 1968, pp. 77–78; Pascu, ed., *Istoria României. Compendiu*, 3rd edition, 1974, p. 68 and map no. 5.

12. *SCIVA*, 25, 2, 1974, p. 318 Nicolae Gudea, a review article about *Dacoromania, Jahrbuch für östliche Latinität*, I, 1973, Freiburg.

13. One part of the lower Danube ceased to be the frontier from 106 to 275 A.D., when Dacia Traiana belonged to the empire.

14. The term "barbarian" is of Greek origin (*barbaroi*) and was used for peoples who spoke a language other than Greek. Later, however, primarily during the age of migrations, all peoples who were neither Roman nor Greek were designated as "barbarian."

15. Hans Jürgens Eggers, *Der römische Import im freien Germanien*, (Hamburg: 1951); *cf.* "die grosse Gesamtkarte."

16. Roman-type fired vessel with a red glaze and imprinted ornamentation.

17. H.J. Eggers, *op. cit.*, p. 53.

18. W.A. von Jenny, *Die Kunst der Germanen im frühen Mittelalter*, (Berlin: 1940), p. 10.

19. J. Wielowiejski, "Die Kontakte Noricums und Pannoniens mit den nördlichen Völkern im Lichte der römischen Importe," in H.J. Dölle, ed., *Römer und Germanen in Mitteleuropa*, (Berlin: 1975), pp. 75–76; *cf.* also G. Witkowski-Sommer, "Spuren römischer Beeinflussung im bildnerischen Schaffen der Germanen" (Gebiet der DDR), in *Römer und Germanen*, 1975, p. 267.

20. G. Witkowski-Sommer, in *Römer und Germanen*, p. 273.

21. Wielowiejski, in *Römer und Germanen*, p. 76.

22. *Ibid.*, pp. 76–77.

23. *Ibid.*, p. 79.

24. Wielowiejski, in *Römer und Germanen*, p. 72.

25. *Ibid.*, p. 70.

26. A. Salamon, "Kaiserzeitliches Fundmaterial aus Nord- und Ostungarn," in *Klio* 51, Berlin-Wiesbaden, p. 327; quoted in D. Gabler, "Zu Fragen der Handelsbeziehungen zwischen den Römern und den Barbaren im Gebiet östlich von Pannonien," in *Römer und Germanen*, p. 92.

27. D. Gabler, in *Römer und Germanen*, p. 107.
28. Sture Bolin, *Fynden av romerska mynt i det fria Germanien* (Finds of Roman Coins in Free Germania], (Lund: 1926), p. 253.
29. *Ibid.*, p. 140.
30. *Ibid.*, p. 142.
31. *Ibid.*, pp. 140–141.
32. *Ibid.*, p. 297.
33. Wielowiejski, in *Römer und Germanen*, p. 73.
34. *Ibid.*, p. 77.; F. Schlette, "Formen des römisch-germanischen Handels," in *Römer und Germanen*, p. 129.
35. Wielowiejski, in *Römer und Germanen*, p. 78.
36. *Ibid.*, p. 79.
37. *Ibid.*, pp. 72–73.
38. S. Bolin, *op. cit.*, pp. 186, 296.
39. Gabler, in *Römer und Germanen*, p. 96.
40. *Ibid.*, p. 102.
41. Eutropius, VIII 6, 1: *Ex toto orbe Romano, infinitas copias hominum transtulerat ad agros et urbes colendas.*
42. Romanian historians are supporters of a rapid process of Romanization of Dacia Traiana: for example, C. Daicoviciu, E. Petrovici, and Gh. Ştefan in *Istoria României*, vol. 1, (Bucharest, 1960) p. 795; Mihail Macrea, *Viaţa în Dacia romană*, 1969, p. 255. Hadrian Daicoviciu, "Dacii şi civilizaţia lor în secolele I î. e.n. - I e.n." in: *Actu Musei Napocensis* V (1968), pp. 51–58; Dumitru Berciu, *De la Burebista la Decebal*, p. 11.
43. *Magyarország története*, [The History of Hungary], (Budapest: 1984), vol. I, p. 240.
44. Eutropius: *abductosque Romanos ex urbibus et agris Daciae, in media Moesia collocavit* [. . . "and taking out the Romans from the towns and fields of Dacia, he settled them in the middle of Moesia"], *Breviarium ab urbe condita*, written between 364 and 378, IX 15, 1. This is confirmed also by Vopiscus (fourth century) in *Scriptores historiae Augustae*, 39, 7.
45. Nicolae Iorga, "Le problème de l'abandon de la Dacie par l'empereur Aurélien," in *Revue historique du sud-est européennes*, I, 1924, pp. 336–337.
46. Vladimir Iliescu, *Provinciam . . . intermisit*, Eutropius, IX 15, 1, in *Revue Roumaine de Linguistique* 15 (1970), pp. 597–600.
47. Jordanes, *Romana* 271.
48. Vladimir Iliescu, "Părăsirea Daciei în lumina izvoarelor literare" [The Abandonment of Dacia in the Light of Literary Sources], in *Studii şi cercetări de istorie veche (SCIV)*, 3, 1971, pp. 425–442.
49. . . . *sublato exercitu et provincialibus reliquit* . . . , Vopiscus, *Vita Aureliani*, 39, 7, in *Scriptores historiae Augustae*.
50. Vasile Pârvan, *Dacia*, fifth edition (Bucharest: 1972), p. 123.
51. *Istoria României. Compendiu*, third edition, Ş. Pascu ed., (Bucharest: 1974), p. 70.
52. *Ibid.*, pp. 70–71; Dumitru Tudor, "Romanizarea Munteniei," *Apulum*, XII, 1971, pp. 111–117.

53. Alexandru Rosetti, *Istoria limbii române, op. cit.*, p. 226.

54. Constantin Daicoviciu ed., *Istoria Românei*, (Bucharest: 1960), pp. 327–329. Ştefan Pascu *et al.*, ed., *Istoria Românei. Compendiu*, 1974, p. 71; András Bodor, "Blocurile cu litere greceşti din cetăţile Dacice," in *Crisia* 2, 1972, pp. 27–35; Dumitru Berciu, "Scriere cu litere latine şi greceşti descoperită la Buridava (Ocniţa), jud. Vîlcea," *SCIVA*, 30, no. 4, 1979, pp. 481–499.

55. *Istoria Romîniei*, C. Daicoviciu, ed., 1960, p. 327. The presence of single letters on pieces of earthenware, for example, can hardly be considered an indication of the spread of "writing" among the population. There can be no question of the significance of writing in the Romanization of a society in which at least the masses of the population are illiterate, as were the Dacians.

56. Dumitru Protase, *Autohtonii în Dacia*, vol. I, *Dacia romană*, (Bucharest: 1980), p. 238.

57. The main points are summarized here on the basis of a review of *La résistance africaine à la romanisation*, (Paris: 1976) by M. Bénabou; "Observaţii privind procesul de romanizare," by Nicolae Gudea, *SCIVA*, 29, 2, pp. 231–240 (1978).

58. Nicolae Gudea, *SCIVA*, 29, 2, 1978, p. 233.

59. *Ibid.*, p. 234.

60. *Ibid.*,

61. András Mócsy, *Gesellschaft und Romanisation in der römischen Provinz Moesia Superior*, (Budapest: 1970), p. 7.

62. *Ibid.*, chapter V. Mócsy gives a detailed analysis of the Romanization of the province of Moesia Superior, which is interesting also from the point of view of Romanization in general and methodology.

63. M. Bénabou, "Résistance et Romanisation en Afrique du Nord sous le Haut-Empire," *Travaux du VIe Congrès International d'Études Classiques*, 1974, p. 374: 1. Romains, 2. Africains réfractaires, 3. le groupe des romanisés partiels.

64. *Cf.*, for example, P.A. Brunt, "The Romanization of the Local Ruling Classes in the Roman Empire," *Travaux du VIe Congrès International d'Études Classiques*, 1974, pp. 161–173; Mócsy, *op. cit.*, p. 249.

65. Volker Bierbrauer, "Jugoslawien seit dem Beginn der Völkerwanderung bis zur slawischen Landnahme," in *Jugoslawien. Integrations-probleme in Geschichte und Gegenwart*, (Göttingen: 1984), p. 67.

66. Slavko Ciglenečki, "Das Weiterleben der Spätantike bis zum Auftauchen der Slawen in Slowenien," *Vortrag an der 26. Internationalen Hochschulwoche 7-11 Oktober 1985 in Tutzing bei München.*

67. Zoltán Székely, "Régi idők vallatása" [The Investigation of Ancient Times], in *Új Élet*, Marosvásárhely, 1981, no. 14, p. 15.

68. *Istoria Românei*, C. Daicoviciu, ed., 1960, vol. I, p. 368.

69. *Ibid.*,

70. Dumitru Protase, *Autohtonii în Dacia* [The Autochthonous Population in Dacia], vol. I, *Dacia romană* (Bucharest: 1980), p. 238.

71. *Ibid.*, pp. 81–82; *Cf.* also Protase, 1966, *op. cit.*

72. Ioan Mitrofan, "Aşezări ale populaţiei autohtone în Dacia Superior" [Settlements of the Autochthonous Population in Dacia Superior], in *Acta Musei Napocensis IX*, 1972, p. 155.

73. Protase, 1980, *op. cit.*, p. 81.

74. Ioan Mitrofan, *op. cit.*, p. 141.

75. Protase, 1980, *op. cit.*, p. 84.

76. *Cf.* Protase, 1980, p. 239. The assumption that the rural areas were also affected by the process of Romanization has proved untenable (D. Tudor, *Oraşe, tîrguri şi sate în Dacia romană*, 1968, p. 8.

77. *Cf.*, for example, Daicoviciu, *Dacica*, (Cluj: 1969), p. 434; Protase, 1980, *op. cit.*, pp. 201–205.

78. Protase, 1980, *op. cit.*, p. 27.

79. András Kerényi, *Die Personennamen von Dazien* (Budapest: 1941), p. 286. *Cf.* G. Schramm, "Frühe Schicksale der Rumänen," in *Zeitschrift für Balkanologie*, vol. XXI/2 1985, p. 234.

80. Certificate for military disbandment.

81. Protase, 1980, *op. cit.*, p. 198.

82. Jan Beneš, *Auxilia Romana in Moesia atque in Dacia. Zu Fragen des römischen Verteidigungssystems im unteren Donauraum und in den angrenzenden Gebieten*, (Prague: 1979), p. 71.

83. C. Daicoviciu, "Problema numărului geto-dacilor," in *Gînd românesc*, Cluj, vol. 2, no. 6, pp. 366–375; in *Dacica*, 1969, p. 17. *Cf.* The extremely low number of *alae* and *cohortes* composed of Dacians in the imperial Roman period, stated by Pàrvan, *Dacia*, Cambridge, p. 190.

84. Protase, 1966, *op. cit.*, pp. 84–102; Protase, 1980, pp. 171–195.

85. Protase, 1980, *op. cit.*, fig. 24 (map), on p. 256.

86. Michael Crawford in *Journal of Roman Studies* 67 (1977), pp. 117–124; see also *Studii şi Cercetări de Numismatică* 7 (1980), p. 51 *et. seq.*

87. Protase, 1980, *op. cit.*, p. 195.

88. Iudita Winkler, in *Studii Clasice*, (Bucharest: 1965), pp. 225–234., quoted in Protase, 1980, p. 194.

89. Protase, 1980, *op. cit.*, p. 34.

90. *Istoria României*, C. Daicoviciu, ed., 1960, p. 268.

91. *Ibid.*, p. 368.

92. Protase, 1980, p. 42. Protase refers to his article in *Acta Musei Napocensis*, V, 1968, p. 509, where essentially the same statement is found.

93. *Ibid.*, p. 77.

94. *Ibid.*, p. 161.

95. *Ibid.*

96. Ioan Glodariu, *Aşezări dacice şi daco-romane la Slimnic* [Dacian and Daco-Roman Settlements at Slimnic], (Bucharest: 1981), p. 39, note 96.

97. *Ibid.*, p. 47, note 123.

98. *Ibid.*, p. 76.

99. *Ibid.*

100. In 1966 Protase noted: "It remains to see whether the settlement from the Latène does not end with the Roman conquest and whether those

few fragments considered Roman and dated to the Roman period were not simply spread there later." Protase, 1966, op. cit., pp. 29–30 (emphasis in the original text).

101. Protase, 1966, p. 106. In his monograph published in 1980, Protase refers to this page but without mentioning the mixing of material from the different periods.

102. Mihail Macrea, Viața în Dacia romană, 1969, p. 473; quoted by Ioan Mitrofan, 1972, p. 143; Protase, 1980, p. 43.

103. Ioan Glodariu, Așezări dacice . . . , op. cit.

104. Ibid., pp. 74–75.

105. Protase, 1980, op. cit., p. 154.

106. Kurt Horedt, "Die spätrömische Siedlungen in Siebenbürgen" (II), Marisia IX, 1979, p. 70. Horedt refers here, as an example, to Pannonia: E.B. Thomas, Römische Villen in Pannonien (Budapest: 1964). See also Protase, 1980, p. 155.

107. Ibid.

108. Protase, 1980, pp. 156–157. This is the case at seven sites: Aiud, Rāhău (Alba County), Deva, Cinciș, Mănerău (Hunedoara County), Chinteni and Bādeni (Cluj County). If one reckons with 40 rural farms, this amounts to about 17% of the total.

109. Protase, 1980, p. 157.

110. András Bodor, in A kolozsvári Bolyai Tudományegyetem Emlékkönyve [The Memorial Volume of the Bolyai University of Kolozsvár], (Cluj-Kolozsvár: 1956), pp. 215–217 and 223; quoted by Protase, 1980, p. 156.

111. Horedt, op. cit., p. 70.

112. Protase, op. cit., 1980, p. 99.

113. Protase cites a number of articles about Pannonia, published in Hungary by A. Mócsy, Gy. Novák, E. Bónis, E. Biró, and T.P. Buócz (Protase, 1976, p. 79, note 154).

114. Max v. Chlingesperg auf Berg: Die römischen Brandgräber bei Reichenhall in Oberbayern (Braunschweig: 1896); quoted by Protase, 1976, p. 79, note 154.

115. Protase, Autohtonii în Dacia, vol. I, Dacia romană (Bucharest: 1980), pp. 101–125.

116. Protase, 1980, op. cit., p. 116.

117. Ibid., pp. 117–118.

118. Ibid., p. 102.

119. Ibid., p. 124.

120. Ibid., p. 104.

121. Ibid., p. 125.

122. Ibid., p. 107.

123. Ibid., p. 103.

124. Ibid., p. 109.

125. Ibid., p. 115.

126. K. Horedt, Acta Musei Apulensis, Apulum, XVI, 1978, p. 234.

127. D. Protase, *Un cimitir dacic din epoca romanǎ la Soporu de Cîmpie* [A Dacian Cemetery from the Roman Time at Soporu de Cîmpie], (Bucharest: 1976), ; Protase, 1980, *op. cit.*, pp. 119–124.

128. *Ibid.*, p. 56 and p. 90, Table 4.

129. K. Horedt in "Die letzten Jahrzehnte der Provinz Dakien in Siebenbürgen" *Apulum* XVI, 1978, p. 233. considers that these very worn coins are not reliable in dating the cemetery to the second century A.D.

130. Protase, 1976, *op. cit.*, p. 65.

131. *Ibid.*, p. 56.

132. Horedt, *op. cit.*, 1978, p. 233.

133. Protase, 1976, *op. cit.*, p. 66.

134. *Ibid.*, p. 63.

135. Hordet, 1978, *op. cit.*, pp. 228–231.

136. *Ibid.*, p. 230.

137. *Ibid.*, pp. 228–229, Figs. 11 and 12 (maps of the cemetery); Protase, 1976, sketches no. I and II (maps of the cemetery).

138. Mihail Macrea, in *Apulum*, VII, 1968, p. 198.

139. Horedt, *Acta Musei Apulensis*, *Apulum*, XVI, 1978, p. 225. Literature on the Carps by Gh. Bichir, *Archaeology and History of the Carpi*, part I-II, Supplementary Series 16, 11 (Oxford: 1976); Dolinescu Ferche Suzana, *Aşezări din secolele III şi VI e.n. în sud-vestul Munteniei. Cercetările de la Dulceanca* [Settlements of the Third and Sixth Centuries A.D. in Southwestern Muntenia. The Investigations at Dulceanca], (Bucharest: 1974); Gh. Bichir, "Relaţiile dintre Sarmaţi şi Daci" [The Relationship Between Sarmatians and Dacians], *SCIVA*, 2, 1970.

140. Horedt, 1978, *op. cit.*, p. 215. five hoards end with the reign of Gordian III and 25 with that of Philippus.

141. Horedt, 1978, *op. cit.*, referring to *Corpus Inscriptionum Latinarum*, III, 1054.

142. Horedt, 1978, *op. cit.*, p. 225.

143. *Ibid.*, p. 233.

144. Cassius Dio, *Roman History*, LXXII, 3, 3. Cf. *Fontes Historiae Daco-Romanae*, vol. II, 1970, p. 704.

145. Protase, 1980, *op. cit.*, 223.

146. *Ibid.*

147. *Ibid.*, pp. 225 and 227, note 25. At Soporu de Cîmpie, Obreja, Locusteni only the jewelry made in the filigree technique is reminiscent of the Carps; and the amphoras, the Sarmatian-type mirrors, and the zoomorph decorations are lacking.

148. Protase, 1980, *op. cit.*, p. 252.

149. *Istoria Romîniei*, C. Daicoviciu, ed., (Bucharest: 1960) p. 391. See also *Istoria României. Compendiu*, Ş. Pascu, red., (Bucharest: 1974), p. 50.

150. Protase, 1980, *op. cit.*, p. 115.

150/a *Ibid.*

151. Protase, 1976, *op. cit.*, p. 57.

152. Protase, 1980, *op. cit.*, p. 99.

153. S. Bolin, 1926, *op. cit.*, pp. 140–141.

154. Of a total of 55 isolated coins found in Carpic sites, 7 originate from cemeteries: 1 is from an urn at Poieneşti, 5 others (4 of bronze and 1 of silver) from the same cemetery; and a silver coin was found in a cemetery at Dochia. Gh. Bichir, *Cultura Carpică* [The Carpic Culture], (Bucharest: 1973), p. 132.

155. Protase, 1980, *op. cit.*, p. 58.

156. Protase, 1966, *op. cit.*, p. 75.

157. *Ibid.*, p. 83, Protase, 1976, p. 77.

158. Protase, 1976, *op. cit.*, p. 32.

159. *Ibid.*, p. 41.

160. Glodariu, 1981, *op. cit.*, p. 49, fig. 25/11 and 25/14, p. 117.

161. Protase, 1980, *op. cit.*, p. 75.

162. The Carps in Moldavia, never dominated by the Roman Empire and not Romanized, adopted Roman earthenware forms in a higher degree: most of their amphorae and many other vessels show a marked Roman influence. The Carpic potters "worked on the Roman models in a creative way" (*Cf.* Gh. Bichir, *Cultura carpică,* 1973, p. 81).

163. Protase, 1976, *op. cit.*, p. 54, with some references to the literature in note 39.

164. La Tène is the name of a village at the Lake Neuchâtel in Switzerland, where a Celtic site with rich material remains weapons, tools, etc., was found. It represents the later period of the Iron Age, marked especially by the Celtic culture that spread over Western and Central Europe during the fifth to the first centuries B.C., designated by the name of this Swiss village. In archaeological literature, the notion "La Tène" was generalized to designate contemporary cultures of other peoples as well: the "Germanic La Tène," the "Iberian La Tène."

165. Protase, 1976, *op. cit.*, p. 56.

166. Protase, 1980, *op. cit.*, pp. 161–162.

167. Protase, 1976, *op. cit.*, p. 81.

168. Haralambie Mihăescu, *La langue latine dans de sud-est de l'Europe* (Bucharest: 1978), *Cf.*, G. Schramm, "Frühe Schicksale der Rumänen" in *Zeitschrift für Balkanologie,* vol. XXI/2 (1985) p. 234, note 21.

169. *Magyarország története* [The History of Hungary], vol. I, (Budapest: 1984), p. 225.

170. Emilian Popescu, *Inscripţiile greceşti şi latine din secolele IV-XIII descoperite în România* [Greek and Latin Inscriptions from the Fourth to Thirteen Centuries Discovered in Romania], (Bucharest: 1976), p. 18. On the Roman inscriptions of Dacia Traiana the following works provide valuable information: *Corpus Inscriptionum Latinarum* (*CIL*), vol. 3; *Inscriptiones Daciae Romanae,* I: Introducere istorică şi epigrafică. Diplomele militare, tăbliţele cerate, ed. by Ion I. Russu (Bucharest: 1975); vol. II: Oltenia şi Muntenia, red. by G. Florescu, C. Petolescu (Bucharest: 1977); vol. III: 1. Dacia Superior, Zona de sud-vest, ed. by I.I. Russu, 1977; 2. Dacia Superior, Ulpia Traiana Dacica Sarmizegethusa, ed. by Russu, 1980; C.C. Petolescu, *Cronica epigrafică*

a României (1975-1980), SCIV, 32, 1981. With regard to E. Popescu's work (*Inscripțiile grecești și latine*) it must be noted that Greek towns were founded in Dobrudja, as along the entire western coast of the Black Sea, over several centuries B.C. and Roman, later Byzantine, domination lasted there until the seventh century. A large part of Popescu's monograph (pp. 35–292) deals with the rich finds of inscriptions from that territory. Most of these are funerary inscriptions. It is obvious that they were made by the local population. Most are in the Greek language, a smaller number in Latin. By contrast, the inscriptions from the period in question found in the rest of present-day Romania are few and contain no references to local people but only short formulae or single words or letters.

On the Greek character of the towns on the shore of the Black Sea see: Dionisie M. Pippidi, A. Ștefan, E. Duroțiu-Boilă, in: "Colloque anglo-roumain d'epigraphie ancienne: Les villes grèques de Scythie Mineure a l'époque romaine", *Dacia* 19, 1975, pp. 141–172.

171. There are only incomplete descriptions about the history and culture of Dacia. A short summary of the Dacian history is given by M. Macrea and D. Tudor, *Epoca sclavagistă romană* (sec. I-III), *Dacia în timpul stăpânirii romane,* in: Istoria României I, Bucharest 1960, pp. 345–476 *Cf., Erdély története,* 1986, *op. cit.,* p. 552.

172. About the date of the abandonment of Dacia see András Bodor, "Împăratul și părăsirea Daciei" [The Emperor and the Abandonment of Dacia], *Studia Univ. Babeș-Bolyai* Ser. Hist. 17, 1972.

173. "abductosque Romanos ex urbibus et agris Daciae, in media Moesia collocavit" [. . . and taking out the Romans from the towns and fields of Dacia, he settled them in the middle of Moesia.] Eutropius, *Ab urbe condita,* IX, 15, 1.

174. Dacia Ripensis (one part of Moesia Superior, in the valley of Timok) and Dacia Mediterranea (one part of Dardania, the present-day eastern Serbia and western Bulgaria).

175. Kurt Horedt, *Siebenbürgen in spätrömischer Zeit* (Bucharest: 1982); "Die städtischen Siedlungen Siebenbürgens in spätrömischer Zeit," *Acta Musei Devensis, Sargetia,* XIV, 1979; "Die spätrömischen Siedlungen in Siebenbür-gen," *Marisia,* IX, 1979.

176. Emanuel Turczynski, *Konfession und Nation. Zur Frühgeschichte der serbischen und rumänischen Nationsbildung* (Düsseldorf: 1976), p. 88, note 242; Konrad Schünemann, *Die Entstehung des Städtewesens in Südosteuropa* (Breslau: 1929), p. 36.

177. Horedt, 1982, *op. cit.,* p. 89.

178. *Ibid.,* p. 90.

179. The "Augustales" were associations concerned with the cult of the emperors in the Roman Empire. Wealthy burghers who belonged to these associations also provided support for the beautification of towns; such, for instance, was the *Aedes Augustalium,* a second century building of Sarmi-zegethusa.

180. Hadrian Daicoviciu, "Etnogeneza românilor," in *Națiunea română,* (Bucharest: 1984), p. 151. Valuable information of Sarmizegethusa is given

by Constantin Daicoviciu, "Sarmizegethusa" in *Realencyclopädie*, suppl. XV, 1974, pp. 599–655.

181. Horedt, 1982, *op. cit.*, p. 61.

182. Joachim Werner, *Reinecke-Festschrift* (Mainz: 1950), p. 154, no. 35, *cf.*, Horedt, "Die städtischen Siedlungen," 1979, *op. cit.*, p. 206, note 13.

183. Horedt, 1982, *op. cit.*, p. 203.

184. *Ibid.*, p. 204.

185. *Ibid.*, p. 62 and p. 153, Fig. 60, 4.

186. *Ibid.*, p. 64.

187. *Ibid.*, p. 205.

188. *Ibid.*

189. *Ibid.*, p. 64.

190. The wall of a small Roman building.

191. Horedt, 1982, *op. cit.*, pp. 66–67, 204.

192. *Ibid.*, p. 69. A synthesis of Porolissum is given by Constantin Daicoviciu, "Porolissum," in *Realencyclopädie*, XXII, 1953, pp. 265–270.

193. *Istoria României*, 1960, p. 620.

194. Dumitru Protase, *Problema continuității în Dacia*, 1966, *op. cit.*, p. 119.

195. Horedt,˅1982, *op. cit.*, p. 69.

195/a Nicolae Gudea, *Acta Musei Porolissensis*, III, 1979, pp. 515–524.

196. Horedt, 1982, *op. cit.*, p. 73.

197. *Ibid.*, p. 213, list of finds no. 7.

198. *Ibid.*, p. 215, list of finds no. 10.

199. Ligia Bârzu, *Continuitatea populației autohtone în Transilvania în secolele IV-V. Cimitirul I de la Bratei* [The Continuity of the Autochthonous Population in Transylvania in the 4th-5th Centuries. Cemetery I at Bratei], (Bucharest: 1973), p. 89.

200. *Cf.*, for example, Protase, 1966, *op. cit.*, p. 107.

201. Horedt, 1982, *op. cit.*, pp. 151–152.

202. *Ibid.*, p. 152.

203. *Ibid.*

204. *Ibid.*, p. 152.

205. *Ibid.*, p. 154 and 216–217, list no. 11.

206. *Ibid.*, p. 165.

207. *Cf.*, the map in Horedt, 1982, *op. cit.*, p. 181, with the area of the Sîntana de Mureş culture and that of the finds of coins.

208. Horedt, 1982, *op. cit.*, p. 73. See further Zoltán Székely, "Korai középkori temetők Délkelet-Erdélyben" [Cemeteries of the Early Middle Ages in Southeastern Transylvania] in *Korunk Évkönyv* [Korunk Yearbook], 1973, pp. 219–228.

209. Horedt, 1982, *op. cit.*, p. 79.

210. *Ibid.*, p. 80.

211. *Ibid.*, p. 81.

212. Horedt, 1982, *op. cit.*, p. 100.

213. *Ibid.*, p. 100.

214. *Ibid.*, p. 102.

215. Ion Nestor, *Revue Roumaine d'Histoire*, 3, 1964, pp. 398–401; *Enzyklopädisches Handbuch zur Ur- und Frühgeschichte Europas*, (Prag: 1966), vol. 1, pp. 159–160; Ion Nestor and Eugenia Zaharia, "Raport preliminar despre săpăturile de la Bratei, jud. Sibiu" [Preliminary Report About the Excavations at Bratei, Sibiu County], in *Materiale şi cercetări arheologice*, 10, 1973, pp. 191–201.

216. Ligia Bârzu, *Continuitatea populaţiei autohtone în Transylvania în secolele IV-V. Cimitirul 1 de la Bratei* [The Continuity of the Autochthonous Population in Transylvania in the 4th to 5th Century. Cemetery 1. at Bratei], (Bucharest: 1973).

217. André Du Nay, 1977; summary of the finds pp. 143–147; a critical discussion pp. 230–231.

218. Further critical discussion by István Bóna, *Archaeológiai Értesítő*, Budapest, 103, 1976; Kurt Horedt, "Die spätrömischen Bestattungen aus Siebenbürgen," in *Studii şi comunicări*. Muzeul Bruckenthal, Sibiu, 21, 1981, 62.

219. Gheorghe Diaconu, "Despre denumirea şi cronologia unor culturi din Dacia romană şi regiunile extracarpatice în mileneul 1 e.n. [About the Designation and the Chronology of Some Cultures in Roman Dacia and in the Transcarpathian Territories During the First Millenium A.D.] in *SCIVA*, 30, 4, 1979, p. 550.

219a. A significant part of the cemetery was destroyed before it could be studied, for a sand-pit (Ligia Bârzu, 1973, p. 9). A severe shortcoming of the description of this cemetery is that it does not indicate in which tomb each of the objects were found; therefore, a horizontal-stratigraphic investigation is not possible. (Horedt, 1982, *op. cit.*, pp. 97–98.) In his recent work, *Siebenbürgen im Frühmittelalter* (Bonn: 1986), published in West Germany, Horedt states that the burial ground of Bratei is clearly Slavic and the assumption that it may be connected with branches of Romanic peoples is incorrect (p. 65).

220. *SCIVA*, 34 (1983), pp. 235–242.

221. Volker Bierbrauer, "Zur chronologischen, soziologischen und regionalen Gliederung des ostgermanischen Fundstoffes des 5. Jahrhunderts in Südosteuropa," in Herwig Wolfram und Falko Daim, *Die Völker an der mittleren und unteren Donau im 5. und 6. Jahrhundert* (Vienna: 1980), p. 132.

222. *Ibid.*, pp. 134–135.

223. *Ibid.*, p. 139.

224. István Kovács, *A marosszentannai népvándorláskori temető. Dolgozatok az Erdélyi Nemzeti Múzeum érem- és régiségtárából*, Kolozsvár. Travaux de la Section numismatique et archéologique du Musée National de Transylvanie, 3, 1912, pp. 250–367.

225. Bierbrauer, 1980, *op. cit.*, p. 133.

226. *Ibid.*, p. 134.

227. Horedt, 1982, *op. cit.*, p. 111.

228. *Ibid.*, p. 208, list 6.

362   Ethnic Continuity in the Carpatho-Danubian Area

229. Protase, 1966, op. cit., p. 117.
230. Horedt, 1982, p. 117.
231. Valuable information on the Sarmatians in Mihály Párducz, Denkmäler der Sarmatenzeit in Ungarn, (Budapest: 1950) vols. 3, Archaeologica Hungarica, 30; Gheorghe Bichir, Les Sarmates sur le territoire de la Roumanie, Actes VIIIᵉ Congr., Belgrade 1971, pp. 275–285; E. Dörner, "Dacii şi Sarmaţii în secolele II-III e.n. în vestul României," Apulum, 9, 1971.
232. The Jaziges, a branch of Sarmatian equestrian nomads, settled in the first decades of our era in the Hungarian Plain. In the first century A.D. their own settlement areas were in the northern part of the Hungarian Plain as well as in the northern part of the territory between the Danube and the Tisza. In the period of the conquest of Dacia the Jaziges lived in the part of the Banat which had not been conquered by the Romans and they were allied with the Romans in wars against the Dacians. Together with the Roxolans they staged attacks in 117 against the Roman borders. The Roxolans, another branch of the Sarmatians, lived on the territory of contemporary Muntenia.
233. Horedt, 1982, op. cit., pp. 104–105.
234. More information on the Carpic material culture in chapter "The Assumed Romanization in Moldavia."
235. Cf., Horedt, 1982, p. 84.
236. Răhău (Rehó) and Cicău (Csákó) in Alba County, Horedt, 1982, p. 85.
237. Horedt, 1982, pp. 86–87; Horedt, "Die spätrömischen Siedlungen in Siebenbürgen," 1979, op. cit., pp. 69–72.
238. Horedt, 1982, p. 172.
239. Ibid., p. 174.
240. Ibid., p. 183.
241. Ibid., p. 182.
242. Ibid.
243. Horedt, 1982, op. cit., p. 176; cf. also Protase, 1966, op. cit., p. 192, Table 3.
244. Constantin Preda, "Circulaţia monedelor romane postaureliene în Dacia [The Circulation of Roman Coins from the Period After Aurelian in Dacia], in SCIVA, Bucharest 1975, p. 441.
245. Constantin Preda and Florentina Preda, "Contribuţia cercetărilor arheologice la cunoaşterea istoriei vechi a României" [The Contribution of the Archaeological Investigations to the Knowledge of the Old History of Romania], in Revista de Istorie, vol. 33, no. 7–8, 1980, p. 1274. In note 223, the authors refer to the following works: Constantin Preda, SCIVA, 26, 1975, 4, pp. 441–485; Kurt Horedt, Contribuţii la istoria Transilvaniei în sec. IV-XIII, (Bucharest: 1958); and Dumitru Protase, Problema continuităţii, op. cit., 1966. See also Constantin Preda, "Circulaţia monedelor bizantine în regiunea carpato-dunăreană" in SCIV, 23, 1972, no. 3, pp. 375–415 and Monedele geto-dacilor, (Bucharest: 1973). Information of the circulation of coins are provided by Michael Crawford in The Journal of Roman Studies, 67 (1977), pp. 117–

124 and in *Studii și Cercetări de Numismatică*, 7 (1980), p. 51 *et. seq.*; see also the short reply of Constantin Preda in *Dacia*, no. 24 (1980), pp. 127–131.

246. Protase, 1966, *op. cit.*, p. 195.

247. Horedt, 1982, p. 179.

248. Nicolae Gudea, "Cîteva observații și note critice cu specială privire la partea istorică a monografiei *Etnogeneza românilor* de Ion I. Russu." [Some Remarks and Critical Notes with Special Reference to the Historical Part of Etnogeneza românilor by Ion I. Russu], in *Acta Musei Napocensis*, XX, 1983, p. 909.

249. Bolin, *Fynden av romerska mynt*, 1926, *op. cit.*, pp. 186, 296.

250. Gabler, in *Römer und Germanen*, 1975, p. 96, Table I, and p. 97, Fig. 4 (map).

251. Protase, 1966, *op. cit.*, p. 193, Fig. 66.

252. Preda, 1975, *op. cit.*, p. 446, Fig. 1.

253. Horedt, 1982, *op. cit.*, p 173, Fig. 66.

254. Protase, 1966, *op. cit.*, p. 197.

255. Horedt, 1982, *op. cit.*, pp. 73–82.

256. Protase, 1966, *op. cit.*, p. 196. *Cf.*, also Horedt, 1982, p. 179.

257. Mihail Macrea, "Monedele și părăsirea Daciei" [The Coins and the Abandonment of Dacia] in *Anuarul Institutului de Studii Clasice*, Cluj, 3, 1936–1940, pp. 300–302, Cluj; quoted by Preda, 1975, *op. cit.*, p. 453.

258. Protase, 1966, p. 198, with two reservations, however: "If we exclude the import of these hoards from the empire into the Daco-Roman territories, and if we disregard some doubts about the integrity and unity of some of them . . ." (p. 197).

259. Preda, 1975, *op. cit.*, p. 453, referring to Macrea, "Monedele și părăsirea Daciei" [The Coins and the Abandonment of Dacia], in *Anuarul Institutului de Studii Clasice*, 3, 1936–1940, pp. 300–302, Cluj.

260. *Ibid.*

261. Horedt, 1982, p. 178.

262. *Ibid.*

263. István Bóna, "Az avar uralom századai" [The Centuries of the Avar Domination], in *Erdély története* [The History of Transylvania], (Budapest: 1986), p. 169.

264. Horedt, 1982, p. 180.

265. *Cf.*, for example, Horedt, 1978, *op. cit.*, p. 215.

266. Protase, 1966, *op. cit.*, p. 184; Preda, 1975, *op. cit.*, p. 443. The low intensity of circulation of coins in the time of the economic crisis in the empire would not prevent this, since hoards usually contain money accumulated during longer periods of time.

267. András Mócsy, *Gesellschaft und Romanisation in der römischen Provinz Moesia Superior*, (Budapest: 1970), p. 259.

268. Kurt Horedt, "Wandervölker und Romanen im 5. bis 6. Jahrhundert in Siebenbürgen," in: Herwig Wolfram, Falko Daim (eds.), *Die Völker an der mittleren und unteren Donau im fünften und sechsten Jahrhundert*, (Vienna: 1980), p. 118.

269. Kurt Horedt, *Siebenbürgen im Frühmittelalter* (Bonn: 1986), p. 53.

270. Horedt, *Contribuţii la istoria Transilvaniei în secolele IV-XIII* (Bucharest: 1958); and Horedt, *Untersuchungen zur Frühgeschichte Siebenbürgens,* (Bucharest: 1958); for supplements have been used the summary of C. Preda: *SCIV,* 23, 1972, and C. Preda: *SCIVA,* 26, 1975; *cf.* Horedt, *Siebenbürgen im Frühmittelalter,* 1986, note 82.

271. *Ibid.*

272. Horedt, *Siebenbürgen im Frühmittelalter,* 1986, p. 53.

273. *Ibid.,* p. 97.

274. *Ibid.,* p. 98.

275. *Ibid.*

276. Horedt, 1982, *op. cit.,* p. 181.

277. References to the literature are found in *Istoria Rominiei,* 1960; E. Lozovan, 1959–62; D. Protase, 1966; K. Horedt, 1982; M. Rusu, 1983–84.

278. Eugen Lozovan, "Aux origines du christianisme Daco-Scythique," in *Geschichte der Hunnen,* by Franz Altheim, 1959–1962, pp. 146–165.

279. Lozovan, 1959–62, *op. cit.,* p. 165.

280. *Istoria României,* vol. I, red. C. Daicoviciu *et al.* (Bucharest: 1960) p. 632.

281. Dumitru Protase, *Problema continuităţii,* 1966, *op. cit.,* p. 141.

282. Kurt Horedt, *Siebenbürgen in spätrömischer Zeit* (Bucharest: 1982), pp. 163–171.

283. Mircea Rusu, "Paleocreştinismul nord-Dunărean şi etnogeneza românilor" [Early Christianity North of the Danube and the Ethnogenesis of the Romanians], in *Anuarul institutului de istorie şi arheologie Cluj-Napoca,* XXVI, 1983–1984, pp. 35–81 and 51, 57.

284. *Ibid.,* p. 40. The towns: Dierna (Orsova), Tibiscum (Jupa, a village), Ulpia Traiana (Sarmizegethusa / Grădişte), Apulum (Alba Iulia), Potaissa (Turda), Napoca (Cluj), and Porolissum (Moigrad). The castra: Mehadia, Gilău, Bologa, Gherla, Românaşi.

285. *Ibid.,* p. 40.

286. Horedt, 1982, *op. cit.,* p. 167. On the objects of Christian character, see also Emilian Popescu, *Inscripţiile greceşti şi latine din secolele IV-XIII descoperite în România, op. cit.,* 1976. An earlier excellent analysis is presented by Ion I. Russu, *Materiale arheologice paleocreştine în Transilvania.* Contribuţii la istoria creş nismului daco-român. *Studii Teologice,* 10, 1958.

287. Horedt, 1982, pp. 218–219, Fundliste B and C.

288. *Ibid.*

289. *Ibid.,* p. 170.

290. *Ibid.*

291. Mircea Rusu, 1983–1984, *op. cit.,* p. 41.

292. *CIL,* III, 1617.

293. Kurt Horedt, "Eine lateinische Inschrift des 4. Jahrhunderts aus Siebenbürgen," *Anuarul Institutului de Studii Clasice,* Cluj-Sibiu, vol. IV, Sibiu, 1941, pp. 10–16; Constantin Daicoviciu, "O senzaţionala descoperire arheologica în Transilvania," *Transilvania,* 72, 8, pp. 575–578, 1941 (in *Dacica,*

1969, p. 522); *Istoria Rominiei*, ed. C. Daicoviciu, 1960, vol. I, p. 632; D. Protase, *Problema continuității*, 1966, *op. cit.*, pp. 144–145; K. Horedt, "Die Fundstelle des Donariums von Biertan, Kr. Sibiu," *Anuarul Institutului de Studii Clasice* (Cluj), 4, 1941–1943, pp. 10–16; and in *Dacia*, N.S., XXIII, 1979, pp. 341–346, Bucharest.

294. Horedt, "Die Fundstelle," 1979, p. 343.

295. Horedt, "Eine lateinische Inschrift," 1941.

296. Daicoviciu (1941) argues that even if Zenovius gave his present to a Gothic community, they must have known Latin and they could learn this language only from a Latin-speaking population in the area (Dacica, 1969, p. 525).

297. Horedt, "Eine lateinische Inschrift," 1941, quoted by Protase, 1966, p. 145.

298. *Archaeológiai Értesítő*, III, Budapest, pp. 252–258, quoted by Protase, 1966, p. 145.

299. Hadrian Daicoviciu, "Ftnogeneza românilor," in *Națiunea română* (Bucharest: 1984), p. 155.

300. István Bóna, in *Erdély története* [The History of Transylvania], *op. cit.*, p. 128.

301. Mircea Rusu, 1983–1984, *op. cit.*, p. 51.

302. *Fontes Historiae Dacoromanae*, vol. II, p. 174. The original Latin text reads as follows: "Inveniuntur autem lapides isti in interiore barbarie Scytharum. Scythiam vero soliti sunt veteres appellare cunctam septemtrionalem plagam, ubi sunt Gothi et Dauni, Venni quoque et Arii usque ad Germanorum Amazonumque regionem."

303. Mircea Rusu, 1983–1984, *op. cit.*, p. 41.

304. Horedt, 1982, *op. cit.*, pp. 151–152.

305. *Ibid.*

308. Walter Pohl, "Die Gepiden und die Gentes an der mittleren Donau nach dem Zerfall des Attilareiches," in *Die Völker an der mittleren und unteren Donau*, 1980, *op. cit.*, p. 270. Literature on the treasure-trove of Szilágysomlyó: Nándor Fettich, "Der zweite Schatz von Szilágysomlyó," in *Arch. Hung.* VIII, Budapest 1932; the treasure-trove of Pietroasa: Radu Harhoiu, *The Treasure from Pietroasa, Romania* (Oxford: 1977). István Bóna, contrary to Horedt and Protase attributed the treasure-trove of Cluj-Someșeni to the Gepidae; K. Horedt und D. Protase, "Ein völkerwanderungszeitlicher Schatzfund aus Cluj-Someșeni, in *Germania* 48, 1970, pp. 89–98.

309. Joachim Werner, "Namensring und Siegelring aus dem gepidischen Fürstengrab von Apahida (Siebenbürgen)," in *Kölner Jahrbuch für Vor- und Frühgeschichte*, 9, 1967/1968. Literature of Apahida I: Henrik Finály, "Der Grabfund von Apahida," in *Ungarische Revue* 1890; Apahida II: K. Horedt and D. Protase, "Das zweite Fürstengrab von Apahida," in *Germania* 50, 1972; Apahida III: Ştefan Matei, "Al treilea mormînt princiar de la Apahida," in *Acta Musei Napocensis*, 19, 1982.

366   Ethnic Continuity in the Carpatho-Danubian Area

310. Valuable data are provided by István Bóna, in *Erdély története, op. cit.*, vol. I, pp. 118–120.

311. On the Goths, the following works provide valuable information: Jordanes (sixth century) *Getica* [The History of the Goths], written in 551, ed. Th. Mommsen, *Monumenta Germaniae Historica*, Hannover 1826 *et. seq.;* Prokopius (sixth century) *Bellum Gothicum*, ed. by J. Haury and G. Wirth (Lipsiae: 1963); Procopius Caesariensis, *De Bello Gothico*, ed. Bonn, *Corpus Scriptorum Historiae Byzantinae* (CSB), ed. Teubner (1905); with English translation in the *Leeb Classical Library*; N. Wagner, *Getica. Untersuchungen zum Leben des Iordanes und zur frühen Geschichte der Goten* (Berlin: 1967); Herwig Wolfram, *Geschichte der Goten* (München: 1979); E. Beninger, *Der westgotisch-alanische Zug nach Mitteleuropa* (Leipzig: 1931); József Hampel, *Altertümer des frühen Mittelalters in Ungarn*, I–III, (Braunschweig: 1905); Ludwig Schmidt, *Die Ostgermanen* (München: 1941); E. A. Thompson, *The Visigoths in the Time of Ulfila* (Oxford: 1966); R. Hachmann, *Die Goten und Skandinavien* (Berlin: 1970).

312. As 300, 325, or only after 376; *cf.* Kurt Horedt, "Wandervölker und Romanen im 5. bis 6. Jahrhundert in Siebenbürgen," in H. Wolfram and F. Daim, *Die Völker and der mittleren und unteren Donau, op. cit.*, p. 117.

313. There are a vast material of literature on the Gepidae: Dezső Csallány, *Archäologische Denkmäler der Gepiden im Mitteldonaubecken (454–568 A.D.), Archaeologica Hungarica 38*, (Budapest: 1961); István Bóna, *Der Anbruch des Mittelalters. Gepiden und Langobarden im Karpatenbecken* (Budapest: 1976); Constantin .C. Diculescu, *Die Gepiden* (Leipzig: 1922); Kurt Horedt, *Untersuchungen zur Frühgeschichte Siebenbürgens* (Bucharest: 1958); Walter Pohl, "Die Gepiden und die Gentes an der mittleren Donau nach dem Zerfall des Attilareiches," in: Herwig Wolfram and Falko Daim, (reds.), *Die Völker an der mittleren und unteren Donau im fünften und sechsten Jahrhundert* (Wien: 1980).

314. Procopius Caesariensis, *Bellum Gothicum, op. cit.*

315. Jordanes, *Getica*, 33.

316. Theophylaktos Simokatta, *Historiae*, VIII, 3; *cf. Fontes Historiae Dacoromanae*, II, 1970, p. 548.

317. Horedt, "Germanen und Romanen in Siebenbürgen," in *Zeitschrift für Siebenbürgische Landeskunde*, 6 (77) Jahrgang, Heft 2/83, p. 176.

318. A list of the settlements is given by Horedt, in *Siebenbürgen im Frühmittelalter, op. cit.*, notes 5, 32, 53, 66, 68, 69, 82, 88, and 89.

319. *Ibid.*

320. On the excavations at Moreşti an excellent and detailed data are provided in: Kurt Horedt, *Moreşti.Grabungen in einer vor- und frühgeschichtlichen Siedlung in Siebenbürgen*, vol. 1 (Bucharest: 1979). For the second phase of the Moreşti culture (Csüged and Csitfalva) see, Kurt Horedt, *Moreşti, vol.2. Grabungen in einer mittelalterlichen Siedlung in Siebenbürgen*, (Bonn: 1984). Between the two phases there are a gap of several centuries. Further literature of Moreşti: Dorin Popescu, "Das gepidische Gräberfeld von Moreşti," *Dacia* 18, 1974, pp. 189–238.

321. The ornamentations are weakly stamped with a wooden implement or die prior to firing. These parts are raised with a matte luster placed over the rough surface. This kind of ceramic appears suddenly during the last two decades of the fourth century. According to recent research this kind of ceramic is to be linked to the Germanic tribes.

322. Horedt, *Moreşti* 1979, op. cit., p. 70.

323. Bóna, *Erdély története, op. cit.*, p. 144.

324. *Ibid.*, p. 163.

325. *Ibid.*, p. 143.

326. Walter Pohl, "Die Gepiden und die Gentes," *op. cit.*, p. 248.

327. Gheorghe Diaconu, in *Dicţionar de istorie veche a României. (Paleoliticsec.X)* [Dictionary of Ancient History of Romania], ed by Dionisie M. Pippidi (Bucharest: 1976) p. 544. It is asserted that Romanic elements were living together with the Gepidae in Transylvania in the fifth and sixth centuries (*Istoria Rominiei*, ed. C. Daicoviciu, vol. I. 1960, p. 711). See further: Constantin Preda and Florentina Preda, 1980, p. 1275.

328. Radu Harhoiu, in *Dicţionar de istorie veche a României, op. cit.*, p. 295.

329. Kurt Horedt, "Das archäologische Bild der romanischen Elemente nach der Räumung Daziens," in *Dacoromania*, I, Jahrbuch für östliche Latinität, Freiburg 1973, p. 144.

330. The argument based on the lack of Gepidic dwelling places on the Hungarian Plain, in contrast to Transylvania, has proven false: such dwelling places have been found in Hungary.

331. Horedt, *Dacoromania* I, 1973, p. 145. It must be remembered, however, that in the current trend of the Romanian historiography the scholar is committed to find "local people," "autochthons," Romans, among the old Germanic population. It is not surprising that even prominent Romanian historians must follow the official prescriptions for writing history.

332. Kurt Horedt, "Germanen und Romanen in Siebenbürgen. Bemerkungen zu einer Besprechung," in *Zeitschrift für Siebenbürgische Landeskunde*, Heft 2/83, p. 174.

333. *Ibid.*, p. 175.

334. Horedt, *Siebenbürgen im Frühmittelalter*, 1986, op. cit. p. 66.

335. Horedt, *Moreşti*, 1979, op. cit., p. 146.

336. István Bóna, "Gepiden an der Theiss—Gepiden in Siebenbürgen", in *Acta Archaeologica Acad. Scient. Hung.* 31, 1979. The reply of Horedt, in *Acta. Arch Acad. Scient. Hung.* 33, 1981, pp. 377–381.

337. Dorin Popescu, "Das gepidische Graberfeld von Moreşti," *Dacia* XVIII, 1974, pp. 189–238.

338. Bóna, "Gepiden an der Theiss ," *op. cit.*, 1979, p. 38.

339. *Ibid.*, p. 46.

340. Horedt, *Moreşti*, 1979, p. 51.

341. Alexandru Rosetti, *Istoria limbii române de la origini până în secolul al XVII-lea* (Bucharest: 1968), p. 242.

342. The exact location of the Nedao River continues to be unknown; opinions on this subject vary: Wolfram, *Goten*, p. 321; Horedt, "Wandervölker

und Romanen," *op. cit.*, p. 118, *cf.*, W. Pohl, "Die Gepiden und die Gentes" in H. Wolfram and F. Daim (eds.), *Die Völker an der mittleren und unteren Donau*, *op. cit.* p. 260, note 62. According to a hypothesis the Nedao River could be the modern Kapos River, a right-side affluent of the Danube (Hermann Schreiben, *I goti*, 1981, p. 192.).

343. W. Pohl, "Die Gepiden und die Gentes," *op. cit.*, p. 264.

344. Hunnic archaeological remnants in Transylvania have been found in Tăuteu (Tóti, Bihar County) and possibly at Moigrad (Mojgrád, Sălaj County). Literature on the Huns: Franz Altheim, *Geschichte der Hunnen*, (Berlin: 1959–1962); Otto Maenchen-Helfen, *The World of the Huns*, (Berkeley: 1973); András Alföldi, *Funde der Hunnenzeit und ihre ethnische Sonderung* (Budapest: 1932); Joachim Werner, *Beiträge zur Archäologie des Attila-Reiches*, (München: 1956).

345. Ludwig Schmidt, *Die Ostgermanen*, (München: 1941), pp. 584–585.

346. For the Avar burial graves in Transylvania see Kurt Horedt, "Die frühgeschichtliche Siedlungslandschaft Siebenbürgens," in *Aluta*, 1980, p. 85.

347. Valuable data on the Avars are provided in: Dezső Csallány, *Archäologische Denkmäler der Awarenzeit in Mitteleuropa. Schrifttum und Fundorte*, (Budapest: 1956); Kurt Horedt, "Avarii în Transilvania," in *SCIV*, 7, 1956; István Bóna, "Die Awaren. Ein asiatisches Reitervolk an der mittleren Donau," in *Awaren in Europa*, (Frankfurt am Main–Nürnberg: 1985); A. Avenarius, *Die Awaren in Europa*, (Bratislava: 1974); Nándor Fettich, "Dunapentelei avar sírleletek" [Avar Cemeteries at Dunapentele], in *Archaeologica Hungarica*, XVIII, Budapest 1936; *Cemeteries of the Avar Period (567–829) in Hungary*, vol. I, É. Garam, I. Kovrig, J. Gy. Szabó, Gy. Török, *Avar Finds in the Hungarian National Museum* (Budapest: 1975); *Avar Cemeteries in Baranya County*, vol. II, A. Kiss (Budapest: 1977).

348. *Magyarország története*, [The History of Hungary], *op. cit.*, 1984, p. 343.

349. More detailed data in György Györffy, *Tanulmányok a magyar állam eredetéről*, [Studies on the Origin of the Hungarian State], (Budapest: 1959).

350. Procopius (or Prokopios Caesarea), *Bellum Gothicum*, 2, 15, 1; 3, 35, 13–22; 8, 25, ed. by J. Haury-G. Wirth (Lipsae: 1963); Jordanes, *Romana et Getica*, V, 35, ed. by Theodor Mommsen (Berlin: 1882); Zdenek Vaňá, *Einführung in die Frühgeschichte der Slawen* (Neumünster: 1970); Francis Dvornik, *Les Slaves. Histoire et civilisation de l'Antiquité aux débuts de l'époque contemporaine* (Paris: 1970); Marija Gimbutas, *The Slavs* (London: 1971); A. P. Vlasto, *The Entry of the Slavs into Christendom. An Introduction of the Medieval History of the Slavs* (Cambridge: 1970);

351. Jordanes, V, 35, *Romana et Getica, op. cit.*

352. Procopius, *Bellum Gothicum, op. cit.*

353. In Serbia the village Negrişori, in Montenegro the two highest mountains, Visitor and Durmitor. There are several Romanian place names in the mountainous area between Niš and Sofia (G. Weigand, *XIII. Jahresbericht des Instituts für rumänische Sprache* [Leipzig: 1908], p. 40 *et. seq.*).

354. Dimitri Obolensky, *The Byzantine Commonwealth, op. cit.*, p. 156.

355. Konstantin Josef Jireček, *Die Heerstrasse von Belgrad nach Constantinopel und die Balkanpässe*, (Prag: 1877), p. 70.

356. Kurt Horedt, "Germanen und Romanen in Siebenbürgen. Bemerkungen zu einer Besprechung," in *Zeitschrift für Siebenbürgische Landeskunde*, 6 (77) Jahrgang, Heft 2/83, pp. 171–176.

357. Georges Sp. Radojičić, "La date de la conversion des Serbes," in *Byzantion* 22 (1952), pp. 253–256.

358. Horedt, *Siebenbürgen im Frühmittelalter, op. cit.*, p. 95.

359. Bóna, *Erdély története, op. cit.*, I, p. 182.

360. *Ibid.*

361. Horedt, *Siebenbürgen im Frühmittelalter*, p. 59.

362. Horedt, *Apulum*, 18, 1980, p. 151.

363. Horedt, "Die Brandgräberfelder der Mediaşgruppe aus dem 7. - 9. Jahrhundert in Siebenbürgen," in *Zeitschrift für Archäologie*, 10, Berlin 1976, pp. 35–57.

364. *Ibid.*, p. 36.

365. *Ibid.*, p. 38.

366. *Ibid.*, p. 41.

367. Dezső Csallány, *Archäologische Denkmäler der Awarenzeit*, 1956, *op. cit.*, pp. 272–279, 273, Table 6:1.

368. Horedt, *Siebenbürgen im Frühmittelalter*, 1986, *op. cit.*, p. 101.

369. Horedt, "Die Brandgräber," 1976, *op. cit.*, p. 46.

370. Dumitru Tudor, "Romanizarea Munteniei," [The Romanization of Wallachia], *Apulum* XII, 1974, p. 116; see further Dan Gh. Teodor, *Teritoriul est-carpatic în veacurile V-XI e.n.*, [The Territory East of the Carpathians in the Fifth to Eleventh Centuries A.D.], (Iaşi: 1978).

371. *Dicţionar de istorie veche a României*, [Encyclopaedia of the Ancient History of Romania], ed. by Dionisie M. Pippidi (Bucharest: 1976), p. 281.

372. Nicolae Gostar, "Vechimea elementului roman la răsărit de Carpaţi," [The Antiquity of the Roman Element East of the Carpathians] in the Romanian Communist Party's ideological and official journal, the *Era Socialistă*, 1979, 6, p. 34.

373. Dan Gh. Teodor, "Romanitatea în Moldova în a doua jumătate a milenului I," [The Roman Population in Moldavia in the Second Half of the First Millennium], in *Era Socialistă*, 1981, 11, p. 36. See further Dan Gh. Teodor, *Teritoriul est-carpatic, op. cit.*

374. Dumitru Tudor, "Romanizarea Munteniei," 1974, *op. cit.*, p. 116; see further Eugenia Zaharia, "Données sur l'archéologie des IVe–XIe siècles sur le territoire de la Roumanie. La culture Bratei et la culture Dridu," in *Dacia*, XV (1971), pp. 286–287.

375. *Istoria României*, ed. C. Daicoviciu, vol. I, 1960, p. 519.

376. *Cf.*, for example, Dumitru Tudor, "Preuves archéologiques attestant la continuité de la domination romaine au nord du Danube après l'abandon de Dacie sous Aurelien (IIIe–Ve siècles)," *Dacoromania* I, 1973, pp. 149–161.

377. *Fontes Historiae Dacoromanae*, vol. II, 1970, pp. 379, 387.

378. Gheorghe Bichir, "Date noi cu privire la romanizarea Munteniei," [New Data About the Romanization of Wallachia], *SCIVA* 29, 3 (1978), p. 385.

379. *Ibid.*, p. 388.

380. *Ibid.*, p. 390.

381. Petre Roman, Suzana Dolinescu-Ferche, "Cercetările de la Ipoteşti (jud. Olt). (Observaţii asupra culturii materiale autohtone din secolul al VI-lea e.n. în Muntenia)." [Researches at Ipoteşti, Olt County. Remarks About the Autochthonous Material Culture of the Sixth Century A.D. in Wallachia], in *SCIVA*, 29, 1, 1978, p. 88.

382. Ptolemaios (Ptolemaeus) Claudius, *Geografiae* III,10,7; *cf.*, *Fontes ad historiam Dacoromaniae pertinentes*, I, (Bucharest: 1964), p. 554. The English translation of Ptolemy's work by E.L. Stevensen (New York: 1932).

383. *Fontes*, I, p. 555, referring to the *Register of Hunt*.

384. *Istoria României*, C. Daicovici (ed.), 1960, vol. I, p. 518.

385. Gheorghe Bichir, *Cultura carpică* [The Carpic Culture], (Bucharest: 1973), p. 153.

386. *Ibid.*, p. 150.

387. *Ibid.*, p. 181.

388. "All the Carps were moved into our territory. The entire Carp population was transferred to Romania." [Roman Empire].

389. Bichir, 1973, *op. cit.*, 70.

390. *Ibid.*, p. 67; the picture on p. 259.

391. *Ibid.*, p. 81.

392. *Ibid.*, p. 79, 83 *et seq.*

393. *Ibid.*, p. 175.

394. *Ibid.*, pp. 127–132.

395. *Ibid.*

396. Silviu Sanie, *Civilizaţia romană la est de Carpaţi şi romanitatea pe teritoriul Moldovei (sec. II. î.e.n.–III. e.n.)* [The Roman Civilization East of the Carpathians and the Romans in the Territory of Moldavia Second Century B.C.–Third Century A.D.], (Iaşi: 1981), p. 93.

397. *Ibid.*, p. 94.

398. *Ibid.*, p. 96.

399. Dan Gh. Teodor, *Continuitatea populaţiei autohtone la est de Carpaţi în secolele VI–XI e.n.*, [The Continuity of the Autochthonous Population East of the Carpathians in the 6th–11th Centuries A.D.], (Iaşi: 1984), pp. 16–17 (with illustrations).

400. Teodor, 1978, *op. cit.*, p. 13.

401. *Ibid.*, p. 17.

402. *Ibid.*, p. 18.

403. *Ibid.*, p. 19.

404. *Ibid.*, p. 21.

405. *Ibid.*, p. 23.

406. *Ibid.*, p. 132.

407. *Ibid.*, pp. 30–31.

408. *Ibid.*, p. 31.

409. *Ibid.*

410. *Istoria României*, ed. C. Daicoviciu, vol. I, 1960, p. 737.

411. Joachim Werner, "Slawische Bügelfibeln des 7. Jahrhunderts," in: *Reinecke Festschrift*, ed. by Gustav Behrens and Joachim Werner, (Mainz: 1950), pp. 150–172.

412. Teodor, 1978, *op. cit.*, p. 43.

413. This is the designation of a Slavic culture found in the region between the middle course of the Dnieper, Rosî and Teasmin rivers and the upper course of the southern Bug (Teodor, 1978, p. 43; referring to articles by D.T. Berezovetz in *Kratkie Soobscenija Institut Arheologii*, Kiev, and in *Materialy i Issledovanija pe Arheologii S.S.S.R*, Moscow, and several other scholars in the Soviet Union).

414. Teodor, 1978, p. 48.

415. *Ibid.*

416. *Ibid.*

417. *Ibid.*, p. 49.

418. *Ibid.*, p. 48.

419. Protase, *Autohtonii în Dacia*, 1980, *op. cit.*, p. 12, note. The note continues as follows: "We use ['"Daco-Roman'"] for its conciseness ("*pentru conciziunea lui*"). Usually, Daco-Roman is said to designate the population of the Romanized Dacians, mixed with the Roman colonists." A similar note is given in Protase, 1976, p. 11, note 2.

420. Silviu Sanie, 1981, *op. cit.*, p. 226.

421. Bichir, 1973, *op. cit.*, p. 178.

422. Sanie, 1981, p. 41.

423. Radu Harhoiu, "Die Kontinuität im Gebiet des heutigen Kumänien," in: H. Wolfram and F. Daim, *Die Völker an der mittleren und unteren Donau*, 1980, *op. cit.*, p. 108.

424. Teodor, 1978, p. 30.

425. *Ibid.*, pp. 40 41: "Unfortunately, it is not yet possible to separate with sufficient certainty the objects found in these dwelling places, and it is thus not possible to state which elements are typical of the autochthons and which are typical of the Slavs."

426. *Ibid.*, p. 17.

427. Dan Gh. Teodor, *Teritoriul est-carpatic în veacurile V–XI e.n. Contribuții arheologice și istorice în problema formării poporului român* [The East Carpathian Territory in the 5th–11th Centuries A.D. Archaeological and Historical Contributions to the Question of the Romanian People's Formation], (Iași: 1978).

428. G. Mihăilă, *Studii de lexicologie și istorie a lingvisticii românești* [Studies of Lexicology and of the History of Romanian Linguistics], (Bucharest: 1973), p. 26. In this same part of Romania, that is, in most of Moldavia, the ancient place names of Slavic origin show an Ukrainian sound pattern, while they otherwise in Romania are mainly of a South Slavic type.

429. Teodor, 1978, *op. cit.*, pp. 48–49.

430. These examples are given by Günter Reichenkron, who refers to Ivan Popović, Petar Skok and Anton Mayer. *Cf.*, G. Reichenkron, "Das Ostromanische," in *Völker und Kulturen Südosteuropas* (München: 1959), p. 158.

431. Ivan Popović, Geschichte der serbokroatischen Sprache, (Wiesbaden: 1960), p. 154.

432. Reichenkron, "Das Ostromanische," op. cit., p. 158.

433. Alexandru Rosetti, Istoria limbii române (Bucharest: 1968), p. 329.

434. Istoria României, ed. C. Daicoviciu, vol. I, (Bucharest: 1960), p. 741.

435. Teodor, 1978, op. cit., p. 33.

436. Dumitru Berciu, Dacoromania (Archaeologia Mundi), (Roma: 1976), p. 148.

437. Ioan Pătruţ, Studii de limba română şi de slavistică [Studies of the Romanian Language and Slavistics], (Cluj: 1974), p. 117. Cf., also, for example, G. Mihăilă, Studii de lexicologie, 1973, op. cit., p. 27; Emil Petrovici, Studii de dialectologie şi toponimie [Studies of Dialectology and Toponymy] (Bucharest: 1970), p. 245; Ion Coteanu, Structura şi evoluţia limbii române (de la origini pînă la 1860) [The Structure and the Evolution of the Romanian Language] (Bucharest: 1981), p. 73.

438. A.P. Vlasto, The Entry of the Slavs into Christendom, 1970, op. cit., p. 308.

439. Gheorghe Diaconu, "Despre denumirea şi cronologia unor culturi din Dacia romană şi regiunile extracarpatice în mileniul I e.n." [About the Designation and Chronology of Some Cultures in Roman Dacia and the Transcarpathian Regions in the First Millennium A.D.] in SCIV, 30, 4, 1979, p. 547.

440. Ibid., p. 550.

441. Ibid., p. 551.

442. Ibid., pp. 551–552.

443. Ibid., pp. 552–553.

444. Edited by Miron Constantinescu et al., 1969, p. 106.

445. Eugenia Zaharia, Săpăturile de la Dridu [The Excavations at Dridu] (Bucharest: 1967). The work of E. Zaharia was published only after Daicoviciu's death, who refuted the Dridu culture. Bulgarian scholars consider the Dridu culture as Bulgaro-Slavic (J. A. Bojilov, "Kultura Dridu i pŭrvoto bulgarskoto carstvo", in Istoričeski pregled 26, 1970, pp. 115–124.).

446. Petre Diaconu–Dumitru Vîlceanu, "Păcuiul lui Soare" [The Name of a Danubian Island], vol. I, Cetatea bizantină (Bucharest: 1972), p. 129.

447. Constantin Daicoviciu, Dacica, Cluj, 1969, p. 552. ("Der Ursprung des rumänischen Volkes im Lichte der neuesten Forschungen und Ausgrabungen," originally published in Forschungen zur Volks-und Landeskunde, Hermannstadt 1967, 10, 2, pp. 5–19). Daicoviciu attempted to oppose to the bias of contemporary Romanian historiographers which becomes ever more remote from scientific requirements. See in particular "Corrigenda" in Acta Musei Napocensis, X 1973, p. 611 et.seq. See further C. Daicoviciu, "Izvoare istorice greşit interpretate" [Misinterpretation of historical sources], in Tribuna (Cluj), 1970, July, August, September, October, November and December.

448. Emperor Constantine VII Porphyrogenitus, De administrando imperio, Greek text ed. by Gyula Moravcsik (Budapest: 1949); a new critical edition in English translation by R.J. Jenkins (Dumbarton Oaks: 1967). Relating to

the texts of Porphyrogenitus referring to the Hungarians, see György Györffy, *A magyarok elődeiről és a honfoglalásról* [About the Ancestors of the Hungarians and About the Conquest], 2nd edition (Budapest: 1975).

449. Valuable informations on the Bulgars are provided in: Gantscho Tzenoff, *Geschichte der Bulgaren und der anderen Südslawen: Von der römischen Eroberung der Balkanhalbinsel an bis zum Ende des neunten Jahrhunderts* (Berlin and Leipzig: 1935); Steven Runciman, *A History of the First Bulgarian Empire* (London: 1930); Ivan Dujčev, "Protobulgares et Slaves," *Annales de l'Institut Kondakov*, Prague, X, 1938, pp. 145–154; Christian Gérard, *Les Bulgares de la Volga et les Slaves du Danube* (Paris: 1939); Robert Lee Wolff, "The Second Bulgarian Empire. Its Origin and History," *Speculum*, XXIV, 1949, pp. 167–206.

450. Imre Boba, *Nomads, Northmen and Slavs. Eastern Europe in the Ninth Century*, (Mouton–The Hague: 1967), p. 77.

451. *Annales Fuldenses*, ed. Friedrich Kurze in: *Mon. Germ. hist. Script. rer. Germ. in usum scholarum* 7, (Berolini: 1891). a. 892.

452. *Magyarország története* [The History of Hungary], vol. I, 1984, p. 371. The Blandiana-B of the first half of the tenth century show connection to the Bijelo Brdo culture.

453. Literature: note 449.

454. Magyar is the name which the Hungarians use to denote themselves. One should speak of Hungarians only from the time of the conquest in the Carpathian Basin.

455. For more detail: *Magyarország története*, 1984, *op. cit.*, vol. I, pp. 326–327.

456. Gyula László, *A kettős honfoglalás* [The Dual Conquest], (Budapest: 1978), p. 92; "A kettős honfoglalásról" [About the Dual Conquest], in *Archaeológiai Értesítő*, Budapest, 1970, 2, 97, pp. 161–190.

457. Samu Szádeczky-Kardoss, "Hitvalló Theophanes az avarokról," [The Confessor Theophanes About the Avars], in: *Antik Tanulmányok*, Budapest, 17 (1970), pp. 121–147; "Kuvrát fiának, Kubernek a története és az avar kori régészeti leletanyag" [The History of Kuvrat's Son Kuber and the Archaeological Material of the Avar Period], in *Antik Tanulmányok*, 15 (1968), pp. 85–87.

458. Horedt, *Siebenbürgen im Frühmittelalter*, 1986, *op. cit.*, p. 176.

459. Gyula Török, "Sopronkőhida IX. századi temetője" [The Ninth Century Cemetery of Sopronkőhida], in: *Fontes Arch. Hung.*, Budapest 1973.

460. István Bóna, "Avar kori települések és Árpád-kori magyar falu a dunaújvárosi Öreghegyen" [Avar Settlements and a Hungarian Village of the Árpád-period at the Öreghegy in Dunaújváros], in: *Fontes Arch. Hung.*, Budapest 1973.

461. György Györffy, *Tanulmányok a magyar állam eredetéről* [Studies on the Origin of the Hungarian State], (Budapest: 1959).

462. Dezső Csallány, in: *Szabolcs Szatmári Szemle*, 1965, pp. 134–148 and *Jósa András Múzeumi Évkönyve*, VIII–IX (1965–66), pp. 33–51; Cf., Gyula László, 1978, *op. cit.*

463. For more detail, see István Bóna, "Az avarok" [The Avars], in *Magyarország története* [The History of Hungary] 1984, I, p. 320, map. no. 25.

464. A fundamental work on the Onogurs: Gyula Moravcsik, "Zur Geschichte der Onoguren" in *Ungarische Jahrbücher*, 10, 1930, pp. 53 *et seq.*

465. The name Székely is used exclusively in Hungarian while in international usage, especially in German, Szekler or Sekler is common. From the vast literature about the origin of the Székelys: Gyula Sebestyén, *A székelyek neve és eredete* [The Name and the Origin of the Székelys], (Budapest: 1897); György Györffy, "A székelyek eredete és településük története" [The Origin of the Székelys and the History of Their Settlements], in *Erdély és népei* [Transylvania and Its Peoples], red. by Elemér Mályusz, (Budapest: 1941); German edition Leipzig 1943.

466. Gyula László–István Rácz, *A nagyszentmiklósi kincs* [The Treasure of Nagyszentmiklós], (Budapest: 1977). A summary about the treasure is given in: J. Banner and I. Jakabffy, *A Közép-Dunamedence régészeti bibliográfiája* [The Archaeological Bibliography of the Middle Danubian Basin], (Budapest: 1954), pp. 445–447; 2, 1961, pp. 200–201. See further S. Szádeczky-Kardoss, *Antik Tanulmányok* [Ancient Studies], 15, 1968, pp. 84–87; Julius Németh, *Die Inschriften des Schatzes von Nagyszentmiklós*, (Budapest: 1932); Gyula László, *Steppenvölker und Germanen*, (Wien, München: 1970).

467. *Magyarország története*, 1984, *op. cit.*, vol. I, p. 344.

468. Originally a nomadic Turkic people originating from Inner Asia, the Khazars built their Khazar Empire on the lower Volga and Don toward the end of the sixth century. The immense Khazar Empire stretched from the Ural Mountains to the steppes of Central Asia and the boundaries of China and comprised various peoples and communities sharing a common language of Turkic origin, Iranians, Bulgars, Finno-Ugrians and others. As of the seventh century the Khazars played an important role in Byzantine politics. In fact, the Byzantines tried to convert them to Christianity. Toward the ninth century the Pechenegs posed a serious threat to the Khazar Empire. In the tenth century the empire disintegrated and its population joined other peoples and became assimilated.

469. Dimitri Obolensky, *The Byzantine Commonwealth. Eastern Europe 500–1453*, (London: 1971), p. 154.

470. Kurt Horedt, "Zur Zeitstellung des Schatzfundes von Sînnicolau Mare (Nagyszentmiklós)," in: *Archäologisches Korrespondenzblatt*, 13, 1983, Heft 4, pp. 503–505; Dezső Csallány range one part of the vessels to the beginning of the eighth century, *Archaeológiai Értesítő*, III, 7–9, 1946–48, p. 361.

471. Joachim Werner, *Der Grabfund von Malaja Pereščepina und Kuvrat, Kagan der Bulgaren* (München: 1984).

472. A list of finds of the Bijelo Brdo culture is provided by Horedt, *Siebenbürgen im Frühmittelalter*, 1986, *op. cit.*, note 275 and 276. Detailed data on the Bijelo Brdo culture are provided in J. Giesler "Untersuchungen zur Chronologie der Bijelo Brdo-Kultur. Ein Beitrag zur Archäologie des 10. und 11. Jahrhunderts im Karpatenbecken," *Praehistorische Zeitschrift* 56, 1981, pp. 3–167.

473. For the excavations of the Zápolya Street (Kolozsvár-Cluj) see, Gyula László, "A Kolozsvár Zápolya utcai temető," *Erdélyi Múzeum*, Kolozsvár, 47, 1942; István Bóna, *Erdély története*, 1986, I, pp. 203–205.

474. Zoltán Székely, "Korai középkori temetők Délkelet-Erdély-ben" [Cemeteries of the Early Middle Ages in Southeastern Transylvania], in *Korunk Évkönyv*, pp. 219–228. A list of tenth century old Hungarian finds in Transylvania is provided by Horedt in *Siebenbürgen im Frühmittelalter*, 1986, note 274. For more detail on this: Bóna, *Erdély története*, 1986, I, pp. 203–217.

475. For the achievements of the year 1964 see, Ştefan Pascu, Mircea Rusu *et al.*, "Cetatea Dăbîca," *Acta Musei Napocensis* (Cluj, later Cluj-Napoca) 5, 1968, pp. 153–202. A critical analysis on this is given by István Bóna, *Archaeológiai Értesítő*, Budapest, 79, 1970.

476. P. Iambor and Şt. Matei, "Cetatea feudală timpurie de la Cluj-Mănăştur" [The Early Feudal Fortress at Cluj-Mănăştur] in *Anuarul Institutului de Istorie şi Arheologie*, Cluj-Napoca, 1975, pp. 291–304. See further Mircea Rusu, "Cetăţile transilvănene din secolele IX–XI şi importanţa lor istorică" [The Transylvanian Fortifications of the 9th–11th Centuries and Their Historical Importance] in *Ziridava*, X, 1978, pp. 159–171.

477. Kurt Horedt, in: *Relations Between the Autochthonous Population and the Migratory Populations on the Territory of Romania*, 1975, *op. cit.*, p. 115.

478. Horedt, *Siebenbürgen im Frühmittelalter*, 1986, pp. 105, 126, 136. There were earthen fortresses excavated throughout Hungary.

479. Mircea Rusu, in: *Relations Between the Autochthonous Population*, 1975, *op. cit.*, p. 212.

480. Bóna, "Der Silberschatz von Darufalva" in *Acta Arch. Hung.* 16 (1964), pp. 154–165.

481. Franz Miklosich, *Die slawischen Ortsnamen aus Apellativen* (Wien: 1874), II, p. 21.

482. Horedt, *Siebenbürgen im Frühmittelalter*, 1986, *op. cit.*, p. 139.

CHAPTER 3

1. Nicolae Gudea, "Cîteva observaţii şi note critice cu specială privire la partea istorică a monografiei *Etnogeneza românilor* de I.I. Russu" [Some Remarks and Critical Notes With Special Reference to the Historical Part of *Etnogeneza românilor* by I.I. Russu], in *Acta Musei Napocensis*, XX, 1983, pp. 903–916.

2. A review about this book was published in a linguistic journal: *Studii şi cercetări lingvistice*, Bucharest, XXXIII, 1982, 3, pp. 278–282.

3. Ion I. Russu, *Etnogeneza românilor. Fondul autohton traco-dacic şi componenţa latino-romanică* [The Ethnogenesis of the Romanians. The Autochthon Thraco-Dacian Ethnical Basis and the Latin-Romance Element], (Bucharest: 1981) p. 155.

4. *Ibid.*, p. 196.

5. Gudea, 1983, p. 904.

6. Liviu Franga, in *Studii şi cercetări lingvistice*, XXXIII (1982), 3, p. 279.

7. Iancu Fischer, *Latina dunăreană* [Danubian Latin], (Bucharest: 1985).

8. *Ibid.*, p. 16.

9. *Ibid.*, p. 20.

10. K. Sandfeld, *Linguistique balkanique* (Paris: 1930); Alexandru Rosetti, *Istoria limbii române* (Bucharest: 1978), 2nd ed., pp. 247–289.

11. *Actes du premier congrès international des linguistes*, (Leiden: 1928), p. 18.

12. Georg Renatus Solta, *Einführung in die Balkanlinguistik mit besonderer Berücksichtigung des Substrats und des Balkanlateinischen*, (Darmstadt: 1980), p. 7.

13. Siegfried Riedl, "Der Artikel im Bulgarischen," in: *1300 Jahre Bulgarien. Studien zum I Internationalen Bulgaristikkongress Sofia 1981*, p. 335, note 47, cf., Trost P., "Zur Kritik der Substrattheorie," in: *Les études balkaniques tchéchoslovaques* III, 1968, p. 48.

14. Alexandru Rosetti, *Étude sur le rhotacisme en roumain*, (Paris: 1924).

15. Matteo Giulio Bartoli, "Das Dalmatische," in: *Schriften der Balkankommission*, vols. IV–V, (Wien: 1906); sardo, dalmatico, albano-romanico. Atti del IV Congr. nazion. dei arti e tradizioni populari, Roma 1942.

16. A presentation of this problem is given, for example, by B.E. Vidos, *Handbuch der romanischen Sprachwissenschaft* (München: 1975), pp. 319–335.

17. Alexandru Rosetti, *Istoria limbii române*, 1986, p. 78.

18. Haralambie Mihăescu, *Limba latină în provinciile dunărene ale Imperiului Roman* [The Latin Language in the Danubian Provinces of the Roman Empire], (Bucharest: 1960).

19. At the official division of the empire in 395 A.D. an eastern and a western part, Dalmatia remained with the western part and Preavalitana (Montenegro and northern Albania) went to the eastern part. The frontier between the two territories went from the gulf of Cattaro to the area west of Belgrade. Since most of Dalmatia belonged for almost another one and a half centuries to the sphere of influence of Rome (in 535 A.D. it was conquered by Byzantium), it was able to take part in several linguistic developments that did not affect the rest of East Latin. Cf., B.E. Vidos, *Handbuch der romanischen Sprachwissenschaft*, first edition 1968, p. 300, referring to M. Valkhoff, *Latijn, Romaans, Roemeens* (Amersfoort: 1932), pp. 18–19.

20. Mihăescu, *Limba latină*, 1960, *op. cit.*, p. 267.

21. *Ibid.*, p. 36.

22. *Ibid.*

23. *Ibid.*, p. 278.

24. *Istoria limbii române*, II, ed. Coteanu et al., (Bucharest: 1969), chapter A, pp. 21–186. The *Istoria limbii române* will henceforth be referred to as the *ILR*.

25. Iancu Fischer, *Latina dunăreană, op. cit.*, p. 6.

26. *Ibid.*, p. 8.

27. There are exceptions to this: Lat. *autumn* Northern Romanian *toamnă*, and others.

28. Mihăescu, *Limba latină*, 1960, *op. cit.*, p. 67; Rosetti, *ILR*, 1968, p. 108.

29. Rosetti, *Istoria limbii române* 1986, pp. 108–109.
30. *Ibid.*, p. 78.
31. V. Väänänen, *Introduction au latin vulgaire*, 3rd edition, 1981, p. 57.
32. Rosetti, *Istoria limbii române* 1986, pp. 119–120.
33. *Ibid.*, pp. 120–121.
34. Väänänen, 1981, *op. cit.*, p. 68.
35. Fischer, *Latina dunăreană*, *op. cit.*, p. 199.
36. Väänänen, 1981, p. 68; Fischer, *op. cit.*, p. 199.
37. Fischer, p. 199.
38. Väänänen, 1981, pp. 69–70.
39. Rosetti, *Istoria limbii române*, 1986, p. 121.
40. Fischer, 1985, *op. cit.*, p. 202.
41. *ILR*, 1969, II, p. 118. The exact number of such words is given: 107.
42. *Ibid.*, p. 123.
43. *Ibid.*, p. 124.
44. *Ibid.*, p. 124 *et seq.*
45. Rosetti, *Istoria limbii române*, 1986, p. 79.
46. *Ibid.*, p. 82.
47. Or are conservative traits as compared to innovations that appeared in the West in those periods. Väänänen's division of the ages of Latin is used here, *cf.*, Väänänen, 1981, p. 13.
48. Väänänen, 1981, *op. cit.*, p. 200. Väänänen quotes C.A. Robson, "L'Appendix Probi et la philologie latine" in: *Le Moyen Âge*, 69, (1963), pp. 37–54. Robson shows that, in contrast to what has been assumed earlier, this text was written "in the Christian centuries, under Lombards, thus, after 568!"
49. Väänänen, 1981, pp. 17–18.
50. Rosetti, *Istoria limbii române*, 1986, p. 104.
51. Mihăescu, 1960, *op. cit.*, p. 96.
52. Rosetti, 1986, *op. cit.*, p. 114.
53. Rosetti, 1986, p. 343, considers that Arumanian *ts* is more recent and developed, as stated by Skok, *Zeitschrift für romanische Philologie*, XLVIII, under Greek influence. (In certain areas of Arumanian, *č* appears).
54. Haralambie Mihăescu, *La langue latine dans le sud-est de l'Europe*, (Bucharest-Paris: 1978), p. 198.
55. Rosetti, 1986, *op. cit.*, pp. 116–117.
56. *Ibid.*
57. Iancu Fischer, "Aspectul linguistic al romanizării Daciei" [The Linguistic Aaspect of the Romanization of Dacia], in *Limba română*, 27, 2, 1978, pp. 190–191. See also I. Fischer, *Latina dunăreană*, 1985, *op. cit.*, pp. 200–201; Rosetti, 1968, *op. cit.*, 136–148.
58. *ILR*, 1969, II, p. 232.
59. Fischer, 1985, *op. cit.*, pp. 201–204; Rosetti, 1968, pp. 148–165.
60. Mihăescu, *Limba latină*, 1960, *op. cit.*, p. 145.
61. *Ibid.*, p. 146.

62. Matilda Caragiu Marioțeanu, *Compendiu de dialectologie, op. cit.,* p. 249.

63. E. Löfstedt, *Late Latin.* Instituttet for sammenlignende kulturforskning, serie A: Forelesninger, XXV (Oslo: 1959), p. 68: "The new system of thought called for and created not a quite new language but certainly new forms of expression."

64. Mihăescu, 1960, *op. cit.,* p. 277.

65. *Cf.,* for example, *Istoria Romîniei,* I (Bucharest: 1960), p. 631.

66. Fischer, 1985, *op. cit.,* p. 54.

67. *Ibid.,* p. 55. The text of *Appendix Probi* is reproduced in Väänänen, 1981, *op. cit.,* pp. 199–203.

68. G. Mihăilă, *Studii de lexicologie și istorie a lingvisticii românești* (Studies of Lexicology and of History of Romanian Linguistics], (Bucharest: 1973), p. 16.

69. Löfstedt, *Late Latin,* 1959, *op. cit.,* p. 17.

70. *ILR,* II, 1969, pp. 15–16.

71. Rosetti, 1986, *op. cit.,* p. 81.

72. Mihăescu, 1960, *op. cit.,* p. 278.

73. Väänänen, *Introduction au latin vulgaire,* 1981, *op. cit.,* p. 83.

74. *ILR* II, 1969, p. 15.

75. H. J. Dölle (red.), *Römer und Germanen in Mitteleuropa,* (Berlin, East Germany: 1975), p. 88.

76. *Ibid.*

77. Mihăescu, 1960, *op. cit.,* pp. 267–268; Rosetti, 1986, *op. cit.,* p. 82; Russu, *Etnogeneza românilor, op. cit.,* p. 199.

78. G. Straka, in *Revue de linguistique romane,* Paris, XXIV, 1960, Livres, comptes rendues sommaires, p. 405.

79. For more detail on this subject in: Werner Bahner, *Das Sprach- und Geschichtsbewusstsein in der rumänischen Literatur von 1780–1880,* (Berlin: 1967).

80. Ion I. Russu, *Etnogeneza românilor* [The Ethnogenesis of the Romanians], (Bucharest: 1981), p. 125. The *Dicționarul explicativ al limbii române,* (Bucharest: 1975) considers that the origin of this word is not known.

81. Russu, *Etnogeneza românilor,* pp. 118–121.

82. *ILR,* pp. 319–320.

83. *The Early History of the Rumanian Language* (Lake Bluff: 1977) p. 47.

84. The details and further literature on the subject can be found in several recent studies: Ivan Popović, *Geschichte der serbokroatischen Sprache* (Wiesbaden: 1960); Ion I. Russu, *Limba traco-dacilor* [The Language of the Thraco-Dacians], (Bucharest: 1967); Id.: *Illirii.Istoria—limba și onomastica—romanizarea* [The Illyrians—History, Language and Onomastics, Romanization], (Bucharest: 1969); Id.: *Etnogeneza românilor* [The Ethnogenesis of the Romanians], (Bucharest: 1981); Georg Renatus Solta, *Einführung in die Balkanlinguistik mit besonderer Berücksichtigung des Substrats und des Balkanlateinischen,* (Darmstad: 1980); Vladimir Georgiev, *The Thracians and Their Language* [in Bulgarian], (Sofia: 1977); Gottfried Schramm, *Eroberer und Eingesessene. Geographische Lehnnamen als Zeugen der Geschichte Südosteuropas im ersten Jahrtausend n. Chr.* (Stuttgart: 1981).

85. Russu, 1981, *op. cit.*, p. 75.

86. Russu, *Illirii*, 1969, *op. cit.*, p. 107. In ancient Indo-European, *kmtom "hundred" was spelled with a palatal *k*. In an ancient Indo-European dialect, this palatal *k* changed to *č* which in certain areas later became *s*. In Avestan (an ancient Iranian idiom), "hundred" is *satem*. Those Indo-European languages, including the Indo-Iranian, Armenian, Albanian, and Balto-Slavic subfamilies, which originate from this dialect with *č* are called "satem languages," the rest, "centum languages."

87. Solta, 1981, *op. cit.*, pp. 119–120. *Cf.*, also Popović, 1960, *op. cit.*, p. 65.

88. *Geographia*, first century B.C.–first century A.D.

89. *Historia*, second century B.C.

90. Russu, 1981, *op. cit.*, p. 79.

91. Detailed data are provided in: Dimiter Detschew (ed.), *Die thrakischen Sprachreste*, (Wien: 1957).

92. Russu, 1981, *op. cit.*, p. 81; in *Limba traco-dacilor*, 1967, pp. 89–130, Thracian (Thraco-Dacian) proper names and lexical elements are given, with assumed etymologies.

92/a Russu, 1981, *op. cit.*, p. 81. In Russu's opinion, the lexical elements from which a consonant shift was deduced are in reality Grecized forms of Thracian names. Other scholars do not agree with this; *cf.*, for example, I. Popović, 1960, *op. cit.*, p. 74, who cites such forms as Μήτοκος - Μήδοκος, Κραςτοvία - Γραςτουία.

93. *ILR*, 1969, *op. cit.*, p. 314.

94. C. Váczy, "Nomenclatura dacică a plantelor la Dioscorides și Pseudo-Apuleius," in: *Acta Musei Napocensis* (Cluj), part IX, 1972, p. 107.

95. Solta, 1980, *op. cit.*, p. 19.

96. *Ibid.*, p. 20.

97. *Ibid.*

98. *ILR*, 1969, pp. 315–316. See further, Dimiter Detschev, *Die thrakischen Sprachreste*, *op. cit.*, pp. 542–565.

99. Ariton Vraciu, *Limba daco-geților* [The Language of the Daco-Getae], (Timișoara: 1980), p. 85.

100. *Geographia*, VII, 3, 10, 3, 13.

101. *ILR*, 1969, p. 318, note 2.

102. *SCIVA*, vol. 28, 1, 1977, p. 15.

103. *Linguistique Balkanique*, II, 1960, pp. 1–19; Vladimir Georgiev, *The Thracians and Their Language* [in Bulgarian], (Sofia: 1977); Solta, 1980, *op. cit.*, p. 117.

104. *Cf.*, the critical discussion by Solta, 1980, *op. cit.*, pp. 117–118.

105. Russu, 1981, *op. cit.*, p. 79.

106. *ILR*, 1969, p. 317.

107. Solta, 1980, *op. cit.*, p. 11.

108. Günter Reichenkron, *Das Dakische (rekonstruiert aus dem Rumänischen)*, (Heidelberg: 1966), p. 92.

108/a Russu, 1981, *op. cit.*, p. 62.

109. *Ibid.*, p. 63.

110. Russu, *Limba traco-dacilor,* 1967, pp. 138–143, has compiled the Thracian lexical data with a probable or assumed sense. The seven words here are from his list.

111. *Ibid.*, p. 112.

112. *ILR,* vol. II, 1969, p. 327 *et. seq.*

113. *Ibid.*, p. 333.

114. Explanatory Dictionary of the Romanian Language, (Bucharest: 1975).

115. The Slavic origin of *zîrnă* is not probable, the meaning of the Slavic word is far from that of *zîrnă* and Romanian *zîrnă* is in its first written forms written with initial *dz* (*Dzărnă,* in a document from Suceava, dated 1488). *Cf,* Rosetti: DR. *zîrnă* "plante vénéneuse," in: *Mélanges linguistiques* (Bucharest: 1977), p. 159; in Rosetti 1985, p. 322.

116. Russu, 1981, *op. cit.,* p. 275.

117. *Ibid.*, p. 323.

118. *Ibid.*, p. 346.

119. *Ibid.*, p. 113.

120. Ovid Densusianu, *Histoire de la langue roumaine,* 1901, I, p. 20, quoted by Russu, 1981, p. 47: "La phonétique et le lexique roumains ne nous offrent aucune particularité qui se trouve en même temps dans les restes de la langue dace, qui nous ont été transmis. Il serait inutile de bâtir des hypothèses fantastiques et de chercher des éléments daciques en roumain. On ne surait toutefois contester l'existence de tels éléments, mais tout philologue doit y renoncer à les admettre là où ils ne peuvent pas être prouvés par la science."

121. Russu, 1981, *op. cit.,* pp. 115–116.

122. *Ibid.*, p. 166.

123. *Ibid.*

124. *Ibid.*, p. 114.

125. Gustav Weigand, "Sind die Albaner die Nachkommen der Illyrer oder der Thraker?," in *Balkan-Archiv,* 3, 1927, pp. 227–251; Dimităr Dečev, *Charakteristik der thrakischen Sprache,* (Sofia: 1952); Id.: *Die thrakischen Sprachreste,* (Wien: 1957); Henrik Barić, "Albanisch, Romanisch und Rumänisch," in: *Godišnjak,* ed. Balkanološki Institut (Sarajevo: 1956), pp. 1–16.

126. An up-to-date presentation of this problem is given by Solta, 1980, *op. cit.,* pp. 108–123.

127. Eqrem Çabej, "L'illyrien et l'albanais," in *Studia Albanica,* VIII, 1, 1970, pp. 157–170.

128. Russu, *Limba traco-dacilor,* 1967, p. 183.

129. Eqrem Çabej, "De quelques problèmes fondamentaux de l'histoire ancienne de l'Albanais," Conférence des études albanologiques, Université d'état de Tirana, Institut d'Histoire et de Linguistique (Tirana: 1962), p. 6.

130. *Ibid.*, p. 14.

131. *Ibid.*

132. Solta, 1980, *op. cit.,* p. 36.

133. Russu, *Illirii, op. cit.,* p. 111. In *Etnogeneza românilor,* 1981, p. 94, a similar statement is found: the phonetics of Albanian agrees with both Illyrian

and Thracian, "but in their lexicology, no common element can be found; the Illyrian and Thraco-Getian grammars [declension and conjugation] are entirely unknown, and the Albanians do not seem to have inherited any cultural element [for example, a proper name or a place name] attested to in the ancient era, in Thracian or in Illyrian."

134. Vladimir Georgiev, *The Thracians and Their Language* (in Bulgarian), (Sofia: 1977), p. 286. *Cf.,* also *ILR,* 1969, p. 317.

135. Gottfried Schramm, *Eroberer und Eingesessene,* 1981, *op. cit.,* p. 34.

136. Ivan Popović, 1960, *op. cit.,* p. 79.

137. Çabej, "Le problème du territoire de la formation de la langue albanaise," in Bull. Association International d'Études Sud-Est Européennes, 1972, 2, pp. 87–89.

138. Popović, 1960, *op. cit.,* p. 84.

139. *Cf.,* for example, Popović, 1960, *op. cit.,* p. 80.

140. *Cf.,* Solta, *op. cit.,* p. 115.

141. Popović, 1960, *op. cit.,* p. 84; Solta, 1980, *op. cit.,* p. 115; Schramm, 1981, *op. cit.,* p. 34.

142. G. Brâncuş, "Albano-romanica, III. Vocala ă în română şi albaneza," [The vowel ă in Romanian and Albanian], in *Studii şi cercetări lingvistice,* XXIV, 3, 1973, Bucharest, p. 294.

143. *Ibid.,* p. 295. A recent presentation of this subject was given by Solta, 1980, pp. 180–183.

144. Solta, 1980, *op. cit.,* p. 184, quoting V. Georgiev, *Linguistique Balkanique* XX, 1977, p. 8.

145. Çabej, "Unele probleme ale istoriei limbii albaneze," in *Studii şi cercetări lingvistice X,* 4, 1959, p. 534; Solta, 1980, *op. cit.,* p. 191.

146. *Ibid.,* p. 193.

147. Çabej, "Unele probleme," *op. cit.,* 1959, p. 531.

148. Solta, 1980, p. 189.

149. *Ibid.,* pp. 195–196.

150. *ILR,* 1969, vol. II, p. 326. The expression "autohton" is used.

151. *Ibid.,* p. 327.

152. Ariton Vraciu, *Limba daco-geţilor, op. cit.,* p. 165.

153. Russu, 1981, *op. cit.,* p. 110.

154. *Ibid.,* p. 111.

155. The method is far from having been generally accepted; *cf.,* for example, C. Tagliavini, *Originile limbilor neolatine,* (Bucharest: 1977), p. 113, note 174; p. 120.

156. Russu, 1981, p. 111.

157. Ariton Vraciu, *Limba daco-geţilor,* 1980, *op. cit.,* p. 88, pp. 57–58, 61, note 3. See also Vasile Arvinte, *Die Rumänen. Ursprung, Volks- und Landesnamen* [The Romanians. Origin, Ethnical- and Landnames], (Tübingen: 1980), pp. 14–15.

158. Russu, 1981, *op. cit.,* p. 112.

159. *Ibid.,* pp. 245–426.

160. Cicerone Poghirc, *ILR*, 1969, *op. cit.*, pp. 319–320; and pp. 327–356; see also *Istoria limbii române*, Florica Dimitrescu *et. al.*, (Bucharest: 1978), p. 72.

161. The Explicative Dictionary of the Romanian Language, (Bucharest: 1975).

162. *ILR*, 1978, p. 73, notes 1 and 2.

163. Vraciu, *Limba daco-geţilor, op. cit.*, pp. 141–142.

164. Russu, 1981, *op. cit.*, p. 132.

165. *Ibid.* The last statement is quite dubious: *brînză* could be connected with Albanian *brëndësa-t*; *zăr* with Albanian *drā* (and *zăr* and *zară* are connected); *urdă* has an Albanian counterpart: *urdhë*, and it is not clear whether it is a loanword or not in Albanian.

166. Russu, 1981, *op. cit.*, p. 132.

167. *Ibid.*, p. 253.

168. *Ibid.*, p. 295.

169. *Ibid.*, p. 355.

170. *ILR*, 1969, vol. II, p. 352.

171. Russu, 1981, *op. cit.*, pp. 244–245.

172. In the following analysis, all numbers given in parentheses and with a question-mark refer to words whose origin from the substratum is considered questionable by Russu.

173. Of which, however, four are questionable. The real number of specific pastoral words not existing in Albanian may thus be even lower.

174. Ion I. Russu, *Dacoromania*, 1973, pp. 191–192; also referring to *Etnogeneza românilor*, 1981.

175. Russu, 1981, pp. 245–426.

176. For example, note 158.

177. Theodor Capidan, *Dacoromania* II, 1921–22, pp. 482–487, quoted by Russu, *Dacoromania* 1973, p. 191; Russu, 1981, p. 135.

178. Russu, *Etnogeneza românilor*, 1981, *op. cit.*, p. 137.

179. *Ibid.*

180. *ILR*, 1978: Viorica Ilea-Pamfil, p. 72.

181. Eqrem Çabej, "Unele probleme ale istoriei limbii albaneze," *op. cit.*, 1959, p. 551: ". . . one can presuppose a non-Latin substratum in the Romanian language, but not in Albanian. What for Romanian can represent the substratum is, for the Albanian language, only an ancient, earlier stage." Vladimir Georgiev (1977, p. 287) also considered that Proto-Albanian was the substratum of Romanian and called this ancient language "Daco-Moesian": "The Daco-Moesian tribes probably infiltrated into the central parts of the Balkan Peninsula (Moesia Superior, Dardania, Dacia Mediterranea, Dacia Ripensis) during the second millennium B.C. (the Dardanians), but also later, in successive waves, during the first millennium B.C. (the Triballes), and even later. Some of these tribes were Romanized during the first centuries A.D. but others were able to preserve their language, which developed under the powerful influence of Latin spoken in the eastern part of the Balkans. This

coexistence of the Romanized and the Proto-Albanian populations continued in the period from fourth to the sixth centuries, when Latin spoken in the eastern part of the Balkan Peninsula began to develop into Romanian."

182. *Cf*, the last sentence in the above note (V. Georgiev, 1977, p. 287): "This coexistence of the Romanized and the Proto-Albanian populations continued in the period from the fourth to the sixth centuries, when Latin spoken in the eastern part of the Balkan Peninsula began to develop into Romanian."

183. The vowel ă and the diphthongs, the phonemes /č/, /ǧ/, /t/, /š/ , existed in this idiom; the definite article appeared after the seventh century. Certain changes that did occur in East Latin developed at this stage in the pronoun as well as in the future tense, with the auxiliary verb *uolo* and the subjunctive with *se* (modern Northern Romanian *să*). A detailed description of Common Romanian, as reconstructed from the present-day Romanian dialects, is given by M. Sala in *ILR*, 1969, vol. II, pp. 189–309.

184. *Cf.*, for example, *ILR*, 1978, p. 76, where the following examples are given: *babă*, "old woman, mother," *boală*, "disease," *nevastă* "married woman, wife," *scump* "expensive, dear, valuable," *sută* "hundred," *rană* "wound," *lopată* "shovel," *plăti* "to pay."

185. *Cf.*, for example, Popović, 1960, *op. cit.*, p. 200. Popović points out that these loans, with "some distortions and changes, prove that there was one single point of borrowing."

186. *Cf.*, for example, Solta, 1980, *op. cit.*, p. 70 and 113.

187. Sextil Pușcariu, *Die rumänische Sprache*, (Leipzig: 1943), p. 396; *Cf.*, Horedt, *Siebenbürgen im Frühmittelalter, op. cit.*, note 259.

188. Alexandru Rosetti, Boris Cazacu, and Ion Coteanu (eds.), (Bucharest: 1965 and 1969).

189. Alexandru Rosetti, (Bucharest: 1968).

190. A. Rosetti, B. Cazacu, and I. Coteanu (eds.), vol. II, pp. 110–116.

191. This list was constructed on the basis of the dictionary of Ernout-Meillet and checked by the authors of *ILR*.

192. *Cf.*, Ovid Densusianu, *Histoire de la langue roumaine*, Opere II, Lingvistica, ed. by V. Rusu *et al.*, (Bucharest: 1975), p. 218.

193. Solta, 1980, *op. cit.*, p. 131.

194. Haralambie Mihăescu, "Les éléments latins de la langue albanaise," I, in: *Revue des études sud-est européennes* 4, Bucharest, 1966, pp. 5–34; II pp. 323–354; quoted p. 27.

195. *Cf.*, for example, Solta, 1980, *op. cit.*, p. 125.

196. Solta, *Einführung in die Balkanlinguistik*, 1980, *op. cit.*, p. 128. Solta also points out that it is wrong to believe that only common innovations are conclusive for the establishment of close relations between different idioms; quoting C. Watkins (*Ancient Indo-European Dialects*, Berkeley and Los Angeles, 1966, p. 30): "At any given stage of language, retentions and innovations are part of the same synchronic structure."

197. Solta, 1980, *op. cit.*, p. 129: "In spite of Mihăescu, the existence of the Albanian-Romanian isoglosses must be admitted."

198. Florica Dimitrescu *et al.* (eds.) *Istoria limbii române*, (Bucharest: 1978), p. 32.

199. Ștefan Pascu, (ed.), *Istoria României. Compendiu*, 3rd ed., 1974, p. 68. Unlike the first edition (1969), this text also includes in the area of formation of Romanian those territories of present-day Romania that never belonged to the Roman Empire (parts of Transylvania and most of Muntenia and Moldavia). We are dealing here with the phenomenon of a contemporary tendency to stretch the linguistic territory over the largest geographic area possible. Among others, for example, Constantin C. Giurescu, Dinu C. Giurescu, *Istoria românilor*, 1975, p. 30.

200. *Cf.*, for example, Florica Dimitrescu *et al.* (eds.), *Istoria limbii române*, (Bucharest: 1978), p. 30.

201. Among others, Ovid Densusianu, Alexandru Philippide, Sextil Puș-cariu. A recent monograph about the Romanian dialects: Matilda Caragiu-Marioțeanu, *Compendiu de dialectologie română (nord-și sud-dunăreană)*, (Bucharest: 1975).

202. Alexandru Rosetti, Sandra Golopenția Eretescu (eds.), "Current Trends in Romanian Linguistics," in *Revue Roumaine de Linguistique*, 23, *Cahiers de Linguistique Théorique et Appliquée*, 15; *History of Romanian*, by Florica Dimitrescu and Mihaela Mancaș, (Bucharest: 1978), pp. 7–8.

203. *Ibid.*

204. Rosetti, *Istoria limbii române*, 1986, *op. cit.*, p. 75; see also Ion Nestor, "Les données arhéologiques et la problème de la formation du peuple roumain," in *Revue Roumaine d'Histoire*, III, 1964, pp. 383–423 and 407–410.

205. Ion I. Russu, 1981, *op. cit.*, p. 166.

206. *Ibid.* Russu returns to the question of terminology on p. 164: "If the terms "Daco-Roman," "Thraco-Dacian," "Carpathian," etc., were frequently used on the preceding pages, they should not be interpreted as a silent pleading for the autochthony and the ethnic-social and territorial "continuity" of the Romanians, are used for the simple reason that they have been in use before and are more convenient and clear, covering certain historical-linguistic notions generally admitted by scholars, notions for which other, more accurate and unequivocal terms have been sought but not found." (Russu, *Etnogeneza românilor*, 1981, p. 164).

207. Iancu Fischer, "Aspectul lingvistic al romanizării Daciei" [The Linguistic Aspect of the Romanization of Dacia], in *Limba română* 27, no. 2, 1978, pp. 189–191.

208. Du Nay, 1978, p. 88.

209. Ion Coteanu, *Structura și evoluția limbii române (de la origini pînă la 1860)* [Structure and Evolution of the Romanian Language (from Its Origins to 1860)], (Bucharest: 1981), p. 74.

210. *Ibid.*

211. *Ibid.*

212. *Cf.*, for example, Alexandru Vulpe, in *Dicționar de istorie veche a României (Paleolitic-sec X)* [Dictionary for the ancient History of Romania], ed. by D.M. Pippidi, (Bucharest: 1976), p. 218: "The last mention of Dacians

Notes 385

is from the fourth century A.D., their language disappeared probably in the sixth to seventh centuries."

213. Cicerone Poghirc, in *ILR*, vol. II, p. 314.

214. Ovid Densusianu, *Opere* [Works], ed. by B. Cazacu, V. Rusu and I. Şerb, II: *Lingvistica. Histoire de la langue roumaine*, (Bucharest: 1975), p. 866.

215. *Cf.*, for example, Rosetti, *Istoria limbii române*, 1968, *op. cit.*, pp. 239–243 with the presentation of earlier theories (mostly of C. Diculescu, G. Giuglea, S. Puşcariu and E. Gamillscheg).

216. Virgiliu Ştefănescu-Drăgăneşti, "A New Look at the Socio-Linguistic and Historical Implications of the Latin Borrowings in Wulfila's Gothic Bible (fourth century A.D.)," in *Forum Linguisticum*, (Lake Bluff, USA), vol. VI, 3, 1982, pp. 265–269.

217. Barbarian peoples of the Roman border-area.

218. Vittoria Corazza, "Le parole latine in gotico," in *Atti della Accadèmia Nazionale dei Lincei* (Roma: 1969), VIII, vol. XIV, Fasc. 1.

219. *Ibid.*, p. 7.

220. *Ibid.*, pp. 77–78.

221. *Ibid.*, p. 80.

222. *Ibid.*, p. 85.

223. This assumption is from Ştefănescu-Drăgăneşti, 1982, *op. cit.*, p. 267.

224. *Ibid.*

225. *Ibid.*, p. 268.

226. *Cf.*, for example, Rosetti, *Istoria limbii române*, 1968; *Istoria limbii române*, ed. A. Rosetti, B. Cazacu and I. Coteanu, vol. II, 1969; for a discussion of the origin of *a gatı*, see p. 341.

227. Eqrem Çabej, "Unele probleme ale istoriei limbii albaneze" [Some Problems of the History of the Albanian Language], in *Studii şi cercetări lingvistice*, 1959 X, p. 531.

228. Ernst Gamillscheg, *Romania Germanica*, vol. II, (Berlin-Leipzig: 1935), p. 245 *et seq.* Gamillscheg also proposed Old Germanic origins for 30 Romanian words.

229. Iorgu Iordan, *Nume de locuri româneşti în Republica Populară Română* [Romanian Place Names in the Romanian People's Republic], (Bucharest: 1952), p. 230, quoting Gustav Kisch who published several studies on Transylvanian place names in the period between the two World Wars.

230. Iordan, 1952, *op. cit.*, p. 230.

231. Rosetti, 1968, *op. cit.*, p. 241.

232. Iordan, 1952, p. 230.

233. *Ibid.*

234. *Ibid.*, p. 231.

235. Rosetti, 1968, p. 240.

236. *Ibid.*, p. 327.

237. *Cf.*, G. Schramm, *Eroberer und Eingesessene*, 1981, *op. cit.*, p. 101; and G. Schramm, "Frühe Schicksale der Rumänen," in *Zeitschrift für Balkanologie*, Band XXI/2, (1985), pp. 236–237. (In the case of a direct borrowing from Latin or Greek, one would expect *aikklēsja* in Gothic.

238. *Istoria limbii române*, ed. by A. Rosetti *et al.*, vol. II, 1969, p. 162.

239. Ştefan Pascu *et al.*, (eds.), *Istoria României. Compendiu*, 1974, p. 94.

240. Konstantin Josef Jireček, *Geschichte der Serben*, vol. I to 1371, (Gotha: 1911), pp. 38–39; a new ed., (Amsterdam: 1967).

241. Pascu (ed.), *Istoria României. Compendiu*, 1974, pp. 75–76.

242. Ion Coteanu, *Structura şi evoluţia limbii române*, 1981, *op. cit.*, p. 73.

243. Dumitru Berciu, *Daco-Romania*, 1976, p. 85.

244. Günter Reichenkron, "Das Ostromanische," in *Völker und Kulturen Südosteuropas*, (München: 1959), p. 167.

245. Berciu, *Daco-Romania*, 1976, p. 138.

246. Ştefan Pascu, (ed.), *Istoria României. Compendiu*, 3rd edition, 1974, p. 77.

247. Mihăescu, *Limba latină în provinciile dunărene*, 1960, *op. cit.*, pp. 35–36.

248. Reichenkron, "Das Ostromanische," *op. cit.*, 1959, p. 169. (referring to S. Puşcariu, *Die rumänische Sprache*, p. 456).

249. Eugen Lozovan, "Aux origines du christianisme daco-scythique," in *Geschichte der Hunnen*, ed. by Franz Altheim (Berlin: 1959–1962), p. 159; with several references to the literature of this cult in the Roman Empire.

250. *Ibid.*, p. 160–161.

251. George Ivănescu, "Les plus anciennes influences de la romanité balkanique sur les Slaves: *luna* "lune," *lunatik* "somnambule," in *Romanoslavica* 1 (1958), pp. 44–51; quoted by Lozovan. 1959–1962, p. 161, note 81.

252. Densusianu, *Histoire de la langue roumaine*, ed. by B. Cazacu *et al.*, (Bucharest: 1975), p. 194.

253. Rosetti, 1986, *op. cit.*, p. 179.

254. *Ibid.*

255. Solta, 1980, *op. cit.*, p. 168.

256. After the appearance of the *Atlas Lingvistic Român*, published first in 1936, Bucharest.

257. Sextil Puşcariu, "Les enseignements de l'Atlas Linguistique de la Roumanie," in *Revue de Transylvanie*, 3, 1, 1936; Puşcariu, "Le rôle de la Transylvanie dans la formation et l'évolution de la langue roumaine," in *La Transylvanie*, Bucharest 1938.

258. *Ibid.*, p. 15.

259. Constantin C. Giurescu, *Istoria Românilor*, (Bucharest: 1935).

260. Puşcariu, "Les enseignements," 1936, pp. 19–20.

261. *Ibid.*, p. 21.

262. Christian Ionescu, *Mică enciclopedie onomastică* [Concise Onomastic Encyclopaedia], (Bucharest: 1975), p. 219.

263. According to W. Meyer-Lübke, *Romanisches Etymologisches Wörterbuch*, 3rd edition, (Heidelberg: 1935), this word is of learned origin, something which was questioned by A. Graur (Cf., *Istoria limbii române*, ed. by A. Rosetti, B. Cazacu, I. Coteanu, (Bucharest: 1969), vol. II, p. 148.

264. Puşcariu, "Le rôle de la Transylvanie," 1938, *op. cit.*, p. 63.

265. *Cf.*, for example, A. Du Nay, 1977, pp. 34–41.

266. B.E. Vidos, *Handbuch der romanischen Sprachwissenschaft*, (München: 1975), translated from Dutch, p. 102.

267. *Ibid.*, p. 101.

268. Matilda Caragiu Marioțeanu, 1975, *op. cit.*, p. 73.

269. *Ibid.*, p. 178.

270. *Ibid.*, p. 177.

271. *Ibid.*, p. 72. Obviously, the existence of words of foreign origin, replacing ancient Latin words in Transylvania (which have been preserved, for example, in Muntenia) "subverts the proposed Latin image of Transylvania," (Rosetti, 1986).

272. Eugen Lozovan, "Byzance et la Romanité Scythique," in: F. Altheim, *Geschichte der Hunnen*, 1959–1962, vol. II, p. 222.

273. *Ibid.*

274. *Ibid.*

275. N. Cartojan, *Istoria literaturii române vechi* [The History of the Old Romanian Literature], 2nd ed (Bucharest: 1980), p. 88.

276. *Ibid.*, p. 89.

277. *Ibid.*

278. Matilda Caragiu-Marioțeanu, *Compendiu de dialectologie*, 1975, *op. cit.*, p. 222.

279. *Ibid.*, p. 238.

280. *Ibid.*, pp. 256–257.

281. *Ibid.*, p. 254.

282. Ernst Gamillscheg, "Über die Herkunft der Rumänen," Sitzungsberichte, (Berlin: 1940), p. 130.

283. *Ibid.*, p. 122.

284. *Ibid.*, p. 131; referring to G. Weigand, Balkan-Archiv I, 31 and 34.

285. Günter Reichenkron, "Die Entstehung des Rumänentums nach den neuesten Forschungen," in *Südost-Forschungen*, XXII, 1963, pp. 61–77.

286. *Cf.*, for example, Rosetti, 1986, *op. cit.*, p. 283.

287. Reichenkron, "Das Ostromanische," 1959, *op. cit.*, p. 169.

288. *Ibid.*, p. 160.

289. Reichenkron, "Vorrömische Bestandteile des Rumänischen," in *Südost-Forschungen*. XIX, 1960, p. 349. An interesting example of the borrowing of a typical Albanian expression by Northern Romanian is given on this page, note 26: Albanian *ha*, "I am eating" + suffix *-me: hame*, "the eating" + the suffix used for the construction of *nomina agentis: -ës: hámës*, "the eater," from which Northern Romanian *hămesi* "to be awfully hungry" (and *hămeseală* "canine appetite").

290. Reichenkron, "Das Ostromanische," 1959, *op. cit.*, p. 169, referring to S. Pușcariu, *Die rumänische Sprache*, p. 456.

291. *Ibid.*, p. 169: "Von Dardania dürfte so einmal die erste Ausbreitung des 'Urrumänentums,' wie man es seit Pușcariu nennt, vollzogen haben."

292. Reichenkron, "Die Entstehung des Rumänentums," 1963, *op. cit.*, p. 66: "Es dürfte vielmehr so sein, dass die meisten der albanisch-rumänischen Wortgleichungen, im Süden der Donau, in der sog. Dardania, als dem südlichen

388 Ethnic Continuity in the Carpatho-Danubian Area

Teil der römischen Provinz Moesia Superior, also etwa im jugoslawischen Mazedonien, entstanden sind."
293. Giurescu, 1975, p. 151.
294. Pascu, (ed.) *Istoria României. Compendiu*, 1974, p. 77.
295. Vasile Arvinte, *Die Rumänen*, 1980, *op. cit.*, p. 27.
296. Eugen Lozovan, "Diachronie et géographie linguistique roumaines," in *Acta Philologica* II, 1959, p. 162.
297. Alexandru Rosetti, *Istoria limbii române de la origini pînă în secolul al XVII-lea* [The History of the Romanian Language From the Origins to the 17th Century], (Bucharest: 1968), p. 214.
298. Ed. by A. Rosetti, B. Cazacu, I. Coteanu (Bucharest: 1969), vol. II.
299. *Istoria limbii române*, ed. by Florica Dimitrescu *et al.*, (Bucharest: 1978).
300. Boris Cazacu, (Bucharest: 1966).
301. *Compendiu de dialectologie română (nord- şi sud-dunăreană)*, (Bucharest: 1975).

CHAPTER 4

1. Emil Petrovici, "La population de la Transylvanie au XIe siècle," in *Revue de Transylvanie*, Sibiu, X, 1944, pp. 71–98.
2. Petrovici, 1944, *op. cit.*, p. 72. In note 4, Petrovici refers to Julius Jung, *Römer und Romanen in den Donauländern* (Innsbruck: 1887), p. 352, note 4: "jene Slaven gehören eben zu den Stammvätern der heutigen Rumänen"; and to Jagić, *Die Kultur der Gegenwart*, Teil I, Abteilung IX, (Berlin-Leipzig: 1908), p. 6. In note 5, Nicolae Drăganu, *Românii în veacurile IX–XIV pe baza toponimiei şi a onomasticei* (Bucharest: 1933), p. 590, and E. Petrovici, in *Dacoromania*, X, p. 276 are quoted.
3. Günter Reichenkron, "Urslavisch ō im Rumänischen," p. 43, in: *Die Welt der Slaven*, V (1960).
4. Theodor Capidan, *Elementul slav în dialectul aromân*, (Bucharest: 1925); *cf.*, Reichenkron, "Urslavisch ō," 1960, *op. cit.*, p. 44.
5. Petrovici, *Dacoromania*, 10, (1941), pp. 128–146; *cf.*, Reichenkron, 1960, *op. cit.*, p. 45.
6. *Ibid.*, p. 44.
7. Alexandru Rosetti, *Istoria limbii române* III: *Limbile slave meridionale* (Bucharest: 1940), p. 58; *cf.*, Reichenkron, 1960, p. 44, note 19.
8. Christo Vasilev, "Bulgarische Sprache. Literatur und Geschichte," in *Südosteuropa Studien*, Heft 27, Neuried 1980.
9. Ivan Duridanov, "Bulgarische Sprache," 1980, *op. cit.*
10. Stefan Kniezsa, *Ungarns Völkerschaften im XI. Jahrhundert*, (Budapest: 1938) p. 9, quoted by Petrovici, 1944, *op. cit.*, p. 75.
11. Petrovici, "La population de la Transylvanie," 1944, *op. cit.*, pp. 75–76.
12. *Ibid.*, p. 77.
13. *Ibid.*, p. 87.

14. Emil Petrovici, "Toponymes roumains d'origine slave présentant le groupe 'voyelle + nasale' pour sl. comm. *ǫ." In: *Studii de dialectologie și toponimie*, Bucharest 1970 (published first in *Balcania*, VII, 1944, pp. 465–474), p. 197, referring to István Kniezsa, *Keletmagyarország helynevei*, 1943, p. 178.

15. *Ibid.*, p. 183.

16. Petrovici refers to Ion Pătruț, "Velarele, labialele și dentalele palatalizate," in *Dacoromania*, X, 1941–43, p. 306 *et seq.*

17. Petrovici, 1970, *op. cit.*, p. 184.

18. Coriolan Suciu, *Dicționar istoric al localităților din Transilvania [Historical Dictionary of the Transylvanian Place Names]*, 2 vols., (Bucharest: 1967), I, p. 196.

19. Petrovici, in *Transilvania*, LXXIII, p. 864, quoted by Kniezsa, 1943, p. 172.

20. Kniezsa, *Keletmagyarország helynevei* [The Place Names of Eastern Hungary], 1943, p. 172.

21. *Ibid.*, p. 284.

22. George Y. Shevelov, *A Prehistory of Slavic. The Historical Phonology of Common Slavic*, (Heidelberg: 1964), pp. 327–328. "It was part of the general trend toward eliminating descending diphthongs, and it was made possible by gradual loss of motivation in vocalis alterations." (*Ibid.*, p. 331).

23. *Ibid.*, p. 331.

24. *Ibid.*, p. 584. This is the background of Kniezsa's statement about the disappearance of the Slavic nasal vowels; see in: *Keletmagyarország helynevei* [The Place Names of Eastern Hungary], in: *Magyarok és Románok* [Hungarians and Romanians], József Deér and László Gáldi (reds.), (Budapest: 1943), p. 120. According to Kniezsa, "because the nasal vowels in the language of the Slavs who lived in contact with the Hungarians disappeared early, by the end of the tenth century, the Slavic place names borrowed by Hungarian indicate that the Hungarians borrowed these names before the disappearance of the nasals, that is, before the end of the tenth century (Dombró, Gambuc, Dombó, Gerend) . . . ." "The Slavs who lived in contact with the Hungarians" were the Slovaks, Czechs, Serbians, Croatians, and Bulgarians. The statement is valid with regard to all these Slavic idioms except Bulgarian. (Kniezsa, p. 120, note 1). "In Bulgarian, however, the nasals were preserved in general throughout the entire Middle Ages; moreover, in certain regions, such as in northeastern Bulgaria and in Macedonia, they are still extant (Oblak, *Mazedonische Studien* [Wien: 1896], p. 19; Miletič, *Das Ostbulgarische*, [Wien: 1880]).. The medieval Bulgarian texts are characterized by the consistent marking of the nasals, which shows their preservation. Also, the Bulgarian texts from Cserged (Cergău, Alba County), which, as shown by their ortography, cannot have been written before the end of the seventeenth century, have preserved the nasals, with the exception of the end-position. *Cf.*, Stefan Mladenov, *Geschichte der bulgarischen Sprache*, (Berlin-Leipzig: 1929), p. 115. Consequently, in areas inhabited by Bulgarians, place names in which nasals appear may have been borrowed after the tenth century as well."

25. G. Mihăilă, "Aspecte teoretice şi istorice ale studierii raporturilor lingvistice vechi slavo-române" [Theoretical and Historical Aspects of the Study of the Ancient Slavo-Romanian Linguistic Contacts], in *Studii şi cercetări lingvistice*, Bucharest, XXXIII, 1982, pp. 65–66. Mihăilă, *Studii de lexicologie şi istorie a lingvisticii româneşti* [Studies of Lexicology and of History of the Romanian Linguistics], (Bucharest: 1973), p. 77: "*ǫ > un: prund, scund; ǫ > ą ăn > în: mîndru* (a more recent reflex, early middle Bulgarian, from the end of the eleventh century to the thirteenth century)." Mihăilă refers here to K. Mirčev, *Istoričeska gramatika na bălgarskija ezik* [Historical Grammar of the Bulgarian Language], 1958, p. 127 *et. seq.*, and to S. B. Bernstein, *Gramatica comparată a limbilor slave* [Comparative Grammar of the Slavic languages], (Bucharest: 1965), p. 222 and 295, a translation into Romanian of Bernstein's work, which appeared in Moscow in 1961 in Russian. Rosetti, *ILR*, 1968, p. 340: "Old Slavic *ǫ* was, in ancient times, rendered as *u* ". . ." "and later, Old Slavic *ǫ* having been changed to *ă* in middle Bulgarian, was rendered in the normal way in Romanian by *î* (< *ă*): *mîndru* Old Slavic *mǫdŭrŭ*, middle Bulgarian *măndŭrŭ* (referring to Petar Skok: *Osnovi romanske lingvistike* [The Basis of Romance Linguistics], [Zagreb: 1940], p. 91).

26. Petrovici, 1944, *op. cit.*, p. 75, note 2; Petrovici refers to L. Miletič, *Sedmogratskitě bălgari*, in "Sbornik za narodni umotvorenija, nauka i knižnina," XIII, (1896), 153 *et. seq*; id., *Sedmogradskitě bălgari i těhnijat ezik*, in "Spisanie na Bălgarskata Akademija na naukitě" kniga XXXIII, klon istoriko-filologicěn i filosofsko-obštestven, 18, Sofija 1926, 1 *et. seq.*

27. Petrovici, "Toponymes roumains," 1970, *op. cit.*, p. 202. Chart no 1 shows the 27 geographical names in which *-în*, (*-îm*) appears in northern Muntenia and Oltenia and the 3 in southern Transylvania. With regard to the importance of this statement, the relevant section is given here in the original:

La dénasalisation des voyelles nasales bulgares a commencé dans certains parlers dès le XII⁰ siècle. Toutefois il y a même aujourd'hui des parlers slaves méridionaux de type oriental (bulgaro-macédonien)—dont celui des Bulgares de Transylvanie, actuellement roumanisés, et quelques parler Bulgares du nord-est, répandus le long de la frontière linguistique bulgaro-roumaine—qui ont conservé la nasalité jusqu'à nos jours⁵⁰. Par conséquent, la conservation de la nasalité dans les toponymes qui figurent sur la carte n°1 ne nous donne aucune indication sur l'époque à laquelle ils ont été empruntés par les Roumains aux Slaves.

It is noteworthy that the article above mentioned of Petrovici, first published in 1958, was republished in 1970 in the collective work Emil Petrovici, *Studii de dialectologie şi toponimie*.

28. Petrovici, 1970, *op. cit.*, p. 77, note 15; p. 78, notes 16, 17, 18.

29. Petrovici, 1944, *op. cit.*, p. 75.

30. *Ibid.*, pp. 79–80.

31. *Ibid.*, p. 79.

32. *Ibid.*

33. Suciu, *Dicţionar istoric,* 1967, II, p. 225. Only "Valea Bistrei" is mentioned by Suciu.

34. Petrovici, 1970, "Istoria poporului român oglindită în toponimie" [The History of the Romanian People Reflected in Toponymy], p. 245; the article was first published in 1964 (in French and in Romanian). The French version was also published, with small changes, under the title "Toponymie et histoire," in *Revue Roumaine d'Histoire,* IV, 1965, no. 1, pp. 1–13. Petrovici refers to the works on geographical names written by Iorgu Iordan, such as *Nume de locuri romîneşti în Republica Populară Română,* 1952, and *Toponimie românească,* 1963.

"The examples of the place names Cîmpulung, Bălgrad, Tîrnava, contradict the theory that the place names are not translated but in case of parallel names in several languages, are created simultaneously in each language on the basis of the same physical or social situation." *(Ibid.,* p. 246).

With regard to the significance of these borrowings, especially that of the river name Tîrnava, and in light of the theory that Transylvania was the most ancient Romanian province, one wonders why this allegedly autochthonous population does not even have names in its own language for the most important rivers in its territory? Rosetti *(ILR,* 1968, p. 328), in fact, commented on this: "The fact that the Romanians have inherited this name proves that they found in that area a Slavic-speaking population [that had] settled there earlier."

Finally, it should be noted that for a long time Romanian toponymic research has devoted itself exclusively to proving the continuity of a Romanized element north of the lower Danube.

35. Ion Moga, *Les roumains de Transylvanie au Moyen Âge,* (Sibiu: 1944), p. 138.

36. *Ibid.*

37. Géza Bárczi, Lóránd Benkő, Jolán Berrár, *A magyar nyelv története* [The History of the Hungarian Language], (Budapest: 1967), p. 151.

38. Kniezsa, *Keletmagyarország helynevei,* 1943, *op. cit.,* p. 209.

39. *Ibid.*

40. Suciu, *Dicţionar istoric,* 1967, vol. I, p. 159.

41. Iorgu Iordan, *Nume de locuri,* 1952, *op. cit.,* p. 26.

42. *Ibid.*

43. *Ibid.*

44. Kniezsa, 1943, *op. cit.,* pp. 224–225.

45. Ion Moga, *Les roumains de Transylvanie au Moyen Âge,* (Sibiu: 1944).

46. Kniezsa, 1943, *op. cit.,* pp. 212–217.

47. V. Frăţilă, "Vechimea unor toponimice din centrul Transylvaniei" [The Ancientness of Certain Place Names in Central Transylvania], in *Limba română* XIX, 1970, pp. 229–238.

48. Suciu, 1968, *op. cit.,* p. 125.

49. *Ibid.*

50. Nicolae Drăganu, *Românii în veacurile IX–XIV pe baza toponimiei și a onomasticei* [The Romanians in the 9th to the 14th Centuries on the Basis of Place Names and Onomastics], (Bucharest: 1933), p. 502; quoted by I. Pătruț, in *Onomastică românească*, (Bucharest: 1980), p. 125.

51. Ioan Pătruț, 1980, p. 123.

52. Iorgu Iordan, *Nume de locuri*, 1952, *op. cit.*, p. 119: "The personal names that become place names only rarely preserve their original form."

53. Frățilă, "Vechimea unor toponimice," 1970, *op. cit.*, p. 233.

54. *Cf.*, Stefan Kniezsa, "Die Gewässernamen des östlichen Karpatenbeckens," in: *Ungarische Jahrbücher*, 23 (1943), pp. 197–198; Lajos Kiss, *Földrajzi nevek etimológiai szótára*, (Budapest: 1978), p. 121; Béla Kálmán, *The World of Names*, (Budapest: 1978), p. 41 and 138.

55. Christian Ionescu, *Mică enciclopedie onomastică*, 1975, p. 165.

56. Frățilă, "Vechimea unor toponimice," 1970, p. 233.

57. Scheiner, *Balkan-Archiv* II, 29; quoted by Kniezsa, *Keletmagyarország helynevei*, 1943, p. 185. The present Romanian name of this village is Broșteni.

58. With regard to Bozko, this is also stated by N.A. Constantinescu, *Dicționarul onomastic românesc*, (Bucharest: 1963), to whom Frățilă refers. Zyn or Sin is of Bulgarian origin, from Bulgarian *sino* "blue." Bozko "personal name" + Hung. *sár* "mud" = "the mud of Bozko"; Zyn "personal name" + *potok* "brook" + *-a* "genitive suffix" = "the brook of Zyn."

59. Iorgu Iordan, *Nume de locuri*, 1952, *op. cit.*, p. 72.

60. *Ibid.*

61. Frățilă, "Vechimea unor," 1970, pp. 235–236.

62. The data about the mentions of this place name in documents are taken from Suciu, *Dicționar istoric*, 1967, *op. cit.*, vol. II, p. 10.

63. *Convorbiri literare*, XI, 1906, p. 295; quoted by Lajos Tamás, *Rómaiak, románok és oláhok Dácia Trajánában* [Romans, Romanians, and Vlachs in Dacia Traiana], (Budapest: 1935), p. 171.

64. Rosetti, *ILR*, 1968, p. 329.

65. Iorgu Iordan, *Toponimie românească*, p. 523; quoted by Frățilă, 1970, p. 236.

66. Aurelian Sacerdoțeanu ("Elemente de continuitate și unitate în istoria medievală a românilor," p. 115, in *Unitate și continuitate în istoria poporului român*, [Bucharest: 1968], quoted by Frățilă, 1970, p. 236, note 24) proposed the etymology Latin *habitatio* "dwelling place" or *habitus* "state" > Romanian *ohaba*. There are two sounds in Ohaba that exclude its being an inherited Latin word in Romanian: *h* and intervocalic *-b-* were not preserved in Romanian, as Frățilă also pointed out.

67. Iorgu Iordan, *Nume de locuri*, 1952, *op. cit.* Iordan gives a great number of examples of the different kinds of place names of which here only a few are given to illustrate the subject.

68. Iordan made the following remark on the frequent appearance of "Traian": I think the presence of the name *Traian* in 12 counties speaks eloquently for the nationalist tendency, coexisting with economic exploration.

69. Iorgu Iordan, *Toponimie românească*, 1963, p. 404.

70. *Ibid.*, p. 340

71. On page one of the original edition of Petru Maior's chief work, *Istoria pentru începutul romînilor în Dacia* [The History of the Beginnings of the Romanians in Dacia], written in the Cyrillic alphabet, the author's name is followed by information about his origin: "de Dicio-Sînmartin."

72. The origin and initial meaning of this name is now forgotten and it may be considered to mean by many speakers *Tre văi* "three valleys." V. Bogrea (*cf.*, Iordan, 1963, p. 494) proposed the derivation of this place name from the personal name *Trivali*, based on the name of the Thracian population in Serbia and in Bulgaria known from ancient sources as *Triballi.*

73. *Cf.*, Silviu Dragomir, *Vlahii din nordul Peninsulei Balcanice în evul mediu* [The Vlachs in the Northern Balkan Peninsula in the Middle Ages], (Bucharest: 1959). A map drawn after Dragomir as well as a list of the appellatives which are on the basis of the Northern Romanian place names and geographical names still extant in the Balkan Peninsula and an English translation are given by Du Nay, 1977, pp. 26–27.

74. Iordan, *Nume de locuri*, 1952, *op. cit.*, p. 123.

75. *Ibid.*

76. *Ibid.*, p. 194.

77. Chirpăr (reg. of Agnetheln, Romanian Agnita) from Transylvanian Saxon Kirpərich = German Kirchberg, and Nocrihi or Nocrich, in the same area, from Transylvanian Saxon Nogrech = German Neukirch (*cf.*, Iordan, 1952, p. 194).

78. Iordan, 1952, p. 213.

79. *Ibid.*, p. 214.

80. *Ibid.*, p. 60.

81. *Ibid.*, p. 73.

82. S. Moldovan and N. Togan, *Dicționarul numirilor de localități · cu proporțiune română din Ungaria* [Dictionary of Place Names With the Romanian Share in Hungary], (Sibiu: 1909).

83. Kniezsa, *Keletmagyarország helynevei*, 1943, *op. cit.*

84. *Cf.*, Iordan, 1952.

85. Iordan, 1952, p. 231. Also *Gărcea, Gârceni* (from Slavic) and *Cuțaoni* (a Romanian pejorative form) appear.

86. Suciu, *Dicționar istoric*, vol. I, 1967, *op. cit.*, p. 424. In other parts of Hungary, there are at least 35 place names containing "*német*" (*cf.*, Elemér Mályusz, in *Századok*, 1939, quoted by T. Nägler, *Die Ansiedlung der Siebenbürger Sachsen*, 1979, p. 182 and map no. 22).

87. Iordan, 1952, *op. cit.*, p. 237.

88. Ștefan Pascu, *Voievodatul Transilvaniei*, I, (Cluj: 1971), p. 82.

89. Emil Petrovici, *Dacoromania*, 10, 1938–1941, p. 266; Ion I. Russu, *Cercetări de lingvistică*, 2, 1957, pp. 263, 266; Gottfried Schramm, "Frühe Schicksale der Rumänen," 1985, *op. cit.*, p. 235; *cf.*, for example, Rosetti, *ILR*, 1968, pp. 227–228.

90. Kniezsa, "Die Gewässernamen," 1943, *op. cit.*, pp. 187–235.

91. A document containing this name and dated to 1306 is a forgery made in the 19th century; *cf.*, Kniezsa, "Die Gewässernamen," 1943, p. 217;

and Suciu, *Dicţionar istoric*, I, 1967, *op. cit.*, p. 166: "document of questionable authenticity."

92. Suciu, 1967, p.166.

93. Kniezsa, "Keletmagyarország helynevei," 1943, *op. cit.*, p. 118.

94. *Ibid.*

95. *Ibid.*, p. 119.

96. *Ibid.*, p. 121.

97. Thomas Nägler, *Die Ansiedlung der Siebenbürger Sachsen,* (Bucharest: 1979), pp. 174–179.

98. Ernst Wagner, *Historisch-statistisches Ortsnamenbuch für Siebenbürgen,* (Köln-Wien: 1977), p. 28; Kniezsa, "Keletmagyarország helynevei," 1943, p. 138.

99. Petrovici, "Toponymes roumains," 1970, p. 195.

100. *Ibid.*, p. 197.

101. Kniezsa, "Keletmagyarország helynevei," 1943, p. 154.

102. Petrovici, 1970, *op. cit.*, p. 196.

103. Mihăilă, *Studii de lexicologie şi istorie a lingvisticii româneşti* [Studies of Lexicology and History of Romanian Linguistics], (Bucharest: 1973), p. 16; Rosetti, *ILR,* 1968, p. 286.

104. Mihăilă, 1973, *op. cit.*, pp. 22–23; Mihăilă, "Aspecte teoretice şi istorice ale studierii raporturilor lingvistice vechi slavo-române" [Theoretical and Historical Aspects of the Study of the Ancient Slavo-Romanian Linguistical Contacts], in *Studii şi cercetări lingvistice,* 33, (1982), p. 65 under the headline: "Miscellanea."

105. Petrovici, "Toponymes roumains," 1970, *op. cit.*, p. 145. See also, Ioan Pătruţ, "Vechimea relaţiilor lingvistice slavo-române," in Pătruţ, *Studii de limba română şi de slavistică,* (Cluj: 1974), pp. 101–123.

106. *Ibid.*

107. Petrovici, 1970, *op. cit.*, p. 74.

108. Mihăilă, *Studii de lexicologie,* 1973, *op. cit.*, p. 13; Mihăilă, "Aspecte teoretice şi istorice," 1982, *op. cit.*, p. 61.

109. Mihăilă, *Studii de lexicologie,* 1973, p. 41.

110. Petrovici, 1970, *op. cit.*, pp. 77–78.

111. *Polnoglasia:* "A linguistic phenomenon characteristic of the Eastern Slavic languages, consisting of the presence of the groups of sound *"oro,"* *"olo,"* *"ere,"* *"ra,"* *"la,"* *"re,"* *"le"* from Old Slavic. From Russian *polnoglasie."* (*Dicţionarul explicativ al limbii române* [DEX], Bucharest, 1975).

112. All the geographical names given by Petrovici, 1970, pp. 77–78, are taken up here. In the fourth, northwestern area, the direct borrowing from Slavic by Romanian is not always certain; Gîmbuţ, for example, was transferred to Romanian from Hungarian, (Petrovici, 1970, p. 197) as also noted elsewhere, and should not be mentioned in the present context.

113. Petrovici, "Toponymes roumains," 1970, *op. cit.*, p. 197: "En examinant la liste des noms de lieux roumains à élément nasal pour sl. comm. *•ǫ* d'origine incontestablement slave, la première constatation qu'on est obligé de faire, c'est que, dans ces toponymes, l'unique traitment de sl. comm. *•ǫ*

est *în*, *îm*, et jamais *un*, *um*." Petrovici stated that the geographical names of Slavic origin in Romania do not show sound characteristics older than Middle Bulgarian: Petrovici, 1970, p. 77, note 15; p. 78, notes 16, 17, 18.

114. Rosetti, *ILR*, 1968, p. 339.

115. *Ibid.*, pp. 340–341; Mihăilă, "Aspecte teoretice," 1982, *op. cit.*, pp. 65–66; Pătruţ, "Vechimea relaţiilor," 1974, *op. cit.*, pp. 244–245.

116. Rosetti, *ILR*, 1968, p. 340.

117. Pătruţ, 1974, p. 243.

118. *Ibid.*, pp. 244–245: "The most ancient Romanian reflex of Slavic *ǫ is *un/um*, which, probably, as also Albanian *un*, must be connected with the stage of Slavic nasal *o*. The corresponding *în/îm*, parallel with Albanian *ën*, reflect probably the stage of Slavic nasal *ã*."

119. Rosetti, *ILR*, 1968, p. 341. See further Oblak, *Mazedonische Studien*, (Wien: 1896) p. 19; Stefan Mladenov, *Geschichte der bulgarischen Sprache* (Berlin-Leipzig: 1929) p. 115.

120. Petrovici, 1970, *op. cit.*, pp. 197–198. This assumption of renewing of the pronunciation, adapting it to the changes in Slavic has been also advanced to explain the fact that most of the Slavic elements of Romanian are of a relatively recent sound pattern. *Cf.*, for example, Rosetti, *ILR*, 1968, p. 288.

121. G. Bárczi, L. Benkő, J. Berrár, *A magyar nyelv története* [The History of the Hungarian Language], (Budapest, 1967), p. 114.

122. *Ibid.*

123. Pătruţ, 1974, p. 245: "The Romanian place names of Slavic origin in which the reflex *în/îm* appears cannot be from before this period [the 11th–12th centuries]."

124. Petrovici, 1970, pp. 199–200. These are the following: Dîmbova (village), Dîmbova (brook), Dîmbova (marsh), Lînga (village), Glîmboaia (brook), Glîmbocul-Fleşti (village), Glîmbocel (village), Glîmbocelu (village), Glîmbocata (brook), Glîmbocata (village), Glîmboca (hamlet of the village Glîmbocata), Glîmbocata (hill near the village of the same name), Glîmbocelul (hamlet of Tîrgul Cîrcinov), Glîmboca (brook, affluent of the river Argeş), Rîncăciov, (river, village, and monastery), Dîmbovicioara (village in Argeş district, the Romanian diminutive of Dîmboviţa), Dîmboviţa (village), Cîmpina (brook), Dîmbovicioara (village in Dîmboviţa district), Dîmboviţa (river), Dîmbovnic (river), Cîmpina (town), Cîmpiniţa (brook flowing through Cîmpina), Dîmbul (brook and village), Dîmbroca (village).

Another three names of this type are found in southern Transylvania: 1. Glîmboca (village in Sibiu County), modern Hungarian Glimboka. In documents: 1322: Honrabach, 1418: *villa* Hunerbach and only beginning with the late sixteenth century (1589) Glemboka; in 1854: Glimboka, Hühnerbach, Glîmboaca (Suciu, 1967, vol. I, p. 266). This name originates from Slavic *glǫboka* "deep" and could be, formally, a direct borrowing from Slavic. Its late mention in the documents suggests, however, that it was created later, possibly by Romanian immigrants from the southern slope of the Southern Carpathians, where several villages bear this name. 2. Glîmboceni, a small river in Hunedoara County not attested to in medieval sources. 3. Glimboca or Glîmboca, modern Hungarian Glimboka, a village in Caraş-Severin County (Krassó-Szörény), which was first attested to (in 1475) as Glamboka; in 1492: Glomboka. These early forms show a Hungarian sound pattern, with -am, -om for Slavic ǫ (Petrovici, 1970, p. 200). (The modern Hungarian name is a recent borrowing from Romanian.) Originally, the name of this village is thus probably a parallel Hungarian and Romanian borrowing from Slavic.

125. Rosetti, *ILR*, 1968, p. 431: Rosetti mentions 35 geographical names of Northern Romanian origin found in Bulgaria, having eliminated those with an Arumanian sound pattern and those that are questionable. He refers to works by Gustav Weigand (for example, *Jahresbericht des Instituts für rumänische Sprache*, [Leipzig: 1909] XV, 88–134); I. Petkanov, "Les éléments romans dans les langues balkaniques," Actes du Xe Congrès international de linguistique et philologie romanes, Strasbourg 1962, Paris 1965, pp. 1167–1172; Ivan Duridanov, in *Sbornik St. Romanski*, 1961, pp. 469–474; and I. Zaimov. A thorough presentation of these geographical names is found in: Silviu Dragomir, *Vlahii din nordul Peninsulei Balcanice în evul mediu* [The Vlachs on the Northern Balkan Peninsula in the Middle Ages], (Bucharest: 1959).

126. Petrovici, 1970, p. 143.

127. *Erdély története* [The History of Transylvania], 1986, vol. I, p. 587. See further Kniezsa, "Keletmagyarország helynevei," 1943, *op. cit.*, p. 124; Béla Kálmán, *The World of Names. A Study in Hungarian Onomatology*, (Budapest: 1978); Lajos Kiss, *Földrajzi nevek etimológiai szótára* [Etymological Dictionary of Geographical Names], (Budapest: 1978). For the early Hungarian historical topography: György Györffy, *Az Árpád-kori Magyarország történeti földrajza* [Historical Geography of Hungary in the Árpád-age], 3 vols., new edition (Budapest: 1987).

128. Kniezsa, *A párhuzamos helynévadás* [Parallel Namegiving], (Budapest: 1944), p. 23.

129. *Ibid.*, p. 20.

130. *Urkundenbuch zur Geschichte der Deutschen in Siebenbürgen*, vol. I, 1191–1342, compiled by Franz Zimmermann and Carl Werner (Hermannstadt: 1892), p. 11, 16, 17, 19, documents 370 no 19. See further Thomas Nägler, *Die Ansiedlung der Siebenbürger Sachsen*, 1979, p. 119. The assumption of Nägler is questionable.

With regard to the settlement of the Transylvanian Germans, it is now generally accepted that they immigrated primarily from middle Franconia (Moselle-Franconia) and the west banks of the Moselle and the Rhine (Cologne, Lüttich, Aachen, Trier, and Luxembourg). A smaller part of them apparently came from Westfalia, Hesse, Bavaria, and Thuringia. An organized settlement of Germans into special areas of Transylvania was started in the mid-twelfth century by King Géza (1141–1162). In 1224 Endre II granted territorial, political, and religious autonomy to the Transylvanian Germans (Saxons) in his so-called "Golden Charter" (*Goldener Brief, Andreanum*). Literature on the settlement and history of the Transylvanian Germans: Georg Eduard Müller, *Die Sächsische Nationsuniversität*, (Hermannstadt: 1928); Otto Mittelstrass,

Beiträge zur Siedlungsgeschichte Siebenbürgens im Mittelalter, (München: 1961); W. Grandjean, *Die Anfänge der Hermannstädter Propstei im Spiegel päpstlicher Urkunden* (Siebenbürgisches Archiv 1971).

131. Wagner, *Historisch-statistisches Ortsnamenbuch,* 1977, *op. cit.,* p. 27.

132. *Ibid.,* p. 47.

133. Thomas Nägler, *Die Ansiedlung,* 1979, *op. cit.,* pp. 174–179.

134. Of the names of "unknown origin," 25 are possibly German, 17 Hungarian, and 8 Slavic. The only name (Reps, Romanian Rupea, Hungarian Kőhalom) considered by Nägler "Romanian? from Latin?" is of neither Latin nor Romanian origin.

135. Kniezsa, "Keletmagyarország helynevei," 1943, p. 249.

136. *Ibid.,* p. 139. There are, of course, several Romanian names borrowed more recently: Reschinar, from Romanian Rășinari, was earlier German Städterdorf; Porkendorf is from Romanian Porcești; Predeal, Fundata, and Kolobitza are also Romanian names borrowed and used today by the Saxons.

137. Mittelstrass, *Beiträge zur Siedlungsgeschichte,* 1961, *op. cit.,* p. 25. Zimmermann and Werner, *Urkundenbuch,* Urkunde: no. 31, pp. 18–20; 1223: *Silva Blacorum et Bissenorum,* Urkunde: no. 43, pp. 32–35.

138. Kniezsa, "Keletmagyarország helynevei," 1943, p. 157.

139. Kniezsa, *A párhuzamos helynévadás* [Parallel Namegiving], (Budapest: 1944), pp. 16–17.

SELECTED
BIBLIOGRAPHY

HISTORICAL SOURCES

Anna Comnena (Komnenē), Alexias, edited by 1. A. *Reifferscheid* 2 vols. (Leipzig: 1884); 2. Alexiade (Règne de l'empereur Alexis I Comnena 1081–1118), translated by Bernard *Leib*, 3 vols. (Paris: 1937–1945).

Annales Fuldenses, ed. by Friedrich *Kurze* in: Mon. Germ. Hist. Script. Rer. Germ. in usum scholarum 7 (Hannover: 1891).

Annales Regni Francorum ab a. 741 usque ad a. 829 qui dicuntur Laurissenses maiores et Einhardi, ed. by Friedrich *Kurze* (Hannover: 1895).

Anonymi (P. Magistri), Gesta Hungarorum, ed. by József *Deér*, in: Scriptores Rerum Hungaricarum ducum regumque stirpis Arpadianae gestarum (Budapest: 1937); Anonymus, Gesta Hungarorum, translated by Dezső *Pais* (Budapest: 1975).

Anonymi Descriptio Europae Orientalis "Imperium Constantinopolitanum, Albania, Serbia, Bulgaria, Ruthenia, Ungaria, Polonia, Bohemia" anno MCCCVIII exarata, ed. by Olgierd *Górka* (Krakow: 1916).

Bartoniek, Emma: Magyar történeti forráskiadványok [Hungarian Historical Sources Publications], (Budapest: 1929).

Cassius Dio (Dio Cassius Cocceianus), Historia Romana.

Choniates (Koniates) Nichetas, Historia, 2 vols., ed. by Johannes Aloys *von Dieten* (Berlin: 1975).

Corpus Inscriptionum Latinarum (*CIL*).

Constantine (Konstantin) *VII Prophyrogenitus*, De administrando imperio, ed. by Gyula *Moravcsik* (Budapest: 1949); a new commentary edition in English translation by R.J.H. *Jenkins* (London: 1962).

Csánki, Dezső: Magyarország történelmi földrajza a Hunyadiak korában [The Historical Geography of Hungary in Hunyadi's Time], vols. I-III and V; the IV. volume by *Fekete Nagy* Antal (Budapest: 1890, 1894, 1897, 1913, and 1941).

Dioscorides, Pedanius Anazarbeus, De materia medica.

Documenta Historiam Valachorum in Hungaria Illustrantia, ed. by Antal *Fekete Nagy* and László *Makkai* (Budapest: 1941).

Documenta Romaniae Historica, C. Transylvania, vol. X. 1351–1355, ed., by Ştefan *Pascu* (Bucharest: 1977).

Documente privind istoria României. Veacul XI, XII și XIII, C. Transilvania, vol. 1, ed. by Eudoxiu *de Hurmuzaki* (Bucharest: 1951).

Fontes Historiae Dacoromanorum, 15 vols., edited by Gheorghe *Popa-Lisseanu* (Bucharest: 1934–1939).

Fontes Historiae Dacoromanae, II, edited by Haralambie *Mihăescu*, Gheorghe *Ștefan*, Radu *Hîncu*, and Vladimir *Iliescu* (Bucharest: 1970).

Fontes Historiae Daco-Romanae III, Scriptores Byzantini, edited by Alexandru *Elian* and Nicolae-Șerban *Tanașoca*, (Bucharest: 1975).

Fontes ad historiam Dacoromaniae pertinentes, I-III, edited by Vladimir *Iliescu*, Virgil C. *Popescu*, Gheorghe *Ștefan*. Institutum Archaeologicum (Bucharest: 1964–1975).

Geographus Ravennas, Ravennatis anonymi Cosmographia et Guidonis Geographia, ed. by Joseph *Schnetz* (Leipzig: 1940).

Glossar zur frühmittelalterlichen Geschichte im östlichen Europa, edited by Jadran *Ferluga*, Manfred *Hellmann*, Herbert *Ludat*. Series A: Latin Names until 900; Series B: Greek Names until 1025 (Wiesbaden: 1973 *et. seq.*).

Gombos, Ferenc Albin: Catalogus Fontium Historiae Hungaricae, I-III. (Budapest: 1937–1938, 1943).

Gyóni, Mátyás: A román történet bizánci forrásai [The Byzantine Sources of the Romanian History], Magyar Tudományos Akadémia I. Oszt. Közl. 5. 1954, pp. 71–78.

Herodotos Halikarnass, Historiae.

Iordanes, Romana et Getica, ed. by Theodor *Mommsen*, in: Mon. Germ. Hist. Auctores antiquissimi, vols. 5/1 (Berlin: 1882) *et. seq.*; *Iordanes*, Romana, ed. by Wilhelm *Martens*, Gotengeschichte und Auszug aus der römischen Geschichte, 3rd. edition (Leipzig: 1913).

Kedrenos, Georgius Cedrenus Ioannis Scylitzae ope, ed. by Immanuel *Bekker*, Corpus Scriptorum Historiae Byzantinae 34 (Bonn: 1938).

Kekaumenos (Cecaumenus), Strategicon et incerti scriptoris De officiis regiis libellus, ed. by B. *Wassiliewsky—V. Jernstedt* (1896; new. edition Amsterdam 1963).

Kinnamos, Ioannes Cinnamus, Epitome rerum ab Ioanne et Alexio Comnensis gestarum, ed. by August *Meinecke*, Corpus Historiae Byzantinae, vol. 26 (Bonn: 1836).

Lenk, von Treuenfeld, Ignaz: Siebenbürgens geographisch-, topographisch-, statistisch-, hydrographisch- und orographisches Lexikon, mittels eines Versuches seiner Landkarten-Beschreibung, 4 vols. (Wien: 1839).

Lukinich, Imre and László *Gáldi*, Documenta Historiam Valachorum in Hungaria Illustrantia usque ad annum 1400 p. Chr., edited by Antal *Fekete Nagy* et László *Makkai* (Budapest: 1941).

Monumenta Germaniae Historica (Hanovrae: 1854).

Monumenta Vaticana historiam regni Hungariae illustrantia. Series I, vols. I-IV, (Budapest: 1885–1891).

Moravcsik, Gyula: Byzantinoturcica I-II. Die byzantinischen Quellen. Der Geschichte der Türkenvölker (Budapest: 1942–1943), 2nd edition Berlin 1958.

Nestor's Chronicle = Povest vremenykh lyet, edited by V.P. *Adrianova* - *Peretts et. al.* Modern Russian translation by D.S. *Lichačev* and B.A. *Romanova*, vol. I (Moscow - Leningrad: 1950). English translation and edition by S.H. Cross and O.P. *Sherbowitz-Wetzor* (Cambridge, Mass.: 1953).

Orbán, Balázs: A Székelyföld leírása [The Description of the Székelys' Land], 6 vols. (Pest: 1868–1873). New edition by Elemér *Illyés* (Firenze-München: 1981).

Ortvay, Tivadar: Magyarország régi vízrajza a XIII-ik század végéig [The Ancient Hydrography of Hungary Until the End of the 13th Century], 2 vols. (Budapest: 1882).

Polybios, Historia.

Popa-Lisseanu, Gheorghe: Izvoarele istoriei românilor [Sources of the History of the Romanians], vols. I, V-VI, and VII (Bucharest: 1934–1935).

Popescu, Emilian: Inscripţiile greceşti şi latine din secolele IV-XIII descoperite în România [Greek and Latin Inscriptions of the 4th–13th Centuries Discovered in Romania], (Bucharest: 1976).

Priskos of Panion (Panites), Fragmenta, in: Historici Minores, ed. by *Dindorf* (Leipzig: 1870); new edition: Fragmenta in Excerptis de legationibus servata, ed. by *De Boor* (Berlin: 1903).

Prokopios Caesarea, De bello Gothico, ed. by James *Maury* and Gerhard *Wirth* (Leipzig: 1963).

Die protobulgarischen Inschriften, ed. by Veselin *Beševliev* (Berlin: 1963).

Ptolemaios Klaudios of Alexandria, Geographia.

Ravennas Anonymus, Geographia, translated by Joseph *Schnetz*, Nomina Germanica 10.

Scriptores Rerum Hungaricarum tempore ducum regumque stirpis Arpadianae gestarum, I–II, ed. by Emericus *Szentpétery* (Budapest: 1937–1938).

Strabón of Amascia, Geographia.

Theophylaktos Simokatta, Historiae, ed. by Immanuel *Bekker* (Bonn: 1834).

Urkundenbuch zur Geschichte der Deutschen in Siebengürgen, vol. I. 1191–1342, vol. II. 1391–1415, compiled by Franz *Zimmermann* and Carl *Werner* (Hermannstadt: 1892–1902).

Veress, Endre (Andrei) (ed.), Bibliografia română-ungară [Romanian-Hungarian Bibliography], (Bucharest: 1931–1935).

BOOKS AND ARTICLES

Alföldi András, "Pannónia rómaiságának kialakulása és történeti kerete" [The Formation and Historical Structure of the Roman Population in Pannonia], Századok, Budapest, LXX, 1936.

————. Zu den Schicksalen Siebenbürgens im Altertum (Budapest: 1944).

Alföldy Géza, Die Personennamen in der römischen Provinz Dalmatia (Heidelberg: 1969).

————. Bevölkerung und Gesellschaft der römischen Provinz Dalmatien, mit einem Beitrag von András Mócsy (Budapest: 1964).

Altheim, Franz, Geschichte der Hunnen, 5 vols., (Berlin: 1959–1962).

Armbruster, Adolf, Romanitatea românilor. Istoria unei idei [The Romanity of the Romanians. The History of an Idea], (Bucharest: 1972).
————. La romanité des roumains. Histoire d'une idée (Bucharest: 1977).
Arumaa, Peeter, Urslavische Grammatik. Einführung in das vergleichende Studium der slavischen Sprachen, 2 vols. (Heidelberg: 1964–1976).
Arvinte, Vasile, Fondul lexical al limbii române în comparație cu celelalte limbii romanice [The Lexical Basis of the Romanian Language in Comparison with Other Romance Languages], (Sinaia: 1971).
————. Die Rumänen. Ursprung, Volks- und Landesnamen [The Romanians. Origin, Ethnical- and Landnames], (Tübingen: 1980).
Assimilation et résistance à la culture gréco-romaine dans le monde ancien. Travaux du VIᵉ Congrès International d'Études Classiques, (Madrid, 1974, București-Paris 1976).
Asztalos, Miklós (ed.), A történeti Erdély [Historic Transylvania], (Budapest: 1936).
Babeș, Mircea, "Unitatea și răspîndirea geto-dacilor în lumina documentelor arheologice (secolele al II-lea î.e.n. - I e.n.)" [The Unity and the Dissemination of the Geto-Dacians in the Light of Archaeological Evidence (2nd Century B.C. - 1st Century A.D.)], SCIVA, 30, 3, 1979, pp. 327–345.
Bahner, Werner, Die lexikalischen Besonderheiten des Frühromanischen in Südosteuropa (Berlin: 1970).
Balla, Lajos, "L'importance des colonisations en Dacie," Acta Classica Univ. Scient. Debrecen, X-XI, 1974–75, pp. 139–143.
Balotă, A., La nasalisation et le rhotacisme dans les langues roumaine et albanaise (Bucharest: 1926).
Banner, János, Jakabffy, Imre, A Közép-Dunamedence régészeti bibliográfiája [The Archaeological Bibliography of the Middle Danubian Basin], (Budapest: 1954); 1954–1959 (Budapest: 1961); 1960–1966 (Budapest: 1968).
Bárczi, Géza, Benkő, Lóránd, Berrár, Jolán, A magyar nyelv története [The History of the Hungarian Language], (Budapest: 1967).
Barić, Henrik, Albanisch, Romanisch und Rumänisch (Sarajevo: 1956).
————. Lingvističke studije (Sarajevo: 1954).
Bartoli, Matteo Giulio, Das Dalmatische. Altromanische Sprachreste von Veglia bis Ragusa und ihre Stellung in der apennino-bulgarischen Romania, 1–2, (Wien: 1906).
Bârzu, Ligia, Continuitatea populației autohtone în Transilvania în secolele IV–V. Cimitirul 1 de la Bratei [The Continuity of the Autochthonous Population in Transylvania in the 4th to 5th Centuries. Cemetery no. 1 at Bratei, (Bucharest: 1973).
————. Continuitatea creației materiale și spirituale a poporului român pe teritoriul fostei Dacii [Continuity of the Material and Spiritual Culture of the Romanian People on the Territory of Former Dacia], (Bucharest: 1979).
————. "Données sur l'archéologie des IVᵉ–XIᵉ siècles sur territoire de la Roumanie. La culture Bratei et la culture Dridu." Dacia, XV, 1971.
————. Săpăturile de la Dridu. Contribuție la arheologia și istoria perioadei de formare a poporului român [The Excavations at Dridu. Contributions

to the Archaeology and the History of the Period of Formation of the Romanian People], (Bucharest: 1967).

Basch, M.H., "Resistance to and Assimilation of Cultural Elements from the Eastern Mediterranean in Pre-Roman Iberia," in: Assimilation et résistance à la culture gréco-romaine dans le monde ancien. Travaux du VIe Congrès International d'Études Classiques, Madrid, septembre 1974.

Battisti, Carlo, Avviamento allo studio del latino volgare, (Bari: 1949).

Bénabou, Marcel, "Résistance et Romanisation en Afrique du Nord sous le Haut-Empire," Assimilation et résistance à la culture gréco-romaine dans le monde ancien. Travaux du VIe Congrès International d'Études Classiques, Madrid, septembre 1974.

Beneš, Jan, Auxilia Romana in Moesia atque in Dacia. Zu den Fragen des römischen Verteidigungssystems im Unteren Donauraum und in den angrenzenden Gebiete (Prague: 1978).

Beninger, Eduard, Der westgotisch-alanische Zug nach Mitteleuropa, Manus Bibliothek 51 (Leipzig: 1931).

Berciu, Dumitru, Dacoromania. Archaeologia Mundi; Enciclopedia Archaeologica (Italian translation), (Roma: 1976).

_____ . "Probleme privind formarea poporului român în lumina cercetării arheologice recente" ["The Problem of the Romanian Ethnogenesis in the Light of Recent Archaeological Researches"], in Revista de Istorie, 28, 1975, no. 8, pp. 1155–1169.

Bernath, Mathias, Habsburg und die Anfänge der rumänischen Nationsbildung. Studien zur Geschichte Osteuropas (Leiden: 1972).

Beševliev, Veselin, Die protobulgarischen Inschriften (Berlin: 1963).

_____ (ed.) Spätgriechische und spätlateinische Inschriften aus Bulgarien (Berlin: 1964).

Bichir, Gheorghe, "Date noi cu privire la romanizarea Munteniei" [New Data About the Romanization of Wallachia], SCIVA, 29, 3, Bucharest 1978, pp. 385–395.

_____ . Cultura carpică [The Carpic Culture], (Bucharest: 1973).

_____ . "La civilisation des Carpes (IIe–IIIe siècle de n.è) à la lumière des fouilles archéologiques de Poiana-Dulcești, de Butnărești et de Pădureni," Dacia, 11, 1967, pp. 177–224.

_____ Archaeology and History of the Carpi, I–II (London: 1976).

Boba, Imre, Nomads, Northmen and Slavs. Eastern Europe in the Ninth Century (The Hague: 1967).

Bodor, András, "Contribuții la problema cuceririi Daciei" [Contributions to the Conquest of Dacia], in AMN, 1, 1964, pp. 137–162.

Bolin, Sture, Fynden av romerska mynt i det fria Germanien. Studier i romersk och äldre germansk historia [Finds of Roman Coins in Free Germania. Studies in Roman and Old German History], (Lund: 1926).

Bóna, István, Der Anbruch des Mittelalters. Gepiden und Langobarden im Karpatenbecken (Budapest: 1976).

_____ . "Gepiden an der Theiss - Gepiden in Siebenbürgen," Acta Arch. Hung. 31, 1979, pp. 9–50.

————. Die Awaren. Ein asiatisches Reitervolk an der mittleren Donau, in: Awaren in Europa (Frankfurt am Main - Nürnberg: 1985).

————. "Das erste Auftreten der Bulgaren im Karpatenbecken," in Studia Turco-Hungarica, 5, 1981.

Bozhilov, Ivan, "Kulturata Dridu i pårvoto bålgarsko tsarstvo" [The Dridu Culture and the First Bulgarian State], Istoricheski Pregled, 1970, no. 4, pp. 115-124.

Branga, Nicolae, Urbanismul Daciei romane [The Urbanism of Roman Dacia], (Timişoara: 1985).

Brâncuş, Gheorghe, "Probleme ale reconstrucţiei elementelor lexicale autohtone în româna comună," in SCL, XVII/2, 1966, pp. 205-218.

Brătianu, Gheorghe, Une énigme et un miracle historique: le peuple roumain (Bucharest: 1937).

Brezeanu, Stelian, "Romani" şi "Blachi" la Anonymus. Istorie şi ideologie politică ["Romans" and "Blachs" in the Work of Anonymus. History and Political Ideology], in Revista de Istorie, vol. 34, 7, 1981, pp. 1313-1340.

Brunt, P.A., "Romanization of the Local Ruling Class in the Roman Empire," in: Assimilation et résistance à la culture gréco-romaine dans le monde ancien. Travaux du VIᵉ Congrès International d'Études Classiques, Madrid, septembre 1974.

Bury, J.B., History of the Eastern Roman Empire, 802-67 (London: 1912).

————. History of the Later Roman Empire I–II (London: 1923).

Çabej, Eqrem, "De quelques problèmes fondamentaux de l'histoire ancienne de l'Albanais," in: Conférence des études albanologiques 15–21 novembre 1962; Université d'Etat de Tirana, Institut d'Histoire et de Linguistique (Publié sous forme de manuscrit).

————. "Unele probleme ale istoriei limbii albaneze" [Some Problems of the History of the Albanian Language], in SCL, X, 4, 1959, pp. 528–560, Cluj.

————. "L'illyrien et l'albanais," in Studia Albanica, VIII, 1, 1970, pp. 157–170.

————. "Zur Charakteristik der lateinischen Lehnwörter im Albanischen," in Revue Roumaine de Linguistique, VII, 1962, pp. 161–199.

————. "Die ältesten Wohnsitze der Albaner auf der Balkaninsel im Lichte der Sprache und der Ortsnamen," in: VII Congresso Internazionale di Scienze Onomastiche. Atti e memorie del Congresso della sezione toponomastica, vol. 1, pp. 241–251.

————. L'illyrien et l'albanais, in: Les Illyriens et la genèse des Albanais (Tirana: 1971), pp. 31–40.

The Cambridge Medieval History, planned by J.B. Bury, edited by J.R. Tanner, C.W. Previté-Orton, Z.N. Brooke, vols. I, II, IV and VIII (Cambridge: 1911, 1913, 1923, vol. VIII 1936).

Capidan, Theodor, "Toponymie macédo-roumaine," in: (ed.) Académie Roumaine: Langue et littérature, Bulletin de la Section littéraire, vol. III, nos. 1–2 (Bucharest: 1972), pp. 31–40.

Capidan, Theodor, Aromânii. Dialectul aromân. Stdiu lingvistic, (Bucharest: 1932).

Caragiu-Marioțeanu, Matilda, Compendiu de dialectologie română (nord- și sud-dunăreană) [Compendium of Romanian Dialectology (North- and South-Danubian)], (Bucharest: 1975).

Carsten, F.L., The Rise of Fascism (London: 1967).

Cazacu, Boris, Studii de dialectologie română (Bucharest: 1966).

Comșa, Maria, "Cu privire la caracterul organizării social-economice și politice de pe teritoriul țării noastre în epoca migrațiilor" [About the Character of the Social-Political Organization in the Territory of Our Country During the Peoples' Migration], in SCIV, 18, 3, Bucharest 1967, pp. 431–442.

_____. "Die bulgarische Herrschaft nördlich der Donau während des IX. und X. Jahrhundert," in Dacia 4, 1960.

Constantinescu, Miron, Daicoviciu, Constantin, Pascu, Ştefan et. al. Istoria României. Compendiu (Bucharest: 1969), 3rd edition 1974.

Corpus Inscriptionum Latinarum (CIL), vol. III contains the Inscriptions of Dacia Romana.

Coteanu, Ion, "Premise pentru stabilirea vocabularului străromânei," in SCL, Bucharest, XVI, 1965, pp. 579–605.

_____. Structura și evoluția limbii române (de la origini pînă la 1860) [The Structure and the Evolution of the Romanian Language (from the Origins to 1860)], (Bucharest: 1981).

Crawford, M. H., Roman Republican Coin Hoards (London: 1969). Remarkable statistics for Dacia. Addition in review by Bucur Mitrea, SCIV, 20, 1969, pp. 508–510.

Crişan, Ion Horațiu, Burebista and His Time (Bucharest: 1978).

_____. "Once More About the Scythian Problem in Transylvania," Dacia, 9, 1965.

_____. Ceramica daco-getică [The Daco-Getian Ceramics], (Bucharest: 1968).

Csallány, Dezső, Archäologische Denkmäler der Gepiden im Mitteldonaubecken (454–568 A.D.), Archaeologica Hungarica 38, (Budapest: 1961).

_____. Archäologische Denkmäler der Awarenzeit in Mitteleuropa. Schrifttum und Fundorte (Budapest: 1956).

Csapody, Csaba, Az Anonymus-kérdés története [The History of the Anonymus's-Problem], (Budapest: 1978).

Les Daces libres aux IIᵉ–IVᵉ siècles de n. ère, in Actes du IIᵉ Congrès International de Thracologie, II, Bucharest, 1980, pp. 232–329.

Dacoromania, ed. by Sextil Pușcariu, I–XI volumes, (Bucharest: 1921–1948).

Daicoviciu, Constantin, Constantinescu, Miron, (eds.), Brève histoire de la Transylvanie (Bucharest: 1965).

_____. Dacica. Collected Works. (Cluj: 1969–1970).

_____. (red.), Istoria României, vol. I, (Bucharest: 1960).

_____. Din istoria Transilvaniei, 2 vols. (Bucharest: 1961).

_____. Petrovici, Emil, Ştefan, Gheorghe, La formation du peuple roumain et de sa langue (Bucharest: 1963).

_____. and Daicoviciu, Hadrian, Sarmizegethusa, 2nd. ed., (Bucharest: 1962).

_____. Hadrian, Dacia de la Burebista la cucerirea romană [Dacia of Burebista to the Roman Conquest], (Cluj: 1972).

Densusianu, Ovid, Opere. Lingvistica. Histoire de la langue roumaine, ed. by B. *Cazacu*, V. *Rusu*, I. *Şerb* (Bucharest: 1975).

Decĕv, Dimităr, Charakteristik der thrakischen Sprache (Sofia: 1952).

————. Die thrakischen Sprachreste (Wien: 1957).

Diaconu, Petre, Les Petchénègues au Bas-Danube (Bucharest: 1970).

Dicţionar enciclopedic romîn [Romanian Encyclopedic Dictionary], (Bucharest: 1962–1966).

Diculescu, Constantin, Die Gepiden (Leipzig: 1922).

Dimitrescu, Florica (ed.), Istoria limbii române. Fonetica, Morfosintaxa, Lexic [The History of the Romanian Language. Phonetics, Morphosyntaxis, Lexicology], (Bucharest: 1978).

Dölle, Hans-Joachim (red.), Römer und Germanen in Mitteleuropa (Berlin: 1975).

Drăganu, Nicolae, Românii în veacurile IX–XIV pe baza toponimiei şi a onomasticei [Romanians in the 9th–14th Centuries on the Basis of the Toponymy and Onomastics], (Bucharest: 1933).

Dragomir, Silviu, Vlahii din nordul Peninsulei Balcanice în evul mediu [The Vlachs of the Northern Balkan Peninsula in the Middle Ages], (Bucharest: 1959).

Dujčev, Ivan, Medioevo bizantino-slavo, vol. 1, (Roma: 1965).

Dumitraşcu, Sever, Teritoriul dacilor liberi din vestul şi nord-vestul României în vremea Daciei romane [The Territory of Free Dacians in Western and Northwestern Romania in the Time of Roman Dacia], (Bucharest: 1978).

Dunăreanu-Vulpe, Ecaterina, Tezaurul de la Pietroasa (Bucharest: 1967).

Du Nay, André, The Early History of the Rumanian Language. Edward Sapir Monograph Series in Language, Culture, and Cognition 3. (Lake Bluff, USA: 1977).

Duridanov, Ivan, Die alten Bevölkerungsverhältnisse Makedoniens auf Grund der Toponymie, in: Actes du Ier Congrès International des Études Balkaniques, VI, (Sofia: 1968), pp. 773–776.

————. "Zur alten slawischen Toponymie Bulgariens," in *Zeitschrift für Slawische Philologie* 29, 1961, pp. 91–102.

Dvornik, Francis, Les Slaves. Histoire et civilisation de l'Antiquité aux débuts de l'époque contemporaine (Paris: 1970).

————. La lutte entre Byzance et Rome à propos de l'Illyricum au IX siècle, in: Études sur l'histoire et sur l'art de Byzance. Mélanges Charles *Diehl*, vol. 1. Histoire (Paris: 1930), pp. 61–80.

Dymond, D.P., Archaeology and History. A Plea for Reconciliation (London: 1974).

East Central and Southeast Europe. A handbook of library and archival resources in North America. Ed. by Paul L. *Horecky* and David H. *Kraus* (Santa Barbara, Calif.: 1977). [The Joint Committee on Eastern Europe Publications series 3.].

Egger, Rudolf, Römische Antike und frühes Christentum. Ausgewählte Schriften, 2 vols. (Klagenfurt: 1963).

Eggers, Hans-Jürgens, Der römische Import im freien Germanien. Band I: Tafeln und Karten, Band II: Text (Hamburg: 1951).

Epigraphical publications, compiled by Nicolae *Gudea:* Beiträge zu einem Literaturnachweis der epigraphischen, das römische Dakien betreffenden Forschung nach 1902. *Arheološki Vestnik* 31, 1980.

Erdély története [The History of Transylvania], red. by Béla *Köpeczi,* László *Makkai,* András *Mócsy,* Zoltán *Szász,* and Gábor *Barta,* vols. I–III. (Budapest: 1986).

Fischer-Galati, Stephen, "Romanian Nationalism," in Peter F. *Sugar* and Ivo J. *Lederer* (eds.), Nationalism in Eastern Europe (Washington: 1969).

Fischer-Galati, Stephen, "The Origins of Modern Romanian Nationalism," in Jahrbücher für Geschichte Osteuropas, ed. by Georg *Stadtmüller,* Neue Folge, band 12/1964 (Wiesbaden: 1964), pp. 48–54.

Fischer, Iancu, Latina dunăreană. Introducere în istoria limbii române [Danubian Latin. Introduction to the History of the Romanian Language], (Bucharest: 1985).

———. "Aspectul lingvistic al romanizării Daciei" [The Linguistic Aspect of the Romanization of Dacia], in *Limba Română,* 27, 2, 1978, pp. 189–191, Bucharest.

Franga, Liviu, "I.I. Russu, Etnogeneza românilor. Fondul autohton traco-dacic și componența latino-romanică, București, Edit. științifică și enciclopedică, 1981, 466 p.," (review), in *SCL,* XXXIII (1982), no. 3, pp. 278–282.

Frățilă, V., "Vechimea unor toponimice din centrul Transilvaniei" [The Ancientness of Certain Place Names in Central Transylvania], in *Limba Română* XIX, Bucharest 1970, pp. 229–238.

Gamillscheg, Ernst, Romania Germanica. Sprach- und Siedlungsgeschichte der Germanen auf dem Boden des Alten Römerreichs, 3 vols. (Berlin-Leipzig: 1934–1936).

———. "Über die Herkunft der Rumänen," in Preuss. Akademie der Wissenschaften. Sitzungsberichte, Philos.-hist. Klasse, (Berlin: 1940), pp. 118–134.

Georgiev, Vladimir, La toponymie ancienne de la Péninsule Balkanique et la thèse méditerranéenne, *Linguistique Balkanique,* III, Fasc. 1, Sofia 1961.

———. The Thracians and Their Language (in Bulgarian), (Sofia: 1977).

———. "L'union linguistique balkanique. L'état actuel de recherches," in *Linguistique Balkanique,* XX, 1–2, 1977, pp. 5–15.

———. Introduzione alla storia delle lingue indoeuropee (Roma: 1966).

———. "Zur dakischen Hydronymie," in Acta Antiqua Acad. Scient. Hungaricae 10 (1962), pp. 115–121.

———. Theiss, Temes, Maros, Szamos (Herkunft und Bildung), in Beiträge zur Namenforschung 12, 1961, pp. 87–95.

———. Văprosi na bălgarskata etimologija (Sofia: 1958).

———. "L'ethnogenèse de la Péninsule Balkanique d'après les données linguistiques," in *L'ethnogenèse,* 1971, pp. 155–170.

Gerov, Boris, "Die lateinisch-griechische Sprachgrenze auf der Balkanhalbinsel," in: Die Sprachen im römischen Reich der Kaiserzeit (Könl-Bonn: 1980).

————— . "Griechisch und Latein in den Ostbalkanländern in römischer Zeit," in: Neue Beiträge zur Geschichte der Alten Welt, vol. 2 Römisches Reich, ed. by Elisabeth Charlotte Welskopf (Berlin: 1965) pp. 233–242.

Gesemann, Gerhard, Haralampieff, Kyrill, Schaller, Helmut (eds.), Bulgarische Sprache, Literatur und Geschichte. Symposium veranstaltet von der Südosteuropa-Gesellschaft mit der Bulgarischen Akademie der Wissenschaften 1978 (Neuried: 1980).

Giurescu, C. Constantin, Istoria românilor din cele mai vechi timpuri pînă astăzi [The History of the Romanians from the Most Ancient Times to the Present], (Bucharest: 1975).

————— . and Giurescu, C. Dinu, Istoria românilor [The History of the Romanians], (Bucharest: 1975).

————— . Istoria României în date (Bucharest: 1972).

Glodariu, Ion, "Aşezarea dacică şi daco-romană de la Slimnic" [The Dacian and Daco-Roman Settlement at Slimnic], in AMN, IX, 1972.

————— . Dacian Trade with the Hellenistic and Roman World (London: 1976).

Gostar, Nicolae, "Vechimea elementului roman la răsărit de Carpaţi" [The Ancientness of the Roman Element East of the Carpathians], in Era Socialistă, vol. LIX, 6, 1979, pp. 34–37.

Grecu, Vasile V., Şcoala Ardeleană şi unitatea limbii române literare [The Transylvanian School and the Unity of the Romanian Literary Language], (Timişoara: 1973).

Gudea, Nicolae, "Ceramica dacică din castrul roman de la Bologa (jud. Cluj)" [The Dacian Ceramics From the Roman Castrum at Bologa (Cluj County)], AMN, VI, 1969, p. 503.

————— . "Vasul cu inscripţie şi simboluri creştine de la Moigrad. Contribuţii la istoria creştinismului daco-roman" [The Vase with Christian Inscription and Symbols from Moigrad. Contributions to the History of Daco-Roman Christianity], Acta Musei Porolissensis, 1979, pp. 515–523.

————— . "Beiträge zu einem Literaturnachweis der epigraphischen, das römische Dakien betreffenden Forschung nach 1902," in: Arheološki Vestnik 31, 1980.

Gyóni, Mathias, "L'oeuvre de Kekaumenos, source de l'histoire roumaine," in Revue d'histoire comparée, XXIIIᵉ année 1945. Nouvelle série, Tome III, no. 1–4, pp. 96–180.

————— . "Les Volochs des Annales primitives de Kiev," in Études slaves et roumaines II, 1949, pp. 56–92.

————— . "La première mention historique des Vlaques des monts Balkans," in Acta Antiqua Hungaricae I, Budapest 1952, 3–4.

Györffy, György, Tanulmányok a magyar állam eredetéről [Studies About the Origin of the Hungarian State], (Budapest: 1959).

————— . "Anonymus Gesta Hungarorumának kora és hitelessége" [The Time and the Authenticity of Anonymus's Gesta Hungarorum], in Irodalomtörténeti közlemények, 1970/1.

————— . "Honfoglalás előtti népek és országok Anonymus Gesta Hungarorumában" [Preconquest Peoples and Countries in the Gesta Hungarorum], in Ethnographia, LXXVI, 1965, Budapest.

————. István király és műve [King Stephen and His Work], (Budapest: 1977).

————. Az Árpád-kori Magyarország történeti földrajza I–III. [The Historical Geography of Hungary of the Árpád-age, I], (Budapest: 1963), new edition 1987.

Haarmann, Harald, Der lateinische Lehnwortschatz im Albanischen. Hamburger Philologische Studien 19, (Hamburg: o.J).

Hachmann, Rolf, Die Goten und Skandinavien (Berlin: 1970).

Hahn, István, "Les relations des peuples d'Europe du nord et du nord-est avec l'empire Romain," in: Comité international des sciences historiques. XVᵉ Congrès international des sciences historiques. Bucharest, 10–17 août 1980. Rapports, II, Chronologie, pp. 37–43.

Hall, Robert A., Jr., External History of the Romance Languages. Foundation of Linguistics Series (ed. C.F. *Hockett*). Comparative Romance Grammar, vol. I. (New York-London-Amsterdam: 1974).

Hampel, József, Altertümer des frühen Mittelalters in Ungarn I–III (Braunschweig: 1905).

Hilczerowna, Zofia, "Le problème de la civilisation de Dridu," in *Slavia Antiqua* 17, 1970, pp. 161–170.

Hitchins, Keith, The Roumanian National Movement in Transylvania, 1780–1849 (Cambridge, Mass.: 1969).

————. Orthodoxy and Nationality. Andreiu Şaguna and the Rumanians of Transylvania, 1846–1873 (Cambridge: Mass.: 1977).

Hóman, Bálint, A Szent László-kori Gesta Ungarorum és XII–XIII századi leszármazói. Forrástanulmány [The Gesta Ungarorum from the Time of Ladislas the Saint and Related Records in the 12th–13th Centuries. A Study of Sources], (Budapest: 1925).

Horedt, Kurt, "Völkerwanderungszeitliche Funde aus Siebenbürgen," in *Germania* 25, 1941.

————. Contribuţii la istoria Transilvaniei în sec. IV–XIII [Contributions to the History of Transylvania in 4th–13th Centuries], (Bucharest: 1958).

————. Siebenbürgen in spätrömischer Zeit (Bucharest: 1982).

————. "Das archäologische Bild der romanischen Elemente nach der Räumung Daziens," in *Dacoromania* I, Jahrbuch für östliche Latinität (Freiburg: 1973), pp. 135–148.

————. "Die städtischen Siedlungen Siebenbürgens in spätrömischer Zeit," in *Sargetia* 14, 1979.

————. "Die letzten Jahrzehnte der Provinz Dakien in Siebenbürgen," in *Apulum* 16, 1978, pp. 211–237.

————. Siebenbürgen im Frühmittelalter (Bonn: 1986).

Hurdubeţiu, Ion, Die Deutschen über die Herkunft der Rumänen (Bucharest: 1977); first ed. Breslau 1943.

Les Illyriens et la genèse des Albanais. Travaux de la session du 3–4 mars 1969, ed. by the Université de Tirana, Institut d'histoire et de linguistique (Tirana: 1971).

Inscriptiones Daciae Romanae: I. Introducere istorică şi epigrafică. Diplomele militare, tăbliţele cerate, red. by I.I. *Russu*, (Bucharest: 1975); II. Oltenia

şi Muntenia, red. by Gr. *Florescu* - C.C. *Petolescu* (Bucharest: 1977); III.
1. Dacia Superior, Zona de sud-vest, red. by I.I. *Russu* (Bucharest: 1977);
III. 2. Dacia Superior, Ulpia Traiana Dacica Sarmizegetusa, red. by I.I.
Russu (Bucharest: 1980). Supplement: C. C. *Petolescu, Cronica epigrafică
a României I* (1975–1980), *SCIV* 32, 1981.

Ionescu, C., Mică enciclopedie onomastică [Concise Onomastic Encyclopedia],
(Bucharest: 1975).

Iordan, Iorgu, Nume de locuri româneşti în Republica Populară Română
(Bucharest: 1952).

————. Toponimie românească (Bucharest: 1963).

————, (ed.) Istoria ştiinţelor în România. Lingvistică (Bucharest: 1975).

Istoria României. Compendiu, ed. by Miron *Constantinescu*, Constantin *Daicoviciu*, and Ştefan *Pascu* (Bucharest: 1974).

Izvoare privind istoria României (Sources Related to the History of Romania)
I., (Bucharest: 1964), II., (Bucharest: 1970).

Jancsó, Benedek, Erdély története [The History of Transylvania], (Cluj-Kolozsvár: 1931).

Jenny von, W. A., Die Kunst der Germanen im frühen Mittelalter (Berlin:
1940).

Jireček, Konstantin Josef, Geschichte der Bulgaren (Prag: 1876).

————. Geschichte der Serben I (bis 1371) and II (bis 1537), (Gotha: 1911,
1918). New ed. (Amsterdam: 1967).

————. Die Romanen in den städten Dalmatiens während des Mittelalters
(Wien: 1901–1904) I-III.

————. Die Heerstrasse von Belgrad nach Constantinopel und die Balkanpässe
(Prag: 1877).

Jokl, Norbert, Studien zur albanischen Etymologie und Wortbildung (Wien:
1911).

Jones, A., The Later Roman Empire (Oxford: 1964).

Kálmán, B., The World of Names. A Study in Hungarian Onomatology
(Budapest: 1978).

Kerényi, András, Die Personennamen von Dazien (Budapest: 1941).

Kiss, Lajos, Földrajzi nevek etimológiai szótára [Etymological Dictionary of
Geographical Names], (Budapest: 1978).

Kniezsa, István, Magyarország népei a XI. században [Peoples of Hungary in
the 11th Century], Szent István Emlékkönyv III, (Budapest: 1938).

————. "Die Gewässernamen des östlichen Karpatenbeckens," in: *Ungarische
Jahrbücher* 23, (Berlin: 1943), pp. 187–235.

————. A párhuzamos helynévadás. Településtörténeti tanulmányok [Parallel
Name-giving. Studies on the History of Settlement], (Budapest: 1944).

————. "Keletmagyarország helynevei" [The Place Names of Eastern Hun-
gary], in: Magyarok és románok [Hungarians and Romanians] József *Deér*,
László *Gáldi* (eds.) (Budapest: 1943).

Koller, Heinrich, "Zur Eingliederung der Slaven in das karolingische Imperium,"
in: Das heidnische und christliche Slaventum II, SS, pp. 33–45, Acta II
Congressus internationalis historiae Slavicae, Salisburgo-Ratisbonensis anno
1967 celebrati.

Kovačević, Jovan, "Les Slaves et la population dans l'Illyricum," in: Berichte über den II. Internationalen Kongress für Slawische Archäologie, vol. 2 (Berlin: 1973), pp. 143–151.

Kovács, István, A marosszentannai népvándorláskori temető [The Cemetery at Marosszentanna of the Peoples' Migration Time]. Dolgozatok az Erdélyi Nemzeti Múzeum érem- és régiségtárából, Kolozsvár. Travaux de la Section numismatique et archéologique du Musée National de Transylvanie, 3, 1912, pp. 250–367.

Krahe, Hans, Die alten balkanillyrischen geographischen Namen auf Grund von Autoren und Inschriften (Heidelberg: 1925).

Kristó, Gyula, Tanulmányok az Árpád-korról [Studies About the Árpád-age], (Budapest: 1983).

László, Gyula, A kettős honfoglalás [The Dual Conquest], (Budapest: 1978).

Lemerle, Paul, "Invasions et migrations dans les Balkans depuis la fin de l'époque romaine jusqu'au VIIIᵉ siècle," in: *Revue Historique*, ccxi, 1954, pp. 265–308.

Löfstedt, E., Late Latin. Instituttet for sammenlignende kulturforskning, serie A: Forelesninger, XXI (Oslo: 1959).

Logoreci, Anton, The Albanians. Europe's Forgotten Survivors (London: 1977).

Lot, Ferdinand, Les invasions barbares et le peuplement de l'Europe. Introduction a l'intelligence des derniers traités de paix (Paris: 1937).

———. La fin du monde antique et le début du Moyen Âge (Paris: 1937).

Lozovan, Eugen, "Diachronie et géographie linguistique Roumaines," in Acta Philologica II, 1959 Roma, pp. 155–169.

———. "Romains et Barbares sur le moyen Danube" in: Franz Altheim, Geschichte der Hunnen II (Berlin: 1960).

Macrea, Mihail, Viaţa în Dacia Romană [Life in Roman Dacia], (Bucharest: 1969).

Macrea, Mihail, Tudor, Dumitru, "Epoca sclavagistă romană (sec. I–III. é.n.). Dacia în tîmpul stăpânirii romană" [The Roman Era of Slavery. (First to third Century A.D.) Dacia in the Time of Roman Domination], in: Istoria României I, (Bucharest: 1960), pp. 345–576.

Magyarország története [The History of Hungary], I–II until 1242, edited by György Székely and Antal Bartha, (Budapest: 1984).

Maior, Petru, Istoria pentru începutul românilor în Dacia [History of the Beginnings of the Romanians in Dacia], I–II. A critical edition by Florea Fugariu and Manole Neagoe (Bucharest: 1970).

Makkai, László, Histoire de Transylvanie (Paris: 1946).

Mályusz, Elemér (ed.), Siebenbürgen und seine Völker (Budapest - Leipzig - Milano: 1943).

Meillet, Antoine and *Vaillant*, André, Le slave commun, 2nd edition (Paris: 1934).

Melich, János, A honfoglaláskori Magyarország [Hungary in the Conquest Time], (Budapest: 1925–29).

Meyer-Lübke, Wilhelm, Romanisches Etymologisches Wörterbuch, 3rd edition (Heidelberg: 1935).

Mihăescu, Haralambie, Limba latină în provinciile dunărene ale Imperiului Roman [The Latin Language in the Danubian Provinces of the Roman Empire], (Bucharest: 1960).

―――. La langue latine dans le sud-est de l'Europe (Bucharest: 1978).

―――. "Les éléments latins de la langue albanaise," in Revue des études sud-est européennes IV, 1966, 1–2, pp. 5–33 and 323–353, vol. II, Bucharest.

Mihăilă, G., Studii de lexicologie şi istorie a lingvisticii româneşti [Studies of Lexicology and of the History of Romanian Linguistics], (Bucharest: 1973).

Mirdita, Zef, "Intorno al problema dell'ubicazione e della identificazione di alcune agglomerati dardani nel tempo preromano," in Posebna izdanja (Sarajevo: 1975).

―――. Problem etnogeneze Albanaca, in Encyclopedia moderna, vol. 5, no. 13 (1970), pp. 30–39.

Mitrofan, Ion, "Descoperiri arheologice la Potaissa" [Archaeological Finds at Potaissa], in AMN, 6, 1969.

―――. "Vestigii in Napoca romana" [Vestiges at Roman Napoca], AMN 13, 1976.

Mittelstrass, Otto, Beiträge zur Siedlungsgeschichte Siebenbürgens im Mittelalter (München: 1961).

Mladenov, Stefan, Geschichte der bulgarischen Sprache (Berlin: 1929).

Mócsy, András, Gesellschaft und Romanisation in der römischen Provinz Moesia Superior (Amsterdam - Budapest: 1970).

Moga, Ion, Les roumains de Transylvanie au Moyen Âge (Sibiu: 1944).

Moldovan, Silviu, Togan, Nicolae, Dicţionarul numirilor de localităţi cu proporţiune română din Ungaria [Dictionary of the Names of Localities with the Romanian Share in Hungary], (Sibiu-Nagyszeben: 1909).

Moravcsik, Gyula, Byzantium and the Magyars (Budapest-Amsterdam: 1970).

Musset, Lucien, Les invasions. Le second assaut contre l'Europe chrétienne (VIIe–XIe siècles), (Paris: 1971).

Nägler, Thomas, Die Ansiedlung der Siebenbürger Sachsen (Bucharest: 1979).

Nandriş, G. and Auty, R., Handbook of Old Church Slavonic, 2 vols. (London: 1959, 1965).

Nandriş, Octave, Phonétique historique du roumain (Paris: 1963), Bibliothèque française et romane, Serie A, vol. 5.

Nationalism in Eastern Europe, ed. by Peter F. Sugar and Ivo J. Lederer (Washington: 1969).

Nestor, Ion, Zaharia, Eugenia, "Raport preliminar despre săpăturile de la Bratei" [Preliminary Report About the Excavations at Bratei], in Materiale X, 1973.

Niculescu, Alexandru, Latinitatea limbii române. Probleme de cronologie relativă (Bucharest: 1978).

Niederhauser, Emil, A nemzeti megújulási mozgalmak Kelet-Európában [The Renewal of National Movements in Eastern Europe], (Budapest: 1977).

Obolensky, Dimitri, The Byzantine Commonwealth. Eastern Europe 500–1453 (London: 1971).

————. "Byzantine Frontier Zones and Cultural Exchanges," XIV Congrès International des Études Byzantines, Bucharest 6–12 septembre 1971. Rapports II, pp. 91–101.

Ostrogorsky, Georg, Geschichte des byzantinischen Staates (München: 1963).

Papahagi, Valeriu, "Originea geografică a aromânilor. Note bibliografice" [The Geographic Origin of the Aromanians. Bibliographic Notes], in *Revista aromânească*, 1929, pp. 56–66.

Párducz, Mihály, Denkmäler der Sarmatenzeit in Ungarn, III, (Budapest: 1950).

Pascu, Ştefan, Voievodatul Transilvaniei [The Duchy of Transylvania], vol. I. 1971, vol. II. 1979 (Cluj-Napoca).

————, (ed.) Istoria României. Compendiu, 3rd ed. (Bucharest: 1974).

————. "Die mittelalterlichen Dorfsiedlungen in Siebenbürgen (bis 1400)," in *Nouvelles études d'Histoire*, Bucharest 1960, pp. 135–148.

Patsch, Carl, Der Kampf um den Donauraum unter Domitian und Traian. Sitzungsberichte der kaiserlichen Akademie der Wissenschaften, philosophische-historische Klasse, vol. 217 (Vienna-Leipzig: 1937).

Pătruţ, Ioan, Studii de limba română şi de slavistică [Studies of the Romanian Language and Slavistics], (Cluj: 1974).

————. Onomastică românească [Romanian Onomastics], (Bucharest: 1980).

Pârvan, Vasile, Dacia, 5th edition (Bucharest: 1972).

Petolescu, Constantin, "Dacii în armata romană" [Dacians in the Roman Army], in *Revista de Istorie*, 1980, 6, pp. 1043–1061.

Petrikovits von, Harald, Der diachronische Aspekt der Kontinuität von der Spätantike zum frühen Mittelalter. Nachrichten der Akademie der Wissenschaften in Göttingen, philosophisch-historische Klasse, 5, 1982.

Petrovici, Emil, "La population de la Transylvanie au XIe siècle," *Revue de Transylvanie X*, Sibiu 1944.

————. Daco-Slava, in: Dacoromania 10, 1943.

————. "Toponymie et histoire," in *Revue roumaine d'Histoire* 4, 1965, pp. 3–13.

————. Studii de dialectologie şi toponimie (Bucharest: 1970), ed. Pătruţ et. al.

Philippide, Alexandru, Originea rominilor, vol. I. 1925, vol. II. 1928, Iaşi.

Pippidi, M. Dionisie (ed.), Dicţionar de istorie veche a României (Paleolitic-sec. X) [Dictionary of the Ancient History of Romania (Paleolitic-tenth Cent.)], (Bucharest: 1976).

Poghirc, Cicerone, "Considérations sur les éléments autochtones de la langue roumaine," in *Revue Roumaine de Linguistique* XII, 1967, pp. 19–36.

————. "L'apport des substrats antiques à l'union linguistique balkanique," in *Linguist Balkanique* XX, 1–2, 1977, pp. 83–87.

————. "Thrace et daco-mésien: langues ou dialects?", in: Thraco-Dacica. Recueil d'études à l'occasion du IIe Congrès International de Thracologie, 1976, edited by Constantin Preda et. al., (Bucharest: 1976) pp. 335–347.

Popescu, Emilian, Inscripţiile greceşti şi latine din secolele IV–XIII descoperite în România [Latin and Greek Inscriptions from the Fourth to Thirteenth Centuries Discovered in Romania], (Bucharest: 1976).

Popescu-Spineni, Marin, România în izvoare geografice şi cartografice [Romania in Geographical and Cartographical Sources], (Bucharest: 1978).

Popović, Ivan, "Bemerkungen über die vorslavischen Ortsnamen in Serbien," in *Zeitschrift für slavische Philologie* 28, (1960) pp. 101–114.

_____. Geschichte der serbokroatischen Sprache (Wiesbaden: 1960).

Preda, Constantin, Monedele geto-dacilor (Geto-Dacian Coins), (Bucharest: 1973).

_____. "Circulaţia monedelor bizantine în regiunea Carpato-Dunăreană" [The Circulation of the Byzantine Coins in the Carpatho-Danubian Area], in *SCIV* 23, 1972, pp. 375–415.

_____. "Circulaţia monedelor romane postaureliene în Dacia" [The Circulation of post-Aurelian Roman Coins in Dacia], in *SCIVA* 26, 4, 1975, pp. 441–485.

_____. and Florentina *Preda*, "Contribuţia cercetărilor arheologice la cunoaşterea istoriei vechi a României" [The Contribution of Archaeological Investigations to the Knowledge About the Early History of Romania], in *Revista de Istorie* 33, 7–8, 1980, pp. 1253–1279.

Prodan, David, Supplex Libellus Valachorum or the Political Struggle of the Romanians in Transylvania During the 18th Century (Bucharest: 1971).

Protase, Dumitru, "Considérations sur les rites funéraires des Daces," in *Revue d'archéologie et d'histoire*, nouvelle série, IV, Bucharest 1962.

_____. Problema continuităţii în Dacia în lumina arheologiei şi numismaticii [The Problem of the Continuity in Dacia in the Light of Archaeology and Numismatics], (Bucharest: 1966).

_____. Riturile funerare la Daci şi Daco-Romani [Funerary Rites of the Dacians and Daco-Romans], (Bucharest: 1971).

_____. "Observaţii asupra aşezărilor rurale din Dacia romană şi postromană (sec. II–VI) pînă la venirea slavilor" [Observations About the Rural Settlements in Roman and post-Roman Dacia (2nd–6th century) Until the Arrival of the Slavs], *Banatica* 1, 1971, p. 93 *et. seq.*

_____. Un cimitir dacic din epoca romană la Soporu de Cîmpie. Contribuţie la problema continuităţii în Dacia [A Dacian Cemetery from the Roman Period at Soporu de Cîmpie. A Contribution to the Problem of Continuity in Dacia], (Bucharest: 1976).

_____. Autohtonii în Dacia, I. Dacia romană (Bucharest: 1980).

Pudić, I., Die Sprachen Jugoslawiens und der Balkansprachbund, in: Actes du Premier Congrès International des Études Balkaniques, vol. 6, Linguistique (Sofia: 1986), pp. 59–69.

Puşcariu, Sextil, Die rumänische Sprache, ihr Wesen und ihre volkliche Prägung (Leipzig: 1943); new edition in Romanian 1976.

_____. "Le rôle de la Transylvanie dans la formation et l'évolution de la langue roumaine," in *La Transylvanie*, (Bucharest: 1938), pp. 37–69.

Realencyclopädie der klassischen Altertumswissenschaft, edited by August Pauly and Georg *Wissowa*. Supplement, vol. 9, pp. 1397–1428, (Stuttgart: 1962).

Reallexikon der germanischen Altertumskunde I (Berlin-New York: 1973).

Reichenkron, Günter, Das Dakische (rekonstruiert aus dem Rumänischen) (Heidelberg: 1966).

——. "Das Ostromanische," in: Völker und Kulturen Südosteuropas. Kulturhistorische Beiträge, vol. I, pp. 153–172, (München: 1959).

——. "Vorrömische Bestandteile des Rumänischen," in *Südost-Forschungen* XIX, 1960, pp. 344–368.

——. "Die Entstehung des Rumänentums nach den neuesten Forschungen," in *Südost-Forschungen* XXII, 1963, pp. 61–77.

Reiter, Norbert, Komparative (= Balkanologische Veröffentlichungen 1) (Berlin: 1979).

Relations Between the Autochthonous Population and the Migratory Populations on the Territory of Romania, edited by Miron *Constantinescu*, Ştefan *Pascu*, Petre *Diaconu* (Bucharest: 1975).

Rohlfs, Gerhard, Die lexikalische Differenzierung der romanischen Sprachen. Versuch einer romanischen Wortgeographie (München: 1954).

Roman, Petre, Ferche, Suzana, "Cercetările de la Ipoteşti (Jud. Olt). (Observaţii asupra culturii materiale autohtone din secolul al VI-lea în Muntenia)" [The Investigations at Ipoteşti (Olt County). (Observations About the Autochthonous Material Culture of the 6th Century in Muntenia)], in *SCIVA* 29, 1, 1978, pp. 73–93.

Romania Germanica. Sprach- und Siedlungsgeschichte der Germanen auf dem Boden des alten Römerreichs, (Berlin-Leipzig: 1934–1935).

Rosetti, Alexandru, Istoria limbii române de la origini pînă în secolul al XVII-lea [The History of the Romanian Language from the Origins to the 17th Century], (Bucharest: 1968), 2nd edition 1978; a definitive edition in 1986.

——. Cazacu, Boris, Coteanu, Ion (eds.), Istoria limbii române, vol. I. 1965, vol. II. 1969, Bucharest.

——. Cazacu, Boris, Onu, Liviu, Istoria limbii române literale. I. De la origini pînă la începutul secolului al XIX- lea. Ediţia nouă, revăzută şi adaugită [The History of the Romanian Literary Language. I. From the Origins to the Beginning of the 19th Century. New edition, revised and added]. (Bucharest: 1971).

——. Golopenţia Eretescu, Sanda (ed.), "Current Trends in Romanian Linguistics," in *Revue Roumaine de Linguistique*, tome XXIII, nos. 1–4; *Cahiers de Linguistique Théorique et Appliquée*, tome XV, nos. 1–2, (Bucharest: 1978).

Runciman, Steven A., A History of the First Bulgarian Empire (London: 1930).

Rura, Michael, J., Reinterpretation of History as a Method of Furthering Communism in Rumania. A Study in Comparative Historiography (Washington, D.C., Georgetown: 1961).

Russu, Ion I., Limba traco-dacilor [The Language of the Thraco-Dacians], 2nd. edition (Bucharest: 1967).

——. Elemente autohtone în limba română. Substratul comun românoalbanez [Autochthonous Elements in the Romanian Language. The Substratum Shared by Romanian and Albanian], (Bucharest: 1970).

——. Die Sprache der Thrako-Daker (Bucharest: 1969).

————. Elemente traco-getice în Imperiul roman și Byzantium [Thraco-Getic Elements in the Roman Empire and Byzantium], (Bucharest: 1976).

————. Illirii. Istoria—limba și onomastica—romanizarea [The Illyrians. History—Language and Onomastics—Romanization], (Bucharest: 1969).

————. Etnogeneza românilor. Fondul autohton traco-dacic și componența latino-romanică [The Ethnogenesis of the Romanians. The Autochthonous Thraco-Dacian Basis and the Latin-Roman Component], (Bucharest: 1981).

Rusu, Mircea, "Castrul roman Apulum și cetatea feudală Alba Iulia" [The Roman Castrum at Apulum and the Feudalistic Fortress at Alba Iulia], in: *Anale.Ist.* I. A. 22 (1979) pp. 47–69.

Sandfeld, K., Linguistique balkanique. Problèmes et résultats (Paris: 1930).

Sanie, Silviu, Civilizația romană la est de Carpați și romanitatea pe teritoriul Moldovei (sec. II î.e.n.-III e.n.) [Roman Civilization East of the Carpathians and Romanity on the Territory of Moldavia (Second Century B.C.-third Century A.D.)], (Iași: 1981).

Schaller, Helmut W., Die Balkansprachen. Eine Einführung in die Balkanphilologie (Heidelberg: 1975).

Scheludko, D., "Lateinische und rumänische Elemente im Bulgarischen," *Balkan-Archiv* III, 1927, pp. 252–289.

Schmidt, Ludwig, Die Ostgermanen (München: 1941).

Schramm, Gottfried, Eroberer und Eingesessene. Geographische Lehnnamen als Zeugen der Geschichte Südosteuropas im ersten Jahrtausend n. Chr. (Stuttgart: 1981).

————. "Frühe Schicksale der Rumänen," in: *Zeitschrift für Balkanologie*, vol. XXI/2 (1985) pp. 223–241.

Schünemann, Konrad, "Die 'Römer' des anonymen Notars," in: *Ungarische Jahrbücher* 1926, pp. 448–457.

Schütz, Joseph, Die geographische Terminologie des Serbokroatischen (Berlin: 1957).

Sedláček, J., "Parallel Phenomena in the Development of the Languages of Southeastern Europe," in *Les Études balkaniques tchécoslovaques* II, (Prague: 1967).

Shevelov, George Y., A Prehistory of Slavic. The Historical Phonology of Common Slavic (Heidelberg: 1964).

Skok, Petar, "Considérations générales sur le plus ancien istro-roman," in: Ort und Wort. Festschrift Jakob Jud (Genf: 1943).

————. La toponymie et la question du substrat et du superstrat (considérations de méthode), in: Premier Congrès International de Toponymie et d'Anthroponymie, Actes et mémoires (Paris: 1938).

Solta, Georg Renatus, Einführung in die Balkanlinguistik mit besonderer Berücksichtigung des Substrats und des Balkanlateinischen (Darmstadt: 1980).

Spinka, Matthew, A History of Christianity in the Balkans. A Study in the Spread of Byzantine Culture Among the Slavs (Chicago: 1933).

Stoicescu, Nicolae, Continuitatea românilor [The Continuity of the Romanians], (Bucharest: 1980).

————. The Continuity of the Romanian People (Bucharest: 1983).

Suciu, Coriolan, Dicționar istoric al localităților din Transilvania [Historical Dictionary of Localities in Transylvania], vol. I. 1967, vol. II. 1968 (Bucharest).

Szádeczky-Kardoss, Samu, "Hitvalló Theophanes az avarokról" [The Confessor Theophanes About the Avars], in: *Antik Tanulmányok* 17, Budapest 1970, pp. 121–147.

Székely, Zoltán, "Materiale ale culturii Sîntana de Mureș din sud-estul Transilvaniei" [Material Remains of the Sîntana de Mureș Culture in Southeastern Transylvania], in *Aluta*, Sfîntu Gheorghe 1969, pp. 7–114.

Tabula Imperii Romani (TIR). A collection of topographical researches and archaeological finds: TIR L-34, Aquincum - Sarmizegethusa-Sirmium (Budapest: 1968); TIR L-35, Romula-Durostorum-Tomis (București: 1969); TIR K-34, Naissus-Dyrrhachion-Scupi-Serdica-Thessalonike (Ljubljana: 1976).

Tagliavini, Carlo, Le origini delle lingue neolatine. Introduzione alla filologia romanza (Bologna: 1964).

————. Originile limbilor neolatine (Bucharest: 1977).

Tamás, Lajos, Rómaiak, románok és oláhok Dacia Trajánában [Romans, Romanians and Vlachs in Dacia Traiana], (Budapest: 1935).

————. Romains, Romans et Roumains dans l'histoire de la Dacie Trajane. Études sur l'Europe Centro-Orientalis 1 (Budapest: 1936).

Temporini, Hildegard and *Haase*, Wolfgang, (eds.)., Aufstieg und Niedergang der römischen Welt. Geschichte und Kultur Roms im Spiegel der neueren Forschung (Berlin-New York: 1977).

Teodor, Dan Gheorghe, Teritoriul est-carpatic în veacurile V–XI e.n. [The Territory East of the Carpathians in the Fifth to Eleventh Centuries A.D.], (Iași: 1978).

————. Continuitatea populației autohtone la est de Carpați în secolele VI–XI. e.n. [The Continuity of the Autochthonous Population East of the Carpathians in the 6th–11th Centuries A.D.], (Iași: 1984).

Tomaschek, Wilhelm, Die alten Thraker. Eine ethnologische Untersuchung vols. 1–2 (Wien: 1893–1894).

Tóth I., Zoltán, "Az erdélyi román nacionalizmus kialakulása" [The Development of Transylvanian Romanian Nationalism], in: Magyarok és románok [Hungarians and Romanians], vol. II edited by *Deér*, J. and *Gáldi*, L. (Budapest: 1944).

Toynbee, Arnold Joseph, Constantine Porphyrogenitus and His World (London: 1973).

Tudor, Dumitru, "Dovezile arheologice despre mențiunea stăpânirii romane la nord de Dunăre după evacuarea aureliană a Daciei (sec. III–V)" [Archaeological Evidence About the Preservation of the Roman Domination North of the Danube After the Abandonment of Dacia by Aurelian (Third to Fifth Centuries)], in *Historica* III, 1974, pp. 93–109.

————. Oltenia romană, 3rd edition (Bucharest: 1968).

Tzenoff, G., Goten oder Bulgaren. Quellenkritische Untersuchung über die Geschichte der alten Skyten, Thrakier und Makedonier (Leipzig: 1915).

————. Die Abstammung der Bulgaren und die Urheimat der Slaven. Eine historisch-philologische Untersuchung über die Geschichte der alten Thrakoillyrer, Skyten, Geten, Hunnen, Kelten u.a. (Berlin-Leipzig: 1930).

————. Geschichte der Bulgaren und der anderen Südslaven: Von der römischen Eroberung der Balkanhalbinsel an bis zum Ende des neunten Jahrhunderts (Berlin-Leipzig: 1935).

Väänänen, Veikko, Introduction au latin vulgaire, 3rd edition (Paris: 1981).

Vaillant, André, Grammaire comparée des langues slaves, vol. I (Paris: 1950).

Valkhoff, Marius, Latijn, Romaans, Roemeens (Amersfoort: 1932).

Vasilev, Chr., "Addenda et Corrigenda zu Sandfelds Linguistique Balkanique," in: Zeitschrift für Balkanologie VI, 1, 1968, pp. 92 et. seq.

————. "Möglichkeiten und Grenzen in der Erforschung der urslawischen Wortgeographie am Beispiel lexikalischer Übereinstimmungen zwischen Serbokroatisch und Westslawisch," in: Wiener Slawistisches Jahrbuch 21 (Wien: 1975), pp. 280–289.

Vasmer, Max, Schriften zur slavischen Altertumskunde und Namenkunde, edited by Herbert Bräuer, 2 vols. (Berlin: 1971).

Vidos, B. E., Handbuch der romanischen Sprachwissenschaft [Handbook of Romance Linguistics], (München: 1975).

Vlasto, A.P., The Entry of the Slavs into Christendom. An Introduction of the Medieval History of the Slavs (Cambridge: 1970).

Vraciu, Ariton, Limba daco-geților [The Language of the Daco-Getae], (Timișoara: 1980).

Vulpe, Alexandru, "Geto-dacii ca unitate etno-istorică în lumea tracă" [The Geto-Dacians as an Ethnic and Historical Unity in the Thracian World], in SCIVA 31, 1, 1980, pp. 5–11.

Vulpe, Radu, Studia thracologica (Bucharest: 1976).

Wagner, Ernst, Historisch-statistisches Ortsnamenbuch für Siebenbürgen. Studia Transylvanica 4 (Köln-Wien: 1977).

Weigand, Gustav, "Sind die Albaner die Nachkommen der Illyrer oder der Thraker?", in Balkan-Archiv III, 1927, pp. 227–251.

Winkler, Judita, "Procesul romanizării în lumina monumentelor epigrafice și sculpturale din așezările rurale ale provinciei Dacia" [The Process of Romanization in the Light of the Epigraphic and Sculptural Monuments from the Rural Settlements of the Province Dacia], SCIVA 25, 4, 1974, pp. 497–515.

————. Der Münzumlauf (Römer in Rumänien), (Köln: 1969).

Wolfram, Herwig, Falko Daim (eds.), Die Völker an der mittleren und unteren Donau im fünften und sechsten Jahrhundert (Wien: 1980).

Wolfram, Herwig, Geschichte der Goten (München: 1979).

Zaharia, Eugenia, Săpăturile de la Dridu. Contribuție la arheologia și istoria perioadei de formare a poporului român [The Excavations at Dridu. A Contribution to the Archaeology and History of the Period of the Romanian Ethnogenesis], (Bucharest: 1967).

_____ . Populația românească în Transilvania în secolele VII–VIII. Cimitirul nr. 2 de la Bratei [The Romanian Population in the 7th–8th Centuries in Transylvania. Cemetery no. 2 at Bratei], (Bucharest: 1977).

_____ . "Données sur l'archéologie des IVe–XIe siècles sur le territoire de la Roumanie. La culture Bratei et la culture Dridu," in *Dacia* XV, 1971, pp. 269–287.

NAME INDEX

421

GAZETTEER

431

SUBJECT INDEX

Albanian language, 223–245, 248–249, 253–255, 380, 382–383
Albanians, 2, 380
Approbatae Constitutiones Regni Transsylvaniae, 41
Avars, 148–151, 153–154, 183, 185–187, 368–369

Bijelo Brdo culture, 187–188, 374
Bulgars, 3, 179–181, 186, 373
Byzantine Empire (Byzantium), 2

Carps, 98, 100, 101, 102, 104, 115, 160–162, 168, 170–171, 358, 370
Catholic Church, 42
Černjachov culture, 114–115
Černjachov-Sîntana de Mureş culture, 110, 116–119, 170–171
Compilatae Constitutiones, 41
Corpus Inscriptionum Latinarum, 357
Cumans, Cumanians, 22, 26, 28, 179, 181, 186, 342

Dacia, 78–80, 107, 359
Dacian language, 215–222, 379–380
Dacians, 2, 35, 102–105, 114–115, 162–163, 170–171, 212
Dacia Traiana, 38, 81–95, 104, 107, 120, 122, 139, 191, 193, 197, 209, 272, 276–277, 352
Daco-Roman continuity, 36–37, 45–46, 169–170
Danubian Principalities, 41
Dardanian language, 213
Diploma Andreanum, 396
Diploma Leopoldinum, 43
Donarium of Biertan, 133–135
Dridu culture, 164, 175–176, 372

Dual Hungarian conquest, 182–184, 373

East Latin, 195–196, 198–201

Gepidae (Gepids), 136, 139–140, 141–148, 149, 150–153, 259, 267, 365–368
Germans (Saxons) of Transylvania, 35–37, 40, 41, 332–333, 344, 396–397
Gesta Hungarorum, 11–30, 46, 52–53, 339–342
Gesta Ungarorum, 14, 18, 20, 178, 340
Getae, 212, 214, 216
Gorodisce culture, 189
Goths, 107, 113–114, 118, 125, 136, 139, 140–141, 160, 168, 171, 261, 267, 366

Humanists, 32–35, 53
Hungarian Chronicle (Magyar Krónika), 19
Hungarian conquest, 153, 176–179, 180
Huns, 51–52, 118, 125, 147–148, 149, 179, 186, 342, 368, 387

Illyrian language, 213
Illyrians, 1, 223–224, 343, 379, 380
Illyricum, 2, 196
Ipoteşti-Cîndeşti-Ciurelu culture, 164, 165, 167, 175–176
Iron Guard, 58–59, 349

Jaziges, 120, 123, 362
Josephinism (Enlightenment), 44–45

438